Deep Learning and Its Applications for Vehicle Networks

Deep Learning (DL) is an effective approach for AI-based vehicular networks and can deliver a powerful set of tools for such vehicular network dynamics. In various domains of vehicular networks, DL can be used for learning-based channel estimation, traffic flow prediction, vehicle trajectory prediction, location-prediction-based scheduling and routing, intelligent network congestion control mechanisms, smart load balancing and vertical handoff control, intelligent network security strategies, virtual smart and efficient resource allocation and intelligent distributed resource allocation methods.

This book is based on the work of world-famous experts on the application of DL to vehicle networks. It consists of the following five parts: (I) *DL for vehicle safety and security:* This part covers the use of DL algorithms for vehicle safety or security. (II) *DL for effective vehicle communications:* Vehicle networks consist of vehicle-to-vehicle and vehicle-to-roadside communications. This part covers how intelligent vehicle networks require a flexible selection of the best path across all vehicles, adaptive sending rate control based on bandwidth availability, and timely data downloads from a roadside base-station. (III) *DL for vehicle control:* The myriad operations that require intelligent control for each individual vehicle are discussed in this part. This also includes emission control, which is based on the road traffic situation, the charging pile load predicted through DL and vehicle speed adjustments based on camera-captured image analysis. (IV) *DL for information management:* This part covers some intelligent information collection and understanding. We can use DL for energy-saving vehicle trajectory control based on the road traffic situation and given destination information; we can also use natural language processing based on the DL algorithm for automatic Internet of Things (IoT) search during driving. (V) *Other applications:* This part introduces the use of DL models for other vehicle controls.

Autonomous vehicles are becoming increasingly popular in society. DL and its variants will play greater roles in cognitive vehicle communications and control. Other machine learning models, such as deep reinforcement learning, will also facilitate the understanding and adjustment of intelligent vehicle behavior. This book will become a valuable reference for your understanding of this critical field.

Deep Learning and Its Applications for Vehicle Networks

Edited by
Fei Hu and Iftikhar Rasheed

CRC Press
Taylor & Francis Group
Boca Raton London New York

CRC Press is an imprint of the
Taylor & Francis Group, an **informa** business

Cover Image: Shutterstock

First edition published 2023
by CRC Press
6000 Broken Sound Parkway NW, Suite 300, Boca Raton, FL 33487-2742

and by CRC Press
4 Park Square, Milton Park, Abingdon, Oxon, OX14 4RN

CRC Press is an imprint of Taylor & Francis Group, LLC

Library of Congress Cataloging-in-Publication Data
Names: Hu, Fei, 1972- editor. | Rasheed, Iftikhar, editor.
Title: Deep learning and its applications for vehicle networks / edited by
Fei Hu and Iftikhar Rasheed.
Description: First edition. | Boca Raton : CRC Press, [2023] | Includes
bibliographical references and index.
Identifiers: LCCN 2022054949 (print) | LCCN 2022054950 (ebook) | ISBN
9781032041377 (hbk) | ISBN 9781032041384 (pbk) | ISBN 9781003190691 (ebk)
Subjects: LCSH: Vehicular ad hoc networks (Computer networks) | Deep
learning (Machine learning)
Classification: LCC TE228.37 .D44 2023 (print) | LCC TE228.37 (ebook) |
DDC 006.3/1--dc23/eng/20230105
LC record available at https://lccn.loc.gov/2022054949
LC ebook record available at https://lccn.loc.gov/2022054950

ISBN: 978-1-032-04137-7 (hbk)
ISBN: 978-1-032-04138-4 (pbk)
ISBN: 978-1-003-19069-1 (ebk)

DOI: 10.1201/9781003190691

Typeset in Times
by SPi Technologies India Pvt Ltd (Straive)

Contents

Preface

The term Deep Learning (DL) describes the set of machine learning algorithms that applies large neural networks with recurrent or convolutional features. In other words, these are Deep Neural Networks (DNNs) for feature generation, learning, classification, and prediction. Currently, DL has been widely utilized by many online services provided by Amazon, Google, and Facebook. DL has a wide range of applications in the domain of the automotive industry, from computer vision processing for autonomous vehicles to intelligent vehicular networks for providing high data rates.

The forthcoming intelligent vehicles will be equipped with a broad range of sensors and actuators, for example, the engine controller, radar, light detection and ranging (LIDAR), and cameras, will enable a vehicle to have knowledge about its surroundings. The vehicles will also incorporate stronger computing capabilities with larger on-board storage devices. This transformation would mean that a traditional vehicular network requires smart processing abilities.

DL will be an effective approach for AI-based vehicular networks and can deliver a powerful set of tools for such vehicular network dynamics. In various domains of vehicular networks, DL can be used for learning-based channel estimation, traffic flow prediction, vehicle trajectory prediction, location-prediction-based scheduling and routing, intelligent network congestion control mechanism, smart load balancing and vertical handoff control, intelligent network security strategies, virtual smart & efficient resource allocation and intelligent distributed resource allocation methods.

This book is a valuable reference or textbook for college students and researchers who want to understand the intelligent vehicle communication systems. It can also be used by industry engineers and technicians for hardware/software design purpose.

This book is based on the work from world-famous experts on the application of DL for vehicle networks. It consists of the following five parts:

Part I. DL for vehicle safety and security: In this part, we have a few chapters to cover the use of DL algorithms for vehicle safety or security. Safety aims to overcome the natural faults to ensure that the autonomous vehicle can correctly recognize the images captured by its camera and adopt the proper actions. For example, a vehicle can realize the road obstacle ahead and apply the brake in a timely manner. Security aims to overcome intentional attacks from adversaries. For example, one may insert falsified sensing signals to the vehicle's RF communication channels to mislead the vehicles; or it pollutes the imaging data to generate wrong DL results. In this part, we will explain how DL can be used to recognize the driver's drowsiness situation. This is also important to vehicle safety.

Part II. DL for effective vehicle communications: Vehicle networks consist of vehicle-to-vehicle and vehicle-to-roadside communications. Intelligent vehicle networks require the flexible selection of the best path across all vehicles, the adaptive sending rate control based on bandwidth availability, timely data downloading from roadside base-station, etc. In this part, we have selected a few chapters on the use of DL for different network layers in V2X networks. For example, in the physical layer, DL can be used for an energy-efficient modulation parameter selections.

Part III. DL for vehicle control: For each individual vehicle, many operations require intelligent control. For example, the brake needs to be applied with different strength levels depending on the distance to the obstacle and current vehicle speed. In this part, we have collected a few chapters on the use of DL for different vehicle operation control: the emission is controlled based on the road traffic situation; the charging pile load is predicted through DL; the vehicle speed is adjusted based on the camera-captured image analysis. There are hundreds of sensors in an autonomous vehicle. All those sensors' data needs to be fused based on efficient data fusion methods. Then DL could be used to further extract interpretable information from the sensor data.

Part IV. DL for information management: This part covers some intelligent information collection and understanding. For example, we can use DL for energy-saving vehicle trajectory control based on the road traffic situation and given destination information; we can also natural language processing based on DL algorithm for automatic internet of things (IoT) search during driving. Vehicle crowdsensing is also a challenging issue since some vehicles do not have incentives to participate in the sensor network. In this part, we will introduce the use of DL for valuable information extraction to better understand road environment.

Part V. Other applications: This part introduces the use of DL models for other vehicle controls. For example, we could use DL to recognize the driver's behavior to determine whether the driver has a clear mind during driving. In this part, we have also discussed the simulator design issues to study the use of DL for computer vision understanding based on the video data collected by the vehicle's cameras.

Autonomous vehicles are becoming more and more popular in easingly society. The DL and its variants will play increasingly important roles in cognitive vehicle communications and control. Other machine learning models such as deep reinforcement learning will also facilitate the intelligent vehicle behavior understanding and adjustment. We expect that this book will become a valuable reference to your understanding of this critical field.

About the Editors

Dr. Fei Hu is a professor in the department of Electrical and Computer Engineering at the University of Alabama. He has published over 10 technical books with CRC Press. His research focus includes cyber security and networking. He obtained his Ph.D. degrees at Tongji University (Shanghai, China) in the field of Signal Processing (in 1999), and at Clarkson University (New York, USA) in Electrical and Computer Engineering (in 2002). He has published over 200 journal and conference papers and books. Dr. Hu's research has been supported by U.S. National Science Foundation, Cisco, Sprint, and other sources. He won the school's President's Faculty Research Award (<1% faculty were awarded each year) in 2020.

Dr. Iftikhar Rasheed is currently working as an assistant professor in the Department of Information and Communication Engineering at The Islamia University of Bahawalpur, Pakistan. He obtained his Ph.D. degree at the University of Alabama, United States of America in the field of Electrical Engineering (in 2020). His research interests include wireless communications, 5G/6G cellular systems, artificial intelligence, vehicle-to-everything (V2X) communications, and Cyber Security. He has published many book chapters and high-quality journal papers.

List of Contributors

Mohd Hasan Ali
The University of Memphis
Memphis, Tennessee

Sadegh Arefnezhad
Graz University of Technology
Graz, Austria

H. M. Abdul Aziz
Kansas State University
Manhattan, Kansas

Erik Balsch
Air Force Research Laboratory
Wright-Patterson Air Force Base
Fairborn, Ohio

Manoj Basnet
The University of Memphis
Memphis, Tennessee

Felipe Bastos
Federal University of Pará
Pará, Brazil

Pedro Batista
Ericsson Research
Kista, Sweden

João Borges
Federal University of Pará
Pará, Brazil

José Nuno A. D. Bueno
University of São Paulo
São Carlos, Brazil

Yang Cao
University of Science and Technology of China
Hefei, China

Hamilton Clouse
Wright-Patterson Air Force Base
Fairborn, Ohio

Ilan Correa
Federal University of Pará
Pará, Brazil

Yue Cui
Tianjin Normal University
Tianjin, China

Sanjoy Das
Kansas State University
Manhattan, Kansas

Mehrdad Dianati
University of Warwick
Coventry, United Kingdom

Ashley Diehl
Wright-Patterson Air Force Base
Fairborn, Ohio

Arno Eichberger
Graz University of Technology
Graz, Austria

Valerio Frascolla
Intel Deutschland GmbH
Neubiberg, Germany

Weichao Gao
Towson University
Towson, Maryland

Bo Gu
Sun Yat-Sen University
Guangzhou, China

Shushi Gu
Harbin Institute of Technology
Shenzhen, China

Mohsen Guizani
Qatar University
Doha, Qatar

Zhaoxia Guo
Sichuan University
Chengdu, China

Karim El Haloui
University of Warwick
Coventry, United Kingdom

Guangjie Han
Hohai University
Changzhou, China

William Grant Hatcher
Towson University
Towson, Maryland

Tao Huang
James Cook University
Cairns, Australia

Valdir Grassi Junior
University of São Paulo
São Carlos, Brazil

Yu Kang
University of Science and Technology of China
and Hefei Comprehensive National Science
Center
Hefei, China

Aldebaro Klautau
Federal University of Pará
Pará, Brazil

Konstantinos Koufos
University of Warwick
Coventry, United Kingdom

Li Bin
Changsha University of Science & Technology
Changsha, China

Silvia Lins
Innovation Center, Ericsson Telecomunicações
São Paulo, Brazil

Yongxin Liu
Auburn University at Montgomery
Montgomery, Alabama

Chao Lu
Towson University
Towson, Maryland

Lucas Barbosa Marcos
University of São Paulo
São Carlos, Brazil

Ben Amor Nader
University of Sfax
Sfax, Tunisia

Abdennour Najmeddine
University of Sfax
Sfax, Tunisia

Ingrid Nascimento
Federal University of Pará
Pará, Brazil

Shuteng Niu
Bowling Green State University
Bowling Green, Ohio

Ailton Oliveira
Federal University of Pará
Pará, Brazil

Peng Jiayi
Changsha University of Science & Technology
Changsha, China

Peng Shurong
Changsha University of Science & Technology
Changsha, China

Gustavo A. Prudencio de Morais
University of São Paulo
São Carlos, Brazil

Zeyad A. H. Qasem
Xiamen University
Xiamen, China

Cheng Qian
Towson University
Towson, Maryland

Houbing Song
Embry-Riddle Aeronautical University
Daytona Beach, Florida

Haixin Sun
Xiamen University
Xiamen, China

Raiyan Talkhani
James Cook University
Cairns, Australia

Ouni Tarek
University of Sfax
Sfax, Tunisia

Marco Henrique Terra
University of São Paulo
São Carlos, Brazil

Jian Wang
University of Tennessee at Martin
Martin, Tennessee

Junfeng Wang
Tianjin University of Technology
Tianjin, China

Jie Wei
The City College of New York
New York, NY

Wei Xiang
La Trobe University
Melbourne, Australia

Zhenyi Xu
University of Science and Technology of China and
    Hefei Comprehensive National Science Center
Hefei, China

Xinxin Yang
Sun Yat-Sen University
Guangzhou, China

Yang Yunhao
Zhejiang University
Hangzhou, China

Wei Yu
Towson University
Towson, Maryland

Guanglin Zhang
Donghua University
Shanghai, China

Zhenyi Zhao
University of Science and Technology of China
Hefei, China

Cong Zhou
University of Warwick
Coventry, United Kingdom

PART I

Deep learning for vehicle safety and security

Deep learning for vehicle safety

1

Raiyan Talkhani and Tao Huang
James Cook University, Cairns, Australia

Shushi Gu
Harbin Institute of Technology (Shenzhen), Shenzhen, China

Zhaoxia Guo
Sichuan University, Chengdu, China

Guanglin Zhang
Donghua University, Shanghai, China

Wei Xiang
La Trobe University, Melbourne, Australia

Contents

DOI: 10.1201/9781003190691-2

1.1 INTRODUCTION

Over the last 30 years, technology in cars has evolved drastically with the introduction of software components to improve the driving experience [1]. By adding traction controls, navigation systems, security systems, airbag deployment systems, and engine management systems, to name just a few, cars have become more reliable to operate, fuel-efficient, and safer for the passengers and drivers [1–4]. Continuous investment is being made to further develop the technology present in the vehicle to improve the driving experience and safety [5]. This has led to further advancements, such as infotainment systems, automatic climate controls, navigation systems, lane change monitoring, cruise control and lane detection [1].

According to the World Health Organization report, vehicle crashes are the main cause of death for children and young people under 30, and approximately 1.2 million people lose their lives annually due to road traffic crashes [6]. The leading causes are due to human error, road conditions, and vehicle faults [7].

This has led to growth in the field of Intelligence Transportation Systems (ITS), with a heavy focus on tools for drivers' aid, autonomous driving, and traffic management [8, 9]. Various technologies have been researched and developed to improve the efficiency and safety of the transportation system. As a result, the

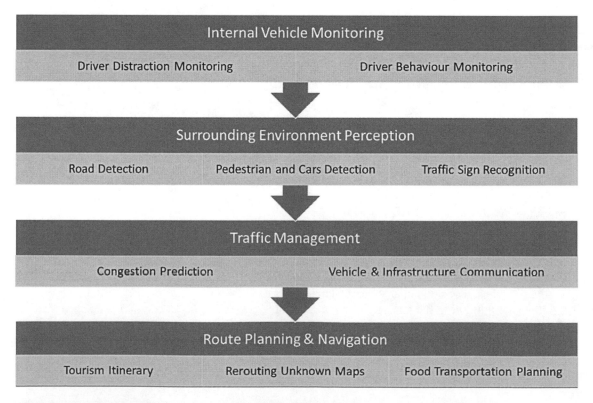

FIGURE 1.1 Different levels and areas where deep learning methods are implemented in ITS.

vehicles and infrastructures will become intelligent and can automatically process different types of events on the road in real time to improve the user travel experiences. A critical motivation of developing various intelligent technologies for the transportation system is that we hope the new technologies can assist drivers in avoiding collisions, staying on track, following the traffic regulations, and avoiding traffic congestions, thereby significantly improving vehicle safety and paving the way for autonomous vehicles [10].

Deep learning has demonstrated its capability in intelligent system design. In addition, deep learning has been demonstrated that it can perform real-time object detection, object recognition, and the optimization of communication networks [11, 12]. This chapter will introduce some recent developments relevant to vehicle safety improvement, such as internal vehicle monitoring, on-road environment monitoring, traffic management, etc. The implementation of the deep learning methods can be achieved in different stages, which are mentioned in Figure 1.1.

1.2 DEEP LEARNING FOR INTERNAL VEHICLE MONITORING

Thanks to the advent of the Internet of Things devices, more sensors (low-price with easy implementation) are now widely used in vehicles. These include the driver monitoring sensors such as cameras, microphones, RPM monitoring and Android-based devices/applications [13–16]. The purpose of the deployment of these devices in vehicles is to detect the states of the drivers. For example, the driver is using a mobile, distracted by passengers, drunk, sick, drowsy or in a normal condition [15]. A distracted driver usually has a delayed reaction to on-road events that the response time can increase by 50% compared to focused driving, thereby dramatically increasing the risks. Therefore, detecting the driver status and mitigating any potential risks in advance can significantly improve driving safety.

1.2.1 Camera-based system

Because of the ease of installing the sensing devices inside the vehicle, considerable research has been carried out to apply deep learning methods to process the sensory data and improve driving safety [14, 17–19]. One common type of deployed sensor in our daily life to monitor the surrounding condition is the camera. Similarly, a camera can be easily installed inside the cockpit to monitor the driver's condition, and the system can alert the driver when distracting behavior is detected inside the vehicle [14]. The development of the deep learning algorithm usually uses pre-collected data to train a designed neural network, rather than the conventional programme that relies on extracted feature manually for detection [20]. Therefore, a labeled large dataset of different types of driver distraction is important for training a designed neural network. Many open datasets can be found on the internet, and interested readers can check the "State Farm Distracted Driver Detection" dataset on Kaggle [21]. There are nine types of distractions in this dataset, as described in Table 1.1, and 2200 RGB images per type of distractions.

TABLE 1.1 Nine types of driver distraction in [21]

Making up	Texting with the right hand	Talking on the phone with the right hand
Talking to passenger	Texting with the left hand	Talking on the phone with the left hand
Drinking	Reaching behind	Operating radio

A modified Visual Geometry Group (VGG) [22] architecture was trained on State Farm Dataset using a cross-entropy loss function. VGG architecture is a form of convolutional neural network used to identify the object of interest present on an image. This experimental setup produced a result of 96.95% accuracy in identifying each class of distraction. This "State Farm Distracted Driver Detection" dataset was used to train a custom deep convolutional neural network (CDCNN) and modified VGG-16 based fine-tuned architecture and achieved an accuracy of 99.64% and 99.73% [16].

1.2.2 Wearable sensor-based system

Wearable sensor technology is another type of system that can be deployed to monitor the driver condition and overcome some drawbacks of the camera-based system. For example, the video captured in a dark environment can be noisy, the camera's view can be accidentally blocked, and the privacy of the driver cannot be protected, etc.

Ziyang et al. [23] investigated the use of wrist wearable sensors. In their study, the participants simulated the driving process on a vehicle simulator. The participants were given clear instructions to act various distracted behaviors. Participants' movements under different types of distraction were captured via surrounding cameras, and the wrist sensor data were recorded simultaneously. The distracted actions collected included talking on the phone, texting, touching the information screen, drinking water, and picking up objects from the passenger seat. The authors then trained a recurrent neural network with long short-term memory (RNN-LSTM) using the collected data. This model achieved an F1-score of 0.85.

Another study [24] used a different type of wearable where, instead of placing the wearable on the participant's wrist, it was placed on their head instead. This was called the Electroencephalogram, where the 32-channel electrode cap is placed around the participant's head, which captures their brain activity. This study used both the participant's brain activity and the spatial information captured using a camera pointed at the driver. The participants performed a driving test on a car simulator, and, at the same time, they were required to complete a series of tasks that would distract their minds. For example, one distraction task performed was to ask the participants to visualize the clock hands in mind and determine if the angle between the hour and minute hands was an acute angle or an obtuse angle. This is to simulate the real-world cases when people fall into deep thinking while driving. A temporal-spatial information network was proposed to extract both the spatial and the temporal features. The model was trained to identify distracted/not distracted binary cases with binary entropy loss function and achieved an accuracy of 92%.

1.2.3 Driver behavior monitoring

A driver's driving behavior can be monitored via various sensors onboard the vehicle. For example, a picture of the driver's behavior can be described by gravity, acceleration, on-board diagnostics (OBDII), rotations per minute (RPM), speed and throttle to create a picture of the driver's behavior [15]. These data can be obtained from both the smartphone of the driver and the engine control unit. Five types of data are collected: 1) Normal driving, 2) aggressive driving, 3) distracted driving, 4) drowsy driving, and 5) drunk driving (Figure 1.2). All of these collected time-series signals were transformed into RGB colour image format, which was used as input data for the convolutional neural network (CNN). Multiple CNN architectures were created with varying numbers of filters and convolutional layers. The best model used two convolutional layers with 32 filters in the first layer and a filter size of 7×7. This model produced an accuracy of 99.99% in predicting the correct number of classes.

The driver monitoring features are limited to classifying the driver behavior and can also be used in driver identification purposes or profiling which user is driving the vehicle [13]. Going one step further,

FIGURE 1.2 Driver cognition and distraction.

these models can also predict the driver's suitability to operate a vehicle based on their current driving conditions compared to their normal driving conditions to minimize the driving safety risk.

1.3 DEEP LEARNING FOR SURROUNDING ENVIRONMENT PERCEPTION

Vehicle safety is affected not only by the driver and passages inside the vehicle but also by the surrounding environment and how the driver reacts to the surrounding environment [25]. Therefore, deep learning-based object detection and identification is an active research field [25, 26]. These objects of interest are classified into potential fields (non-moving road objects such as stationary vehicles or sidewalks) or kinetic fields (moving objects such as other vehicles and pedestrians) [25]. The research goal is to detect the surrounding environment in real time and assist the drivers in decision-making [27] and thereby to improve road safety and reduce road accidents. Furthermore, the development of this technology is essential to the realization of fully autonomous vehicles [27, 28].

1.3.1 Road detection

In some single-vehicle accidents, the vehicle runs off the road, falls in a river, or hit a building or a tree. Therefore, it is crucial that the vehicle only drives on the designated road, thereby detecting the drivable area is a prerequisite for decision-making and planning a safe trajectory [29]. Chen et al. [30] addressed this issue by identifying the road's drivable surface and identifying the boundaries of the road based on camera inputs. The authors adapted a deep convolutional neural network (DCNN) and introduced an RBNet architecture to achieve this goal. Firstly, a serial of convolutional blocks outputs is processed via convolutional filters and concatenated to form a feature vector. Then a two-branch structure is used. One branch is designated to detect the surface of the road, and the other branch is designated to detect the boundary of the road. Finally, the two branch outputs are fused to produce the final output. The architecture was evaluated on a KITTI road detection benchmark [31]. In their work, 289 images were used for training, and 290 images were used for testing. The main evaluation metrics used for comparison are maximum F1-measure (MaxF) and average precision (AP). Their proposed RBNet achieved 94.97% for MaxF and 91.49% AP.

In order to further improve the detection accuracy, other types of sensors are used on the vehicle to detect the surroundings. Caltagirone et al. [29] used data generated by both cameras and light detection and ranging (LiDAR) sensors to detect roads. The drawback of a stand-alone camera system is that it can only produce a reliable 2D sense of the surrounding environment semantically and lack accurate depth information of surroundings. On the other hand, LiDAR sends out pulsed laser beams and process the received reflected of the beams to generate a 3D model of the surrounding environment [32]. The sensed LiDAR data is an unstructured and sparse point cloud. This point cloud data can be fused with the camera image to form a more accurate spatial representation of the surrounding environment with semantic information. In order to integrate the LiDAR data with the camera image in the process, a multi-modal system could be designed to fuse the two streams of data in raw level or feature level for the road detection. The designed neural network is based on the convolutional neural network (FCN), and the performance is evaluated using the KITTI road detection benchmark, and further improved the MaxF score to 96.03%.

1.3.2 Vehicle surrounding environment detection

The usual vehicle accidents involve crashes into other vehicles, pedestrians due to distracted driving or missed traffic lights and signs. Thus, it is crucial to detect various types of objects on the roads. The problem arises when the objects of interest are small, partially occluded, the object's surface has light reflection, or the images are captured in various light conditions [27]. Pham and Jeon [27] proposed models that focused on identifying objects such as cars, pedestrians and cyclists. A two-steam CNN architecture, termed DeepStereoOP, was proposed to simultaneously process the RGB image data and depth features. The outputs of the two process branches were concatenated and further processed by fully connected layers. These models were trained on the KITTI object detection dataset [31], where 3712 images were used for training, and 3769 images were used for validation. Easy, moderate, and hard, these three difficulty levels are defined based on the object height, occlusion, and truncation. For the easy level, their design outperformed all other compared neural networks and achieved AP 93.04% for cars, AP 81.82% for pedestrians and AP 79.58% for cyclists.

In addition to vehicles, pedestrians, and cyclists, road signs are crucial for safe driving [33]. Road signs are designed to be easy for people to recognize under varying conditions and give instructions to the driver about the maximum speed information, road conditions, and risks in the coming road segmentation. However, there are many variations of the road signs, such as color and design pattern. To address the challenges brought by these variations, Islam et al. [34] proposed a two-phase deep learning architecture. The first stage was used to detect the presence of the road sign, and the second stage was used to identify the information on the road sign. The first stage used hybrid color segmentation algorithms to take advantage of the road signs' design. The second stage consists of a neural network trained to recognize ten different types of most occurring road signs: Caution! Hump, Towing Zone, No Entry, Speed Limit, Keep Left, Give Way, Traffic Lights Ahead, Stop, Pedestrian Crossing, Keep Right. The traffic sign data were collected using dash camera by recording videos while driving on the Malaysian highway and a sample of 100 images were taken for each type of road sign. In addition, the LISA dataset [35] is used. Out of the 1000 images collected, 700 were used for training, 150 for validation and 150 for testing the model, achieved an average of 99.9% accuracy.

The road sign is usually clean and can be easily identified. However, in some cases, the road sign can become dirty or partially covered by random stickers. Usually, it is not hard for a human to identify the road sign in these circumstances. However, this brings a challenge for the deep learning algorithm [33, 36]. Misidentified road signs can endanger vehicle safety, especially for fully autonomous vehicles. To investigate this issue, Yang et al. proposed a targeted attention attack (TAA) deep learning model that utilized a soft attention map to identify the crucial pixels and discard the rest of the pixels [33, 36]. Once the image is segmented, it is now used as an input for a 92-layered Residual Attention Network (RAN) followed by CNN that was used to identify the road signs. The RAN and CNN were trained separately.

TABLE 1.2 Challenging driving environment

CATEGORY	PHENOMENON
Camera	Dark current noise, readout noise, photon shot noise
Driving	Zoom, motion, OutFocus. (Any changes to the physical state of the object due to motion of the vehicle)
Weather	Snow, frost, fog, light, light, and moisture.
System	Whitening (Moisture in lens), data format, and resolution.

Two datasets were used in the experiment, and the images of road signs were not balanced. The first dataset used was LISA [35], which contained 7855 images of 26 different road signs collected from multiple cameras placed in different vehicles driving around in the United States. The second dataset, GTSRB [37], contained 51,840 images of 43 different road signs from the roads in Germany. The authors achieved an attack success rate (ASR) of 86.7% on stop signs and 36.7% on pedestrian crossing signs.

1.3.3 Object detection in challenging environments

The everyday driving for most of us seems easy. However, some drivers may need to drive vehicles through harsh environments. For example, it can be a fieldwork journey. In this case, the data captured by sensors can be noisy [38]. To address this issue, Kim et al. proposed a two-phase deep learning architecture. The first phase consisted of an adversarial defence module (ADM) and the second phase consisted of a DenseNet. The ADM module has an adversarial defence mechanism that can help reduce the computational cost and assist in multi-scale feature extraction in a harsh environment. The DenseNet used successive feature concatenation with applied pixel shuffle to achieve the feature detection [38, 39]. The COCO2015 dataset [40] and BDD100k [41] dataset were used in the model training. These datasets contained images in various challenging conditions mentioned in Table 1.2 and the proposed algorithm achieved a mean average precision of 43.7% for generic object detection and a mean average precision of 39.0% for driving conditions.

1.4 DEEP LEARNING FOR TRAFFIC MANAGEMENT

Traffic is another critical factor that affects vehicle safety. In heavy traffic, drivers are more likely to make mistakes compared to light traffic. In addition, road accidents are more likely to happen in some weather conditions, such as heavy rain or snow. Therefore, efficient dynamic traffic management is necessary to minimize vehicle accidents so that people can travel safely [42]. Well-managed traffic can improve road safety and reduce carbon emissions as cars spend less time on the road. With the advent of modern technology, there was an explosion in relevant data collecting, such as GPS tracking, traffic radar readings, social media, and traffic cameras, to allow deep learning-based big data analysis for traffic management [42, 43].

1.4.1 Traffic flow modelling

Hossein and Khalid [43] proposed an end-to-end deep learning methodology for real-time traffic management by identifying congestion in real time. By identifying the traffic congestion allows the traffic department to redirect the traffic flows to alleviate the congestion. The input to the deep learning model is the observation of the traffic flow, and the model's output is the recommended traffic management scheme. The input and output were paired for training purposes. The model's input is processed as 2D images, with one dimension representing the observation in time intervals and the other dimension representing the road links. The pixels in the image represent the corresponding traffic speed at a given time on a given road link. The output was an array of vectors in vector form, and each vector represents a control device with binary values for control purposes. Due to the challenges of collecting the real-world dataset for training, a laboratory-generated dataset is used for training purposes. In addition, a real-time traffic network simulation model was designed to simulate the traffic. The designed deep learning architecture consists of feature maps, a pooling layer, and a fully connected network layer. Their work found out that the more the dataset is used for training, the traffic can be managed more efficiently and thus reduce more travel time.

Chen et al. [44] proposed a novel fuzzy deep convolutional network (FDCN) that integrated with the adaptively generated fuzzy rules to predict the traffic flow. There are two data paths in the designed architecture. One path is the fuzzy network, and one is the deep convolution network. The outputs of the two paths are fused together for prediction. The proposed deep learning architecture was evaluated on the real Beijing taxicab trajectory dataset, and a cross-entropy loss function was used. The authors found out that the stacked residual units determine the number of layers in the proposed FDCN architecture. In addition, multi-step ahead prediction has been experimented within this work. The experiment's outcome showed that the predicted traffic flow was aligned to the observed traffic flow and performs well in medium to high traffic flows. The proposed FDCN model achieved an RMSE of 0.3037 and an MRE of 0.2045 with a 20-layer structure.

Weather conditions are also affecting the traffic condition on-road and should be considered in the study. Therefore, some researches have been carried out to integrate the weather data in the deep learning algorithms to improve the dynamic prediction accuracy of the traffic flow [45]. The gated recurrent neural (GRU) network is used in this study for the prediction of the traffic flow. The inputs of the GRU network is a constructed 3D data matrix that contains both the weather and the traffic conditions. A designed neural network termed deep GRU recurrent neural network (DGRNN) is proposed. The final prediction layer is a fully connected layer. The used dataset is extracted from the Caltrans performance measurement system (PeMS) [46], and the weather data is from the National Oceanic and Atmospheric Administration (NOAA) repository [47]. Multiple variations of DGRNN were experimented in this study, and the best performance was achieved with a two-hidden layer structure and 500 hidden units at each layer. This structure achieved a mean squared error (MSE) of 3.76×10^{-5}, a mean absolute error (MAE) of 0.0079, and a root-mean-squared error (RMSE) of 0.0019.

1.4.2 Vehicle and infrastructure communications

To achieve effective traffic management, the prediction of the traffic flow is the first step. The next step is to inform the vehicles on the road about the road conditions and give drivers warnings or advice on an alternative route. Furthermore, the traffic management system can coordinate the road management system to guide vehicles to alleviate traffic congestion. To achieve these operations, reliable and fast communication between the vehicle to vehicle (V2V) and between the vehicle to infrastructure (V2I) are required [48, 49], as shown in Figure 1.3. The quality of service (QoS) of communication is critical to improving the safety of the vehicles. The advantage of having V2V communication is that there is minimum latency when it comes to exchanging information, which could prevent traffic accidents [50]. V2I communication, on the other hand, is about communicating with Roadside Units (RSU). RSU is a device placed at certain intervals along the roadside that is used to store relevant information regarding the road and the traffic [51]. It can be used to manage the traffic flow and improve vehicle safety by sending information about the road condition to the vehicles [48]. However, with the increased number of vehicles on the road, having a satisfactory communication infrastructure is difficult to implement without ballooning cost of the infrastructure, so the problem will always be limited resources.

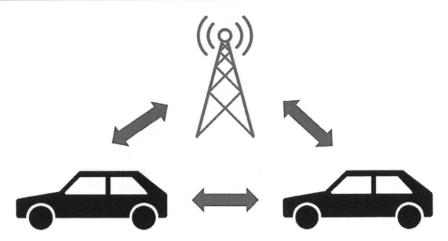

FIGURE 1.3 Illustration of V2V and V2I communication.

To address this issue, an example study by Ning et al. [49] introduced a deep reinforcement learning based traffic control system using the 5G network. Reinforcement learning is different from supervised learning. It rewards the desired behaviour but punishes undesired behaviour [52]. The work in [49] focused on the resource allocation for Mobile Edge Computing (MEC) and caching problems in the context of the Internet of Connected Vehicles (IoCVs). The authors designed a joint system where the base station and the RSU collaboratively transmit the data to the vehicles. Furthermore, a joint optimization problem was formulated to maximize the operator's revenue and also the quality of experience of the vehicles. The experiment is carried out based on the real traffic data in Hangzhou, China. The proposed DDPG-based scheme, which combines a Deep Neural Network and the Actor-Critic structure, has been demonstrated can achieve a satisfactory result.

Other than the existing resource allocation problems, other factors, such as service coverage, RSU migration, and service allocation, are also critical factors that affect the vehicles' quality of experience. In [48], the authors considered these factors and proposed a quality of service (QoS) index based on the service delay, packet error rate, and system usage rate. In addition, a deep learning-inspired RSU Service Consolidation (RSC) Approach was proposed. Two models were used in this approach: the RSU-migration model and the linear-programming-based multicast model. This proposed DL-RSC approach achieved a service reliability rate of 71%, the quality of experience of the vehicles increased by 67%, and the delay rate was reduced by 18%.

1.5 DEEP LEARNING-BASED ROUTE PLANNING AND NAVIGATION

In previous sections, we discussed how deep learning could help the driver focus on the driving task, help the driver avoid crashes, and help the road authority better manage the traffic flows. All these can reduce vehicle risk and improve the safety of the driving experience. Besides the factors discussed in these sections, better route planning and navigation can also improve vehicle safety. This section explores how deep learning methods can assist vehicles plan and navigating/planning routes through road networks. A good route plan can improve vehicle safety and reduce travel time [53]. However, in the real world, navigation and route planning are complex due to the dynamic of the external environment, such as changed road conditions due to slow traffic, road closure, etc. [54].

1.5.1 Route planning for travellers

Two ways are currently being used in the route planning task. The first method is to find the shortest distance between two points by calculating the total geographical distance among different points [55, 56]. The second method uses historically routing data from various drivers, which is known as route recommendations modelling [57, 58]. One can also combine these two methods and form a hybrid model [59, 60]. However, the existing method is not flexible and can only plan for a single route. To address this issue, Huang et al. [53] proposed a multi-task deep travel route planning (MDTRP) framework that use rich supporting data to achieve effective route planning. The focus of this study were the tourists or new visitors to a city who wish to explore local attractions without spending their time stuck in traffic. To ensure this attribute in the model, MDTRP uses long short-term memory (LSTM) and multi-layer perceptron (MLP) modules to learn from historical travel data of places travelled by tourists.

The dataset was created by extracting information from Flickr [61], where tourists geotag images of local attractions in six different cities, including Toronto, Vienna, Edinburgh, Glasgow, Budapest, and Osaka. Between 7,000 to 40,000 images were collected from each city, recording around 30 attractions from each, and between 1,000 and 6,000 travel sequences from each. This information is then combined with the order in which the said tourists travel to different local attractions. The model was then used to recommend the next attraction, plan routes, and must-visit places. The authors compared two cases: general route planning and "must-visit" planning. For both cases, the proposed model gave satisfying performances.

1.5.2 Route planning for food transportation

Another area where route planning is critical is the food delivery route planning to ensure the food reaches the plate while it is still fresh [62]. In addition, in some cases, the map used for route planning may be outdated or missing. Liu et al. addressed this challenging problem using the historical GPS data by the food delivery drivers to train a deep inverse reinforcement learning (IRL) model. The dataset used was obtained from the Meituan-Dianping Group, which consisted of 4,974,003 trajectories collected between January and September 2019 by delivery drivers in Xiamen, Fujian Province in China. The authors improved the F1 score on distance by 8% when the map information is unknown, compared to the model in [63].

1.5.3 Dynamic routing with unknown map

However, road networks keep evolving, rarely remaining the same over time, from road blocks due to construction or traffic jams. Han and Yilmaz [54] addressed this issue by visually understanding the environment, i.e. recognizing the road signs and updating the route plan. By using the double-critic Q learning network (DCQLN) model based on the deep reinforcement learning model trained using a dataset collected by placing iPhones in moving vehicles in and around the Ohio State University Campus. A model was then tested to see how it responds to changes in the environment, where it outperformed the existing models in recognizing the changes on the road and updating the maps. This study is limited as it only looks into responding to changes to the driving surfaces to update or reroute the vehicle.

1.6 CONCLUSIONS

In this chapter, we have reviewed the recent development of deep learning technology that can improve vehicle safety. ITS is designed to improve vehicle safety and make the transportation system more efficient [64–69]. The improvement can be carried out from various aspects – for example, internal vehicle condition monitoring, road environment monitoring, traffic management, and routing. Various deep learning algorithms were explored in these tasks, such as LSTM, CNN, reinforcement learning, and variations of them. These researches demonstrated that deep learning effectively identifies the distracted driver, objects on the road, and traffic signs, and predicts traffic flows. However, when a vehicle is in high-speed mode, how fast and reliably to detect these factors that affect vehicle safety needs additional research. In addition, the related privacy and security issues are still open research questions [70]. Nevertheless, once these technologies are mature enough to be used in the real world, it is going to result in much safer driving conditions with reduced human error and improved the flow of traffic.

REFERENCES

[1] R. Coppola, and M. Morisio, "Connected car: technologies, issues, future trends," *ACM Computing Surveys*, vol. *49*, no. 3, pp. 1–36, 2016, doi: 10.1145/2971482.

[2] A. S. Mutschler "How to make autonomous vehicles reliable," *Semiconductor Engineering on Test, Measurement and Analytics*, September 11, 2017. https://semiengineering.com/will-autonomous-vehicles-be-reliable/

[3] K. A. Abu Kassim, L. Arokiasamy, M. H. Md Isa, and C. H. Ping, "Intention to purchase safer sar: an application of theory of planned behavior," *Global Business and Management Research*, vol. *9*, no. 1, p. 188, 2017.

[4] A. Alberini, V. Di Cosmo, and A. Bigano, "How are fuel efficient cars priced? Evidence from eight EU countries," *Energy Policy*, vol. *134*, p. 110978, 2019, doi: 10.1016/110978

[5] A. Parment, *Auto Brand: Building Successful Car Brands for the Future*, London: Kogan Page Limited, 2014.

[6] S. Shrivastava, and P. Shrivastava, "Global reduction in the incidence of deaths dssociated with road traffic Injuries: World Health Organization," *MAMC Journal of Medical Sciences*, vol. *5*, no. 3, pp. 152–153, 2019.

[7] M. A. Nzegwu, and C. O. Nzegwu, "Review of causes of road traffic accidents in Benin city, Nigeria: a 1-year study, August 2003-July 2004," *Emergency medicine Australasia*, vol. *19*, no. 1, pp. 77–78, 2007.

[8] T. Mine, A. Fukuda, and S. Ishida, "The unconscious learning effect on driver attention," In Tsunenori Mine, Akira Fukuda, & Shigemi Ishida (Eds.), *Intelligent Transport Systems for Everyone's Mobility*, Singapore: Springer, 2019, pp. 3–13.

[9] R. I. Meneguette, R. E. De Grande, and A. A. F. Loureiro, "Intelligent transportation systems," In Rodolfo I. Meneguette, Robson E. De Grande, & Antonio A. F. Loureiro (Eds.), *Intelligent Transport System in Smart Cities Aspects and Challenges of Vehicular Networks and Cloud*, 1st ed. 2018. ed., Cham: Springer International Publishing, 2018, pp. 147–166.

[10] G. Dimitrakopoulos, L. Uden, and I. Varlamis, "Part five: the future of ITS applications," *The Future of Intelligent Transport Systems*, Amsterdam: Elsevier, 2020.

[11] L. Xiao, Y. Zhang, W. Gao, D. Xu, and C. Li, "An object perception and positioning method via deep perception learning object detection," *Concurrency and Computation*, 2021, doi: 10.1002/cpe.6203.

[12] Y. Xu, D. Dong, W. Xu, and X. Liao, "SketchDLC: a sketch on distributed deep learning communication via trace capturing," *ACM Transactions on Architecture and Code Optimization*, vol. *16*, no. 2, pp. 1–26, 2019.

[13] Z. Halim, R. Kalsoom, S. Bashir, and G. Abbas, "Artificial intelligence techniques for driving safety and vehicle crash prediction," *The Artificial Intelligence Review*, vol. *46*, no. 3, pp. 351–387, 2016.

[14] A. A. Khalid, and Z. Mohammed, "Detecting driver distraction using deep-learning approach," *Tech Science Press on Computers, Materials & Continua*, vol. *68*, no. 1, pp. 689–704, 2021.

[15] M. Shahverdy, M. Fathy, R. Berangi, and M. Sabokrou, "Driver behavior detection and classification using deep convolutional neural networks," *Elsevier on Expert Systems with Applications*, vol. *149*, p. 113240, 2020.

[16] A. Gumaei, M. Al-Rakhami, M. M. Hassan, A. Alamri, M. Alhussein, M. A. Razzaque, and G. Fortino, "A deep learning-based driver distraction identification framework over edge cloud," *Springer on Neural Computing & Applications*, 2020, doi: 10.1007/s00521-020-05328-1.

[17] M. Gjoreski, M. Gams, M. Lustrek, P. Genc, J. U. Garbas, and T. Hassan, "Machine learning and end to end deep learning for monitoring driver distractions from physiological and visual signals," *IEEE Access*, vol. *8*, pp. 70590–70603, 2020.

[18] M. García-García, A. Caplier, and M. Rombaut, "Sleep deprivation detection for real time driver monitoring using deep learning," In A. Campilho, F. Karray, B. ter Haar Romeny (Eds.), *Lecture Notes in Computer Science*, *Springer International Publishing*, Cham: Springer, 2018, pp. 435–442. doi: 10.1007/978-3-319-93000-8_49.

[19] A. Ş. Şener, I. F. Ince, H. B. Baydargil, I. Garip, and O. Ozturk, "Deep learning based automatic vertical height adjustment of incorrectly fastened seat belts for driver and passenger safety in fleet vehicles," *Proceedings of the Institution of Mechanical Engineers. Part D, Journal of Automobile Engineering*, vol. *236*, pp. 639–654, 2021.

[20] I. Goodfellow, Y. Bengio, and A. Courville, "Introduction," *Deep Learning*, Cambridge, MA: MIT Press, 2016.

[21] *State Farm Distracted Driver Detection*, Kaggle, 2016, Available: https://www.kaggle.com/c/state-farm-distracted-driver-detection [Accessed Jan 2021].

[22] K. Simonyan, and A. Zisserman, "Very deep convolutional Networks for large scale image recognition", *arXiv [cs.CV]*, 2015.

[23] X. Ziyang, L. Li, and X. Xu, "Recognition of driving distraction using driver's motion and deep learning," *IIE Annual Conference Proceedings*, pp. 949–954, 2020.

[24] G. Li, W. Yan, S. Li, X. Qu, W. Chu, and D. Cao, "A temporal spatial deep learning approach for driver distraction detection based on EEG signals," *IEEE Transactions on Automation Science and Engineering*, vol. *19*, pp. 1–13, 2021.

[25] J. Wang, J. Wu, and Y. Li, "The driving safety field based on driver vehicle road interactions," *IEEE Transactions on Intelligent Transportation Systems*, vol. *16*, no. 4, pp. 2203–2214, 2015.

[26] L. Wan, Y. Sun, L. Sun, Z. Ning, and J. J. P. C. Rodrigues, "Deep learning based autonomous vehicle super resolution DOA estimation for safety driving," *IEEE Transactions on Intelligent Transportation Systems*, vol. *22*, no. 7, pp. 4301–4315, 2021.

[27] C. C. Pham, and J. W. Jeon, "Robust object proposals re-ranking for object detection in autonomous driving using convolutional neural networks," *Signal Processing: Image Communication*, vol. *53*, pp. 110–122, 2017.

[28] R. K. Jurgen, "Major design and test collaborations," *Autonomous Vehicles For Safer Driving*, Warrendale, PA: Society of Automotive Engineers, 2013.

[29] L. Caltagirone, M. Bellone, L. Svensson, and M. Wahde, "LIDAR camera fusion for road detection using fully convolutional neural networks," *Robotics And Autonomous Systems*, vol. *111*, pp. 125–131, 2019.

[30] Z. Chen, and Z. Chen, "RBNet: a deep neural network for unified road and road boundary detection," *Lecture Notes in Computer Science, Springer International Publishing*, 2017, pp. 677–687.

[31] A. Geiger, P. Lenz, and R. Urtasun, "Are we ready for autonomous driving? The KITTI vision benchmark suite," *Proceedings of IEEE Conference on Computer Vision and Pattern Recognition*, 2012, pp. 3354–3361.

[32] Z. Chen, "Chapter One," *Application of Airborne liDAR Data in the Modelling of 3d Urban Landscape Ecology*, Newcastle upon Tyne, England: Cambridge Scholars Publishing, 2017.

[33] X. Yang, W. Liu, S. Zhang, W. Liu, and D. Tao, "Targeted attention attack on deep learning models in road sign recognition," *IEEE Internet of Things Journal*, vol. *8*, no. 6, pp. 4980–4990, 2021.

[34] K. T. Islam, and R. G. Raj, "Real-time (vision based) road sign recognition using an artificial neural network," *Sensors (Basel, Switzerland)*, vol. *17*, no. 4, pp. 853, 2017.

[35] A. Mogelmose, M. M. Trivedi, and T. B. Moeslund, "Vision based traffic sign detection and analysis for intelligent driver assistance systems: perspectives and survey," *IEEE Transactions on Intelligent Transportation Systems*, vol. *13*, no. 4, pp. 1484–1497, 2012.

[36] O. E. Johnson, and A. M. Adebayo, "Effect of safety education on knowledge of and compliance with road safety signs among commercial motorcyclists in Uyo, Southern Nigeria," *Ghana Medical Journal*, vol. *45*, no. 3, pp. 89–96, 2011.

[37] J. Stallkamp, M. Schlipsing, J. Salmen, and C. Igel, "Man vs. computer: benchmarking machine learning algorithms for traffic sign recognition," *Neural Networks*, vol. *32*, pp. 323–332, 2012.

[38] Y. Kim, H. Hwang, and J. Shin, "Robust object detection under harsh autonomous driving environments," *IET Image Processing*, vol. *16*, pp. 958–971, 2021.

[39] T. Li, W. Jiao, L.-N. Wang, and G. Zhong, "Automatic DenseNet sparsification," *IEEE Access*, vol. *8*, pp. 62561–62571, 2020.

[40] T.-Y. Lin, M. Maire, S. Belongie, J. Hays, P. Perona, D. Ramanan, P. Dollár, and C. L. Zitnick, "Microsoft COCO: common objects in context," *Lecture Notes in Computer Science, Springer International Publishing*, pp. 740–755, 2014.

[41] H. C. Fisher Yu, X. Wang, W. Xian, Y. Chen, F. Liu, V. Madhavan, and T. Darrell, "BDD100K: a diverse driving dataset for heterogeneous multitask learning," *Proceedings of IEEE Conference on Computer Vision and Pattern Recognition (CVPR)*, 2020, pp. 2633–2642.

[42] Y. Lv, Y. Duan, W. Kang, Z. Li, and F.-Y. Wang, "Traffic flow prediction with big data: a deep learning approach," *IEEE Transactions on Intelligent Transportation Systems*, vol. *16*, no. 2, pp. 865–873, 2015.

[43] H. Hashemi, and K. Abdelghany, "End to end deep learning methodology for real time traffic network management: deep learning for real-time traffic network management," *Wiley on Computer-Aided Civil And Infrastructure Engineering*, vol. *33*, no. 10, pp. 849–863, 2018.

[44] W. Chen, J. An, R. Li, L. Fu, G. Xie, M. Z. A. Bhuiyan, and K. Li, "A novel fuzzy deep-learning approach to traffic flow prediction with uncertain spatial–temporal data features," *Elsevier on Future Generation Computer Systems*, vol. *89*, pp. 78–88, 2018.

[45] D. Zhang, and M. R. Kabuka, "Combining weather condition data to predict traffic flow: a GRU-based deep learning approach," *IET Intelligent Transport Systems*, vol. *12*, no. 7, pp. 578–585, 2018.

[46] *Caltrans Performance Measurement System (PeMS)*, California Department of Transportation, 2011. Available: https://pems.dot.ca.gov/ [Accessed Jan 2021].

[47] *Weather Radar*, National Oceanic and Atmospheric Administration, 2018. Available: https://www.noaa.gov/ [Accessed Jan 2021].

[48] M. S. Mekala, G. Dhiman, R. Patan, S. Kallam, K. Ramana, K. Yadav, and A. O. Alharbi, "Deep learning influenced joint vehicle to infrastructure and vehicle to vehicle communication approach for internet of vehicles," *Wiley on Expert Systems*, vol. *39*, p. e12815, 2021.

[49] Z. Ning, K. Zhang, X. Wang, M. S. Obaidat, L. Guo, X. Hu, B. Hu, Y. Guo, B. Sadoun, and R. Y. K. Kwok, "Joint computing and caching in 5G envisioned internet of vehicles: a deep reinforcement learning based traffic control system," *IEEE Transactions on Intelligent Transportation Systems*, vol. *22*, no. 8, pp. 5201–5212, 2021.

[50] T. Abbas, K. Sjöberg, J. Karedal, and F. Tufvesson, "A measurement based shadow fading model for vehicle to vehicle network simulations," *International Journal of Antennas and Propagation*, vol. 2015, pp. 1–12, *2015*.

[51] Q. I. Ali, "Event driven duty cycling: an efficient power management scheme for a solar-energy harvested road side unit," *IET Electrical Systems in Transportation*, vol. *6*, no. 3, pp. 222–235, 2016.

[52] R. S. Sutton, and A. G. Barto, "3. reinforcement learning problem," *Reinforcement Learning: An Introduction*, Cambridge, MA: MIT Press, 1998.

[53] F. Huang, J. Xu, and J. Weng, "Multi task travel route planning with a flexible deep learning framework," *IEEE Transactions on Intelligent Transportation Systems*, vol. *22*, no. 7, pp. 3907–3918, 2021.

[54] Y. Han, and A. Yilmaz, "Dynamic routing for navigation in changing unknown maps using deep reinforcement learning," *ISPRS Annals of The Photogrammetry, Remote Sensing and Spatial Information Sciences*, pp. 145–150, 2021, doi: 10.5194/isprs-annals-V-1-2021-145-2021.

[55] I. R. Brilhante, J. A. Macedo, F. M. Nardini, R. Perego, and C. Renso, "On planning sightseeing tours with TripBuilder," *Elsevier on Information Processing & Management*, vol. *51*, no. 2, pp. 1–15, 2015.

[56] B. Alves Beirigo, and A. Gustavo dos Santos, "A parallel heuristic for the travel planning problem," *International Conference on Intelligent Systems Design and Applications (ISDA)*, 2015, pp. 283–288.

[57] L. Chen, L. Zhu, J. Cao, G. Zhu, and Y. Ge, "Travel recommendation via fusing multi auxiliary information into matrix factorization," *ACM Transactions on Intelligent Systems and Technology*, vol. *11*, no. 2, pp. 1–24, 2020.

[58] S. Jiang, X. Qian, T. Mei, and Y. Fu, "Personalized travel sequence recommendation on multi source big social media," *IEEE Transactions on Big Data*, vol. *2*, no. 1, pp. 43–56, 2016.

[59] Z. Yu, H. Xu, Z. Yang, and B. Guo, "Personalized travel package with multi point of interest recommendation based on crowdsourced user footprints," *IEEE Transactions on Human-Machine Systems*, vol. *46*, no. 1, pp. 151–158, 2016.

[60] C. Zhang, H. Liang, K. Wang, and J. Sun, "Personalized trip recommendation with POI availability and uncertain traveling time," *Conference on Information and Knowledge Management*, pp. 911–920, 2015.

[61] K. H. Lim, J. Chan, C. Leckie, and S. Karunasekera, "Personalized trip recommendation for tourists based on user interests, points of interest visit durations and visit recency," *Knowledge and Information Systems*, vol. *54*, no. 2, pp. 375–406, 2017.

[62] S. Liu, H. Jiang, S. Chen, J. Ye, R. He, and Z. Sun, "Integrating Dijkstra's algorithm into deep inverse reinforcement learning for food delivery route planning," *Transportation Research. Part E, Logistics and Transportation Review*, vol. *142*, p. 102070, 2020.

[63] M. Wulfmeier, P. Ondruska, and I. Posner, "Maximum entropy deep inverse reinforcement learning." *arXiv: Learning*, 2015.

[64] Z. Xiong, H. Sheng, W. Rong, and D. E. Cooper, "Intelligent transportation systems for smart cities: a progress review," *Science China Information Sciences*, vol. *55*, no. 12, pp. 2908–2914, 2012.

[65] V. Nazário Coelho, I. Machado Coelho, T. A. Oliveira, and L. S. Ochi, *Smart and Digital Cities From Computational Intelligence to Applied Social Sciences*, 1st ed. 2019. ed., Cham: Springer International Publishing, 2019.

[66] M. J. Thornbush, and O. Golubchikov, "Introduction," *Sustainable Urbanism in Digital Transitions: From Low Carbon to Smart Sustainable Cities*, Cham: Springer International Publishing AG, 2019.

[67] H. B. Aladi, S. Saha, A. Kurian, and A. Basu, "Predictive analytics for safer smart cities," *2017 International Conference On Smart Technologies For Smart Nation (SmartTechCon)*, pp. 1010–1017, 2017.

[68] F. Arena, and D. Ticali, "The development of autonomous driving vehicles in tomorrow's smart cities mobility," *AIP Conference Proceedings*, vol. *2040*, no. 1, p. 140007. AIP Publishing LLC, 2018.

[69] A. Boukerche, and M. Sha, "Design guidelines on deep learning based pedestrian detection methods for supporting autonomous vehicles," *ACM Computing Surveys*, vol. *54*, no. 6, pp. 1–36, 2021.

[70] B. Rinner, and T. Winkler, "Privacy-protecting smart cameras," *International Conference on Distributed Smart Cameras*, pp. 1–5, 2014.

Deep learning for driver drowsiness classification for a safe vehicle application

2

Sadegh Arefnezhad and Arno Eichberger

Institute of Automotive Engineering, Graz University of Technology, Graz, Austria

Contents

DOI: 10.1201/9781003190691-3

2.1 INTRODUCTION

2.1.1 Importance of drowsiness detection

Drowsiness is an intermediate condition that fluctuates between alertness and sleep. It reduces the consciousness level and prevents a person from responding quickly to important road safety issues [1]. The American Automobile Association (AAA) has reported that about 24% of 2,714 drivers that participated in a survey admitted to being extremely drowsy while driving, at least once in the previous month [2]. In 2017, the National Highway Transportation Safety Administration (NHTSA) also reported 795 fatalities in traffic accidents that involve drowsy driving [3]. It has also been reported that drowsy driving has caused about 2.5% of fatal accidents from 2011 through 2015 in the USA, and it is estimated to have produce an annual economic loss of USD230 billion [4]. Klauer et al. have found in their study that drowsy drivers contributed to 22–24% of crashes or near-crash risks [5]. Similarly, the German Road Safety Council (DVR) has reported that drowsy drivers have caused one in every four fatal highway crashes [6]. In a study carried out in 2015, it was reported that the average prevalence of falling asleep while driving in the previous two years was about 17% in 19 European countries [7]. The results of these studies emphasize the importance of detecting drowsiness early enough to initiate preventive measures. Drowsiness detection systems are intended to warn the drivers before an upcoming level of drowsiness gets critical to prevent drowsiness-related accidents. The difficulty of classifying driver vigilance in an *accurate*, *robust*, and *predictive* manner is a delicate task, which is also manifested in the highly diverging numbers in accident statistics, as presented above. *Accuracy* here means that the amount of false-positive classifications of driver drowsiness is below an acceptable threshold. *Robustness* means that, even in the case of loss of signals that are used to monitor driver vigilance, the system should still be able to classify drowsiness, albeit at a reduced level of accuracy. *Prediction* means that the classification method can differentiate a reasonable number of drowsiness levels to detect driver inattentiveness early enough to carry out countermeasures.

2.1.2 Application in future automated vehicles

Intelligent systems that automate motor vehicle driving on the roads are being introduced to the market step-wise. The Society of Automotive Engineers (SAE) issued a standard defining six levels, ranging from no driving automation (level 0) to full driving automation (level 5) [8]. While the SAE levels 0–2 require that an attentive driver carries out (or at least monitors) the dynamic driving task, in the SAE level 3 of automated driving, drivers will be allowed to do a secondary task, allowing the system to control the vehicle under limited conditions, e.g., on a motorway. However, the automation system has to hand back the vehicle guidance to the driver whenever it can no longer control the state of the vehicle. However, the handover of vehicle control to a drowsy driver is not regarded as safe. Therefore, the system should be informed about the state of the driver.

Recent studies have also shown that automated driving can lead to a higher level of drowsiness in drivers. For example, Ahlström et al. [9] studied the influence of level 2 of automated driving (partial automation) on the driver's vigilance state. They developed a test procedure that includes four different conditions: daytime-manual, daytime-automated, night-time-manual, and night-time-automated. Various indicators of drowsiness were measured in that study during driving tests, including heart rate and blink duration. Results showed that drivers experienced higher drowsiness levels in the night-time-automated driving in comparison to other driving conditions. However, according to the results, automated driving had no significant influence on the drowsiness level in the daytime tests when the drivers were alert and had a full night's sleep before starting the test. In another study, Schömig et al. [10] evaluated the influence of performing a secondary task during automated driving on the drowsiness level. Their test procedure included three different driving tests: (1) manual driving (no automation), (2) automated driving (no need for any input from the driver), and (3) automated driving while performing a secondary task (answering some quiz questions).

The results show that in the first two driving tests (manual driving and automated driving without secondary task) drowsiness becomes gradually higher, but in the third test (automated driving with the secondary task) the drowsiness level is approximately constant. These results highlight the influence of performing a secondary task during automated driving in order to prevent drowsiness in drivers.

Automation levels according to SAE Level 3 had been prevented from market introduction until 2021 because of a lack of certification standards. Those standards are needed to homologate vehicles that feature the delicate take-over procedure between automated and human vehicle control in certain circumstances. Therefore, driver monitoring was legally required for the first time from 2021 onwards in the UN regulation 157 for Automated Lane Keeping Systems (ALKS),[1] requiring an observation of the availability of the driver for take-over scenarios. The availability of the driver is monitored by confirming two out of three attentiveness criteria: (a) driver gaze direction is confirmed as primarily looking at the road ahead; (b) driver gaze direction is being confirmed as looking at the rear-view mirrors; or (c) driver head movement is confirmed as primarily directed towards the driving task. Drowsiness is not explicitly mentioned in this standard, again as a consequence of the challenging task to classify driver attentiveness in an *accurate*, *robust*, and *predictive* manner.

Legal standards require a minimum set of requirements for vehicle certification. The vehicle manufacturer, depending on its philosophy, tends to over-fulfill certification standards with in-house targets, and accurate, robust, and predictive driver monitoring will be one important aspect of this.

2.2 DRIVER DROWSINESS DETECTION METHODS

2.2.1 Subjective measures

Subjective measures determine the drowsiness using questionnaires that drivers fill in to report their levels of vigilance. One of the most commonly used subjective scales for drowsiness is the Karolinska Sleepiness Scale (KSS) [11], which is a nine-point scale that each scale describes the driver's vigilance. Table 2.1 presents the scales of KSS. As this table shows, this scale varies from extremely alert to very sleepy conditions. The KSS was validated using objective scores derived by brain activities in [12]. Results show that sleepiness can be measured using the relationship between brain signals and the KSS. The results of [13] also show that median reaction time and alpha and theta power densities of brain signals are highly correlated with the KSS. Another subjective measure that is also used in the literature is the Stanford Sleepiness Scale (SSS) [14]. This measure has seven different scales, which are presented in Table 2.2. As this table presents, this scale changes from feeling active to no longer fighting sleep. Arnedt et al. [15] studied the relationship between different scales of the SSS and the lateral position and speed variation of the car.

TABLE 2.1 Karolinska Sleepiness Scale (KSS) [11]

RATING	VERBAL DESCRIPTION
1	Extremely alert
2	Very alert
3	Alert
4	Fairly alert
5	Neither alert nor sleepy
6	Some signs of sleepiness
7	Sleepy, but no effort to keep alert
8	Sleepy, some effort to keep alert
9	Very sleepy, great effort to keep alert, fighting sleep

TABLE 2.2 Stanford Sleepiness Scale (SSS) [14]

RATING	VERBAL DESCRIPTION
1	Feeling active, vital, alert, or wide awake
2	Functioning at high levels, but not at peak; able to concentrate
3	Awake, but relaxed; responsive but not fully alert
4	Somewhat foggy, let down
5	Foggy; losing interest in remaining awake; slowed down
6	Sleepy, woozy, fighting sleep; prefer to lie down
7	No longer fighting sleep, sleep onset soon; having dream-like thoughts

These subjective sleepiness measures have been widely used in the literature as ground truth for different levels of the driver's vigilance. For example, Meng et al. [16] and Friedrichs and Yang [17], Wang and Xu [18], used the KSS to define the ground truth for three levels of drowsiness: (1) Alert: $1 \leq KSS \leq 6$, (2) Moderately drowsy: $KSS = 7$, and (3) Extremely drowsy: $KSS = 8–9$.

2.2.2 Objective measures

2.2.2.1 Input sources for driver drowsiness detection

Input sources that have been exploited to design a driver drowsiness detection system can be categorized into three main groups: 1) vehicle-based data, 2) facial-based data, and 3) biosignals. The following sections will explain each of these data sources and some of the corresponding recent studies to develop a driver drowsiness detection system.

- Facial-based data: Three main facial-based sources that are widely used in the literature for driver drowsiness detection are eyelid opening value, pupil diameter, and mouth state [19–23]. This type of data is collected using an installed camera inside the cabin and different image processing techniques were applied to the captured images for detecting the driver's eyes and mouth [24]. This type of data can be collected non-invasively without attaching any sensor to the driver's body. However, the quality of these data depends on the light and weather conditions [25, 26]. Previous studies also show that wearing sunglasses can decrease the accuracy of the systems designed based on the eye's status [26].
- Biosignals: Biosignals that have been commonly employed for driver drowsiness detection include electroencephalography (EEG) [27–31], electrocardiography (ECG) [32–36], electromyography (EMG) [37–39], electrooculography (EOG) [40–42], electrodermal (EDA) [43], and respiration [44–47]. These types of data can obtain a better accuracy for the detection of drowsiness onset than other resources. Therefore, preventive measures and warnings can be activated in a timely manner before showing extreme signs of drowsiness [48]. However, biosignals are usually contaminated by different noise sources such as motion artifacts from the driver's body and device noise [49]. Furthermore, biosignals are collected by connecting some electrodes to the driver's body. Some researchers proposed non-intrusive data collection methods but their accuracy is relatively low [50].
- Vehicle-based data: Researchers have utilized vehicle-based data to design non-invasive driver drowsiness detection systems. The most frequently exploited vehicle-based data for this goal include lateral and longitudinal accelerations, steering wheel angle, steering wheel angular velocity, yaw angle, lateral deviation from road center-line, and speed [51–56]. These types of data can be collected using installed sensors such as accelerometers, gyroscopes, and lane-detection

cameras [57]. Vehicle-based data can only be used to monitor the driver's drowsiness in manual driving since the drivers insert no input into the vehicle in the automated mode [58, 59]. The accuracy of the systems based on vehicle-based data also depends on the driving skills and road conditions [60].

The next subsection explains the recent deep learning methods which have been employed for driver drowsiness detection based on different data source types.

2.2.3 Deep learning methods

- Deep learning methods applied to the facial-based data:

To build a driver drowsiness detection system using facial-based data, Convolutional Neural Networks (CNN) have been widely used in the literature to detect the driver's face and eyes. For example, Zhao et al. [61] employed a multi-task cascaded convolutional network (MTCNN) [62] for face detection. This network returns the region of interest (ROI) that includes the position of the nose, left and right corners of the mouth, and left and right eyes in the driver's facial bounding box. Figure 2.1 shows the performance of the MTCNN for face and ROI detection. After ROI detection, it was used to calculate two drowsiness indicators: (1) PERcentage of eyelid CLOSure (PERCLOS) and (2) Mouth Opening Degree (MOP). PERCLOS presents the proportion of time that eyes are more than 80% closed in a specific interval (e.g. 1 minute) [63–65]. Similar to PERCLOS, MOP also shows the percentage of mouth closure in a specific interval [66]. These indicators were used as input to a classifier to detect open/close eye and open/close mouth.

Transfer learning has also been commonly used in vision-based methods [67]. In transfer learning, a previously trained neural network is fine-tuned to be used for solving a similar problem. This technique reduces the amount of data that is needed to train the deep neural network for obtaining satisfying performance with regard to the new problem [67]. Nojiri et al. [21] employed the AlexNet [68] and GoogLeNet [69] to apply the transfer learning for recognition of eye status in the presence of eye makeup. The images of right and left eyes in open and closed states were inserted into the deep networks as inputs for eye status recognition. Results showed that Support Vector Machine (SVM) trained by Histogram of Oriented Gradient (HOG)-based features outperformed both AlexNet and GoogLeNet in terms of misrecognition.

Naurois et al. [70] proposed a method based on different types of data including physiological measurements (such as heart rate and respiration rate), vehicle-based data (such as steering angle and lateral distance from road centerline), and facial-based data (such as head positions and blink duration). Moreover, participant information (such as sleep quality, driving frequency, and the number of coffee cups per day), and driving time (the duration of the driving test from the beginning of the session in a minute) were also recorded before and during the driving tests. The Observer Rating of Drowsiness (ORD) was utilized based on the recorded videos of driving tests as the ground truth for two levels of driver's vigilance: alert and drowsy. An Artificial Neural Network (ANN) with two hidden layers trained by the Levenberg–Marquardt algorithm was employed for drowsiness classification. Different combinations of

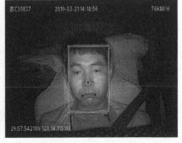

FIGURE 2.1   Face and ROI detection using MTCNN [61][2].

the collected data were used as inputs to the ANN. Results showed that using the collected data together with Participant Information (PI) and Driving Time (DT) improved the classification accuracy of the ANN. For example, the Mean Square Error (MSE) of the ANN trained with vehicle-based data was reduced from 0.69 to 0.23 when the same data were used as inputs together with both PI and DT. The smallest MSE of 0.22 was achieved when facial-based data together with PI and DT were used as inputs. According to the results, the MSE was higher when all collected data together with PI and DT were inputs to the ANN.

The combination of CNN and Bidirectional Long-Short Term Memory (BiLSTM) networks was proposed in [22] for drowsiness detection using recorded videos during driving tests where CNN was used to extract the eye-based features and BiLSTM classified the eyes' status in two different classes: open or closed. The InceptionV3 [71] was used as the CNN feature extractor from eyes' images. Results showed that using the BiLSTM as the eyes' status classifier provided a higher accuracy (94%) than using only the Softmax Layer of InceptionV3 without BiLSTM (85%).

Dua et al. [72] developed an ensemble method based on deep CNNs for the classification of driver's facial movements into four classes: non-drowsiness, drowsiness with eye blinking, yawning, and nodding. Their method consists of four various deep CNNs: AlexNet [68], VGG-FaceNet [73], FlowImageNet [74], and ResNet [75]. Hand gestures, head movements, and facial expressions were used as inputs to these networks. The output of every network was used as inputs to a Softmax classifier to classify the driver drowsiness. Results showed that this method achieved a classification accuracy of about 85%. Phan et al. [76] developed two methods based on the processing of the drivers' face images. In the first method, two blink and yawn features were extracted from images using CNN, and the drowsiness labels (drowsy or awake) were defined based on the predefined thresholds for every feature. In the second approach, two networks of ResNet-50V2 [77] and MobileNet-v2 [78] were used to extract features from input images by taking the advantage of transfer learning. Results showed that the first method achieved the classification accuracy of 83% for two classes of alert and drowsy. However, using the second method and applying the transfer learning by ResNet-50V2 and MobileNet-v2 provided the accuracy of 96.1% and 97.3%, respectively.

One of the main problems with facial-based systems is their low performance in face detection when the driver wears glasses or sunglasses. To remove this drawback, Huynh et al. [79] proposed a semi-supervised classification method based on 3d CNN. In their method, features of input images of the drivers' faces were extracted by applying a 3d CNN with 20 input frames of 64×64 pixels in every iteration. The extracted features were used as inputs to the classifier. Gradient boosting in the Xgboost library [80] was used as the classifier that provides two output classes: alert and drowsy. Results showed that this method achieved the drowsiness classification accuracies of 89.12%, 91.36%, and 84.16% for barefaced, glasses, and sunglasses situations, respectively.

2.2.3.1 Deep learning methods applied to the biosignals

Three main biosignals that have been widely used in the literature for driver drowsiness detection are electrocardiogram (ECG), electrooculogram (EOG), and electroencephalogram (EEG) signals. A combination of CNN and Bidirectional Long-Short-Term-Memory (Bi-LSTM) networks was applied in [81] to EEG signals. In that study, drowsiness was classified into five different levels. These levels were defined using the KSS values reported by participants. The EEG signals were first preprocessed using band-pass filtering and Independent Component Analysis (ICA) for artifact rejection. Then, a CNN was employed to extract the spatial features from segmented EEG signals. Finally, a Bi-LSTM network was used to consider the characteristic of long-term dependencies of extracted features using CNN. A Softmax layer was also utilized as the last layer of the network as a classification layer. Results showed that this method achieved an accuracy of 69% for five levels and 87% for two levels of drowsiness. Figure 2.2 shows the architecture of the proposed network in [81] for drowsiness classification.

Chaabene et al [82] also developed a method using CNN applied to EEG data for drowsiness detection. An Infinite Impulse Response (IIR) filter was utilized for pre-processing of the EEG data to remove the eye blinks and muscle activities. Subsequently, the filtered EEG data was transformed to the frequency domain using Fast Fourier Transform (FFT). In that study, the Alpha-Theta waves (5–9 Hz) of two

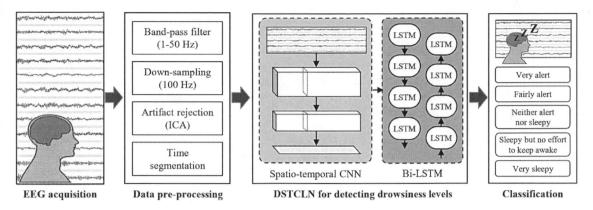

FIGURE 2.2 Flowchart of the proposed method in [81] for drowsiness classification[3].

occipital (O1 and O2) electrodes and two temporal (T7 and T8) electrodes were used as inputs to a CNN that included a dropout layer to reduce the risk of over-fitting. Data augmentation techniques were also applied to the training set of input data to generate more samples and improve the training progress. The results showed that this approach obtained an accuracy of about 90% for binary classification.

Hajinoroozi et al. [83] used the combination of the Restricted Boltzmann Machine (RBM) and CNN (RCNN) to detect the driver's drowsiness using EEG channels. In that study, the reaction time of the driver to steer the car back to the right lane after preplanned lateral deviations during a simulator-based test. If the reaction time is less than 0.7 sec, the driver was considered alert. The driver was also considered drowsy if the reaction time was larger than 2.1 sec. Thirty EEG channels were collected from every driver and an RCNN was trained for every channel. Finally, a bagging classifier was used to classify the drowsiness using extracted features using RCNNs. Results showed that this method outperformed the conventional CNN and deep fully connected networks as well as traditional classifiers (support vector machine and lane discriminative analysis). Based on the results, this method obtained an accuracy of about 82% for binary drowsiness detection.

Stacked auto-encoders with Softmax layers were used in [84] to design a binary classifier for drowsiness. In that study, only two EEG electrodes of O1 and O2 were collected from 62 subjects. The Discrete Cosine Transform (DCT) was first employed to transform the EEG signals to the frequency domain. The DCT outputs were inserted into the first auto-encoder as inputs. The first auto-encoder was trained to reproduce the same DCT specifications. Then, the output of the first encoder was removed to obtain its "code" features. These features were then used as the inputs to the second auto-encoder to obtain the more abstract features of the DCT data. Finally, the whole network was fine-tuned using the back-propagation technique and the results were inserted into a Softmax layer that reported the driver vigilance level as a binary output. Figure 2.3 shows the flowchart of the proposed method in [84].

Ma et al. [31] developed a method using the combination of Principal Component Analysis (PCA) and deep learning for drowsiness detection using EEG channels. In that study, the EEG data were first pre-processed by applying the downsampling from 500 Hz to 200 Hz and band-pass filtering from 0.1 to 45

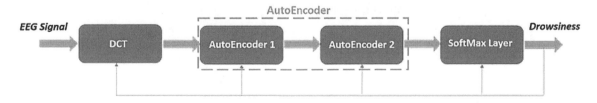

FIGURE 2.3 The proposed method in [84] for drowsiness detection using EEG channels applying stacked auto-encoders[4].

Hz. This band-pass filtering removed the slow drift, high-frequency noise, and powerline interference. To reduce the computation complexity to train the deep network, PCA was applied for extracting the important features from EEG data and reducing its dimension. The outputs of PCA were used as inputs to the PCANet model. In the PCANet, first, a sliding window is used to centralize the data covered by the window by reducing the mean of the corresponding EEG data. The output of this centralization is then used to apply the PCA filtration on every input matrix. Finally, Support Vector Machine (SVM) and K-Nearest Neighbors (KNN) were employed as two widely applied classifiers to evaluate the extracted features from PCANet for driver drowsiness classification. Results showed that this methodology achieved a classification accuracy of about 95% using SVM and 89% for KNN. Figure 2.4 shows the flowchart of the proposed method in [31].

A combination of sparse-deep belief networks (sparse-DBN) and autoregressive modeling were used in [85] to detect driver drowsiness using the EEG data collected from 43 participants. In that study, autoregressive modeling was used to extract features from the EEG data. Extracted features were inserted as inputs to a sparse-DBN which was trained in the greedy layer-wise manner. Two Restricted Boltzmann Machines (RBM) were used in the structure of the sparse-DBN. The first RBM was trained in an unsupervised way to produce a generative model while the second RBM was used as a supervised classifier. After pre-training of each RBM, the whole model was fine-tuned by the backpropagation method. Results showed that this method classified the driver's vigilance into two classes of fatigue and alert with an accuracy of about 93%.

Gao et al. [86] proposed a combination of the multiplex recurrent network and CNN and applied it to 30 EEG signals for drowsiness classification. In that study, a combination of facial-based observations and reported KSS values were used to define the ground truth of drowsiness. The data were first downsampled from 1000 to 200 Hz and filtered by a band-pass filter from 1 to 50 Hz. The ICA was also used in this step to remove the movement artifacts from EEG data. After the pre-processing step, the recurrence network of each channel was reconstructed separately. In the recurrence network, every data point is considered as a node and the two nodes are connected if they are closer than a proximity threshold to each other. The mutual information of every two layers of the recurrence network was then computed to construct the

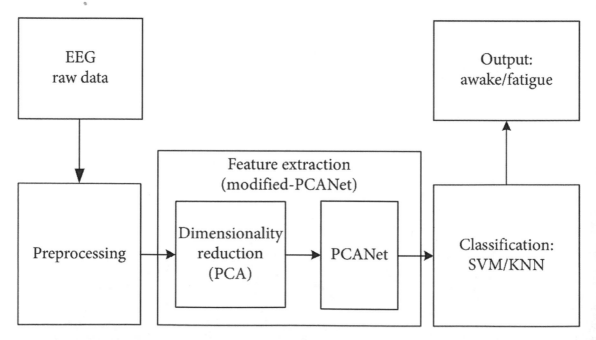

FIGURE 2.4 The proposed method in [31] for drowsiness classification uses the combination of neural network and PCA technique[5].

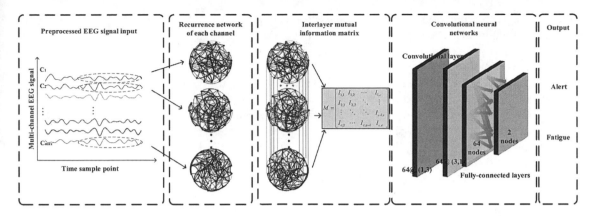

FIGURE 2.5 Proposed method in [86] to classify the drowsiness using EEG data applying a combination recurrence network with CNN[6].

mutual information matrix with the size 30×30. This matrix was used as input to a CNN instead of the original EEG data that can decrease the training time of the CNN and improve its performance. This CNN has a Softmax layer as its last layer that outputted the two states of the driver: alert and fatigue. Figure 2.5 shows the flowchart of the method proposed in [86]. The results showed that this method classified the drowsiness with an average accuracy of about 93%.

Reprinted from [86], with the permission of AIP Publishing, License number: 5411930966185.

Ren et al. [28] proposed a methodology based on Radial Basis Function (RBF) applied to the 32 channels of EEG data with a sampling frequency of 500 Hz. In that study, a fourth-order Butterworth band-pass filtering (1–45 Hz) was used to remove the high-frequency noise and slow drifts. To extract features from pre-processed EEG data, PCA was employed for dimensionality reduction. The first 10 principal components of every segmented EEG data were selected as features. Using this method, every segment of EEG data with the size of 32×2000 was transformed to a matrix with the size of 32×10. These matrices were inserted as inputs to the RBF network that was used as a classifier. The results showed that this approach achieved an average accuracy of about 93% for binary classification of drowsiness.

Similar approaches were also used to estimate the drivers' cognitive workload. For example, Tjolleng et al. [87] developed a method based on ECG signals using neural networks to classify the driver's workload into three different levels: low, medium, and high. In that study, three time-domain features (mean of beat-to-beat intervals, standard deviation of beat-to-beat intervals, and root mean squared of adjacent beat-to-beat intervals) together with three frequency-domain features (power in low frequency, power in high frequency, and ratio of these two powers of beat-to-beat intervals) were extracted from ECG data. Two significant features that provided the most discriminative powers for workload classes were selected for every driver among all features. The selected features were normalized using median values for every driver to mitigate the influence of individual differences between participants on the system's performance. The selected features were utilized as inputs to an ANN model that was constructed using one input layer with 2 nodes, one hidden layer with 15 nodes and sigmoid activation function, and one output layer with 3 nodes that returned three levels of workload. Results showed that the proposed method achieved the training and test accuracies of about 95% and 82%, respectively.

Recurrence plots (RP) of ECG signals were used in [88] to design a wearable drowsiness detection system for drivers. In that study, the heartbeats were first detected from ECG data. The beat-to-beat values which were too different from their 10 data points in their neighborhood were replaced with the average of that points. Three different RPs of beat-to-beat intervals were produced using detected heartbeats, including Bin-PR, Cont-PR, and ReLU-PR. The Bin-RP was generated by binarization of the difference between two beat-to-beat intervals by setting a pre-specified threshold. If the difference was less than the threshold the corresponding pixel in the RP was set to 1; otherwise it was set to 0. The Cont-PR is similar to the Bin-RP without applying the threshold. The corresponding pixel in the Cont-RP was equal to the exact value of the difference between every two data points. The ReLU-PR was produced by applying the ReLU function to the Cont-PR image. By applying the ReLU, the corresponding pixel in the ReLU-PR was set to zero if the difference was smaller than the threshold, otherwise, it would be equal to the exact difference value. Figure 2.6 shows an example for each type of RPs. Three types of RP were separately used as inputs to the VGG19 network where the parameters of the initial three convolution blocks were frozen and the last two blocks were trained using produced RPs. Figure 2.7 shows the structure of the used network in [88]. According to the results, the proposed method ReLU-RP provided better accuracy than two other RPs that was about 70%. Results also presented that this method outperformed the conventional classifiers such as KNN and SVM which were trained using extracted features from ECG signals.

Siddiqui et al. [89] developed a method for drowsiness detection based on respiration rate collected using impulsive radio ultra-wideband (IR-UWB) radar. This radar system measured the chest movements of the 40 drivers. The collected respiration rate per minute data was used as input in different machine learning methods such as SVM, logistic regression (LR), and Multilayer Perceptron (MLP). Results showed that the SVM outperformed the other classification methods with an accuracy of about 87%.

Wavelet scalogram images of the ECG data were used as inputs to a deep CNN in [90] to classify the drowsiness into three classes: alert, moderately drowsy, and extremely drowsy. To improve the performance of the deep CNN, the Bayesian optimization method was applied to estimate the optimal hyperparameters of the network (e.g. learning rate and dropout probability). Since the database was imbalanced, a weighted Softmax layer was used as the last layer of the network. Wavelet scalogram images were also produced using the Morse wavelet [91]. Drowsiness classification was performed for the two driving modes of automated and manual. Results showed that this approach received a balanced accuracy of about 77% and 79% for manual and automated modes, respectively. The performance of this method was compared with the random forest and KNN classifiers trained by extracted features from HRV

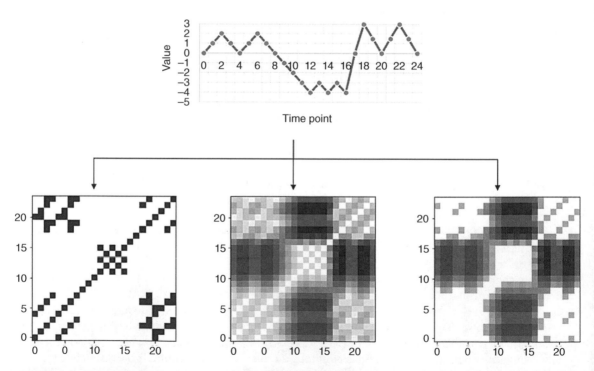

FIGURE 2.6   Examples of recurrence plot (RP) extracted from ECG signals for driver drowsiness detection [88]: Bin-RP (left), Cont-RP (middle), and ReLU-RP (right)[7].

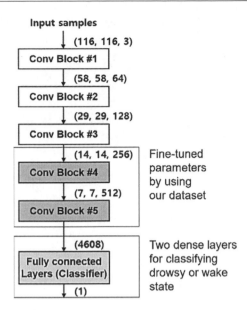

Input samples

Conv Block #1 — (116, 116, 3)

(58, 58, 64)

Conv Block #2

(29, 29, 128)

Conv Block #3

(14, 14, 256) — Fine-tuned parameters by using our dataset

Conv Block #4

(7, 7, 512)

Conv Block #5

(4608) — Two dense layers for classifying drowsy or wake state

Fully connected Layers (Classifier)

(1)

FIGURE 2.7 The architecture of the fine-tuned VGG19 model used in [88] to classify the driver drowsiness using the recurrence plot of the ECG data[8].

data. Results showed that the best accuracy obtained by these traditional classifiers was 62% and 64% for manual and automated modes, respectively. Therefore, the deep learning approach can significantly outperform the classical method based on the HRV data for the classification of driver drowsiness. The same deep learning approach has been applied to the eyelid data in [92] for manual and automated driving. Results showed that the balanced accuracy of classification is 80.5% and 79.8% for the manual and automated modes when only eyelid data were used for classification. A soft ensemble method was also used in [92] to fuse the data of the two different systems designed based on ECG and eyelid data. Results showed that this ensemble method can outperform both of the system that use only one input source. The balanced accuracy of the ensemble classifier was 81.1% and 80.2% for manual and automated modes, respectively.

2.3 COMPARISON OF METHODS

Different data sources have been used by researchers to detect or classify drowsiness levels in drivers. Each one of these data sources has its own advantages and disadvantages over other sources. Biosignals usually are more accurate than other data to detect the early stages of drowsiness in drivers. However, new wearable or contactless devices need more development to increase the popularity of drowsiness detection using biosignals such ECG and EEG in drivers. Vehicle-based systems are non-invasive for drivers and data can be collected using implemented sensors on the car such as GPS, camera, and Inertial Measurement Units (IMU). However, this type of data cannot be used to detect drowsiness in conditional levels of automated driving (SAE levels 3). On the other hand, facial-based data can be used in image processing methods to detect drowsiness but this type of system usually warns the drive when critical signs of drowsiness such as yawning and head nodding are obvious. Therefore, they can be too slow to warn the driver in a timely manner to prevent accidents. Moreover, the performance of the face detection algorithms can be degraded during the nighttime and when drivers wear glasses, sunglasses, or a scarf.

When biosignals are used as inputs to the drowsiness detection systems, the individual difference between drivers should also be taken into account to design a user-specific system that provides higher accuracy than a general system which is designed for the average range of drivers. This system personalization can be performed using the transfer learning technique which transfers what has been learnt by the general system to the personalized system applying fine-tuning to the parameters of the general system.

Researchers also used the different numbers of classes to classify drivers' drowsiness. Most of the previous works only consider two classes: alert and drowsy. These works usually achieved a higher classification accuracy than other papers that used 3 to 5 classes. However, when only two classes are considered for drowsiness, it is more difficult for the classifier to distinguish the onset of the drowsiness and warn the driver accordingly.

Taking into account that the quantity and quality of the dataset and its preprocessing will have a major influence, we compared the drowsiness detection results of the 44 previous works in Table 2.3. This table provides the used signal, used method, provided accuracy (Acc.), and the number of classes reported in the corresponding paper (No. C.). As this table shows, 35 papers (79.5%) used only two classes, 8 papers (18.2%) used three classes, and only one paper used 5 classes for the driver drowsiness classification. The median of the accuracy for the papers presented in Table 2.3 is about 87% with the first and third quartiles of 78.6% and 93.8%, respectively. The median represents more or less the achievable accuracy when transferring research into application in the vehicle.

TABLE 2.3 Comparison between different drowsiness detection systems proposed in the literature

NO.	REF.	USED SIGNAL	METHOD	ACC. (%)	NO. C.
1	[79]	Facial images	3D CNN	87.5	2
2	[72]	Facial expressions	VGG-facenet	87.1	2
3	[72]	Yawning with hand gestures	Transfer learning: AlexNet, VGG-FaceNet, FlowImageNet and ResNet	87.0	2
4	[22]	Eyelid movements	CNN-BILSTM	94.0	2
5	[76]	Facial expressions	ResNet-50V2	96.1	2
6	[76]	Facial expressions	MobileNet-v2	97.3	2
7	[81]	EEG channels	CNN-BILSTM	69.0	5
8	[81]	EEG channels	CNN-BILSTM	87.0	2
9	[82]	EEG data (O1, O2, T7, and T8)	CNN	90.0	2
10	[83]	EEG; 30 channels	channel-wise CNN (CCNN)	82.0	2
11	[87]	ECG-based time and frequency features	Three-layer feed-forward neural network	82.0	3
12	[88]	ECG	CNN trained by recurrence plots of heart rate variability data	70.0	2
13	[93]	Facial expressions	Modified LeNet	97.0	2
14	[94]	Facial expressions and head position	fusion system for drowsiness detection based on blinking measurement and the 3D head pose estimation	87.0	3
15	[95]	Steering wheel angle	Approximated entropy of steering wheel angle	78.0	2
16	[16]	Steering wheel angle	MultilevelOrdered Logit (MOL)	72.92	3

(Continued)

TABLE 2.3 (Continued)

NO.	REF.	USED SIGNAL	METHOD	ACC. (%)	NO. C.
17	[17]	Steering wheel angle	Shallow neural network	73.5	**3**
18	[54]	Steering wheel angle	Random forest classifier applied to the raw steering data	79.0	2
19	[52]	Steering wheel angle	Meta-ensemble learning for three sets of features	86.1	2
20	[96]	Heart rate variability	Linear Discriminative Analysis (LDA)	65.5	2
21	[96]	Heart rate variability and respiration	LDA	78.5	2
22	[97]	Heart rate variability	Wavelet analysis and SVM classifier	95.0	2
23	[1]	Heart rate variability	SVM classifier	70.0	2
24	[1]	Heart rate variability and One EEG channel	SVM classifier	81.0	2
25	[27]	EEG channels (MIT/BIH Polysomnographic data set)	Hermite decomposition for feature extraction and extreme learning machine as a classifier	91.7	2
26	[28]	EEG channels	Two-Level Learning Hierarchy Radial Basis Function	92.71	2
27	[4]	EEG channels from MIT/BIH Polysomnographic database [98]	LDA for feature selection and shallow neural network as a classifier	85.5	2
28	[99]	EEG channels	Mahalanobis distance from the alert model derived from the distribution of Alpha and Theta bands	76.7	2
29	[39]	EMG and ECG signals	Mahalanobis distance (MD) discriminator	86.7	2
30	[44]	Respiration signal measured by plethysmography belt	Thoracic Effort Derived Drowsiness index (TEDD)	93.4	2
31	[45]	Respiration signal measured by thermal imaging	SVM classifier	90.0	2
32	[20]	Face images from the DROZY database [100]	Eye Aspect Ratio (EAR) inserted to SVM classifier	94.4	2
33	[101]	Facial images (eyelid distances)	Multi-timescale temporal CNN	Timescale; 5sec.: 70.7 10sec.: 85.4 30sec.: 89.9 60sec.: 94.2	2
34	[102]	Eye and mouth features	Combination of CNN and kernelized correlation filters	92	2
35	[103]	Facial expressions	Deep belief network	96.7	**3**
36	[104]	Heart rate variability	Shallow neural network	90.0	2
37	[105]	Facial images	Eye Aspect Ratio (EAR) inserted to SVM classifier	94.8	2

(Continued)

TABLE 2.3 (Continued)

NO.	REF.	USED SIGNAL	METHOD	ACC. (%)	NO. C.
38	[106]	EEG channels from MIT/ BIH Polysomnographic database [98]	Genetic Algorithm based Support Vector Machine (GA-SVM)	89.5	2
39	[107]	R-R intervals derived from ECG data	Combination of AutoEncoders and LSTM	86.0	2
40	[108]	EEG channels from MIT/ BIH Polysomnographic database [98]	Optimized Tunable Q Wavelet Transform	96.1	2
41	[90]	ECG data	CNN trained by Wavelet Scalogram images	78.0	**3**
42	[90]	ECG data	Random forest trained by HRV features	64.0	**3**
43	[56]	Steering wheel data	Adaptive neuro-fuzzy feature selector and SVM classifier	98.1	2
44	[109]	Vehicle data: steering wheel data, lateral deviation, lateral acceleration, yaw rate, and steering angular velocity	Combination of CNN and LSTM (CNN-LSTM)	96.0	**3**

Note: Ref.: Reference; Acc.: Accuracy; No. C.: Number of Classes of Drowsiness.

2.4 SUMMARY AND OUTLOOK

This chapter summarized the state-of-the-art drowsiness detection using deep learning methods. Drowsiness is a deficit in the human driving task that results in a certain amount of road accidents. However, the accident research delivers divergent numbers, because it is obviously difficult for the researcher to rate the individual level of drowsiness and relate it to accident causation.

But challenges in drowsiness classification are also present in research and can be summarized by accuracy, robustness, and prediction. For the sake of accuracy, the classification shall deliver only a small amount of false positives, and it should still work robustly whenever a sensor signal is lost and a reasonable number of different levels of drowsiness should be detected to predict oncoming driver unavailability.

Drowsiness classifications are applied in manual driving, usually delivering a coffee cup warning to communicate oncoming drowsiness to the driver. The classification relies mostly on vehicle-based signals such as the steering angle or the deviation of the car from the middle of the road. Countermeasures in manual driving are related to the responsibility of the driver to take a break or not. Therefore, high potentials for road safety are related to automated driving. In case the driver is no longer needed (SAE J3017 levels 4 and 5), monitoring of the driver is also not needed but will be introduced in a more distant future. However, SAE level 3 systems will be introduced in the near future, and monitoring the driver attentiveness will be a legal requirement. But again, the challenges in classifying drowsiness in an accurate, predictive manner remain high.

Deep learning using different data sources, including vehicle-based data (steering angle, mid-lane deviation, etc.), facial data (eyelid movement), and biosignals (heart rate), offer the highest potential in achieving the aforementioned targets. The chapter summarized the different methods using deep learning and the related results in achieving accuracy robustness and prediction. It also presents the difficulties in obtaining signals from various data sources, pre-processing them, and finding an adequate deep learning method. As Table 2.3 represents, most of the papers only proposed a binary classification using different data sources. Therefore, more research work is needed regarding the detection of the onset of drowsiness in drivers considering a higher number of classes. Moreover, the quality of the recorded data in the real world can have a significant influence on the performance of the system. Therefore, to design a robust driver system, its accuracy should be investigated for different configurations of data sources.

NOTES

1   https://unece.org/transport/documents/2021/03/standards/un-regulation-no-157-automated-lane-keeping-systems-alks

2   Copyright © 2020 Zuopeng Zhao et al. This is an open access article distributed under the Creative Commons Attribution License, which permits unrestricted use, distribution, and reproduction in any medium, provided the original work is properly cited.

3   This is an open access article distributed under the Creative Commons Attribution License which permits unrestricted use, distribution, and reproduction in any medium, provided the original work is properly cited.

4   This is an open access article distributed under the Creative Commons Attribution License which permits unrestricted use, distribution, and reproduction in any medium, provided the original work is properly cited.

5   Copyright © 2019 Yuliang Ma et al. This is an open access article distributed under the Creative Commons Attribution License, which permits unrestricted use, distribution, and reproduction in any medium, provided the original work is properly cited.

6   Reprinted from [86], with the permission of AIP Publishing; License No. 5184880137550.

7   This is an open access article distributed under the Creative Commons Attribution License which permits unrestricted use, distribution, and reproduction in any medium, provided the original work is properly cited.

8   This is an open access article distributed under the Creative Commons Attribution License which permits unrestricted use, distribution, and reproduction in any medium, provided the original work is properly cited.

REFERENCES

[1] M. Awais, N. Badruddin, and M. Drieberg, "A hybrid approach to detect driver drowsiness utilizing physiological signals to improve system performance and wearability," *Sensors*, vol. *17*, no. 9, 2017, doi: 10.3390/s17091991.

[2] AAA Foundation for Traffic Safety, "2019 Traffic Safety Culture Index (Technical Report), June 2020," Washington, DC, Jun. 2020. [Online]. Accessed: January 2021. Available: https://aaafoundation.org/2019-traffic-safety-culture-index/

[3] National Highway Traffic Safety Administration, "Traffic safety facts: 2017 fatal motor vehicle crashes: overview," NHTSA's National Center for Statistics and Analysis, 1200 New Jersey Avenue SE., Washington DOT HS 812 603, Oct. 2018. Accessed: April 14 2021. [Online]. Available: https://crashstats.nhtsa.dot.gov/Api/Public/ViewPublication/812603

[4] A. G. Correa, L. Orosco, and E. Laciar, "Automatic detection of drowsiness in EEG records based on multimodal analysis," *Medical Engineering & Physics*, vol. *36*, no. 2, pp. 244–249, 2014, doi: 10.1016/j.medengphy.2013.07.011.

[5] S. Klauer, V. Neale, T. Dingus, Jeremy Sudweeks, and D. J. Ramsey, "The prevalence of driver fatigue in an urban driving environment: results from the 100-car naturalistic driving study," In *Proceedings of the 2005 International Conference on Fatigue Management in Transportation Operations*. 2005.

[6] Fraunhofer-Gesellschaft, *Eyetracker warns against momentary driver drowsiness - Press Release Oktober 12*, 2010. [Online]. (Accessed: April 14 2021). Available: https://www.fraunhofer.de/en/press/research-news/2010/10/eye-tracker-driver-drowsiness.html

[7] M. Gonçalves et al., "Sleepiness at the wheel across Europe: a survey of 19 countries," *Journal of Sleep Research*, vol. *24*, no. 3, pp. 242–253, 2015, doi: 10.1111/jsr.12267.

[8] T. Inagaki and T. B. Sheridan, "A critique of the SAE conditional driving automation definition, and analyses of options for improvement," *Cognition, Technology & Work*, vol. *21*, no. 4, pp. 569–578, 2019, doi: 10.1007/s10111-018-0471-5.

[9] C. Ahlström, R. Zemblys, H. Jansson, C. Forsberg, J. Karlsson, and A. Anund, "Effects of partially automated driving on the development of driver sleepiness," *Accident; Analysis and Prevention*, vol. *153*, p. 106058, 2021, doi: 10.1016/j.aap.2021.106058.

[10] N. Schömig, V. Hargutt, A. Neukum, I. Petermann-Stock, and I. Othersen, "The interaction between highly automated driving and the development of drowsiness," *Procedia Manufacturing*, vol. *3*, pp. 6652–6659, 2015, doi: 10.1016/j.promfg.2015.11.005.

[11] A. Shahid, K. Wilkinson, S. Marcu, and C. M. Shapiro, "Karolinska sleepiness scale (KSS)," in *STOP, THAT and One Hundred Other Sleep Scales*, A. Shahid, ed., New York: Springer, 2012, pp. 209–210. [Online]. Available: https://link.springer.com/chapter/10.1007/978-1-4419-9893-4_47

[12] G. R. Poudel, C. R. H. Innes, and R. D. Jones, "Distinct neural correlates of time-on-task and transient errors during a visuomotor tracking task after sleep restriction," *NeuroImage*, vol. *77*, pp. 105–113, 2013, doi: 10.1016/j.neuroimage.2013.03.054.

[13] K. Kaida et al., "Validation of the Karolinska sleepiness scale against performance and EEG variables," *Clinical Neurophysiology: Official Journal of the International Federation of Clinical Neurophysiology*, vol. *117*, no. 7, pp. 1574–1581, 2006, doi: 10.1016/j.clinph.2006.03.011.

[14] A. Shahid, K. Wilkinson, S. Marcu, and C. M. Shapiro, "Stanford sleepiness scale (SSS)," in *STOP, THAT and One Hundred Other Sleep Scales*, A. Shahid, ed., New York: Springer, 2012, pp. 369–370.

[15] J. Arnedt, G. J. Wilde, P. W. Munt, and A. W. MacLean, "How do prolonged wakefulness and alcohol compare in the decrements they produce on a simulated driving task?," *Accident Analysis & Prevention*, vol. *33*, no. 3, pp. 337–344, 2001, doi: 10.1016/S0001-4575(00)00047-6.

[16] M. Chai, S.-W. Li, W.-C. Sun, M.-Z. Guo, and M.-Y. Huang, "Drowsiness monitoring based on steering wheel status," *Transportation Research Part D: Transport and Environment*, vol. *66*, pp. 95–103, 2019, doi: 10.1016/j.trd.2018.07.007.

[17] F. Friedrichs and B. Yang, "Drowsiness monitoring by steering and lane data based features under real driving conditions," in *2010 18th European Signal Processing Conference*, 2010, pp. 209–213. [Online]. Available: https://ieeexplore.ieee.org/document/7096521

[18] X. Wang and C. Xu, "Driver drowsiness detection based on non-intrusive metrics considering individual specifics," *Accident Analysis & Prevention*, vol. *95*, pp. 350–357, 2016, doi: 10.1016/j.aap.2015.09.002.

[19] H.-T. Choi, M.-K. Back, and K.-C. Lee, "Driver drowsiness detection based on multimodal using fusion of visual-feature and bio-signal," in *2018 International Conference on Information and Communication Technology Convergence (ICTC)*, Jeju, Oct. 2018, pp. 1249–1251.

[20] C. B. S. Maior, M. J. D. C. Moura, J. M. M. Santana, and I. D. Lins, "Real-time classification for autonomous drowsiness detection using eye aspect ratio," *Expert Systems with Application*, vol. *158*, p. 113505, 2020, doi: 10.1016/j.eswa.2020.113505.

[21] N. Nojiri, X. Kong, L. Meng, and H. Shimakawa, "Discussion on machine learning and deep learning based makeup considered eye status recognition for driver drowsiness," *Procedia Computer Science*, vol. *147*, pp. 264–270, 2019, doi: 10.1016/j.procs.2019.01.252.

[22] S. P. Rajamohana, E. G. Radhika, S. Priya, and S. Sangeetha, "Driver drowsiness detection system using hybrid approach of convolutional neural network and bidirectional long short term memory (CNN_BILSTM)," *Materials Today: Proceedings*, vol. *45*, pp. 2897–2901, 2021, doi: 10.1016/j.matpr.2020.11.898.

[23] A. Moujahid, F. Dornaika, I. Arganda-Carreras, and J. Reta, "Efficient and compact face descriptor for driver drowsiness detection," *Expert Systems with Application*, vol. *168*, p. 114334, 2021, doi: 10.1016/j.eswa.2020.114334.

[24] X. Fan, B.-C. Yin, and Y.-F. Sun, "Yawning detection for monitoring driver fatigue," in *International Conference on Machine Learning and Cybernetics, 2007: [ICMLC 2007]; 19–22 August 2007, Hong Kong, China*, Hong Kong, China, 2007, pp. 664–668.

[25] M. Golz, D. Sommer, U. Trutschel, B. Sirois, and D. Edwards, "Evaluation of fatigue monitoring technologies," *Somnologie*, vol. *14*, no. 3, pp. 187–199, 2010, doi: 10.1007/s11818-010-0482-9.

[26] L. M. Bergasa, J. Nuevo, M. A. Sotelo, R. Barea, and M. E. Lopez, "Real-time system for monitoring driver vigilance," *IEEE Transactions on Intelligent Transportation Systems*, vol. *7*, no. 1, pp. 63–77, 2006, doi: 10.1109/TITS.2006.869598.

[27] S. Taran and V. Bajaj, "Drowsiness detection using adaptive hermite decomposition and extreme learning machine for electroencephalogram signals," *IEEE Sensors Journal*, vol. *18*, no. 21, pp. 8855–8862, 2018, doi: 10.1109/JSEN.2018.2869775.

[28] Z. Ren et al., "EEG-based driving fatigue detection using a two-level learning hierarchy radial basis function," *Frontiers in Neurorobotics*, vol. *15*, p. 618408, 2021, doi: 10.3389/fnbot.2021.618408.

[29] M. Awais, N. Badruddin, and M. Drieberg, "Driver drowsiness detection using EEG power spectrum analysis," in *IEEE Region 10 symposium, 2014: IEEE TENSYMP 2014; 14–16 April 2014, Kuala Lumpur, Malaysia*, Kuala Lumpur, Malaysia, 2014, pp. 244–247.

[30] F. Lin, L. Ko, C. Chuang, T. Su, and C. Lin, "Generalized EEG-based drowsiness prediction system by using a self-organizing neural fuzzy system," *IEEE Transactions on Circuits and Systems I: Regular Papers*, vol. *59*, no. 9, pp. 2044–2055, 2012, doi: 10.1109/TCSI.2012.2185290.

[31] Y. Ma et al., "Driving fatigue detection from EEG using a modified PCANet method," *Computational Intelligence and Neuroscience*, vol. *2019*, p. 4721863, 2019, doi: 10.1155/2019/4721863.

[32] M. Hendra, D. Kurniawan, R. V. Chrismiantari, T. P. Utomo, and N. Nuryani, "Drowsiness detection using heart rate variability analysis based on microcontroller unit," *Journal of Physics: Conference Series*, vol. *1153*, p. 12047, 2019. [Online]. Available: https://iopscience.iop.org/article/10.1088/1742-6596/1153/1/012047

[33] F. Abtahi, A. Anund, C. Fors, F. Seoane, and K. Lindecrantz, "Association of drivers' sleepiness with heart rate variability: a pilot study with drivers on real roads," in *IFMBE proceedings, 1680-0737, Volume 65, EMBEC & NBC 2017: Joint Conference of the European Medical and Biological Engineering Conference (EMBEC) and the Nordic-Baltic Conference on Biomedical Engineering and Medical Physics (NBC), Tampere, Finland, June 2017 / Hannu Eskola, Outi Väisänen, Jari Viik, Jari Hyttinen (Eds.)*, H. Eskola, O. Väisänen, J. Viik, and J. Hyttinen, Eds., Singapore: Springer, 2018, pp. 149–152. [Online]. Available: https://link.springer.com/chapter/10.1007%2F978-981-10-5122-7_38

[34] K. Fujiwara et al., "Heart rate variability-based driver drowsiness detection and its validation with EEG," *IEEE Transactions on Biomedical Engineering*, vol. *66*, no. 6, pp. 1769–1778, 2019, doi: 10.1109/TBME.2018.2879346.

[35] S.-J. Jung, H.-S. Shin, and W.-Y. Chung, "Driver fatigue and drowsiness monitoring system with embedded electrocardiogram sensor on steering wheel," *IET Intelligent Transport Systems*, vol. *8*, no. 1, pp. 43–50, 2014, doi: 10.1049/iet-its.2012.0032.

[36] S. Arefnezhad, A. Eichberger, M. Fruhwirth, C. Kaufmann, and M. Moser, "Driver drowsiness classification using data fusion of vehicle-based measures and ECG signals," in *2020 IEEE International Conference on Systems, Man, and Cybernetics (SMC)*, Toronto, ON, Canada, Oct. 2020, pp. 451–456.

[37] M. Akin, M. B. Kurt, N. Sezgin, and M. Bayram, "Estimating vigilance level by using EEG and EMG signals," *Neural Computing and Applications*, vol. *17*, no. 3, pp. 227–236, 2008, doi: 10.1007/s00521-007-0117-7.

[38] V. Balasubramanian and K. Adalarasu, "EMG-based analysis of change in muscle activity during simulated driving," *Journal of Bodywork and Movement Therapies*, vol. *11*, no. 2, pp. 151–158, 2007, doi: 10.1016/j.jbmt.2006.12.005.

[39] R. Fu and H. Wang, "Detection of driving fatigue by using noncontact EMG and ECG signals measurement system," *International Journal of Neural Systems*, vol. *24*, no. 3, p. 1450006, 2014, doi: 10.1142/S0129065714500063.

[40] D. Chen, Z. Ma, B. C. Li, Z. Yan, and W. Li, "Drowsiness detection with electrooculography signal using a system dynamics approach," *Journal of Dynamic Systems, Measurement, and Control*, vol. *139*, no. 8, 2017, doi: 10.1115/1.4035611.

[41] T. C. Chieh, M. M. Mustafa, A. Hussain, S. F. Hendi, and B. Y. Majlis, "Development of vehicle driver drowsiness detection system using electrooculogram (EOG)," in *2005 1st International Conference on Computers, Communications, & Signal Processing with Special Track on Biomedical Engineering*, Kuala Lumpur, Malaysia, Nov. 2005, pp. 165–168.

[42] S. M. R. Noori and M. Mikaeili, "Driving drowsiness detection using fusion of electroencephalography, electrooculography, and driving quality signals," *Journal of Medical Signals and Sensors*, vol. *6*, no. 1, pp. 39–46, 2016. [Online]. Available: https://pubmed.ncbi.nlm.nih.gov/27014611

[43] D. Malathi, J. D. D. Jayaseeli, S. Madhuri, and K. Senthilkumar, "Electrodermal activity based wearable device for drowsy drivers," *Journal of Physics: Conference Series*, vol. *1000*, p. 12048, 2018.

[44] F. Guede-Fernández, M. Fernández-Chimeno, J. Ramos-Castro, and M. A. García-González, "Driver drowsiness detection based on respiratory signal analysis," *IEEE Access*, vol. *7*, pp. 81826–81838, 2019, doi: 10.1109/ACCESS.2019.2924481.

[45] S. E. H. Kiashari, A. Nahvi, H. Bakhoda, A. Homayounfard, and M. Tashakori, "Evaluation of driver drowsiness using respiration analysis by thermal imaging on a driving simulator," *Multimedia Tools and Applications*, vol. *79*, no. 25, pp. 17793–17815, 2020, doi: 10.1007/s11042-020-08696-x.

[46] J. Solaz et al., "Drowsiness detection based on the analysis of breathing rate obtained from real-time image recognition," *Transportation Research Procedia*, vol. *14*, pp. 3867–3876, 2016, doi: 10.1016/j.trpro. 2016.05.472.

[47] C. Yang, X. Wang, and S. Mao, "Respiration monitoring with RFID in driving environments," *IEEE Journal on Selected Areas in Communications*, vol. *39*, no. 2, pp. 500–512, 2021, doi: 10.1109/JSAC.2020.3020606.

[48] A. Sahayadhas, K. Sundaraj, and M. Murugappan, "Detecting driver drowsiness based on sensors: a review," *Sensors (Basel, Switzerland)*, vol. *12*, no. 12, pp. 16937–16953, 2012, doi: 10.3390/s121216937.

[49] E. Michail, A. Kokonozi, I. Chouvarda, and N. Maglaveras, "EEG and HRV markers of sleepiness and loss of control during car driving," in *2008 30th Annual International Conference of the IEEE Engineering in Medicine and Biology Society*, Vancouver, BC, Aug. 2008, pp. 2566–2569.

[50] H. J. Baek, G. S. Chung, K. K. Kim, and K. S. Park, "A smart health monitoring chair for nonintrusive measurement of biological signals," *IEEE Transactions on Information Technology in Biomedicine*, vol. *16*, no. 1, pp. 150–158, 2012, doi: 10.1109/TITB.2011.2175742.

[51] A. D. McDonald, J. D. Lee, C. Schwarz, and T. L. Brown, "A contextual and temporal algorithm for driver drowsiness detection," *Accident Analysis & Prevention*, vol. *113*, pp. 25–37, 2018, doi: 10.1016/j.aap.2018.01.005.

[52] J. Krajewski, D. Sommer, U. Trutschel, D. Edwards, and M. Golz, "Steering wheel behavior based estimation of fatigue," in *Proceedings of the 5th International Driving Symposium on Human Factors in Driver Assessment, Training, and Vehicle Design : Driving Assessment 2009*, Big Sky, Montana, USA, 2009, pp. 118–124. [Online]. Available: https://ir.uiowa.edu/drivingassessment/2009/papers/18/

[53] M. Ingre, T. Akerstedt, B. Peters, A. Anund, and G. Kecklund, "Subjective sleepiness, simulated driving performance and blink duration: examining individual differences," *Journal of Sleep Research*, vol. *15*, no. 1, pp. 47–53, 2006, doi: 10.1111/j.1365-2869.2006.00504.x.

[54] A. D. McDonald, J. D. Lee, C. Schwarz, and T. L. Brown, "Steering in a random forest: ensemble learning for detecting drowsiness-related lane departures," *Human Factors*, vol. *56*, no. 5, pp. 986–998, 2014, doi: 10.1177/0018720813515272.

[55] S. Arefnezhad, S. Samiee, A. Eichberger, M. Frühwirth, C. Kaufmann, and E. Klotz, "Applying deep neural networks for multi-level classification of driver drowsiness using Vehicle-based measures," *Expert Systems with Application*, vol. *162*, p. 113778, 2020, doi: 10.1016/j.eswa.2020.113778.

[56] S. Arefnezhad, S. Samiee, A. Eichberger, and A. Nahvi, "Driver drowsiness detection based on steering wheel data applying adaptive neuro-fuzzy feature selection," *Sensors (Basel, Switzerland)*, vol. *19*, no. 4, 2019, doi: 10.3390/s19040943.

[57] A. Eskandarian and A. Mortazavi, "Evaluation of a smart algorithm for commercial vehicle driver drowsiness detection," in *2007 IEEE Intelligent Vehicles Symposium*, 2007, pp. 553–559.

[58] M. Burghardt, R. Wimmer, C. Wolff, and C. Womser-Hacker, eds., "A robust drowsiness detection method based on vehicle and driver vital data,". in *Mensch und Computer 2017 - Workshopband*. Regensburg: Gesellschaft für Informatik: Gesellschaft für Informatik e.V, 2017. Accessed: November 9 2021.

[59] J. Schmidt, C. Braunagel, W. Stolzmann, and K. Karrer-Gauss, "Driver drowsiness and behavior detection in prolonged conditionally automated drives," in *2016 IEEE Intelligent Vehicles Symposium (IV 2016): Gotenburg, Sweden, 19-22 June 2016*, Gotenburg, Sweden, 2016, pp. 400–405.

[60] R. Jabbar, K. Al-Khalifa, M. Kharbeche, W. Alhajyaseen, M. Jafari, and S. Jiang, "Real-time driver drowsiness detection for android application using deep neural networks techniques," *Procedia Computer Science*, vol. *130*, pp. 400–407, 2018, doi: 10.1016/j.procs.2018.04.060.

[61] Z. Zhao, N. Zhou, L. Zhang, H. Yan, Y. Xu, and Z. Zhang, "Driver fatigue detection based on convolutional neural networks using EM-CNN," *Computational Intelligence and Neuroscience*, vol. *2020*, p. 7251280, 2020, doi: 10.1155/2020/7251280.

[62] K. Zhang, Z. Zhang, Z. Li, and Y. Qiao, "Joint face detection and alignment using multitask cascaded convolutional networks," *IEEE Signal Processing Letters*, vol. *23*, no. 10, pp. 1499–1503, 2016, doi: 10.1109/ LSP.2016.2603342.

[63] D. Dinges and R. Grace, "Perclos: A valid psychophysiological measure of alertness as assessed by psychomotor vigilance," US Department of Transportation: Federal Highway Administration FHWA-MCRT-98-006, Oct. 1998. Accessed: November 9 2021. [Online]. Available: https://rosap.ntl.bts.gov/view/dot/113

[64] R. J. Hanowski, D. S. Bowman, A. Alden, W. W. Wierwille, and R. J. Carroll, "PERCLOS+: development of a robust field measure of driver drowsiness," in *15th World Congress on Intelligent Transport Systems and ITS America's 2008 Annual Meeting*. Accessed: November 9 2021. [Online]. Available: https://trid.trb.org/ View/904975

[65] D. Sommer and M. Golz, "Evaluation of PERCLOS based current fatigue monitoring technologies," *Annual International Conference of the IEEE Engineering in Medicine and Biology Society. IEEE Engineering in Medicine and Biology Society. Annual International Conference*, vol. *2010*, pp. 4456–4459, 2010, doi: 10.1109/IEMBS.2010.5625960.

[66] H. Tsuda, A. A. Lowe, H. Chen, J. A. Fleetham, N. T. Ayas, and F. R. Almeida, "The relationship between mouth opening and sleep stage-related sleep disordered breathing," *Journal of Clinical Sleep Medicine*, vol. *07*, no. 02, pp. 181–186, 2011, doi: 10.5664/jcsm.28107.

[67] C. Tan, F. Sun, T. Kong, W. Zhang, C. Yang, and C. Liu, "A survey on deep transfer learning," in *LNCS sublibrary. SL 1, Theoretical Computer Science and General Issues, vol. 11140, Artificial Neural Networks and Machine Learning -- ICANN 2018: 27th International Conference on Artificial Neural Networks, Rhodes, Greece, October 4–7, 2018, Proceedings. Part II / Věra Kůrková, Yannis Manolopoulos, Barbara Hammer, Lazaros Iliadis, Ilias Maglogiannis (eds.)*, V. Kůrková, Y. Manolopoulos, B. Hammer, L. S. Iliadis, and I. G. Maglogiannis, Eds., Cham, Switzerland: Springer, 2018, pp. 270–279.

[68] A. Krizhevsky, I. Sutskever, and G. E. Hinton, "ImageNet classification with deep convolutional neural networks," *Communications of the ACM*, vol. *60*, no. 6, pp. 84–90, 2017, doi: 10.1145/3065386.

[69] C. Szegedy et al., "Going deeper with convolutions," Sep. 2014. [Online], In *Proceedings of the IEEE conference on computer vision and pattern recognition*, pp. 1–9. 2015. Available: https://arxiv.org/pdf/1409.4842

[70] C. J. de Naurois, C. Bourdin, A. Stratulat, E. Diaz, and J.-L. Vercher, "Detection and prediction of driver drowsiness using artificial neural network models," *Accident Analysis & Prevention*, vol. *126*, pp. 95–104, 2019, doi: 10.1016/j.aap.2017.11.038.

[71] C. Szegedy, V. Vanhoucke, S. Ioffe, J. Shlens, and Z. Wojna, "Rethinking the inception architecture for computer vision," Dec. 2015. [Online], In *Proceedings of the IEEE conference on computer vision and pattern recognition*, pp. 2818–2826. 2016. Available: https://arxiv.org/pdf/1512.00567

[72] M. Dua, R. Shakshi S. R. Singla, and A. Jangra, "Deep CNN models-based ensemble approach to driver drowsiness detection," *Neural Computing & Applications*, vol. *33*, no. 8, pp. 3155–3168, 2021, doi: 10.1007/s00521-020-05209-7.

[73] O. M. Parkhi, A. Vedaldi, and A. Zisserman, "Deep face recognition," in *Procdings of the British Machine Vision Conference 2015*, Swansea, pp. 41.1–41.12.

[74] J. Donahue et al., "Long-term recurrent convolutional networks for visual recognition and description," Nov. 2014. [Online], *Proceedings of the IEEE conference on computer vision and pattern recognition*, pp. 2625–2634. 2015. Available: https://arxiv.org/pdf/1411.4389

[75] K. He, X. Zhang, S. Ren, and J. Sun, "Deep residual learning for image recognition," Dec. 2015. [Online], In *Proceedings of the IEEE conference on computer vision and pattern recognition*, pp. 770–778. 2016. Available: https://arxiv.org/pdf/1512.03385.

[76] A.-C. Phan, N.-H.-Q. Nguyen, T.-N. Trieu, and T.-C. Phan, "An efficient approach for detecting driver drowsiness based on deep learning," *Applied Sciences*, vol. *11*, no. 18, p. 8441, 2021, doi: 10.3390/app11188441.

[77] K. He, X. Zhang, S. Ren, and J. Sun, "Identity mappings in deep residual networks," in *LNCS sublibrary: SL6 - Image processing, computer vision, pattern recognition, and graphics, 9905-9912, Computer vision - ECCV 2016: 14th European Conference, Amsterdam, The Netherlands, October 11–14, 2016 : proceedings / Bastian Leibe, Jiri Matas, Nicu Sebe, Max Welling (eds.)*, F. Leibe, Ed., Cham, Switzerland: Springer, 2016, pp. 630–645.

[78] A. G. Howard et al., "MobileNets: efficient convolutional neural networks for mobile vision applications," Apr. 2017. [Online]. Available: https://arxiv.org/pdf/1704.04861

[79] X.-P. Huynh, S.-M. Park, and Y.-G. Kim, "Detection of driver drowsiness using 3D deep neural network and semi-supervised gradient boosting machine," in *LNCS sublibrary. SL 6, Image processing, computer vision, pattern recognition, and graphics, vol. 10118, Computer vision -- ACCV 2016 Workshops: ACCV 2016 International Workshops, Taipei, Taiwan, November 20–24, 2016, Revised selected papers. Part III / Chu-Song Chen, Jiwen Lu, Kai-Kuang Ma (eds.)*, C.-S. Chen, J. Lu, and K.-K. Ma, Eds., Cham, Switzerland: Springer, 2017, pp. 134–145.

[80] T. Chen and C. Guestrin, "XGBoost: a scalable tree boosting system," 34, Mar. 2016. [Online], iN *Proceedings of the 22nd acm sigkdd international conference on knowledge discovery and data mining*, pp. 785–794. 2016. Available: https://arxiv.org/pdf/1603.02754

[81] J.-H. Jeong, B.-W. Yu, D.-H. Lee, and S.-W. Lee, "Classification of drowsiness levels based on a deep spatio-temporal convolutional bidirectional LSTM network using electroencephalography signals," *Brain Sciences*, vol. *9*, no. 12, p. 348, 2019, doi: 10.3390/brainsci9120348.

[82] S. Chaabene, B. Bouaziz, A. Boudaya, A. Hökelmann, A. Ammar, and L. Chaari, "Convolutional neural network for drowsiness detection using EEG signals," *Sensors (Basel, Switzerland)*, vol. *21*, no. 5, p. 1734, 2021, doi: 10.3390/s21051734.

[83] M. Hajinoroozi, Z. Mao, and Y. Huang, "Prediction of driver's drowsy and alert states from EEG signals with deep learning," in *2015 IEEE 6th International Workshop on Computational Advances in Multi-Sensor Adaptive Processing (CAMSAP)*, Cancun, Mexico, Dec. 2015, pp. 493–496.

[84] F. Rundo et al., "An innovative deep learning algorithm for drowsiness detection from EEG signal," *Computation*, vol. *7*, no. 1, p. 13, 2019, doi: 10.3390/computation7010013.

[85] R. Chai et al., "Improving EEG-based driver fatigue classification using sparse-deep belief networks," *Frontiers in Neuroscience*, vol. *11*, p. 103, 2017, doi: 10.3389/fnins.2017.00103.

[86] Z.-K. Gao, Y.-L. Li, Y.-X. Yang, and C. Ma, "A recurrence network-based convolutional neural network for fatigue driving detection from EEG," *Chaos*, vol. *29*, no. 11, p. 113126, 2019, doi: 10.1063/1.5120538.

[87] A. Tjolleng et al., "Classification of a driver's cognitive workload levels using artificial neural network on ECG signals," *Applied Ergonomics*, vol. *59*, Pt A, pp. 326–332, 2017, doi: 10.1016/j.apergo.2016.09.013.

[88] H. Lee, J. Lee, and M. Shin, "Using wearable ECG/PPG sensors for driver drowsiness detection based on distinguishable pattern of recurrence plots," *Electronics*, vol. *8*, no. 2, p. 192, 2019, doi: 10.3390/electronics8020192.

[89] H. U. R. Siddiqui et al., "Non-invasive driver drowsiness detection system," *Sensors (Basel, Switzerland)*, vol. *21*, no. 14, p. 4833, 2021, doi: 10.3390/s21144833.

[90] S. Arefnezhad, A. Eichberger, M. Frühwirth, C. Kaufmann, M. Moser, and I. V. Koglbauer, "Driver monitoring of automated vehicles by classification of driver drowsiness using a deep convolutional neural network trained by scalograms of ECG signals," *Preprints*, 2021, doi: 10.20944/preprints202111.0230.v1.

[91] J. M. Lilly and S. C. Olhede, "Higher-order properties of analytic wavelets," *IEEE Transactions on Signal Processing*, vol. *57*, no. 1, pp. 146–160, 2009, doi: 10.1109/TSP.2008.2007607.

[92] S. Arefnezhad, "Evaluation of driver performance in semi-automated driving by physiologic, driver behaviour and video-based Sensors," PhD Thesis, Institute of Automotive Engineering, Graz University of Technology, Graz, Austria, 2021.

[93] A. Sinha, R. P. Aneesh, and S. K. Gopal, "Drowsiness detection system using deep learning," in *2021 Seventh International conference on Bio Signals, Images, and Instrumentation (ICBSII)*, Chennai, India, Mar. 2021, pp. 1–6.

[94] B. Akrout and W. Mahdi, "Spatio-temporal features for the automatic control of driver drowsiness state and lack of concentration," *Machine Vision and Applications*, vol. *26*, no. 1, pp. 1–13, 2015, doi: 10.1007/s00138-014-0644-z.

[95] Z. Li, S. E. Li, R. Li, B. Cheng, and J. Shi, "Online detection of driver fatigue using steering wheel angles for real driving conditions," *Sensors (Basel, Switzerland)*, vol. *17*, no. 3, 2017, doi: 10.3390/s17030495.

[96] J. Vicente, P. Laguna, A. Bartra, and R. Bailón, "Drowsiness detection using heart rate variability," *Medical & Biological Engineering & Computing*, vol. *54*, no. 6, pp. 927–937, 2016, doi: 10.1007/s11517-015-1448-7.

[97] G. Li and W.-Y. Chung, "Detection of driver drowsiness using wavelet analysis of heart rate variability and a support vector machine classifier," *Sensors (Basel, Switzerland)*, vol. *13*, no. 12, pp. 16494–16511, 2013, doi: 10.3390/s131216494.

[98] A. L. Goldberger et al., "PhysioBank, PhysioToolkit, and PhysioNet: components of a new research resource for complex physiologic signals," *Circulation*, vol. *101*, no. 23, pp. E215–20, 2000, doi: 10.1161/01.cir.101.23.e215.

[99] L. Chin-Teng, C. Che-Jui, L. Bor-Shyh, H. Shao-Hang, C. Chih-Feng, and W. I-Jan, "A real-time wireless brain-computer interface system for drowsiness detection," *IEEE Transactions on Biomedical Circuits and Systems*, vol. *4*, no. 4, pp. 214–222, 2010, doi: 10.1109/TBCAS.2010.2046415.

[100] Q. Massoz, T. Langohr, C. Francois, and J. G. Verly, "The ULg multimodality drowsiness database (called DROZY) and examples of use," in *2016 IEEE Winter Conference on Applications of Computer Vision (WACV)*, Lake Placid, NY, USA, Mar. 2016, pp. 1–7.

[101] Q. Massoz, J. G. Verly, and M. van Droogenbroeck, "Multi-timescale drowsiness characterization based on a video of a driver's face," *Sensors (Basel, Switzerland)*, vol. *18*, no. 9, 2018, doi: 10.3390/s18092801.

[102] W. Deng and R. Wu, "Real-time driver-drowsiness detection system using facial features," *IEEE Access*, vol. *7*, pp. 118727–118738, 2019, doi: 10.1109/ACCESS.2019.2936663.

[103] L. Zhao, Z. Wang, X. Wang, and Q. Liu, "Driver drowsiness detection using facial dynamic fusion information and a DBN," *IET Intelligent Transport Systems*, vol. *12*, no. 2, pp. 127–133, 2018, doi: 10.1049/iet-its.2017.0183.

[104] M. Patel, S. Lal, D. Kavanagh, and P. Rossiter, "Applying neural network analysis on heart rate variability data to assess driver fatigue," *Expert Systems with Appliation*, vol. *38*, no. 6, pp. 7235–7242, 2011, doi: 10.1016/j.eswa.2010.12.028.

[105] F. You, X. Li, Y. Gong, H. Wang, and H. Li, "A real-time driving drowsiness detection algorithm with individual differences consideration," *IEEE Access*, vol. *7*, pp. 179396–179408, 2019, doi: 10.1109/ACCESS.2019.2958667.

[106] H. Wang, L. Zhang, and L. Yao, "Application of genetic algorithm based support vector machine in selection of new EEG rhythms for drowsiness detection," *Expert Systems with Appliation*, vol. *171*, p. 114634, 2021, doi: 10.1016/j.eswa.2021.114634.

[107] H. Iwamoto, K. Hori, K. Fujiwara, and M. Kano, "Real-driving-implementable drowsy driving detection method using heart rate variability based on long short-term memory and autoencoder," *IFAC-PapersOnLine*, vol. *54*, no. 15, pp. 526–531, 2021, doi: 10.1016/j.ifacol.2021.10.310.

[108] S. K. Khare and V. Bajaj, "Optimized tunable Q wavelet transform based drowsiness detection from electroencephalogram signals," *IRBM*, 2020, doi: 10.1016/j.irbm.2020.07.005.

[109] S. Arefnezhad, S. Samiee, A. Eichberger, M. Frühwirth, C. Kaufmann, and E. Klotz, "Applying deep neural networks for multi-level classification of driver drowsiness using vehicle-based measures," *Expert Systems with Application*, vol. *162*, p. 113778, 2020, doi: 10.1016/j.eswa.2020.113778.

A deep learning perspective on Connected Automated Vehicle (CAV) cybersecurity and threat intelligence

3

Manoj Basnet and Mohd Hasan Ali
The University of Memphis, Memphis, Tennessee

Contents

DOI: 10.1201/9781003190691-4

3.1 INTRODUCTION

The connected and autonomous vehicle (CAV) is the next-generation mobility service—powered by intelligent automation and robust communication—aimed at replacing human-maneuvered vehicles with the software agent matching or even exceeding the human-level intelligence, control, and agility with the least decision errors possible. US National Safety Council (NSC) [1] reported a 24 % spike in roadway death rates from 2019 despite the number of miles driven dropping by 13%, the highest increment in 96 years in the US since 1924. Most of the time, these fatalities are the result of human error. The NSC has estimated that in the year 2020 4.8 million additional roadway users were seriously injured, with an estimated cost of $474 billion. The next generation of transportation and mobility envisions a safe, reliable, agile, automated, trustworthy, and service-based mobility architecture. The architecture should be able to eliminate human errors by using intelligent decision-making software agents based on the situational and behavioral information collected by sensors and transceivers through communication. Apart from that, the service-based architecture removes the concept of vehicle ownership and includes more diversity, such as the disabled and older people. CAV is the evolving technology to achieve the envisioned goals of future mobility and transportation.

Today's vehicles are not simply electromechanical entities but also complex software agents with electronics [2]. Within this context, the term connected means the vehicle exchanges data between the systems and networks (to other vehicles and infrastructures) for predictive maintenance, dynamic insurance policy, passenger information, fleet management, comfort, and situational and behavioral awareness [3]. Fully autonomous means the vehicle conducts dynamic driving tasks automatically in real time without the driver's intervention [4].

The connected vehicle generates 25 GB of data per hour, even at a lower level of autonomy. Integrating RADAR, LIDAR, Camera, Ultrasonics, Motion sensors, GNSS, and IMU into the vehicle can generate 40 Gbit/s data leading up to 380 TB to 5100 TB of data in a year [5]. This wealth of high-volume, high-speed data needs a gigantic level of storage, intense computation, and astute processing. As the data volume vehemently upsurges, software, hardware, data privacy, and security issues become increasingly important. Increased connectivity elevates the attack surfaces of the CAV, while automation lacks the sophisticated human-level agility and intelligence for threat mitigation. The inherent vulnerabilities of this technology come from the untested supply chain, such as hardware, software, and infrastructures.

Deep learning has been unprecedentedly successful in deciphering the complex nonlinear spatiotemporal pattern of highly stochastic data. Given the data's volume, veracity, and velocity, deep learning could be handy in designing cyberattack detection and mitigation in the CAV environment. Figure 3.1. shows

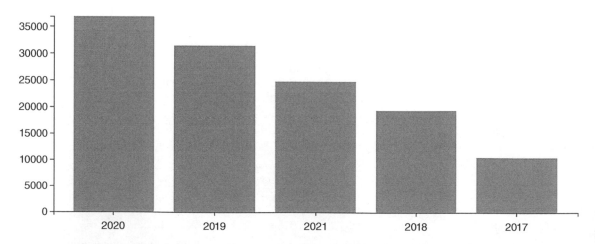

FIGURE 3.1   The number of publications on connected automated vehicles over the last five years.

the current trends of publications queried under "(((ALL=(Connected Vehicle)) OR ALL=(Automated vehicle)) AND ALL=(Cybersecurity)) OR ALL=(Deep learning)" in the web of science for 2017 through 2020. This has produced a result of 127,042 publications so far, with growing interest every year.

This chapter deals with the deep learning perspective on CAV cybersecurity and threat intelligence. In addition, we proposed novel end-to-end deep CNN-LSTM-based computational intelligence for cyber-attack detection and classification in the CAV ecosystem. The proposed model has been successfully trained, tested, and evaluated on the CAV-KDD dataset and compared against other deep learning models such as Deep Neural Networks (DNN) and Convolutional Neural Networks (1D-CNN), Long-Short Term (LSTM). The proposed model outperformed the aforementioned deep learning models in terms of various performance metrics and increased model complexity.

3.2 CAV TECHNOLOGICAL ENABLERS: AUTOMATION AND CONNECTIVITY

The key technological enablers for CAV are Automation and Connectivity. The vehicle driving automation system performs either part or all of the dynamic driving tasks (DDT). The Society of Automotive Engineers (SAE) defined the six levels of automation for vehicles ranging from no automation (Level 0) to full automation (Level 5) in its 2021 release [6]. In Levels 0–2, the driver drives the entire or part of DDT, while in levels 3–5, ADS performs the entire DDT upon engagement. Figure 3.2. shows the overall

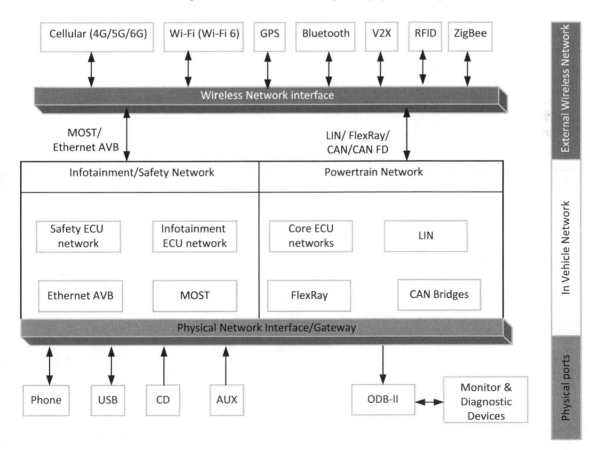

FIGURE 3.2 Connectivity of the CAV.

connectivity architecture with a wireless network interface, physical interface, and In-vehicle network in between. The CAV is co-evolving with next-generation network architectures and communication protocols. It can exploit the latency, speed, and bandwidth of recent cellular communication such as 5G. The recent advancement in Wi-Fi 6 could be used in place of high user density. Also, inbuilt GPS has been widely used for navigation. Moreover, Bluetooth, RFID, ZigBee, and V2X communication have extended the range of connectivities and applications. The in-vehicle network has mainly a high-speed infotainment system for information dissemination and entertainment; and a Powertrain network for core functionalities of the vehicle. These are mainly composed of electronic control units (ECUs) connected through local control area network (CAN) buses. The physical network interface provides ports to connect the phone, USB, CD, and AUX from the infotainment system and ODB-II from the powertrain system. This ODB-II can be extended via physical or wireless network interfaces to the vehicle's OEM, drivers, and computerized intelligence. Previous advances in connectivity and automation have enabled the following vehicle functionalities as per the US Department of Transportation (DoT) [7].

a) Collision warning: forward collision warning, lane departure warning, rear cross-traffic warning, and blind-spot warning.
b) Collision intervention: automatic emergency braking, pedestrian automatic emergency braking, automatic rear braking, and blind-spot intervention.
c) Driving control assistance: adaptive cruise control, lane-centering, and lane-keeping assistance.
d) Additional systems: Automatic high beams, backup camera, and automatic crash notification.

3.3 CAV THREAT LANDSCAPE AND THREAT INTELLIGENCE

Threat intelligence begins with an identification of the assets and then finding the weighted utility to the assets, i.e., threat landscape. Assets are entities that have specific utilities and hence add values to the system. The value comes from the cost of creating it and the competition to make it readily available. Therefore, from a game-theoretic perspective, there is always competition to exploit the utility, i.e., the risk of biased usage, which creates vulnerabilities. An attacker can exploit the vulnerabilities by using social engineering and reverse engineering. The electromechanical vehicle, while adopting the evolving network architecture and automation—so-called CAV—migrates all the vulnerabilities related to the processes, protocols, supply chains, and software from the incumbent technologies. Furthermore, CAV has vulnerabilities or risks originating from communication, automation, IT, OT, and physical system. Here, we will briefly explain the cyber vulnerabilities of low-level sensors [8] and vehicle control modules.

3.3.1 In-vehicle (low-level sensor) cyber vulnerabilities

1. GPS: The transparent architecture of GPS, its open standard, and free accessibility are the main reasons for generating spoofing and jamming attacks on GPS.
2. Inertial measurement units (IMUs) provide velocity, acceleration, and orientation data by using accelerometers and gyroscopes. The gyroscope and inclination sensors measure the road gradient and adjust the speed accordingly for safe maneuvering. The spoofed data can generate a false control signal for speed control. Also, the jamming of the sensors may disrupt the vehicle's autonomous speed adjustment.
3. Engine control sensor: These sensors monitor the dynamics of the engine, such as temperature, airflow, exhaust gas, and engine knock, and are connected to CAN.

4. Tire Pressure Management System (TPMS): TPMS has not been used in decision-making but is physically accessible to outsiders.
5. LiDAR sensors: are used to generate the 3D map of the vehicle's environment for localization, obstacle avoidance, and navigation. Laser beams can fool liDAR sensors.
6. Cameras (stereo- or mono-vision) and infrared systems are used for static and dynamic obstacle detection, object recognition, and 360-degree information with other sensor fusions. Cameras contain the charge-coupled device (CCD) or complementary Metal Oxide Semiconductor (CMOS) sensor that can be partially disabled from a 3- meter distance using low-powered lasers.

3.3.2 Vehicle control modules

All modern vehicles use engine control units (ECU) to acquire, process, and control electronic signals. ECUs are roughly categorized into powertrain, safety systems, body control, and data communications. The powertrain is the brain of the ECU, which controls transmissions, emissions, charging systems, and control modules. Safety systems are responsible for collision avoidance, airbag deployment, active braking, etc. Body control controls the electric windows, AC, mirrors, immobilizer, and locking. Data communications control the communication between different communication modules. The networking of ECUs can be done through either CAN buses or FlexRay. The key ECUs in CAV in descending order of importance are as follows [8, 9].

a) Navigation control module (NCM)
b) Engine control module (ECM)
c) Electronic brake control module (EBCM)
d) Transmission control module (TCM)
e) Telematics module with remote commanding
f) Body control module (BCM)
g) Inflatable restraint module (IRM)
h) Vehicle vision system (VVS)
i) Remote door lock receiver
j) Heating, ventilation, and air conditioning (HVAC)
k) Instrument panel module
l) Radio and entertainment center

3.3.3 Security analysis of CAV threats

CAV can have around 100 million lines of code across 50–70 ECUs. As the number of lines of code grows, it becomes unfeasible to perform careful security implications. Some security incidences and their analysis are presented here [3].

a) Remotely control a vehicle: The attacker exploits the vulnerability in the cellular system and lands on the infotainment system. In most vehicles, the infotainment system has a driver with information such as service schedules, tire pressure, etc. The infotainment system has a connection with the CAN bus that connects all the ECUs. Therefore, it is possible to enter through the infotainment system and inject or spoof malicious signals. For e.g., ECUs controlling steering or brake.
b) Disable the vehicle: exploiting flaws in authentication, authorization, and access control in smart devices and apps to activate AC, windows, and windshield to drain the battery.
c) Remotely unlock the vehicle/theft: exploit known vulnerabilities in the keyless entry system using SDR. In 2020, hackers remotely unlocked the car door and started the engine in the

Mercedes Benz-E class. The manufacturer generally uses symmetric keys between the key fob, entry system, and ignition keys. An attacker can sniff the radio frequency between the key fob and entry system either by brute force or as a man-in-the-middle attack. Later the symmetric key can be compromised by replay attack or reverse engineering. The problem becomes enormous when some leading vehicle manufacturers used the same master cryptographic keys along the model line.

d) Safety conditions: Panic attacks such as Mobileye and the Tesla X hack fooled the autopilot system to trigger the brakes and steer into an oncoming vehicle.

e) Vehicle tracking/monitoring: extract patterns or fingerprints from the data.

f) Weaponizing the vehicle.

g) Malware: bots for crypto-jacking or DDoS.

h) Ransomware could be a huge problem to be dealt with in the future CAV.

i) Distribution of illicit goods.

3.3.4 Attack surfaces

The orthodox electromechanical vehicles, while adapting to the evolving network architecture, communications, and AI-powered automation, also carry all the vulnerabilities of incumbent technologies.

CAV also inherits elevated attack surfaces and attack vectors with elevated sophistication. These attack vectors are the specific methods, paths, or processes through which the CAV can be exploited. Insider threats such as the Levandowski trade secret trial between Waymo and Uber [10], Cyberattack into V2X communications [11], Sensor spoofing and exploitation [12], Dumpster diving for data: acting as a honeypot, Supply chain, and third-party risks are some of the prominent threats in the CAV ecosystem. Figure 3.3. enlists the prime attack surfaces.

3.3.5 Organizational risks to CAV ecosystem

The organizational risks imposed on the CAV ecosystem are well documented in [13]. The convergence of IT security, OT security, and physical security is challenging in any cyber-physical system, including the CAV ecosystem. The interconnections, interactions, and co-impacts of attack on these eccentric systems should be analyzed and evaluated. Dealing with big data (high volume, high speed, high variety) and extracting inferences in the CAV ecosystem requires high computational capacity, storage, and processing to deal with the multimodal data from different sensors. Data communication between multiple nodes, servers, and systems impose security and privacy risks. The divergent nature of stakeholders, such as different vendors of CAV, OEM, ITS, V2X, and its data privacy policy, might not allow CAV actors to collaborate in threat detections and mitigations. The cyber-physical security protocols, enterprise policies, and regulations still have to go a long way in the CAV ecosystem.

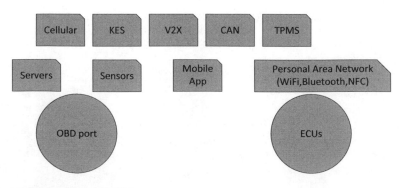

FIGURE 3.3 Key attack surfaces of CAV.

3.4 CAV THREAT MITIGATION: ANOMALY DETECTION AND CLASSIFICATION WITH DEEP LEARNING

"Deep Learning is building a system by assembling parameterized modules into a (possibly dynamic) computation graph and training it to perform a task by optimizing the parameters using a gradient-based method," as quoted by Yann Le Cunn, ACM Turing awardee and a pioneer in deep learning at the AAAI-20 event [14]. Graphs can be defined dynamically by input-dependent programs. Output computation may not necessarily be the feedforward; it might be some minimizing energy functions (inference model) [15]. The designer has complete freedom to choose learning paradigms such as supervised, reinforced, self-supervised/unsupervised, and objective functions such as classification, prediction, and reconstruction. Often limitations of supervised learning are mistakenly seen as limitations of deep learning. If the cake is intelligence, self-supervised learning is the bulk of the cake, supervised learning is the icing, and RL is the cherry on the cake. The next revolution in AI won't be supervised nor reinforced [16].

Deep learning has been an exciting paradigm for anomaly detection and classification in various cyber-physical realms, such as industrial control systems, smart grids, SCADA-controlled systems, etc. [17]. Now specific state-of-the-art applications of deep learning in CAV cybersecurity are summarized. In [18], Generative Adversarial Network-based IDS has been used to detect the anomaly in ECU by analyzing the CAN message frame, specifically the message identifier and frequency. The dataset was recorded from the OBD-II port of an undefined vehicle. The authors modified the firefly algorithm to find the optimal structure of the Generator network. Finally, they claimed the superior accuracy of the proposed model to the PSO- and GA- optimized GAN. However, the paper does not have much information regarding the training time, data size, data samples, computational complexity, etc.

In [19], a deep learning-based LSTM autoencoder was implemented to design IDS for CAN and central network gateways using car hacking and UNSW-NB15 datasets. Statistical features such as total count, mean, and standard deviation are extracted from the network packets. The proposed model claimed to outperform some of the decision tree and SVM-based classifiers. It's unlikely to claim the DL model can detect zero-day attacks since the supervised ML model cannot detect and classify the data that have never been trained.

In [20], authors use GAN for designing IDS capable of learning unknown attacks in the in-vehicle network. They extracted the CAN bus data for normal and attack using Raspberry Pi and simple hardware in the OBD-II port. Instead of converting all the CAN data to an image (making real-time detection at stake due to increased processing), only CAN IDs are converted into the image by using one-hot encodings. For training, the first discriminator uses the normal and abnormal CAN images extracted from the actual vehicle, while the second discriminator uses normal and random noise. The generator and discriminator compete to increase their performance, and the second discriminator can detect fake images similar to real CAN images. The proposed model, however, has used only CAN IDs as the main feature to identify the attack from the non-attack. Converting data into images hinders the real-time detection of IDS. Also, the model can't detect operational flaws from the attack.

In [21], ResNet-inspired DCNN has been used for the sequence learning of broadcasted CAN IDs using the same dataset as in [20]. However, they are more interested in finding the pattern in the sequence of IDs rather than individual IDs. 29 bits IDs are recorded for every 29 consecutive IDs forming a 29x29 grid image ready to go into the DCNN and correspondingly labeled as an attack or no attack. They claimed that the DCNN seems to be more efficient in sequence learning than LSTM for this problem. This model needs high computational power and cannot detect unknown attacks.

Yu [22] proposed a novel self-supervised Bayesian Recurrent Autoencoder to detect adversarial trajectory in Sybil attacks targeting crowdsourced navigation systems. It uses time-series features of vehicle trajectories and embeds the trajectories in a latent distribution space as multivariate random variables using an encoder-reconstructor. This distribution is used to reconstruct the authentic trajectories and compared with the input to evaluate the credibility score. The author claimed that this model improves the baseline model by at least 76.6%.

3.5 FRONTIERS IN DEEP LEARNING (ADVANCEMENT AND FUTURE)

The challenges of deep learning: Supervised models require the extensive labeling of data, while reinforcement learning requires a very large number of interactions. Very slight modifications in fewer pixels and even a small change in rules in the environment can err the model. The inefficacy of the deep learning-based models is rooted in the assumption of "independent and identically distributed (i.i.d)" data. This assumes that the training data capture all the stochasticity of the real dynamic environment and that observations are independent of each other. To capture the dynamics of the changing environment, the learner model should evolve accordingly. Deep learning models are data-hungry; future deep learning should be envisioned to learn with fewer samples and fewer trials. For that model should correctly and broadly understand the environment before learning the tasks. Deep learning models are very poor at abstraction, and reasoning needs an enormous amount of data to learn a simple task. Symbolic AI has proven to be much better at reasoning and abstraction. Deep learning models are good at providing end-to-end solutions but miserable at breaking them down into interpretable and modifiable subtasks.

Currently, deep learning is said to have achieved system I natural intelligence, i.e., just achieving associative or mapping intelligence. For example, a human driver navigates to the neighborhood with visual cues that have been used a hundred times before without looking up at the direction or map. Also, while navigating to the new environment, he could use a map, direction, reasoning, and logic to get to the destination. The first is the system I cognition, while the second is system II cognition [23].

The pioneer deep learning scientists pointed out the following roadmaps for the future AI to be more conscious (system II cognition) at NeurIPS 2019:

- Handling the out-of-distribution (o.o.d) nonstationarity in the environment
- Systematic generalization
- Consciousness prior
- Meta-learning and localized change hypothesis for causal discovery
- Cosmopolitan DL architectures

3.5.1 Meta-learning

When we start learning some new tasks, we simply do not start from scratch; instead, we try to use prior experiences ($\theta_i \in \Theta$) from the prior known tasks ($t_j \in T$), where Θ is the discrete, continuous, or mixed configuration space, and T is the set of all known tasks. For example, a human driver can easily drive in a completely new environment. Along the way to learning specific tasks the human brain also learns how it is learning. If applied to learning new tasks, these prior learning experiences from the tasks could bring one step closer to getting system II's cognitive power. As a result, this new model would quickly learn the new tasks with sparse data. Meta-learning, or learning to learn, is the science of transferring learning experiences and meta-data from broader tasks to learn a new task with the least information in the least possible time [24]. The meta-data embody the prior learning tasks and the learned models in terms of exact algorithm configurations, hyperparameters, network architectures, and the resulting performance metrics such as accuracy, training time, FAR, F1-score, and prior weights, and measurable properties of tasks (meta-features). Once meta-data is collected, a machine needs to extract and transfer knowledge of the meta-data to search for the optimal models to solve the new tasks. Paper [24] explains how meta-learners learn from the model evaluations, such as task-independent recommendations, configurations of space design, and its transfer techniques, including surrogate models and warm, started to multitask learning. Unlike the base learner, where the model adapts to the fixed a priori or fixed parameterized biases, meta-learners dynamically choose the correct biases [25].

The meta-learning tends to transfer knowledge learned from different environments to learn a new task with the least training as opposed to data-hungry supervised learning heavily biased due to i.i.d assumption. The evolution of transfer learning may help the machine achieve system II cognition as the human. The working principle of the meta-learning algorithm is presented below.

Step 1: Make a set of prior known tasks: $t_j \in T$

Step 2: Make a set of configurations resulting from the learning task t_j such as hyperparameter settings, network architecture, and so on: $\theta_i \in \Theta$

Step 3: Prior evaluation measures (accuracy, FAR, training time, cross-validation) of each configuration θ_i to task t_j: $P_{i,j}(\theta_i, t_j)$

Step 4: Assign a set of all prior scalar evaluations $P_{i,j}(\theta_i, t_j)$ of configuration θ_i on task t_j to P: P = {$P_{i,j}(\theta_i, t_j)$}

Step 5: evaluate the performance $P_{i,new}$ on new task t_{new} and assign it to P_{new}: P_{new} = {$P_{i,new}$}

Step 6: Now the meta-learner L is trained on P' to predict recommended configurations Θ^*_{new} for new task t_{new}, where $P' = P \cup P_{new}$

Step 7: L is the learning algorithm derived from meta-learning to learn a new task

3.5.2 Federated learning

Federated learning (FL) is a machine learning framework where multiple nodes collaboratively train a model with local data under the orchestration of the centralized service provider/server [26]. Each node does not transfer or share locally stored data; instead it transfers the focused updates for immediate aggregation. A learning model can harness privacy, security, regulatory and economic benefits [27]. In FL, we define N set of CAVs ready to collaborate {V_1, …., V_N} from different vendors with corresponding decentralized and isolated data {D_1, …., D_N}. The conventional ML/DL model pulls up all the data $D = D_1 \cup$ …. $\cup D_N$ and train the learning model L with D. In contrast, FL does not pulls up data D instead it share some model inference/parameters to train the learning model L.

The future CAV industry is envisioned with numerous CAVs from multiple vendors. With the lack of fully developed protocol standards, cross-vendor trust issues discourage data sharing among competing vendors. The various FL application in the CAV domain can be found in [28–31]. Article [28] describes how a piece of falsified information from a single CAV could disrupt the training of the global model. [29] proposed the dynamic federated proximal (DFP)-based FL framework for designing the autonomous controller of the CAV. DFP is said to account for the mobility of CAVs, wireless fading channels, and non-iid and unbalanced data. While solving the privacy leakage problem, FL has some inherent vulnerabilities, such as model inversion, membership inference, etc. [30] proposed Byzantine-fault-tolerant (BFT) decentralized FL with privacy preservation in the CAV environment. Blockchain-based FL for CAV operations is proposed in [31]. Non-iid data distributions among multiple nodes, unbalanced datasets, and communication latency are some of the challenges being solved in FL [26, 27, 32].

3.6 END-TO-END DEEP CNN-LSTM ARCHITECTURE FOR CAV CYBERATTACK DETECTION

This chapter proposes the novel deep CNN-LSTM architecture for attack detection and classification in the CAV environment, as per Figure 3.4. Generally, CNN can learn the high dimensional spatial information of the feature space and may fail to capture distant temporal correlation. LSTM, on the other hand, can capture the temporal correlation by learning the sequence. Thus, the stacked model can learn the spatio-temporal features of the learning problem. The CNN-LSTM model is expected to perform better by learning the huge data's hierarchical feature representations and long-term temporal dependencies.

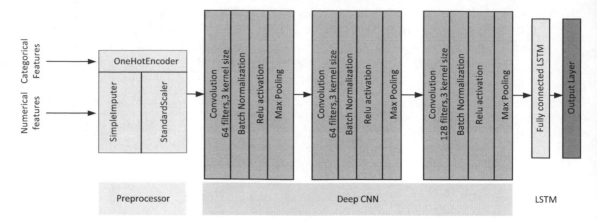

FIGURE 3.4   Proposed end-to-end deep CNN-LSTM architecture.

The proposed end-to-end Deep CNN-LSTM architecture pipeline has a pre-processor, a deep CNN layer, a fully connected LSTM, and an output layer.

a) Pre-processor: The pre-processor transforms the features into a machine-learning-compatible format. Most of the dataset contains mixed features such as numerical (integer, float) and categorical (nominal, ordinal) datatypes. Deep learning algorithms perform the computation only in integer or float features. Therefore, all the categorical features should be transformed into numerical forms. OneHotEncoder transforms the nominal features into binary formats. However, the high cardinality features would be encoded with elevated dimensionality. The SimpleImputer transformer deals with the dataset's missing values for numerical features. Moreover, the standard scaler standardizes the features by implementing zero mean and unit variance. Finally, the preprocessor outputs the features ready to fetch to the Deep CNN architecture.

b) Deep CNN architecture: This layer is generally implemented to extract the spatial information using its kernel and present the high-level features. Being able to capture the local patterns, 1D CNN is the popular algorithm for time series classification/regression successfully tested in natural language processing, the audio industry, and anomaly detection [33]. The *1D convolution layer* creates 64 convolution kernels of size three that convolve with the inputs over a single spatial or temporal dimension. The filters determine the dimensionality of output space, while the kernel determines the length of the 1D convolution window. The *Batch Normalization Layer* normalizes the filter's output using the mean and standard deviations of the current batch of inputs. The activation function used is *ReLu* for solving the exploding and vanishing gradient of its other compatriots, such as sigmoid tanh [34]. *MaxPolling1D* downsamples the normalized filters' output by taking the maximum value over the spatial window of pool size four that extracts the high-level features. This marks the completion of a single block of deep CNN architecture, and we have added a similar block twice to extract more high-level features.

c) Fully connected LSTM: The 1D CNN generally extracts the local temporal information, and it is hard to capture all the long-term sequential correlations. That is where fully connected *LSTM* comes in handy to capture long-term sequential relations. The details of the LSTM model are explained in our previous journal work [35]. The LSTM layer has 64 LSTM units.

d) Output layer: The output layer has three nodes—belonging to three different classes—to evaluate the probability of the sample belonging to each class. The probability sums to one with the highest probability indicating the predicted class taken care of by the *softmax* [36] activation function. For one-hot encoded output classes, *categorical cross-entropy* [37] is used.

3.6.1 Performance analysis

3.6.1.1 Dataset

The CAV-KDD dataset is adapted from the KDD99 [38] dataset, a well-known benchmark for intrusion detection. KDD99 dataset includes normal connections data and simulated attack data in a military network environment. Authors of [4] adapted by using 10% of KDD99 train data and 10% of KDD99 test data to form the CAV-KDD train and test dataset. The train data and test data are mutually exclusive, meaning the model has never experienced the test data during model fitting. There are three kinds of data; normal data refers to the normal packets, Neptune and Smurf refer to the simulated DoS attacks. The reason for choosing only these three types is that deep learning models are data-hungry and need huge sample data to capture the distribution of the dataset. Further, we pre-process and refine the dataset that will be implementable in a deep learning environment. Table 3.1 represents the distribution of the dataset while training and testing the CNN-LSTM. 30 % of training data is held to validate the model for the hyperparameter tuning. Table 3.2 indicates the class imbalance in the CAV train—20% belonging to the Normal category, 22% belonging to the Neptune attack, and 58% belonging to the Smurf attack—inherently induces data biases in the learning model. Figure 3.5 presents the variance captured by the singular values over the 20 samples, interpreted as the information captured by the prominent features. The four singular values, i.e., four prime features, can contribute to 92.90% of data variance. Singular value decomposition (SVD) is the popular dimensionality reduction technique that projects the m-dimensional data (m-columns/features) into a subspace with m or fewer dimensions without losing the essence of the original data [38].

Principal component analysis (PCA) is the dimensionality reduction technique that uses the SVD to project data from hyperspace to lower dimensional space and extract the matrix's dominant patterns [39]. Figure 3.6. presents the PCA with two principal components over the 90,000 data samples showing tightly overlapped subspaces. In this notion, it's hard for any linear classifier to draw the nonlinear boundaries between different classes. Therefore, a nonlinear classifier such as deep learning could be handy. Deep learning is handy when one expects minimal or no feature selections since it can make good decisions with hyperdimensional feature space (Table 3.1).

TABLE 3.1 Evolution of driving automation [7, p. 30]

LEVEL OF DRIVING AUTOMATION	ROLE OF USER	ROLE OF AUTOMATION SYSTEM
Level 0- No driving Automation	Driver always performs the entire DDT.	No DDT at all, safety warning and some other momentary emergency intervention in some cases
Level 1- Driver Assistance	Driver supervises the driving automation, performs all other DDT, determines when to engage or disengage the driving automation, and controls the entire DDT upon requirement or desire.	ADS, while engaged, executes either longitudinal or lateral vehicle motion control subtask and hand over the control to the driver upon immediate intervention.
Level 2-Partial Driving Automation	Driver supervises the driving automation, performs all other DDT, determines when to engage or disengage the driving automation, and controls the entire DDT upon requirement or desire.	ADS, upon engagement, execute both longitudinal and lateral vehicle motion control subtask and disengages upon driver request.
Level 3-Conditional Driving Automation	Driver, while ADS is not engaged, verifies the operational readiness of the ADS, and decides whether to engage ADS or not. Once ADS got engaged, the driver becomes DDT fallback-ready user. Though ADS is engaged, a user is always receptive to user intervention requests and DDT performance-relevant failures. Moreover, a user is always there for risk assessment and ADS disengagement.	ADS, while disengaged, permits the operations only within its operational design domain (ODD). Users can immediately take control upon the request. ADS, while engaged, perform the entire DDT within its ODD, transmits intervention requests to the DDT fallback-ready user when ODD limits are reached or when DDT performance-relevant failures are detected.

(Continued)

TABLE 3.1 (Continued)

LEVEL OF DRIVING AUTOMATION	ROLE OF USER	ROLE OF AUTOMATION SYSTEM
Level 4-High Driving Automation	Driver, while ADS is not engaged, verifies the operational readiness of the ADS, and decides whether to engage ADS or not. Once ADS got engaged, the driver becomes a passenger. Upon ADS engagement, the passenger does not perform DDT or DDT fallback or risk assessment. A passenger may disengage the ADS and become the driver and perform the DDT after ODD limits have been reached.	ADS, while disengaged, permits the operations only within its operational design domain (ODD). ADS, while engaged, perform the entire DDT within its ODD, It may prompt the passenger to resume operations of the vehicle near the ODD limits. Also, It performs DDT fallback transitions upon user request to achieve minimal risk or under DDT-relevant system failures or reaching the ODD limits. It may cause some delay for the disengagement.
Level 5- Full Driving Automation	Driver, while ADS is not engaged, verifies the operational readiness of the ADS, and decides whether to engage ADS or not. Once ADS got engaged, the driver becomes a passenger. Upon ADS engagement, the passenger need not perform DDT or DDT fallback or risk assessment. A passenger may disengage the ADS, becomes the driver, and performs the risk assessment.	ADS, while not engaged, permits engagement of ADS under driver manageable all road conditions. ADS, while engaged, perform all the DDT, performs automatic DDT fallback transitions to minimal risk condition upon DDT performance -relevant failures or user request to achieve minimal risk condition. ADS got disengaged only when it achieves minimal risk conditions, or a driver is performing the DDT. It may cause some delay for the disengagement.

3.6.1.2 Evaluation metrics

The end-to-end deep CNN-LSTM architecture uses accuracy, precision, recall, and F1-score to assess the performance of the classifier model. In this work, to quantify the performance of the proposed detection method, some performance metrics have been considered, such as accuracy, precision, recall, and F-1 score (defined below) from the confusion matrix. The confusion matrix generally reflects how efficiently a particular machine/algorithm classifies the actual data. It is the most ubiquitous matrix for the performance evaluation of the classifier, which is shown in Table 3.3, where the meaning of TP, FP, FN, and TN are described below (Table 3.2).

- True-positive (TP): correctly classified intrusion,
- False-positive (FP): non-intrusive behavior wrongly classified as an intrusion,
- False-negative (FN): intrusive behavior wrongly classified as non-intrusive,
- True-negative(TN): correctly classified non-intrusive behavior.

Accuracy: It estimates the correctly classified data out of all datasets. The higher the accuracy, the better the ML model. (Accuracy $\in = [0, 1]$)

$$\text{Accuracy} = \frac{TP + TN}{TP + TN + FP + FN} \tag{1}$$

TABLE 3.2 Confusion matrix

ACTUAL CLASS↓\PREDICTED CLASS→	ANOMALY	NORMAL
Anomaly	TP	FN
Normal	FP	TN

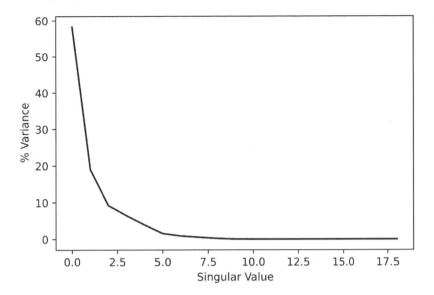

FIGURE 3.5   Variance captured by the Singular values.

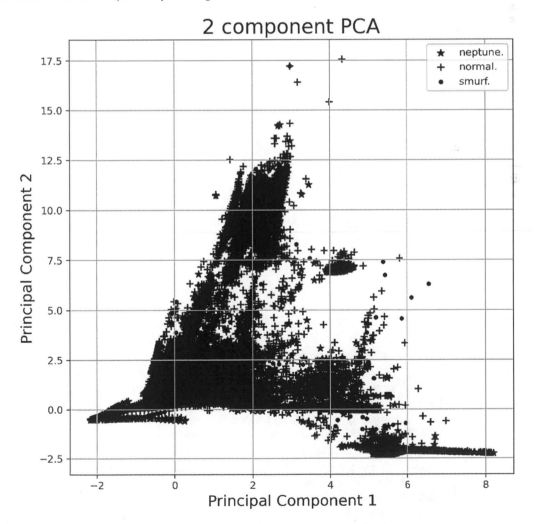

FIGURE 3.6   Principal component analysis.

TABLE 3.3 Performance metrics

ALGORITHMS	PRECISION	RECALL	F1-SCORE	AUC	ACCURACY
DNN	99.70%	99.50%	99.60%	99.82%	99.64%
CNN	99.84%	99.62%	99.73%	99.99%	99.75%
LSTM	92.41%	96.29%	93.85%	99.95%	93.89%
CNN-LSTM	99.85%	99.73%	99.74%	99.99%	99.75%

Precision: It estimates the ratio of correctly classified attacks to the number of all identified attacks. Precision represents the repeatability and reproducibility of the model (Precision $\in = [0, 1]$). The higher the precision, the better the ML model.

$$Precision = \frac{TP}{TP + FP} \tag{2}$$

True positive rate/Recall: It estimates the ratio of a correctly classified anomaly to all anomaly data. A higher value is desired to be a better ML model and is given by: (Recall $\in = [0, 1]$)

$$Recall = \frac{TP}{TP + FN} \tag{3}$$

F1-Score/Measure: It is the harmonic mean of precision and recall. A higher value of the F1 score represents the good ML model ($F1 - score \in = [0, 1]$) and given by

$$F1 - score = 2 * \frac{Precision * Recall}{Precison + Recall} \tag{4}$$

AUC: Area under the curve (AUC) tells the model's degree of separability. Higher the AUC better the model's separability.

3.6.2 Results and discussions

The experiments have been carried out in Intel® Core™ i7 2.6 GHz CPU with 16 GB RAM computer. The Anaconda Navigator 2.0.4 hosts JupyterLab 3.0.14, where algorithms are written in Python 3.8.8 of notebook 6.3.0. Our end-to-end deep CNN-LSTM model architecture is clearly explained, including the number and size of convolution filters, kernel size, numbers and size of pooling layers, batch normalization layers, fully connected LSTM layer, and output layer, as in section 6. For the comparison purpose, along with the CNN-LSTM, we created Deep Neural Network (DNN), Convolution Neural Network (CNN), and Long-Short Term Memory (LSTM). The models' performance metrics are evaluated under similar constraints, such as the same train and test data, hyperparameters, batch size, etc. Apart from that, all our deep learning models run for 10 epochs taking a batch of size 500 while training and all the models are tested with a batch size of 20. 30% of the train data has been held out for validation so that one can tune the hyperparameters. The trained model has never experienced the features from the test data during the training, so the models don't over-parameterize and memorize.

Figure 3.7. presents the progression of training and validation accuracies and training and validation losses along the epochs. The training was so smooth that within 680 steps of the first epoch, our proposed model achieved successive training and validation accuracies of 91.80% and 99.98%, with successive losses of 0.3231 and 0.0052. The average training time per epoch was 95.1 seconds. The best model from the training has achieved 99.99% accuracy on validation data. This model can be trained up to just two epochs to get more than 99% training and validation accuracies.

Table 3.3 compares the precision, recall, f1-score, AUC, and testing accuracy of different deep learning algorithms against the proposed CNN-LSTM. The proposed CNN-LSTM model has achieved

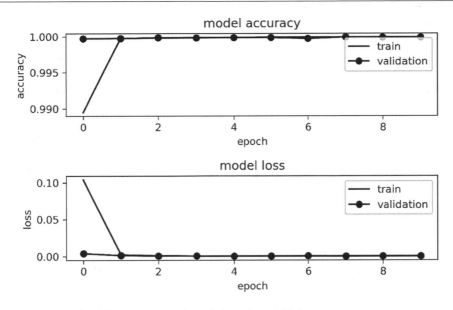

FIGURE 3.7   Training and validation progression of deep CNN-LSTM.

the highest precision, recall, f1-score, AUC, and testing accuracy, i.e., more than 99% in each metric among other implemented algorithms. 1D CNN algorithm has achieved almost similar AUC and accuracy as the proposed CNN-LSTM algorithm. For similar setups with two hidden layers and 64 hidden nodes, LSTM is found to be the most inferior in terms of all other performance metrics, with the exception of the AUC. All the performance metrics for DNN, CNN, and CNN-LSTM were found to perform excellently with more than 99% evaluation metrics. This justifies the superior performance of our proposed deep CNN-LSTM algorithm. Similarly, Table 3.5. presents the proposed model's classwise performance, where the model exhibits an almost 100% precision score for the samples from all three classes. The resulting recall and f1-score is almost 100% for Smurf and Neptune, with 99% for samples from a normal class (Tables 3.3 and 3.4).

Figure 3.8. presents the multiclass confusion matrix where each block has the number of samples with a percentage belonging to that block. The last row indicates the actual samples belonging to those classes, while the last column represents the predicted samples using the proposed algorithm. The numbers and percentages in off-diagonal columns are misclassified samples. The highest misclassification rate of the proposed is 0.23% for the Smurf attack, which is 640 out of 164,091 samples. This implicit misclassification, i.e., bias, came from the data distribution because Smurf got almost 58.04% of total samples for the testing model got similar bias because of similar data distribution in training. This bias in classifying Smurf resulted in a false alarm of normal class, i.e., there is a Smurf attack, but the model will predict it as a normal event. However, this error is less than 0.23%, which is very small. But for high-sensitivity CAV attack detection, upsampling and downsampling can help achieve equal data distribution while training the model. Overall, the proposed model has outstanding performance metrics, almost 100%.

TABLE 3.4   Classwise performance evaluation of the proposed DCNN-LSTM model

LABEL	PRECISION	RECALL	F1-SCORE	SUPPORT
Smurf	1.00	1.00	1.00	164091
Normal	1.00	0.99	0.99	60590
Neptune	1.00	1.00	1.00	58001

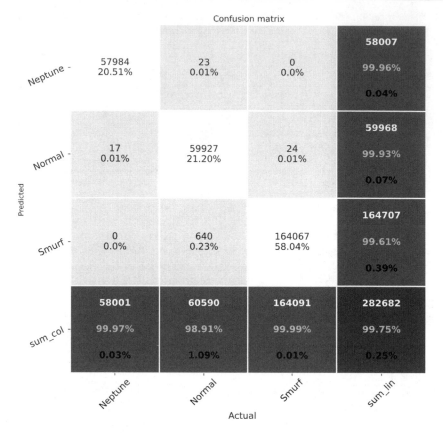

FIGURE 3.8 Confusion matrix of deep CNN-LSTM.

3.7 CONCLUSION

With the luxury of automation and connectivity, CAV inherits most of the cyber-physical vulnerabilities of incumbent technologies, including evolving network architectures, wireless communications, and AI-assisted automation. This chapter sheds light on cyber-physical vulnerabilities and risks that originated in IT, OT, and the physical domains of the CAV ecosystem, eclectic threat landscapes, and threat intelligence. To deal with the security threats embedded in high-speed, high-dimensional, multimodal data and assets of eccentric stakeholders of the CAV ecosystem, this chapter presents and analyzes state-of-the-art deep learning-based threat intelligence for attack detection. Since deep learning itself has been evolving to attain superior cognition and intelligence, it would also directly impact threat intelligence. The collaborative learning platform of deep learning, federated learning, can share threat intelligence without the need to share the data between divergent stakeholders of the CAV ecosystem. Also, deep learning for CAV has still to work on meta-learning for robust and swift generalization under the dynamic environment and out of distribution data context. The frontiers in deep learning and the challenges have been included in the chapter. We have proposed, trained, and tested the deep CNN-LSTM model for CAV threat intelligence; assessed and compared the performance of the proposed model against other deep learning algorithms such as DNN, CNN, and LSTM. Our results indicate the superiority of the proposed model, although DNN and 1d-CNN also achieved more than 99% of accuracy, precision, recall, f1-score, and AUC on the CAV-KDD dataset. The performance of deep CNN-LSTM comes with increased model complexity and cumbersome hyperparameter tuning. Still, there are open challenges to deep learning adoption in the CAV cybersecurity paradigm due to costlier implementations and training, the lack of adequately developed protocols and policies, poorly defined privileges between stakeholders, adversarial threats to the deep learning model, and poor generalizability of the model under out of data distributions.

REFERENCES

[1] National Safety Council "Motor Vehicle Deaths in 2020 Estimated to be Highest in 13 Years, Despite Dramatic Drops in Miles Driven - National Safety Council." https://www.nsc.org/newsroom/motor-vehicle-deaths-2020-estimated-to-be-highest (accessed July 21, 2021).

[2] F. Falcini and G. Lami, "Deep Learning in Automotive: Challenges and Opportunities," in *Software Process Improvement and Capability Determination*, vol. *770*, A. Mas, A. Mesquida, R. V. O'Connor, T. Rout, and A. Dorling, Eds. Cham: Springer International Publishing, 2017, pp. 279–288. doi: 10.1007/978-3-319-67383-7_21.

[3] Emyr Thomas of BAE Systems "Security Challenges for Connected and Autonomous Vehicles," *BAE Systems | Cyber Security & Intelligence*. https://www.baesystems.com/en/cybersecurity/feature/security-challenges-for-connected-and-autonomous-vehicles (accessed September 12, 2021).

[4] Q. He, X. Meng, R. Qu, and R. Xi, "Machine Learning-Based Detection for Cyber Security Attacks on Connected and Autonomous Vehicles," *Mathematics*, vol. *8*, no. 8, p. 1311, 2020, doi: 10.3390/math8081311.

[5] Simon Wright "Autonomous Cars Generate more than 300 TB of data per year," *Tuxera*, 2021. https://www.tuxera.com/blog/autonomous-cars-300-tb-of-data-per-year/ (accessed July 21, 2021).

[6] SAE International "J3016C: Taxonomy and Definitions for Terms Related to Driving Automation Systems for On-Road Motor Vehicles - SAE International." https://www.sae.org/standards/content/j3016_202104/ (accessed August 24, 2021).

[7] National Highway Traffic Safety Administration "Automated Vehicles for Safety | NHTSA." https://www.nhtsa.gov/technology-innovation/automated-vehicles-safety (accessed August 25, 2021).

[8] S. Parkinson, P. Ward, K. Wilson, and J. Miller, "Cyber Threats Facing Autonomous and Connected Vehicles: Future Challenges," *IEEE Transactions on Intelligent Transportation Systems*, vol. *18*, no. 11, pp. 2898–2915, 2017, doi: 10.1109/TITS.2017.2665968.

[9] A. M. Wyglinski, X. Huang, T. Padir, L. Lai, T. R. Eisenbarth, and K. Venkatasubramanian, "Security of Autonomous Systems Employing Embedded Computing and Sensors," *IEEE Micro*, vol. *33*, no. 1, pp. 80–86, 2013, doi: 10.1109/MM.2013.18.

[10] N. Statt, "Self-Driving Car Engineer Anthony Levandowski Pleads Guilty to Stealing Google Trade Secrets," *The Verge*, 2020. https://www.theverge.com/2020/3/19/21187651/anthony-levandowski-pleads-guilty-google-waymo-uber-trade-secret-theft-lawsuit (accessed September 12, 2021).

[11] Z. El-Rewini, K. Sadatsharan, D. F. Selvaraj, S. J. Plathottam, and P. Ranganathan, "Cybersecurity challenges in vehicular communications," *Vehicular Communications*, vol. *23*, p. 100214, 2020, doi: 10.1016/j.vehcom.2019.100214.

[12] J. Shen, J. Y. Won, Z. Chen, and Q. A. Chen, "Demo: Attacking Multi-Sensor Fusion based Localization in High-Level Autonomous Driving," in *2021 IEEE Security and Privacy Workshops (SPW)*, 2021, pp. 242–242. doi: 10.1109/SPW53761.2021.00039.

[13] Stefan Marksteiner and Ma Zhendong, "Cybersecurity for Connected and Autonomous Vehicles," p. 36, 2019.

[14] Rossi Francesca "AAAI 2020 Conference | Thirty-Fourth AAAI Conference on Artificial Intelligence." *Proceedings of the Third Central European Cybersecurity Conference*, pp. 1–3, 2019, https://aaai.org/Conferences/AAAI-20/ (accessed September 12, 2021).

[15] Y. Bengio, Y. Lecun, and G. Hinton, "Deep Learning for AI," *Communications of the ACM*, vol. *64*, no. 7, pp. 58–65, 2021, doi: 10.1145/3448250.

[16] Hinton Geoff, Yann Le Cunn, and Bengio Yoshua, *AAAI 20/AAAI 2020 Keynotes Turing Award Winners Event/Geoff Hinton, Yann Le Cunn, Yoshua Bengio*, 2020. [Online Video]. https://www.youtube.com/watch?v=UX8OubxsY8w (accessed September 12, 2021).

[17] M. Basnet, S. Poudyal, M. H. Ali, and D. Dasgupta, "Ransomware Detection Using Deep Learning in the SCADA System of Electric Vehicle Charging Station," *ArXiv210407409 Cs Eess*, 2021. [Online]. http://arxiv.org/abs/2104.07409 (accessed June 04, 2021).

[18] A. Kavousi-Fard, M. Dabbaghjamanesh, T. Jin, W. Su, and M. Roustaei, "An Evolutionary Deep Learning-Based Anomaly Detection Model for Securing Vehicles," *IEEE Transactions on Intelligent Transportation Systems*, vol. *22*, no. 7, pp. 4478–4486, 2021, doi: 10.1109/TITS.2020.3015143.

[19] J. Ashraf, A. D. Bakhshi, N. Moustafa, H. Khurshid, A. Javed, and A. Beheshti, "Novel Deep Learning-Enabled LSTM Autoencoder Architecture for Discovering Anomalous Events From Intelligent Transportation Systems," *IEEE Transactions on Intelligent Transportation Systems*, vol. *22*, no. 7, pp. 4507–4518, 2021, doi: 10.1109/TITS.2020.3017882.

[20] E. Seo, H. M. Song, and H. K. Kim, "GIDS: GAN based Intrusion Detection System for In-Vehicle Network," *2018 16th Annual Conference on Privacy, Security and Trust PST*, pp. 1–6, 2018, doi: 10.1109/PST.2018.8514157.

[21] H. M. Song, J. Woo, and H. K. Kim, "In-vehicle network intrusion detection using deep convolutional neural network," *Vehicular Communications*, vol. *21*, p. 100198, 2020, doi: 10.1016/j.vehcom.2019.100198.

[22] J. J. Q. Yu, "Sybil Attack Identification for Crowdsourced Navigation: A Self-Supervised Deep Learning Approach," *IEEE Transactions on Intelligent Transportation Systems*, vol. *22*, no. 7, pp. 4622–4634, 2021, doi: 10.1109/TITS.2020.3036085.

[23] D. Kahneman, *Thinking, Fast and Slow*, 1st edition. New York: Farrar, Straus and Giroux, 2013.

[24] J. Vanschoren, "Meta-Learning: A Survey," *ArXiv181003548 Cs Stat*, 2018. [Online]. http://arxiv.org/abs/1810.03548 (accessed: August 30, 2021).

[25] R. Vilalta and Y. Drissi, "A Perspective View and Survey of Meta-learning," *Artificial Intelligence Review*, vol. *18*, pp. 77–95, 2002.

[26] P. Kairouz et al., "Advances and Open Problems in Federated Learning," *ArXiv191204977 Cs Stat*, 2021. [Online]. http://arxiv.org/abs/1912.04977 (accessed August 31, 2021).

[27] Y. Zhao, M. Li, L. Lai, N. Suda, D. Civin, and V. Chandra, "Federated Learning with Non-IID Data," *ArXiv180600582 Cs Stat*, 2018. [Online]. http://arxiv.org/abs/1806.00582 (accessed August 31, 2021).

[28] R. A. Mallah, G. Badu-Marfo, and B. Farooq, "Cybersecurity Threats in Connected and Automated Vehicles based Federated Learning Systems," *ArXiv210213256 Cs*, 2021. [Online]. http://arxiv.org/abs/2102.13256 (accessed August 31, 2021).

[29] T. Zeng, O. Semiari, M. Chen, W. Saad, and M. Bennis, "Federated Learning on the Road: Autonomous Controller Design for Connected and Autonomous Vehicles," *ArXiv210203401 Cs Eess*, 2021. [Online]. http://arxiv.org/abs/2102.03401 (accessed August 31, 2021).

[30] J.-H. Chen, M.-R. Chen, G.-Q. Zeng, and J. Weng, "BDFL: A Byzantine-Fault-Tolerance Decentralized Federated Learning Method for Autonomous Vehicles," *IEEE Transactions on Vehicular Technology*, pp. 1–1, 2021, doi: 10.1109/TVT.2021.3102121.

[31] Y. Fu, F. R. Yu, C. Li, T. H. Luan, and Y. Zhang, "Vehicular Blockchain-Based Collective Learning for Connected and Autonomous Vehicles," *IEEE Wireless Communications*, vol. *27*, no. 2, pp. 197–203, 2020, doi: 10.1109/MNET.001.1900310.

[32] M. Mohri, G. Sivek, and A. T. Suresh, "Agnostic Federated Learning," in *International Conference on Machine Learning*, 2019, pp. 4615–4625. [Online]. https://proceedings.mlr.press/v97/mohri19a.html (accessed August 31, 2021).

[33] W. Tang, G. Long, L. Liu, T. Zhou, J. Jiang, and M. Blumenstein, "Rethinking 1D-CNN for Time Series Classification: A Stronger Baseline," *ArXiv200210061 Cs Stat*, 2021. [Online]. Available: http://arxiv.org/abs/2002.10061 (accessed September 7, 2021).

[34] M. Basnet and M. H. Ali, "Deep Learning-based Intrusion Detection System for Electric Vehicle Charging Station," in *2020 2nd International Conference on Smart Power Internet Energy Systems (SPIES)*, 2020, pp. 408–413. doi: 10.1109/SPIES48661.2020.9243152.

[35] M. Basnet and Mohd H. Ali, "Exploring Cybersecurity Issues in 5G Enabled Electric Vehicle Charging Station with Deep Learning," *IET Generation, Transmission & Distribution*, p. gtd2.12275, 2021, doi: 10.1049/gtd2.12275.

[36] A. Martins and R. Astudillo, "From Softmax to Sparsemax: A Sparse Model of Attention and Multi-Label Classification," in *International Conference on Machine Learning*, 2016, pp. 1614–1623. [Online]. https://proceedings.mlr.press/v48/martins16.html (accessed September 8, 2021).

[37] Z. Zhang and M. Sabuncu, "Generalized Cross Entropy Loss for Training Deep Neural Networks with Noisy Labels," in *Advances in Neural Information Processing Systems*, 2018, vol. *31*. [Online]. https://proceedings.neurips.cc/paper/2018/hash/f2925f97bc13ad2852a7a551802feea0-Abstract.html (accessed: September 8, 2021).

[38] M. E. Wall, A. Rechtsteiner, and L. M. Rocha, "Singular Value Decomposition and Principal Component Analysis," in *A Practical Approach to Microarray Data Analysis*, D. P. Berrar, W. Dubitzky, and M. Granzow, Eds. Boston, MA: Springer US, 2003, pp. 91–109. doi: 10.1007/0-306-47815-3_5.

[39] S. Wold, K. Esbensen, and P. Geladi, "Principal Component Analysis," *Chemometrics and Intelligent Laboratory Systems*, vol. *2*, no. 1, pp. 37–52, 1987, doi: 10.1016/0169-7439(87)80084-9.

PART II

Deep learning for vehicle communications

Deep learning for UAV network optimization

4

Jian Wang
University of Tennessee at Martin, Martin, Tennessee

Yongxin Liu
Auburn University at Montgomery, Montgomery, Alabama

Shuteng Niu
Bowling Green State University, Bowling Green, Ohio

Houbing Song
Security and Optimization for Networked Globe Laboratory (SONG Lab), Embry-Riddle Aeronautical University, Daytona Beach, Florida

Contents

DOI: 10.1201/9781003190691-6

4.1 INTRODUCTION

The 2nd generation (2G) cellular networking provides both voice and text services. The 3rd generation (3G) cellular networking retains the voice and text service link and adds one more link to provide a general packet radio service (GPRS). As the deployments of base stations (BSs) and manufacturers increase dramatically, the 4th generation long-term evolution (4G LTE) cellular communication will come to the public. In the 4G LTE, the researchers and engineers have taken a great deal of effort to exploit the potential of 4G LTE. Compared with 2G and 3G, various novel and practical approaches have been proposed to refine the spectrum efficiency and quality of services (QoS). As cellular networking evolves, a 5th generation new radio (5G NR) is developing. Implementing 5G NR on a large scale stimulates the new revolutions in many fields, including health care and self-driving vehicles. Compared with 4G LTE, 5G NR has more enhancements in many aspects, such as latency [1], spectrum efficiency [2], traffic capacity [3], connection density [4], experienced throughput [5] and network efficiency [6].

Network slicing separates the hardware into multiple virtual networks according to different applications, services, and purposes. The operators can deploy multiple and specific networks in the same physical hardware to maximize networking usage [7]. Beamforming and Multiple Input and Multiple Output (MIMO) were considered two fundamentals to advance the communication capacity in 4G LTE. In 5G NR, these two key technologies are implemented to achieve higher traffic capacity and connection density [8]. Simultaneously, 5G NR adopts cloud computing [9, 10] and edge computing [11] to enhance experimented throughput, which is affected by networking latency seriously. Once the construction of networks has finished, 5G NR will be ready to connect everything [12]. Naturally, the evolution of 5G NR fuels the development of the Internet of Things (IoT). The massive BSs are the fundamental to the massive deployment of IoT, which connects everything, including vehicles, mobile devices, and Unmanned Aerial Vehicles (UAVs). The comparison between 1G, 2G, 3G, 4G, and 5G is shown in Table 4.1.

With the growth of novel control technologies, manufacturing, and battery, UAVs have developed over several years and have provided an impetus to many technical revolutions in various fields such as agriculture and power plants [13]. UAV can carry spray pesticides to cure the diseases of crops which are caused by pests or a lack of appropriate nutrition. Workers can steer UAV to detect if the power line connects well

TABLE 4.1 Comparison between 1G, 2G, 3G, 4G, and 5G

COMPARISON	SWITCHING	CORE NETWORKING	MULTIPLEXING	DATA BANDWIDTH
1G	Circuit	PSTN	FDMA	2.4 Kb/s
2G	Circuit & Packets	PSTN	TDMA/CDMA	64 Kb/s
3G	Packets	Packet N/W	CDMA	2 Mb/s
4G LTE	All packets	Packet N/W & PSTN	CDMA	100 Mb/s
5G NR	All packets	Internet	CDMA	1 Gb/s

remotely so that the workers do not have to climb the tower and reduce labor consumption. Although UAV accelerates the development of many fields, the limitations of conventional communication still constrain its flexibility and capacities such as flight range and fleet connection. The majority of UAV communication is based on remote radio controllers. These radio controllers support Direct Sequential Spread Spectrum (DSSS) and Frequency Hopping Spread Spectrum (FHSS) [14]. The maximum flight range is constrained by the controllers' transmitter power [15]. In addition, videos, images, and other operation information are delivered in different links, which needs to carry different transceivers to receive information. Point-to-point communication cannot guarantee QoS and is vulnerable to external interference. The other approach is to connect UAV to cellular networking. The cellular BSs take the place of the controllers' transceivers and transmits the data with cellular networking. Many researchers spent their efforts to improve the cellular-connected UAV [16–18]. The cellular-connected UAV is shown in Figure 4.1. Due to the data rates in 2G and 3G, most cellular-connected UAV research focuses on integrating and enhancing 4G LTE. Their work primarily considers UAV as a platform that relays data transmission. Simultaneously, UAV networking is separated from the ground IoT. The operators need to have specific equipment to access UAV networking and bridge the networking to terrestrial networking [19, 20]. As a result of 4G LTE, the cellular-connected UAV has not been applied on a large scale [21]. Compared with 4G LTE, 5G NR can satisfy the requirement of UAV on mobile communication. The trade-off in 4G LTE may be eliminated under 5G NR. The comparison between 4G LTE and 5G NR is depicted in Table 4.2.

Following the revolution in computing capacity, Artificial Intelligence (AI) went through the winter [22] and had been going to blossom. As novel computing approaches advance, AI has already been implemented into many fields to provide intelligent services for workers and machines. The AI-based implementations have apparent effects on the enhancement in different fields, stimulating many people to engage in AI research. Deep learning (DL), a subset of AI, has been implemented continuously to

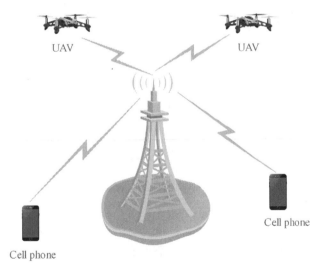

FIGURE 4.1   Cellular-connected UAV.

TABLE 4.2 Comparison of performance between 4G and 5G

COMPARISON	HANDOVER	USER PLANE LATENCY	CONTROL PLAN LATENCY	SUPPORTED MAXIMUM COUPLING LOSS
4G LTE	49.5 ms	20 ms	100 ms	140 dB
5G NR	0 ms	1 ms	10 ms	164 dB

accelerate machine production. Among many DL-enabled approaches, Reinforcement Learning (RL) is one of the most promising approaches to help UAV acquire knowledge from interaction with the environment. The DL contains three parts: supervised learning, unsupervised learning, and RL. Some researchers have applied RL to UAV optimization, which can replace the conventional approaches, like PID, to achieve a more robust and accurate control [23].

DL-enabled UAV networking can achieve more sufficient networking services from inter- and intra-networking which can provide the UAV networking with more capacities to finish the complex missions which have high requirements of collaborations and corporations, both simultaneously and sequentially. With ultra-high frequencies carriers, 5G NR can provide ultra wide-band wireless communication for UAV networking with the sacrifice of transmission range and energy divergence which attracts many researchers to make efforts to amend the tradeoff to extend the reliance of 5G NR-enabled UAV networking. With reliable wide-band wireless communication, the feasible throughput of UAV networking can assure QoS for UAV, which is critical to the perception and complement of mission from remote terminals in real time. The instantaneous feedback and intrusion loops between remote terminals and swarm UAS networking on the light is essential to the complex mission complement. Concurrently, the trained RL can allocate the network resources to improve the communication quality of UAV fleet [24, 25]. The RL implementations on UAV prove that the DL-enabled approaches are promising methods to improve UAV networking under the era of 5G. Due to the advantages of learning from interaction, RL can assure robust optimization for UAV swarm networking. Comparable with the distributed UAV swarm networking, Multi-Agent Reinforcement Learning (MARL) can improve the throughput of UAV swarm networking. Each UAV as an agent is formulated to MARL to achieve the optimal throughput and coverage and maximization of long-term rewards [26]. MARL optimizes the movement of UAV with offline exploration and online learning [27]. The joint optimization combining offline and online movements can optimize throughput for UAV networking and cellular networking.

This chapter principally provides a comprehensive review of DL for UAV networking throughput enhancement. Section 4.2 presents the key categories for UAV networking throughput enhancement. Section 4.3 demonstrates the routing enhancing for UAV networking throughput. DL-enabled routing approaches for the throughput enhancement will be presented. With optimal routing generation, section 4.4 mainly presents UAV networking construction, which includes UAV swarm networking construction and DL-enabled UAV swarm networking throughput enhancement. Section 4.5 presents DL-enabled UAV networking throughput enhancement in resource allocation and scheduling.

4.2 KEY CATEGORIES FOR UAV NETWORKING THROUGHPUT ENHANCEMENT

With the development of cellular networking, UAV networking can deploy on a large scale with QoS. The categories of UAV networking throughput enhancement are listed as follows:

- *Routing: Routing can provide the efficient packet delivery for connections. The robustness and efficiency of routing in UAV networking can reduce the latency and improve the QoS of UAV networking on the various implementations of UAVs. Due to the flexibility, UAV networking needs to interact with the status of QoS and maintain the routing connectivity with DL.*
- *Relay: Connections in UAV networking depend on relay to extend the range of packet delivery. The qualities of relay determine the stability of UAV networking throughput.*
- *Bandwidth: With the advanced communication implementations, UAV networking can achieve higher throughput with optimal spectrum usage and high QoS assurance.*
- *Coverage: With efficient energy consumption and spectrum multiplexing, UAV networking throughput can be achieved for uploading and downloading connections. An energy-efficient approach promotes each UAV communication coverage to intensify the service to users.*

TABLE 4.3 Categories of UAV networking throughput enhancement

CATEGORIES	SPECIFIC ASPECTS	REFERENCES
Relay	1. Uploading speed 2. Low Bit Error Rate (BER)	[28]
Routing	1. Access point 2. Handovers 3. Link selection 4. Traffic estimation	[25]
Bandwidth	1. Spectrum usage 2. QoS assurance	[29]
Coverage	1. Energy consumption 2. Spectrum multiplexing	[30]
Interference	1. Link selection 2. Scheduling	[31]
Scheduling	1. Active link selection 2. Link orders allocation	[27]

- *Interference: Interference enhancement principally reduces the latency for each link in UAV networking. The interference reduction on each link can improve the success rate of packet delivery for multiple hops.*
- *Scheduling: Scheduling for different sets of active links in UAV networking can reduce collisions in the same time slots which decrease the interference in different routing and reduce packet delivery rate (PDR). With the networking status derived from UAV networking, DL can generate the status of the networking and leverage RL policies to improve the throughput of UAV networking* (Table 4.3).

4.3 ROUTING ENHANCEMENT FOR UAV NETWORKING THROUGHPUT

UAV networking stimulates the evolution of UAV swarms and plays a vital role in the UAV fleet [32]. Reliable and efficient routing algorithms can provide low delays and packet losses for the services [33]. The UAV networking routing algorithms can find the shortest cost for the delivery. The characteristics of Flying Ad hoc Networks (FANET) pose a challenge for the routing algorithms. To enhance the throughput of FANET routing, the researchers proposed many FANET-oriented routing algorithms to improve FANET. According to the based models, the UAV networking routing algorithms have three categories (depicted as Figure 4.2): 1) Position-based routing algorithms; 2) Topology-based routing algorithms; 3) Swarm-based routing algorithms. In the Position-based routing algorithms, the routing algorithms can be sorted into two main categories: 1) Multiple path-based algorithms; 2) Single path-based algorithms. The topology-based algorithms can be sorted into three categories according to the methods of response: 1) Proactive; 2) Reactive; 3) Hybrid.

4.3.1 Position-based routing

The position-based routing protocols are based on the geographic positions. The UAV finds the destination before delivery, which is like the hot potato routing protocol. The UAV forwards the packets to the

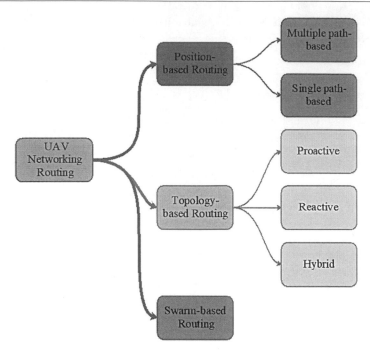

FIGURE 4.2   UAV networking routing.

neighbors. After that, the neighbors identify the packet destination and forward it to the next hop. The position-based routing can be sorted into two categories: 1) single path-based; 2) multiple path-based.

4.3.1.1 Single path-based

The single path-based approaches are efficient and straightforward in path discovery. There is only one valid path that leads to the destination. The UAV checks the packets' destination and forwards it to the next hop until the packets find the destination. The single path-based algorithms are efficiency and lower overheads for the whole distributed system [34–36]. However, it poses a challenge to the system for maintenance. The dynamic topology may cause one link to be invalid, and for all of the communication links to crash [37].

4.3.1.2 Multiple path-based

Due to the weak reliability in the single path-based approaches, the researchers tried the multiple path-based approaches [38]. UAV can get the packets with the same destinations simultaneously, and the bandwidth has been enlarged remarkably. However, the path discovery with multiple paths also has some technical problems that generate loops in the path discovery. The loops cause the path to decrease the efficiency of the packet delivery [39]. Ad hoc on-demand distance vector (AODV) can prevent the loop problem [40, 41]. The multiple path-based approaches can provide reliable connections and broader bandwidth. Nevertheless, path discovery processing costs much overhead and causes a loop in the path.

4.3.2 Topology-based routing

The topology-based routing algorithms are mainly based on the centralized routing protocols, such as optimized link state routing (OLSR) [42], and the decentralized routing protocols, distance vector (DV) routing protocols [43]. These two routing algorithms are fundamental to networking construction. The topology-based routing algorithms are dependent on the topology updating and the path information. The nodes find the paths for delivery according to the link status.

4.3.2.1 Proactive

The current proactive routing protocols are based mainly on OLSR. UAV acquires the complete information of the network before it executes the path discovery. The efficiency of delivery is high once the path discovery is completed [44]. The proactive approaches have the advantages of path discovery and resource allocation. However, the control mechanism is centralized, which needs much overhead for management. The management costs much power and computation resources [45].

4.3.2.2 Reactive

The reactive routing protocols allow UAV to find a path for delivery, which are based on DV routing [46]. Among the DV routing, AODV is the most practical and successful protocol [47]. The AODV protocols do not need to maintain the complete link information periodically. The UAV can request routing when needed. The reactive routing protocols can adapt to the dynamic topology of UAV networking. However, the reactive approaches occupy much overhead of the system, which lacks delivery efficiency [48].

4.3.2.3 Hybrid

The proactive approaches and the reactive approaches have apparent disadvantages and advantages. Some researchers have combined these two advantages to propose hybrid approaches. The hybrid approaches can have efficient path discovery and better performance for the dynamic topology [49]. However, the hybrid approaches have not been deployed on a large scale. Resource allocation and routing management pose a big challenge for the control system [50].

4.3.3 Swarm-based routing

Swarm-based routing algorithms are rare. Due to the expense involved, the swarm-based routing is not mature. The research of the swarm-based routing focuses on ant colony algorithms. The researchers leveraged ant colony algorithms to find the best path for communication [51]. Apart from the ant colony algorithms, the bee colony algorithms are also implemented into the UAV swarms [52]. The swarm-based routing algorithms are reliable, efficient, and robust to the dynamic topology [53]. However, the initialization of swarm-based routing algorithms takes a long time, and the maintenance is hard to finish. The distributed routing algorithms for UAV networking are mainly based on AODV [54, 55]. The authors compared AODV and OLSR in FANET with the simulator of NS-2 [56]. The evaluation shows that OLSR is not suitable for highly dynamic and low-density networking. In the research of [47], the evaluation shows that the time consumption of AODV on the initial path discovery stage is overwhelmed. Furthermore, the authors, in [47], concluded that the path discovery stage on the AODV can decrease the stability of FANET. An optimization is proposed to implement Dijkstra to extend the transmitting buffer. The results show that the optimization can reduce the latency between end-to-end communication [57].

In terms of the centralized routing algorithms, the main weakness of OLSR is overhead for topology maintenance in real time. Based on the weakness, many researchers made a relative modification on OLSR to satisfy the requirements of communication. With constraints of the related speed between nodes, the authors in [36] proposed a predictive OLSR (P-OLSR) which predicts the transmission load and adjusts transmission count in real time. Their evaluation shows that the P-OLSR outperforms OLSR and BABEL. Apart from the speed, the authors, in [44], proposed mobility and load-aware OLSR (ML-OLSR) for FANET. Compared with OLSR, the simulations show that ML-OLSR can achieve lower end-to-end delay and high PDR. Similar research in [42], a multidimensional perception and energy awareness OLSR (MPEAOLSR) is proposed. The MPEAOLSR can improve PDR, reduce packet loss rate and end-to-end delay regarding node link time, link layer congestion, and node residual energy.

Flexibility is a distinctive advantage of UAV swarm, but also a significant disadvantage of UAV swarm. The UAV swarm has more freedom to complete missions, which poses an immense challenge to UAV swarm networking. Due to the dynamic topology of UAV networking, the authors optimized the search space for a cube-based space region partition (CSRP) [58]. Their evaluations show that this partition could improve the performance of the average delay, packet delivery, and delay jitter. The main drawback is that it sacrifices the flexibility of UAV swarm. CSRP guarantees efficiency and low latency underneath the stability of networking. In [59], the authors acquire geographic information to enhance routing efficiency. The routing collects localization and executes routing path in direction greedily. Their simulation shows that directional delivery can improve the performance of packet delivery ratio, average delay, and routing overhead. The combination of greedy perimeter stateless routing (GPSR) and AODV is proposed in [46] and optimized with particle swarm optimization (PSO). This combination could improve PDR on the greedy routing stage and the flooding path-discovery stage.

4.3.4 DL-enabled routing for UAV networking

The 5G NR is impending to assist the evolution of UAV swarm networking. The compact and affordable nodeB devices can be implemented into the mobile devices to extend the scale of 5G NR from the ground to the aerial [60]. The current research of 5G NR on routing focuses on the optimization of multiple resources allocation [61], and multiple combined problems resolving [62] of new characteristics of 5G NR and the conventional issues [63]. Signal-to-Noise Ratio (SNR) and Reference Signal Received Quality (RSRQ) are implemented in order to enhance the detection of beam alignment of mmWave 5G, which can improve the capacity of each beam connection. With the combined prediction of target localization and mobility, the link-weight-based routing can achieve an optimal route to transmit packets with Huffman coding for security [64]. With the optimization of channel quality and resource block allocation, the base stations can achieve the maximization of the cellular spectrum with multiple paths for routing [65]. The advantage of the optimization are that it can provide device-to-device (D2D) communication when a small set of base stations is invalid [66]. As the most critical issue of 5G NR in all fields, joint optimization of virtual networking function (VNF) placement and multicast traffic routing has severe effects on the quality and the stability of links generated between nodes in the 5G NR networking [67]. A mixed-integer linear programming (MILP) model can formulate the joint optimization of the multicast traffic routing and VNF placement with the minimum provisioning cost on VNF and links. Since the MILP is an NP-hard problem, the combination of single-path routing and multi-path routing can enhance the efficiency and the accuracy of problem resolving remarkably [68]. Like [68], an integer linear programming (ILP) model [69] can formulate the problem of the joint multicast routing and OFDM resource allocation problem in D2D networking with consideration of limit spectrum reusing half-duplex operation and contiguity in the resource block allocations. A two-stage optimization performs pre-admittance filtering to detect networking states and extends the reduced ILP model with the branch-and-cut method. With network slice (NS) selection and routing, a framework for enabling the negotiation, selection, and assignment of NSs can improve QoS with static, dynamic, and hybrid routing in 5G networking [70]. At the same time, a fast request routing distributes traffic demands among source nodes intelligently, and routes flow through intermediate nodes strategically. The joint optimization focuses mainly on source direction and flow routing in mobile networking with built-in content sources. The evaluation shows the maximum link utilization can extend significantly [71].

With the bandwidth of 5G NR, the minor errors on links can degrade the communication between heterogeneous networking and devices [72]. The links' quality is critical to the security in the upper layers. The UAV swarm networking is dependent on the quality of links, including aerial networking and ground networking. The combination of wireless sensor networking (WSN) and mobile ad hoc networking

(MANET) can improve routing efficiency for disasters response. The combined 2-layer routing can generate paths via WSN or MANET according to the packets in the delivery and the states of emergency [73]. The dynamic environment requires the stability of links' quality. A routing and resource allocation (RRA) scheme based on self-organizing feature maps (SOM) can reorder the link set to achieve the optimal quality of service in the multi-core networks [74]. Assisted by ultra-dense networking (UDN), a particle swarm optimization can optimize the routing discovery and enhance PDR, throughput, and energy saving, which improves the reliability and QoS of 5G NR [75].

Apart from the reliability, the delay between end-to-end devices is also essential in 5G NR, especially in the packets' delivery of UAV swarm networking. An anchorless routing is enhanced with Locator/ID Separation Protocol (LISP). The control plane can achieve the optimal delay and provide services for user plane nodes [76]. Fueled by DL, Q-learning optimizes the nodes selection and generates the shortest paths, which maximizes throughput with the avoidance of congested network nodes [77]. A deep RL-based autonomous synchronous signal routing leverages a DNN to learn the policy of the minimum link asymmetry. With the optimal result, the time synchronization can assist the remote controller to maintain the balance between the synchronous services request and network resources allocation with reduction of end-to-end latency [78].

The impending trend of 5G NR on every device stimulates the evolution of UAV swarm networking from many aspects [79]. However, there are still many issues waiting for researchers to explore and solve. The reliability, elasticity, and flexibility of UAV swarm networking require deep research on 5G NR [80]. The 5G NR based UAV swarm networking can extend the scale and the flexibility on a large scale.

4.4 UAV NETWORKING CONSTRUCTION

The advancement of UAV networking stimulates the evolution of the UAV swarm and plays a vital role in the development of the UAV fleet [32]. Reliable and efficient routing algorithms can provide lower number of delays and packet losses for services [33]. The architectures of UAV swarm networking mainly focus on FANET, which is like MANET and Vehicle Ad hoc Networking (VANET). However, unlike MANET and VANET, FANET has more flexibility and dynamics. The FANET poses a challenge for the current routing algorithms [81], which mostly are not suitable for deployment on a large scale.

4.4.1 UAV swarm networking construction

The UAV swarm consists of multiple small UAVs on a large scale (shown as Figure 4.3). The UAV swarm has advantages of flexibility, light weight, and mobility, enabling the UAV swarm to deploy in specific areas on a large scale. The UAV swarm can split into different swarms to finish the different parts of the mission collaboratively. Based on the requirement of missions, different UAV swarms can play various roles to finish specific missions. The information exchanged between different swarms can improve the accuracy of mission execution. Location sharing in real time can reduce the collisions drastically. Based on cellular networking, the UAV swarm can form the networking to execute the mission assigned from the mobile devices [82]. The controllers can change the UAV swarm networking architecture with the ground terminal and maintain the networking status remotely. The evaluation shows that the coordination protocol can improve communication precision under different speeds. To enhance collision avoidance, the signal strength to measure the position distribution of neighbors is implemented into UAV swarm networking. With the onboard inertial measurement unit (IMU), the UAV swarm can coordinate itself to maintain the performance of networking [83]. The standard configurations are limited to the computational capacities which constrain the UAV swarm networking on throughput, latency, and reliability. The onboard computer enhances the UAV swarm, which focuses on the open-source platform of 3DR [84]. OLSR explores the

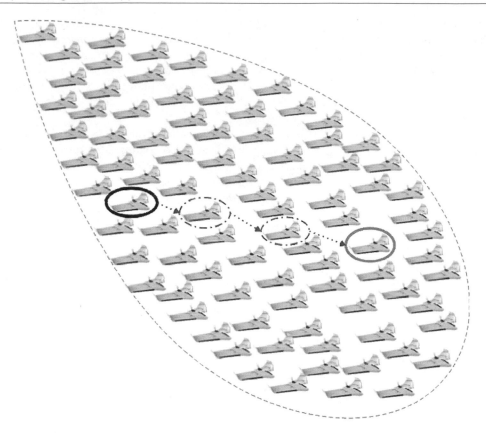

FIGURE 4.3   Routing enhancement for UAV networking enhancement.

potential of the UAV swarm in the tactic scenarios [85]. Their evaluation shows that OLSR can construct proper communication in constraint environments effectively. For the tactical scenarios, there are many uncertainties. The interference and obstacle distributions are dynamic, which is hard to predict and avoid. Inspired by free space optical (FSO), the full-duplex antennas improve the freedom of beam steering. With random beam selection, UAV swarm networking can accelerate networking construction. However, the disadvantage of FSO are the overheads of the system. The overwhelming overheads limit FSO deployment on a large scale, which sluggish UAV swarm networking formation control in real time. To improve the performance of the formation control for UAV swarm networking, the distributed consensus approach enhances the formation-tracking precision of the UAV swarm networking. The second-order discrete neighbor information constructs the consensus to satisfy the requirement of UAV swarm networking [86]. The dynamic nature of the UAV swarm poses a challenge to formation control. Based on the dynamic nature of the UAV swarm, the distributed flocking model can improve the controllability and improve the output of UAV swarm networking. However, the bio-inspired paradigm is still hard to implement into the UAV swarm. The simplifications of some functions with master–slave mode can satisfy UAV swarm networking [87].

With Software Defined Networking (SDN), UAV swarm networking also benefits from FANET. The SDN integrates Micro Unmanned Aerial Vehicles (MUAVs) into FANET, which can extend the flexibility of UAV swarm networking. Enabled with Mobile Edge Computing (MEC), MUAVs can be an effective subtle for UAV swarm [88]. To improve the reliability, the SDN can explore the networking updating strategy. With the maximization of reliability and multiple paths generation, UAV swarm networking can reduce the overhead of the system and increase the updating frequency [89]. The resilient construction can improve the robustness of UAV swarm networking. To re-organize the UAV swarm networking, the authors proposed a swarm intelligent-based and damage-resilient mechanism. By identifying the damage phase of UAV swarm networking, the UAV swarm can adjust the way points to re-organize the lost connections to the UAV swarm networking. Their evaluation shows that the outstanding convergence speed and communication overhead than the conventional approaches [90]. An autonomic approach constructs a collaborative swarm networking that can provide a reliable overlay service [91]. The collaborative swarm networking can defend against the flash floods and attacks. With the optimized area coverage, self-organization of mesh networks for UAV swarm networking is enabled [92]. With received signal strength indication (RSSI), the UAV swarm can form the networking by adjusting localization. Optimized by the genetic algorithms, the proposed approach can achieve better connectivity and swarm spreading. The UAV swarm networking constructions are mainly on the formation and routing control constrained with the overhead. The conventional approaches can achieve the optimal performance under the limited population. Due to the centralized architecture, the conventional approaches can attain optimal controllability, which is vulnerable to crashes and connection fluctuations. A decentralized and elastic routing architecture is critical to the heterogeneous UAV swarm networking, which can obtain reliable and continuous connections under the dynamic nature.

4.4.2 DL-enabled UAV swarm networking enhancement

The UAV swarm networking has advantages of distribution, low overheads, and proactiveness. These advantages give promising opportunities to deploy a UAV swarm on a large scale. Some enhancements improve UAV swarm networking. A node aggregation is applied to enhance data ferrying inside UAV swarm networking [93] in the tactical defense networking scenarios. The dynamic topology leads to the uncertainty of UAV swarm networking. Based on the dynamic topology and time-varying link conditions, link status is optimized by a deep Q-learning model [94]. With the optimal links, UAV swarm networking can achieve more throughput efficiency (shown as Figure 4.4). An online genetic algorithm [95] optimizes the movement of the UAV swarm, which can reduce the overheads and improve the survival in a complex environment. Due to the limitation of on-board energy, the Channel State Information for Transmitter (CSIT) maximizes the energy allocation of UAV swarm networking [96]. With two subtle optimizations separated from energy optimization, UAV swarm networking can achieve the maximum optimization of energy efficiency globally. A spectrum management architecture maximizes the spectrum utilization of cellular networking [97].

Further, the conventional approaches of cellular networking of resource allocation are based on being station-oriented, which cannot balance the users' requirement in their coverage. A user-oriented cellular networking coverage architecture achieves seamless service support to mobile users [98]. The evaluation shows that the gain of coverage is at least 30% higher than under conventional approaches. Due to the probability of aggression, the security on UAV swarm networking is critical to public property and safety. The large-scale Channel State Information (CSI) for the power allocation [99] enhances the security of connections inside UAV swarm networking. With constraints of transmission power, the proposed approach can improve the secure throughput to mitigate eavesdropping. The current UAV swarm networking lacks adaptability and flexibility to satisfy the dynamics of data flow. An AODV based SDN architecture [100] explored UAV swarm networking routing, which simultaneously establishes control and data planes. During the connection construction, they embedded the security verification to enhance the security for UAV networking and ground IoT. Their evaluation shows that the throughput of swarm UAV networking is improved significantly. Simultaneously, to reduce the overhead securely, the authors leverage the Random Networking Coding (RNC) to reduce the hop selection. Their evaluation shows that RNC can decrease the delay and violation probabilities effectively [101]. Apart from the penetration to the typical UAV swarm, the malicious UAV in the restricted areas needs to be escorted. To escort the malicious UAV, a UAV swarm with a defense system can detect, intercept, and capture the malicious UAV [102]. The whole process contains the clustering phase, formation phase, chase phase, and escort phase. In the previous phases, the UAV swarm detected the malicious UAV with the networking construction. In the last phase, they leveraged the collision-avoidance to escort the malicious to restricted zones. The conventional

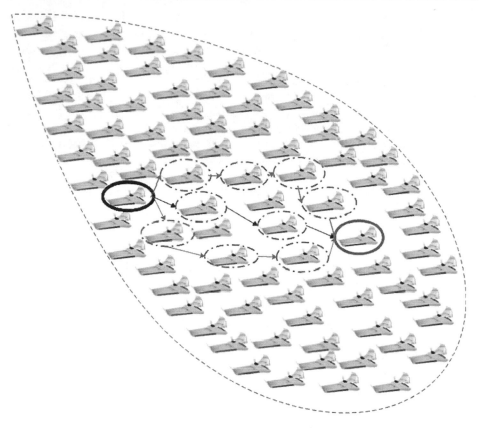

FIGURE 4.4   Multiple routing enhancement for UAV networking throughput.

enhancement approaches made significant contributions to the deployment of UAV swarm networking. The DL enhanced UAV swarm networking can provide services of the relay, rescue, and data gathering. However, constraint with overhead, throughput, and latency, the conventional approaches are complicated to implement to inter-UAV swarm networking on a large scale. The optimal connections between the heterogeneous UAV swarm networking can allow multiple mission executions feasible and ubiquitous. To overcome the dynamic nature of UAV swarm networking, a large scale deployment of UAV swarm networking requires the routing to be flexible, reliable, elastic, and energy saving.

4.5 DL-ENABLED UAV NETWORKING THROUGHPUT

Due to the life span of the UAV swarm, the throughput optimization is significant to maximize the profits of each cruise. Optimizing throughput for UAV swarm networking mainly focuses on trajectory, deployment, and energy consumption. With 5G NR, the UAV swarm can achieve more sophisticated missions and provide reliable and efficient assistance to the IoT services. As Figure 4.5 shows, two UAV networking can leverage communication volume to exchange information and collaborate with each other to finish complex missions. To maximize data-ferrying services, the authors leveraged the optimal trajectory to reduce the flight time between the source and the destination. The optimization of time allocation enhances the connection time to mitigate the packet error rate. The experiment shows that the proposed paradigm can achieve practical throughput for scattered nodes ferrying communication [103]. Simultaneously, similar work [104] optimized the trajectory, transmit power, and mobility of UAV jointly to maximize the

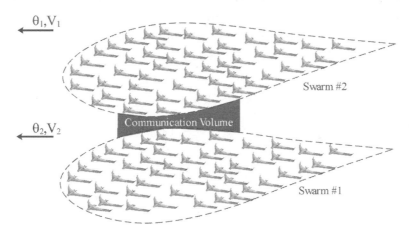

θ_1, V_1

θ_2, V_2

Swarm #2

Communication Volume

Swarm #1

FIGURE 4.5 Collaboration between UAV networking.

throughput between UAV and mobile users. The trajectory optimization for the UAV swarm networking is based on path loss modeling, which mainly maximizes connections time between UAV and desired ground devices.

Besides the trajectory optimization, there are also those scenarios that need UAV swarms to keep stable in topology, providing stable connections for the ground devices and the packet delivering. These scenarios need deployment optimization for UAV swarm networking. With optimal path loss and channels, the networking can provide the maximum throughput for ground services. To optimize the deployment for the broken links, grid condition estimations to feed Deep Q-learning, and Deep Q-learning outputs the optimal link for the packet delivery underneath the dynamic topology of UAV swarm networking [94]. Concurrently, global optimization of packet delivery priority through three networking layers (application layer, networking layer, and physical layer) improves the overall networking capacity. The authors formulated the optimization of flight altitude, energy consumption, and traveling time into a non-convex and nonlinear problem [105]. They leveraged the optimal 3D deployment to achieve maximum throughput and solved the problem with the aid of Lagrangian dual relaxation, interior-point, and subgradient projection. An optimal deployment of UAV swarm aids cellular networking [106]. The authors formulated the maximization of throughput between UAV and cellular networking and resolve the problem with a selection of UAV in the relay queuing. The evaluation shows that the proposed optimization can achieve outstanding gain at low SNR environments.

Optimal energy consumption approaches can extend the life span of UAV swarm networking on the execution. The extended life span helps the networking to achieve better throughput for ground devices. To extend the communication coverage and system performance, the maximization of throughput with the subjection to energy consumption and transmit power was formulated [107]. To solve this problem, the authors optimized the transmit power of secondary users and the mobile relay. Moreover, the evaluation showed promising potentials. With the wireless charging stations, ground solar panels provide energy to UAV. Joint optimization of energy and throughput between UAV and ground devices was formulated. Concurrently, an optimization of balance energy bought, energy sold, and throughput revenue resolves the problem [108]. Another joint optimization of user association, admission control, and power allocation to achieve the maximization of throughput for cloud radio access network (C-RAN), which is critical to UAV swarm networking [109]. Similarly, MARL optimizes the UAV's path and time resource allocation jointly to achieve the maximum throughput between UAV and IoT devices. The policy reinforces each agent to achieve local optimization [110]. A long-term resource allocation can achieve the maximum throughput for the UAV networking with MARL. The evaluation shows a good tradeoff strike between the throughput gain and the information exchange overhead [111]. The trajectory and power allocation are critical to UAV swarm networking. MARL enhances the trajectory of UAV and power allocation to achieve the maximum throughput between UAV and ground users [112]. The evaluation shows that the networking utility and system overhead can be optimized jointly. With the feedback and UAV fusion node, the distributed RL approach improves the throughput allocation and the utility of the whole system [25]. The distributed RL mitigate the security threat with congestion of spectrum and hopping of frequencies. However, the optimization is difficult to be achieved in the training significantly.

The conventional RL approaches deploy Q-learning or Deep Q-learning Network (DQN) into UAV swarm networking and achieve the local and the global optimization for the throughput. DQN reduces the time consumption on the relaying and obtains seamless video offloading services [113]. A liquid Q-learning predicted the users' requests and states. With the predication, the corresponding deployment of UAV with specific content can aid the throughput of users [114]. With Markov Decision Processing (MDP), DQN can achieve the minimum energy consumption for data aggregation [115]. Based on the real-time interaction and historical data, Q-learning amended the relaying power to reduce the bit error rate and energy consumption. The amendment can defend against the random jamming attacks [116]. With services of seamless cellular networking, actor-critic algorithms learn the vehicle movement environment to obtain the signal coverage and the dynamic nature of vehicles. The actor-critic algorithms can handle the continuous action space. The simulations show the average throughput for the vehicle can rise. However, the algorithms consume too much energy when the throughput requirement increases [117]. To extend the range of 5G NR, the UAV swarm with network slice can extend the accessing scale for the networking. The extension can provide computing aid for the UAV swarm networking. The computing aid is under job offloading which minimizes the energy consumption and queuing delay [118]. The private BSs can only provide services to the specific UAV, which lacks coordination between different BSs. The throughput between the BSs and the UAV cannot satisfy the massive networking requirement. A two-level architecture optimized the BSs' behaviors and achieved long term payoffs. The self-interested and independent behaviors on the lower level finish the noncooperation sub games and the cooperative game [119]. As the number of users increases, the algorithm loses the efficiency of the instantaneous payoff.

4.5.1 DL-enabled allocation for throughput enhancement

An optimization problem was decomposed into two suboptimizations which obtain 1) communication scheduling and power allocation and 2) trajectory optimization to achieve a better throughput between UAV and ground terminals [120]. A similar thought [121] focuses on the optimal adjustment of trajectory generation and speed control. By applying the alternating optimization and successive convex programming, a local optimization for UAV and ground users can be achieved [122]. The optimal trajectory of mobile relaying can enhance the throughput for UAV networking. With the fixed trajectory of relaying, power allocation optimization extends the throughput maximization. Furthermore, based on the allocated power, the trajectory achieved the maximum throughput [123]. Aiming to maximize the uplink throughput, a trajectory optimization maximized the throughput [124]. Better performances were achieved [125] which optimized UAV trajectories, the scheduling for uplinks and downlinks [126], and power allocations jointly. The block coordinate descent and successive convex approximation enhanced the throughput [127]. The optimal trajectory can enable UAV to obtain good channel states and energy savings so that the UAV can achieve the optimal throughput for ground devices. The main flaws are the mobility and flexibility.

The achievable rate of MIMO cognitive radio systems [128] requires enhancement on UAV relaying. The constraint with power allocation, energy consumption, and channel interference, and power optimization can improve the throughput between UAV and ground users (Primary and Secondary) [129, 130]. To achieve resilience of UAV swarm networking, a deep Q-learning deployed UAV to rescue the broken links dynamically. The deployment of relay nodes is optimized based on QoS and link conditions. The deep Q learning can achieve the efficient throughput [94]. A power splitting-based relaying protocol for packets forwarding [131] can generate a strategy of amplification and forwarding for the UAV networking. Joint optimization of bandwidth allocation, power consumption, and trajectories [132] can improve the spectrum efficiency and the average end-to-end throughput. With resource allocations, UAV can achieve the extensive QoS, enabling more complicated implementation. However, the machine learning-enabled approaches still cannot enlarge the scale deployment of UAV swarm networking. For cognitive UAV networking, the optimization of three-dimensional location and spectrum sensing duration [133] divided the problem into two convex sub-problems [134] to improve the throughput weighted and location weighted sum to solve the non-convex problem. The optimized time slots can achieve maximum throughput for disaster-affected area [135] and multiple areas services [108]. The throughput maximization and Grid-connected Micro Generation (GMG) energy consumption should keep balance. An optimization maximized the profit which contains mission plans, action associations, and optimal balance between GMG and UAV [136]. Additional parameters obtaining uplink power control and resource allocation for the wireless energy and information transfer were considered in Wireless Powered Communication Networking (WPCN) system to achieve efficiency [104, 137]. The evaluation [132] shows the cyclical time division multiple access schemes can keep throughput between UAV and users stable as the delay tolerance increases. With the reduction of latency between the ground devices [138] and UAV in the flight, the networking can be extended to a larger scale which is still a constraint within dozens. The delay tolerance can improve the access of ground devices to UAV swarm networking for multiple missions simultaneously.

Joint optimization of time allocation, reflection coefficient, and UAV trajectories maximized the system throughput backscatter device with UAV harvesting [139]. To extend the communication coverage and system performance, a power control algorithm [107] improved the throughput for the relaying networking for secondary users in UAV-assisted cellular networking. The spread spectrum transmission [140] can reduce the requirement of system synchronizations. The spread spectrum collected different channels and fused the data to achieve a more accurate estimation. A throughput optimization for cache-enabled UAV [141] can improve the throughput between UAV and IoT, which obtains deployment optimization and probabilistic caching placement [141]. The Markov chain decided the nodes' mode and optimized the trajectory of UAV with a greedy algorithm [142]. The Markov chain can achieve the maximization of system throughput for UAV investigation. Multiple targets optimization can enable UAV swarm networking to achieve optimization globally with the sacrifice of time consumption and computational resources. The evaluation shows that the proposed approach can achieve better throughput than conventional optimizations. However, the program is too complex, which is not suitable to deploy on a large scale. The combination of optimal trajectory, resource allocation, and multiple targets optimization can improve the throughput of the networking from different aspects. However, these approaches are not feasible to improve the throughput of UAV swarm networking on a large scale. The throughput of UAV networking focuses on the networking and ground devices that rarely contain the throughput of the heterogeneous UAV swarms on a large scale. The previous research can be a valuable reference for the extension of UAV swarm networking on a large scale. The hierarchical architectures of UAV swarms can help ground terminals achieve efficient controllability with the sacrifice of resilience and flexibility. Based on the fluid UAV swarms, a more compatible communication paradigm for heterogeneous UAV swarm networking is needed.

4.5.2 DL-enabled scheduling for throughput enhancement

With beamforming, UAV swarm networking can have directional connections precisely for packets delivery. Moreover, UAV swarm networking can achieve the minimization of energy consumption and information leakage [143]. With optimal beam steering management, beamforming can execute optimal beams for connections and reduce interference. With beamforming, the distributed and decentralized architecture can have directional connections and the minimum interference. Based on MIMO, multiple links can be scheduled in time division or frequency division for the throughput maximization of UAV swarm networking. Extending 5G NR can provide heterogeneous UAV swarm networking feasibility, flexibility, and reliability. The surging demands of enhancement for UAV swarm accelerate the evolution of networking. With a hierarchical game model for optimization of D2D and UAVs, predictable dynamic matching market addressed UAV selection and time allocation. A congestion game can solve the channel access problem

[144]. A self-organized collision discovery mechanism avoided the unavailable topology information and information exchange to hinder slot access [145]. Another way [146] to address the access problem, Direction of Arrival (DOA), can provide the relative position and channel gain for estimation. Mixed-integer nonlinear programming (MINLP) can enhance the capability of self-recovering. UAV learning of deployment and association maximize the sum-rate of networking. 'Learn-As-You-Fly' can optimize the balance of bandwidth, QoS, position deployment, and altitude allocation. Firstly, a distributed matching-based association can balance bandwidth allocation and QoS. Secondly, K-means helps UAVs to address the deployment of UAVs. Finally, game-theoretic approach maximizes the limited interference sum-rate [147]. Simultaneously, a deep Q-learning model can determine the optimal link between two UAV nodes. A locally optimal position of UAV can enhance the overall network with an optimization algorithm [94]. However, the interference between the ground nodes and UAV swarm networking is critical to QoS. A two-phase transmission protocol can leverage cellular networking and D2D to mitigate the interference between ground devices and UAV swarms [148].

Cellular networking is the most potent approach to integrate UAV swarm networking into National Airspace System (NAS) to enhance the connectivity, reliability, and flexibility [19]. A fully-fledged drone-based 3D cellular network incorporated users and UAVs in different altitudes to reduce the latency. The optimal deployment of UAV base stations achieves the maximum coverage for ground users [149, 150]. The optimal estimation of distribution for ground users and base stations can achieve the minimization of 3D cell association. With the minimum latency, the optimal uplink sum rate can enhance the QoS of UAV swarm networking. A cooperative UAV sense-and-send protocol enables UAV-to-X communication. An analysis of cellular networking serving UAV and ground users is on user and network-level performance [151]. The joint optimization of sub channel allocation and UAV speed can solve three sub-problems of UAV-to-user channel allocation, UAV-to-UAV channel allocation, and UAV speed control [19, 152]. A 3D positioning for aerial base stations can optimize transmit power allocation for all the nodes in the uplink, downlink, and the combination of uplink and downlink [153]. Simultaneously, an optimal spectrum sharing can achieve the minimum rate for UAVs' and users' uplinks [152]. With joint optimization of user association, spectrum allocation, and content caching [154], a liquid state machine can predict the users' request distribution with limited information. The machine can deploy UAVs with optimal resource allocation strategies to maximize the serving associations with feasible throughput [114].

5G NR-enabled UAV swarm networking benefits from Non-Orthogonal Multiple Access (NOMA) which provides higher receiving power and enhanced spectrum efficiency for mobile users. A MIMO NOMA (MIMO-NOMA)-assisted UAV networking [155] to achieve higher SNR slopes for mobile users. With tractable analytical upper bounds for Line of Sight (LoS) and Non-Line of Sight (NLoS), the interference to the paired NOMA users can be zero. Concurrently, a UAV-assisted NOMA networking provides services to ground users simultaneously with joint optimization of UAV trajectory and NOMA precoding [156]. The NOMA extends the association to users under the explosive data traffic [157]. A formulation of UAV swarm networking with OMA and NOMA was transformed into a tractable problem and solved with penalty dual decomposition to maximize the minimum average rate among ground users under OMA and NOMA [158]. A user-centric and a UAV-centric strategy can provide analytical expression and enhancement for the coverage in the scenario of imperfect Successive Interference Cancellation (ipSIC) [159]. The throughput of UAV swarm networking is critical to QoS and safety. To reduce Small-cell Base Stations (SBS), UAVs were facilitated with caches and assist offloading requests to SBS. The assistance can improve the throughput for mobile users [160]. Joint optimization of UAV deployment, caching placement, and user association can maximize QoS [161]. Joint optimization of time allocation and position can maximize the uplink throughput for ground users [162] and nodes [163]. With the minimization of propulsion energy and operation cost, joint optimization of UAV trajectory, sensor node of wake-up time allocation, and transmitting power can achieve the propulsion energy consumption and operation cost [164]. A tractable 3D model can evaluate the average downlink with 5G NR and satisfy high throughput requirement [165]. To overcome information leakage and increase transmission reliability, an optimization for multi-hop re- laying networking [166] can enhance the throughput of UAVs networking with the optimization of coding rates, transmit power, and hops [107]. With machine learning, the probability of spatial false alarm and spatial missed detection can formulate the distribution of active UAVs. The distribution can assist the stochastic geometry to generate the coverage probability of D2D [167] and UAV networking. A dynamic fly- hover-transmit scheme can determine UAVs' mobility and transmitting power (wireless information transfer, wireless energy transfer, and silent) to maximize UAVs' sum-throughput overall ground terminals [168].

4.5.2.1 Scheduling for UAV networking

Currently, UAV networking scheduling mainly focuses on resource allocation and task management, which maximizes the UAV networking and minimizes the consumption of resource allocations. A buffer-aware transmission scheduling can enhance UAV relay networks and minimize the energy consumption of ground devices. The optimal link selections can reduce the retransmission and minimize the energy consumption on ground devices and UAV networking [169]. The optimal user selection can minimize energy consumption, overflow, and throughput fairness. However, the optimization is an NP-complete problem that is hard to converge.

Similarly, a successive convex approximation solved the joint optimization on trajectory and user schedule. With finite energy consumption, the optimization can maximize the user scheduling with the sacrifice of the flexibility and the alternative orders [170]. Different from the previous approximations, optimum scheduling for the beaconing period saved energy consumption in the game theory framework. With interaction, an equilibrium learning framework optimized UAVs' actions to reach equilibrium. The equilibrium is with the current status and the history under no knowledge of the component information [171]. The UAV reaches the Nash equilibrium without knowledge of others' information which can reduce the burden of the computation. However, the Nash equilibrium consumes too much time and leads to fluctuations of the system. Integration of coordinated and uncoordinated approaches optimized the device association, sub channel allocation, power allocation, and the deployment of UAV to maximize energy efficiency [172]. The association was constructed based on the allocation of sub-channels and the devices can get the association when the transmission gain is satisfied. The main drawback is that the processing is inefficient and cannot achieve the global optimization. The maximization of energy usage extends the lifespan of the UAV networking and provides support to the QoS of networking.

Due to the dynamic UAV networking, a light and optimum link selection approach is crucial to QoS. Dynamic optimization adjusted the deployment of UAV and establish the optimum connections via UAV delivery. The dynamic optimization leveraged proportional integral derivative (PID) to control the movement and achieved the optimum delay-tolerance links. The links are constraints to the speed and the response of UAV [173]. A proportional fairness scheduling enhanced the balance between service fairness and ergodic capacity. Without CSI, the scheduling obtains the flexible deployment for UAV implementations which surpass the conventional approaches [174]. After that, a formula of integer linear programming [175] solved the optimal transmission scheduling problem, which is based on an optimization of link selection. A cross entropy calculation solved the selection of the optimum links that can optimize the average throughput. But the calculation is restricted by the successive interference cancellation.

With optimization of task allocation and deployment, the UAV networking can extend on a large scale. Optimum scheduling for UAV aid relay networking improved the long-term average throughput for the users and provided seamless relay services for the moving and static UAVs [176]. The proposed scheduling can aid relay networking without information exchange. However, the position estimation is dependent on the global position system (GPS) seriously. With the flexible networking architecture, a dynamic fault-tolerant task scheduling mitigated the failure nodes and realized the rapid resilience for the internal scheduling [177]. Compared with Max-min throughput algorithms, the dynamic fault-tolerant task scheduling achieved more flexibility and reliability for connections. A flexible network scheduling can enhance the cluster task scheduling dynamically. The fuzzy theory membership degree can satisfy the constraints of mission requirements for the scheduling [178]. The previous work can solve the dynamic scheduling, which has high computation requirements and is hard to deploy in practical scenarios. Joint optimization of association control scheduling, tasks and resources allocations, and UAV deployment exploited block coordination and successive convex approximation [179]. The joint optimization can optimize the multiple parameters and minimize the maximum computation latency. However, the joint optimization has high time consumption and overhead for the cloud and edge computing system. The local and cloud computations vary significantly in static net- working and mobile wireless networking. With limited power allocation, the distributed scheduling achieved optimal task allocations with the stochastic network optimization and the distributed correlated scheduling [180].

4.5.2.2 DL-enabled scheduling for UAV networking

RL can achieve the hyper parameters with DL and robust performance on the throughput enhancement for UAV networking. The RL-enabled scheduling approaches to achieve outstanding performances on networking optimizations and workflow management. Compared with the conventional scheduling approaches, the RL-enabled scheduling shows more robust, resilient, and globally optimum capacities with deep neural network (DNN). With DNN, RL obtains global optimizations on the enhancement of QoS quickly with optimal convergence at high speed. To achieve safe and QoS awareness on the Internet of Vehicles (IoV), a DQN learned optimum scheduling for the extended lifetime of the battery-powered IoV. The agent learns the environment with the feeding of experience and the realization of a successful scheduling policy [181]. Compared with the random search, greedy searching approaches, the DQN-enabled approach surpassed the completed request, mean delay, and lifetime. A softmax multiple classifiers-enabled DQN (S-DQN) escalates the optimization of the scheduling strategy derived from MDP with constraints of delay, cost, and energy [182] to enhance the QoS of the diversified communication services. S-DQN can achieve the global optimizations on throughput and E2E delay in SDN. However, S-DQN is vulnerable to the jitters in the system. To improve QoS for ultra-reliable low latency communication (URLLC) and reduce the packets loss, RL-based deterministic policy optimized the scheduling of bandwidth allocation and overlapping positions with the considerations of channel variations and URLLC arrivals [183]. The RL-based deterministic policy improved the reliability of eMBB and URLLC with system-wide balance simultaneously. However, the performance declines as the access increase, which is hard to implement on a large scale. A joint user scheduling and beam selection minimized the delay with MARL [184, 185] and satisfies the instantaneous QoS. The scheduling achieves optimization with the local observations; however, it is hard to have a global optimization. To enhance QoS in the deterministic network services, an RL leveraged predictive data and reward configuration to optimize the flow scheduling, which has a good performance on the QoS. However, the system is suffering from the overwhelming overhead. To obtain an optimum scheduling workflow, a temporal fusion pointer network-based RL improved the QoS of the multi-objective workflow scheduling with the historical actions and the acceleration of asynchronous advantage actor critic (A3C) [186]. Similarly, to improve the QoS of home's access point (AP), an RL-based control and scheduling can enable the AP to schedule the arriving multimedia traffic with the desired QoS. The scheduling has a global optimization with a long training processing [187].

Optimal resource allocation can maximize the networking capacity and reduce resource consumption. To solve the conflicts of multiple objectives scheduling, a DQN-enabled MARL generates optimal scheduling for the multiple-workflows over infrastructure-as-a-service clouds. The MARL leverages a game model balance to find a correlated equilibrium for the make span and cost criteria [188]. To derive an optimal time scheduling mechanism for throughput enhancement, a double DQN (DDQN) obtains a global optimization for the policy rendering in a RF powered backscatter cognitive radio network [189]. The DDQN can obtain outstanding performance on the average throughput with different packet arrival probabilities and busy time slots. However, the DDQN shows a weak decline once the busy time slots increase. To address the radio resource scheduling for 5G networking, an advantage pointer critic deep RL enhanced the frequency allocation to users. The policy gradient optimization can enhance the throughput and fairness index [190]. A proportional fair (PF) scheduling-enabled deep RL [191] achieved a higher speed convergence than direct and dual learning. A deep RL framework can solve the online scheduling optimization on a large scale [192]. The related and regularized stacked autoencoder can compress and represent high dimensional informational channel quality in reduced state space with unsupervised learning.

Based on the tight searching space, an adaptive h-mutation accelerated the optimization with preserved and prioritized experience replaying. With the MDP of transmission reliability, a resource scheduling leveraged DQN to maximize the reliability with the joint constraints of transmission mode, relay selection, and the allocations of time and power [193].

To enhance the efficiency and quality, RL accelerates the management of task allocation and achieves the robust, resilience, and flexibility performance. To solve the ineffective management for the edge nodes, an SDN-based dynamic task scheduling leveraged deep RL to solve the task assignments and the scheduling, which minimizes the network latency and improves the efficiency of energy [194]. To solve the inappropriate allocation of the resource, RL-based cluster-enabled cooperative scheduling improved the efficiency and reliability of vehicular networking and maximized the throughput of networking, which refines the efficiency of the vehicular networking and the reliability with RL-based transmission [195]. To reduce the latency of the edge computing networking, an A3C-based cloud-edge collaboration scheduling solved the NP-hard optimization of minimizing task scheduling for cloud edge networking. The A3C-enabled approach surpasses DQN and RL-G on the convergence speed, however, it has an increasing task failure rate when task density is extensive. It is essential to satisfy the intelligent scheduling on the packet transmission for ultra-reliable low latency communication. An SDN-based scheduling leveraged a generative adversarial network (GAN) to determine the action space generated from DDQN with consideration of states prediction [196]. RL-based dynamic task scheduling addresses an MDP problem to improve the efficiency of task execution for the multifunction radar network [197].

4.6 CONCLUSIONS

In this chapter, we have provided a comprehensive review on DL-enabled throughput enhancement for UAV networking. With the enhancement of 5G NR, UAV networking can form multiple swarms to finish complex missions. The missions have high requirements with regard to the accuracy of performance, collaboration, and corporation. Deep learning can improve UAV networking from routing, resource allocation, and scheduling. The assurance of QoS and performance of UAV networking can improve the deployment of UAV swarms on a large scale and benefits many applications in different fields.

REFERENCES

[1] T. Yang, J. Zhao, T. Hong, W. Chen, and X. Fu, "Automatic identification technology of rotor UAVs based on 5G network architecture," in *2018 IEEE International Conference on Networking, Architecture and Storage (NAS)*, pp. 1–9, 2018.

[2] J. Wang, A. Jin, D. Shi, L. Wang, H. Shen, D. Wu, L. Hu, L. Gu, L. Lu, Y. Chen, J. Wang, Y. Saito, A. Benjebbour, and Y. Kishiyama, "Spectral efficiency improvement with 5G technologies: results from field tests," *IEEE Journal on Selected Areas in Communications*, vol. *35*, pp. 1867–1875, 2017.

[3] T. O. Olwal, K. Djouani, and A. M. Kurien, "A survey of resource management toward 5G radio access networks," *IEEE Communications Surveys Tutorials*, vol. *18*, pp. 1656–1686, third quarter 2016.

[4] Y. Wang, Z. Zhang, P. Zhang, Z. Ma, and G. Liu, "A new cloud-based network framework for 5G massive internet of things connections," in *2017 IEEE 17th International Conference on Communication Technology (ICCT)*, pp. 412–416, 2017.

[5] Z. Na, Y. Wang, M. Xiong, X. Liu, and J. Xia, "Modeling and throughput analysis of an ADO-OFDM based relay-assisted VLC system for 5G networks," *IEEE Access*, vol. *6*, pp. 17586–17594, 2018.

[6] X. Ge, J. Yang, H. Gharavi, and Y. Sun, "Energy efficiency challenges of 5G small cell networks," *IEEE Communications Magazine*, vol. *55*, pp. 184–191, May 2017.

[7] R. Vannithamby and S. Talwar, "Distributed Resource Allocation in 5G Cellular Networks," In *Towards 5G: Applications, Requirements and Candidate Technologies.* Wiley, 2017, pp. 129–161, doi: 10.1002/9781118979846.ch8.

[8] F. W. Vook, A. Ghosh, and T. A. Thomas, "Mimo and beamforming solutions for 5G technology," in *IEEE MTT-S International Microwave Symposium (IMS2014)*, pp. 1–4, 2014.

[9] D. Wubben, P. Rost, J. S. Bartelt, M. Lalam, V. Savin, M. Gorgoglione, A. Dekorsy, and G. Fettweis, "Benefits and impact of cloud computing on 5G signal processing: flexible centralization through cloud-ran," *IEEE Signal Processing Magazine*, vol. *31*, pp. 35–44, 2014.

[10] T. X. Tran, A. Hajisami, P. Pandey, and D. Pompili, "Collaborative mobile edge computing in 5G Net- works: new paradigms, scenarios, and challenges," *IEEE Communications Magazine*, vol. *55*, pp. 54–61, 2017.

[11] M. Agiwal, A. Roy, and N. Saxena, "Next generation 5G wireless networks: a comprehensive survey," *IEEE Communications Surveys Tutorials*, vol. *18*, no. 3, pp. 1617–1655, 2016.

[12] V. P. Subba Rao and G. S. Rao, "Design and modelling of an affordable UAV based pesticide sprayer in agriculture applications," in *2019 Fifth International Conference on Electrical Energy Systems (ICEES)*, pp. 1–4, 2019.

[13] X. Liu, L. Hou, and X. Ju, "A method for detecting power lines in UAV aerial images," in *2017 3rd IEEE International Conference on Computer and Communications (ICCC)*, pp. 2132–2136, 2017.

[14] M. Edrich and R. Schmalenberger, "Combined dsss/fhss approach to interference rejection and navigation support in UAV communications and control," in *IEEE Seventh International Symposium on Spread Spectrum Techniques and Applications*, vol. *3*, pp. 687–691, 2002.

[15] A. Volkert, H. Hackbarth, T. J. Lieb, and S. Kern, "Flight tests of ranges and latencies of a threefold redundant c2 multi-link solution for small drones in vll airspace," in *2019 Integrated Communications, Navigation and Surveillance Conference (ICNS)*, pp. 1–14, 2019.

[16] T. Zeng, M. Mozaffari, O. Semiari, W. Saad, M. Bennis, and M. Debbah, "Wireless communications and control for swarms of cellular-connected UAVS," in *2018 52nd Asilomar Conference on Signals, Systems, and Computers*, pp. 719–723, 2018.

[17] W. Mei, Q. Wu, and R. Zhang, "Cellular-connected UAV: uplink association, power control and inter- ference coordination," in *2018 IEEE Global Communications Conference (GLOBECOM)*, pp. 206–212, 2018.

[18] H. Hellaoui, O. Bekkouche, M. Bagaa, and T. Taleb, "Aerial control system for spectrum efficiency in UAV-to-cellular communications," *IEEE Communications Magazine*, vol. *56*, pp. 108–113, 2018.

[19] S. Zhang, H. Zhang, B. Di, and L. Song, "Cellular UAV-to-x communications: design and optimization for multi-UAV networks," *IEEE Transactions on Wireless Communications*, vol. *18*, pp. 1346–1359, 2019.

[20] G. Xu, J. Wang, L. Yuan, and H. Zhang, "Cooperative UUB control of elastic UAV formation adapting flight speed," in *Proceedings of 2014 IEEE Chinese Guidance, Navigation and Control Conference*, pp. 2231–2235, 2014.

[21] M. Lauridsen, L. C. Gimenez, I. Rodriguez, T. B. Sorensen, and P. Mogensen, "From LTE to 5G for connected mobility," *IEEE Communications Magazine*, vol. *55*, pp. 156–162, 2017.

[22] J. Hendler, "Avoiding another AI winter," *IEEE Intelligent Systems*, vol. *23*, pp. 2–4, 2008.

[23] T. Sugimoto and M. Gouko, "Acquisition of hovering by actual UAV using reinforcement learning," in *2016 3rd International Conference on Information Science and Control Engineering (ICISCE)*, pp. 148–152, 2016.

[24] Q. Wang, W. Zhang, Y. Liu, and Y. Liu, "Multi-UAV dynamic wireless networking with deep reinforce- ment learning," *IEEE Communications Letters*, vol. *23*, pp. 1–1, 2019.

[25] A. Shamsoshoara, M. Khaledi, F. Afghah, A. Razi, and J. Ashdown, "Distributed cooperative spectrum sharing in UAV networks using multi-agent reinforcement learning," in *2019 16th IEEE Annual Consumer Communications Networking Conference (CCNC)*, pp. 1–6, 2019.

[26] J. Cui, Y. Liu, and A. Nallanathan, "The application of multi-agent reinforcement learning in UAV networks," in *2019 IEEE International Conference on Communications Workshops (ICC Workshops)*, pp. 1–6, 2019.

[27] S. E. Hammami, H. Afifi, H. Moungla, and A. Kamel, "Drone-assisted cellular networks: a multi-agent reinforcement learning approach," in *ICC 2019 - 2019 IEEE International Conference on Communications (ICC)*, pp. 1–6, 2019.

[28] L. Xiao, X. Lu, D. Xu, Y. Tang, L. Wang, and W. Zhuang, "Uav relay in vanets against smart jamming with reinforcement learning," *IEEE Transactions on Vehicular Technology*, vol. *67*, pp. 4087–4097, May 2018.

[29] C. H. Liu, Z. Chen, J. Tang, J. Xu, and C. Piao, "Energy-efficient UAV control for effective and fair communication coverage: a deep reinforcement learning approach," *IEEE Journal on Selected Areas in Communications*, vol. *36*, pp. 2059–2070, 2018.

[30] U. Challita, W. Saad, and C. Bettstetter, "Interference management for cellular-connected UAVS: a deep reinforcement learning approach," *IEEE Transactions on Wireless Communications*, vol. *18*, pp. 2125–2140, April 2019.

[31] Y. Cao, L. Zhang, and Y. Liang, "Deep reinforcement learning for user access control in UAV networks," in *2018 IEEE International Conference on Communication Systems (ICCS)*, pp. 297–302, 2018.

[32] M. Y. Arafat and S. Moh, "A survey on cluster-based routing protocols for unmanned aerial vehicle networks," *IEEE Access*, vol. 7, pp. 498–516, 2019.

[33] O. S. Oubbati, A. Lakas, F. Zhou, M. Gu̇nes, and M. B. Yagoubi, "A survey on position-based routing protocols for flying ad hoc networks (fanets)," *Vehicular Communications*, vol. 10, pp. 29–56, 2017.

[34] D. Medina, F. Hoffmann, F. Rossetto, and C. Rokitansky, "A geographic routing strategy for north atlantic in-flight internet access via airborne mesh networking," *IEEE/ACM Transactions on Networking*, vol. 20, pp. 1231–1244, 2012.

[35] L. Lin, Q. Sun, S. Wang, and F. Yang, "A geographic mobility prediction routing protocol for ad hoc UAV network," in *2012 IEEE Globecom Workshops*, pp. 1597–1602, 2012.

[36] S. Rosati, K. Kruz· Elecki, L. Traynard, and B. R. Mobile, "Speed-aware routing for UAV ad-hoc net- works," in *2013 IEEE Globecom Workshops (GC Wkshps)*, pp. 1367–1373, 2013.

[37] E. Kuiper and S. Nadjm-Tehrani, "Geographical routing with location service in intermittently connected manets," *IEEE Transactions on Vehicular Technology*, vol. 60, pp. 592–604, 2011.

[38] M. Iordanakis, D. Yannis, K. Karras, G. Bogdos, G. Dilintas, M. Amirfeiz, G. Colangelo, and S. Baiotti, "Ad-hoc routing protocol for aeronautical mobile ad-hoc networks," in *Fifth International Symposium on Communication Systems, Networks and Digital Signal Processing (CSNDSP)*, pp. 1–5, Citeseer, 2006.

[39] R. Shirani, M. St-Hilaire, T. Kunz, Y. Zhou, J. Li, and L. Lamont, "On the delay of reactive-greedy- reactive routing in unmanned aeronautical ad-hoc networks," *Procedia Computer Science*, vol. 10, pp. 535–542, 2012. ANT 2012 and MobiWIS 2012.

[40] E. Sakhaee and A. Jamalipour, "A new stable clustering scheme for pseudo-linear highly mobile ad hoc networks," in *IEEE GLOBECOM 2007 - IEEE Global Telecommunications Conference*, pp. 1169–1173, 2007.

[41] J. Maxa, M. S. Ben Mahmoud, and N. Larrieu, "Joint model-driven design and real experiment-based validation for a secure UAV ad hoc network routing protocol," in *2016 Integrated Communications Navigation and Surveillance (ICNS)*, pp. 1E2-1–1E2-16, 2016.

[42] S. Y. Dong, "Optimization of OLSR routing protocol in UAV ad hoc network," in *2016 13th International Computer Conference on Wavelet Active Media Technology and Information Processing (IC- CWAMTIP)*, pp. 90–94, 2016.

[43] P. E. I. Dorathy and M. Chandrasekaran, "Distance based dual path ad hoc on demand distance vector routing protocol for mobile ad hoc networks," in *2017 4th International Conference on Advanced Computing and Communication Systems (ICACCS)*, pp. 1–6, 2017.

[44] Y. Zheng, Y. Wang, Z. Li, L. Dong, Y. Jiang, and H. Zhang, "A mobility and load aware olsr routing protocol for UAV mobile ad-hoc networks," in *2014 International Conference on Information and Communications Technologies (ICT 2014)*, pp. 1–7, 2014.

[45] A. V. Leonov, G. A. Litvinov, and D. A. Korneev, "Simulation and analysis of transmission range effect on AODV and OLSR routing protocols in flying ad hoc networks (fanets) formed by mini-UAVS with different node density," in *2018 Systems of Signal Synchronization, Generating and Processing in Telecommunications (SYNCHROINFO)*, pp. 1–7, 2018.

[46] F. Wang, Z. Chen, J. Zhang, C. Zhou, and W. Yue, "Greedy forwarding and limited flooding based routing protocol for UAV flying ad-hoc networks," in *2019 IEEE 9th International Conference on Electronics Information and Emergency Communication (ICEIEC)*, pp. 1–4, 2019.

[47] A. V. Leonov and G. A. Litvinov, "About applying aodv and olsr routing protocols to relaying network scenario in fanet with mini-UAVS," in *2018 XIV International Scientific-Technical Conference on Actual Problems of Electronics Instrument Engineering (APEIE)*, pp. 220–228, 2018.

[48] A. V. Leonov and G. A. Litvinov, "Considering aodv and olsr routing protocols to traffic monitoring scenario in fanet formed by mini-UAVS," in *2018 XIV International Scientific-Technical Conference on Actual Problems of Electronics Instrument Engineering (APEIE)*, pp. 229–237, 2018.

[49] V. Ramasubramanian, Z. J. Haas, and E. G. Sirer, "Sharp: a hybrid adaptive routing protocol for mobile ad hoc networks," in *Proceedings of the 4th ACM International Symposium on Mobile Ad Hoc Networking & Computing, MobiHoc '03*, (New York, NY, USA), pp. 303–314, Association for Computing Machinery, 2003.

[50] L. Gupta, R. Jain, and G. Vaszkun, "Survey of important issues in UAV communication networks," *IEEE Communications Surveys & Tutorials*, vol. 18, no. 2, pp. 1123–1152, 2015.

[51] Y. Yu, L. Ru, W. Chi, Y. Liu, Q. Yu, and K. Fang, "Ant colony optimization based polymorphism-aware routing algorithm for ad hoc UAV network," *Multimedia Tools and Applications*, vol. 75, pp. 14451–14476, 2016.

[52] A. V. Leonov, "Application of bee colony algorithm for fanet routing," in *2016 17th International Conference of Young Specialists on Micro/Nanotechnologies and Electron Devices (EDM)*, pp. 124–132, 2016.

[53] S. S. Manvi, M. S. Kakkasageri, and C. V. Mahapurush, "Performance analysis of AODV, DSR, and swarm intelligence routing protocols in vehicular ad hoc network environment," in *2009 International Conference on Future Computer and Communication*, pp. 21–25, 2009.

[54] J. Wang, N. Juarez, E. Kohm, Y. Liu, J. Yuan, and H. Song, "Integration of sdr and uas for malicious wi-fi hotspots detection," in *2019 Integrated Communications, Navigation and Surveillance Conference (ICNS)*, pp. 1–8, 2019.

[55] Q. Zhang, M. Jiang, Z. Feng, W. Li, W. Zhang, and M. Pan, "IOT enabled UAV: Network architecture and routing algorithm," *IEEE Internet of Things Journal*, vol. 6, no. 2, pp. 3727–3742, 2019.

[56] A. V. Leonov and G. A. Litvinov, "Applying AODV and OLSR routing protocols to air-to-air scenario in flying ad hoc networks formed by mini-UAVS," in *2018 Systems of Signals Generating and Processing in the Field of on Board Communications*, pp. 1–10, 2018.

[57] A. Rovira-Sugranes and A. Razi, "Predictive routing for dynamic UAV networks," in *2017 IEEE Inter- national Conference on Wireless for Space and Extreme Environments (WiSEE)*, pp. 43–47, 2017.

[58] P. Zhang, Q. Zhang, M. Jiang, and Z. Feng, "Cube based space region partition routing algorithm in UAV networks," in *2017 23rd Asia-Pacific Conference on Communications (APCC)*, pp. 1–6, 2017.

[59] M. Y. Arafat and S. Moh, "Location-aided delay tolerant routing protocol in UAV networks for post-disaster operation," *IEEE Access*, vol. 6, pp. 59891–59906, 2018.

[60] A. Kumari, R. Gupta, S. Tanwar, and N. Kumar, "A taxonomy of blockchain-enabled softwarization for secure UAV network," *Computer Communications*, vol. 161, pp. 304–323, 2020.

[61] A. Mathur, K. Panesar, J. Kim, E. M. Atkins, and N. Sarter, "Paths to autonomous vehicle operations for urban air mobility," in *AIAA Aviation 2019 Forum*, p. 3255, 2019.

[62] N. Kumar, J. J. P. C. Rodrigues, and N. Chilamkurti, "Bayesian coalition game as-a-service for content distribution in internet of vehicles," *IEEE Internet of Things Journal*, vol. 1, no. 6, pp. 544–555, 2014.

[63] J.Á. Flores Granados, J. Mongay Batalla, and C. Togay, "Redundant localization system for automatic vehicles," *Mechanical Systems and Signal Processing*, vol. 136, p. 106433, 2020.

[64] I. Rasheed, F. Hu, Y. Hong, and B. Balasubramanian, "Intelligent vehicle network routing with adaptive 3D beam alignment for mmWave 5G-based V2X communications," *IEEE Transactions on Intelligent Transportation Systems*, vol. 22, pp. 2706–2718, 2020.

[65] Y. Liu, J. Wang, H. Song, J. Li, and J. Yuan, "Blockchain-based secure routing strategy for airborne mesh networks," in *2019 IEEE International Conference on Industrial Internet (ICII)*, pp. 56–61, 2019.

[66] A. V. Bastos, C. M. Silva, and D. C. da Silva, "Assisted routing algorithm for d2d communication in 5G wireless networks," in *2018 Wireless Days (WD)*, pp. 28–30, 2018.

[67] N. Kumar, S. Misra, J. J. P. C. Rodrigues, and M. S. Obaidat, "Coalition games for spatio-temporal big data in internet of vehicles environment: a comparative analysis," *IEEE Internet of Things Journal*, vol. 2, no. 4, pp. 310–320, 2015.

[68] O. Alhussein, P. T. Do, J. Li, Q. Ye, W. Shi, W. Zhuang, X. Shen, X. Li, and J. Rao, "Joint VNF placement and multicast traffic routing in 5G core networks," in *2018 IEEE Global Communications Conference (GLOBECOM)*, pp. 1–6, 2018.

[69] S. Alwan, I. Fajjari, and N. Aitsaadi, "Joint multicast routing and OFDM resource allocation in LTE-D2D 5G cellular network," in *NOMS 2018 - 2018 IEEE/IFIP Network Operations and Management Symposium*, pp. 1–9, 2018.

[70] V. K. Choyi, A. Abdel-Hamid, Y. Shah, S. Ferdi, and A. Brusilovsky, "Network slice selection, assignment and routing within 5G networks," in *2016 IEEE Conference on Standards for Communications and Networking (CSCN)*, pp. 1–7, 2016.

[71] J. He and W. Song, "Evolving to 5G: a fast and near-optimal request routing protocol for mobile core networks," in *2014 IEEE Global Communications Conference*, pp. 4586–4591, 2014.

[72] X. Yue, Y. Liu, J. Wang, H. Song, and H. Cao, "Software defined radio and wireless acoustic networking for amateur drone surveillance," *IEEE Communications Magazine*, vol. 56, pp. 90–97, 2018.

[73] D. Hrabcak, L. Dobos, and J. Papaj, "The concept of 2-layer routing for wireless 5G networks and beyond," in *2019 29th International Conference Radioelektronika (RADIOELEKTRONIKA)*, pp. 1–5, 2019.

[74] Q. Yao, H. Yang, B. Yan, B. Bao, A. Yu, and J. Zhang, "Routing and resource allocation leveraging self- organizing feature maps in multi-core optical networks against 5G and beyond," in *2020 International Wireless Communications and Mobile Computing (IWCMC)*, pp. 857–860, 2020.

[75] D. D. Misra and K. Kumar Sarma, "Cooperative routing mechanism in the 5G ultra dense network," in *2018 5th International Conference on Signal Processing and Integrated Networks (SPIN)*, pp. 721–725, 2018.

[76] K. Fukui, K. Tsubouchi, and S. Iwashina, "A comparative study on anchorless routing in 5G system," in *2019 International Conference on Information Networking (ICOIN)*, pp. 424–426, 2019.

[77] C. V. Murudkar and R. D. Gitlin, "Optimal-capacity, shortest path routing in self-organizing 5G networks using machine learning," in *2019 IEEE 20th Wireless and Microwave Technology Conference (WAMICON)*, pp. 1–5, 2019.

[78] A. Yu, B. Yu, H. Yang, Q. Yao, J. Zhang, and M. Cheriet, "Deep reinforcement learning based time synchronization routing optimization for C-ROFN in beyond 5G," in *2020 International Wireless Communications and Mobile Computing (IWCMC)*, pp. 865–867, 2020.

[79] V. Yazıcı, U. C. Kozat, and M. O. Sunay, "A new control plane for 5G network architecture with a case study on unified handoff, mobility, and routing management," *IEEE Communications Magazine*, vol. 52, no. 11, pp. 76–85, 2014.

[80] T. Alladi, V. Chamola Naren, and N. Kumar, "Parth: a two-stage lightweight mutual authentication protocol for UAV surveillance networks," *Computer Communications*, vol. 160, pp. 81–90, 2020.

[81] K. Kumar, S. Kumar, O. Kaiwartya, A. Sikandar, R. Kharel, and J. L. Mauri, "Internet of unmanned aerial vehicles: Qos provisioning in aerial ad-hoc networks," *Sensors*, vol. 20, no. 11, p. 3160, 2020.

[82] B. J. Olivieri de Souza and M. Endler, "Coordinating movement within swarms of UAVS through mobile networks," in *2015 IEEE International Conference on Pervasive Computing and Communication Workshops (PerCom Workshops)*, pp. 154–159, 2015.

[83] O. Shrit, S. Martin, K. Alagha, and G. Pujolle, "A new approach to realize drone swarm using ad-hoc network," in *2017 16th Annual Mediterranean Ad Hoc Networking Workshop (Med-Hoc-Net)*, pp. 1–5, 2017.

[84] S. Enge˙braten, K. Glette, and O. Yakimenko, "Networking-enabling enhancement for a swarm of cots drones," in *2018 IEEE 14th International Conference on Control and Automation (ICCA)*, pp. 562–569, 2018.

[85] Y. Jiang, Z. Mi, H. Wang, X. Wang, and N. Zhao, "The experiment and performance analysis of multi-node UAV ad hoc network based on swarm tactics," in *2018 10th International Conference on Wireless Communications and Signal Processing (WCSP)*, pp. 1–6, 2018.

[86] L. He, Y. Hou, X. Liang, J. Zhang, and P. Bai, "Time-varying formation tracking control for aircraft swarm with switching directed sympathetic networks," in *2019 IEEE 3rd Information Technology, Networking, Electronic and Automation Control Conference (ITNEC)*, pp. 199–204, 2019.

[87] M. Chen, F. Dai, H. Wang, and L. Lei, "Dfm: A distributed flocking model for UAV swarm networks," *IEEE Access*, vol. 6, pp. 69141–69150, 2018.

[88] W. Yang, Y. Wang, and J. Yuan, "Network construction in tactical UAV swarms with fsoc array antennas," in *2019 IEEE 3rd Information Technology, Networking, Electronic and Automation Control Conference (ITNEC)*, pp. 779–785, 2019.

[89] X. Zou, n. LV, K. Chen, and H. Wang, "A network updates scheme for software-defined airborne network of the aviation swarm," in *2019 3rd International Conference on Electronic Information Technology and Computer Engineering (EITCE)*, pp. 345–354, 2019.

[90] M. Chen, H. Wang, C. Chang, and X. Wei, "SIDR: a swarm intelligence-based damage-resilient mechanism for UAV swarm networks," *IEEE Access*, vol. 8, pp. 77089–77105, 2020.

[91] R. Lua and W. K. Ng, "Autonomic swarms for regenerative and collaborative networking," in *9th IEEE International Conference on Collaborative Computing: Networking, Applications and Worksharing*, pp. 40–49, 2013.

[92] L. Ruetten, P. A. Regis, D. Feil-Seifer, and S. Sengupta, "Area-optimized UAV swarm network for search and rescue operations," in *2020 10th Annual Computing and Communication Workshop and Conference (CCWC)*, pp. 0613–0618, 2020.

[93] R. Hunjet, B. Fraser, T. Stevens, L. Hodges, K. Mayen, J. C. Barca, M. Cochrane, R. Cannizzaro, and J. L. Palmer, "Data ferrying with swarming uas in tactical defence networks," in *2018 IEEE International Conference on Robotics and Automation (ICRA)*, pp. 6381–6388, 2018.

[94] A. M. Koushik, F. Hu, and S. Kumar, "Deep Q-learning-based node positioning for throughput-optimal communications in dynamic UAV swarm network," *IEEE Transactions on Cognitive Communications and Networking*, vol. 5, no. 3, pp. 554–566, 2019.

[95] G. Leu and J. Tang, "Survivable networks via UAV swarms guided by decentralized real-time evolutionary computation," in *2019 IEEE Congress on Evolutionary Computation (CEC)*, pp. 1945–1952, 2019.

[96] C. Liu, W. Feng, Y. Pei, J. Wang, Y. Chen, and N. Ge, "Energy efficiency optimization for UAV swarm-enabled aerial small cell networks," in *2020 International Conference on Computing, Networking and Communications (ICNC)*, pp. 561–566, 2020.

[97] Z. Feng, L. Ji, Q. Zhang, and W. Li, "Spectrum management for mmwave enabled UAV swarm networks: challenges and opportunities," *IEEE Communications Magazine*, vol. 57, no. 1, pp. 146–153, 2019.

[98] W. Huang, J. Peng, and H. Zhang, "User-centric intelligent UAV swarm networks: performance analysis and design insight," *IEEE Access*, vol. 7, pp. 181469–181478, 2019.

[99] X. Wang, W. Feng, Y. Chen, and N. Ge, "Power allocation for UAV swarm-enabled secure networks using large-scale csi," in *2019 IEEE Global Communications Conference (GLOBECOM)*, pp. 1–6, 2019.

[100] C. Guerber, N. Larrieu, and M. Royer, "Software defined network based architecture to improve security in a swarm of drones," in *2019 International Conference on Unmanned Aircraft Systems (ICUAS)*, pp. 51–60, 2019.

[101] H. Song, L. Liu, S. Pudlewski, and E. S. Bentley, "Random network coding enabled routing in swarm unmanned aerial vehicle networks," in *2019 IEEE Global Communications Conference (GLOBECOM)*, pp. 1–6, 2019.

[102] M. R. Brust, G. Danoy, P. Bouvry, D. Gashi, H. Pathak, and M. P. Gon çalves, "Defending against intrusion of malicious UAVS with networked UAV defense swarms," in *2017 IEEE 42nd Conference on Local Computer Networks Workshops (LCN Workshops)*, pp. 103–111, 2017.

[103] C. Cheng, P. Hsiao, H. T. Kung, and D. Vlah, "Maximizing throughput of UAV-relaying networks with the load-carry-and-deliver paradigm," in *2007 IEEE Wireless Communications and Networking Conference*, pp. 4417–4424, 2007.

[104] S. Ahmed, M. Z. Chowdhury, and Y. M. Jang, "Energy-efficient UAV-to-user scheduling to maximize throughput in wireless networks," *IEEE Access*, vol. *8*, pp. 21215–21225, 2020.

[105] S. Chou, A. Pang, and Y. Yu, "Energy-aware 3D unmanned aerial vehicle deployment for network throughput optimization," *IEEE Transactions on Wireless Communications*, vol. *19*, no. 1, pp. 563–578, 2020.

[106] S. K. Singh, K. Agrawal, K. Singh, C. Li, and W. Huang, "On UAV selection and position-based throughput maximization in multi-UAV relaying networks," *IEEE Access*, vol. *8*, pp. 144039–144050, 2020.

[107] H. Li and X. Zhao, "Throughput maximization with energy harvesting in UAV-assisted cognitive mobile relay networks," *IEEE Transactions on Cognitive Communications and Networking*, vol. *7*, pp. 197–209, 2020.

[108] L. Chiaraviglio, F. D'Andreagiovanni, W. Liu, J. Gutierrez, N. Blefari-Melazzi, K. R. Choo, and M. Alouini, "Multi-area throughput and energy optimization of UAV-aided cellular networks powered by solar panels and grid," *IEEE Transactions on Mobile Computing*, vol. *20*, pp. 2427–2444, 2020.

[109] M. Ali, Q. Rabbani, M. Naeem, S. Qaisar, and F. Qamar, "Joint user association, power allocation, and throughput maximization in 5G H-CRAN networks," *IEEE Transactions on Vehicular Technology*, vol. *66*, no. 10, pp. 9254–9262, 2017.

[110] J. Tang, J. Song, J. Ou, J. Luo, X. Zhang, and K. Wong, "Minimum throughput maximization for multi-UAV enabled wpcn: a deep reinforcement learning method," *IEEE Access*, vol. *8*, pp. 9124–9132, 2020.

[111] J. Cui, Y. Liu, and A. Nallanathan, "Multi-agent reinforcement learning-based resource allocation for UAV networks," *IEEE Transactions on Wireless Communications*, vol. *19*, no. 2, pp. 729–743, 2020.

[112] N. Zhao, Z. Liu, and Y. Cheng, "Multi-agent deep reinforcement learning for trajectory design and power allocation in multi-UAV networks," *IEEE Access*, vol. *8*, pp. 139670–139679, 2020.

[113] K. Zheng, Y. Sun, Z. Lin, and Y. Tang, "Uav-assisted online video downloading in vehicular networks: a reinforcement learning approach," in *2020 IEEE 91st Vehicular Technology Conference (VTC2020- Spring)*, pp. 1–5, 2020.

[114] M. Chen, W. Saad, and C. Yin, "Liquid state machine learning for resource and cache management in lte-u unmanned aerial vehicle (UAV) networks," *IEEE Transactions on Wireless Communications*, vol. *18*, no. 3, pp. 1504–1517, 2019.

[115] M. Yi, X. Wang, J. Liu, Y. Zhang, and B. Bai, "Deep reinforcement learning for fresh data collection in UAV-assisted iot networks," in *IEEE INFOCOM 2020 - IEEE Conference on Computer Communi- cations Workshops (INFOCOM WKSHPS)*, pp. 716–721, 2020.

[116] W. Wang, X. Lu, S. Liu, L. Xiao, and B. Yang, "Energy efficient relay in UAV networks against jam- ming: a reinforcement learning based approach," in *2020 IEEE 91st Vehicular Technology Conference (VTC2020- Spring)*, pp. 1–5, 2020.

[117] M. S. Shokry, D. Ebrahimi, C. Assi, S. Sharafeddine, and A. Ghrayeb, "Leveraging UAVS for coverage in cell-free vehicular networks: a deep reinforcement learning approach," *IEEE Transactions on Mobile Computing*, vol. *20*, pp. 2835–2847, 2020.

[118] G. Faraci, C. Grasso, and G. Schembra, "Reinforcement-learning for management of a 5G network slice extension with UAVS," in *IEEE INFOCOM 2019 - IEEE Conference on Computer Communications Workshops (INFOCOM WKSHPS)*, pp. 732–737, 2019.

[119] A. Asheralieva and D. Niyato, "Hierarchical game-theoretic and reinforcement learning framework for computational offloading in UAV-enabled mobile edge computing networks with multiple service providers," *IEEE Internet of Things Journal*, vol. *6*, no. 5, pp. 8753–8769, 2019.

[120] Y. Xu, L. Xiao, D. Yang, Q. Wu, and L. Cuthbert, "Throughput maximization in multi-UAV enabled communication systems with difference consideration," *IEEE Access*, vol. *6*, pp. 55291–55301, 2018.

[121] L. Xie, J. Xu, and R. Zhang, "Throughput maximization for UAV-enabled wireless powered communication networks," *IEEE Internet of Things Journal*, vol. *6*, no. 2, pp. 1690–1703, 2019.

[122] W. Shi, H. Zhou, J. Li, W. Xu, N. Zhang, and X. Shen, "Drone assisted vehicular networks: architecture, challenges and opportunities," *IEEE Network*, vol. *32*, no. 3, pp. 130–137, 2018.

[123] Y. Zeng, R. Zhang, and T. J. Lim, "Throughput maximization for UAV-enabled mobile relaying systems," *IEEE Transactions on Communications*, vol. *64*, no. 12, pp. 4983–4996, 2016.

[124] L. Xie, J. Xu, and R. Zhang, "Throughput maximization for UAV-enabled wireless powered communication networks - invited paper," in *2018 IEEE 87th Vehicular Technology Conference (VTC Spring)*, pp. 1–7, 2018.

[125] M. Hua, L. Yang, C. Pan, and A. Nallanathan, "Throughput maximization for full-duplex UAV aided small cell wireless systems," *IEEE Wireless Communications Letters*, vol. *9*, no. 4, pp. 475–479, 2020.

[126] N. Zhang, S. Zhang, P. Yang, O. Alhussein, W. Zhuang, and X. S. Shen, "Software defined space-air-ground integrated vehicular networks: challenges and solutions," *IEEE Communications Magazine*, vol. *55*, no. 7, pp. 101–109, 2017.

[127] L. Xie, J. Xu, and Y. Zeng, "Common throughput maximization for UAV-enabled interference channel with wireless powered communications," *IEEE Transactions on Communications*, vol. *68*, no. 5, pp. 3197–3212, 2020.

[128] J. Li, G. Lei, G. Manogaran, G. Mastorakis, and C. X. Mavromoustakis, "D2D communication mode selection and resource optimization algorithm with optimal throughput in 5G network," *IEEE Access*, vol. *7*, pp. 25263–25273, 2019.

[129] L. Sboui, H. Ghazzai, Z. Rezki, and M. Alouini, "On the throughput of cognitive radio mimo systems assisted with UAV relays," in *2017 13th International Wireless Communications and Mobile Computing Conference (IWCMC)*, pp. 939–944, 2017.

[130] J. Wang, Y. Liu, S. Niu, and H. Song, "5G-enabled optimal bi-throughput for UAS swarm networking," in *2020 International Conference on Space-Air-Ground Computing (SAGC)*, pp. 43–48, 2020.

[131] M. Hua, C. Li, Y. Huang, and L. Yang, "Throughput maximization for UAV-enabled wireless power transfer in relaying system," in *2017 9th International Conference on Wireless Communications and Signal Processing (WCSP)*, pp. 1–5, 2017.

[132] J. Fan, M. Cui, G. Zhang, and Y. Chen, "Throughput improvement for multi-hop UAV relaying," *IEEE Access*, vol. *7*, pp. 147732–147742, 2019.

[133] X. Liang, W. Xu, H. Gao, M. Pan, J. Lin, Q. Deng, and P. Zhang, "Throughput optimization for cognitive UAV networks: A three-dimensional-location-aware approach," *IEEE Wireless Communications Letters*, vol. *9*, no. 7, pp. 948–952, 2020.

[134] J. M. Batalla, M. Kantor, C. X. Mavromoustakis, G. Skourletopoulos, and G. Mastorakis, "A novel methodology for efficient throughput evaluation in virtualized routers," in *2015 IEEE International Conference on Communications (ICC)*, pp. 6899–6905, 2015.

[135] L. Chiaraviglio, L. Amorosi, F. Malandrino, C. F. Chiasserini, P. Dell'Olmo, and C. Casetti, "Optimal throughput management in uav-based networks during disasters," in *IEEE INFOCOM 2019 - IEEE Conference on Computer Communications Workshops (INFOCOM WKSHPS)*, pp. 307–312, 2019.

[136] L. Chiaraviglio, F. D'andreagiovanni, R. Choo, F. Cuomo, and S. Colonnese, "Joint optimization of area throughput and grid-connected microgeneration in UAV-based mobile networks," *IEEE Access*, vol. *7*, pp. 69545–69558, 2019.

[137] J. Park, H. Lee, S. Eom, and I. Lee, "UAV-aided wireless powered communication networks: trajectory optimization and resource allocation for minimum throughput maximization," *IEEE Access*, vol. *7*, pp. 134978–134991, 2019.

[138] G. Manogaran, C.-H. Hsu, B. S. Rawal, B. Muthu, C. X. Mavromoustakis, and G. Mastorakis, "Isof: Information scheduling and optimization framework for improving the performance of agriculture systems aided by industry 4.0," *IEEE Internet of Things Journal*, vol. *8*, no. 5, pp. 3120–3129, 2021.

[139] M. Hua, L. Yang, C. Li, Q. Wu, and A. L. Swindlehurst, "Throughput maximization for UAV-aided backscatter communication networks," *IEEE Transactions on Communications*, vol. *68*, no. 2, pp. 1254–1270, 2020.

[140] A. Giorgetti, M. Lucchi, M. Chiani, and M. Z. Win, "Throughput per pass for data aggregation from a wireless sensor network via a UAV," *IEEE Transactions on Aerospace and Electronic Systems*, vol. *47*, no. 4, pp. 2610–2626, 2011.

[141] B. Jiang, J. Yang, H. Xu, H. Song, and G. Zheng, "Multimedia data throughput maximization in internet-of-things system based on optimization of cache-enabled UAV," *IEEE Internet of Things Journal*, vol. *6*, no. 2, pp. 3525–3532, 2019.

[142] K. Krishnamoorthy, M. Pachter, and P. Chandler, "Maximizing the throughput of a patrolling UAV by dynamic programming," in *2011 IEEE International Conference on Control Applications (CCA)*, pp. 916–920, 2011.

[143] P. Dinh, T. M. Nguyen, S. Sharafeddine, and C. Assi, "Joint location and beamforming design for cooperative UAVS with limited storage capacity," *IEEE Transactions on Communications*, vol. *67*, no. 11, pp. 8112–8123, 2019.

[144] D. Liu, Y. Xu, J. Wang, J. Chen, Q. Wu, A. Anpalagan, K. Xu, and Y. Zhang, "Opportunistic utilization of dynamic multi-UAV in device-to-device communication networks," *IEEE Transactions on Cognitive Communications and Networking*, vol. *6*, no. 3, pp. 1069–1083, 2020.

[145] K. Yao, J. Wang, Y. Xu, Y. Xu, Y. Yang, Y. Zhang, H. Jiang, and J. Yao, "Self-organizing slot access for neighboring cooperation in UAV swarms," *IEEE Transactions on Wireless Communications*, vol. *19*, no. 4, pp. 2800–2812, 2020.

[146] D. Fan, F. Gao, B. Ai, G. Wang, Z. Zhong, Y. Deng, and A. Nallanathan, "Channel estimation and self-positioning for UAV swarm," *IEEE Transactions on Communications*, vol. *67*, no. 11, pp. 7994–8007, 2019.

[147] H. El Hammouti, M. Benjillali, B. Shihada, and M. Alouini, "Learn-as-you-fly: a distributed algorithm for joint 3d placement and user association in multi-UAVS networks," *IEEE Transactions on Wireless Communications*, vol. *18*, no. 12, pp. 5831–5844, 2019.

[148] Y. Han, L. Liu, L. Duan, and R. Zhang, "Towards reliable UAV swarm communication in d2d-enhanced cellular network," *IEEE Transactions on Wireless Communications*, vol. *20*, pp. 1567–1581, 2020.

[149] M. Mozaffari, A. Taleb Zadeh Kasgari, W. Saad, M. Bennis, and M. Debbah, "Beyond 5G with UAVS: foundations of a 3d wireless cellular network," *IEEE Transactions on Wireless Communications*, vol. *18*, pp. 357–372, 2019.

[150] P. Wang, C. Chen, S. Kumari, M. Shojafar, R. Tafazolli, and Y. Liu, "HDMA: hybrid D2D message authentication scheme for 5G-enabled vanets," *IEEE Transactions on Intelligent Transportation Systems*, vol. *22*, pp. 1–10, 2020.

[151] M. M. Azari, F. Rosas, and S. Pollin, "Cellular connectivity for UAVS: network modeling, performance analysis and design guidelines," *IEEE Transactions on Wireless Communications*, vol. *18*, pp. 3366–3381, 2019.

[152] M. M. Azari, G. Geraci, A. Garcia-Rodriguez, and S. Pollin, "UAV-to-UAV communications in cellular networks," *IEEE Transactions on Wireless Communications*, vol. *19*, no. 9, pp. 6130–6144, 2020.

[153] M. A. Ali and A. Jamalipour, "Uav placement and power allocation in uplink and downlink operations of cellular network," *IEEE Transactions on Communications*, vol. *68*, no. 7, pp. 4383–4393, 2020.

[154] J. Ji, K. Zhu, D. Niyato, and R. Wang, "Probabilistic cache placement in UAV-assisted networks with d2d connections: performance analysis and trajectory optimization," *IEEE Transactions on Communications*, vol. *68*, no. 10, pp. 6331–6345, 2020.

[155] T. Hou, Y. Liu, Z. Song, X. Sun, and Y. Chen, "Multiple antenna aided noma in UAV networks: a stochastic geometry approach," *IEEE Transactions on Communications*, vol. *67*, no. 2, pp. 1031–1044, 2019.

[156] K. Wang, P. Xu, C. M. Chen, S. Kumari, M. Shojafar, and M. Alazab, "Neural architecture search for robust networks in 6G-enabled massive IOT domain," *IEEE Internet of Things Journal*, vol. *8*, pp. 5332–5339, 2020.

[157] D. Zhai, H. Li, X. Tang, R. Zhang, Z. Ding, and F. R. Yu, "Height optimization and resource allocation for noma enhanced UAV-aided relay networks," *IEEE Transactions on Communications*, vol. *69*, pp. 962–975, 2020.

[158] F. Cui, Y. Cai, Z. Qin, M. Zhao, and G. Y. Li, "Multiple access for mobile-UAV enabled networks: joint trajectory design and resource allocation," *IEEE Transactions on Communications*, vol. *67*, no. 7, pp. 4980–4994, 2019.

[159] T. Hou, Y. Liu, Z. Song, X. Sun, and Y. Chen, "Exploiting noma for UAV communications in large-scale cellular networks," *IEEE Transactions on Communications*, vol. *67*, no. 10, pp. 6897–6911, 2019.

[160] N. Zhao, F. Cheng, F. R. Yu, J. Tang, Y. Chen, G. Gui, and H. Sari, "Caching UAV assisted secure transmission in hyper-dense networks based on interference alignment," *IEEE Transactions on Communications*, vol. *66*, no. 5, pp. 2281–2294, 2018.

[161] T. Zhang, Y. Wang, Y. Liu, W. Xu, and A. Nallanathan, "Cache-enabling UAV communications: Network deployment and resource allocation," *IEEE Transactions on Wireless Communications*, vol. *19*, no. 11, pp. 7470–7483, 2020.

[162] Y. Sun, Z. Ding, and X. Dai, "A user-centric cooperative scheme for UAV-assisted wireless networks in malfunction areas," *IEEE Transactions on Communications*, vol. *67*, no. 12, pp. 8786–8800, 2019.

[163] J. Wang, Y. Liu, and H. Song, "Counter-unmanned aircraft system(s) (c-uas): state of the art, challenges, and future trends," *IEEE Aerospace and Electronic Systems Magazine*, vol. *36*, no. 3, pp. 4–29, 2021.

[164] C. Zhan and Y. Zeng, "Aerial-ground cost tradeoff for multi-UAV-enabled data collection in wireless sensor networks," *IEEE Transactions on Communications*, vol. *68*, no. 3, pp. 1937–1950, 2020.

[165] W. Yi, Y. Liu, Y. Deng, and A. Nallanathan, "Clustered UAV networks with millimeter wave com- munications: a stochastic geometry view," *IEEE Transactions on Communications*, vol. *68*, no. 7, pp. 4342–4357, 2020.

[166] H. Wang, Y. Zhang, X. Zhang, and Z. Li, "Secrecy and covert communications against UAV surveillance via multi-hop networks," *IEEE Transactions on Communications*, vol. *68*, no. 1, pp. 389–401, 2020.

[167] M. Monemi and H. Tabassum, "Performance of UAV-assisted D2D networks in the finite block-length regime," *IEEE Transactions on Communications*, vol. *68*, no. 11, pp. 7270–7285, 2020.

[168] Y. L. Che, Y. Lai, S. Luo, K. Wu, and L. Duan, "Uav-aided information and energy transmissions for cognitive and sustainable 5G networks," *IEEE Transactions on Wireless Communications*, vol. *20*, pp. 1668–1683, 2020.

[169] Y. Emami, K. Li, and E. Tovar, "Buffer-aware scheduling for UAV relay networks with energy fairness," in *2020 IEEE 91st Vehicular Technology Conference (VTC2020-Spring)*, pp. 1–5, 2020.

[170] Z. Wang, W. Xu, D. Yang, and J. Lin, "Joint trajectory optimization and user scheduling for rotary- wing UAV-enabled wireless powered communication networks," *IEEE Access*, vol. *7*, pp. 181369–181380, 2019.

[171] S. Koulali, E. Sabir, T. Taleb, and M. Azizi, "A green strategic activity scheduling for UAV networks: a sub-modular game perspective," *IEEE Communications Magazine*, vol. *54*, no. 5, pp. 58–64, 2016.

[172] H. Yang and X. Xie, "Energy-efficient joint scheduling and resource management for UAV-enabled multicell networks," *IEEE Systems Journal*, vol. *14*, no. 1, pp. 363–374, 2020.

[173] J. Kwon and S. Hailes, "Scheduling UAVS to bridge communications in delay-tolerant networks using real-time scheduling analysis techniques," in *2014 IEEE/SICE International Symposium on System Integration*, pp. 363–369, 2014.

[174] H. Kong, M. Lin, W.-P. Zhu, H. Amindavar, and M.-S. Alouini, "Multiuser scheduling for asymmetric FSO/RF links in satellite-UAV-terrestrial networks," *IEEE Wireless Communications Letters*, vol. *9*, no. 8, pp. 1235–1239, 2020.

[175] Y. Zheng and K.-W. Chin, "Link scheduling for data collection in SIC-capable UAV networks," in *2019 29th International Telecommunication Networks and Applications Conference (ITNAC)*, pp. 1–6, 2019.

[176] J. Baek, S. I. Han, and Y. Han, "User scheduling for non-orthogonal transmission in UAV-assisted relay network," in *2017 IEEE 28th Annual International Symposium on Personal, Indoor, and Mobile Radio Communications (PIMRC)*, pp. 1–5, 2017.

[177] T. Duan, W. Wang, T. Wang, X. Chen, and X. Li, "Dynamic tasks scheduling model of UAV cluster based on flexible network architecture," *IEEE Access*, vol. *8*, pp. 115448–115460, 2020.

[178] T. Duan, W. Wang, T. Wang, M. Huang, X. Li, and H. He, "Dynamic tasks scheduling model for UAV cluster flexible network architecture," in *2020 3rd International Conference on Unmanned Systems (ICUS)*, pp. 78–83, 2020.

[179] S. Mao, S. He, and J. Wu, "Joint UAV position optimization and resource scheduling in space-air-ground integrated networks with mixed cloud-edge computing," *IEEE Systems Journal*, vol. *15*, pp. 3992–4002, 2020.

[180] W. Sun, "Distributed optimal scheduling in UAV swarm network," in *2021 IEEE 18th Annual Consumer Communications Networking Conference (CCNC)*, pp. 1–4, 2021.

[181] R. F. Atallah, C. M. Assi, and M. J. Khabbaz, "Scheduling the operation of a connected vehicular network using deep reinforcement learning," *IEEE Transactions on Intelligent Transportation Systems*, vol. *20*, no. 5, pp. 1669–1682, 2019.

[182] T. Yang, J. Li, H. Feng, N. Cheng, and W. Guan, "A novel transmission scheduling based on deep reinforcement learning in software-defined maritime communication networks," *IEEE Transactions on Cognitive Communications and Networking*, vol. *5*, no. 4, pp. 1155–1166, 2019.

[183] J. Li and X. Zhang, "Deep reinforcement learning-based joint scheduling of EMBB and URLLC in 5G networks," *IEEE Wireless Communications Letters*, vol. *9*, no. 9, pp. 1543–1546, 2020.

[184] C. Xu, S. Liu, C. Zhang, Y. Huang, and L. Yang, "Joint user scheduling and beam selection in mmwave networks based on multi-agent reinforcement learning," in *2020 IEEE 11th Sensor Array and Multichannel Signal Processing Workshop (SAM)*, pp. 1–5, 2020.

[185] G. Dartmann, H. Song, and A. Schmeink. *Big Data Analytics for Cyber-Physical Systems: Machine Learning for the Internet of Things*. ISBN: 9780128166376. Elsevier, 2019, pp. 1–360.

[186] B. Wang, H. Li, Z. Lin, and Y. Xia, "Temporal fusion pointer network-based reinforcement learning algorithm for multi-objective workflow scheduling in the cloud," in *2020 International Joint Conference on Neural Networks (IJCNN)*, pp. 1–8, 2020.

[187] S. Aroua, G. Quadrio, Y. Ghamri-Doudane, O. Gaggi, and C. E. Palazzi, "Qos-aware reinforcement learning for multimedia traffic scheduling in home area networks," in *GLOBECOM 2020 - 2020 IEEE Global Communications Conference*, pp. 1–6, 2020.

[188] Y. Wang, H. Liu, W. Zheng, Y. Xia, Y. Li, P. Chen, K. Guo, and H. Xie, "Multi-objective work- flow scheduling with deep-q-network-based multi-agent reinforcement learning," *IEEE Access*, vol. *7*, pp. 39974–39982, 2019.

[189] T. T. Anh, N. C. Luong, D. Niyato, Y.-C. Liang, and D. I. Kim, "Deep reinforcement learning for time scheduling in rf-powered backscatter cognitive radio networks," in *2019 IEEE Wireless Communications and Networking Conference (WCNC)*, pp. 1–7, 2019.

[190] F. AL-Tam, A. Mazayev, N. Correia, and J. Rodriguez, "Radio resource scheduling with deep pointer networks and reinforcement learning," in *2020 IEEE 25th International Workshop on Computer Aided Modeling and Design of Communication Links and Networks (CAMAD)*, pp. 1–6, 2020.

[191] J. Wang, C. Xu, Y. Huangfu, R. Li, Y. Ge, and J. Wang, "Deep reinforcement learning for scheduling in cellular networks," in *2019 11th International Conference on Wireless Communications and Signal Processing (WCSP)*, pp. 1–6, 2019.

[192] F. Jiang, K. Wang, L. Dong, C. Pan, and K. Yang, "Stacked autoencoder-based deep reinforcement learning for online resource scheduling in large-scale mec networks," *IEEE Internet of Things Journal*, vol. 7, no. 10, pp. 9278–9290, 2020.

[193] Y.-H. Xu, G. Yu, and Y.-T. Yong, "Deep reinforcement learning-based resource scheduling strategy for reliability-oriented wireless body area networks," *IEEE Sensors Letters*, vol. 5, no. 1, pp. 1–4, 2021.

[194] B. Sellami, A. Hakiri, S. Ben Yahia, and P. Berthou, "Deep reinforcement learning for energy-efficient task scheduling in sdn-based iot network," in *2020 IEEE 19th International Symposium on Network Computing and Applications (NCA)*, pp. 1–4, 2020.

[195] Y. Xia, L. Wu, Z. Wang, X. Zheng, and J. Jin, "Cluster-enabled cooperative scheduling based on rein- forcement learning for high-mobility vehicular networks," *IEEE Transactions on Vehicular Technology*, vol. 69, no. 11, pp. 12664–12678, 2020.

[196] F. Naeem, S. Seifollahi, Z. Zhou, and M. Tariq, "A generative adversarial network enabled deep distributional reinforcement learning for transmission scheduling in internet of vehicles," *IEEE Transactions on Intelligent Transportation Systems*, vol. 22, pp. 4550–4559, 2020.

[197] L. Xu, and T. Zhang, "Reinforcement learning based dynamic task scheduling for multifunction radar network," in *2020 IEEE Radar Conference (RadarConf20)*, pp. 1–5, 2020.

State-of-the-art in PHY layer deep learning for future wireless communication systems and networks

5

Konstantinos Koufos, Karim El Haloui and Cong Zhou
University of Warwick, Coventry, United Kingdom

Valerio Frascolla
Intel Deutschland GmbH, Neubiberg, Germany

Mehrdad Dianati
University of Warwick, Coventry, United Kingdom

Contents

DOI: 10.1201/9781003190691-7

5.1 INTRODUCTION

The recent advances on programmable wireless networks using software-defined networking principles and network function virtualization (SDN/NFV), together with the ongoing breakthroughs in machine learning, artificial intelligence (AI/ML) and computational capabilities, set a stage where future communication networks can thrive. The next generation of wireless communication systems is expected to penetrate across various vertical industries, offering highly heterogeneous services with stringent requirements over the same unified physical infrastructure, while keeping both OpEx and CapEx low (see Figure 5.1). Unsurprisingly, extensive data collection, big data analytics and AI/ML are indispensable enablers in realising the goal of automation, orchestration, and performance optimization of such a complex ecosystem, see the vision papers in [1–6]. During the past few years, the ongoing activities by several organizations

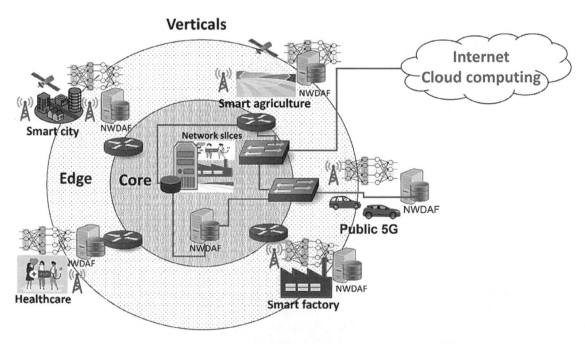

FIGURE 5.1 The deployment of a unified physical infrastructure (core network) reduces the total CapEx and OpEx compared to the deployment of dedicated networks for each vertical and allows identifying profitable use cases. Edge computing is employed for satisfying the requirements of time-critical services. Big data analytics with AI/ML through the NWDAF is used at the core network for dynamic assignment of network slices to verticals and at the edge for analysing various KPIs and optimising the operation at the RAN. For presentation clarity, the figure illustrates the connections to the cloud and the core network only for one of the verticals (smart agriculture).

and standardization bodies in the telecommunication sector, led by 3GPP, ETSI ENI (ETSI experiential networking intelligence), ETSI ZSM (ETSI zero-touch network and service management), and O-RAN Alliance, confirm the pivotal role that AI/ML will play in next generation communication networks.

The standard development organizations and the telecommunication industry have so far joined forces to resolve vendor inter-operability issues by leveraging open interfaces and develop AI/ML-based solutions that operate on long timescales. For instance, 3GPP has introduced in Rel-15 the network data analytics function (NWDAF) for the instantiation, orchestration, and management of network slices [7]. In addition, the ETSI ENI committee has designed a system, which provides intelligent recommendations for network management to another system, e.g., a mobile network operator (MNO) [8]. Furthermore, the ETSI ZSM committee has developed a generalised functional reference architecture of future communication networks that supports high levels of autonomy, self-healing, and self-optimization [9]. And, finally, the O-RAN Alliance has introduced closed control loops at the RAN, i.e., the near-real-time and the non-real-time RAN intelligent controllers (RICs), operating respectively at timescales between 10ms and 1000ms and more than 1000ms [10]. More contextually, the non-real-time RIC is mostly about instantiation of network slices and optimization of RAN policies, while the real-time RIC handles spectrum management, traffic steering and admission control, to name a few.

While embedding AI/ML in network functions that operate at long timescales is of paramount importance, several organizations and major research projects are actively working on the real-time RIC by providing ML-assisted operation at the PHY layer, i.e., at timescales less than 10ms (the frame duration in the 5G NR). To give some representative examples, in 2017 the ITU-T study group launched the focus group on ML for future networks including 5G (FG-ML5G), which has listed ML-based channel modelling, channel prediction and link adaptation optimization as important use cases for future networks [11]. We provide an updated review of research activities in these important areas in Sections 5.5 and 5.7. Furthermore, the ongoing project ARIADNE, funded by the European H2020 research framework, investigates the potential of using reflecting intelligent surfaces (RIS) for implementing the high data-rate backhaul of millimetre-wave (mm-wave) small cell networks in the D-band (130–174.8 GHz) [12]. As explained in Subsection 5.8.3, the ML-based optimization of phase shifters in RIS is a research topic that is worth pursuing. The expected operations of future wireless networks in higher-frequency spectrums such as mm-wave frequencies and THz bands make the well-validated understanding of sub-6GHz wireless communications inadequate and superfluous. New techniques should be developed for channel equalization and symbol detection in higher frequencies and high doppler channels [13, 14], and as it is explored in Sections 5.3 and 5.4, AI/ML can assist in this direction.

Motivated by the aforementioned potentials, in this book chapter, we aim to provide the interested readers with a comprehensive analysis and review of the most recent progress in the use of data-driven and ML-based approaches at the PHY layer in the study of modern communication systems and networks. Before that, an overview of related survey articles is provided.

5.1.1 Related survey papers

The overview studies in [15–18] focus on ML techniques for cognitive radio-based vehicular ad hoc networks (CR-VANETs) [15], wireless sensor networks (WSNs) [16], the Internet-of-Things (IoT) for smart cities [17] and industrial IoT [18]. These surveys are certainly important as the transportation and IoT sectors would significantly benefit from the 5G and 6G ecosystems. In the same vein, the authors in [19, 20] present an overview of ML techniques encountered in self-organised cellular networks, including self-configuration of operational and radio parameters, self-optimization, and self-healing. Likewise, the study in [21] reviews artificial neural networks (ANNs) for optimising various aspects of wireless networks capitalising on unmanned aerial vehicles (UAVs). Resource allocation and content caching for wireless virtual reality, failure detection, target surveillance, and user activity classification for IoT are also summarised in [21].

TABLE 5.1 Taxonomy of survey articles on intelligent communications & networking

			TAXONOMY OF SURVEY ARTICLES	
APPLICATION-ORIENTED			LAYERING-ORIENTED	ML-ORIENTED
WSN	[16]	PHY	[22] [23] [24] [25, 26] [27]	[28, 29]
IoT	[17] [18]	MAC	[23] [30] [31] [24] [25] [26] [27]	
VANET	[15]	NET	[32] [24, 32] [25] [26] [27]	
Cellular	[19] [20]	Edge	[23]	
UAV	[21]			

The surveys in [26, 27] adopt a different approach without explicitly considering use cases, but, instead, separate research contributions based on the protocol layer where the ML component operates (see Table 5.1). The authors in [22] have compiled a critical review of ML algorithms at the PHY layer with an emphasis on MIMO systems and hardware imperfections due to RF and power amplifier nonlinearities. At the MAC layer, intelligent power control and resource allocation in OFDMA downlink are explored in [23, 30], respectively. In addition, the review paper in [31] presents an in-depth analysis of ML-based approaches at the MAC layer, including spectrum, backhaul, and cache management. In the network layer, intelligent base station clustering, switching control, mobility management, user association, and routing are treated, while in the application layer, intelligent localization is considered [31]. An overview of distributed ML techniques at the edge, such as the recently recommended federated learning by 3GPP, is also included in [23]. The authors in [32] mainly discuss the use of ML techniques for fundamental network layer issues, which are related to network slicing, such as traffic prediction and classification, congestion control, fault/QoS management and network security.

The survey paper [24] is another extensive review of ML-empowered wireless communications covering all protocol layers and stressing the importance of collecting data analytics at the edge for time-critical services. The mainstream open-source libraries and platforms for NN deployment and training are presented, which is of interest to communications engineers starting to explore ML platforms. The study in [25] is a short review of ML-enabled RAN that highlights essential points, including channel estimation, symbol detection, channel coding, and dynamic spectrum access at RAN layer 1 and 2, while fault recovery, energy optimization, and the formation of cell sectors are reviewed at RAN layer 3. The activities of O-RAN Alliance and the recommendations in 3GPP Release 16 towards an intelligent RAN and 5G core are acknowledged. In [33], one may find a detailed overview of new features introduced by 3GPP Releases 16 and 17, but the treatment of data analytics is limited.

Another way to organise AI/ML techniques applied to wireless communication networks is to consider the employed learning method such as supervised, unsupervised, reinforcement, and deep learning. This taxonomy is followed in [28] and can be beneficial for those with a keen interest in the learning methods and advancements brought along in this area. In our view, deep reinforcement learning is of particular interest in wireless networks as it can be used for distributed intelligent decision-making in the face of uncertainty, as detailed in [29]. Finally, the authors in [34] present an overview of ongoing standardization activities, trends in the industry and major research projects on intelligent communications and networking.

5.1.2 Summary of this chapter

The remainder of this chapter is organised as follows. In Section 5.2, we divide the state-of-the-art into purely data-driven and model-aided ML techniques, as suggested by Renzo et. al. [35]. In Section 5.3, we review deep learning methods for symbol detection, including model-aided auto-encoders and sequential detectors. Intelligent channel equalization and prediction are presented in Section 5.4 and 5.5, respectively. ML-assisted channel coding and link adaptation are the topics of Sections 5.6 and 5.7, respectively. In Section 5.8, we discuss AI/ML methods for enhancing the signal detection performance using spectrum sensing, convolutional neural networks (CNNs) for automatic modulation classification and intelligent radio environment using reflecting surfaces. Note that while the standardization efforts on intelligent communications are mostly focused on cellular systems, the implementation of signal processing functions using machine learning techniques is pervasive to other wireless technologies such as WLAN and Zigbee. In Section 5.9, we have included a review of performance evaluation techniques of wireless networks combining machine learning and stochastic geometry based on performance metrics pertinent to the PHY layer. We conclude this chapter in Section 5.10.

5.2 DATA-DRIVEN ML METHODS FOR TRANSCEIVER OPTIMIZATION

The long-established systematic approach in the study and design of general communications systems, and, more specifically, wireless transceivers, is to decompose them into functional blocks. Each block is studied independently and optimised in a disarticulated manner leading to suboptimal transceiver designs. With the advent of ML/AI, new revolutionary paradigms and techniques, that lead to spectacular advances across many fields, can be leveraged to bring forward new architectures and potentially allow to design optimal transceivers.

The overarching principle of a communication system is to receive a faithful copy of what is transmitted. In this end, using ML, the complete system can be seen as a single unit and be optimised to learn the optimal system mapping between source and received symbols. In the literature, this approach is also known as pure data-driven technique [35]. It replaces all signal processing blocks, c.g., modulation, channel coding, phase correction, error correction, matched filtering, etc., into a purely data-driven autoencoder which learns how to map source symbols to adapted signal waveforms robust to channel corruption together with an optimal decoding scheme at the receiver.

The decomposition into several blocks of the communication chain can be leveraged by incorporating domain expert knowledge into the design of a block. At times, a tradeoff, between optimality and mathematical tractability, is necessary. Accurate mathematical models can be devised but these may lead to high-order computational complexity problems and restrict their usage if real-time operation is required [22]. Furthermore, accurate models are not always achievable and might not capture the whole complexity coming, for example, from hardware imperfections or other non-linearities [35]. Nevertheless, we will shortly see below that imperfect models can still provide "good-enough" solutions, which can serve as initialization vectors in ML algorithms, and thus, reduce their training time.

In Section 5.2.1, we review key studies on ML-based design at the PHY layer using pure data-driven techniques. Then, in Section 5.2.2 we discuss another approach for optimising the transceiver design where ML and mathematical modelling work together and mutually benefit from each other.

5.2.1 Data-driven approach for end-to-end transceiver optimization

A natural ML architecture that fits the structure of a transceiver is the autoencoder, which is composed of an encoder, the transmitter, and a decoder, the receiver. The difference of a communications system autoencoder architecture is the insertion of extra layers in-between the encoder and decoder to model the channel [36]. Different channel profiles from the additive white Gaussian noise (AWGN) to more complex channels can be modelled this way [37].

The channel, and, in particular, its gradient, must be known to carry out backpropagation and train the NN at the transmitter. This condition poses the following challenges:

- The channel used for training must be similar to the actual channel where communication takes place.
- The channel transfer function must be differentiable.

Provided that these constraints are met, the autoencoder can be trained over all possible source messages using gradient descent. Unlike other ML applications, due to the random nature of the wireless channel, overfitting is likely not an issue here [38]. With sufficient training, the transmitter can learn a robust and accurate mapping of the source output to transmitted symbols, whilst the receiver trains its NN to implement, for instance, maximum likelihood decoding of the received symbols. Usually, a softmax activation function is the last layer of a NN performing classification tasks. Its output can then be interpreted as a probability mass function over the set of transmitted symbols [39] and thus, the softmax activation function is tailored to receivers implementing soft decoding.

Transceivers designed as autoencoders perform equally as traditional designs [36, 37] demonstrating that ML techniques can provide alternative solutions. Yet, many challenges can preclude the adoption of autoencoders as practical solutions. These are related to aspects of training and to the explicability of NNs in general. On the one hand, a requirement for training is the full differentiability of the weights of the NN as a function of the neurons which is not guaranteed and is rarely the case for channels because of the following reasons.

- Firstly, the channel displays non-deterministic characteristics due to noise or its fading profiles.
- Secondly, there might be signal processing blocks, such as quantification, that are by essence non-differentiable.
- And lastly, some blocks may be poorly understood or inaccurate, e.g., the frequency response of power amplifiers.

The above-mentioned issues make the learning challenging as traditional learning techniques become inoperative. On the other hand, explainability of NN is crucial to understand the relationship between the network architecture and the required end-to-end performance. Unlike conventional methods, explainability and insight is lost completely when employing purely data-driven autoencoders.

To mitigate the impact of small discrepancies between the actual channel and the model used for training, the study in [38] has enhanced the performance of a wireless system designed as an autoencoder by dividing the training phase into two stages. Firstly, the autoencoder is trained offline on a stochastic channel model which should closely approximate the actual channel. Secondly, online collected pilots are used to fine-tune the NN at the receiver using supervised learning. The technique of using an already trained NN and tune it is known in the literature as transfer learning. In this case, the knowledge of the transfer function is required in the first stage of the training and only a partial transfer learning is performed to fine-tune the receiver to the actual channel but not the transmitter.

To enhance the transmitter's performance, one may separate the NNs of the transmitter and receiver and iteratively optimise them during training [40]. Firstly, given the parameters of the transmitter's NN, the receiver's weights are fine-tuned using supervised learning. Next, given the receiver's weights, the transmitter can explore various symbol mappings and receive the quality of each mapping (the value of the loss function) over a feedback channel. Essentially, the autoencoder has been replaced by a supervised learning method at the receiver and a reinforcement learning method at the transmitter. In this way, a channel model is no longer required at the cost of implementing a feedback link. Practical implementations using software-defined radios have indicated that the training is robust to noisy feedback channels with SNRs higher than 6 dB [41].

Other solutions to overcome the unknown channel impairments involve the use of generative adversarial networks (GANs) [42] and channel gradient estimation using perturbation techniques [43]. Firstly, it is noted that the lack of a channel model does not affect at all the training of the receiver provided that the loss function is differentiable, and that the receiver is aware of the data sent for training. Next, a model of the actual channel can be generated through training using a GAN, or the gradient of the channel can be numerically approximated using stochastic optimization. Finally, given the channel generator or the approximated channel gradients, a backpropagation algorithm can be applied to propagate and calculate gradients from the receiver to the transmitter through the channel, and, thus, allowing us to train the NN at the transmitter. After all, the system designer should evaluate the cost of implementing a feedback channel [40, 41], the required time and cost of training a GAN over the communication channel [42], and the required complexity to estimate the gradients using stochastic optimization [43]. All these techniques achieve similar performance in AWGN and Rayleigh block fading channels with supervised learning assuming perfect channel knowledge. Unfortunately, scalability to long block lengths and time variations of the channel remain open issues in all the above studies.

Even though the training of NNs is mostly executed offline, the required amount of labelled data and the training time should not be overlooked. All sources of randomness need to be represented within the training set, which inevitably increases its size. Also, note that measurement campaigns and data labelling are costly. These, in turn, could seriously impede the deployment of such methods. One way to reduce the training time is to incorporate expert knowledge into ML. The study in [36] is perhaps the first to employ this technique in the PHY layer and suggest splitting the NN at the receiver into two NNs: The first equalizes the channel and the second soft decodes the received symbols. The study in [36] has inspired numerous follow-up studies suggesting the integration of mathematical models into ML for PHY layer processing.

5.2.2 Model-aided data-driven methods for modular transceiver optimization

The main idea behind model-aided ML transceiver design is to keep the modular structure of the transceiver and use ML to optimise only some of the signal processing blocks, especially those involving complicated computations, or for which some simplifications are assumed to make them mathematically tractable. As compared to the traditional model-based framework, there are two noticeable improvements: (i) the computational time could be reduced once the NN is trained; and (ii) the performance could be enhanced if the employed models are just approximations. As compared to end-to-end data-driven techniques, the training time and the need for available labelled datasets decreases in the model-aided approach [44]. Also, according to transfer learning, imperfect or inaccurate models can be used advantageously in the ML process flow to initialise ML weights and reduce further the training time. Then, ML training can fine-tune the weights obtained by the selected models. For an overview of the model-aided ML at the PHY layer, readers can refer to [44].

A detailed per-block review of model-based data-driven techniques for intelligent transceiver design follows in the next sections.

5.3 DEEP LEARNING FOR SYMBOL DETECTION

In this section, the body of literature demonstrates that incorporating simple expert knowledge, e.g., the properties of Orthogonal Frequency Division Multiplexing (OFDM) transmitted waveforms, into the design of autoencoders and NN-based receivers can simplify their operation and enhance the symbol detection performance compared to the baseline model-based schemes.

5.3.1 Incorporating expert knowledge into autoencoders

It is well known that in OFDM with cyclic prefix, frame synchronization is achieved with an autocorrelation-based peak detector given the size of the Fast Fourier Transform (FFT) and the length of the cyclic prefix. Therefore, OFDM communication systems, designed as autoencoders, do not need a separate NN at the receiver to track sampling errors [45]. OFDM can also transform the signal model from wideband to narrowband, simplifying the equalization process. Therefore, at the transmitter's side, it becomes easier to learn a constellation mapping (or precoding) which counteracts the impact of channel effects. For instance, the autoencoder designed in [41] shapes a non-symmetrical and non-centred constellation, which is robust to channel distortions, thereby bypassing the need of inserting pilots in the transmitted signals. As a result, a separate NN at the receiver for single-tap channel equalization is not needed either. Autoencoders can therefore eliminate the need of pilots, thus increasing the useful data rate and reducing the overall implementation complexity for OFDM-based systems. Furthermore, the study in [45] does not apply a separate NN for correcting the carrier frequency offset either with negligible impact on the bit error ratio (BER). On the contrary, in traditional model-based systems, single-tap equalization using dedicated pilots, carrier frequency offset compensation and OFDM symbol detection are separately done.

Unfortunately, the robustness of OFDM to frequency selectivity does not come without cost. The combined effect of the Inverse Fast Fourier Transform (IFFT) block and the non-linearity of the power amplifier may result in detrimental signal distortion. In [46], the encoder learns to map source symbols onto constellation points for each subcarrier so that a loss function, which equals the weighted sum of the BER and the peak-to-average-power-ratio (PAPR), is kept low. The proposed scheme outperforms conventional PAPR reduction schemes and achieves a lower bit error ratio (BER) than the classical OFDM in Rayleigh fading channels with AWGN. However, the study in [46] does not assess the performance with a realistic model for the power amplifier, and therefore one cannot draw solid conclusions about the autoencoder's performance.

Another source of signal distortion (inter-carrier interference) in OFDM is the quantification at the receiver. Quantification prevents end-to-end training of the autoencoder because it essentially inserts a non-differentiable layer before signal detection, as illustrated in Figure 5.2. One way to overcome this limitation is presented in [41, 47], where the encoder and decoder are alternatively trained without knowing the channel at the transmitter. In this architecture, the decoder can be normally trained using supervised learning and some algorithm for backpropagation without explicitly considering the channel. In [41], the

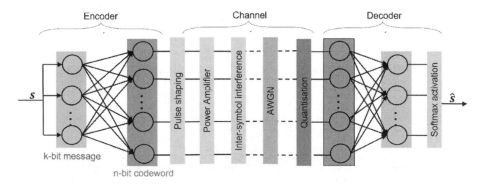

FIGURE 5.2 Block diagram of an auto-encoder with the channel incorporating linear effects (inter-symbol interference, AWGN), non-linear distortions (pulse shaping, power amplifier) and a non-differentiable layer modelling quantification preventing end-to-end training of the encoder.

encoder is trained using reinforcement learning based on rewards calculated at the receiver and fed back to the transmitter. Therefore, unlike the decoder, the training of the encoder is essentially done on-line, which is the penalty paid for an agent (the transmitter) operating in unknown environments.

5.3.2 Implementing NNs at the receiver

An auto-encoder optimises both ends of a communication link, but its training overhead can be significant. When the required resources for training become prohibitively high, an alternative approach suggests implementing symbol detection using a NN only at the receiver. The transmitter generates a standard OFDM waveform, and at the receiver the (offline) learning phase is done over a class of channel models with known statistical properties, which should have a similar distribution to the actual channels (see Figure 5.3). The minimum mean squared error (MMSE) equaliser, see [48], with one pilot every eight subcarriers experiences much higher BER than the deep neural network (DNN)-based receiver designed in [49]. This is because the MMSE-based receiver with this proportion of pilots is not able to estimate the channel perfectly, while the DNN extracts more accurate information about the channel during training. Similarly, the DNN-based receiver outperforms MMSE over non-linear distorted channels due to waveform clipping in [49]. With many pilots, the BER performances of DNN and MMSE are comparable. Nevertheless, the DNN does not need to estimate the channel state information (CSI), and it learns to decode the transmitted symbols only based on the received data, resulting in a much simpler implementation at the cost of offline training.

To accelerate training, the study in [50] cascades two NNs at the receiver, instead of one fully-connected deep neural network (FC-DNN) and incorporates expert knowledge to initialise the NN weights. The first NN has a single layer and performs channel equalization, while the second NN is a bidirectional long short-term memory (LSTM) for symbol detection. To initialise their weights, the NNs use linear-MMSE for channel estimation and zero-forcing for symbol detection. Then, the DNNs are trained to refine the coarse initial inputs. The proposed method achieves the same BER performance, as reported in [49], but is ten times faster with a weights reduction of eight. This example demonstrates that carefully embedding expert knowledge into data-driven techniques, e.g., by transfer learning, could be rewarding.

MIMO detection is another area where incorporating expert knowledge into ML can offer clear benefits using the idea of deep unfolding [51]. In particular, iterative algorithms for MIMO detection, like the

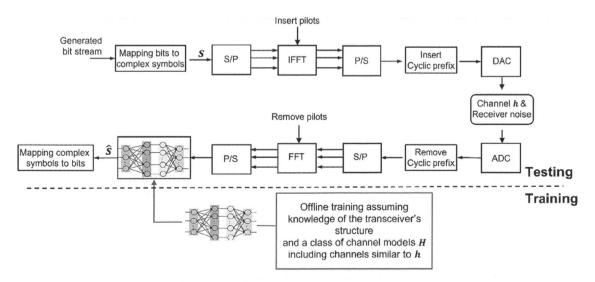

FIGURE 5.3 Block diagram of an OFDM communication system with symbol detection implemented using a FC-DNN which is trained offline using a class of channel models. S/P stands for serial-to-parallel.

projected gradient descent in [52], can be unfolded such that each iteration is associated with a hidden layer. Deep unfolding can simplify the detector's implementation if the iterations involve simple operations. In [52], the NN-based detector achieves competitive performance, in terms of symbol error rate, over independent and identically distributed (iid) Gaussian channels to state-of-art algorithms like approximate message passing (AMP) and semidefinite relaxation, but with 30 times less running time. Despite this promising result, the associated NN involves a few million weights and is not flexible to changes in constellation size, requiring either training anew or will suffer from significant performance degradation with link adaptation. Under highly correlated channels, it also performs clearly worse than semidefinite relaxation. In the same vein, the study in [53] unfolds the AMP algorithm and employs linear MMSE for channel equalization. As a result, it reduces the number of trainable parameters and leads to stronger robustness to modulation order, imperfect CSI, and channel correlation than [52]. However, the authors in [54] claim that the performance of the NN designed in [53] is poor compared to (optimal) maximum likelihood decoding (MLD) when tested with 3GPP spatially correlated channels. To solve this issue, the authors devise an architecture that does not amplify the noise under correlated channels, and report symbol error rates within 1.5 dB from MLD.

All studies [52–54] have adopted the idea of deep unfolding to incorporate expert knowledge into ML. In Section 5.6, we will see that belief propagation decoding of polar and low-density parity check (LDPC) codes is another area where iterative algorithms are unfolded and represented as NNs, simplifying the operation of the decoder.

5.3.3 Sequential detectors using ML

One of the main sources of received signal quality degradation for wideband transmissions is inter-symbol interference (ISI). Naturally, a CNN-based equaliser can capture the effects of ISI on the received signal samples better than a FC-DNN, because each neuron gets input only from a limited set of nearby nodes from the previously hidden layer. In [55], a seven-layer CNN-based equaliser yields smaller BER than a five-layer DNN-based equaliser, especially at high SNRs. Apart from achieving lower BER, the subject CNN, despite having more hidden layers, has in fact fewer weights than the DNN, resulting also in less training time. Therefore, including basic domain features into the selection of the NN's architecture can reduce the complexity of channel equalization.

In wireless channels with ISI, the Viterbi algorithm is a popular technique for sequential symbol detection [56]. It is optimal, in terms of BER, for stationary and causal channels with finite memory and a known statistical relationship between the input and the output of the channel. In practice, this relation distribution might be poorly estimated, especially in time-varying channels or might not be available at all. In this case, the performance of the Viterbi decoding algorithm significantly degrades. To cope with imperfect CSI in multi-tap channels, the authors in [57] have suggested recurrent neural networks (RNNs), where the multiple delayed copies of a symbol are encoded into the states of an RNN. Furthermore, Viterbinet, a FC-NN which learns the log-likelihood ratios (LLRs) of the received signal sample for all possible transmitted sequences of symbols, has been implemented in [58]. The receiver needs to know the channel memory length and the constellation size, which are much easier to obtain or estimate than the CSI. Apart from the ML-based computation of the LLRs, the rest of the detector employs the classical Viterbi algorithm (see Figure 5.4).

In Figure 5.5 it is illustrated that the symbol error performance of Viterbinet in ISI channels with AWGN approaches that of Viterbi decoding when the channels used for training and testing are identical, compare the blue and red curve over there. Moreover, when the Viterbinet is trained over a class of channels, emulating imperfect knowledge of the CSI at the receiver, it clearly outperforms Viterbi decoding operating at the same level of channel uncertainty, compare the green and black curves in Figure 5.5. Moreover, Viterbinet shows good resilience to the SNR used for training as illustrated in Figure 5.6 and 5.7. Nevertheless, Figure 5.6 and 5.7 indicate that the SNR hyperparameter used for training can clearly impact the performance of Viterbinet.

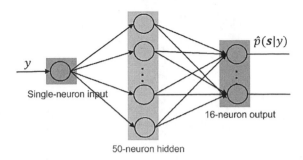

FIGURE 5.4   Viterbinet learns to estimate only the LLR of the received signal sample y for all possible transmitted sequences of symbols s. For channel memory length $l = 4$ and BPSK modulated symbols, we have $s = (s_1\ s_2\ s_3\ s_4)$ with $s_i \in \{-1, 1\}\ \forall\ i$. In our implementation of Viterbinet, we use a NN with just a single hidden layer and we do not estimate the marginal probability of the channel output $\hat{p}(y)$. The 16-neuron output layer applies a softmax activation to estimate the conditional probabilities while other layers apply ReLU. The total number of trainable parameters is less than 1 000.

In block-fading time-varying channels, the performance of Viterbinet can be enhanced by integrating an on-line learning module, which can track the changes in the channel and update the weights accordingly [58]. For this purpose, error detection and forward error correction must be implemented at the receiver to ensure that the received codeword is decoded correctly. In that case, the corrected symbols and the associated decoder input can be used to re-train the NN. This method is known as meta-learning and reduces the BER by successfully correcting discrepancies between the actual fading channel and the fading model used for training [58].

5.4 CHANNEL ESTIMATION USING ML

While in the previous section we discussed NN architectures that jointly perform channel equalization and symbol detection, in this section, we review ML techniques tailored to channel estimation. The authors in [59] investigate channel estimation in a challenging environment combining time- and frequency-selective fading. They initialise the DNN using (truncated) normally distributed random weights and a model-based method, e.g., pilot transmission along with traditional least-squares (LS) estimation at the receiver. Then, they iteratively fine-tune the weights with supervised learning (see Figure 5.8). This method tracks the amplitude and phase of channels unseen during training better than linear MMSE yielding lower BERs. One reason for the improved performance is that the DNN can learn the time correlations in the channel from the previously estimated CSIs.

The study in [60] treats the time-frequency response of a fast-fading channel as a 2d image. The unknown pixels are estimated from the constellation of pilots in the image, which are assumed to be perfectly known at the receiver. The CNN-based algorithm achieves a lower mean squared error (MSE) than MMSE, if the latter estimates the channel correlation matrix from the received signal samples. For a detailed review of channel equalization methods using DNNs and CNNs, see the review papers [22, 61] and the references therein. Recurrent neural networks (RNNs), that can sequentially process the received signal samples, have also been proposed for adaptive channel equalization since the early 1990s [62]. RNN-based equalisers perform well under both linear and nonlinear channels and outperform traditional linear equalisers provided that the channel has deep spectral nulls or suffers from nonlinear distortions [63].

The study in [64] utilises meta-learning that can rapidly adapt to channels which were not experienced in the training phase. Different categories of channels constitute different classes, where a class can be,

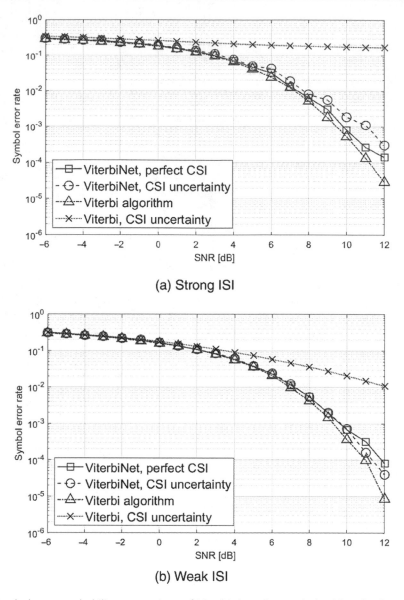

(a) Strong ISI

(b) Weak ISI

FIGURE 5.5   Symbol error probability comparison of Viterbi decoding and Viterbinet in channels with strong and weak ISI at various SNRs. The power delay profile is $\sum_{\tau=1}^{l} e^{-\gamma(\tau-1)}$ with $\gamma = 0.1$ modelling strong ISI (a), and $\gamma = 1$ modelling weak ISI (b). To simulate Viterbi decoding with CSI uncertainty, we corrupt the power delay profile with additive white Gaussian noise that has variance equal to 0.2. Training Viterbinet with CSI uncertainty is carried out over 100 realizations of corrupted power delay profiles with a block of 50 generated symbols in each realization. For testing Viterbinet, 50 000 transmitted symbols are simulated in a single simulation run using the power delay profile. We have used cross-entropy loss provided by the Adam optimiser. The learning rate is 0.01, the number of epochs is 100 and the mini batch size is 27. See also the caption of Figure 5.4 for the structure of the NN and more details on parameter settings.[1]

for example, the Rayleigh fading channel trained at few Doppler frequencies. The main idea is that the meta-learner can identify, from only a few pilots, the class that resembles the most to the actual channel and construct a good enough initialization vector for training. It is shown in [64] that the meta-learner can outperform in terms of BER the DNN-based equaliser in [49], when the two schemes are compared in

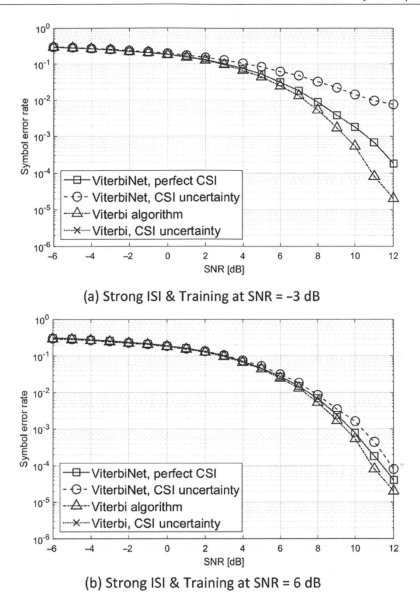

(a) Strong ISI & Training at SNR = −3 dB

(b) Strong ISI & Training at SNR = 6 dB

FIGURE 5.6 Finding a good value for the SNR hyperparameter to train Viterbinet. A single SNR is used for training under strong ISI $\gamma = 1$. The SNR used for training is −3 dB (a), and 6 dB (b). See the caption of Figure 5.5 for the rest of parameter settings. The blue curve is included for comparison purposes as it represents a bound on the performance.

unseen nonlinear channels, e.g., slow fading Rayleigh, where traditional approaches like the least-squares and MMSE do not perform well either. Meta-learning is also used in [65], but in a different context. This study considers sporadic transmissions of IoT, where, due to the limited number of pilots per device, the base station cannot reliably estimate the E2E channel, including the effects of fading and power amplifier, for each device. Therefore, it uses previously received pilots from other devices as meta-data, for fast training of the new device.

Linear MMSE is typically used for downlink channel estimation in MIMO systems, but its performance degrades when the pilot length becomes smaller than the number of transmit antennas [66], or the number of RF chains at the receiver is limited [67]. Another issue in Frequency Division Duplex (FDD)

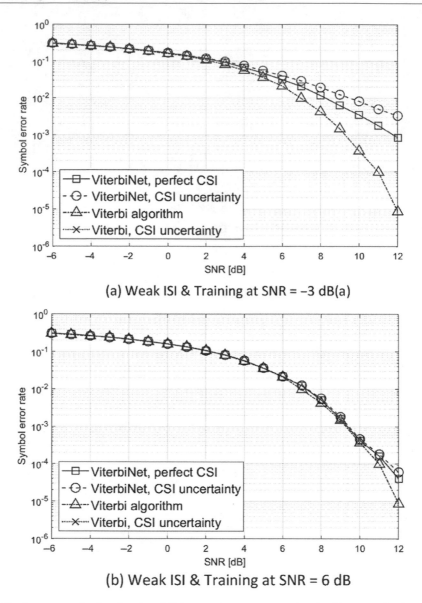

(a) Weak ISI & Training at SNR = –3 dB(a)

(b) Weak ISI & Training at SNR = 6 dB

FIGURE 5.7   Finding a good value for the SNR hyperparameter to train Viterbinet. A single SNR is used for training under weak ISI $\gamma = 0.1$. The SNR used for training is −3 dB (a), and 6 dB (b). See the caption of Figure 5.5 for the rest of parameter settings.

MIMO is the feedback of estimated CSIs to the base station, which can create an excessive signalling overhead when the number of transmit antennas gets large. The 5G NR Rel-15 supports two codebook-based CSI feedback schemes, which essentially quantify the acquired CSIs, striking a balance between the accuracy of received CSIs at the base station and the signalling overhead. For massive MIMO systems, type-II CSI feedback including both the amplitude of CSI and the beam direction may still incur a high overhead [68].

A typical model-based method to deal with excessive CSI feedback assumes channel sparsity in the feedback link and uses a compressive sensing algorithm; however, in practice, the propagation channels are often not sparse. The authors of [69] propose CsiNet, which reduces the CSI overhead using an

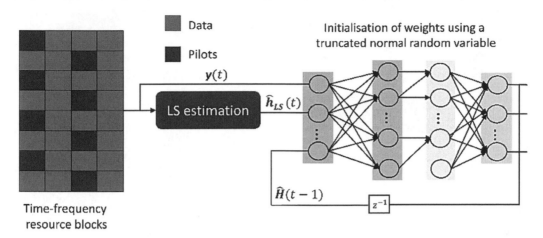

FIGURE 5.8 A block diagram for the training process for DNN-based channel estimation used in [59]. At time *t*, the inputs to the NN are the vector of the received symbols y(*t*), the least-square channel estimate $\hat{h}_{LS}(t)$ based on the transmitted pilot sequence, and the output of the NN in the previous timestep $\hat{H}(t-1)$. The latter allows to track the channel variations. For illustration simplicity, the vector inputs to the NN are shown as inputs to a single neuron. The *z*-transform z^{-1} is used to indicate delay by one time step.

autoencoder in the feedback link for CSI compression at the encoder (the receiver) and reconstruction at the decoder (the transmitter). Their idea mimics the operation of compressive sensing but achieves lower MSE between the original and the recovered channels than state-of-art compressive sensing methods. For a detailed review of deep learning (DL)-based methods for CSI feedback compression, see [23].

5.5 CHANNEL PREDICTION IN FREQUENCY- AND TIME-DOMAIN USING ML

ML-aided channel prediction has been listed as an important use case for emerging wireless networks by ITU FG-ML5G.[2] In this direction, the studies in [70, 71] design DNNs, which learn to predict the downlink CSI from the uplink CSI, eliminating the need for receiver feedback, essentially imitating a TDD system by learning some sort of weaker channel reciprocity between the frequency bands used for uplink and downlink communication. The intuition is that in (massive) MIMO systems the uplink and downlink channels experience nearly the same scatterers and physical propagation paths and, thus, there must exist a high correlation in the amplitude of their CSIs. On the other hand, the phases of the CSIs between uplink and downlink are uncorrelated [72]. In [71], ray-tracing simulations are executed for the uplink and downlink of a MISO system with 128 antennas and 200 paths. It is illustrated that the DNN-based prediction of downlink CSIs performs well, especially when the propagation paths have small angular spreads.

Another issue in adaptive communication schemes is that the received CSI might become quickly outdated, resulting in suboptimal link adaptation, erroneous transmit antenna selection, etc. Outdated CSI can become a major problem when the channel has a relatively short coherence time, e.g., in high-speed railway and vehicular communications. The traditional model-based approach to handle this issue is to consider the wireless channel as an autoregressive process and use time-series predictions, e.g., a Kalman filter, to feedback the estimated subsequent, instead of the current, CSI to the transmitter [73]. Unfortunately, autoregressive models suffer from error propagation at long-range predictions. Additionally, they require the precise knowledge of either the autocorrelation function or the Doppler spectrum (the power spectral

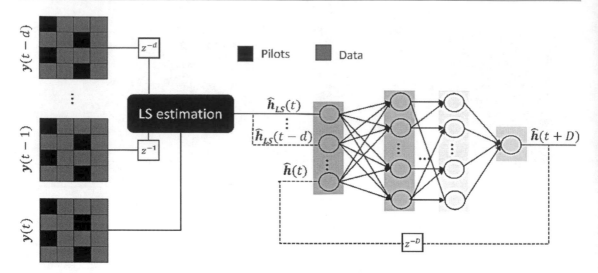

FIGURE 5.9 The trained NN takes as input the least-square channel estimation $\hat{h}_{LS}(t-i)$ based on the received pilot sequence at time $(t - i)$, $i = 0, 1, \ldots d$ and the predicted channel $\hat{h}(t)$ at time t to predict the channel at time $(t + D)$. For illustration simplicity, the vector inputs/outputs to the NN are shown as inputs/ outputs to a single neuron. The z-transform z^{-j} is used to indicate delay by j time steps.

density) of the channel. Finally, they can only exploit temporal correlations and, thus, perform suboptimally in MIMO channels, which can exhibit both spatial and temporal correlations.

The use of ML can help alleviate the problem of outdated CSI at the cost of training. Temporal correlations in the fading channel can be predicted using RNNs which are well-known good predictors for time series. By adapting the number of neurons in the input layer to the number of transmitting, receiving antennas, and the input delay, RNNs can simultaneously learn spatial and temporal correlations [74]. Furthermore, RNNs can predict long-range channel correlations by feeding the predicted channel output after the required time delay as an input to the NN (see Figure 5.9). Finally, in frequency selective channels, RNNs can be combined with the traditional block-type pilot arrangement in OFDM systems that uses interpolation to estimate the CSI for all subcarriers from a known constellation of pilots. In [75], the designed RNN leverages temporal and spatial channel correlations and, thus, consistently outperforms Kalman filters in terms of BER under the 3GPP extended vehicular and typical urban channel models in a 4 x 1 MIMO system.

5.6 CHANNEL CODING USING AI/ML

In future heterogeneous wireless networks, different services will have very diverged latencies, connectivity and throughput requirements. These requirements shall determine the performance constraints the channel codes must meet, in terms of error correction capability, decoding latency, and implementation complexity. Therefore, the selection of coding schemes for 5G and beyond is likely to be application-specific [76]. Note that advances in channel coding can deliver significant cost enhancements for mobile network operators (MNOs).[3]

The block-based structure of LDPC codes allows for a much more efficient parallelization than that for Turbo codes, which opens up communication systems to new applications and services by reducing latency. Therefore, LDPC codes have replaced Turbo coding in the data plane of 5G NR with codeword lengths in the order of 10 000 bits. Polar codes outperform other candidate coding schemes at short packets, 100–1000 bits, and they have been adopted for the control plane of enhanced mobile broadband (eMBB) and the physical broadcast channel, offering negligible BER at low code rates. However, the high complexity of successive cancellation for decoding polar codes at practical block lengths justifies the use of LDPC codes in 5G New-Radio (NR) [77].

Naturally, decoding can be viewed as a classification task, which can be addressed by a neural network (NN). One key strength of NNs vs. many traditional decoding schemes is their linear architecture and avoidance of iterative calculations. Thus, NNs can simplify decoding without sacrificing much on the block error rate (BLER). On the downside, their main bottleneck and limitation are the high training time required once scaled to practical block lengths. This scalability issue partly explains why most attempts to integrate channel coding with DNNs have, so far, used short polar codes.

The study in [78] implements DNN-based decoding of ½ rate polar codes with block length $N = 16$ in AWGN. A three-layer (128, 64, 32) DNN with 2^{18} training epochs attains a BER almost identical to (optimal) map a posteriori (MAP) decoding. To optimise the signal-to-noise ratio (SNR) hyperparameter used for training, the following two points are observed: at high SNRs, the NN does not learn how noise corrupts data, and at low SNRs, noise corrupts data so much that the NN cannot distil the encoding structure. An SNR equal to 1 dB is finally chosen for the training phase, and, during testing, the DNN maintains its performance close to MAP decoding for all considered SNRs. Another promising finding is that the DNN generalises well to unseen codewords during training, i.e., it can learn the encoding rule only from a limited set of codewords, but without approaching the performance of MAP decoder in that case. Unlike polar codes, it has been observed that the generalization property does not hold for unstructured codes, e.g., LDPC and random coding. It is worth mentioning that even for polar codes, the generalization property has only been confirmed for block lengths up to $N = 32$, and thus, might not hold in practice.

To extend the operation of DNN-based decoding to larger blocks, the study in [79] adopts expert knowledge, i.e., the belief propagation (BP) decoding of polar codes and partitions the encoding graph into multiple independent blocks. Each block contains only a part of the codeword and is associated with a single DNN. Similar to [78], each DNN has three hidden layers and individually decodes its part of the codeword nearly at MAP performance. Afterwards, all the decoded bits propagate through the remaining stages of the BP graph to generate the estimated codeword. Different blocks can vary in size, but they should all be small enough to be successfully replaced by NNs. Finally, the DNN with $N = 128$ bits and eight blocks attain similar BER to BP at significantly lower latency, as it completely avoids iterations. The latency–complexity tradeoff can be controlled through the selection of the number and sizes of blocks.

Despite their good error-correction performance, the latency of Turbo codes is prohibitively high for some time-sensitive applications such as those supported by 5G ultra-reliable and low-latency communications (uRLLC). The study in [80] designs the Turbonet, a DL NN integrated into the max-log-MAP turbo decoder leveraging the iterative structure of Turbo codes and replacing each iteration by a DNN decoding unit. The DNN only estimates the extrinsic LLRs through supervised learning, while preserving the rest of the standard Turbo decoder architecture. This idea resembles that of Viterbinet [58], where the NN only replaces the calculation of LLRs for all possible transmitted sequences of symbols using supervised learning too. A Turbonet with three DNNs outperforms the max-log-MAP algorithm that uses three iterations in terms of BER and approaches the performance of the log-MAP decoder while reducing the computation time 10-fold [80]. Finally, the Turbonet generalises well for unseen SNRs and code rates.

The studies discussed so far implement DNNs to optimise the decoding performance. However, RNNs can naturally model sequential codes, e.g., convolutional and Turbo codes. The states of the RNN are essentially the cell states of the (convolutional) decoder determined by the previously seen bits. We have already seen in [57] that RNNs can outperform the Viterbi algorithm for (uncoded) symbol detection over multi-tap channels with imperfect CSI. In [81], a 100-bit and ½ rate recursive systematic convolutional code is trained at 0 dB in the AWGN channel and shows excellent generalization capabilities to other SNRs and block lengths during testing. Finally, some further studies using NNs to construct efficient channel codes are summarised in [22].

5.7 INTELLIGENT LINK ADAPTATION

Link adaptation in Long-Term Evolution (LTE) utilises static look-up tables that map each modulation-and-coding-scheme (MCS) to a channel quality indicator (CQI). The user equipment (UE) estimates the downlink signal-to-interference and noise ratio (SINR) for each subcarrier and selects the MCS that maximises its rate for BLER not exceeding some threshold (10% is used in LTE). To calculate the BLER, the UE consults link-level SNR vs. BER curves, which are pre-calculated assuming a specific channel model. The UE feedbacks the selected MCS, in the form of CQI, to the base station, and the latter adapts the MCS using the look-up table which is also sent back to the UE. The main issue in the above process is that link adaptation does not consider the actual channel where communication takes place, potentially leading to inaccurate MCS selections. In addition, the UE only periodically feedbacks the CQI to the base station to reduce signalling overhead. As a result, in time-varying channels such as those experienced in vehicular communications, the received CQI might be outdated, compromising spectral efficiency [82, 83].

To mitigate the issue of outdated CQI, outer-loop link adaptation (OLLA) is incorporated into 5G NR. According to OLLA, the mapping of SINR to CQI in the look-up table is continuously adapted using offsets that are calculated based on the received hybrid automatic repeat request (HARQ) negative or positive acknowledgements (see Figure 5.10). Besides, ML techniques have been suggested for outdated CQIs mostly utilising reinforcement learning [84], because, otherwise, the required amount of training time and data labelling becomes enormous. Reinforcement learning (RL), and especially Markov decision processes, are excellent decision-making tools in discrete-time stochastic environments complying with the Markovian property, i.e., the next environment state solely depends on the current state-action pair.

The system model in [85] uses OFDM, and the environmental state is described by the (discretised) average SNR across all subcarriers. The action is the selected MCS, and the reward is the throughput that the agent will experience. Under coloured interference, the agent, in the long run, can achieve higher expected spectral efficiency than the standard method based on the look-up tables. Nevertheless, calculating the average SNR as in [85] might not be optimal when the channel coherence bandwidth is larger than the bandwidth occupied by the considered block of subcarriers; Optimising the MCS over a set of correlated subcarriers is considered in [83]. In [86], a cognitive heterogeneous network is considered, where the primary system learns the interference pattern of secondary users with DRL, and, based on the predicted interference, selects the MCS maximising its expected discounted rate. Finally, in [87], a multi-user MIMO mm-wave system with link adaptation using supervised learning is considered. The UE learns to select the modulation order and the spatial multiplexing or diversity order that maximises its throughput based on the estimated SNR. For an overview of supervised learning techniques for adaptive modulation and coding (AMC), including k nearest-neighbours and support vector machines see [55].

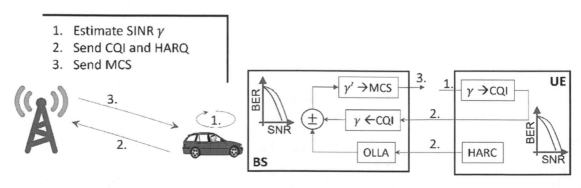

FIGURE 5.10 Schematic diagram for downlink outer-loop link adaptation (OLLA).

To sum up, the B5G/6G networks will need more flexible and agile AMC than the standard look-up tables because of the diversified service requirements and the highly unpredictable channel and interference conditions, which are difficult to model or even simulate. AI/ML, and particularly DRL, is a promising option for better adaptability of the MCS to the actual environment and service type.

5.8 INTELLIGENT RADIOS

Even though emerging wireless networks will operate at mm-wave, visible light, and THz frequencies, where a vast amount of spectrum is still unoccupied, it is necessary to utilise sub-6 GHz frequencies as efficiently as possible, owing to their favourable wireless propagation conditions. A significant volume of research and implementation have been already carried out using software-defined radios that can opportunistically exploit unoccupied spectrum using spectrum sensing and geolocation databases [88, 89]. Soon, AI/ML-empowered radios will apply sophisticated techniques, uncovering hidden spectrum usage patterns and enhancing spectrum utilization efficiency [90]. Furthermore, with the recent invention of reconfigurable metamaterials, not only the transceiver but also the environment can be controlled, programmed, and adapted through AI/ML. Next, we review some of the key AI/ML-based methods for cooperative spectrum sensing, automatic wireless signal classification, and reconfigurable intelligent surfaces (RIS).

5.8.1 Intelligent spectrum sensing

Spectrum sensing aims to identify unoccupied spectrum chunks in space and/or time that can be used opportunistically by unlicensed (or secondary) systems. This mitigates spectrum scarcity under the constraint that the generated disturbances to the licensed (or primary) users can be tolerated. The main hurdle of using spectrum sensing for secondary spectrum access is its reliability under multipath fading and shadowing, yielding the well-known hidden node problem. The secondary user may not detect the primary signals due to a deep fade, and erroneously perceive the spectrum as unoccupied, generating unacceptable interference levels to the licensed users. Cooperative spectrum sensing (CSS) may alleviate the hidden node problem and reduce the spectrum sensing tasks per user [91].

Naturally, the spectrum occupancy statistics vary in both space and time. The topology of the secondary network, e.g., due to mobility, is also subject to change. As a result, the traditional CSS schemes using hand-engineered fixed decision rules become quickly suboptimal. Instead of casting spectrum sensing as an m-ary hypothesis testing problem, it is equivalent to view it as a classification task and apply ML to maintain a good performance in time-varying environments. The study in [92] suggests various unsupervised (k-means, Gaussian mixture models) and supervised learning (K-nearest-neighbours and support vector machines) methods, which improve the detection performance at the cost of training. The training module should be activated only when the environment changes but maintaining an up-to-date dataset by continuously collecting and storing spectrum data measurements is costly. The study in [93] suggests using GANs to generate new labelled data for a given environment and a combination of GANs with autoencoders to generate new datasets when the environment changes.

Secondary users located close to each other naturally experience correlated propagation path loss to the primary users. A CNN can exploit such correlations by learning the appropriate convolutional kernels. If there are multiple spectrum bands available for sensing, the CNN is fed with a two-dimensional matrix, where each row contains the spectrum sensing outcomes for a secondary user across the different frequencies. It is expected that closely located rows of the matrix correspond to closely located users. Then, the CNN can leverage both spatial and spectral correlations. The receiver-operating-characteristic (ROC) curve of the CNN-based CSS scheme upper-bounds that of the traditional K-out-of-N hard decision rule at the cost of training, increased computational time and knowledge of the secondary user locations [94]. Overall, the supervised learning techniques appear to attain the best detection performance at the cost of labelled data.

The distribution of sensing measurements across multiple secondary users and spectrum bands can be used to uncover more secondary spectrum usage opportunities while keeping low the energy cost per user [95]. When a user must sense very wide bandwidths, sampling at the Nyquist rate might not be possible due to hardware limitations. Compressive sensing leverages signal sparsity over the considered frequency range and allows sub-Nyquist sampling rates without losing much signal information [96]. Traditionally, the expected value of occupancy over the entire wideband spectrum is calculated, yielding suboptimal performance when spectrum utilization considerably varies from one spectrum band to the other. To obtain better spectrum occupancy statistics, the study in [97] proposes ML to take advantage of the inherent temporal correlations in spectrum usage that allow the user to make more accurate predictions of spectrum utilization per block. In this way, the required number of collected samples becomes adaptive and reflects the real-time spectrum activity. Finally, the recent advances in spectrum sensing using ML may complement existing methods and standards for secondary spectrum access using geolocation databases [98].

5.8.2 Automatic signal recognition using CNNs

Signal recognition may refer to modulation classification, e.g., analog vs. digital, PSK vs. QAM, or wireless signal classification, e.g., WiFi vs. Zigbee, or Bluetooth waveforms. It is an important enabler for intelligent radio because it allows adapting the transmission parameters to the wireless carriers in the vicinity of the transceiver. For instance, automatic signal recognition can yield more sophisticated interference control, more efficient dynamic spectrum access and improved spectrum monitoring than simplistic signal detection.

Automatic modulation classification has been a well-researched topic over the past three decades, see [99] for an overview, which has been recently flourished by the adoption of ML techniques in wireless communications [55]. The conventional approaches utilise maximum likelihood or feature-based detection for modulation discrimination. The maximum likelihood detection computes the conditional PDF of the received data for each candidate modulation scheme and results in optimal classification provided that the channel impairments are perfectly known. In practice, expectation-maximization algorithms are adopted to estimate the latent variables, e.g., the CSI [61]. The (sub-optimal) feature-based classifications rely on the higher-order cumulants of modulation schemes, and they are much simpler to implement [100].

CNNs are expected to be more effective than other ML techniques for modulation classification because they can successfully extract features from multi-dimensional and highly unstructured data. The study in [101] has produced a large dataset of radio signals using software-defined radios and applied CNNs to discriminate among 24 modulation schemes in various SNRs and channel conditions, including carrier frequency offsets, various symbol rates, AWGN, and multipath fading channels. It has shown that CNNs outperform complicated probabilistic and feature-based classifiers. Naturally, CNNs can implement image-based modulation identification on constellation diagrams, signal distributions and spectrograms [102]. These techniques can further enhance the classification accuracy even at low SNRs, but they require extra resources for data transformation and visualization.

5.8.3 Intelligent radio environment

Intelligent radios can help deal with the problem of spectrum scarcity; however, the forthcoming services in 5G/6G wireless networks create spectrum demands which are unlikely to be satisfied in sub-6 GHz frequency bands. The mm-wave and THz frequency spectrum are largely unoccupied and conducive to high data rate applications but unfortunately subject to high attenuation. At the same time, deploying relays to enhance the signal quality at the receiver is costly because it requires extra RF chains and signal-processing, analog-to-digital (ADC) and digital-to-analog (DAC) converters, and power amplifiers. Also, it is well-known that relays suffer from high self-interference in full-duplex mode and halving the achievable data rates in half-duplex operation. On the contrary, reflectors made of a massive number of inexpensive antennas or nearly passive meta-materials do not have these limitations [103].

Metamaterial-based reflecting surfaces, hereafter referred to as reflecting intelligent surfaces (RIS), are man-made electromagnetic structures that are very thin, large in transverse size, and exhibit properties not found in nature. They consist of sub-wavelength artificial scattering particles (meta-atoms arranged in a grid-like structure with sub-wavelength grid distance), which can be fabricated to alter the electro-magnetic waves impinged upon them in a desirable way, e.g., reflecting the incoming waves toward the intended direction without necessarily complying with Snell's law, see [104] for a detailed overview. Once configured, they do not require any power supply to operate, justifying their naming after nearly passive reflectors. The breakthrough of using RIS in wireless networks came when it became possible to control and customise the RIS operation through software. For instance, the RIS can be programmed to apply time-varying transformations to the incident waves (absorption, refraction, beamforming) depending on the CSIs. In principle, the use of RIS extends the concepts of software-defined networking and radio to include a programmable environment too. Note that controlling the environment might be particularly useful when there are limited options for transceiver optimization, e.g., in single antenna low-power IoT.

Due to their conformal geometry, the RIS can coat sizeable parts of ceilings, furniture, windows, and buildings. The study in [105] suggests a planar meta-material, the HyperSurface tile, which also carries a lightweight IoT device capable of receiving commands from a central gateway to control its electro-magnetics response, e.g., the phase shifts applied to the incoming wave so that, for instance, all multipath components add coherently at the receiver. Due to the combined effect of the large surface aperture with reflecting beamforming, the received power approximately scales proportionally to N^2 where N is the number of the tiles [106]; Recall that in massive MIMO the received power scales only linearly with the number of transmit antennas. It has been shown that the RIS can create local hotspots, help cancel inter-ference, improve spectrum sharing and enhance physical layer security [103, 107, 108] (see Figure 5.11). For instance, a RIS can turn a low-rank into a full-rank channel by introducing rich-scattering propagation towards the receiver [103].

Even though the analytical models for RIS have just started to gain maturity [109], and the experi-mental setups are so far limited [110], researchers have been already investigating the application of AI/ML in RIS-empowered wireless networks [104]. They envision that both the transceiver and the radio environment would be controlled and optimised through AI/ML in future communication networks [35].

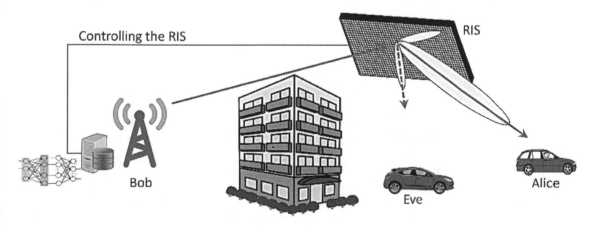

FIGURE 5.11 Illustration of the smart radio environment. A RIS is used to enhance non-line-of-sight com-munication in urban vehicular networks with physical layer security. The main beam is directed to Alice and artificial noise is transmitted towards Eve. The RIS is controlled from the base station which employs a DNN that learns to design the phase shifts.

The study in [111] estimates the direct and the cascade channels for each user with supervised learning; however, the phase shifts between each reflecting element and the user are assumed to be perfectly known. In practice, the major problem in RIS-assisted communication is the design of phase shifts. For instance, using the configuration described in [111], a RIS equipped with low-cost devices capable of sensing and reporting back to a gateway enables a centralised controller to learn the CSIs of both channels, i.e., base station to RIS and RIS to mobile users. After sufficient training, a DNN can optimally control the reflecting phases in real-time, which reduces the controller's complexity [112]. Nevertheless, due to the large number of reflecting elements, the challenge lies in the huge training overhead. To tackle this problem, a combination of compressive sensing and DL is suggested in [113].

5.9 ML FOR SYSTEM-LEVEL PERFORMANCE EVALUATION OF WIRELESS NETWORKS

The traditional approach for assessing the system-level performance of wireless networks have been simulations and simplified models for the deployment and interference, e.g., the hexagonal grid for the locations of base stations and the Wyner model for modelling inter-cell interference [114]. With the advent of heterogeneous networks due to hot spots and nonuniform population densities, the traditional models become less accurate as they do not capture the irregular network structure. In this direction, during the past two decades, tools from stochastic geometry have been employed to obtain tractable solutions for random networks at low computational complexity [115]. Recent advances have also paved the way towards analytical methods that describe the statistical distribution of the network-wide performance, provided that the underlying point processes are ergodic [116–118].

While the analysis using stochastic geometry accounts for various sources of randomness, including the locations and activities of transmitters and the wireless fading channel, simplified assumptions are often adopted for the sake of tractability, leading to erroneous results, as they cannot capture the entire complexity of the wireless system. For example, the coverage probability in interference-limited Poisson networks with nearest base station association, single-antenna network entities, and Rayleigh fading is found to be independent of the transmit power level and the density of base stations. Furthermore, due to this independence, the ergodic area spectral efficiency (ASE) with link adaptation is found to increase linearly with the density of base stations, and thus, it diverges in the ultra-dense limit [115]. Both results do not reflect the reality of typical network deployments. The study in [119] argues that the divergence of ASE is due to the misuse of the power-law propagation pathloss model, which is inaccurate for small to medium distances. Using a fitted stretched-exponential pathloss function instead, the authors find that the ASE is a non-decreasing function of the base station density and reaches a plateau in the ultra-dense regime. While the adopted model results in tractable expressions for the ASE, this might not always be the case for other performance metrics. Therefore, the integration of stochastic geometry with data-driven approaches can be promising [120, 121]. Nevertheless, engaging ML tools into the system-level performance evaluation of wireless networks is still in its infancy.

The authors in [122] observe that the coverage probability of a randomly selected user in Poisson cellular networks is well-approximated by the sigmoid function. Then, they train a NN to fit the sigmoid to the input parameters which are the base station density, operation threshold, pathloss exponent, and the standard deviation and correlation distance of shadowing. The suggested method lacks scalability as it is a pure data-driven technique, but it incorporates details, e.g., the shadowing correlation distance, that are not taken care of by existing models. The study in [123] first derives a mathematical expression for the subject question, i.e., the secrecy outage probability of the ground-to-air communication link in the presence of aerial colluding eavesdroppers. Then, it generates labelled datasets using this expression and trains a NN to predict the performance given the input parameters. It turns out that the NN can compute the performance metric 1000 times faster than the mathematical expression at the cost of reduced explainability.

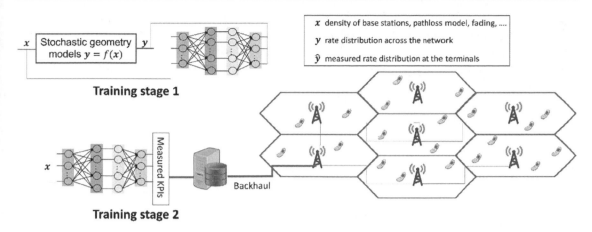

FIGURE 5.12   Transfer learning combining mathematical models based on stochastic geometry and rate measurements at the user terminals for training a DNN that estimates the distribution of user rates across the network. The trained NN at stage 1 is used to initialise the training at stage 2.

Deep transfer learning is perhaps the most promising way to integrate ML into stochastic geometry to improve the accuracy and complexity of the system-level performance evaluation of future wireless networks. In [124], a NN is trained to optimise the transmit power level of base stations given their density. The weights are initialised using the closed-form expression derived in [125] to accelerate training. Then, the weights are fine-tuned using limited measurement data to correct model imperfections. In this study, model imperfections may stem from an inaccurate power consumption model during training or an imprecise deployment model for the base stations, which is likely closer to a repulsive than a Poisson point process [126]. The need for measurement data is significantly reduced with deep transfer learning because the largest portion of the training dataset is generated using a mathematical expression. It is expected to witness more examples of deep transfer learning in this area sooner than later, e.g., refining the distribution of per-link reliability across the network, also known as the meta-distribution of the rate or SINR, with limited rate measurements at mobile terminals (see Figure 5.12).

5.10 CONCLUSIONS

It is undeniable that, at multiple times, ML/AI have demonstrated excellent performance levels for channel estimation, channel prediction, channel coding, etc. These novel techniques can prove essential in the design of RAN intelligent control loops at short timescales for future networks. The role of ML/AI at the PHY layer was also part of an ITU-T initiative devised to trigger the exploration of ML techniques for future networks with the aim to indisputably set the stage of future research activities within public institutions, universities, and the private sector. In this book chapter, we have explored key discoveries and headways that will forge the future of a symbiotic relationship between AI and communication systems whilst focusing on critical and pivotal applications, e.g., channel estimation, channel prediction, and channel coding. Of particular interest is the control of reflecting intelligent surfaces using ML and how it can help in mm-wave vehicular communication in urban areas with strong attenuation. Nevertheless, ML/AI, and more particularly deep learning methods, often lack the crucial characteristic of explicability to shed vital light on their intrinsic mechanisms. This weakness is not only suffered by purely data-driven methods but also by NNs serving at the heart of model-aided modular transceivers. This lack of visibility of the internal mechanisms limits fundamental advances in the design of NNs to improve performances or extend their scope of applications [127]. Techniques based on transfer learning are executed in an ad-hoc fashion and still lack explicability. It was also noted that optimal NN parameters and architecture seem partially disconnected from the parameters of each use case. This seemingly disparage observation calls for innovative solutions to not only tackle the explainability but also more generally the trustworthiness of NNs to increase their adoption and acceptance by mobile network operators, and other stakeholders.

NOTES

1   Our simulation results for Viterbinet are generated by modifying the code based on Yoav Cohen's work shared on GitHub https://github.com/yoavchoen/ViterbiNet-in-Python
2   https://www.itu.int/en/ITU-T/focusgroups/ml5g/Pages/default.aspx
3   https://www.accelercomm.com/news/193m-savings-with-improvements-in-5g-radio-signal-processing

REFERENCES

[1] Li, R., et al., Intelligent 5G: When cellular networks meet artificial intelligence. *IEEE Wireless Communications*, 2017. **24**(5): pp. 175–183.
[2] Letaief, K.B., et al., The roadmap to 6G: AI empowered wireless networks. *IEEE Communications Magazine*, 2019. **57**(8): pp. 84–90.
[3] You, X., et al., Towards 6G wireless communication networks: Vision, enabling technologies, and new paradigm shifts. *Science China Information Sciences*, 2021. **64**(1): pp. 1–74.
[4] Zhao, Y., et al., A comprehensive survey of 6g wireless communications. arXiv preprint arXiv:2101.03889, 2020.
[5] Shahraki, A., et al., A comprehensive survey on 6G networks: Applications, core services, enabling technologies, and future challenges. arXiv preprint arXiv:2101.12475, 2021.
[6] Bhat, J.R. and S.A. Alqahtani, 6G Ecosystem: Current status and future perspective. *IEEE Access*, 2021. **9**: pp. 43134–43167.
[7] Kekki, Sami, et al., *ETSI, 5G; 5G System; Network Data Analytics Services; Stage 3, in 3GPP TS 29.520 version 15.3.0*. 2019, ETSI. p. 11.
[8] Frost, Lindsay, et al., *ETSI, ENI System Architecture*. 2019, ETSI.
[9] ZSM, *ETSI Zero-touch Network and Service Management (ZSM) Introductory white paper* 2017.
[10] Alliance, O., *O-RAN Use Cases and Deployment Scenarios*. White Paper, 2020.
[11] FG-ML5G, I.-T., *Use cases for machine learning in future networks including IMT-2020, Supplement 55 (Technical report)*. 10/2019.
[12] SAP, Compagna, Luca, and Pasic, Aljosa, Deliverable 6.3 Identification of Future Emerging Issues/Topics (Final Version). 2015.
[13] Raghavan, V. and J. Li, Evolution of physical-layer communications research in the post-5G era. *IEEE Access*, 2019. **7**: pp. 10392–10401.
[14] Dean, T.R., et al., Rethinking modulation and detection for high Doppler channels. *IEEE Transactions on Wireless Communications*, 2020. **19**(6): pp. 3629–3642.
[15] Hossain, M.A., et al., Comprehensive survey of machine learning approaches in cognitive radio-based vehicular ad hoc networks. *IEEE Access*, 2020. **8**: pp. 78054–78108.
[16] Kumar, D.P., T. Amgoth, and C.S.R. Annavarapu, Machine learning algorithms for wireless sensor networks: A survey. *Information Fusion*, 2019. **49**: pp. 1–25.
[17] Mahdavinejad, M.S., et al., Machine learning for internet of things data analysis: A survey. *Digital Communications and Networks*, 2018. **4**(3): pp. 161–175.

[18] Khalil, R.A., et al., Deep learning in the industrial internet of things: Potentials, challenges, and emerging applications. *IEEE Internet of Things Journal*, 2021. **8**: pp. 11016–11040.

[19] Wang, X., X. Li, and V.C. Leung, Artificial intelligence-based techniques for emerging heterogeneous network: State of the arts, opportunities, and challenges. *IEEE Access*, 2015. **3**: pp. 1379–1391.

[20] Klaine, P.V., et al., A survey of machine learning techniques applied to self-organizing cellular networks. *IEEE Communications Surveys & Tutorials*, 2017. **19**(4): pp. 2392–2431.

[21] Chen, M., et al., Artificial neural networks-based machine learning for wireless networks: A tutorial. *IEEE Communications Surveys & Tutorials*, 2019. **21**(4): pp. 3039–3071.

[22] Zhang, C., et al., Artificial intelligence for 5G and beyond 5G: Implementations, algorithms, and optimizations. *IEEE Journal on Emerging and Selected Topics in Circuits and Systems*, 2020. **10**(2): pp. 149–163.

[23] Gündüz, D., et al., Machine learning in the air. *IEEE Journal on Selected Areas in Communications*, 2019. **37**(10): pp. 2184–2199.

[24] Zhang, C., P. Patras, and H. Haddadi, Deep learning in mobile and wireless networking: A survey. *IEEE Communications Surveys & Tutorials*, 2019. **21**(3): pp. 2224–2287.

[25] Shafin, R., et al., Artificial intelligence-enabled cellular networks: A critical path to beyond-5G and 6G. *IEEE Wireless Communications*, 2020. **27**(2): pp. 212–217.

[26] Mao, Q., F. Hu, and Q. Hao, Deep learning for intelligent wireless networks: A comprehensive survey. *IEEE Communications Surveys & Tutorials*, 2018. **20**(4): pp. 2595–2621.

[27] Ali, S., et al., *6G White Paper on Machine Learning in Wireless Communication Networks*. arXiv preprint arXiv:2004.13875, 2020.

[28] Wang, J., et al., Thirty years of machine learning: The road to Pareto-optimal wireless networks. *IEEE Communications Surveys & Tutorials*, 2020. **22**(3): pp. 1472–1514.

[29] Luong, N.C., et al., Applications of deep reinforcement learning in communications and networking: A survey. *IEEE Communications Surveys & Tutorials*, 2019. **21**(4): pp. 3133–3174.

[30] You, X., et al., AI for 5G: research directions and paradigms. *Science China Information Sciences*, 2019. **62**(2): pp. 1–13.

[31] Sun, Y., et al., Application of machine learning in wireless networks: Key techniques and open issues. *IEEE Communications Surveys & Tutorials*, 2019. **21**(4): pp. 3072–3108.

[32] Boutaba, R., et al., A comprehensive survey on machine learning for networking: Evolution, applications and research opportunities. *Journal of Internet Services and Applications*, 2018. **9**(1): pp. 1–99.

[33] Ghosh, A., et al., 5G evolution: A view on 5G cellular technology beyond 3GPP release 15. *IEEE access*, 2019. **7**: pp. 127639–127651.

[34] Koufos, K., et al., Trends in intelligent communication systems: Review of standards, major research projects, and identification of research gaps. *Journal of Sensor and Actuator Networks*, 2021 **10**: p. *60*.

[35] Zappone, A., et al., Model-aided wireless artificial intelligence: Embedding expert knowledge in deep neural networks for wireless system optimization. *IEEE Vehicular Technology Magazine*, 2019. **14**(3): pp. 60–69.

[36] O'Shea, T. and J. Hoydis, An introduction to deep learning for the physical layer. *IEEE Transactions on Cognitive Communications and Networking*, 2017. **3**(4): pp. 563–575.

[37] O'Shea, T.J., K. Karra, and T.C. Clancy. Learning to communicate: Channel auto-encoders, domain specific regularizers, and attention. in *2016 IEEE International Symposium on Signal Processing and Information Technology (ISSPIT)*. 2016. IEEE.

[38] Dörner, S., et al., Deep learning based communication over the air. *IEEE Journal of Selected Topics in Signal Processing*, 2017. **12**(1): pp. 132–143.

[39] Goodfellow, I., Y. Bengio, and A. Courville, *Deep Learning* 2016: MIT Press. https://www.deeplearningbook.org/

[40] Aoudia, F.A. and J. Hoydis. End-to-end learning of communications systems without a channel model. in *2018 52nd Asilomar Conference on Signals, Systems, and Computers*. 2018. IEEE.

[41] Aoudia, F.A. and J. Hoydis, Model-free training of end-to-end communication systems. *IEEE Journal on Selected Areas in Communications*, 2019. **37**(11): pp. 2503–2516.

[42] Ye, H., et al. Channel agnostic end-to-end learning based communication systems with conditional GAN. in *2018 IEEE Globecom Workshops (GC Wkshps)*. 2018. IEEE.

[43] Raj, V. and S. Kalyani, Backpropagating through the air: Deep learning at physical layer without channel models. *IEEE Communications Letters*, 2018. **22**(11): pp. 2278–2281.

[44] He, H., et al., Model-driven deep learning for physical layer communications. *IEEE Wireless Communications*, 2019. **26**(5): pp. 77–83.

[45] Felix, A., et al. OFDM-autoencoder for end-to-end learning of communications systems. in *2018 IEEE 19th International Workshop on Signal Processing Advances in Wireless Communications (SPAWC)*. 2018. IEEE.

[46] Kim, M., W. Lee, and D.-H. Cho, A novel PAPR reduction scheme for OFDM system based on deep learning. *IEEE Communications Letters*, 2017. **22**(3): pp. 510–513.

[47] Balevi, E. and J.G. Andrews, One-bit OFDM receivers via deep learning. *IEEE Transactions on Communications*, 2019. **67**(6): pp. 4326–4336.

[48] Van De Beek, J.-J., et al. On channel estimation in OFDM systems. in *1995 IEEE 45th Vehicular Technology Conference. Countdown to the Wireless Twenty-First Century*. 1995. IEEE.

[49] Ye, H., G.Y. Li, and B.-H. Juang, Power of deep learning for channel estimation and signal detection in OFDM systems. *IEEE Wireless Communications Letters*, 2017. **7**(1): pp. 114–117.

[50] Gao, X., et al., ComNet: Combination of deep learning and expert knowledge in OFDM receivers. *IEEE Communications Letters*, 2018. **22**(12): pp. 2627–2630.

[51] Hershey, J.R., J.L. Roux, and F. Weninger, Deep unfolding: Model-based inspiration of novel deep architectures. arXiv preprint arXiv:1409.2574, 2014.

[52] Samuel, N., T. Diskin, and A. Wiesel, Learning to detect. *IEEE Transactions on Signal Processing*, 2019. **67**(10): pp. 2554–2564.

[53] He, H.T., et al., Model-Driven Deep Learning for MIMO Detection. *IEEE Transactions on Signal Processing*, 2020. **68**: pp. 1702–1715.

[54] Khani, M., et al., Adaptive neural signal detection for massive MIMO. *IEEE Transactions on Wireless Communications*, 2020. **19**(8): pp. 5635–5648.

[55] Luo, F.-L., *Machine Learning for Future Wireless Communications*. 2020: John Wiley & Sons Ltd. https://www.wiley.com/en-pk/Machine+Learning+for+Future+Wireless+Communications-p-9781119562306

[56] Forney, G.D., The viterbi algorithm. *Proceedings of the IEEE*, 1973. **61**(3): pp. 268–278.

[57] Farsad, N. and A. Goldsmith, Neural network detection of data sequences in communication systems. *IEEE Transactions on Signal Processing*, 2018. **66**(21): pp. 5663–5678.

[58] Shlezinger, N., et al., ViterbiNet: A deep learning based Viterbi algorithm for symbol detection. *IEEE Transactions on Wireless Communications*, 2020. **19**(5): pp. 3319–3331.

[59] Yang, Y., et al., Deep learning-based channel estimation for doubly selective fading channels. *IEEE Access*, 2019. **7**: pp. 36579–36589.

[60] Soltani, M., et al., Deep learning-based channel estimation. *IEEE Communications Letters*, 2019. **23**(4): pp. 652–655.

[61] Pham, Q.-V., et al., Intelligent radio signal processing: A contemporary survey. arXiv preprint arXiv: 2008.08264, 2020.

[62] Kechriotis, G., E. Zervas, and E.S. Manolakos, Using recurrent neural networks for adaptive communication channel equalization. *IEEE Transactions on Neural Networks*, 1994. **5**(2): pp. 267–278.

[63] Burse, K., R.N. Yadav, and S. Shrivastava, Channel equalization using neural networks: A review. *IEEE transactions on systems, man, and cybernetics, Part C (Applications and Reviews)*, 2010. **40**(3): pp. 352–357.

[64] Mao, H., et al. RoemNet: Robust meta learning based channel estimation in OFDM systems. in *ICC 2019-2019 IEEE International Conference on Communications (ICC)*. 2019. IEEE.

[65] Park, S., et al., Learning to demodulate from few pilots via offline and online meta-learning. *IEEE Transactions on Signal Processing*, 2020. **69**: pp. 226–239.

[66] Kang, J.-M., C.-J. Chun, and I.-M. Kim, Deep learning based channel estimation for MIMO systems with received SNR feedback. *IEEE Access*, 2020. **8**: pp. 121162–121181.

[67] He, H., et al., *Deep learning-based channel estimation for beamspace mmWave massive MIMO systems*. IEEE Wireless Communications Letters, 2018. **7**(5): pp. 852–855.

[68] Onggosanusi, E., et al., Modular and high-resolution channel state information and beam management for 5G new radio. *IEEE Communications Magazine*, 2018. **56**(3): pp. 48–55.

[69] Wen, C.-K., W.-T. Shih, and S. Jin, Deep learning for massive MIMO CSI feedback. *IEEE Wireless Communications Letters*, 2018. **7**(5): pp. 748–751.

[70] Arnold, M., et al. Towards practical FDD massive MIMO: CSI extrapolation driven by deep learning and actual channel measurements. in *2019 53rd Asilomar Conference on Signals, Systems, and Computers*. 2019. IEEE.

[71] Yang, Y., et al., Deep learning-based downlink channel prediction for FDD massive MIMO system. *IEEE Communications Letters*, 2019. **23**(11): pp. 1994–1998.

[72] Liu, Z., L. Zhang, and Z. Ding, Overcoming the channel estimation barrier in massive MIMO communication via deep learning. *IEEE Wireless Communications*, 2020. **27**(5): pp. 104–111.

[73] Baddour, K.E. and N.C. Beaulieu, Autoregressive modeling for fading channel simulation. *IEEE Transactions on Wireless Communications*, 2005. **4**(4): pp. 1650–1662.

[74] Jiang, W. and H.D. Schotten. *Multi-antenna fading channel prediction empowered by artificial intelligence*. in *2018 IEEE 88th Vehicular Technology Conference (VTC-Fall)*. 2018. IEEE.

[75] Jiang, W. and H.D. Schotten, Neural network-based fading channel prediction: A comprehensive overview. *IEEE Access*, 2019. **7**: pp. 118112–118124.

[76] Shao, S., et al., Survey of turbo, LDPC, and polar decoder ASIC implementations. *IEEE Communications Surveys & Tutorials*, 2019. **21**(3): pp. 2309–2333.

[77] Arikan, E., Channel polarization: A method for constructing capacity-achieving codes for symmetric binary-input memoryless channels. *IEEE Transactions on information Theory*, 2009. **55**(7): pp. 3051–3073.

[78] Gruber, T., et al. On deep learning-based channel decoding. in *2017 51st Annual Conference on Information Sciences and Systems (CISS)*. 2017. IEEE.

[79] Cammerer, S., et al. Scaling deep learning-based decoding of polar codes via partitioning. in *GLOBECOM 2017-2017 IEEE Global Communications Conference*. 2017. IEEE.

[80] He, Y., et al., Model-driven DNN decoder for turbo codes: Design, simulation, and experimental results. *IEEE Transactions on Communications*, 2020. **68**(10): pp. 6127–6140.

[81] Kim, H., et al., Communication algorithms via deep learning. arXiv preprint arXiv:1805.09317, 2018.

[82] Bruno, R., A. Masaracchia, and A. Passarella. Robust adaptive modulation and coding (AMC) selection in LTE systems using reinforcement learning. in *2014 IEEE 80th Vehicular Technology Conference (VTC2014-Fall)*. 2014. IEEE.

[83] Blanquez-Casado, F., M.D.C.A. Torres, and G. Gomez, Link adaptation mechanisms based on logistic regression modeling. *IEEE Communications Letters*, 2019. **23**(5): pp. 942–945.

[84] Yun, S. and C. Caramanis. Reinforcement learning for link adaptation in MIMO-OFDM wireless systems. in *2010 IEEE Global Telecommunications Conference GLOBECOM 2010*. 2010. IEEE.

[85] Leite, J.P., P.H.P. de Carvalho, and R.D. Vieira. A flexible framework based on reinforcement learning for adaptive modulation and coding in OFDM wireless systems. in *2012 IEEE Wireless Communications and Networking Conference (WCNC)*. 2012. IEEE.

[86] Zhang, L., et al., Deep reinforcement learning-based modulation and coding scheme selection in cognitive heterogeneous networks. *IEEE Transactions on Wireless Communications*, 2019. **18**(6): pp. 3281–3294.

[87] Satyanarayana, K., et al., Multi-user hybrid beamforming relying on learning-aided link-adaptation for mmWave systems. *IEEE Access*, 2019. **7**: pp. 23197–23209.

[88] Mitola, J. and G.Q. Maguire, Cognitive radio: Making software radios more personal. *IEEE Personal Communications*, 1999. **6**(4): pp. 13–18.

[89] Haykin, S., Cognitive radio: Brain-empowered wireless communications. *IEEE Journal on Selected Areas in Communications*, 2005. **23**(2): pp. 201–220.

[90] Qin, Z. and G.Y. Li, Pathway to intelligent radio. *IEEE Wireless Communications*, 2020. **27**(1): pp. 9–15.

[91] Liang, Y.-C., et al., Sensing-throughput tradeoff for cognitive radio networks. *IEEE Transactions on Wireless Communications*, 2008. **7**(4): pp. 1326–1337.

[92] Thilina, K.M., et al., Machine learning techniques for cooperative spectrum sensing in cognitive radio networks. *IEEE Journal on Selected Areas in Communications*, 2013. **31**(11): pp. 2209–2221.

[93] Davaslioglu, K. and Y.E. Sagduyu. Generative adversarial learning for spectrum sensing. in *2018 IEEE International Conference on Communications (ICC)*. 2018. IEEE.

[94] Lee, W., M. Kim, and D.-H. Cho, Deep sensing: Cooperative spectrum sensing based on convolutional neural networks. arXiv preprint arXiv:1705.08164, 2017.

[95] Koufos, K., K. Ruttik, and R. Jantti, Distributed sensing in multiband cognitive networks. *IEEE Transactions on Wireless Communications*, 2011. **10**(5): pp. 1667–1677.

[96] Candès, E.J. Compressive sampling. in *Proceedings of the international congress of mathematicians*. 2006. Madrid, Spain.

[97] Khalfi, B., A. Zaid, and B. Hamdaoui. When machine learning meets compressive sampling for wideband spectrum sensing. in *2017 13th International Wireless Communications and Mobile Computing Conference (IWCMC)*. 2017. IEEE.

[98] Koufos, K., K. Ruttik, and R. Jäntti. *Controlling the interference from multiple secondary systems at the TV cell border*. in *2011 IEEE 22nd International Symposium on Personal, Indoor and Mobile Radio Communications*. 2011. IEEE.

[99] Dobre, O.A., et al., Survey of automatic modulation classification techniques: Classical approaches and new trends. *IET Communications*, 2007. **1**(2): pp. 137–156.

[100] Zhu, Z. and A.K. Nandi, *Automatic Modulation Classification: Principles, Algorithms and Applications*. 2015: John Wiley & Sons. https://www.wiley.com/en-us/Automatic+Modulation+Classification:+Principles,+Algorithms+and+Applications-p-9781118906491

[101] O'Shea, T.J., T. Roy, and T.C. Clancy, Over-the-air deep learning based radio signal classification. *IEEE Journal of Selected Topics in Signal Processing*, 2018. **12**(1): pp. 168–179.

[102] Wang, Y., et al., Data-driven deep learning for automatic modulation recognition in cognitive radios. *IEEE Transactions on Vehicular Technology*, 2019. **68**(4): pp. 4074–4077.

[103] Basar, E., et al., Wireless communications through reconfigurable intelligent surfaces. *IEEE Access*, 2019. **7**: pp. 116753–116773.

[104] Di Renzo, M., et al., Smart radio environments empowered by reconfigurable AI meta-surfaces: An idea whose time has come. *EURASIP Journal on Wireless Communications and Networking*, 2019. **2019**(1): pp. 1–20.

[105] Liaskos, C., et al., A new wireless communication paradigm through software-controlled metasurfaces. *IEEE Communications Magazine*, 2018. **56**(9): pp. 162–169.

[106] Wu, Q. and R. Zhang, Towards smart and reconfigurable environment: Intelligent reflecting surface aided wireless network. *IEEE Communications Magazine*, 2019. **58**(1): pp. 106–112.

[107] Akyildiz, I.F., A. Kak, and S. Nie, 6G and beyond: The future of wireless communications systems. *IEEE Access*, 2020. **8**: pp. 133995–134030.

[108] Tan, X., et al. Increasing indoor spectrum sharing capacity using smart reflect-array. in *2016 IEEE International Conference on Communications (ICC)*. 2016. IEEE.

[109] Di Renzo, M., et al. Analytical modeling of the path-loss for reconfigurable intelligent surfaces–anomalous mirror or scatterer? in *2020 IEEE 21st International Workshop on Signal Processing Advances in Wireless Communications (SPAWC)*. 2020. IEEE.

[110] Tang, W., et al., Wireless communications with reconfigurable intelligent surface: Path loss modeling and experimental measurement. *IEEE Transactions on Wireless Communications*, 2020. **20**(1): pp. 421–439.

[111] Elbir, A.M., et al., Deep channel learning for large intelligent surfaces aided mm-wave massive MIMO systems. *IEEE Wireless Communications Letters*, 2020. **9**(9): pp. 1447–1451.

[112] Gao, J., et al., Unsupervised learning for passive beamforming. *IEEE Communications Letters*, 2020. **24**(5): pp. 1052–1056.

[113] Taha, A., M. Alrabeiah, and A. Alkhateeb, Enabling Large Intelligent Surfaces With Compressive Sensing and Deep Learning. *IEEE Access*, 2021. **9**: pp. 44304–44321.

[114] Xu, J., J. Zhang, and J.G. Andrews, On the accuracy of the Wyner model in cellular networks. *IEEE Transactions on Wireless Communications*, 2011. **10**(9): pp. 3098–3109.

[115] Andrews, J.G., F. Baccelli, and R.K. Ganti, A tractable approach to coverage and rate in cellular networks. *IEEE Transactions on Communications*, 2011. **59**(11): pp. 3122–3134.

[116] Haenggi, M., The meta distribution of the SIR in Poisson bipolar and cellular networks. *IEEE Transactions on Wireless Communications*, 2015. **15**(4): pp. 2577–2589.

[117] Kalamkar, S.S. and M. Haenggi, The spatial outage capacity of wireless networks. *IEEE Transactions on Wireless Communications*, 2018. **17**(6): pp. 3709–3722.

[118] Koufos, K. and C.P. Dettmann, The meta distribution of the SIR in linear motorway VANETs. *IEEE Transactions on Communications*, 2019. **67**(12): pp. 8696–8706.

[119] Al Ammouri, A., J.G. Andrews, and F. Baccelli, SINR and throughput of dense cellular networks with stretched exponential path loss. *IEEE Transactions on Wireless Communications*, 2017. **17**(2): pp. 1147–1160.

[120] Hmamouche, Y., M. Benjillali, and S. Saoudi. On the role of stochastic geometry in sixth generation wireless networks. in *2020 10th International Symposium on Signal, Image, Video and Communications (ISIVC)*. 2021. IEEE.

[121] Hmamouche, Y., et al., New trends in stochastic geometry for wireless networks: A tutorial and survey. *Proceedings of the IEEE*, 2021. **109**: pp. 1200–1252.

[122] El Hammouti, H., M. Ghogho, and S.A.R. Zaidi. A machine learning approach to predicting coverage in random wireless networks. in *2018 IEEE Globecom Workshops (GC Wkshps)*. 2018. IEEE.

[123] Bao, T., et al., Secrecy outage performance of ground-to-air communications with multiple aerial eavesdroppers and its deep learning evaluation. *IEEE Wireless Communications Letters*, 2020. **9**(9): pp. 1351–1355.

[124] Zappone, A., M. Di Renzo, and M. Debbah, Wireless networks design in the era of deep learning: Model-based, AI-based, or both? *IEEE Transactions on Communications*, 2019. **67**(10): pp. 7331–7376.

[125] Di Renzo, M., et al., System-level modeling and optimization of the energy efficiency in cellular networks—A stochastic geometry framework. *IEEE Transactions on Wireless Communications*, 2018. **17**(4): pp. 2539–2556.

[126] Nakata, I. and N. Miyoshi, Spatial stochastic models for analysis of heterogeneous cellular networks with repulsively deployed base stations. *Performance Evaluation*, 2014. **78**: pp. 7–17.

[127] Lechner, M., et al., Neural circuit policies enabling auditable autonomy. *Nature Machine Intelligence*, 2020. **2**(10): pp. 642–652.

Deep learning-based index modulation systems for vehicle communications

6

Junfeng Wang
Tianjin University of Technology, Tianjin, China

Yue Cui
College of Computer and Information Engineering, Tianjin Normal University, Tianjin, China

Zeyad A. H. Qasem and Haixin Sun
School of Information Science and Engineering, Xiamen University, Xiamen, China

Guangjie Han
College of Internet of Things Engineering, Hohai University, Changzhou, China

Mohsen Guizani
Qatar University, Doha, Qatar

Contents

DOI: 10.1201/9781003190691-8

6.1 INTRODUCTION

The communication systems of the next generation must serve a huge number of human and non-human users, so wireless communications are constantly evolving towards increasingly complex systems due to required increases of throughput, mobility, and ubiquity. Additionally, the Internet of Things (IoT), which is considered to be one of the main promising advantages of the next generation, raises other challenging tasks related to the energy efficiency as the sensors are usually battery-based and the source of power is not always available. To that aim, new advanced techniques will be employed such as cell-free multi-input multi-output (MIMO), index modulation (IM), advanced/distributed beam-forming, new waveforms, etc. However, the explosion in the number of devices and the increasing variety of verticals (application domains) raise significant challenges to the signal processing in terms of performance, optimization and complexity. Specifically, up to 28 billion smart devices are expected to be connected across the world by the year 2021 [1]. The traditional model-based optimizations are less and less applicable as we enter the realm of communication systems whose environments are more and more complicated. Therefore, recent trends show the interest of researchers towards the amalgam of various technologies such as integration of sensors and embedded systems with cyber-physical systems (CPS), vehicle-to-vehicle (V2V) communication systems, vehicle-to-infrastructure (V2I) communication systems, and 5G wireless systems with the IoT as a center [2].

With regard to physical layer, providing a higher data rate practically becomes a challenging task due to the limited available bandwidth compared over the huge number of users. Although extensive studies focus on the enhancement of spectral and energy efficiency, that the majority of those studies consider idealistic conditions at the receiving end which is not always applicable as many other issues are also usually raised, such as significant multipath spread, the limited available bandwidth, poor physical link quality, and time-varied channels caused by Doppler effects. Generally, two main modulation techniques are employed: single-carrier and multi-carrier modulations [3]. One signal frequency is exploited in single-carrier mode to transmit the information bits while multi-carrier modulation divides the total frequency into several subcarriers, and each subcarriers is dedicated to transmit a part of data stream simultaneously.

On one hand, single-carrier modulation is advantageous over multi-carrier modulation in terms of: 1) peak to average power ration (PAPR), which is very low in single-carrier modulation. That advantage is very attractive for using low-cost devices and for the stability of systems; 2) the robustness of single-carrier modulation against frequency shift and phase noise is much more than multi-carrier, which makes the time and frequency synchronizations easier specially in communication systems whose channels are harsh [4], 3) single-carrier modulation has been found effective to cope with the inter-symbol interference (ISI) because of the use of adaptive equalizer, i.e., a decision feedback equalizer with a recursive least squares algorithm [4] and it was demonstrated that the use of correcting coding can provide a communication with better quality [5]. Although those are advantages in a single-carrier system, equalizing and estimating parameters of the channel with higher complicated processing is still required to guarantee the communication reliability. Hence, multicarrier modulation is introduced to solve those issues, it can mitigate the bandwidth limitation and delay spread of wide channel resulted in the ISI in the case of a single-carrier system with less processing required. Multicarrier modulation system can equalize the channel at significantly less complexity but, unfortunately, the significant Doppler effect leads to severe inter-carrier interference (ICI) [6, 7].

The MIMO systems have been provided to cope with the issue of limited data rate of communication systems, including multiuser MIMO [8] and conventional single-user MIMO [9, 10]. Multiuser MIMO systems separate every user's signal transmitted from each antenna spatially, whereas the single-user MIMO was originally conceived to improve the overall data rate in a communication channel. Both the single-user MIMO and the multiuser MIMO are limited by the co-channel interference in the rich multipath environment [11] and the physical size of the device. In order to solve the impact of co-channel interference, a combination of MIMO and code division multiplexing access is investigated. An orthogonal code is assigned to each user leading to overcoming the co-channel interference at the expense of data rate.

Recently, the IM has been presented to deal with the issue of the ICI in multi-carrier systems [12–15], energy efficiency and inter-user interference in direct sequence spread spectrum (DSSS) [16–18], and inter-antennas interference in the MIMO systems [19]. Spatial Modulation (SM) [20] is proposed as an alternative solution for the conventional MIMO technology; it is intended to enhance the utilization of spectral efficiency by transmitting more data bits via the index of the active antennas plus the physical transmitted bits. Unfortunately, the data rate offered by the SM is still limited compared to the alternative MIMO schemes and it cannot currently support the next generation of communication systems. Many other techniques have been proposed to increase the transmitted mapped data of the SM techniques through conveying the same transmitted physical bits either by separating the real and imaginary part independently or by using one or more active antennas [19, 21–23]. Unfortunately, both MIMO and SM techniques are also restricted by the physical size of the device and the available hardware space.

Recently, orthogonal frequency division multiplexing indexed modulation (OFDM-IM) [12–15] is presented to solve the issue of the ICI and the limited spectral efficiency of the scheme of OFDM by dividing the information bits into physical data bits and indexed data bits. The physical data bits are modulated and transmitted via some activated subcarriers out of the available subcarriers, and the indexed data bits are transmitted using the index of those active subcarriers. Therefore, the activation of some subcarriers leads to a reduction of the ICI and an improvement in spectral efficiency in low- to medium-data rate systems [24]. In rapidly time-varying channels, less activated sub-carriers and better bit error rate (BER) performance have been obtained compared to conventional OFDM [14], but this has happened at the expense of the achieved data rate. The OFDM-IM inherits the same issue of a high PAPR problem [24]. Moreover, the random activation of subcarriers following the incoming information bits makes the estimation of the channel infeasible. Channel estimation-based OFDM-IM was proposed in [25] by inserting fixed subcarriers at the end of each sub-group for transmitting the pilots' symbols, but this method will limit the spectral efficiency in the OFDM-IM dramatically in the double selective channel since the subgroups of subcarriers indexing will become very short, leading to limitation in the data bits transmitted by the indices of subcarriers. Additionally, in high modulation order, the OFDM-IM becomes useless since it cannot produce the same data rate of conventional OFDM.

On the other hand, coded index modulation-spread spectrum (CIM-SS) and generalized coded index modulation-spread spectrum (GCIM-SS) [17, 18] have been proposed to improve the spectral efficiency and energy efficiency in the DSSS systems. Similar to the OFDM-IM, the information bits are divided into physical data bits and indexed data bits. The physical data bits are modulated via any digital modulation (e.g., binary phase shift keying (BPSK) modulation) while the indexed information bits are transmitted through the index of spreading code selected to spread the modulated physical information bits. Although this technique provides a data rate that is comparable with the DSSS, unfortunately, the wrong detection of the index of spreading code leads to wrong decisions on whole transmitted bits. That is very probable in communication systems whose channel is harsh as the orthogonality of spreading code will certainly be lost.

Deep learning (DL) has been recently employed for the IM as a low-complex efficient detector at the receiving end and for enhancing the performance and avoiding the deterioration due to the wrong detection of spreading code in the CIM-SS [16, 26–28]. Different DL designs have been presented for the IM having a tradeoff between performance and complexity. Additionally, the low-complexity receiver based on the DL is also researched to enhance the energy efficiency in the V2V commination systems.

In this chapter, we start the study of the V2V and V2I communication systems. Then, the applications of the DL for the IM is introduced, including the multicarrier, the single-carrier and the MIMO modulation systems. The effects of the IM on energy efficiency have also been studied. Finally, the conclusions are presented in the last section.

6.2 V2V AND V2I COMMUNICATIONS

The V2V/V2I communication systems are high-speed wireless networks where each moving device, such as a car, smart traffic signals, or any other nodes, can exchange such information with other nodes located in the same range of communication radio in real time. The information could be related to the location, braking, information about environment, and so on. The V2V/V2I communication systems can be regarded as mesh networks [29, 30], whose applications can be adopted for many applications, including environmental monitoring, media sharing, motorcycle detection, and disaster prevention. Figure 6.1 [31] shows a visual representation of the vehicle communications. Supported connected vehicle technology (CVT) safety applications based on the V2V/V2I communications require rapid acquisition, low latency with high reliability, and the highest security and privacy standards [32]. In order to fulfill that requirement, dedicated short-range communication (DRSC) has been assigned to the V2V/V2I by the Federal Communications Commission. However, the DRSC is still insufficient to support the CVT applications, but other wireless technologies can also be accessible for the CVT applications. The V2I differs from the V2V with respect to the manner in which the data are exchanged between the vehicles and road

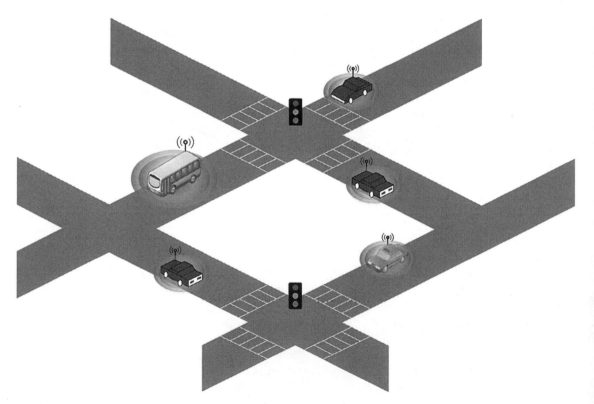

FIGURE 6.1 Scenarios of vehicle communications.

(Adapted from [31].)

infrastructure. Infrastructure components, such as lane markings, road signs, and traffic lights, can wirelessly provide information to the vehicle, and vice versa.

Power consumption in vehicle communications is one of the most critical factors to be considered during the system design since nodes are usually battery-based, and it becomes difficult to recharge them due to the environmental difficulties or the sustainability of the power source [19]. The IM has been presented as an alternative solution, which transmits the majority of information bits with free energy consumption for the V2V/V2I systems [33], but the higher computational complexity at the receiving end leads to increased energy consumption. Therefore, the DL-based IM is one of the candidate solutions to provide communication systems with enhanced power consumption and less computational complexity.

6.3 DEEP LEARNING-BASED INDEX MODULATION SYSTEMS

The DL [34] has been recently applied in wireless communication systems to jointly estimate the channel and detect the received signal [35] and also to reduce the PAPR effect [36]. In the IM communications, the DL was employed to achieve low-complexity detection for the OFDM-IM [27], CIM-SS [16], and SM systems [26, 37].

6.3.1 Multicarrier-based index modulation systems

Recently, different approaches have been introduced to implement IM for multi-carrier modulation [38, 39]. The OFDM-IM is the most common scheme transmitting the information bits physically by any digital modulations and also by the index of active subcarriers used to transmit the physical information bits.

6.3.1.1 Transmitter of system model with OFDM-IM

The general process of the OFDM-IM is shown in Figure 6.2. However, many other extensions have been presented based on that approach, but they are still following the same process with only different methods of mapping the bits, such as performing the IM on real and imaginary parts of modulated data separately. Let B be the stream of information bits to be transmitted within one symbol whose number of subcarriers is N. In order to enable the detection at the receiving end by avoiding the high resulted complexity, B is first divided into G groups, and each group $g \in \{1, \cdots, G\}$ has b bits; $b = B / G$ which is transmitted via a subgroup of subcarriers N_o. The IM is performed within b bits by activating only k out of N_o. The bit splitter divides the information bits in each group g into two sub-groups, $P_1^{(g)}$ and $P_2^{(g)}; b^{(g)} = P_1^{(g)} + P_2^{(g)}.P_1^{(g)}$ represents the indexed information bits transmitted via the index of the activate subcarriers, that can be applied by a look-up table or combinatorial mapping [14]. For example, a look-up table is shown in Table 6.1 for $N_o = 4$ and $k = 2$. While $P_2^{(g)}$ are physically modulated and mapped into a symbol $s^{(g)} \in \chi$, and χ represents any M-ary digital modulations having unit average power, then transmitted via those activated subcarriers. Therefore, $P_2^{(g)} = k \log_2(M)$, where k is the number of active subcarriers in each group g. Additionally, $P_1^{(g)}$ can be expressed as $P_1^{(g)} = \left\lfloor \log_2 \binom{N_o}{k} \right\rfloor$, where $\lfloor . \rfloor$ denotes the floor operator. The resulted vector of mapping the $s^{(g)}$ on k when taking the second and third subcarriers to be active is $x^{(g)} = \left[0, s_1^{(g)}, s_2^{(g)}, 0 \right]$. The $N \times 1$ OFDM-IM data block is generated by obtaining x^g for all g as follows:

$$X = \left[x^{(1)}, x^{(2)}, \ldots \ldots, x^{(G)} \right]. \tag{6.1}$$

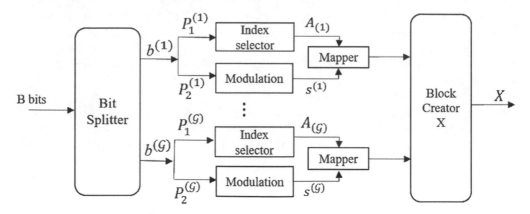

FIGURE 6.2 Transmitter in the OFDM-IM system model.

TABLE 6.1 A look-up table for $N_o = 4$, $k = 2$ and $P_1 = 2$

INDEX BITS	INDICES A_G
[0 0]	{1, 2}
[0 1]	{1, 3}
[1 0]	{1, 4}
[1 1]	{2, 3}

Therefore, the number of bits transmitted via one OFDM-IM symbol in that case can be expressed as:

$$\gamma = \mathcal{G}\left(k \log_2\left(M \right) + \left\lfloor \log_2\binom{N_o}{k} \right\rfloor \right). \tag{6.2}$$

The equivalent number of bits transmitted via the conventional OFDM scheme is $\gamma_{\text{OFDM}} = N\log_2(M)$. However, the less k in (6.2), the better the performance of the OFDM-IM, but that is at the expense of the achieved data rate. Similarly, when increasing k the performance will be deteriorated and the indexed information bits will also be decreased. When increasing M, the OFDM-IM cannot reach the data rate of the conventional OFDM approach. Therefore, the OFDM-IM can achieve comparable performance over conventional OFDM only at the low to medium data rate [40].

6.3.1.2 Traditional detection scheme

The signal X is processed similar to the conventional OFDM. The received signal can be written as:

$$y = h * \underline{X} + v, \tag{6.3}$$

where h, $*$ and $\underline{X}$ denote the channel impulse response, circular convolution, and the time-domain signal equivalent to X after performing the inverse Fourier transform and adding the cyclic prefix as guard interval, respectively. v represents the additive white Gaussian noise (AWGN).

At the receiving end, maximal likelihood (ML) detector is considered to be the optimal detector where the physical and indexed information bits are detected jointly. When considering perfect knowledge of the channel at the receiving end, the frequency-domain received signal obtained by discarding the guard interval and performing Fast Fourier Transform (FFT) can be given by:

$$Y = HX + V,\tag{6.4}$$

where Y and H denote the frequency-domain received signal and the frequency-domain impulse response of the channel, respectively, and V the AWGN in the frequency domain. Therefore, the ML detector can be applied for each group g to estimate the physical and indexed information bits jointly as follows:

$$\left(\hat{X},\hat{i}\right) = \arg\min_{s,i}\left\|Y - H_iX\right\|_2^2,\tag{6.5}$$

where $\hat{X}$ and $\hat{i}$ denote estimates of the transmitted symbol and index of active subcarriers, respectively, and $\|.\|$ is the two norm of a vector operation.

The resulting complexity yielded by the ML detector includes looking for the minimum Euclidean distance among all possible realizations. The resulted computational complexity of ML detector for each group g is cM^k, where $c = 2^{P_1^{(g)}}$.

6.3.1.3 Deep learning-based detector

The DL has been implemented in the OFDM-IM for detecting the indexed and physical information bits jointly with less complexity and with an almost similar performance to that of the ML detector. The DL is only used for detection; the channel effect must first be recovered using any type of equalizer. We have adopted here zero forcing equalizer. Hence, the guard interval is first discarded from the received signal y, and the output of the FFT operation is forwarded into the equalizer to obtain the frequency-domain received signal as follows:

$$\hat{X} = \frac{Y}{H}.\tag{6.6}$$

As explained earlier, the vector X contains G groups and index operations are performed within each group g. Thus, every group g will be fed up into the input layer of the DL model to be processed and get the bits carried by each group in the output of the DL model.

6.3.1.3.1 Deep learning model   The DL detector model is shown in Figure 6.3. The fully-connected (FC) nonlinear layers are only required to detect the modulated and indexed bits of the OFDM-IM, including the first input layer with $3N_o$ nodes, the hidden layer corresponds to Q nodes tuned as a tradeoff between the complexity and performance, and the output layer whose size is set based on the number bits b of each group g. At the hidden layer, the rectifier linear unit (Relu) is utilized as $f_{Relu}(x) = \max(x,0)$, and the sigmoid function (Sig) is utilized in the output layer with $f_{Sig}(x) = \dfrac{1}{1+e^{-x}}$ to estimate the transmitted bits of each group $\hat{b}^{(g)}$. Since the output of the sigmoid function lies between 0 and 1, a threshold set to decide whether the output is 0 or 1. We set 0.5 as a threshold and decided the output is 0 if the output less than 0.5 and 1 otherwise. It's worth mentioning that the deep neural network (DNN) output can be expressed as:

$$\hat{b}^{(g)} = f_{sig}\left(\wp_2\, f_{\tanh}\left(\wp_1\hat{x}^{(g)} + \beta_1\right) + \beta_2\right),\tag{6.7}$$

Where $\wp_1$, β_1, and $\wp_2$, β_2 are the weights and bias of the first and the second hidden layers, respectively. $\hat{b}^{(g)}$ is the output of the DNN corresponding to the data bits carried by each group g, including the physical modulated bits and indexed bits. Therefore, the input data in the input layer is a concatenation of $Re\left(\hat{x}^{(g)}\right)$, $Im\left(\hat{x}^{(g)}\right)$ and $\left|\hat{x}^{(g)}\right|^2$ of each $\hat{x}^{(g)}$ extracted from the equalized data symbols $\hat{X}$, $Re(.)$ and $Im(.)$ are the real part and imaginary part of $(.)$, respectively. The output is the estimated information bits carried physically and via index of subcarriers; it means that digital demodulation is no longer required.

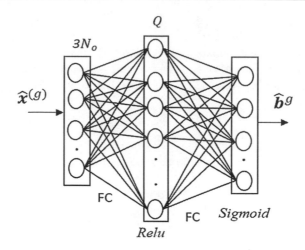

FIGURE 6.3   Deep learning model.

Additionally, the DL detector does not need to retrain during the test stage, providing significant reduction of complexity at the receiving end.

6.3.1.3.2 Training procedure

The DNN model needs to be trained offline before using as a detector. In the training stage, we generate random data sequence where different transmitted data frames are generated randomly. The collected received signal is equalized as in (6.6). By utilizing these collected data, DNN training is processed to minimize the difference between the DL model outputs and the original transmitted data bits. The loss function is defined as:

$$f\left(x_b^{(g)}, \hat{x}_b^{(g)}, \theta\right) = \frac{1}{b^{(g)}} \left\| x_b^{(g)} - \hat{x}_b^{(g)} \right\|^2. \tag{6.8}$$

In (6.8), $x_b^{(g)}$ denotes the original data bits of transmitted within the group g whose length is $b^{(g)}$. Most importantly, the offline training process is independent of the channel due to the pre-processing of the channel shown in Subsection 6.3.1.

In the training stage, the adaptive moment estimation, which is an advanced updated algorithm based on stochastic gradient descent, is adopted. Therefore, the parameter $\theta = [\wp, \mathfrak{f}]$ can be updated:

$$\theta^+ := \theta - \alpha \nabla f\left(x_b^{(g)}, \hat{x}_b^{(g)}, \theta\right), \tag{6.9}$$

where α indicates the learning rate and ∇ is the gradient operator.

The DL-based receiver is very sensitive to the used signal-to-noise ratio (SNR) ρ_{train}, so it is selected carefully to let the DL-based detector be able to work well at any other SNR [27]. Herein, we set $\rho_{train} = 10\ dB$ which gives good performance during the test stage for any SNR value.

6.3.1.3.3 Online deployment

The online deployment of the DL can be performed after the offline training using the optimized θ. Therefore, the received data is pre-processed and then put into the DNN to estimate the transmitted bits in real time. In other words, the proposed DL-based detector doesn't need extra training for updating the parameter θ. Most importantly, the detector achieves better results with cancelling the inter-block interference effects and without extra training for the DNN model.

The complexity of the DL model is calculated at the online deployment as the training stage is performed offline. The input layer of the DL model has constant length following the length of $x^{(g)}$, and also that applicable for the output layer which also has a length equal to b. The hidden layer Q can be modified either vertically or horizontally to have a tradeoff between the complexity and the performance. Setting the hidden layer Q horizontally means having more layers, and setting it vertically means modifying the number of nodes of the hidden layers. The complexity of DL based detector is analyzed in [27] in function of runtime where it's found that one of the main advantages of employing the DL detector is its complexity doesn't depend on the modulation order M nor the number of active subcarriers. But, to achieve enhanced performance, the size Q must be increased leading to higher computational complexity. It's also mentioned In [27] that increasing Q leads to better BER performance at the expense of computational complexity. The structure of this receiver can be considered as a combination of model-based and DL-based model since the channel effects must be recovered before processing the received data by the DL. Unless, the DL model becomes channel-dependent which means training stage must be done again to track the channel variation which results of higher complexity at the receiving end.

6.3.2 Single-carrier based index modulation systems

The IM is also implemented for the DSSS communication systems leading to an increase in energy efficiency [17] as well as avoiding the inter-users interference in harsh channels. In higher modulation order, the IM can be implemented to carry more indexed information bits in both real and quadrature parts having more spectral efficiency [18]. At the receiving end, maximal ratio combining (MRC) is implemented to detect the physical and indexed information bits with less computational complexity and less susceptibility to the channel estimation error [41]. One of the main problems in using the MRC is the sensitivity of detecting the spreading code, where wrong detection for the index of the spreading code might lead to fault detection of whole transmitted information bits. Particularly, in such environment with time-varied channel where the orthogonality of spreading code will be certainly lost. Therefore, to enable the implementation of that scheme into harsh communication environments, the DL has been adopted at the receiving end to jointly detect the physical and indexed information bits jointly.

6.3.2.1 Transmitter of system model with CIM-SS

The structure of the transmitter of the CIM-SS is shown in Figure 6.4. Assume that a group of data bits stream g is needed to be transmitted, it is divided into two groups, including the first group g_1 which represents the physical information bits and the second group g_2 denoting the index information bits. Unlike the OFDM-IM, the CIM-SS carries the majority of bits via the index of spreading code; it is very useful for communication environments where inter-users interference is critical. The first group, g_1, is modulated by using any digital modulation such as the BPSK resulting the modulated signal s. The second bits group is conveyed via the index of selected spreading code based on the Hadamard-Walsh matrix $\mathcal{W} = \{\mathfrak{w}_1, \cdots \cdots, \mathfrak{w}_N\}$, where $\mathcal{N}$ is the length of Walsh spreading code. The maximum number of bits can be transmitted using the index of spreading codes as in the conventional CIM-SS, $\log_2(\mathcal{N})$. The signal of the CIM-SS can be expressed by considering a DSSS system with one user and K symbols sequence for each user as in [42]. The spread spectrum code of the user is $\mathfrak{w}_n(t)$ with $T_{\mathfrak{w}}$ chip duration and the data bit duration is T_s. Then, the spreading factor can be expressed as $M = \dfrac{T_S}{T_{\mathfrak{w}}}$. Therefore, the CIM-SS signal can be expressed as:

$$x(t) = \sum_{k=1}^{K} \sum_{m=1}^{M} s_k \mathfrak{w}_{q,m} g(t - kmT_{\mathfrak{w}}), \tag{6.10}$$

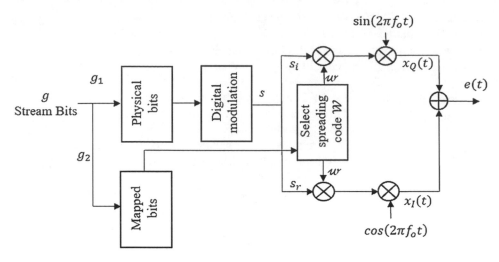

FIGURE 6.4   Transmitter in the CIM-SS system model.

where $\mathbb{W}_{q,m}$ denotes the qth Walsh code selected to carry the mapped data bits via index of the spreading code, and $g(t - kmT_a)$ is the unit rectangular function.

On the other hand, when employing quadrature modulation order such as quadrature phase shift keying (QPSK), the GCIM can be employed for carrying additional information bits via the index of spreading code. For example, the modulated information bits are $s=s_r + js_i$, where s_r represents the real part of modulated data s, s_i is the imaginary part, and $j = \sqrt{-1}$. Therefore, the index selected code to spread s_r is used to carry indexed information bits as well as the index selected code to spread s_i. In that case, the GCIM-SS signal can be written as:

$$x(t) = \sum_{k=1}^{K}\sum_{m=1}^{M}\left(s_r\hat{w}_{qr,m}g(t - kmT_a) + js_i\hat{w}_{qi,m}g(t - kmT_a)\right),\tag{6.11}$$

where $\mathbb{W}_{qr,m}$ and $\mathbb{W}_{qi,m}$ are the qth Walsh code selected to carry the mapped data bits through the index of the spreading codes used to spread the real and imaginary parts of modulated information bits, respectively.

Therefore, the maximum achievable data rate of the CIM and GCIM can, respectively, be expressed as:

$$\gamma_{CIM} = \log_2 M + \log_2 \mathcal{N},\tag{6.12}$$

$$\gamma_{GCIM} = 2\times\log_2 M + 2\times\log_2 \mathcal{N},\tag{6.13}$$

where M is the modulation order used for transmitting the physical modulated bits. When assuming same modulation order in both CIM and GCIM, the GCIM transmits double physical information bits as both real and imaginary parts of the constellation mapping will carry information bits.

6.3.2.2 Conventional detection scheme

After transmitting the $x(t)$ via a channel, the received signal can be expressed as:

$$y(t) = x(t)*h + v.\tag{6.14}$$

In communication systems where the channel is harsh, h need to be first estimated and recovered to be able to detect the transmitted information bits. Therefore, the MRC detector can be applied for detecting

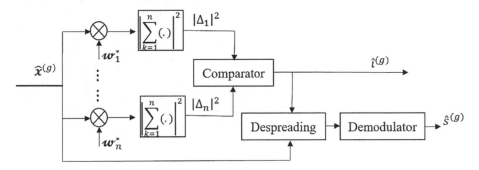

FIGURE 6.5   Detector for CIM based on MRC.

the physical and indexed information bits. The received estimated signal $\hat{x}(t)$ is passed through an MRC detector shown in Figure 6.5. The output of l-th code, $l \in \{1,\dots \mathcal{N}\}$, is given by:

$$\partial_l = \sum_{n=1}^{\mathcal{N}} \hat{x}(t) \hat{w}_l. \tag{6.15}$$

g_2 is detected by selecting the maximum square absolute value, that is:

$$\widehat{w}_q = \arg\max_l \left| \partial_l \right|^2. \tag{6.16}$$

g_1 is detected by dispreading the $\hat{x}(t)$ using the selected spreading code based on (6.14), and then the $\hat{s}$ is demodulated using constellated digital modulation.

6.3.2.3 Deep learning-based detection

The receiver of the CIM-SS based on the DL can also be utilized only after recovering the channel effects. Unless, the DL model must be increased to enable the detection task at the receiving end, which leads to higher computational complexity. Therefore, the DL model can only be employed for detecting the transmitted information bits without performing the estimation tasks. It is useful for the vehicle communication systems as transmitting only one user leads first to avoid the inter-users interference and the energy efficiency will be improved. However, the complexity will be little bit higher than that of the MRC detector as we will explain later.

The deep learning detector model is similar to Figure 6.3 except for different number of nodes in each layer. The input layer contains $2\mathcal{N}$ nodes representing the real and imaginary parts of the estimated signal $\hat{x}(t)$, which are concatenated and fed up into the input layer of the DL model. Moreover, the number of nodes in the output layer is equal to the number of bits carried in the bit stream g. Therefore, only the hidden layer can be tuned to have a tradeoff between the complexity and performance. At the hidden layer, $f_{Relu}(x) = \max(x,0)$ is utilized, and $f_{Sig}(x) = \dfrac{1}{1+e^{-x}}$ is employed in the output layer. A threshold of 0.5 is set to detect whether the output bit will be 0 or 1. The DNN output can be expressed as:

$$\hat{g} = f_{sig}\left(\wp_2\, f_{\tanh}\left(\wp_1 \hat{x}(t) + \mathfrak{f}_1\right) + \mathfrak{f}_2\right). \tag{6.17}$$

The input data in the input layer is a concatenation of $Re\left(\hat{x}(t)\right)$ and $Im\left(\hat{x}(t)\right)$. The output is the estimated information bits carried physically and via index of spreading code; it means that no digital demodulation is required anymore.

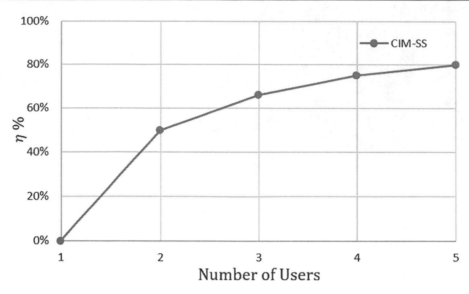

FIGURE 6.6 Energy efficiency performance with different number of users.

The rest of the process is performed similar to the DL model explained in Subsection 6.3.1. Implementing DL for the CIM-SS is a promising technique in vehicle communications within complicated communication environment. Figure 6.6 shows the performance of the energy efficiency when using the CIM-SS over the conventional DSSS with different number of users. Apart from the inter-users interference avoided by using the IM, the energy efficiency is also improved significantly. In communication environment where recharging the devices is difficult, that technique becomes very promising. The computational complexity of the CIM-SS based on the DL is still acceptable as the training stage can also be performed offline. Therefore, the complexity includes the multiplications and summation is required for test stage. The required real operation R_T of the DL-based detector is expressed as:

$$R_T = (2NQ + Qd).$$ (6.18)

In (6.18), d is the number of bits carried by the group g.

6.3.3 Multi-input multi-output based index modulation systems

The IM has been employed for the MIMO systems to avoid the inter-antennas interference resulting in the SM systems [20], and then many other extensions have been presented in literature [19, 21–23]. The SM carries the physical and index information bits. The physically transmitted information bits are modulated and transmitted by active antenna out of the available antennas. While the index of active antenna is used to transmit the indexed of information bits. The DL has been also applied into the MIMO systems with the IM at the receiving end to either reduce the computational complexity or improve the spectral efficiency.

6.3.3.1 System model and related works

Five categories can be classified for spatial modulation technique (SMT) schemes. First, the SMT schemes only transmit data via the index of active antennas without any modulated physical data such as space shift keying modulation (SSK) [43, 44] and generalized space shift keying (GSSK) [45]. Second, the SMT schemes transmit physical information bits by any digital modulation and indexed information bits via the index of active antenna used to transmit the physical information such as the SM [20, 46, 47], the GSM and the FGSM [19, 22, 48]. Third, the SMT schemes separately transmit the real part and the imaginary part of modulated information bits and transmit indexed information bits via the index of antennas transmitting the real part and also indexed information bits via the index of antennas transmitting the imaginary part such as quadrature spatial modulation (QSM), fully quadrature spatial modulation (FQSM) [49] and differential quadrature spatial modulation (DQSM) and generalized quadrature spatial modulation (GQSM) [23, 49, 50]. Fourth, the SMT schemes transmit physical information bits following such constellation via such antennas and another physical information bits using another type of constellation, and use the index of antennas to transmit additional indexed information via the index of active antennas [21, 51]. That means at least two antennas must be activated simultaneously to transmit the information bits based on different constellation mapping. Finally, the SMT schemes transmit indexed information bits via the index of transmit antennas as well as additionally indexed information bits via a spreading code used to spread the physical information bits [26, 52, 53].

In the first group, the SSK [43, 44] transmits the signal via one antenna out of the available antennas carrying the indexed information bits via the index of that antenna. In other words, no modulated information bits are transmitted in the SSK. The achievable data rate of the SSK is expressed as:

$$\gamma_{SSK} = \log_2(N_t),\tag{6.19}$$

where N_t is the number of available antennas.

The GSSK [45] activates a subset of antennas out of the available antennas instead of only one antennas. Also, the signal is transmitted, which means only indexed information bits are transmitted in this scheme. The achievable data rate of the GSSK is:

$$\gamma_{GSSK} = \left\lfloor \log_2 \binom{N_t}{N_s} \right\rfloor,\tag{6.20}$$

where N_s denotes the number of active antennas.

In the second classification, the transmitted signal is no longer known, but the information bits are modulated and then transmitted via the active antenna, e.g., the SM activate one antenna out of the available antennas transmitting the modulated information bits, and the index of the active antenna is used to transmit additional information bits. Therefore, the achievable data rate of the SM can be written as:

$$\gamma_{SM} = \log_2(M) + \log_2(N_t).\tag{6.21}$$

Similar to the GSSK, the GSM transmits the modulated data via a set of antennas out of the available antennas. The achievable data rate of the GSM is:

$$\gamma_{GSM} = \log_2(M) + \left\lfloor \log_2 \binom{N_t}{N_s} \right\rfloor.\tag{6.22}$$

The FGSM [19] combines the SM and the GSM by transmitting the modulated information bits via one or more antennas and the index of the antennas is employed for the additional information bits. The achievable data rate of the FGSM can be read as:

$$\gamma_{FGSM} = \log_2(M) + \left\lfloor \log_2 \sum_{k=1}^{N_t} \binom{N_t}{N_s} \right\rfloor = \log_2(M) + N_t - 1.\tag{6.23}$$

In the third classification, the modulated information bits are not transmitted via one or more antennas at once, but the real and imaginary parts are separated and the index of antennas transmitting them is used to transmit additional indexed information bits. The QSM [23] transmits the real part of the modulated information bits via one antenna out of the available antennas; the index of that antenna carries indexed information bits. Similarly, the index of imaginary part of the modulated information bits is transmitted via another antenna out of the available antennas, and the index of that antenna is used also to transmit additional indexed information bits. In this way, the achieved data rate of the QSM will be increased, which can be written as:

$$\gamma_{QSM} = \log_2(M) + \log_2(N_t)^2. \tag{6.24}$$

The same idea of the GSM has been applied for the resulting scheme called GQSM [23, 49, 50]. The real part of the signal is transmitted via a set of transmit antennas instead of one single transmit antenna used in the QSM, and the same for the imaginary part. By this way, the achievable data rate increases, and receiver complexity increases as well. Therefore, the achieved data rate of the GQSM can be read as:

$$\gamma_{GQSM} = \log_2(M) + 2\left\lfloor \log_2\binom{N_T}{N_u} \right\rfloor. \tag{6.25}$$

On the other hand, the DQSM [23, 49, 50] transmits the real and imaginary parts of the constellated data via the permutations of the active antennas. On the transmitter side of this scheme, the perfect knowledge of channel is no longer required, transmitted data thus depend on the current and previous data block, and its achievable data rate is expressed as follows:

$$\gamma_{DQSM} = N_t \log_2(M) + \left\lfloor \log_2(N_t!) \right\rfloor, \tag{6.26}$$

where (!) is the factorial operator.

In the FQSM [49], the real part of the modulated information bits is transmitted via one or more antennas out of the available transmitting antennas, and the same is for the imaginary part. This leads to a substantial increase in the indexed information bits. The achieved data rate of the FQSM is expressed as:

$$\gamma_{FQSM} = \log_2(M) + 2\left\lfloor \log_2 \sum_{k=1}^{N_t}\binom{N_t}{N_s} \right\rfloor = \log_2(M) + 2(N_t - 1). \tag{6.27}$$

In the fourth group, two different constellations are employed for transmitting physical information bits, and indexed information bits are transmitted through the index of active antennas, e.g., EFGSM [21], whose data rate can be read as:

$$\gamma_{EFGSM} = \log_2(M) + \left\lfloor \log_2 \sum_{k=2}^{N_T}\binom{N_T}{N_s} \right\rfloor + \log_2\left(\frac{M}{2}\right). \tag{6.28}$$

Finally, in the last classification, the modulated bits are first spread using such orthogonal codes. The index of the spreading code is employed for carrying indexed information bits, and spread information bits are transmitted via one or more antennas and the index of the active antennas is dedicated to transmit additional information bits. An example of the SMT schemes is fully generalized spatial modulation spread spectrum (FGSM-SS), where the real and imaginary information bits are spread by a spreading code whose indices are carrying indexed information bits, and then the resulted information bits are transmitted via one or more active antennas out of the available antennas. The achieved data rate of the FGSM-SS is:

$$\gamma_{FGSM-SS} = \log_2(M) + 2\log_2(\mathcal{N}) + (N_t - 1), \tag{6.29}$$

where $\mathcal{N}$ denotes the length of the spreading code.

Generally, at the receiving end, the ML detector is considered at the optimal detector to detect the indexed and physical information bits jointly.

6.3.3.2 Deep learning-based SMTs

In the DL-based SMT scheme, the transmitters are designed as well as the ones mentioned above. Furthermore, the DL-based receivers have been implemented to avoid the higher computational complexity resulting from the ML detector, especially for these SMTs with higher achieved data rate. For example, when it increases the data rate by extending the transmitted indexed information bits, the complexity of the ML detector will be increased exponentially.

The DL-based detector was employed to decrease the higher computational complexity resulting from increasing the data rate by the index of the spreading code. The receiver can be considered a combination of model-based and DL-based components since the channel effects are first recovered and compensated. Then, the DL is adopted to overcome the explosion of computational complexity due to the length of spreading codes. The same DL model in Figure 6.3 is employed, where the number of nodes in the input layer is set to $2\mathcal{N}\mathcal{N}_t$ as the spreading codes of the transmitted signal have been performed for the real and imaginary parts separately. Therefore, the real and imaginary parts are concatenated before inserting them into the DL model, and the transmission of the spread signal is done via unknown transmitting antennas. Moreover, the signal coming from all antennas is analysed to perform joint detection using the DL with less computational complexity.

In [54], complex-valued convolutional neural network (CV-CNN) mode is presented to avoid the higher computational complexity of the GSM scheme. In that work, auto-encoder based CV-CNN has been employed, where the channel and the noise are considered in the encoder side. Then, at the receiving end, the received signal is processed by the decoder. The disadvantage of this detector is achieving a complexity reduction of only 14.7% at the expense of deterioration of the BER performance. Furthermore, the channel cannot be estimated and recovered due to the complex communication environments. In order to overcome it, enhanced CV-CNN has been presented in [55] to further decrease the computational complexity, and considering the channel and noise in the encoder has been solved, where it is also difficult to recover the channel effects in hard communication environments by traditional techniques.

In [56], machine learning and DL techniques with adaptive SM systems were presented. The K-nearest neighbors and support vector machine algorithms were first employed to decrease the computational complexity resulted of using the ML detector. Then, the DNN based multi-label classifier was also employed for adaptive SM scheme. Despite the reduction of complexity, it's always at the expense of loss in BER performance, and idealistic conditions are always assumed at the receiving end. It means that further investigations with practical channels and communication environments are needed.

6.3.3.3 Performance analysis on energy efficiency of vehicle communications with IM

In vehicle communications, energy efficiency is one of the main critical issues to deal with as the vehicles are usually battery-based and sometimes it becomes too complicated to recharge those vehicles in such communication environments. Reducing the computational complexity at the receiving end using the DL can lead to the decrease of the power consumption. Also, the use of the IM has a promising potential on the power consumption. Figure 6.7 shows the performance of different SMTs on energy efficiency when assuming a rate of 10 bit per channel use (bpcu). It's worth mentioning that the first group mentioned previously, e.g., the SSK and the GSSK transmit the information bits only by the index of antennas, which leads to a limited transmitted bpcu; that restricts having different energy efficiency like others in Figure 6.7. It's straightforward to notice that increasing the information bits transmitted by the index of antennas leads to better enhancement of energy efficiency.

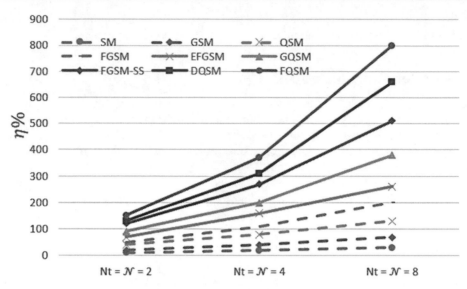

FIGURE 6.7   Performance of energy efficiency of different SMTs.

6.4 CONCLUSIONS

The IM has a promising improvement on energy efficiency as more information bits are transmitted with energy-free consumption, which makes it an attractive solution for vehicle communication systems. The more indexed information bits that are transmitted, the more energy efficiency is gained. Despite the loss of energy efficiency due to the ML higher computational complexity at the receiving end, the DL can replace the ML detector with less computational complexity and almost similar achieved performance. The DL-based detectors must be used at the receiving end after recovering the environment effects. Otherwise the energy efficiency performance will be deteriorated as the training stage of the DL model must be done again to track the channel variation at the receiving end. The design of the complete DL receiver which will handle the environmental effects and detection complexity is a very interesting study, which might lead to numerous promising performance results.

REFERENCES

[1] P. Bhoyar, P. Sahare, S. B. Dhok, and R. B. Deshmukh, "Communication technologies and security challenges for internet of things: A comprehensive review," *AEU-International Journal of Electronics and Communications*, vol. *99*, pp. 81–99, 2019.

[2] K. Shafique, B. A. Khawaja, F. Sabir, S. Qazi, and M. Mustaqim, "Internet of things (IoT) for next-generation smart systems: A review of current challenges, future trends and prospects for emerging 5G-IoT scenarios," *IEEE Access*, vol. *8*, pp. 23022–23040, 2020.

[3] T. Jiang, D. Chen, C. Ni, and D. Qu, *OQAM/FBMC for future wireless communications: principles, technologies and applications.* Academic Press, 2017. https://www.elsevier.com/books/oqam-fbmc-for-future-wireless-communications/jiang/978-0-12-813557-0

[4] Y. Han, Y. Chen, B. Wang, and K. R. Liu, "Time-reversal massive multipath effect: a single-antenna "massive MIMO" solution," *IEEE Transactions on Communications*, vol. *64*, no. 8, pp. 3382–3394, 2016.

[5] H. Ramchandran and D. L. Noneaker, "Iterative equalization and decoding for high-data-rate frequency-hop spread-spectrum communications," *IEEE Military Communications Conference*, vol. 2, pp. 934–940, 2004.

[6] H. A. Leftah and S. Boussakta, "Novel OFDM based on C-transform for improving multipath transmission," *IEEE Transactions on Signal Processing*, vol. *62*, no. 23, pp. 6158–6170, 2014.

[7] P. Robertson and S. Kaiser, "The effects of Doppler spreads in OFDM (A) mobile radio systems," *IEEE VTS 50th Vehicular Technology Conference*, vol. *1*, pp. 329–333, 1999.

[8] S. Schwarz, R. W. Heath, and M. Rupp, "Single-user MIMO versus multi-user MIMO in distributed antenna systems with limited feedback," *EURASIP Journal on Advances in Signal Processing*, vol. 2013, no. 1, p. 54, *2013*.

[9] E. Telatar, "Capacity of multi-antenna Gaussian channels," *European Transactions on Telecommunications*, vol. *10*, no. 6, pp. 585–595, 1999.

[10] G. J. Foschini, "Layered space-time architecture for wireless communication in a fading environment when using multi-element antennas," *Bell Labs Technical Journal*, vol. *1*, no. 2, pp. 41–59, 1996.

[11] L. Giangaspero, L. Agarossi, G. Paltenghi, S. Okamura, M. Okada, and S. Komaki, "Co-channel interference cancellation based on MIMO OFDM systems," *IEEE Wireless Communications*, vol. *9*, no. 6, pp. 8–17, 2002.

[12] R. Abu-Alhiga and H. Haas, "Subcarrier-index modulation OFDM," *IEEE International Symposium on Personal, Indoor and Mobile Radio Communications, PIMRC*, vol. *1*, pp. 177–181, 2009.

[13] D. Tsonev, S. Sinanovic, and H. Haas, "Enhanced subcarrier index modulation (SIM) OFDM," *IEEE GLOBECOM Workshops, GC Wkshps 2011*, pp. 728–732, 2011.

[14] E. Başar, Ü. Aygölü, E. Panayırcı, and H. V. Poor, "Orthogonal frequency division multiplexing with index modulation," *IEEE Transactions on Signal Processing*, vol. *61*, no. 22, pp. 5536–5549, 2013.

[15] E. Basar, "Index modulation techniques for 5G wireless networks," *IEEE Communications Magazine*, vol. *54*, no. 7, pp. 168–175, 2016.

[16] Z. A. Qasem, H. A. Leftah, H. Sun, J. Qi, J. Wang, and H. Esmaiel, "Deep learning-based code indexed modulation for autonomous underwater vehicles systems," *Vehicular Communications*, vol. *28*, p. 100314, 2021.

[17] G. Kaddoum, M. F. A. Ahmed, and Y. Nijsure, "Code index modulation: A high data rate and energy efficient communication system," *IEEE Communications Letters*, vol. *19*, no. 2, pp. 175–178, 2015.

[18] G. Kaddoum, Y. Nijsure, and H. Tran, "Generalized code index modulation technique for high-data-rate communication systems," *IEEE Transactions on Vehicular Technology*, vol. *65*, no. 9, pp. 7000–7009, 2016.

[19] H. S. Hussein, H. Esmaiel, and D. Jiang, "Fully generalised spatial modulation technique for underwater communication," *Electronics Letters*, vol. *54*, no. 14, pp. 12–13, 2018.

[20] R. Y. Mesleh, H. Haas, and S. Sinanovi, "Spatial modulation," *IEEE Transactions on Vehicular Technology*, vol. *57*, no. 4, pp. 2228–2241, 2008.

[21] Z. A. H. Qasem, H. Esmaiel, H. Sun, J. Wang, Y. Miao, and S. Anwar, "Enhanced fully generalized spatial modulation for the internet of underwater things," *Sensors*, vol. *19*, no. 7, pp. 1519–1519, 2019.

[22] T. L. Narasimhan, P. Raviteja, and A. Chockalingam, "Generalized spatial modulation in large-scale multiuser MIMO systems," *IEEE Transactions on Wireless Communications*, vol. *14*, no. 7, pp. 3764–3779, 2015.

[23] R. Mesleh, S. Member, S. S. Ikki, and H. M. Aggoune, "Quadrature spatial modulation," *IEEE Transactions on Vehicular Technology*, vol. *9545*, no. c, pp. 1–5, 2014.

[24] N. Ishikawa, S. Sugiura, and L. Hanzo, "Subcarrier-index modulation aided OFDM-will it work?," *IEEE Access*, vol. *4*, pp. 2580–2593, 2016.

[25] Y. Acar, S. A. Çolak, and E. Başar, "Channel estimation for OFDM-IM systems," *Turkish Journal of Electrical Engineering & Computer Sciences*, vol. *27*, pp. 1908–1921, 2019.

[26] Z. A. Qasem, H. Esmaiel, H. Sun, J. Qi, and J. Wang, "Deep learning-based spread-Spectrum FGSM for underwater communication," *Sensors*, vol. *20*, no. 21, p. 6134, 2020.

[27] T. Van Luong, Y. Ko, N. A. Vien, D. H. Nguyen, and M. Matthaiou, "Deep learning-based detector for OFDM-IM," *IEEE Wireless Communications Letters*, vol. *8*, no. 4, pp. 1159–1162, 2019.

[28] A. A. Marseet and T. Y. Elganimi, "Fast detection based on customized complex valued convolutional neural network for generalized spatial modulation systems," *IEEE Western New York Image and Signal Processing Workshop (WNYISPW)*, vol. *1*, pp. 1–5, 2019.

[29] S. Eckelmann, T. Trautmann, H. Ußler, B. Reichelt, and O. Michler, "V2V-communication, lidar system and positioning sensors for future fusion algorithms in connected vehicles," *Transportation Research Procedia*, vol. *27*, pp. 69–76, 2017.

[30] M. Belkheir, Z. Qasem, M. Bouziani, and A. Zerroug, "Ad Hoc network lifetime enhancement by energy optimization," *Ad Hoc Sensors Wireless Networks*, vol. *28*, no. 1–2, pp. 83–95, 2015.

[31] J. Harding et al., "Vehicle-to-vehicle communications: readiness of V2V technology for application," United States, National Highway Traffic Safety Administration, 2014.

[32] M.-S. Kim, S. Lee, D. Cypher, and N. Golmie, "Fast handover latency analysis in proxy mobile IPv6," *IEEE Global Telecommunications Conference*, pp. 1–5, 2010.

[33] X. Cheng, M. Wen, L. Yang, and Y. Li, "Index modulated OFDM with interleaved grouping for V2X communications," *17th International IEEE Conference on Intelligent Transportation Systems (ITSC)*, pp. 1097–1104, 2014.

[34] J. Schmidhuber, "Deep learning in neural networks: an overview," *Neural networks*, vol. *61*, pp. 85–117, 2015.

[35] H. Ye, G. Y. Li, and B.-H. Juang, "Power of deep learning for channel estimation and signal detection in OFDM systems," *IEEE Wireless Communications Letters*, vol. *7*, no. 1, pp. 114–117, 2017.

[36] M. Kim, W. Lee, and D.-H. Cho, "A novel PAPR reduction scheme for OFDM system based on deep learning," *IEEE Communications Letters*, vol. *22*, no. 3, pp. 510–513, 2017.

[37] M. H. Khadr, I. Walter, H. Elgala, and S. Muhaidat, "Machine learning-based massive augmented spatial modulation (ASM) for IoT VLC systems," *IEEE Communications Letters*, vol. *25*, no. 2, pp. 494–498, 2020.

[38] Z. A. Qasem, H. A. Leftah, H. Sun, J. Qi, and H. Esmaiel, "X-transform time-domain synchronous IM-OFDM-SS for underwater acoustic communication," *IEEE Systems Journal*, pp. 1–12, 2021.

[39] J. Wang et al., "On orthogonal coding-based modulation," *IEEE Communications Letters*, vol. *24*, no. 4, pp. 816–820, 2020.

[40] J. Zheng and H. Lv, "Peak-to-average power ratio reduction in OFDM index modulation through convex programming," *IEEE Communications Letters*, vol. *21*, no. 7, pp. 1505–1508, 2017.

[41] Q. Li, M. Wen, E. Basar, and F. Chen, "Index modulated OFDM spread spectrum," *IEEE Transactions on Wireless Communications*, vol. *17*, no. 4, pp. 2360–2374, 2018.

[42] L.-J. Liu et al., "An underwater acoustic direct sequence spread spectrum communication system using dual spread spectrum code," *Frontiers of Information Technology & Electronic Engineering*, vol. *19*, no. 8, pp. 972–983, 2018.

[43] J. Jeganathan, A. Ghrayeb, L. Szczecinski, and A. Ceron, "Space shift keying modulation for MIMO channels," *IEEE Transactions on Wireless Communications*, vol. *8*, no. 7, pp. 3692–3703, 2009.

[44] M. Di Renzo and H. Haas, "Space shift keying (SSK) modulation with partial channel state information: optimal detector and performance analysis over fading channels," *IEEE Transactions on Communications*, vol. *58*, no. 11, pp. 3196–3210, 2010.

[45] J. Jeganathan, A. Ghrayeb, and L. Szczecinski, "Generalized space shift keying modulation for MIMO channels," *IEEE 19th International Symposium on Personal, Indoor and Mobile Radio Communications*, pp. 1–5, 2008.

[46] M. Di Renzo, H. Haas, and P. M. Grant, "Spatial modulation for multiple-antenna wireless systems: A survey," *IEEE Communications Magazine*, vol. *49*, no. 12, pp. 182–191, 2011.

[47] A. Mohammadi and F. M. Ghannouchi, "Single RF front-end MIMO transceivers," *IEEE Communications Magazine*, vol. *49*, no. 12, pp. 104–109, 2011.

[48] A. Younis, N. Serafimovski, R. Mesleh, and H. Haas, "Generalised spatial modulation," *Conference Record - Asilomar Conference on Signals, Systems and Computers*, pp. 1498–1502, 2010.

[49] H. S. Hussein, M. Elsayed, U. S. Mohamed, H. Esmaiel, and E. M. Mohamed, "Spectral efficient spatial modulation techniques," *IEEE Access*, vol. *7*, pp. 1454–1469, 2018.

[50] R. Mesleh, S. Althunibat, and A. Younis, "Differential quadrature spatial modulation," *IEEE Transactions on Communications*, vol. *65*, no. 9, pp. 3810–3817, 2017.

[51] C. C. Cheng, H. Sari, S. Sezginer, and Y. T. Su, "New signal designs for enhanced spatial modulation," *IEEE Transactions on Wireless Communications*, vol. *15*, no. 11, pp. 7766–7777, 2016.

[52] F. Çögen, E. Aydin, N. Kabaoğlu, E. Bagar, and H. Ilhan, "A novel MIMO scheme based on code-index modulation and spatial modulation," *26th Signal Processing and Communications Applications Conference (SIU)*, pp. 1–4, 2018.

[53] E. Aydin, F. Cogen, and E. Basar, "Code-index modulation aided quadrature spatial modulation for high-rate MIMO systems," *IEEE Transactions on Vehicular Technology*, vol. *68*, no. 10, pp. 10257–10261, 2019.

[54] A. Marseet and F. Sahin, "Application of complex-valued convolutional neural network for next generation wireless networks," *IEEE Western New York Image and Signal Processing Workshop (WNYISPW)*, pp. 1–5, 2017.

[55] A. A. Marseet and T. Y. Elganimi, "Fast detection based on customized complex valued convolutional neural network for generalized spatial modulation systems," *IEEE Western New York Image and Signal Processing Workshop (WNYISPW)*, pp. 1–5, 2019.

[56] P. Yang, Y. Xiao, M. Xiao, Y. L. Guan, S. Li, and W. Xiang, "Adaptive spatial modulation MIMO based on machine learning," *IEEE Journal on Selected Areas in Communications*, vol. *37*, no. 9, pp. 2117–2131, 2019.

Deep reinforcement learning applications in connected-automated transportation systems

7

H. M. Abdul Aziz and Sanjoy Das
Kansas State University, Manhattan, Kansas

Contents

DOI: 10.1201/9781003190691-9

7.1 INTRODUCTION

The last decade has experienced unprecedented transformation in mobility technologies, most notably, the connected and automated vehicles (CAVs) and shared-use services (e.g., ride-hailing, ride-sharing, and bike-sharing). Connectivity and automation are paving the future of transportation—modes, infrastructure, and services. The envisioned connected and automated transportation networks will have vehicles, infrastructures, and road users communicating, sharing data, and cooperating to achieve the desired safety, mobility, environmental goals [1]. The Society of Automotive Engineers (SAE) defines six levels (from zero to five) of automation based on driving functionality and the role of human drivers. Level 0–2 vehicles are equipped with driving support features to assist human drivers. The automated driving systems (ADSs) are introduced from level-3 CAVs, and only level-5 CAVs are to fully autonomous in all environmental conditions—generally defined by the operational design domain (ODD). According to the SAE J3016, an ODD *defines operating conditions under which a given ADS or feature thereof is specifically designed to function, including, but not limited to, environmental, geographical, and time-of-day restrictions, and/ or the requisite presence or absence of specific traffic or roadway characteristics* [2]. The ODD specifies (as described by the manufacturer or the ADS software system developer) the technical capabilities of an ADS—algorithms, sensing, use cases, business models, operational boundaries, and risk management strategies [3]. The ADS features are highly dependent on artificial Intelligence (AI) and relevant machine learning (ML) techniques. At the same time, the CAV environment offers opportunities to build machine-learning-based applications to improve the safety, mobility, and carbon impact of transportation systems

The last few years have witnessed rapid progress in AI and ML—methodologies and applications. In particular, *deep neural networks* (DNNs) have been established as a powerful tool to solve a wide variety of real-world problems whose complexities had previously been considered too daunting to be addressed through algorithmic means. These tasks were either left unaddressed or, wherever possible, assigned to human-level decisions. Nowadays, DNNs can match and even outperform human performance levels. As a direct consequence, there has been a proliferation of the use of DNNs in a diverse variety of real-world applications, including direct applications in connected and automated transportation. The vehicle-to-everything communications coupled with the ADS technologies will be ubiquitous in future transportation systems. It's no surprise that both academic researchers and industry stakeholders (ADS developers— *Waymo, Zoox,* and automobiles—Ford, GM, Audi) have shown extensive interests in applying DNN or its variants to develop CAV applications, and there has been a surge in the use of DNNs in a plethora of ADS tasks. One attractive feature of DNNs is their ability to learn from experience to improve their overall performance. Lately, there has been significant academic interest in *reinforcement learning* (RL) combined with DNN. RL allows the DNN to interact with the outside world, enhancing their performances through trial and error, relying entirely on a simple set of reward/penalty signals as feedback.

The applications of DNN within the context of connected and automated transportation systems are abundant. This chapter will focus on a specific subarea of DNN, the *deep reinforcement learning* (DRL), which aims to provide an overview of the theoretical aspects and review of the ADS tasks and connected-vehicle applications that explicitly utilize DRL.

7.1.1 Chapter organization

The remainder of this chapter is organized as follows. The next section provides deeper insights—theoretical aspects—into deep reinforcement learning. At the onset, the section briefly introduces classical reinforcement learning as a primary machine learning paradigm. Next, DNN architectures for RL are elaborated at greater length. While avoiding rigorous mathematical details, the section outlines, in a formulaic manner, the essential steps needed in various RL algorithms that are used to train DNNs. Afterward, we describe the data environment within a connected and automated environment. The following two sections explore DRL applications in the CAV landscape. Finally, we conclude the chapter with a brief discussion on the challenges and future research direction regarding applying DRL techniques in CAV applications.

7.2 DEEP REINFORCEMENT LEARNING: THEORY AND BACKGROUND

7.2.1 (Deep) reinforcement learning: a brief history

Machine learning involves a mathematical model with its own set of adjustable parameters, such as the weights in a neural network. The model can be trained to perform any desired task following an algorithm that iteratively fine-tunes these parameters for optimal performance. Supervised learning is used in classification and regression tasks; it involves the presence of a supervisor that provides the learning model with the desired output for every input. On the other hand, unsupervised learning, which is designed to discover hidden features in the data, does not involve any such supervisor. In addition to the supervised and unsupervised learning, reinforcement learning (RL) is the third core paradigm in machine learning. RL involves reward signals that are provided to the learning model. In this sense, reinforcement learning may be construed as intermediate between supervised and unsupervised learning [4]. In RL, the learning model, which shall be hitherto referred to as the agent, exerts a degree of control over an external environment through a sequence of actions. The instantaneous state of the environment is either fully or partially observable to the agent. The reward signals, which are numerical values, indicate the overall desirability of the environment's state. Without any loss of generality, it will be assumed that the higher the reward, the better the environmental condition.

The genesis of RL can be traced back to the seminal work of Richard Bellman [5], who introduced dynamic programming as a general tool for optimal control problems. He proposed an expression that defined the value of a state of the environment in terms of the immediate as well as the expected future rewards. In the same year [6], Bellman also formulated the concept of a Markov Decision Process (MDP) that was meant to address discrete control problems. Bellman's ideas eventually led to the formulation for a slew of value-based approaches for RL. In 1960, Ron Howard [7] formulated policy-based RL approaches. It was not until 1983 that these methods were combined under the actor-critic architecture [8]. In 1988, Richard Sutton [9] devised the temporal-difference class of reinforcement learning algorithms. The book *Reinforcement Learning: An Introduction* co-authored by him is perhaps the most significant one on the topic [10].

Q-learning [11] was an important breakthrough that provided the basis for online RL approaches. Another landmark in RL was achieved in 1994, with the introduction of the TD-Gammon algorithm [12] that was able to exceed human-level performance in playing the game of backgammon. TD-Gammon was also one of the earliest uses of a neural network for RL. AlphaGo [13] was one of the first successful uses of a deep neural network (DNN) in RL. AlphaGo was able to defeat a human professional Go player in [14]. A version of AlphaGo was introduced in [15] that could train itself without human intervention.

Since its inception deep reinforcement learning (DRL) has been successfully applied to a wide variety of complex domains. In the field of robotics, it has been used in tasks such as navigation [16], arm manipulation and trajectory tracking [17], object grasping [18], motion planning [19], and for air delivery and flight control of unmanned aircraft systems [20]. Further, it has found many applications in communications and networking, including cybersecurity [21], mobile edge caching [22], and sensor networks [23]. In energy systems, DRLs have been applied to home management applications [24], smart distribution systems [25], medical decision systems [26], and agriculture [27].

7.2.2 Classical reinforcement learning

The state space of the environment will be denoted as $\mathbb{S}$ and the agent's action space as $\mathbb{A}$. At each discrete time instance t, the current state $s_t \in \mathbb{S}$ of the environment is perceived by the agent, which then implements an action $a_t \in \mathbb{A}$. The environment then responds with an immediate reward $r_t \in \mathcal{R}$ and transitions to the next state s_{t+1} with a probability $p(s_{t+1} \mid s_t, a_t)$.

As the reward signal r_t is based on s_t and a_t, we consider a reward function $r : \mathbb{S} \times \mathbb{A} \rightarrow \mathcal{R}$. Figure 7.1 illustrates the overall framework. It must be noted that modeling the reward function in this manner a simplification of the general situation where r_t also depends on s_{t+1}. Furthermore, it is generally stochastic (as in transportation applications) and represents a probability distribution. In *model-based* RL, the agent models the environmental transition probabilities and reward function. During online training, in many RL algorithms, the agent learns the model online by maintaining a count of all transitions taking place and rewards received.

TABLE 7.1 List of acronyms

ADS	AUTOMATED DRIVING SYSTEM
AV	Automated Vehicle
CAV	Connected and Automated Vehicle
CNN	Convolutional Neural Network
CV	Connected Vehicles
DACN	Deep Actor-Critic Network
DDPG	Deep Deterministic Policy Gradient
DRL	Deep Reinforcement Learning
DNN	Deep Neural Network
DPN	Deep Policy Network
DQN	Deep Q-Network
DOT	Department of Transportation
GPU	Graphics Processing Unit
LSTM	Long Short Term Memory
MDP	Markov Decision Process
ODD	Operational Design Domain
POMDP	Partially Observed Markov Decision Process
PPO	Proximal Policy Optimization
RL	Reinforcement Learning
TL	Transfer Learning
TRPO	Trust Region Policy Optimization

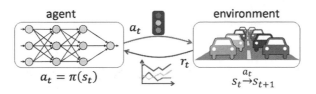

FIGURE 7.1 Reinforcement Learning Framework. The agent-environment interaction shown, pertains to time instance *t*. The transition to the next state is also shown.

Model-based RL has been used in [28] for an internet of vehicles application. However, in most CAV applications, the environment is too complex to be amenable to mathematical modeling. *Model-free* RL is better suited for such situations; accordingly, this chapter focusses on model free, online reinforcement learning.

Instead of greedily aiming to improve the immediate reward r_t at every time instance t, the agent may be trained to seek a higher sum of the immediate and all future, discounted rewards $R_t = r_t + \gamma r_{t+1} + \gamma^2 r_{t+2} + \ldots$, which is termed the *return*. It is evident that the return can be expressed recursively as,

$$R_t = r_t + \gamma R_{t+1} \tag{7.1}$$

The quantity $\gamma \in [0, 1]$ is called the *discount* factor. This lookahead feature of taking into account future rewards prevents the agent from learning greedy actions that, while fetching large instantaneous rewards, may adversely affect the environment later on. The environment-agent interactive process is hereafter assumed to begin at time $t = 0$ and terminate at $t = T$, the *time horizon*. Unless $T < \infty$, the discount γ must be strictly less than unity so that the returns R_t remain bounded. The 5-tuple $(\mathbb{S}, \mathbb{A}, p, r, \gamma)$ defines the MDP. Although the initial state s_0 is fixed in some applications (such as games), in other applications it usually follows some stochastic distribution. If so, due to notational convenience, $p_0(s)$ will be used to denote the initial state distribution of the environment (p_0 is subsumed by p in MDP $(\mathbb{S}, \mathbb{A}, p, r, \gamma)$).

The entire sequence of states, actions, and rewards is referred to as an *episode* represented as ε, so that $\varepsilon = s_0 \xrightarrow{a_0, r_0} s_1 \xrightarrow{a_1, r_1} s_2 \cdots \xrightarrow{a_{T-1}, r_{T-1}} s_T$. For instance, in the lane-changing application proposed in [29], an episode consists the states, actions, and rewards at uniformly spaced discrete time instances, from the initiation of lane merging until the merging is accomplished. The sequence of actions is based on the *policy* that the agent follows. This policy can be either deterministic or stochastic. A deterministic policy is a mapping $\pi : \mathbb{S} \rightarrow \mathbb{A}$, so that $a_t = \pi(s_t)$. Figure 7.1 illustrates at some time instance t, the interaction between an agent following a deterministic policy π, and its environment. The agent implements an action $a_t = \pi(s_t)$, and receives a reward r_t, while the environment transitions from s_t to another state s_{t+1}. *Policy evaluation* refers to RL, where the policy π is known *a priori* and remains fixed. The purpose of such approaches is to evaluate the policy's efficacy or to assign numerical values to the environment's states (discussed later). In *policy improvement* RL, the goal is to learn the *optimal policy* π^*, i.e. the policy that maximizes the expected return $\mathbb{E}_{\pi^*}[R_0]$.

A deterministic optimal policy might not exist in some application domains. For instance, the optimal policy of an agent trained to play the game of rock–paper–scissors, is to randomly pick any of the three available actions with an equal probability of 1/3. In many situations, a deterministic policy, although possible, might not necessarily be a judicious choice. As an example, a deterministic routing policy in a road network would be rendered ineffective during repair work resulting in some roads being closed to traffic. Under these circumstances, a stochastic policy is implemented to allow the agent to randomize actions.

Stochastic policies are indispensable in model-free RL during the training process. It endows the agent with the ability to explore the environment, occasionally picking a previously untried action in order to see if it eventually leads to a better policy. Without adequate exploration, the RL algorithm may converge prematurely to a suboptimal policy. Conversely, incorporating too much exploitation slows down the algorithm's convergence. In machine learning, striking the right tradeoff between them is the well-known *exploration–exploitation dilemma* [30]. A stochastic policy $\pi : \mathbb{S} \rightarrow [0,1]^{|\mathbb{A}|}$ is a probability distribution over $\mathbb{A}$ so that $a_t \sim \pi(s_t)$.

RL algorithms fall under two basic classes: (i) *value-based* RL, and (ii) *policy-based* RL. For the purpose of policy evaluation, value-based RL can quantify the merit of either states or a state-action pairs by assigning values to them. The goal of value-based RL for policy evaluation is to obtain the best estimates of these values. In policy-free RL, the agent's policy is directed toward maximizing these values. On the other hand, policy-based RL directly learns the desired policy. The *actor-critic* method combines features of both classes.

7.2.2.1 Value-based RL

The Markov (or 'memoryless') property of the MDP shows that this expected return is independent of the prior history of the episode, i.e. $\mathbb{E}_\pi[R_t \mid s_t] = \mathbb{E}_\pi[R_t \mid s_t, s_{t-1}, a_{t-1}, \ldots, s_0]$. Here, $\mathbb{E}_\pi[\bullet]$ represents the expectation of its argument when all actions are determined from π. Accordingly, when the environment is at any state s_t, the prior history of how it arrived there can be ignored. The *value* of a state $s \in \mathbb{S}$ under π is defined as the expected return when starting from that state,

$$v^\pi(s) \triangleq \mathbb{E}_\pi[R_t \mid s_t = s]. \tag{7.2}$$

From an online RL standpoint, it is more useful to evaluate the expected returns for all available actions $a \in \mathbb{A}$ from the state s, including ones that deviate from the underlying policy. The *Q-value* (or state-action value) of such a state-action pair (s, a) under policy π is this expected return when implementing the evaluative action a from state s. Denoting this as $q^\pi(s, a)$,

$$q^\pi(s,a) \triangleq \mathbb{E}_\pi[R_t \mid s_t = s, a_t = a] \tag{7.3}$$

At any time instance t, when the environment is at the state s_t, the agent can implement several possible actions as a_t, with each of them fetching a different expected return R_t. The optimal action from would be to pick the one that maximizes it. In other words, from s_t the optimal action a_t^* would be the one with the highest Q-value. Moreover, the optimal value of the state is the highest Q-value. Ignoring the time subscript, and assuming for simplicity, a deterministic policy, we arrive at the following pair of expressions,

$$\pi^*(s) = \operatorname*{argmax}_a q^*(s,a), \tag{7.4a}$$

$$v^*(s) = \max_a q^*(s,a). \tag{7.4b}$$

The quantity $q^*(\bullet)$ is the Q-value of its arguments under π^*. The first of the above expressions can be interpreted as the definition of the optimal policy π^*.

Tabular Q-learning is applicable when the states as well as the actions are discrete and small in number, in which case all Q-values are stored in an $|\mathbb{S}| \times |\mathbb{A}|$ array. It is used for policy improvement. The array is initially filled with zeros or small random values and the environment is at s_0. In each iteration of the RL process, suppose the environment is in the state s. The agent proceeds by picking an action a, leading to the transition $s \xrightarrow{a,r} s'$ where r is the reward, and s', the environment's next state. In order to explore the action space, the agent does not always pick the action a greedily. The tabular entry is updated as per in accordance with the learning step shown below,

$$q(s,a) \leftarrow (1-\eta)q(s,a) + \eta\{r + \gamma \max_{a'} q(s',a')\}. \tag{7.5}$$

The parameter η ($0 < \eta \ll 1$) is the *learning rate*. The second term $r + \gamma \max_{a'} q(s', a')$ appearing to the right in this expression is the *target value*. Since the above learning step implements policy-free learning, the target value that any tabular entry $q(s, a)$ is incremented toward the target value uses a max operation that is independent of any policy. Banach's fixed point theorem [30] shows that the tabular entries $q(s, a)$ converge to their optimal values $q^*(s, a)$.

In *SARSA* [10], which is the policy evaluation counterpart of Q-learning, the policy π is known beforehand. SARSA is used to only evaluate the quality $q^\pi(s, a)$ of each state-action pair (s, a) under π. Therefore, in the learning step in SARSA corresponding to (7.1), the term $\max_{a'} q(s', a')$ is replaced with $q^\pi(s', a')$, the expression analogous to (7.5) for SARSA is given below,

$$q(s,a) \leftarrow (1-\eta)q(s,a) + \eta \left\{ r + \gamma q \left(s', \pi(s') \right) \right\}. \tag{7.6}$$

Observe that in (7.6), from the next state s', instead picking the action that maximizes the Q-value, SARSA adheres to the policy π.

In order to incorporate exploration in RL, the agent must follow a stochastic policy. The ϵ-*greedy policy* is such a policy that is used widely. Given any such policy π, the expression shown below yields the conditional probability of picking an action a from a state s,

$$\pi(a \mid s) = \begin{cases} 1-\epsilon, a \leftarrow \operatorname{argmax}_a q(s,a); \\ |\mathbb{A}|^{-1} \epsilon, a \leftarrow \operatorname{random}(\mathbb{A}). \end{cases} \tag{7.7}$$

So the agent picks an action from $\mathbb{A}$, randomly and with a uniform probability of ϵ, and greedily with probability of $1 - \epsilon$. It is always a good idea to lower the parameter ϵ steadily so that as learning progresses, the agent becomes increasingly exploitative. This method is used in [31]. In [32], where driver behavior is modeled using Q-learning, a modified version of the ϵ-greedy method is used, where actions are picked from amongst the scenario-dependent feasible ones only. Curiosity-driven exploration is suggested in [33] as an enhancement to ϵ-greedy search. Here, the agent receives an additional reward whenever its action leads to an infrequently visited environmental state. It has also been applied to train DNNs (discussed later) in other CAV applications involving DRL [34]). The *softmax policy* is another popular method to incorporate randomness. The expression below shows the conditional probability of action a being selected from state s under π,

$$\pi(a \mid s) = \left[\sum_{a'} e^{\tau^{-1} q(s,a')} \right]^{-1} e^{\tau^{-1} q(s,a')}. \tag{7.8}$$

Clearly, the probability of picking an action is proportional to the exponential of its Q-value; thereby biasing the *Softmax* policy toward better actions. The *Boltzmann parameter* τ is steadily lowered so that the policy gets increasingly exploitative as the training progresses.

7.2.2.2 Policy-based RL

Initialized with an arbitrary policy π, RL proceeds in two steps [10]. The first step involves policy evaluation. Its purpose is to learn either Q-values $q^\pi(s, a)$ of state-action pairs (s, a), or the *state values*, $v^\pi(s) = \max_a q^\pi(s, a)$. The latter step implements policy improvement. It uses the learned values to refine the policy π. The two steps are implemented in an iterative manner until the policy cannot be refined any further. An advantage of policy-based learning is that once the policy stabilizes, further training until all Q-values converge is not required. Although seldom applied directly, as discussed later in this section, schemes that extend policy based methods to train DNNs have met with remarkable success in a wide range of CAV problems.

7.2.3 Deep reinforcement learning

Tabular RL is suitable only when $\mathbb{S}$ and $\mathbb{A}$ are finite and have small enough cardinalities to be computationally tractable. In continuous environments, the states and/or actions must be discretized for tabular storage, leading to a drop in performance. A more effective way to circumvent this bottleneck is through parametrization. Linear parametrization has been a popular choice in many applications. Suppose each environmental state s is represented in terms of some $D \times 1$ feature vector $\boldsymbol{\varphi}(s)$, where $\varphi : \mathbb{S} \to \mathcal{R}^D$, the value of state s can be approximated as $v(s) \approx \theta^{\mathrm{T}}\boldsymbol{\varphi}(s)$, where θ is an $D \times 1$ vector of weights. Value-based RL reduces to the problem of estimating θ. Although linear parametrization is not common in CAV applications, it has been used in [35] for driver modeling.

Unlike linear parameters, DNNs can capture nonlinear relationships very well. It is not surprising that most recent CAV applications use DNNs. *Deep Q-networks* (DQNs) use DNNs for Q-learning or SARSA. They are equipped to handle continuous state spaces. However, the action space must be discrete and small enough to be computationally tractable. On the other hand, *deep policy networks* (DPNs), which are policy-based RL methods, can deal with continuous actions. Hereafter, the symbol θ shall be used to represent the set of weights and biases of a DNN.

Figure 7.2 illustrates various DNN arrangements for RL. Figure 7.2. (left) shows a DQN arrangements with separate inputs for the feature vector of state s and the action a, and a single output $q^\theta(s, a)$. Actions can be coded using unary notation (e.g. 0001, 0010, 0100, 1000). The drawback of this arrangements is that it needs to be run multiple times, once for each action a. Figure 7.2 (middle) depicts another DQN arrangements whose sole input is the state s. It provides as outputs, the Q-values $q(s, a)$ for every possible action a. Figure 7.2 (right) illustrates the overall arrangements of a DPN; its output is $\pi^\theta(s)$. In order to reflect their dependence on θ, all quantities are show with superscripts.

7.2.3.1 Deep Q-networks

In DQNs, the target value, $r + \gamma \max_{a'} q^\theta(s', a')$ is identical to that in (7.5) (or (7.6) for policy evaluation). The DNN's parameter θ is updated to minimize the squared error between the learned $q^\theta(s, a)$ and the new target. The corresponding update rule when using gradient descent is expressed in the following manner,

$$\theta \leftarrow \theta - \eta \left(r + \gamma \max_{a'} q^\theta \left(s', a' \right) - q^\theta \left(s, a \right) \right) \nabla_\theta q^\theta \left(s, a \right). \tag{7.9}$$

The *neural fitted Q* algorithm [36] is a straightforward implementation of gradient descent training using the scheme shown in Figure 7.2 (top, right).

Unlike in tabular Q-learning, where each update as in (**7.5**) moves $q^\theta(s, a)$ closer to the target, any increment to θ in a DQN also causes the target value to shift. Such *nonstationary target* behavior is due to the proximity of s' and s in $\mathbb{S}$, the states being temporally separated by only a single time step. This issue can be dealt with readily by training the DQN using target values from an older copy of itself in memory, referred to as the *target network*.

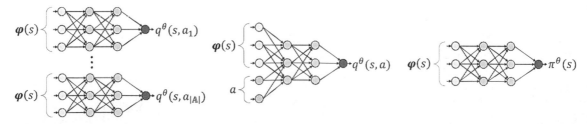

FIGURE 7.2   Deep Neural Networks. Shown are two possible DQN schemes (left, middle) as well as a DPN scheme (right).

Another closely related problem arising when updating θ as per (7.4) after every transition is the correlation of temporal sequences of training samples. This often leads to undesirable oscillatory behavior or even divergence, an effect that can be removed through *experience replay*. During each round of training, as a first step the neural network agent is allowed to interact with the environment while θ is held constant. Observed transition samples $s \xrightarrow{a,r} s'$ are stored in a *replay buffer* $\mathcal{D}$. It must be ensured that a sufficiently large number of samples (from one of more episodes) have been stored before initiating the next step, which involves training the DNN. The samples in $\mathcal{D}$ are shuffled randomly to decorrelate samples, after which any supervised DNN algorithm can be used, possibly using minibatch training. More efficient DNN training algorithms (e.g. ADAM) can be used instead of vanilla gradient descent. After enough training epochs have been carried out, $\mathcal{D}$ is flushed for the next round. The process is repeated until the desired level of performance is achieved, although in many domains it may be carried on indefinitely. Figure 7.3 illustrates the typical arrangement using a replay buffer.

Overestimation of Q-values [Has10] is a problem frequently encountered in stochastic environments that is introduced by the maximization operation. Google DeepMind [13] rectifies this problem by storing an older copy of the primary DNN with parameter set θ as the target DNN. If θ and θ' are the weight parameters of the primary and target DNNs, increments in θ are proportional to $(r + \gamma \max_{a'} q^{\theta'}(s', a') - q^{\theta}(s, a))\nabla_{\theta}q^{\theta}(s, a)$. The target network is updated periodically using Polyak averaging as $\theta' \leftarrow (1 - \tau)\theta' + \tau\theta$ where τ is a training parameter usually set to $\tau = 1$. The target DNN is updated only after the primary DNN has undergone a significant amount of training. The most common DQN architecture uses primary and target DNNs as well as a buffer $\mathcal{D}$. The samples in $\mathcal{D}$ are drawn by running the target network against the environment.

Double DQN [37] eliminate overestimation by using two separate DNNs, say A and B with parameters θ_A and θ_B, which are trained independently of one another. The samples in $\mathcal{D}$ may be drawn using the averaged output $\frac{1}{2}\left(q^{\theta_A} + q^{\theta_B}\right)$. While training the DNNs, a sample is drawn at random from $\mathcal{D}$ without replacement. Updates to θ_A are done in accordance with (7.4), but with the maximization operation carried out using the outputs of DNN B and vice versa. In other words, the gradient direction $\nabla_{\theta_A}q^{\theta}_A(s, a)$ is scaled by a factor $\eta(r + \gamma \max_{a'} q^{\theta}_B(s', a') - q^{\theta}_A(s, a))$. In a parallel manner, maximums of q^{θ}_A are used to update θ_B. During each iteration, double DQN randomly picks either θ_A or θ_B to update. It may be noted that both A and B may be implemented with their own primary and target DNNs, so that the overall architecture incorporates four DNNs with identical structures albeit different weights.

Dueling DQN architectures [38] divide $q^{\theta}(s, a)$ into two terms, the state value $v^{\theta}(s)$, and the state-action *advantage* $A^{\theta}(s, a)$ is the difference between them. Since $q^{\theta}(s, a) = \mathbb{E}_{\pi}[R_t \mid s_t = s, a_t = a]$ and $v^{\theta}(s) = \mathbb{E}_{\pi}[R_t \mid s_t = s]$, the advantage of action a in state s, $A^{\theta}(s, a)$ is the expected gain in the return obtained by picking action a over the policy π_{θ}. The DNN architecture consists of an input layer for the state s, that after a few initial hidden layers, splits into two separate pathways, each of which is a fully connected DNN. Using the symbols θ_V and θ_A for the weight parameters of the pathways. The scalar output of the value pathway is the state's value, $v^{\theta}_V(s)$. The output of the advantage pathway is an $|\mathbb{A}|$ dimensional

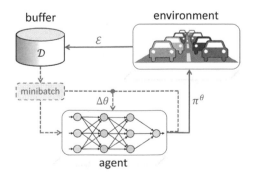

FIGURE 7.3 DRL with Replay Buffer. The pathways pertaining to agent's interaction with the environment (solid blue) and during training (dashed red) are shown.

vector comprising of the advantages $A^\theta_A(s, a)$ of all available actions in $\mathbb{A}$. The Q-value is obtained as

$$q^\theta(s,a) = v^\theta(s) - |\mathbb{A}|^{-1} \sum_{a'} A^\theta(s,a').$$

7.2.3.2 Deep policy networks

Unlike the earlier methods, DPNs [39] do not require the use of Q-values. The agent is usually incorporated as a neural network (see Figure 7.2 (right)). Such a policy network is directly trained to provide the optimal action for each state. DPNs can be used even in complex situations where $\mathbb{S}$ and $\mathbb{A}$ are infinite (continuous states and actions). It uses returns $R(\mathcal{E}) = \sum_t \gamma^t r_t$ of episodes $\mathcal{E}$ as the objective function for maximization. Moreover, strong theoretical convergence guarantees have been established [40].

Policy learning algorithms to train DPNs are based on the *policy gradient theorem* [40]. Consider a random variable x whose distribution is parametrized by θ such that. Let $f(x)$ be an arbitrary function of x, not necessarily differentiable. With a few simple algebraic steps, it can be established that the gradient of the expected value of the function, $\nabla_\theta \mathbb{E}_\theta[f(x)]$ is equal to $\mathbb{E}_\theta[f(x)\nabla_\theta \log p_\theta(x)]$ (the operator $\mathbb{E}_\theta[\bullet] \equiv \mathbb{E}_{x \sim p_\theta}[\bullet]$ is the expected value of its argument when $x \sim p_\theta$). Observe that the derivative of $f(x)$ does not appear in the expression, which is remarkable from the standpoint of reinforcement learning. Let us treat an entire episode $\mathcal{E}$ as an instance of the random variable x and the total return that the agent receives from $\mathcal{E}$ as the function $R(\mathcal{E})$, the summation being carried out over all time instances in $\mathcal{E}$. Since the return function is intrinsic to the external environment, its gradient is inaccessible to the learning algorithm. On the other hand, the policy π_θ is fully parametrized in terms of the DNN weights θ. The next paragraph discusses how the gradient of the expected log-probability of $\mathcal{E}$ can be used in DNN training algorithms.

Using the rules of probability, it can be seen that the joint probability of $\mathcal{E}$ is the product of the probabilities of all transitions $s_t \xrightarrow{a_t} s_{t+1}$ in $\mathcal{E}$, so that $p_\theta(\mathcal{E}) = \prod_t \pi_\theta(a_t \mid s_t)p(s_{t+1} \mid s_t, a_t)$. Furthermore, since the transition probabilities $p(s_{t+1} \mid s_t, a_t)$ are independent of θ, it can be shown that the gradient $\nabla_\theta \log p_\theta(\mathcal{E}) = \sum_t \nabla_\theta \log \pi_\theta(a_t \mid s_t)$. Under these circumstances, the gradient $\nabla_\theta \mathbb{E}_\theta[R(\mathcal{E})]$ ($\mathbb{E}_\theta[\bullet] \equiv \mathbb{E}_{\mathcal{E} \sim \pi_\theta}[\bullet]$) of the expected return can be expressed as $\mathbb{E}_\theta\left[R(\mathcal{E})\sum_t \nabla_\theta \log \pi_\theta(a_t \mid s_t)\right]$. This is the policy gradient theorem. Each gradient term $\nabla_\theta \log \pi_\theta(a_t \mid s_t)$ can be readily computed using backpropagation.

The policy gradient theorem shows that θ can be incremented using stochastic gradient ascent according to the update rule,

$$\theta \leftarrow \theta + \eta \mathbb{E}_\theta\left[R(\mathcal{E})\sum_t \nabla_\theta \log \pi_\theta(a_t \mid s_t)\right]. \tag{7.10}$$

The expectation $\mathbb{E}_\theta[\bullet]$ can be estimated by generating a statistically large number of samples of the form $s_t \xrightarrow{a_t, r_t} s_{t+1}$, from the environment while holding θ fixed, storing them in the buffer $\mathcal{D}$, and then using the sample mean as the variables' expected value. From (7.10), it is seen that gradients of the log probabilities of all action a_t in $\mathcal{E}$ are weighted by the episode's total return $R(\mathcal{E})$. In this manner, episodes with higher returns are given higher weightage. Therefore, it makes intuitive sense that training the DPN produces policies with increasingly higher returns.

It can be noticed that the summation in (7.10) is carried out over a temporal sequence, with $\nabla_\theta \log \pi_\theta(a_t \mid s_t)$ being the term at any given time instance t in this summation. Each term is weighed by the same factor $R(\mathcal{E})$. However, at every time instance t, the return $R(\mathcal{E})$ can be split into two components,

$\sum_{t'=0}^{t-1} \gamma^{t'} r_{t'}$ and $\gamma^t \sum_{t'=t}^{T-1} \gamma^{t'-t} r_{t'}$, which the 'past' and 'future' returns. As the agent applies action a_t only at the instance t, this past history is irrelevant. The REINFORCE algorithm [39] uses only the future component $R_t(\mathcal{E}) = \sum_{t'=t}^{T-1} \gamma^{t'-t} r_{t'}$ of the total return as the weight of $\nabla_\theta \log \pi_\theta(a_t \mid s_t)$,

$$\theta \leftarrow \theta + \eta \mathbb{E}_\theta \left[\sum_t R_t(\mathcal{E}) \nabla_\theta \log \pi_\theta(a_t \mid s_t) \right]. \tag{7.11}$$

Often, the return $R(\mathcal{E})$ is very sensitive to small perturbations in θ. Recent policy gradient methods use *natural gradients* [41] involve pre-multiplying the gradient with the inverse of the Fisher information matrix $\mathbf{F}_\theta$. Increments to θ are in proportion to $\mathbf{F}_\theta^{-1} \nabla_\theta \mathbb{E}_\theta [R(\mathcal{E})]$. Since $\mathbf{F}_\theta$ is analogous to the Hessian matrix in parameter space, DNN training algorithms using the natural gradient can be interpreted as second-order methods, whereas (7.10) and (7.11) are instances of first-order algorithms. *Trust region policy optimization* (TRPO) [42] and *proximal policy optimization* (PPO) [43] are two popular variants of natural gradient-based DNN training, where increments in θ are restricted within a small region where the second-order approximation of $R(\mathcal{E})$ is valid. TRPO uses a constraint to impose this restriction, whereas PPO uses a penalty term for this purpose. Within the CAV domain, PPO has been used in [31, 44], whereas the performances of both TRPO and PPO have been compared in [45]. Yet another significant CAV application reporting the use of PPO is [46].

In order to estimate $\mathbb{E}_\theta$, policy learning uses sample averages of episodes stored in its buffer $\mathcal{D}$. A limiting factor of any DPN algorithm's effectiveness is the high sample variances. For example, unless the variable $R_t(\mathcal{E})$ is centered around the origin, directly implementing (7.11) is likely to yield a significantly high value of the variance, $\text{var}_\theta \left[\sum_t R_t(\mathcal{E}) \nabla_\theta \log \pi_\theta(a_t \mid s_t) \right]$. Fortunately, this issue can be readily alleviated by replacing the gradients' weights $R_t(\mathcal{E})$ with $R_t(\mathcal{E}) - R_B$, where R_B is the *baseline*. It can be shown that this modification, while lowering variance does not introduce any statistical bias in the estimate. Constant baselines have been addressed in [47, 48] whereas action dependent baselines have been considered more recently in [49]. [50] compares several baselines for autonomous driving in urban areas.

7.2.3.3 Deep actor-critic networks

Deep actor-critic network (DACN) architectures take a different approach to reduce variance. There are two DNNs – an *actor* and a *critic*. Both networks in DACN can be trained simultaneously using samples drawn from $\mathcal{D}$. Let θ_A and θ_C be their weight parameters which can be incremented from each sample. Consider any such sample that pertains to time instance t so that the state and action are s_t and a_t. The expected return from this state and action pair, $\mathbb{E}[R_t(\mathcal{E}) \mid s_t, a_t]$ is the output of the critic, so that $q^{\theta_C}(s_t, a_t) = \mathbb{E}_{\theta_C}[R_t(\mathcal{E}) \mid s_t, a_t]$. Since we are dealing with a single time instance, the summation over time in (7.11) can be dropped. The actor's parameter can then be incremented in the following manner where η_A is the actor's step size,

$$\theta_A \leftarrow \theta_A + \eta_A q^{\theta_C}(s_t, a_t) \nabla_{\theta_A} \log \pi_{\theta_A}(a_t \mid s_t). \tag{7.12a}$$

Since the critic's function is to provide estimates the of the return with the existing policy and not towards improving the latter, the target value used to update θ_C parallels that used in SARSA. The following expression shows the critic's update rule,

$$\theta_C \leftarrow \theta_C + \eta_C \left(r_t + q^{\theta_C}(s_{t+1}, a_{t+1}) - q^{\theta_C}(s_t, a_t) \right) \nabla_{\theta_C} q^{\theta_C}(s_t, a_t). \tag{7.12b}$$

The *deep deterministic policy gradient* (DDPG) RL extends DACN to deterministic policies. In many CAV applications, the DRL have to be endowed with the capability to handle spatial images. The initial layers of the underlying DNNs incorporate *convolutional neural networks* (CNNs) for this purpose. Examples of the use of CNN layers in DRL in CAV applications are [51–53]. Processing *temporal* patterns can be accomplished by incorporating one or more recurrent neural network layers. Long Short Term Memory (LSTM) layers are the predominant choice in CAV applications [54]). Autoencoder DNNs have been used in [55].

DDPG has been found to be useful in several other CAV applications, as in [56–62]. In [63], DDPG has been used within a multi-agent framework (discussed later). The A2C approach – DACN that uses the advantage function discussed earlier, has been used in [64] and in [65]. The closely related A3C has been used in [66]. In [67], A3C is applied to maximize the aggregate income of an EV aggregator, which are shared by wind farms. The well-known Shapley value borrowed from game theory, is used to distribute the money in an equitable manner.

7.2.4 Formulating (deep) reinforcement learning for CAV application

In the present context, the environment's states, the set of actions available to the agent, and the reward function are application-specific and the efficacy of the RL algorithm depends, to a large extent, on how accurately they represent the specific CAV application. For instance, autonomous vehicle parking is addressed in [68], where the state is determined from a combination of driver behavior (modeled using Gaussian mixtures) as well as spatial knowledge of the parking vicinity. Further, DRL is used for automated merging of an on-ramp vehicle to the destination lane in [69]. The environment's states are determined from the coordinates, speed, acceleration, size, and heading of three vehicles—the on-ramp vehicle, as well as the ones preceding and following it in the destination lane. The five actions at the agent's disposal are 'acceleration', 'deceleration', 'left', 'right' and 'auto-pilot'. The reward function takes into account the relative position of the merging vehicle and the optimal position in its destination lane. In a similar application [70], the states comprise the position and velocity of the lane-changing vehicle as well as those of the vehicles preceding and following it in its own lane, as well as the adjacent left and right lanes. In another CAV application [29], the state representation incorporates the positions, velocities, and directions of vehicles and pedestrians, as well as the position and sizes of roadblocks. Each action consists of real values of acceleration and steering direction. Reward signals take into account safety, driving direction accuracy and urgency of lane change. Collisions incur high penalty (negative reward). In [71], which considers lane changing within a broader scope, actions fall into three groups: 'throttle', 'brake' and 'steering'. Reward signals are based on number of lane changes needed to get to the destination as well as on collision. In a more elaborate application [72] that involves providing edge computing services to autonomous vehicles, as well as vehicle route planning, the reward signals incorporate service delays and migration costs as well as vehicular routing times.

Later sections in this chapter will explore CAV applications utilizing the DRL techniques. In-depth coverages of CAV related DRL applications can be found in [73, 74]. Surveys of DRL applications for motion planning and driving of autonomous vehicles appear in [75, 76]. For theoretical considerations, the reader is referred to [4, 77].

7.3 DATA ENVIRONMENT IN CAV NETWORKS

Connected and automated vehicular networks offer a rich data environment to utilize for machine learning algorithm development. The section will discuss the basic elements of connectivity in a CAV environment, along with a brief overview of the sensing system in AVs. The US DOT [78] broadly describes the connected vehicle environment as a set of technologies that enable vehicle-to-vehicle (V2V), vehicle-to-infrastructure (V2I), and vehicle-to-everything (V2X) data exchange and communications for applications aiming at improving the safety, mobility, and environmental sustainability of transportation systems.

7.3.1 Benefits

Besides the cellphone-based services (e.g., navigation, infotainments) the sensors linked to the Controller Area Network (CAN) Bus and the Electric Control Unit (ECU) can be used for data sharing and communications. A connected vehicle environment can provide information including time stamp, position (latitude, longitude), heading angle, speed, lateral acceleration, longitudinal acceleration, yaw rate, throttle position, brake status, turn signal status, steering angle, headlight status, wiper status, external temperature, vehicle length, vehicle width, vehicle mass, and bumper height.

Vehicle-to-everything, also known as the V2X technology, connects the elements of a transportation network—vehicles, pedestrians, bicyclists, roadside units, traffic signals, and edge-computing assets. The US DOT describes the V2X technology as an ecosystem of cooperative communications and each new generation of technology should adapt to fit within the ecosystem—interoperability, compatibility with legacy application, and adoption by the IOOs and automotive manufacturers. The vehicle-based sensor system (irrespective of the automation level of the vehicle) cannot ensure 360-degree sensing environment and all possible communications—infrastructure, persons, and other edge computing resources. Thus, it is important to have cooperative ITS enabled by the V2X technologies.

V2X sensors can complement the deficiencies caused by the lack of a full 360-degree vision. Also, we need to find the role of ADAS (Advanced Driver Assistance Systems) regarding complementing the "brain" of the car. V2X environment can accommodate multiple classes of sensors, including Radar, camera, LiDAR, Ultrasonic, V2X wireless sensors, HD/3D maps, precise positioning (GNSS—Global Navigation Satellite Systems positioning, dead reckoning, VIO). Dedicated Short Range Communication (DSRC) is one of the most adopted V2X technologies out there. DSRC uses the 75 MHz band of the 5.9 GHz spectrum and operates based on the IEEE 802.11p standards mostly for the latency-critical V2X applications such as collision avoidance. The more recent Cellular-V2X (C-V2X) technology [79] can take at least four forms of C-V2X: (i) Vehicle-to-Infrastructure, (ii) Vehicle-to-Network, (iii) Vehicle-to-Vehicle (V2V), and Vehicle-to-Person (V2P). (This may include pedestrians, bicyclists, other vulnerable users). In the case of V2V and V2I, generally PC5 Air-Interface is used and V2N uses the LTE Uu Air interface. Latency-sensitive applications (e.g., safety) uses the PC5 interface (communication range 100m or more).

Most existing connected vehicle-based safety and mobility applications follow the SAE J2735 standard message set (see Figures 7.4 and 7.5). Primary message sets include Basic Safety Message (BSM), Signal Phase and Timing (SPaT), Map Data (MAP), Signal Request Message (SRM), Priority Status Message (PSM), and Roadside Alert (RSA). Figure 7.4 provides more details on the message sets—what data are available and being shared. The Basic Safety Message (BSM) has been widely used for safety-critical applications. BSM has two parts: BSM-1, which is broadcasted by the connected vehicles in all cases and the BSM-2, which is only exchanged at specific events—when ABS (Antilock Braking System) is activated. Generally, the range of BSM transmission is about 1000 meters. Since the latency and coverage of CV data vary with the type of applications (safety vs. speed harmonization), the DSRC-based communication is often augmented with the cellular data. Figure 7.5 describes the type and specifications of the data available through the BSM sets.

7.3.2 Data generated by AVs

The data generated by AVs—quality, quantity, and frequency—is mostly dictated by the level of automation as defined by the Society of Automotive Engineers (SAE) [2]. The lower level of automation requires

Signal Phase and Timing (SPat) Message
Message ID: 02
Data exchange rate: 10 Hz (10 times per second)
Intersection ID: Intersection identification number
Lanes Count: Number of movement states (Phases/Stages)
Movement State: Current signal state information
Name of the movement (e.g., Northbound Through and Right Turn), Total number of lanes served by each movement, . Signal status, Current state of Pedestrian phase, . Remaining time of current signal phase. Vehicle count, Pedestrian detection and pedestrian count
Priority: The active priority state data
Preempt: The active preemption state data

Map Data Message (MAP)
Message ID:
Data exchange rate: 1Hz (1 time per second)
Intersection ID: Intersection identification number
RefPoint: The GPS Reference point)
Approaches: Defines an approach with a set of incoming and outgoing lane(s)
Lanes: ID, width, lane attributes, node list (a lane can have multiple nodes), and connection
Nodelist: A sequence of coordinates that creates a path for each lane.

Signal Request Message (SRM)
Message ID: 14
MsgCount: Provides a sequence number for data stream; MsgCount is only updated when message
SignalRequest: Data element with: Intersection ID, Vehicle approach lane (InLane), vehicle egressing lane (OutLane), Vehicle type, Canceling Request
Timeofservice: The time point in future when service is requested to start
Endofservice: The time point in future when the service is requested to end
Transitstatus: Information whether the vehicle is a transit priority class type
VehicleIdent: Additional information on vehicle identification
VehicleVIN: Vehiclename, VIN number, vehicle class
Vehicle Data: The BSM message data blob--BSM part 1

Priority Status Message
Message ID:
Intersection ID: identification number
Number of active priority request
ActiveRequestTable: Information on each active request including:
1. Request number
2. Vehicle ID
3. Vehicle type
4. Inbound Lane

Roadside Alert (RSA)
Example: Accident ahead, EMS in the area, work zone ahead
TypeEvent: ITIS codes iof common events
Priority: Urgency of the message
Position: Event position (Crash), speed and heading (emergency responders)

FIGURE 7.4   Message sets in connected vehicle environment.

BSM (Basic Safety Message) 10Hz, High Availability and Low Latency, Channel 172	
BSM (Part-1) [Mandatory]	**BSM (Part-2) [Optional]**
DSRC_MessageID: What kind of message, <02> for BSM; MsgCount: sequence number incremented with packets	EventFlags: Occurence of an event: Hard Brake, Hazard Lights, Emergency Response Vehicles, Stop Line Violation, and so on.
TemporaryID: Randomly assigned ID and held constant for few minutes to correlate the stream of BSM packets	PathHistory: Vehicle location history: formatted as "Bread Crumbs", the path can be presented as piecewise linear fashion
DSecond: Current time with resolution of 1 millisecond	PathPrediction: Indicates the path a sender expects to travers
Latitude, Longitude: Geographic location with 0.1 micro degree	RTCMPackage: GPS correction data in the RTCM style based on the number of satellites in view
Elevation: Position above or below sea level with 0.1 meter resolution	
PostionalAccuracy: On standard deviation position error along both semi-major and semi-minor axes and the heading of the semi-major	
TransmissionAndSpeed: Vehicle gear (transmission settings) and vehicle speed with 1 cm/second resolution	
Heading: Heading of vehicle motion relative to compass North; Resolution 1/80 degree	
SteeringWheelAngle: Position relative to compass north, resolution 1.5 degree	
AccelerationSet4Way: Longitudinal, Lateral, Vertical acceleration, and Yaw rate: Angular velocity of rotation around a vertical axis (related to stability)	
BrakeSystemStatus: Whether braking is active on any set of wheels; Status of the systems: Traction control, Anti-lock brakes, Stability control, Brake Boost, and Auxiliary Brakes	
VehicleSize: Vehicle length and width with 1 cm resolution	

FIGURE 7.5   Data specification in the Basic Safety Message (BSM).

fewer sensing and actuation needs as described by the dynamic driving tasks (DDTs). Compared to SAE level-2 AV (equipped with features such as cooperative adaptive cruise control, lane keep assist, and parking assistance), a SAE level-5 AV will have at least thirty additional sensors to complete DDT in a safe and efficient manner. The sensing components include (not limited to) ultrasonic, RADAR, LiDAR, standard cameras, long range and stereo cameras, and dead reckoning sensors. Table 7.2 shows the average data generation capability, range, vision radius, and common applications of various sensing systems in Avs [80–82]. According to [83], estimates that an AV is capable of producing about 1.4 terabytes every hour of operations. DRL frameworks can leverage these datasets for training and validation for specific applications (see section YZ).

7.4 DEEP REINFORCEMENT LEARNING APPLICATIONS: CONNECTED VEHICLES

The research area applying DRL techniques to solve problems in connected transportation systems is relatively new and continuously expanding with the progress in the algorithms and data availability. We expect to see extensive applications of the DRL in CV applications in the near future as the nation embraces the CV technology and infrastructure units are built for comprehensive deployment. [84] surveyed DRL applications in general transportation research. In general, transportation researchers have applied RL techniques for signal control [85–90], routing [91–94], dynamic speed control [95–97], and minimizing fuel consumption [98]. Deep-learning-based applications are also used either within the cyberphysical system or smart cities frameworks [73, 99–101]. [54] utilized RL and Transfer Learning (TL) together to generate high-performance LSTM predictors for traffic flow and trajectories. [102] proposed a long-term traffic flow prediction algorithm that uses a graph convolutional policy network based on RL to tackle the challenge of data sparsity.

TABLE 7.2 Properties of different sensing systems in autonomous vehicles

SENSOR CLASS/TYPE	AVERAGE NUMBER OF SENSORS	COMMON TASKS/ ASSISTANCE	RANGE (DISTANCE, IN METERS)	FIELD OF VISION (IN DEGREES)	DATA GENERATED MBITS/S/SENSOR
RADAR (Short, Long, and Medium Range)	4–6	Measuring distance and position of obstacles, motion planning	50–250	18–80	0.1–15
LiDAR	1–5	Measure distance, object detection	150–200	360	20–100
Ultrasonic (Sound waves)	8–16	Measuring distance to obstacles at short range	3–5		< 0.01
Camera	6–12	Detection of lane markings, road signs, traffic lights	3–200	90	500–3500
Vehicle motion, GNSS, Internal Measurements Unit (IMU)	NA	Geolocation, localization, motion planning	NA	NA	< 0.1

7.4.1 Lane changing and assistance

Lateral control of vehicles is a complex decision-making task in general, considering the dynamic traffic environment and interaction with other vehicles on the road [103, 104]. The applications include lane-keeping assistance, lane-changing decision-making, and merging at conflict points (e.g., ramps, interchanges). Initially, the data availability and communications in the connected vehicle environment led to significant research regarding lane selection and assistance algorithms for connected vehicles [105, 106]. The section will explore the DRL applications in three areas: lane-changing, ramp-merging, and lane assistance.

Within the context of DRL, the primary action in a lane-changing process is to decide whether to stay on the existing lane or change the lane (left or right). The decision also depends on the situation—mandatory vs. discretionary lane changing [103]. At a fine-grained view, the action space may also include acceleration, deceleration, and gap-acceptance criteria. The state space is generally built with information about the surrounding traffic—position (ego and neighbors), relative speed, headways, and upstream-downstream conditions (e.g., near signalized intersections, locations with possible end of lanes). The reward functions generally target efficiency (speed, throughput, and delay) and safety (collision avoidance) metrics. DRL techniques are applied for cooperative multi-agent lane-changing [107], merging decision accounting for unconnected vehicles [108], minimizing impact on the flow after merging [109]. [69] applied both DQN and dueling DQN with alternate linear and ReLu layers. Although the dueling DQN architecture contains more hidden layers deeper, the results in [69] indicate that it converges significantly faster than the DQN, which amounts to an overall reduction in computational overheads.

7.4.2 Traffic signal control

The traffic signal control can be formulated as an MDP and can be solved with RL techniques [85–90, 110, 111]. The existing algorithms in the literature vary in dimensions, including state representation, action set, single vs. multi-agent control, and scale of deployment (isolated vs. network of intersections) [73, 84, 112]. Researchers have utilized images to represent discrete traffic state [113], queue length or density [114], and visual configuration [115]. The DRL applications mostly focused on scalability and efficiency. [51] proposed integrated DQN and Recurrent Neural Network (converting network layers to LSTM layers) for signal control optimization in a small *two by two* grid. [116] developed DACN-based algorithm with reward functions accounting for traffic flow and delay. [117] developed a DQN-based algorithm for signal control in partially detected traffic environment. [56] developed cooperative DDPG enabled DQN-based control for grid-like large-scale networks. [64] proposed an advantage-actor-critic DRL-based multi-agent signal control system for a large-scale network with results from a synthetic grid and a real-world network. [52] developed DQN-based algorithm for isolated signalized intersections that involves a dynamic discount factor within the iterative Bellman equation. In a similar effort, Autoencoder-based DRL [55] is developed for signalized isolated intersection control optimization. [115] compared DDPG and value-function-based signal control algorithm for isolated intersection with snapshots (vector of raw pixels) of traffic environment from a traffic simulator. [53] applied graph convolutional neural network to develop CNN-DQN based signal control. [114] proposed a cooperative double Q-learning method within the multi-agent framework for large-scale applications and studied the convergence properties with stochastic traffic demands. In another study, asynchronous DRL to accommodate large-scale optimization [113]. [57] developed twin-delayed DDPG algorithm for the joint policy optimization of signal controls and CAVs. [118] developed cooperative group-based multi-agent learning algorithm that leverages V2I and I2I (RSU and controllers) data-sharing and -coordination capabilities.

7.4.3 Traffic flow optimization

DRL techniques are also applied to traffic flow optimization, including routing, stability control of flows, and congestion pricing problems. The flow optimization in transportation networks is a well-studied problem. Accordingly, the literature is quite rich. We only focuses on the DRL-based applications within the CAV landscape—leverages connectivity or data within the flow optimization framework. Existing studies include applications such as dynamic speed control [119], energy management with optimizing traffic oscillation [120], managing stop-and-go waves (shockwave control) [121], Langrangian control to minimize the effect of congestion bottlenecks [122], driving fast through heterogeneous traffic without unnecessary lane changes [123], and dynamic lane pricing [124].

[125] leveraged a double DQN to develop spatio-temporal DRL for optimizing mobility-on-demand services. The proposed *STRide* framework accounts for the distribution of supply-demands, ride preferences and service-providers' revenue maximization. [126] applied DRL to combine traffic signal control and re-routing of vehicles in a connected environment. [72] developed a multi-agent DRL algorithm to optimize communication resource allocation and routing of CAVs. A two-branch convolution-based deep Q-network is built to couple service migration and mobility optimization (joint rewards) and executed in a distributed manner. [127] integrated combinatorial optimization and DRL techniques for the ride-sourcing problems—balancing waiting time and the optimal request-driver matching. They investigated four DRL algorithms—delayed multi-agent deep Q learning, delayed multi-agent actor-critic, delayed multi-agent Proximal Policy Optimization, and delayed multi-agent actor-critic with experience replay.

Efforts are also made toward traffic flow optimization (routing, speed harmonization, and path planning) with energy and environmental goals. [128] applied twin-delayed deep deterministic policy gradient technique to implement eco-driving with limited connectivity among vehicles and infrastructure assets. [58] proposed a hybrid deep Q-learning and policy gradient method considering longitudinal (acceleration and deceleration) and lateral control (lane-changing) to minimize fuel consumptions. [129] developed a POMDP-based actor-critic DRL algorithm to design optimal speed and power usage profiles-based leveraging the connectivity and mapping information in a CAV environment. [130] built a deep learning-based trajectory-planning algorithm for eco-approach and departure with two components: trajectory feasibility checker and a speed predictor for the next time step. [131] proposed deep reinforcement learning build an eco-driving velocity planner for a plug-in hybrid electric vehicle and compared with adaptive cruise controllers. Other efforts include eco-approach and departure near signalized intersections [132] and eco-driving on freeway sections [133].

7.4.4 Rail and maritime transportation

DRL has some applications in the area of automatic train operation systems—optimal speed curves without manual operations. [59] developed smart train operation algorithms utilizing DDPG and normalized advantage function and evaluated the performance with respect to manual train operations of the Yizhuang Line of the Beijing Subway. [134] optimized communication-based-train control using DQN to minimize profile tracking errors and energy consumption. DRL techniques have also been applied in autonomous ship (water vessel) navigation—path planning and collision avoidance. [135] applied TL and DRL to find steering policies for three classes: mariner, container, and tanker vessels. [136] developed a DQN-based algorithm with reward functions integrating obstacle avoidance, target approaching, speed modification, and attitude correction. [46] applied a DRL-based controller using PPO to solve collision avoidance for autonomous maritime vessels. [137] surveyed the recent advancements—autonomous operations and techniques—relevant to maritime surface ships.

7.4.5 Data communications, computing, and networking

[138] proposed an integrated DRL-based framework to optimize networking, caching, and computing (resource allocations) in a connected vehicle environment. DQN is used to find the optimal resource allocation policy accounting for multiple services. [139] developed a DDPG-based algorithm to address

multi-agent power allocation control in general device-to-device (D2D) communications within the context of connected automated vehicular networks. In [140] a DQN with experience replay is used for mobile edge computing resource allocation in an internet of vehicles. Minibatch training of a DNN has been used in [141] for optimal scheduling operations for communication between mobile intelligent vehicles and a centralized agent that controls IoT gateways. This approach reports introduces batchwise normalization of rewards to eliminate oscillations, thus helping stabilize the convergence of stochastic gradient descent. [142] proposed Neural Network for Data rate and transmission power (NNDP) leveraging DRL to optimize data rate and transmission power in V2V communications. [63] developed a Multi-Agent Deep Deterministic Policy Gradient for dynamic controller assignment in an IoV environment and compared both the cooperative and the non-cooperative behavior of RL agents. [143] leverages DRL technique to solve the edge-computing resource allocation problem. The proposed distributed multi-agent learning scheme aims to minimize vehicular task offloading cost in complex vehicular networks. [144] developed a sequential heterogeneous user-central cluster migration strategy in connected vehicle networks (communication among devices and vehicles) that utilizes model-free DRL architecture. In an application involving vehicular edge computing networks [143], an aggregation algorithm is used to divide delivery vehicles into groups, with an agent assigned to each group. A coordination graph is used for to coordination between agents, which are trained using DDPG.

7.4.6 DRL applications for cybersecurity

[145] proposed a Deep Sanitization Reinforcement Learning algorithm to assure data security (privacy and protecting sensitive information) in connected vehicle networks (CAVs interact with the other devices in the network), focusing on improving the trust in CAVs. [146] applied DQN to improve the quality-of-service (QoS) of connected vehicular networks considering data transfer among vehicles, RSUs, and gateways. The developed DRL focused on energy consumption, latency of the information, and the overall safety of the transportation services. In order to maintain vehicular privacy, [145] proposes 'deep sanitization RL' that incorporates a sanitization step in each DQN training cycle. Multiperiod operations are handled in the same study by including LSTM layers within the DNN agent architecture. [34] developed a DQN-based trust management method, namely the software-defined trust-based VANET architecture for vehicular networks to find the optimal communication link policy and improve data forwarding, link quality, and security of the vehicular network communications. [147] proposed a DRL-based control framework for CAVs acting as a mobile-based station to optimize network coverage near high demand locations (shopping malls, near stadiums, and terminals).

7.5 DEEP REINFORCEMENT LEARNING APPLICATIONS: AUTOMATED DRIVING SYSTEMS

Automated driving system applications—specific to the levels of automation [2] and the allocation of dynamic driving tasks (DDT)—profoundly rely on machine learning-based algorithms. The spur in this research area has been substantially inspired from the advancement in CAV technologies as well as the emergence of computational power to handle *big data*. Principal components of an ADS include mapping and localization, scene representation, motion planning, control, and actuation [2, 148]. DRL has been used in ADS applications, including dynamic path planning (collision avoidance and control optimization), navigation without local mapping (complex intersections, merging, diverging), predicting the intent of vulnerable users (e.g., pedestrians, bicyclists), and lateral control (lane keeping and lane changing) [149, 150]. We limit our scope to the surface AVs only using the existing road networks.

While formulating the DRL model, researchers have used ego-vehicle position (relative to neighbor vehicles and infrastructure assets), speed, lane configuration, sensor-produced 2D aerial view, and traffic environment (geometry and anticipated trajectories) to represent the state [151]. The availability of AV-related data has been a challenge for the training and validation of DRL models. DRLs have leveraged simulation tools (as external environment) such as CARLA [152], *DeepDrive* [153], *Gazebo* [154], Constellation [155], and *flow* [156] to generate training data and scenarios. Reward functions for AV specific applications are generally customized based on the DDT and the DRL framework—model vs. model-free, training, data, and targeted policy. Existing studies have defined reward functions to minimize travel delay, avoid collisions, maximizing stability and comfort while satisfying safety requirements, and risk minimization [84, 149, 150].

7.5.1 Motion planning

The studies focusing on motion planning and control of CAVs are diverse and utilized diverse forms of machine learning algorithms (in addition to the DRL techniques). [157, 158] explored the existing motion planning and control algorithms relevant to CAVs. This section only explores the DRL specific efforts. [29] integrated DQN and expert systems to develop a hybrid guidance system for AVs. A vehicular blockchain technology was applied to ensure the privacy and data security regarding the CAV rule-sharing and building mechanism of the knowledge base for the expert systems [159] compared Monte-Carlo Tree Search and DQN-based techniques for the overtaking (passing) decision-making of AVs. They proposed the *SafeRL* algorithm that considers risk-taking behavior and speeding in the reward function. [160] developed end-to-end ADS utilizing DRL integrated with a sequential latent environment model and validated the model with CARLA simulator. [60] developed DRL-based autonomous braking decision making allowing multi-reward functions within the DDPG framework. DRL methodologies are also applied within the car-following modeling approaches ([161, 162] [163, 164]). [165] proposes a novel Deep Scenes architecture for ADS which learns complex interaction-aware scene representations based on Deep Sets and Graph Convolutional Networks and developed the Graph-Q and DeepScene-Q off-policy reinforcement learning algorithms. [166] utilized DQN for autonomous braking system design and applied the algorithms for scenarios involving AVs encountering pedestrians in an urban environment. Recent efforts involves utilizing both discrete (e.g., DQN) and continuous (e.g., actor-critic DDPG) action set for autonomous driving [61], DQN with filtered experiences [167], DQN in a mixed traffic environment with experience replay [168], identity- and position-based dynamic coordination graph within the DRL framework [169], utilizing planning-feature-based deep behavior decision method [170].

Navigation through intersections—signalized, non-signalized, roundabouts—has been identified as a major challenge within the AV motion planning research area. [62] proposed a DDPG-based algorithm for optimal trajectories through signalized intersection. [171] applied DQN for navigating signalized intersection with limited information about the environment. [172] demonstrated the *zero-shot transfer* of an autonomous driving policy from simulation to the University of Delaware's scaled smart city with adversarial multi-agent reinforcement learning. The DRL-based control policies were experimented in real-world roundabout. Other applications include merging at ramps for AVs [173], overtaking maneuvers [174], highway junction path-planning [175], and moving around the parking lots [176].

7.5.2 Lateral control

Deep learning-focused ADS research became more prolific in recent years [73, 149]. DRL-based algorithms are commonly applied for lateral control—lane changing, lane keeping, and lane assistance—of CAVs. [177] developed a double DQN algorithm for speed and lane-changing decisions of autonomous truck-trailers. [178] proposed DQN-based lane-changing decision algorithm for the AVs which uses Q-function approximator with closed-form greedy policy. [179] demonstrated effectiveness of the DDPG-based DRL (trained using both simulation and real-world data) technique for the lane-following task. [180] proposed collision-free lane-changing decision model with and without speed adjustments with inverse reinforcement learning [181] using DQN. [182] jointly considered high-level lateral and low-level rule-based trajectory decisions within a DQN framework. [183] applied DRL to develop autonomous lane-changing algorithms for dynamic and uncertain traffic environments with partially unobservable system states.

7.5.3 Safety

It is critical to account for safety in the design and development of ADS. The National Highway Transportation Safety Administration (NHTSA) emphasizes trustworthy deployment AVs to build public confidence in large-scale ADS deployment [1]. NHTSA highlighted four aspects regarding Voluntary Safety Self-Assessments (VSSA) of AV testing and deployments: (a) safety considerations of ADSs, (b) communicating and collaborating with the State Department of Transportation (DOT) units, (c) support to self-establish of industry safety norms, and (d) development of public trust, and acceptance through transparent testing and deployment of ADSs. Researchers have developed DRL-based AV modules that inherently integrate the safety aspects into rewards, state, and policy preferences. [184] proposed *SafeDAgger* algorithm for end-to-end autonomous driving with the capability of predicting error between reference policy and ground truth actions. [185] applied DRL for long-term driving strategy accounting for the unpredicted behavior of agents (other vehicles and pedestrians). A Survival-Oriented-Reinforcement-Learning (SORL) was proposed, which can be integrated with the DDPG algorithm. [186] focused on optimal driving performance with collision avoidance integrating DRL and safety-based control. For a comprehensive review, the readers are referred to [149, 187].

7.6 CHALLENGES AND FUTURE DIRECTIONS

The recent efforts to apply DRL techniques to solve problems within the connected and automated transportation domain have revealed several challenges which have yet to be addressed. Commonly experienced obstacles include the lack of training and validation data, the need for heavy computing (e.g., GPU-based) resources, and challenges in the optimization of hyperparameters. Further, the sensitivity of DRL algorithms to hyperparameters leads to the issue of reproducing results and replicating the methodology of the DRL-based solutions. This section provides an overview of the challenges and future directions regarding DRL research specific to the CAV related applications.

7.6.1 Transferability to real-world applications

The lack of ground truth data (*e.g.*, real-world deployment of CAV applications) is a major challenge to the success of DRL algorithms. Most existing studies used simulation-based synthetic data for training and validation [84, 188]. This leads to the issue of transferability of the DRL algorithms from a laboratory setting to real-world applications. Consider the autonomous driving task of avoiding collision with a pedestrian. The developed DRL algorithms in the laboratory setting may not be able to be trained for all possible complex situations one might find in real-world traffic environments. Therefore, the transferability to the real-world deployment warrants rigorous training and testing in a real-world environment with a continuous learning feedback. In addition to the lack of real-world training data, current CAV literature does not offer comprehensive benchmarking data for CAV-specific problems (e.g., signal control, autonomous lane changing, and routing) that can be used to evaluate the performance of advanced DRL algorithms.

The data environment in connected and automated transportation networks is highly stochastic and depends on the sensing capability as well as the overall market share of equipped vehicles. Therefore, the resolution and quantity of available data will vary among transportation networks—both spatially and temporally. Moreover, the DRL algorithm may perform differently because of under- or over-trained agents. For instance, a DRL model which is trained to solve traffic signal optimization problem may not be readily transferrable to similar networks of signalized intersections because of the data environment heterogeneity and non-compatible connectivity. This underscores the need for the DRL models be adaptive to the data environment by design to reflect desired learning rate and quality of solution.

7.6.2 Representation of traffic environment

The transportation system optimization and control problems (e.g., routing, signal control) are traditionally formulated with explicit hard constraints—capacity of lane, speed limit, and movements during a red light. These constraints are enforced by explicit mathematical expressions [189] or simulation parameters [110]. Conversely, most DRL-based algorithms incorporate constraints by introducing penalty functions in the reward structure [84, 112, 188] and this may not guarantee the non-violation of the constraints compared with a mathematical optimization- or micro-simulation-based approach. Further, modeling and integrating multi-modal traffic—pedestrians, bicyclists, e-scooters, wheel-chairs—into an DRL framework is not straightforward and have not been explored widely in the existing literature. Although simulation tools such as CARLA [152] can accommodate some of the features, a scalable multi-agent DRL framework requires significant computational resources and data handling capacity. This is a potential avenue for future research.

7.6.3 Formulating reward functions

Defining and formulating reward functions within a DRL model for CAV applications (e.g., motion planning and lane-changing) has been identified as a major challenge in most studies [84, 188]. One potential reason is the lack of a good understanding of the desired behavior of the autonomous vehicles in mixed traffic consisting of pedestrians, traffic signals, roadside units, and neighboring CAVs. The formulation of an appropriate reward function has typically been aimed at eliciting the optimal policy. Existing studies applied methodologies including reward shaping [190, 191], inverse reinforcement learning [192–194], and intrinsic motivation [195] to address this challenge. A hybrid architecture integrating human (expert demonstration) and CAVs into the learning process can be used to generate suitable reward functions. Moreover, it is critical to formulate reward functions for CAV applications accounting for the trustworthiness of services and the safety perception of the human users. Next, we briefly describe the above-mentioned approaches.

Existing studies have focused on supplementing rewards with an additional component that penalizes undesirable phenomena encountered during the training process, such as incorporating heuristics and penalizing oscillations. This approach, referred to as *reward shaping* [196], has begun to be exploited in CAV applications [180, 190, 191]. An alternate approach is to enable the DRL to infer a suitable reward function using human behavior as the model. This approach, called *inverse reinforcement learning* [181], has been explored in recent CAV research [192, 194, 197, 198]. However, none of them make use of the most recent DNN approaches for inverse RL. For instance, in [35] only linear weights have been considered to form reward signals from state features. Entropy-based approaches [199], which have shown to be very effective, have not been applied to the CAV domain.

Finally, some CAV applications of DRL should be treated within a *multi-objective* framework. In [200] multi-objective optimization has been used to simultaneously maximize coverage and fairness. In this model, a set of autonomous cars as service providers for other users. Cars move in a spatial grid to maximize coverage. However, there is a need for these cars to maintain connectivity between themselves. As the entire spatial grid cannot be covered at any time, a fairness objective is introduced. However, the reward function is obtained merely by the addition of separate terms for fairness and coverage. Combining multiple objectives using linear weights have long been discarded in optimization theory in favor of Pareto optimal approaches [201, 202].

7.6.4 Multi-agent DRL in CAV environment

Several CAV applications involve the use of multiple agents that must learn in coordination with one another. The most straightforward approach would be to treat the joint actions of all agents as a single vector action. Unfortunately, except for simple toy applications, such a method would lead to combinatorial explosion, rendering them useless for large-scale applications in connected and automated transportation networks. Another challenge arises when the reward signals or environment states vary across the agents making the system inherently heterogeneous. Moreover, RL techniques for such situations must adhere to communication limitations between the agents. Multi-agent reinforcement learning is a relatively nascent research topic that lies at the interface between RL and game theory [203]. A recent article [204] provides a broad review of multi-agent DRL.

Of late, there have been several instances of multi-agent DRLs being used in CAV applications. An actor-critic architecture has been used in [63] with multiple actor agents. The DDPG algorithm has been applied in this setting. However, this research incorporates only a single critic. Thus, it does not represent a fully distributed multi-agent framework that a real-world CAV application would necessitate. In a ride-sharing application that also applies DRL within a multi-agent setting, the matching algorithm that is applied to identify pairs of passengers and drivers operates in a centralized manner. An interesting feature of the proposed architecture is that simultaneous cooperation and competition between driver agents have been considered. RL for traffic light control to alleviate congestion in city-wide traffic has been taken up in [65]. However, the shared objective of all agents is to minimize the sum total of all vehicular delays. It can be seen that although multi-agent DRL is being actively investigated in representative CAV applications, the myriad of challenges of true multi-agent scenarios has yet to be taken up.

7.6.5 Partial state observability

Most existing studies focusing on DRL algorithms assume full-state observability in a CAV environment. It is more likely that we will be dealing with a partially observed state in a real-world traffic environment. The lack of a fully observable traffic state may originate in several ways. First, the sensing ability of CAVs may defect under adverse weather conditions or simply due to technological limitations (less-than-perfect perception of the surrounding world). Second, the presence of un-connected vehicles (in mixed traffic) that do not share information with neighboring vehicles and the infrastructure units will not allow a fully observed traffic state. Third, cooperative-driving automation applications may not be able to perceive the decision-making process of all agents (e.g., human drivers not willing to coordinate for energy-optimal speed harmonization). The performance of CAV applications can be suboptimal with partial state observability [205–208]. Within the context of the RL framework, the decision-making problem in CAV applications with a partially observed traffic environment can be formulated as a partially observable Markov decision process (POMDP). DRL techniques have been applied to solve POMDPs—partially observed game screens in Atari [209], Deep Variational Reinforcement Learning for *Mountain Hike* and *flickering Atari* games [210], navigation of UAVs in unknown environments [211], driver inspection and maintenance planning [212]. The CAV application domain needs to expand to address the POMDPs through DRL techniques.

REFERENCES

[1] NHTSA, *"Automated Driving Systems: A Vision for Safety 2.0,"* Washington, DC, United States, 2017. [Online]. Available: https://www.nhtsa.gov/document/automated-driving-systems-20-voluntary-guidance.

[2] SAE J3016, "Taxonomy and definitions for terms related to driving automation systems for on-road motor vehicles," 2021.

[3] SAE Industry Technologies Consortia, "AVSC best practice for describing opertational design domain: Conceptual framework and Lexicon," 2020.

[4] V. François-Lavet, P. Henderson, R. Islam, M. G. Bellemare, and J. Pineau, "An introduction to deep reinforcement learning," *Found. Trends Mach. Learn.*, vol. *11*, no. 3–4, pp. 219–354, 2018, doi: 10.1561/2200000071.

[5] R. Bellman, *Dynamic Programming.* Princeton, 1957. https://press.princeton.edu/books/paperback/9780691146683/dynamic-programming.

[6] R. Bellman, "A Markovian decision process," *J. Math. Mech.*, vol. *6*, no. 5, pp. 679–684, 1957, [Online]. Available: http://www.jstor.org/stable/24900506

[7] R. Howard, *Dynamic Programming and Markov Processes.* Cambridge, MA: MIT Press, 1960.

[8] A. G. Barto, R. S. Sutton, and C. W. Anderson, "Neuronlike adaptive elements that can solve difficult learning control problems," *IEEE Trans. Syst. Man. Cybern.*, vol. *SMC-13*, no. 5, pp. 834–846, 1983, doi: 10.1109/TSMC.1983.6313077.

[9] R. S. Sutton, "Learning to predict by the method of temporal differences," *Mach. Learn.*, vol. *3*, pp. 9–44, 1988, [Online]. Available: https://link.springer.com/content/pdf/10.1007/BF00115009.pdf

[10] R. S. Sutton and A. G. Barto, "Reinforcement learning: An introduction," *UCL,Computer Sci. Dep. Reinf. Learn. Lect.*, p. 1054, 2018, doi: 10.1109/TNN.1998.712192.

[11] C. J. C. H. Watkins, "Learning from delayed rewards," England, 1989. [Online]. Available: http://www.cs.rhul.ac.uk/~chrisw/new_thesis.pdf

[12] G. Tesauro, "TD-Gammon, a self-teaching Backgammon program, achieves master-level play," *Neural Comput.*, vol. *6*, no. 2, pp. 215–219, 1994, doi: 10.1162/neco.1994.6.2.215.

[13] V. Mnih et al., "Human-level control through deep reinforcement learning," *Nature*, vol. *518*, no. 7540, pp. 529–533, 2015, doi: 10.1038/nature14236.

[14] D. Silver et al., "Mastering the game of Go with deep neural networks and tree search," *Nature*, vol. *529*, no. 7587, pp. 484–489, Jan. 2016, doi: 10.1038/nature16961.

[15] D. Silver et al., "Mastering the game of Go without human knowledge," *Nature*, vol. *550*, no. 7676, pp. 354–359, 2017, doi: 10.1038/nature24270.

[16] F. Zeng, C. Wang, and S. S. Ge, "A survey on visual navigation for artificial agents with deep reinforcement learning," *IEEE Access*, vol. *8*, pp. 135426–135442, 2020, doi: 10.1109/ACCESS.2020.3011438.

[17] T. Zhang and H. Mo, "Reinforcement learning for robot research: A comprehensive review and open issues," *Int. J. Adv. Robot. Syst.*, vol. *18*, no. 3, p. 172988142110073, 2021, doi: 10.1177/17298814211007305.

[18] M. Q. Mohammed, K. L. Chung, and C. S. Chyi, "Review of deep reinforcement learning-based object grasping: Techniques, open challenges, and recommendations," *IEEE Access*, vol. *8*, pp. 178450–178481, 2020, doi: 10.1109/ACCESS.2020.3027923.

[19] H. Sun, W. Zhang, R. Yu, and Y. Zhang, "Motion planning for mobile robots—focusing on deep reinforcement learning: A systematic review," *IEEE Access*, vol. *9*, pp. 69061–69081, 2021, doi: 10.1109/ACCESS.2021.3076530.

[20] K. Li, K. Zhang, Z. Zhang, Z. Liu, S. Hua, and J. He, "A UAV Maneuver decision-making algorithm for autonomous airdrop based on deep reinforcement learning," *Sensors*, vol. *21*, no. 6, p. 2233, 2021, doi: 10.3390/s21062233.

[21] T. T. Nguyen and V. J. Reddi, "Deep reinforcement learning for cyber security." 2019, [Online]. Available: https://arxiv.org/abs/1906.05799.

[22] H. Zhu, Y. Cao, W. Wang, T. Jiang, and S. Jin, "Deep reinforcement learning for mobile edge caching: Review, new features, and open issues," *IEEE Netw.*, vol. *32*, no. 6, pp. 50–57, Nov. 2018, doi: 10.1109/MNET.2018.1800109.

[23] N. C. Luong et al., "Applications of deep reinforcement learning in communications and networking: A survey," *IEEE Commun. Surv. Tutorials*, vol. *21*, no. 4, pp. 3133–3174, 2019, doi: 10.1109/COMST.2019.2916583.

[24] K. Mason and S. Grijalva, "A review of reinforcement learning for autonomous building energy management," *Comput. Electr. Eng.*, vol. *78*, pp. 300–312, Sep. 2019, doi: 10.1016/j.compeleceng.2019.07.019.

[25] D. Zhang, X. Han, and C. Deng, "Review on the research and practice of deep learning and reinforcement learning in smart grids," *CSEE J. Power Energy Syst.*, vol. *4*, no. 3, pp. 362–370, Sep. 2018, doi: 10.17775/CSEEJPES.2018.00520.

[26] S. Liu, K. C. See, K. Y. Ngiam, L. A. Celi, X. Sun, and M. Feng, "Reinforcement learning for clinical decision support in critical care: Comprehensive review," *J. Med. Internet Res.*, vol. *22*, no. 7, p. e18477, Jul. 2020, doi: 10.2196/18477.

[27] D. Elavarasan and P. M. D. Vincent, "Crop yield prediction using deep reinforcement learning model for sustainable agrarian applications," *IEEE Access*, vol. *8*, pp. 86886–86901, 2020, doi: 10.1109/ACCESS.2020.2992480.

[28] D. Wang, Q. Zhang, J. Liu, and D. Yao, "A novel QoS-Aware grid routing protocol in the sensing layer of internet of vehicles based on reinforcement learning," *IEEE Access*, vol. *7*, pp. 185730–185739, 2019, doi: 10.1109/ACCESS.2019.2961331.

[29] Y. Fu, C. Li, F. R. Yu, T. H. Luan, and Y. Zhang, "Hybrid autonomous driving guidance strategy combining deep reinforcement learning and expert system," *IEEE Trans. Intell. Transp. Syst.*, vol. *19*, no. 4, pp. 1–14, 2021, doi: 10.1109/TITS.2021.3102432.

[30] I. J. Sledge and J. C. Príncipe, "Trading utility and uncertainty: Applying the value of information to resolve the exploration–exploitation dilemma in reinforcement learning," in *Handbook of Reinforcement Learning and Control. Studies in Systems, Decision and Control*, vol. *325*, Derya Cansever, Frank L. Lewis, Kyriakos G. Vamvoudakis, Yan Wan, Eds. Cham: Springer, 2021, pp. 557–610.

[31] J. Aznar-Poveda and J. Garcia-Haro, "Simultaneous data rate and transmission power adaptation in V2V communications: A deep reinforcement learning approach," *IEEE Access*, vol. *PP*, p. 1, 2021, doi: 10.1109/ACCESS.2021.3109422.

[32] J. Guo, S. Cheng, and Y. Liu, "Merging and diverging impact on mixed traffic of regular and autonomous vehicles," *IEEE Trans. Intell. Transp. Syst.*, vol. *22*, no. 3, pp. 1639–1649, 2021, doi: 10.1109/TITS.2020.2974291.

[33] B. Hu and J. Li, "An edge computing framework for powertrain control system optimization of intelligent and connected vehicles based on curiosity-driven deep reinforcement learning," *IEEE Trans. Ind. Electron.*, vol. *68*, no. 8, pp. 7652–7661, 2021, doi: 10.1109/TIE.2020.3007100.

[34] D. Zhang, F. R. Yu, R. Yang, and L. Zhu, "Software-defined vehicular networks with trust management: A deep reinforcement learning approach," *IEEE Trans. Intell. Transp. Syst.*, pp. 1–15, 2020, doi: 10.1109/tits.2020.3025684.

[35] M. F. Ozkan and Y. Ma, "Modeling driver behavior in car-following interactions with automated and human-driven vehicles and energy efficiency evaluation," *IEEE Access*, vol. *9*, pp. 64696–64707, 2021, doi: 10.1109/ACCESS.2021.3075194.

[36] M. Riedmiller, "Neural fitted Q iteration – first experiences with a data efficient neural reinforcement learning method," in *Machine Learning, ECML 2005*, Springer, 2005, pp. 317–328.

[37] H. van Hasselt, A. Guez, and D. Silver, "Deep reinforcement learning with double Q-learning," *Proc. AAAI Conf. Artif. Intell.*, vol. *30*, no. 1, Mar. 2016, Accessed: October 15, 2021. [Online]. Available: https://ojs.aaai.org/index.php/AAAI/article/view/10295

[38] Z. Wang, T. Schaul, M. Hessel, H. Van Hasselt, M. Lanctot, and N. De Frcitas, "Dueling network architectures for deep reinforcement learning," *33rd International Conference on Machine Learning, ICML 2016*, 2016, vol. *4*, pp. 2939–2947, Accessed: September 26, 2021. [Online]. Available: http://arxiv.org/abs/1511.06581

[39] R. J. Williams, "Simple statistical gradient-following algorithms for connectionist reinforcement learning," *Mach. Learn.*, vol. *8*, no. 3–4, pp. 229–256, 1992, doi: 10.1007/BF00992696.

[40] R. S. Sutton, D. A. McAllester, S. P. Singh, and Y. Mansour, "Policy gradient methods for reinforcement learning with function approximation," *Advances in Neural Information Processing Systems*, 2000, pp. 1057–1063.

[41] J. Peters and S. Schaal, "Reinforcement learning of motor skills with policy gradients," *Neural Networks*, vol. *21*, no. 4, pp. 682–697, 2008, doi: 10.1016/j.neunet.2008.02.003.

[42] J. Schulman, S. Levine, P. Abbeel, M. Jordan, and P. Moritz, "Trust region policy optimization," *Proceedings of the 32nd International Conference on Machine Learning, PMLR*, 2015, vol. *37*, pp. 1889–1897, [Online]. Available: http://proceedings.mlr.press/v37/schulman15.pdf

[43] J. Schulman, F. Wolski, P. Dhariwal, A. Radford, and O. Klimov, "Proximal policy optimization algorithms," 2017, Accessed: September 26, 2021. [Online]. Available: http://arxiv.org/abs/1707.06347

[44] S.-S. Lee and S. Lee, "Resource allocation for vehicular fog computing using reinforcement learning combined with heuristic information," *IEEE Internet Things J.*, vol. *7*, no. 10, pp. 10450–10464, 2020, doi: 10.1109/JIOT.2020.2996213.

[45] Y. Guan, Y. Ren, S. E. Li, Q. Sun, L. Luo, and K. Li, "Centralized cooperation for connected and automated vehicles at intersections by proximal policy optimization," *IEEE Trans. Veh. Technol.*, vol. *69*, no. 11, pp. 12597–12608, 2020, doi: 10.1109/TVT.2020.3026111.

[46] M. El-Dairi and R. J. House, "COLREGs-compliant multiship collision avoidance based on deep reinforcement learning," *IEEE Access*, pp. 165344–165364, 2020, doi: https://doi.org/10.1109/ACCESS.2020.3022600

[47] H. Kimura and S. Kobayashi, "Reinforcement learning for continuous action using stochastic gradient ascent," in *Intelligent Autonomous Systems*, vol. *5*, 1998, pp. 288–295,.

[48] P. Marbach and J. N. Tsitsiklis, "Simulation-based optimization of Markov reward processes," *IEEE Trans. Automat. Contr.*, vol. *46*, no. 2, pp. 191–209, 2001, doi: 10.1109/9.905687.

[49] P. S. Thomas and E. Brunskill, "Policy gradient methods for reinforcement learning with function approximation and action-dependent baselines." 2017, [Online]. Available: https://arxiv.org/abs/1706.06643

[50] J. Chen, S. E. Li, and M. Tomizuka, "Interpretable end-to-end urban autonomous driving with latent deep reinforcement learning," *IEEE Trans. Intell. Transp. Syst.*, pp. 1–11, 2021, doi: 10.1109/TITS.2020.3046646.

[51] S. Shi and F. Chen, "Deep recurrent Q-learning method for area traffic coordination control," *J. Adv. Math. Comput. Sci.*, vol. *27*, no. 3, pp. 1–11, 2018, doi: 10.9734/JAMCS/2018/41281.

[52] C.-H. Wan and M.-C. Hwang, "Value-based deep reinforcement learning for adaptive isolated intersection signal control," *IET Intell. Transp. Syst.*, vol. *12*, no. 9, pp. 1005–1010, 2018, doi: 10.1049/IET-ITS.2018.5170.

[53] T. Nishi, K. Otaki, K. Hayakawa, and T. Yoshimura, "Traffic signal control based on reinforcement learning with graph convolutional neural nets," *IEEE Conf. Intell. Transp. Syst. Proceedings, ITSC*, vol. *2018-November*, pp. 877–883, 2018, doi: 10.1109/ITSC.2018.8569301.

[54] M. Karimzadeh et al., "Reinforcement learning-designed LSTM for trajectory and traffic flow prediction," pp. 1–6, 2021, doi: 10.1109/WCNC49053.2021.9417511.

[55] L. Li, Y. Lv, and F.-Y. Wang, "Traffic signal timing via deep reinforcement learning," *IEEE/CAA J. Autom. Sin.*, vol. *3*, no. 3, pp. 247–254, 2016, doi: 10.1109/JAS.2016.7508798.

[56] T. Tan, F. Bao, Y. Deng, A. Jin, Q. Dai, and J. Wang, "Cooperative deep reinforcement learning for large-scale traffic grid signal control," *IEEE Trans. Cybern.*, vol. *50*, no. 6, pp. 2687–2700, 2020, doi: 10.1109/TCYB.2019.2904742.

[57] H. Zhu, Z. Wang, F. Yang, Y. Zhou, and X. Luo, "Intelligent traffic network control in the era of internet of vehicles," *IEEE Trans. Veh. Technol.*, vol. *9545*, no. c, pp. 1–16, 2021, doi: 10.1109/TVT.2021.3105478.

[58] Q. Guo, O. Angah, Z. Liu, and X. Ban (Jeff), "Hybrid deep reinforcement learning based eco-driving for low-level connected and automated vehicles along signalized corridors," *Transp. Res. Part C Emerg. Technol.*, vol. *124*, p. 102980, 2021, doi: 10.1016/J.TRC.2021.102980.

[59] K. Zhou, S. Song, A. Xue, K. You, and H. Wu, "Smart train operation algorithms based on expert knowledge and reinforcement learning," *IEEE Trans. Syst. Man, Cybern. Syst.*, pp. 1–12, 2020, doi: 10.1109/tsmc.2020.3000073.

[60] Y. Fu, C. Li, F. R. Yu, T. H. Luan, and Y. Zhang, "A decision-making strategy for vehicle autonomous braking in emergency via deep reinforcement learning," *IEEE Trans. Veh. Technol.*, vol. *69*, no. 6, pp. 5876–5888, 2020, doi: 10.1109/TVT.2020.2986005.

[61] A. Sallab, M. Abdou, … E. P.-E., and undefined 2017, "Deep reinforcement learning framework for autonomous driving," *ingentaconnect.com*, 2017, doi: 10.2352/ISSN.2470-1173.2017.19.AVM-023.

[62] M. Zhou, Y. Yu, and X. Qu, "Development of an efficient driving strategy for connected and automated vehicles at signalized intersections: A reinforcement learning approach," *IEEE Trans. Intell. Transp. Syst.*, vol. *21*, no. 1, pp. 433–443, 2020, doi: 10.1109/TITS.2019.2942014.

[63] T. Yuan, W. R. da Neto, C. E. Rothenberg, K. Obraczka, C. Barakat, and T. Turletti, "Dynamic controller assignment in software defined internet of vehicles through multi-agent deep reinforcement learning," *IEEE Trans. Netw. Serv. Manag.*, vol. *18*, no. 1, pp. 585–596, 2021, doi: 10.1109/TNSM.2020.3047765.

[64] T. Chu, J. Wang, L. Codeca, and Z. Li, "Multi-agent deep reinforcement learning for large-scale traffic signal control," *IEEE Trans. Intell. Transp. Syst.*, vol. *21*, no. 3, pp. 1086–1095, Mar. 2020, doi: 10.1109/TITS.2019.2901791.

[65] T. Wang, A. Hussain, L. Zhang, and C. Zhao, "Collaborative edge computing for social internet of vehicles to alleviate traffic congestion," *IEEE Trans. Comput. Soc. Syst.*, pp. 1–13, 2021, doi: 10.1109/TCSS.2021.3074038.

[66] Q. Qi et al., "Scalable parallel task scheduling for autonomous driving using multi-task deep reinforcement learning," *IEEE Trans. Veh. Technol.*, vol. *69*, no. 11, pp. 13861–13874, 2020, doi: 10.1109/TVT.2020.3029864.

[67] Y. Pan, W. Wang, Y. Li, F. Zhang, Y. Sun, and D. Liu, "Research on cooperation between wind farm and electric vehicle aggregator based on A3C algorithm," *IEEE Access*, vol. *9*, pp. 55155–55164, 2021, doi: 10.1109/ACCESS.2021.3071803.

[68] F. Y. Wang, N. N. Zheng, D. Cao, C. M. Martinez, L. Li, and T. Liu, "Parallel driving in CPSS: A unified approach for transport automation and vehicle intelligence," *IEEE/CAA J. Autom. Sin.*, vol. *4*, no. 4, pp. 577–587, 2017, doi: 10.1109/JAS.2017.7510598.

[69] O. Nassef, L. Sequeira, E. Salam, and T. Mahmoodi, "Building a lane merge coordination for connected vehicles using deep reinforcement learning," *IEEE Internet Things J.*, vol. *8*, no. 4, pp. 2540–2557, 2021, doi: 10.1109/JIOT.2020.3017931.

[70] J. Liu, W. Zhao, and C. Xu, "An efficient on-ramp merging strategy for connected and automated vehicles in multi-lane traffic," *IEEE Trans. Intell. Transp. Syst.*, pp. 1–12, 2021, doi: 10.1109/TITS.2020.3046643.

[71] Y. Fu, C. Li, F. R. Yu, T. H. Luan, and Y. Zhang, "An autonomous lane-changing system with knowledge accumulation and transfer assisted by vehicular blockchain," *IEEE Internet Things J.*, vol. *7*, no. 11, pp. 11123–11136, Nov. 2020, doi: 10.1109/JIOT.2020.2994975.

[72] Q. Yuan, J. Li, H. Zhou, T. Lin, G. Luo, and X. Shen, "A joint service migration and mobility optimization approach for vehicular edge computing," *IEEE Trans. Veh. Technol.*, vol. *69*, no. 8, pp. 9041–9052, 2020, doi: 10.1109/TVT.2020.2999617.

[73] A. Haydari and Y. Yilmaz, "Deep reinforcement learning for intelligent transportation systems: A survey," *IEEE Trans. Intell. Transp. Syst.*, pp. 1–22, 2020, doi: 10.1109/TITS.2020.3008612.

[74] N. Parvez Farazi, B. Zou, T. Ahamed, and L. Barua, "Deep reinforcement learning in transportation research: A review," *Transp. Res. Interdiscip. Perspect.*, vol. *11*, p. 100425, 2021, doi: 10.1016/J.TRIP.2021.100425.

[75] S. Aradi, "Survey of deep reinforcement learning for motion planning of autonomous vehicles," *IEEE Trans. Intell. Transp. Syst.*, pp. 1–20, 2020, doi: 10.1109/TITS.2020.3024655.

[76] B. R. Kiran et al., "Deep reinforcement learning for autonomous driving: A survey," *IEEE Trans. Intell. Transp. Syst.*, pp. 1–18, 2021, doi: 10.1109/TITS.2021.3054625.

[77] K. Arulkumaran, M. P. Deisenroth, M. Brundage, and A. A. Bharath, "Deep reinforcement learning: A brief survey," *IEEE Signal Process. Mag.*, vol. *34*, no. 6, pp. 26–38, Nov. 2017, doi: 10.1109/MSP.2017.2743240.

[78] US Department of Transportation, "Intelligent Transportation Systems - Connected Vehicle Benefits," 2020. Accessed: October 08, 2021. [Online]. Available: https://www.its.dot.gov/cv_basics/cv_basics_what.htm

[79] I. Qualcomm Technologies, "C-V2X Congestion Control Study (80-PE732-74 Rev. AA)," 2020.

[80] J. Vargas, S. Alsweiss, O. Toker, R. Razdan, and J. Santos, "An overview of autonomous vehicles sensors and their vulnerability to weather conditions," *Sensors*, vol. *21*, no. 16, pp. 1–22, 2021, doi: 10.3390/s21165397.

[81] D. J. Yeong, G. Velasco-Hernandez, J. Barry, and J. Walsh, "Sensor and sensor fusion technology in autonomous vehicles: A review," *Sensors*, vol. *21*, no. 6, pp. 1–37, 2021, doi: 10.3390/s21062140.

[82] S. Campbell et al., "Sensor technology in autonomous vehicles: A review," *29th Irish Signals Syst. Conf. ISSC 2018*, pp. 1–4, 2018, doi: 10.1109/ISSC.2018.8585340.

[83] S. Heinrich and L. Motors, "Flash memory in the emerging age of autonomy," in *Flash Memory Summit*, 2017, pp. 1–10, [Online]. Available: https://www.flashmemorysummit.com/English/Collaterals/Proceedings/2017/20170808_FT12_Heinrich.pdf

[84] N. Parvez Farazi, B. Zou, T. Ahamed, and L. Barua, "Deep reinforcement learning in transportation research: A review," *Transp. Res. Interdiscip. Perspect.*, vol. *11*, no. March, p. 100425, 2021, doi: 10.1016/j.trip.2021.100425.

[85] Y. Wu, H. Chen, and F. Zhu, "DCL-AIM: Decentralized coordination learning of autonomous intersection management for connected and automated vehicles," *Transp. Res. Part C Emerg. Technol..*, vol. *103*, no. November 2018, pp. 246–260, 2019, doi: 10.1016/j.trc.2019.04.012.

[86] C. Cai, C. K. Wong, and B. G. Heydecker, "Adaptive traffic signal control using approximate dynamic programming," *Transp. Res. Part C Emerg. Technol.*, vol. *17*, no. 5, pp. 456–474, Oct. 2009, doi: 10.1016/j.trc.2009.04.005.

[87] D. Mguni, J. Jennings, S. V. Macua, E. Sison, S. Ceppi, and E. M. de Cote, "Coordinating the crowd: Inducing desirable equilibria in non-cooperative systems," no. Id, 2019, [Online]. Available: http://arxiv.org/abs/1901.10923

[88] M. Abdoos, N. Mozayani, and A. L. C. Bazzan, "Traffic light control in non-stationary environments based on multi agent Q-learning," *Intell. Transp. Syst. (ITSC), 2011 14th Int. IEEE Conf.*, pp. 1580–1585, 2011.

[89] L. Kuyer, S. Whiteson, B. Bakker, and N. Vlassis, "Multiagent reinforcement learning for urban traffic control using coordination graphs," in *Machine Learning and Knowledge Discovery in Databases*, vol. *5211*, W. Daelemans, B. Goethals, and K. Morik, Eds. Springer Berlin/Heidelberg, 2008, pp. 656–671.

[90] S. El-Tantawy, B. Abdulhai, and H. Abdelgawad, "Design of reinforcement learning parameters for seamless application of adaptive traffic signal control," *J. Intell. Transp. Syst.*, vol. *18*, no. 3, pp. 227–245, 2013.

[91] A. L. C. Bazzan and R. Grunitzki, "A multiagent reinforcement learning approach to en-route trip building," *Proc. Int. Jt. Conf. Neural Networks*, vol. *2016-Octob*, pp. 5288–5295, 2016, doi: 10.1109/IJCNN.2016.7727899.

[92] J. J. Q. Yu, W. Yu, and J. Gu, "Online vehicle routing with neural combinatorial optimization and deep reinforcement learning," *IEEE Trans. Intell. Transp. Syst.*, vol. *20*, no. 10, pp. 3806–3817, 2019, doi: 10.1109/TITS.2019.2909109.

[93] K. Zhang, F. He, Z. Zhang, X. Lin, and M. Li, "Multi-vehicle routing problems with soft time windows: A multi-agent reinforcement learning approach," *Transp. Res. Part C Emerg. Technol.*, vol. *121*, p. 102861, Dec. 2020, doi: 10.1016/J.TRC.2020.102861.

[94] I. Bello, H. Pham, Q. V. Le, M. Norouzi, and S. Bengio, "Neural combinatorial optimization with reinforcement learning," *5th Int. Conf. Learn. Represent. ICLR 2017 - Work. Track Proc.*, 2019.

[95] F. Zhu and S. V. Ukkusuri, "Accounting for dynamic speed limit control in a stochastic traffic environment: A reinforcement learning approach," *Transp. Res. Part C Emerg. Technol.*, vol. *41*, pp. 30–47, 2014, doi: 10.1016/j.trc.2014.01.014.

[96] Y. Zhang, P. Sun, Y. Yin, L. Lin, and X. Wang, "Human-like autonomous vehicle speed control by deep reinforcement learning with double Q-learning," *IEEE Intell. Veh. Symp. Proc.*, vol. *2018-June*, pp. 1251–1256, 2018, doi: 10.1109/IVS.2018.8500630.

[97] C. Lu, J. Huang, L. Deng, and J. Gong, "Coordinated ramp metering with equity consideration using reinforcement learning," *J. Transp. Eng. Part A Syst.*, vol. *143*, no. 7, p. 04017028, 2017, doi: 10.1061/JTEPBS.0000036.

[98] S. M. A. B. Al Islam, H. M. A. Aziz, H. Wang, and S. E. Young, "Minimizing energy consumption from connected signalized intersections by reinforcement learning," 2018.

[99] X. Liu, H. Xu, W. Liao, and W. Yu, "Reinforcement learning for cyber-physical systems," *Proc. - IEEE Int. Conf. Ind. Internet Cloud, ICII 2019*, pp. 318–327, 2019, doi: 10.1109/ICII.2019.00063.

[100] Z. WeiHua, G. Vikash, and L. Zhenhui, "Recent advances in reinforcement learning for traffic signal control," *ACM SIGKDD Explor. Newsl.*, vol. *22*, no. 2, pp. 12–18, 2021, doi: 10.1145/3447556.3447565.

[101] Y. Wang, D. Zhang, Y. Liu, B. Dai, and L. H. Lee, "Enhancing transportation systems via deep learning: A survey," *Transp. Res. Part C Emerg. Technol.*, vol. *99*, pp. 144–163, 2019, doi: 10.1016/J.TRC.2018.12.004.

[102] H. Peng et al., "Dynamic graph convolutional network for long-term traffic flow prediction with reinforcement learning," *Inf. Sci. (Ny).*, vol. *578*, pp. 401–416, 2021, doi: 10.1016/J.INS.2021.07.007.

[103] T. Toledo, C. F. Choudhury, and M. E. Ben-Akiva, "Lane-changing model with explicit target lane choice," *Transp. Res. Rec. J. Transp. Res. Board*, vol. *1934*, no. 1, pp. 157–165, 2005, doi: 10.1177/0361198105193400117.

[104] M. Ben-Akiva, C. Choudhury, and T. Toledo, "Integrated lane-changing models," *Transp. Simul. Beyond Tradit. Approaches*, pp. 61–74, 2019, doi: 10.1201/9780429093258-4.

[105] F. Aubeck, T. Oetermann, G. Birmes, and S. Pischinger, "Lane change driver assistance system for online operation optimization of connected vehicles," *2019 IEEE Intell. Transp. Syst. Conf. ITSC 2019*, pp. 2887–2894, 2019, doi: 10.1109/ITSC.2019.8917535.

[106] D. Tian, G. Wu, P. Hao, K. Boriboonsomsin, and M. J. Barth, "Connected vehicle-based lane selection assistance application," *IEEE Trans. Intell. Transp. Syst.*, vol. *20*, no. 7, pp. 2630–2643, 2019, doi: 10.1109/TITS.2018.2870147.

[107] C. Chen, J. Qian, H. Yao, J. Luo, H. Zhang, and W. Liu, "Towards comprehensive maneuver decisions for lane change using reinforcement learning," 2018.

[108] O. Nassef, L. Sequeira, E. Salam, and T. Mahmoodi, "Deep reinforcement learning in lane merge coordination for connected vehicles," in *IEEE International Symposium on Personal, Indoor and Mobile Radio Communications, PIMRC*, 2020, vol. 2020-Augus, doi: 10.1109/PIMRC48278.2020.9217273.

[109] I. Nishitani, H. Yang, R. Guo, S. Keshavamurthy, and K. Oguchi, "Deep merging: Vehicle merging controller based on deep reinforcement learning with embedding network," *Proc. - IEEE Int. Conf. Robot. Autom.*, pp. 216–221, 2020, doi: 10.1109/ICRA40945.2020.9197559.

[110] F. Zhu, H. M. A. Aziz, X. Qian, and S. V. Ukkusuri, "A junction-tree based learning algorithm to optimize network wide traffic control: A coordinated multi-agent framework," *Transp. Res. Part C Emerg. Technol.*, vol. *58*, 2015, doi: 10.1016/j.trc.2014.12.009.

[111] H. M. A. Aziz, F. Zhu, and S. V. Ukkusuri, "Learning-based traffic signal control algorithms with neighborhood information sharing: An application for sustainable mobility," *J. Intell. Transp. Syst. Technol. Planning, Oper.*, vol. *22*, no. 1, pp. 40–52, 2018, doi: 10.1080/15472450.2017.1387546.

[112] H. Wei, G. Zheng, V. Gayah, and Z. Li, "Recent advances in reinforcement learning for traffic signal control," *ACM SIGKDD Explor. Newsl.*, vol. *22*, no. 2, pp. 12–18, 2021, doi: 10.1145/3447556.3447565.

[113] W. Genders and S. Razavi, "Asynchronous n-step Q-learning adaptive traffic signal control," *J. Intell. Transp. Syst. Technol. Planning, Oper.*, vol. *23*, no. 4, pp. 319–331, 2019, doi: 10.1080/15472450.2018.1491003.

[114] X. Wang, X. Ke, Z. Qiao, and X. Chai, "Large-scale traffic signal control using a novel multiagent reinforcement learning," *IEEE Trans. Cybern.*, vol. *51*, no. 1, pp. 174–187, 2021, doi: 10.1109/TCYB.2020.3015811.

[115] S. S. Mousavi, M. Schukat, and E. Howley, "Traffic light control using deep policy-gradient and value-function-based reinforcement learning," *IET Intell. Transp. Syst.*, vol. *11*, no. 7, pp. 417–423, Sep. 2017, doi: 10.1049/IET-ITS.2017.0153.

[116] M. Coskun, A. Baggag, and S. Chawla, "Deep reinforcement learning for traffic light optimization," *IEEE Int. Conf. Data Min. Work. ICDMW*, vol. *2018-November*, pp. 564–571, Feb. 2019, doi: 10.1109/ICDMW.2018.00088.

[117] R. Zhang, A. Ishikawa, W. Wang, B. Striner, and O. K. Tonguz, "Using reinforcement learning with partial vehicle detection for intelligent traffic signal control," *IEEE Trans. Intell. Transp. Syst.*, vol. *22*, no. 1, pp. 404–415, Jan. 2021, doi: 10.1109/TITS.2019.2958859.

[118] T. Wang, J. Cao, and A. Hussain, "Adaptive traffic signal control for large-scale scenario with cooperative group-based multi-agent reinforcement learning," *Transp. Res. Part C Emerg. Technol.*, vol. *125*, no. February, p. 103046, 2021, doi: 10.1016/j.trc.2021.103046.

[119] Y. Wu, H. Tan, L. Qin, and B. Ran, "Differential variable speed limits control for freeway recurrent bottlenecks via deep actor-critic algorithm," *Transp. Res. Part C Emerg. Technol.*, vol. *117*, 2020, doi: 10.1016/J.TRC.2020.102649.

[120] X. Qu, Y. Yu, M. Zhou, C. T. Lin, and X. Wang, "Jointly dampening traffic oscillations and improving energy consumption with electric, connected and automated vehicles: A reinforcement learning based approach," *Appl. Energy*, vol. *257*, 2020, doi: 10.1016/J.APENERGY.2019.114030.

[121] A. R. Kreidieh, C. Wu, and A. M. Bayen, "Dissipating stop-and-go waves in closed and open networks via deep reinforcement learning," *IEEE Conf. Intell. Transp. Syst. Proceedings, ITSC*, vol. *2018*-November, pp. 1475–1480, Dec. 2018, doi: 10.1109/ITSC.2018.8569485.

[122] E. Vinitsky, K. Parvate, A. Kreidieh, C. Wu, and A. Bayen, "Lagrangian control through Deep-RL: Applications to bottleneck decongestion," *IEEE Conf. Intell. Transp. Syst. Proceedings, ITSC*, vol. *2018-November*, pp. 759–765, 2018, doi: 10.1109/ITSC.2018.8569615.

[123] Z. Bai, W. Shangguan, B. Cai, and L. Chai, "Deep reinforcement learning based high-level driving behavior decision-making model in heterogeneous traffic," *Chinese Control Conf. CCC*, vol. *2019-July*, pp. 8600–8605, 2019, doi: 10.23919/CHICC.2019.8866005.

[124] V. Pandey, E. Wang, and S. D. Boyles, "Deep reinforcement learning algorithm for dynamic pricing of express lanes with multiple access locations," *Transp. Res. Part C Emerg. Technol.*, vol. *119*, no. August, p. 102715, 2020, doi: 10.1016/j.trc.2020.102715.

[125] S. He and K. G. Shin, "Spatio-temporal capsule-based reinforcement learning for mobility-on-demand coordination," *IEEE Trans. Knowl. Data Eng.*, vol. *4347*, no. c, pp. 1–1, 2020, doi: 10.1109/tkde.2020.2992565.

[126] A. Mushtaq, I. U. Haq, M. U. Imtiaz, A. Khan, and O. Shafiq, "Traffic flow management of autonomous vehicles using deep reinforcement learning and smart rerouting," *IEEE Access*, vol. *9*, pp. 51005–51019, 2021, doi: 10.1109/ACCESS.2021.3063463.

[127] J. Ke, F. Xiao, H. Yang, and J. Ye, "Learning to delay in ride-sourcing systems: A multi-agent deep reinforcement learning framework," *IEEE Trans. Knowl. Data Eng.*, vol. *4347*, no. 5, pp. 1–1, 2020, doi: 10.1109/tkde.2020.3006084.

[128] M. Wegener, L. Koch, M. Eisenbarth, and J. Andert, "Automated eco-driving in urban scenarios using deep reinforcement learning," *Transp. Res. Part C Emerg. Technol.*, vol. *126*, no. January, p. 102967, 2021, doi: 10.1016/j.trc.2021.102967.

[129] Z. Zhu, S. Gupta, A. Gupta, and M. Canova, "A deep reinforcement learning framework for eco-driving in connected and automated hybrid electric vehicles," pp. 1–12, 2021, [Online]. Available: http://arxiv.org/abs/2101.05372

[130] G. Wu, F. Ye, P. Hao, D. Esaid, K. Boriboonsomsin, and M. J. Barth, "Deep learning-based eco-driving system for battery electric vehicles publication date data availability," 2019. doi: 10.7922/G2NP22N6.

[131] A. Pozzi, S. Bae, Y. Choi, F. Borrelli, D. M. Raimondo, and S. Moura, "Ecological velocity planning through signalized intersections: A deep reinforcement learning approach," *Proc. IEEE Conf. Decis. Control*, vol. *2020-December*, pp. 245–252, 2020, doi: 10.1109/CDC42340.2020.9304005.

[132] S. R. Mousa, S. Ishak, R. M. Mousa, J. Codjoe, and M. Elhenawy, "Deep reinforcement learning agent with varying actions strategy for solving the eco-approach and departure problem at signalized intersections," *Transp. Res. Rec.*, vol. *2674*, no. 8, pp. 119–131, 2020, doi: 10.1177/0361198120931848.

[133] Y. Jiang, "Vision-based eco-oriented driving strategies for freeway scenarios using deep reinforcement learning," University of California, Riverside, 2020.

[134] L. Zhu, Y. He, F. R. Yu, B. Ning, T. Tang, and N. Zhao, "Communication-based train control system performance optimization using deep reinforcement learning," *IEEE Trans. Veh. Technol.*, vol. *66*, no. 12, pp. 10705–10717, 2017, doi: 10.1109/TVT.2017.2724060.

[135] A. B. Martinsen and A. M. Lekkas, "Curved path following with deep reinforcement learning: Results from three vessel models," *Ocean. 2018 MTS/IEEE Charleston, Ocean 2018*, 2019, doi: 10.1109/OCEANS.2018.8604829.

[136] Y. Cheng and W. Zhang, "Concise deep reinforcement learning obstacle avoidance for underactuated unmanned marine vessels," *Neurocomputing*, vol. *272*, pp. 63–73, 2018, doi: 10.1016/j.neucom.2017.06.066.

[137] L. Wang, Q. Wu, J. Liu, S. Li, and R. R. Negenborn, "State-of-the-art research on motion control of maritime autonomous surface ships," *J. Mar. Sci. Eng.*, vol. *7*, no. 12, 2019, doi: 10.3390/JMSE7120438.

[138] Y. He, N. Zhao, and H. Yin, "Integrated networking, caching, and computing for connected vehicles: A deep reinforcement learning approach," *IEEE Trans. Veh. Technol.*, vol. *67*, no. 1, pp. 44–55, 2018, doi: 10.1109/TVT.2017.2760281.

[139] K. K. Nguyen, T. Q. Duong, N. A. Vien, N. A. Le-Khac, and L. D. Nguyen, "Distributed deep deterministic policy gradient for power allocation control in D2D-based V2V communications," *IEEE Access*, vol. *7*, pp. 164533–164543, 2019, doi: 10.1109/ACCESS.2019.2952411.

[140] G. Wang and F. Xu, "Regional intelligent resource allocation in mobile edge computing based vehicular network," *IEEE Access*, vol. *8*, pp. 7173–7182, 2020, doi: 10.1109/ACCESS.2020.2964018.

[141] R. F. Atallah, C. M. Assi, and M. J. Khabbaz, "Scheduling the operation of a connected vehicular network using deep reinforcement learning," *IEEE Trans. Intell. Transp. Syst.*, vol. *20*, no. 5, pp. 1669–1682, 2019, doi: 10.1109/TITS.2018.2832219.

[142] J. Aznar-Poveda, A.-J. Garcia-Sanchez, E. Egea-Lopez, and J. Garcia-Haro, "Simultaneous data rate and transmission power adaptation in V2V communications: A deep reinforcement learning approach," *IEEE Access*, vol. *PP*, pp. 1–1, 2021, doi: 10.1109/access.2021.3109422.

[143] K. Zhang, J. Cao, and Y. Zhang, "Adaptive digital twin and multi-agent deep reinforcement learning for vehicular edge computing and networks," *IEEE Trans. Ind. Informatics*, vol. *3203*, no. c, pp. 1–1, 2021, doi: 10.1109/tii.2021.3088407.

[144] Y. Lin, Z. Zhang, Y. Huang, J. Li, F. Shu, and L. Hanzo, "Heterogeneous user-centric cluster migration improves the connectivity-handover trade-off in vehicular networks," *IEEE Trans. Veh. Technol.*, vol. *69*, no. 12, pp. 16027–16043, 2020, doi: 10.1109/TVT.2020.3041521.

[145] U. Ahmed, J. C.-W. Lin, and G. Srivastava, "Privacy-preserving deep reinforcement learning in vehicle ad hoc networks," *IEEE Consum. Electron. Mag.*, vol. *2248*, no. c, pp. 1–1, 2021, doi: 10.1109/mce.2021.3088408.

[146] R. F. Atallah, C. M. Assi, and M. J. Khabbaz, "Scheduling the operation of a connected vehicular network using deep reinforcement learning," *IEEE Trans. Intell. Transp. Syst.*, vol. *20*, no. 5, pp. 1669–1682, 2019.

[147] Z. Chen, C. H. Liu, and R. Wang, "Learning to navigate connected autonomous cars for long-term communication coverage," *IT Prof.*, vol. *20*, no. 6, pp. 46–53, 2018, doi: 10.1109/MITP.2018.2876923.

[148] L. Claussmann, M. Revilloud, D. Gruyer, and S. Glaser, "A review of motion planning for highway autonomous driving," *IEEE Trans. Intell. Transp. Syst.*, vol. *21*, no. 5, pp. 1826–1848, 2020, doi: 10.1109/TITS.2019.2913998.

[149] B. R. Kiran et al., "Deep reinforcement learning for autonomous driving: A survey," *IEEE Trans. Intell. Transp. Syst.*, pp. 1–18, 2021, doi: 10.1109/TITS.2021.3054625.

[150] V. Talpaert et al., "Exploring applications of deep reinforcement learning for real-world autonomous driving systems," *VISIGRAPP 2019 - Proc. 14th Int. Jt. Conf. Comput. Vision, Imaging Comput. Graph. Theory Appl.*, vol. *5*, pp. 564–572, 2019, doi: 10.5220/0007520305640572.

[151] E. Leurent, Y. Blanco, D. Emov, and O.-A. Maillard, "A survey of state-action representations for autonomous driving," 2018, [Online]. Available: https://hal.archives-ouvertes.fr/hal-01908175

[152] A. Dosovitskiy, G. Ros, F. Codevilla, A. Lopez, and V. Koltun, "CARLA: An open urban driving simulator," in *1st Conference on Robot Learning (CoRL 2017)*, 2017, no. CoRL, pp. 1–16, [Online]. Available: http://arxiv.org/abs/1711.03938

[153] C. Quiter and M. Ernst, "Deepdrive/Deepdrive: 2.0," 2018. https://deepdrive.voyage.auto/.

[154] N. Koenig and A. Howard, "Design and use paradigms for Gazebo, an open-source multi-robot simulator," *2004 IEEE/RSJ Int. Conf. Intell. Robot. Syst.*, vol. *3*, pp. 2149–2154, 2004, doi: 10.1109/iros.2004.1389727.

[155] NVIDIA, "NVIDIA DRIVE Constellation," 2020. https://developer.nvidia.com/drive/drive-constellation.

[156] C. Wu, A. R. Kreidieh, K. Parvate, E. Vinitsky, and A. M. Bayen, "Flow: A modular learning framework for mixed autonomy traffic," *IEEE Trans. Robot.*, pp. 1–17, 2021, doi: 10.1109/TRO.2021.3087314.

[157] B. Paden, M. Čáp, S. Z. Yong, D. Yershov, and E. Frazzoli, "A survey of motion planning and control techniques for self-driving urban vehicles," *IEEE Trans. Intell. Veh.*, vol. *1*, no. 1, pp. 33–55, 2016, doi: 10.1109/TIV.2016.2578706.

[158] L. Claussmann, M. Revilloud, D. Gruyer, and S. Glaser, "A review of motion planning for highway autonomous driving," *IEEE Trans. Intell. Transp. Syst.*, vol. *21*, no. 5, pp. 1826–1848, May 2020, doi: 10.1109/TITS.2019.2913998.

[159] S. Mo, X. Pei, and C. Wu, "Safe reinforcement learning for autonomous vehicle using Monte Carlo Tree search," *IEEE Trans. Intell. Transp. Syst.*, pp. 1–8, 2021, doi: 10.1109/TITS.2021.3061627.

[160] J. Chen, S. E. Li, and M. Tomizuka, "Interpretable end-to-end urban autonomous driving with latent deep reinforcement learning," *IEEE Trans. Intell. Transp. Syst.*, pp. 1–11, 2021, doi: 10.1109/TITS.2020.3046646.

[161] M. Zhu, X. Wang, and Y. Wang, "Human-like autonomous car-following model with deep reinforcement learning," *Transp. Res. Part C Emerg. Technol.*, vol. *97*, pp. 348–368, Dec. 2018, doi: 10.1016/j.trc.2018.10.024.

[162] G. Bacchiani, D. Molinar, and M. Patander, "Microscopic traffic simulation by cooperative multi-agent deep reinforcement learning," *Proc. Int. Jt. Conf. Auton. Agents Multiagent Syst. AAMAS*, vol. *3*, pp. 1547–1555, 2019.

[163] Y. Ye, X. Zhang, and J. Sun, "Automated vehicle's behavior decision making using deep reinforcement learning and high-fidelity simulation environment," *Transp. Res. Part C Emerg. Technol.*, vol. *107*, pp. 155–170, Oct. 2019, doi: 10.1016/J.TRC.2019.08.011.

[164] A. Keselman, S. Ten, A. Ghazali, and M. Jubeh, "Reinforcement learning with A* and a deep heuristic," 2018, Accessed: September 26, 2021. [Online]. Available: http://arxiv.org/abs/1811.07745

[165] M. Huegle, G. Kalweit, M. Werling, and J. Boedecker, "Dynamic interaction-aware scene understanding for reinforcement learning in autonomous driving," *Proc. - IEEE Int. Conf. Robot. Autom.*, pp. 4329–4335, 2020, doi: 10.1109/ICRA40945.2020.9197086.

[166] H. Chae, C. M. Kang, B. Do Kim, J. Kim, C. C. Chung, and J. W. Choi, "Autonomous braking system via deep reinforcement learning," *IEEE Conf. Intell. Transp. Syst. Proceedings, ITSC*, vol. *2018-March*, pp. 1–6, 2018, doi: 10.1109/ITSC.2017.8317839.

[167] W. Xia, H. Li, and B. Li, "A control strategy of autonomous vehicles based on deep reinforcement learning," *Proc. - 2016 9th Int. Symp. Comput. Intell. Des. Isc. 2016*, vol. *2*, pp. 198–201, 2016, doi: 10.1109/ISCID.2016.2054.

[168] K. Makantasis, M. Kontorinaki, and I. Nikolos, "Deep reinforcement-learning-based driving policy for autonomous road vehicles," *IET Intell. Transp. Syst.*, vol. *14*, no. 1, pp. 13–24, Jan. 2020.

[169] C. Yu et al., "Distributed multiagent coordinated learning for autonomous driving in highways based on dynamic coordination graphs," *IEEE Trans. Intell. Transp. Syst.*, vol. *21*, no. 2, pp. 735–748, Feb. 2020, doi: 10.1109/TITS.2019.2893683.

[170] L. Qian, X. Xu, Y. Zeng, and J. Huang, "Deep, consistent behavioral decision making with planning features for autonomous vehicles," *Electron. 2019, Vol. 8, Page 1492*, vol. *8*, no. 12, p. 1492, 2019, doi: 10.3390/ELECTRONICS8121492.

[171] D. Isele, R. Rahimi, A. Cosgun, K. Subramanian, and K. Fujimura, "Navigating occluded intersections with autonomous vehicles using deep reinforcement learning," in *Proceedings - IEEE International Conference on Robotics and Automation*, 2018, pp. 2034–2039, doi: 10.1109/ICRA.2018.8461233.

[172] B. Chalaki et al., "Zero-shot autonomous vehicle policy transfer: From simulation to real-world via adversarial learning," *IEEE Int. Conf. Control Autom. ICCA*, vol. *2020-October*, pp. 35–40, 2020, doi: 10.1109/ICCA51439.2020.9264552.

[173] P. Wang and C. Y. Chan, "Formulation of deep reinforcement learning architecture toward autonomous driving for on-ramp merge," *IEEE Conf. Intell. Transp. Syst. Proceedings, ITSC*, vol. *2018-March*, pp. 1–6, 2018, doi: 10.1109/ITSC.2017.8317735.

[174] D. C. K. Ngai and N. H. C. Yung, "A multiple-goal reinforcement learning method for complex vehicle overtaking maneuvers," *Intell. Transp. Syst. IEEE Trans.*, vol. *12*, no. 2, pp. 509–522, 2011.

[175] K. Kashihara, "Deep Q learning for traffic simulation in autonomous driving at a highway junction," *2017 IEEE Int. Conf. Syst. Man, Cybern. SMC 2017*, vol. *2017-January*, pp. 984–988, 2017, doi: 10.1109/SMC.2017.8122738.

[176] A. Folkers, M. Rick, and C. Buskens, "Controlling an autonomous vehicle with deep reinforcement learning," *IEEE Intell. Veh. Symp. Proc.*, vol. *2019-June*, pp. 2025–2031, 2019, doi: 10.1109/IVS.2019.8814124.

[177] C. J. Hoel, K. Wolff, and L. Laine, "Automated speed and lane change decision making using deep reinforcement learning," *IEEE Conf. Intell. Transp. Syst. Proceedings, ITSC*, vol. *2018-November*, pp. 2148–2155, 2018, doi: 10.1109/ITSC.2018.8569568.

[178] P. Wang, C. Y. Chan, and A. De La Fortelle, "A reinforcement learning based approach for automated lane change Maneuvers," *IEEE Intell. Veh. Symp. Proc.*, vol. *2018-June*, pp. 1379–1384, 2018, doi: 10.1109/IVS.2018.8500556.

[179] A. Kendall et al., "Learning to drive in a day," *Proc. - IEEE Int. Conf. Robot. Autom.*, vol. *2019-May*, pp. 8248–8254, 2019, doi: 10.1109/ICRA.2019.8793742.

[180] S. Sharifzadeh, I. Chiotellis, R. Triebel, and D. Cremers, "Learning to drive using inverse reinforcement learning and deep q-networks," 2016, Accessed: September 26, 2021. [Online]. Available: https://arxiv.org/abs/1612.03653

[181] S. Arora and P. Doshi, "A survey of inverse reinforcement learning: Challenges, methods and progress," *Artif. Intell.*, vol. *297*, p. 103500, 2021.

[182] J. Wang, Q. Zhang, D. Zhao, and Y. Chen, "Lane change decision-making through deep reinforcement learning with rule-based constraints," *Proc. Int. Jt. Conf. Neural Networks*, vol. *2019*-July, 2019, doi: 10.1109/IJCNN.2019.8852110.

[183] A. Alizadeh, M. Moghadam, Y. Bicer, N. K. Ure, U. Yavas, and C. Kurtulus, "Automated lane change decision making using deep reinforcement learning in dynamic and uncertain highway environment," *2019 IEEE Intell. Transp. Syst. Conf. ITSC 2019*, pp. 1399–1404, 2019, doi: 10.1109/ITSC.2019.8917192.

[184] J. Zhang and K. Cho, "Query-efficient imitation learning for end-to-end simulated driving," *Proc. AAAI Conf. Artif. Intell.*, vol. *31*, no. 1, 2017, Accessed: September 27, 2021. [Online]. Available: https://ojs.aaai.org/index.php/AAAI/article/view/10857

[185] S. Shalev-Shwartz, S. Shammah, and A. Shashua, "Safe, multi-agent, reinforcement learning for autonomous driving," arXiv Prepr. arXiv1610.03295v1, p. 13, 2016, Accessed: September 27, 2021. [Online]. Available: https://arxiv.org/abs/1610.03295v1

[186] X. Xiong, J. Wang, F. Zhang, and K. Li, "Combining deep reinforcement learning and safety based control for autonomous driving," 2016, Accessed: September 27, 2021. [Online]. Available: https://arxiv.org/abs/1612.00147v1

[187] J. García Fern, and O Fernández, "A comprehensive survey on safe reinforcement learning," *J. Mach. Learn. Res.*, vol. *16*, no. 42, pp. 1437–1480, 2015, Accessed: September 27, 2021. [Online]. Available: http://jmlr.org/papers/v16/garcia15a.html

[188] B. R. Kiran et al., "Deep reinforcement learning for autonomous driving: A survey," *IEEE Trans. Intell. Transp. Syst.*, 2021, doi: 10.1109/TITS.2021.3054625.

[189] H. M. A. Aziz and S. V. Ukkusuri, "Unified framework for dynamic traffic assignment and signal control with cell transmission model," *Transp. Res. Rec.*, vol. *2311*, pp. 73–84, 2012.

[190] B. De Villiers and D. Sabatta, "Hindsight reward shaping in deep reinforcement learning," *2020 Int. SAUPEC/RobMech/PRASA Conf. SAUPEC/RobMech/PRASA 2020*, 2020, doi: 10.1109/SAUPEC/RobMech/PRASA48453.2020.9041058.

[191] P. Mannion, S. Devlin, J. Duggan, and E. Howley, "Reward shaping for knowledge-based multi-objective multi-agent reinforcement learning," *Knowl. Eng. Rev.*, vol. *33*, pp. 1–29, 2018, doi: 10.1017/s0269888918000292.

[192] S. Sharifzadeh, I. Chiotellis, R. Triebel, and D. Cremers, "Learning to drive using inverse reinforcement learning and deep Q-networks," 2016, Accessed: September 26, 2021. [Online]. Available: http://arxiv.org/abs/1612.03653

[193] B. Piot, M. Geist, and O. Pietquin, "Bridging the gap between imitation learning and inverse reinforcement learning," *IEEE Trans. Neural Networks Learn. Syst.*, vol. *28*, no. 8, pp. 1814–1826, 2017, doi: 10.1109/TNNLS.2016.2543000.

[194] D. Hadfield-Menell, A. Dragan, P. Abbeel, and S. Russell, "Cooperative inverse reinforcement learning," *Adv. Neural Inf. Process. Syst.*, no. Nips, pp. 3916–3924, 2016.

[195] S. Singh, A. G. Barto, and N. Chentanez, "Intrinsically motivated reinforcement learning," *Adv. Neural Inf. Process. Syst.*, vol. *2*, no. 2, pp. 70–82, 2005.

[196] M. Grzes and D. Kudenko, "Theoretical and empirical analysis of reward shaping in reinforcement learning," in *2009 International Conference on Machine Learning and Applications*, 2009, pp. 337–344.

[197] A. Dosovitskiy, G. Ros, F. Codevilla, A. Lopez, and V. Koltun, "CARLA: An open urban driving simulator," no. CoRL, pp. 1–16, 2017, [Online]. Available: http://arxiv.org/abs/1711.03938

[198] B. Mariusz et al., "End to end learning for self-driving cars." 2016, [Online]. Available: arxiv:1604.07316.

[199] B. D. Ziebart, A. L. Maas, J. A. Bagnell, A. K. Dey, and others, "Maximum entropy inverse reinforcement learning," *Aaai*, 2008, vol. *8*, pp. 1433–1438.

[200] Z. Chen, C. H. Liu, and R. Wang, "Learning to navigate connected autonomous cars for long-term communication coverage," *IT Prof.*, vol. *20*, no. 6, pp. 46–53, 2018, doi: 10.1109/MITP.2018.2876923.

[201] A. Abels, D. Roijers, T. Lenaerts, A. Nowé, and D. Steckelmacher, "Dynamic weights in multi-objective deep reinforcement learning," in *Proceedings of the 36th International Conference on Machine Learning, PMLR*, 2019, vol. *97*, pp. 11–20.

[202] C. Liu, X. Xu, and D. Hu, "Multiobjective reinforcement learning: A comprehensive overview," *IEEE Trans. Syst. Man, Cybern. Syst.*, vol. *45*, no. 3, pp. 385–398, 2015, doi: 10.1109/TSMC.2014.2358639.

[203] S. Gronauer and K. Diepold, *Multi-agent Deep Reinforcement Learning: A Survey*, no. 0123456789. Springer Netherlands, 2021.

[204] A. Oroojlooy and D. Hajinezhad, "A review of cooperative multi-agent deep reinforcement learning." 2019, [Online]. Available: https://arxiv.org/abs/1908.03963

[205] H. M. Aziz, H. Wang, and S. Young, "Investigating the impact of connected vehicle market share on the performance of reinforcement-learning based traffic signal control," no. June, 2019, [Online]. Available: https://www.osti.gov/biblio/1566974

[206] S. M. A. B. Al Islam, A. Hajbabaie, and H. M. A. Aziz, "A real-time network-level traffic signal control methodology with partial connected vehicle information," *Transp. Res. Part C Emerg. Technol.*, vol. *121*, no. September, p. 102830, 2020, doi: 10.1016/j.trc.2020.102830.

[207] N. J. Goodall, B. Park (Brian), and B. L. Smith, "Microscopic estimation of arterial vehicle positions in a low-penetration-rate connected vehicle environment," *J. Transp. Eng.*, vol. *140*, no. 10, p. 04014047, 2014, doi: 10.1061/(ASCE)TE.1943-5436.0000716.

[208] C. M. Day and Darcy M. Bullock, "Opportunities for detector-free signal offset optimization with limited connected vehicle market penetration: A proof-of-concept study," no. 16, pp. 1–21, 2015.

[209] M. Hausknecht and P. Stone, "Deep recurrent q-learning for partially observable MDPs," *AAAI Fall Symp. - Tech. Rep.*, vol. FS-15-06, pp. 29–37, 2015.

[210] M. Igl, L. Zintgraf, T. A. Le, F. Wood, and S. Whiteson, "Deep variational reinforcement learning for POMDPs," *35th Int. Conf. Mach. Learn. ICML 2018*, vol. *5*, pp. 3359–3375, 2018.

[211] X. Z. Chao Wang, J. Wang, and X. Zhang, "Autonomous navigation of UAV in large-scale unknown complex environment with deep reinforcement learning," *2017 IEEE Global Conference on Signal and Information Processing (GlobalSIP), IEEE*, pp. 858–862, 2017.

[212] C. P. Andriotis and K. G. Papakonstantinou, "Deep reinforcement learning driven inspection and maintenance planning under incomplete information and constraints," *Reliab. Eng. Syst. Saf.*, vol. *212*, no. February, p. 107551, 2021, doi: 10.1016/j.ress.2021.107551.

PART III

Deep learning for vehicle control

Vehicle emission control on road with temporal traffic information using deep reinforcement learning

8

Zhenyi Xu
University of Science and Technology of China, Hefei, China
Hefei Comprehensive National Science Center, Hefei, China

Yang Cao
University of Science and Technology of China, Hefei, China

Yu Kang
University of Science and Technology of China, Hefei, China
Hefei Comprehensive National Science Center, Hefei, China

Zhenyi Zhao
University of Science and Technology of China, Hefei, China

DOI: 10.1201/9781003190691-11

Contents

8.1 INTRODUCTION

Traffic emissions released by vehicles contain harmful substances, such as carbon monoxide (CO), carbon dioxide (CO_2), nitrogen oxides (NO_x), hydrocarbons (HC) and particulate matters (PM2.5), which have a great impact on the public health. The increased vehicle usage significantly aggravate the urban air pollution. According to the China Vehicle Environmental Management Annual Report (2018), in 2017 total CO emission is up to 33.273 million tons, HC is 4.071 million tons, and NOx is 5.743 million tons. In some of the Chinese megalopolises, such as Beijing, Shanghai, Shenzhen, the vehicle emission share rate of PM2.5 is approximately 13.5%–41%. Therefore, it is necessary to study traffic emission control to help relevant government departments make proper traffic control policies [1] and reasonable traffic planning [2].

In recent years, there have been a lot of studies focusing on the issue of vehicle emission management. Most of the existing traffic emission control works can be classified into feedback control based approach and traffic management based approach.

The feedback control-based method needs to establish a macroscopic traffic flow model and a microscopic traffic emission model for the controller to predict traffic emissions from traffic networks. Zhang et al. [3] presented a discrete traffic flow model and designed a delay-feedback controller to suppress traffic jam and decrease traffic emission. Shu et al. [4] proposed an integrated macroscopic traffic model to predict the traffic flow states and the emissions released by every vehicle at different operational conditions and designed the model predictive controller to reduce both travel delays and traffic emissions. Shuai et al. [5] used multi-class macroscopic traffic flow and emission models for MPC for traffic networks to achieve a balanced tradeoff between total time spent and total emissions. Uzunova et al. [6] proposed the adoption of a non-integer robust control approach to analyse the speed and density variations due to perturbations on the road and to assure robust performances for the traffic velocity and evaluated pollution factor of CO_2 emissions of the controlled and uncontrolled model. However, the macroscopic traffic flow model and induced control strategy is definitely inaccurate.

The traffic management-based approach focuses mainly on the traffic speed and flow regulation in order to reduce the traffic emissions of the entire traffic networks. Panis et al. [7] consider the effect of active speed management on traffic-induced emissions, suggesting that vehicle acceleration and deceleration are important factors in determining traffic induced emission. Li et al. [8] proposed an optimal dynamic credit charge scheme to redistribute the traffic flows to attain mobility and emission goals.

Duell et al. [9] presented a novel framework to estimate city-wide vehicle environmental effects that integrate a dynamic traffic assignment model with the novel application of a vehicle energy consumption model. Miles et al. [10] proposed a decision support system (DSS) that uses an underlying traffic model to inform an atmospheric dispersion model. Bel et al. [11] used quantile regression to evaluate whether speed management policies have been successful in promoting cleaner air, not only in terms of average pollutant levels but also during high and low pollution episodes. De Blasiis et al. [12] presented an integrated simulation tool to analyse the effects of traffic flow conditions on the pollutants' emissions. Panis et al. [13] analysed different traffic types (urban versus highway traffic) with different modelling approaches (microscopic versus macroscopic) to examines the impact of speed management policies on emissions. Carslaw et al. [14] used Generalized Additive Models to describe how emissions from individual vehicles vary depending on their driving conditions, taking account of variable interactions and time-lag effects, and quantified the impact that vehicle speed control has on-vehicle emissions of CO_2 by road type, fuel type and driver behaviour. Dijkema et al. [15] studied the lowering of the maximum speed limit effects on reducing traffic-related air pollution. The traffic management-based approach designed the traffic control strategies based on the history traffic flow information, which is an offline strategy with time-lag effect.

And with the rapid development of traffic data collection and artificial intelligence techniques, some studies are shifting to use deep reinforcement learning (RL) approaches on traffic management. The RL learns directly from the interactions between states and actions through episodes, the agents take optimal actions according to the long-term accumulation of rewards. In this chapter, we present a deep reinforcement learning emission control strategy, which automatically learns the optimal traffic flow and speed limits to reduce traffic emission on the target road segment based on the temporal traffic information. The main contributions of this study are as follow:

1) We proposed a road vehicle emission control reinforcement learning model to establish the relationship of emissions and traffic information. And a compound emission environment state space is designed to leverage the emission temporal dependencies. Moreover, to deal with the large state and action space, a deep return valuation network (DQN) is applied to estimate the optimal long-term value function.
2) The proposed approach is evaluated on real-world vehicle emission data in Hefei. The results demonstrate the effectiveness of the proposed approach against baseline methods.

8.2 RELATED WORK

There are some published works on traffic control in transportation field, i.e. traffic lights control, traffic flow optimization, and vehicle speed regulation. Li et al. [16] applied the deep reinforcement learning method to design a signal timing plan by implicitly modeling the control actions and the change of system states. Nishi et al. [17] developed a RL-based traffic signal control method that employs a graph convolutional neural network to cope with broader traffic demand. Walraven et al. [18] solved the traffic optimization problem with reinforcement learning, where the traffic congestion on the highway is reduced. Li et al. [19] incorporated the reinforcement learning technique in variable speed limit control strategies to reduce system travel time at freeway bottlenecks. Chao et al. [20] proposed an indirect reinforcement learning model based on Dyna-Q architecture to manage incident-induced congestion for ramp control. A more general application of reinforcement learning in this domain can be found in Cruciol et al. [21], where different reward functions are investigated for decision-making in air traffic flow management with several stakeholders. Xu et al. [22] proposed a deep spatio-temporal framework with multisource urban data to predict the vehicle emissions in region scale. Yau et al. [23] reviews various RL models and algorithms applied to traffic signal control in the aspects of the representations of the RL model (i.e., state, action, and reward), performance measures, and complexity to establish a foundation for further investigation in this research field.

TABLE 8.1 Notations

NOTATION	DESCRIPTION
EF	An emission episode
TA	Traffic agent to conduction emission
tv_t	Traffic volume at time t (V/h)
ts_t	Traffic average speed at time t (km/h)
Π	Traffic agent control policy

8.3 OVERVIEW

8.3.1 Preliminary

The main notations used in this chapter are shown in Table 8.1.

Traffic Agent: The traffic agent *TA* has the factors of traffic volume *tv*, and traffic average speed *ts*, which is the main body to interact with the emission environment.

Emission Episode: An emission episode *EF* is a period emission sequence in a day, in which the total vehicle emission we want to minimize. The emission consists of fuel, CO, HC, and NO at each time interval, which can be defined as $EF_t = \{Fuel_t, CO_t, HC_t, NO_t\}$. And the sequences of emissions are all normalized respectively. In our problem, the length of emission episode is 24 hours, and the time interval is 1 hour.

8.3.2 Traffic data insight

Figure 8.1(a) and (b) show the daily speed and traffic volume distribution heatmap of the history traffic data. We find that in the morning rush hours, e.g. 10 a.m., the traffic pattern is with low speed and high traffic volume which easily contributes to high vehicle emissions, as can be seen in Figure 8.1(c).

8.3.3 Problem formulation

Problem: Given the history emission episodes *EF*, and traffic agent factors *TA*, design a control policy π to minimize the total emission amount in an episode while ensuring a normal traffic volume, as shown in Figure 8.2.

8.4 METHODOLOGY

Obtaining the history emission episodes, a reinforcement learning-based model (EFRL) is proposed to minimize the total emission in the episode by learning traffic agent control policy.

8.4.1 Framework

As shown in Figure 8.3, our model consists of two phases, offline learning and online controlling.

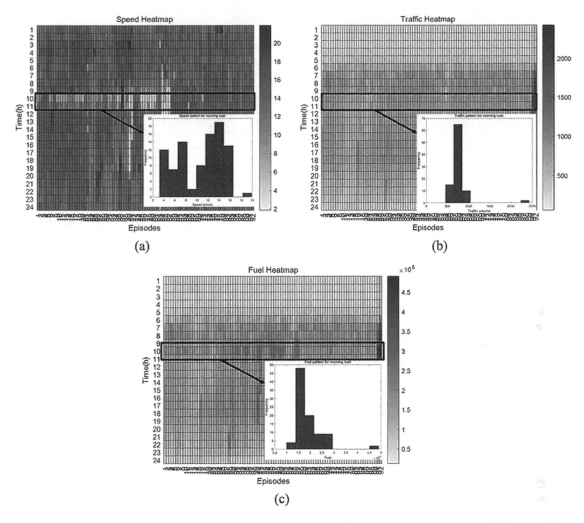

FIGURE 8.1 Daily traffic and emission distribution: (a) low speed in the morning rush hours; (b) high traffic in the morning rush hours; (c) high emissions in the morning rush hours.

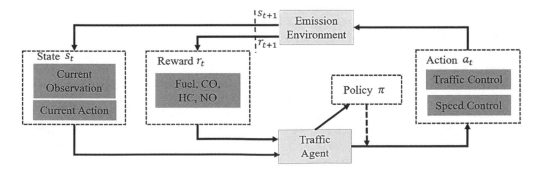

FIGURE 8.2 Emission control policy problem definition.

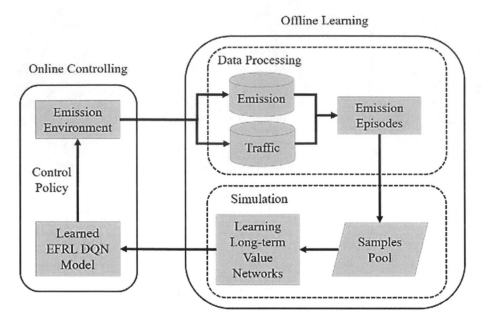

FIGURE 8.3   The system framework of EFRL.

Data Processing Given the original vehicle emission measurements and traffic-related information from the emission remote sensing systems (emission environment), the EFRL structures the batched data into states s_t for generating the emission episodes.

Simulation In traffic emission variation process, there are interactions between vehicle emission and traffic information. Therefore, to train and evaluate a dynamic traffic emission model, a system simulator is required to simulate the system dynamics under repositions. During the simulation phase, the samples pool derived from the real emission dataset to train our EFRL model. Specifically, the emission environment states, the traffic agent's coordination actions and immediate reward at each time step are used to train our EFRL DQN model for estimating the long-term value function, from which the coordination optimal traffic controlling policy can be inferred.

Online Controlling After the offline learning phase, we obtain the trained EFRL DQN model, which returns optimal traffic control policy with traffic flow limits and vehicle speed limits suggestions to reduce vehicle emissions.

8.4.2 EFRL model

A reinforcement learning model (Sutton et al. 1998) is usually defined as a six tuple model, i.e. (S, A, T, R, π, γ), where S is the state space of environment, A is the action space of agents, T is the transition probability which an agent took action a given state s_t will transit to the next state s_{t+1}, R represents the immediate reward after taking action under a specific state, i.e. $r_t(s_t, a_t)$, π is a policy $S \times A \rightarrow \pi$, describing the probability to take an action given a specific state, γ is a time discount parameter. The agent tries to select actions so that the sum of the discounted rewards it receives in the future is maximized, an action has long-term rewards, G_t, defined as Equation (8.1)

$$G_t = r_t + \gamma \cdot r_{t+1} + \gamma^2 \cdot r_{t+2} + \cdots + \gamma^k \cdot r_{t+k} \tag{8.1}$$

where $t + k$ is the final time step.

The objective of reinforcement learning is to learn an optimal policy π such that given state s_t, and taken action a_t, the agent is able to receive the maximum expected long-term discounted reward. The optimal long-term value function is defined as Equation (8.2)

$$Q^*(s_t, a_t) = \max E_\pi(G_t \mid s_t, a_t, \pi) \tag{8.2}$$

Bellman equation is usually adopted to calculate Equation (8.2), which is defined as

$$Q^*(s_t, a_t) = E_{st+1}\left(r_t + \gamma \cdot \max Q^*(s_{t+1}, a_{t+1}) \mid s_t, a_t\right) \tag{8.3}$$

Given the optimal long-term value of each action by each state, we can get the optimal policy with Equation (8.4)

$$a^*_t = \arg\max Q^*(s_t, a_t) \tag{8.4}$$

Based on the traditional reinforcement learning theory, we can formulate the emission control model as following concepts.

Observation Each time the traffic agent requires new control, it has a real-time observation of the current emission environment. The observation is defined to include the emission environment states, and the traffic agent states. For the emission environment states, which includes current emission states EF_t, and the predicted emission $\widehat{EF}_t$ in the next period. For the traffic agent states, which includes the current observations of traffic volume $tv_{o,t}$, and traffic average speed $ts_{o,t}$. An observation can be denoted as $O_t = (EF_t, \widehat{EF}_t, tv_{o,t}, ts_{o,t})$.

Action The action of the traffic agent is denoted as a vector describing the traffic volume limits and the traffic average speed limits, which is can be represented as $a_t = (tv_t, ts_t)$. For example, action $a_1 = (120, 40)$ denotes that the current traffic volume is limited to 120 V/h and the vehicle speed is limited to 40 km/h on the target road segment in the next hour.

State The state of the emission environment is defined as interleaved sequences of observations and actions com bined with current time, which can be denoted as $s_t = (O_{t\_k}, a_{t\_k}, \cdots, O_{t\_1}, a_{t\_1}, O_t, t)$, k is the observation time lag. And k is set to 1 in this work.

Immediate reward To control the emission of an episode at low level while ensuring a quite traffic volume. The immediate reward is defined as a combination gain of emission and traffic volume $r_t = G_I(EF_t - EF_{t+1}) + G_I(tv_{t+1} - tv_t)$ after taking action a_t under s_t and transiting to s_{t+1} in period (t,t+1]. And the definition of G_I is as

$$G_I(x) = \begin{cases} 1, x > 0 \\ -1, \text{otherwise} \end{cases} \tag{8.5}$$

Optimal value network Defining the EFRL model, we can design DQN to estimate the optimal long-term value function (Equation 8.3), i.e. $Q^*(S, A, \theta): S A Q^*$, where otherwise θ are the learning parameters. Our EFRL model is optimized by minimizing the Bellman equation square error, the objective function is formulated as

$$\min_\theta L = \mathbb{E}\left[\left(Q^*(s_t, a_t, \theta) - Q^*_{target}(s_t, a_t, \theta^-)\right)^2\right]$$

$$= \mathbb{E}\left[\left(Q^*(s_t, a_t, \theta) - \left(r^t + \gamma \cdot \max_{a_{t+1}} Q^*_{target}(s_t, a_t, \theta^-)\right)\right)^2\right] \tag{8.6}$$

And the pseudo algorithm for training the optimal long- term value network is detailed in Algorithm 8.1.

ALGORITHM 8.1 EFRL DQN training algorithm

Require:

1: Sample replay buffer D; emission episodes $EF = \{EF^1, EF^2, \dots, EF^N\}$; episode length T; behavior network parameter θ; target network parameter θ^-.

Return:

Learned EFRL DQN model $Q^*(\theta)$

2: $D \leftarrow \varnothing$ //Initialize the replay buffer D

3: Random initialize $Q^*(S, A, \theta), \theta^- \leftarrow \theta$

4: **for** each episode EF^i $(1 \leq i \leq N)$ **do**

5: **for** each time step t$(1 \leq i \leq N)$ **do**

6: random select an action a_t with probability $\epsilon \in [0, 1]$ // ϵ is a parameter for exploration

7: otherwise select $a_t = \underset{a \in A}{\arg\max} Q^*(s_t, a, \theta)$

8: the traffic agent executes action a_t and transits to next state s_{t+1}, receiving reward r_t.

9: storing new sample (s_t, a^t, s_{t+1}, r_t) to D

10: sample random minibatch (s_t, a^t, s_{t+1}, r_t) from D

11: $Q^*\left(s_t, a, \theta\right) = Q^*_{target}\left(s_t, a, \theta^-\right)$

12: minimize L (Equation 8.6)

13: $\theta^- \leftarrow \theta$

14: **end for**

15: **end for**

8.5 EXPERIMENTS

8.5.1 Data and setup

The proposed method is implemented in a high-performance server with GeForce GTX 1080Ti GPU.

And we use real-world road segment to evaluate the emission control reinforcement learning model. Specifically, we collect emission data from vehicle remote sensing systems deployed on a main road in Hefei, which is authorized by Hefei Environmental Protection Bureau. As a sensor station may not have records sometimes, the missing entries are filled by average value. And the data details are summarized in Table 8.2.

TABLE 8.2 Experimental emission datasets

DATASET	MEASUREMENT
Location	Hefei
Time Span	2017/5/1–2017/7/31
Time interval	1 hour
Evaluation stations	4
Pollutants measurements	Fuel, CO, HC, NO
Traffic volume	$[0,3512]$ (V • h^{-1})
Vehicle speed	$[0,77.9]$ (km • h^{-1})
Available time interval	2091 (117 missing)

8.5.2 Baselines and metric

To evaluate the performance of the proposed EFRL model, we compare it with the following baselines:

Random policy (RP) This emission control policy means that the traffic agent selects a random action for traffic volume and traffic average speed limits policy each time.

Monte Carlo (MC) MC estimates optimal actions based on experience episodes without complete knowledge of the environment [24]. With this strategy, the traffic agent revises its policy and value estimates based on emission episodes experience.

Q-learning (QL) The QL is the most commonly used reinforcement learning algorithms [25, 26]. The QL agent chooses the optimal action based on the largest Q-value.

Metric evaluation To evaluate the EFRL control policy, we compare the total emission in average episode with the baseline policies. The average episode emission is defined as follows.

$$EF_{k,\text{average}} = \sum_{i=1}^{N}\sum_{t=1}^{T}\frac{1}{N}EF_k(i,t) \tag{8.7}$$

where k *Fuel, CO, HC, NO,* N is the total emission episodes, T is the episode length.

8.5.3 Results

In the emission policy evaluation experiment, we used the policy algorithms as described in the previous section to run different traffic emission simulations with traffic and speed control. Figure 8.4 show the total emissions of different emission controlling policies. And the emission reduction ratio respect to the total emission without controlling policy is shown in Table 8.3, the emission reduction is little while taking the random policy. Moreover, the policies perform unstably on different pollution, i.e. MC and QL performs well on CO, HC reduction, MC and QL achieve similar results on NO reduction. And our EFRL achieves the best results on all pollution reduction.

The traffic statistics of different policies are shown in Table 8.4 and Figure 8.5, comparing with the non-control pol- icy and random policy, the reinforcement learning-based approaches are more stable on

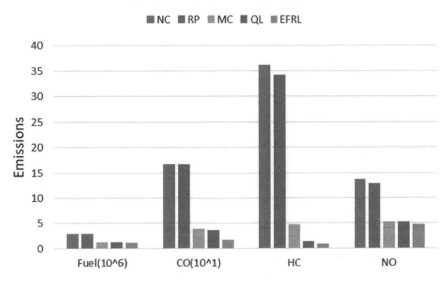

FIGURE 8.4 Emission controlling comparison.

TABLE 8.3 Emission reduction comparison on average episode

CONTROL POLICY	FUEL (%)	CO (%)	HC (%)	NO (%)
RP	↑ 1.28	↑ 0.11	↓ 5.54	↓ 6.01
MC	↓ 56.42	↓ 76.86	↓ 86.95	↓ 61.93
QL	↓ 59.34	↓ 78.08	↓ 96.38	↓ 62.37
EFRL	↓ 62.39	↓ 89.54	↓ 97.72	↓ 65.56

TABLE 8.4 Traffic volume speed models

MODELS	TRAFFIC VOLUME		SPEED	
	MEAN	STD	MEAN	STD
None control	569.02	278.29	11.55	1.87
RP	576.33	276.50	11.53	1.85
MC	316.89	122.39	11.58	0.53
QL	303.40	89.09	11.57	0.46
EFRL	266.85	81.99	11.15	1.46

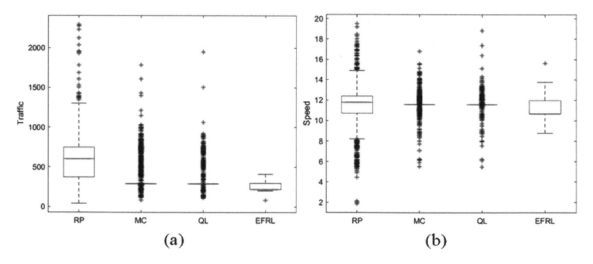

FIGURE 8.5 Policy quality comparison on Fuel: (a) traffic volume distribution; (b) traffic speed distribution.

the traffic volume and speed control. We can find that the EFRL policy can significantly reduce the traffic emission in average episode while ensuring a quite normal traffic volume and speed.

And to evaluate the training performance of EFRL, Figure 8.6 shows the total reward of training iterations. We can find that as the training process, there is an increasing trend of total reward.

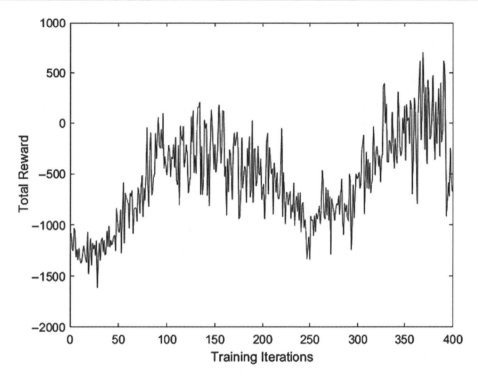

FIGURE 8.6   Total reward of training iterations.

8.6 CONCLUSION

In this chapter, we solved the traffic emission management based on a deep reinforcement learning model, namely EFRL. Different from the existing works which leverage the macroscopic traffic flow model and microscopic traffic emission model to simulate the emission environment, the EFRL directly learned from the history emission sequence, and used a compound emission state to capture the system temporal dependencies. To deal with the large state and action space, a DQN is applied to estimate the optimal long-term value function. The proposed policy is evaluated on real-world vehicle emission data in Hefei. And the comparing result demonstrated the effectiveness of the proposed method.

In the future, we will extend the single road segment control policy to other spatiotemporal emission controlling on a regional scale.

REFERENCES

[1] Pe´rez, P., Trier, A., and Reyes, J. (2000). Prediction of pm2.5 concentrations several hours in advance using neural networks in santiago, chile. *Atmospheric Environment*, *34*(8), 1189–1196.

[2] Xu, Z., Kang, Y., and Cao, Y. (2020). Emission stations location selection based on conditional measurement gan data. *Neurocomputing*, *388*, 170–180.

[3] Zhang, L.D. and Zhu, W.X. (2015). Delay-feedback control strategy for reducing CO_2 emission of traffic flow system. *Physica A: Statistical Mechanics and its Applications*, *428*, 481–492.

[4] Shu, L., Schutter, B.D., Zegeye, S.K., Hellendoorn, H., and Xi, Y. (2013). Integrated urban traffic control for the reduction of travel delays and emissions. *IEEE Transactions on Intelligent Transportation Systems*, *14*(4), 1609–1619.

[5] Shuai, L., Hellendoorn, H., and Schutter, B.D. (2017). Model predictive control for freeway networks based on multi-class traffic flow and emission models. *IEEE Transactions on Intelligent Transportation Systems*, *18*(2), 306–320.

[6] Uzunova, M., Losero, R., Lauber, J., and Djemai, M.(2012). Traffic velocity control for evaluation the impact of gases emissions: Case study of toll plaza. In *International Symposium on Environment Friendly Energies & Applications*.

[7] Panis, L.I., Broekx, S., and Liu, R. (2006). Modelling instantaneous traffic emission and the influence of traffic speed limits. *Science of the Total Environment*, *371*(1C3), 270–285.

[8] Li, Y., Ukkusuri, S.V., and Fan, J. (2018). Managing congestion and emissions in transportation networks with dynamic carbon credit charge scheme. *Computers & Operations Research*, *99*, 90–108.

[9] Duell, M., Levin, M., and Waller, S. (2014). Urban vehicle energy consumption for policy evaluation: Impact of electric vehicles. In *19th International Conference of Hong Kong Society for Transportation Studies: Transportation and Infrastructure, HKSTS 2014*, 271–278.

[10] Miles, A., Zaslavsky, A., and Browne, C. (2018). Iot-based decision support system for monitoring and mitigating atmospheric pollution in smart cities. *Journal of Decision Systems*, *27*, 56–67.

[11] Bel, G., Bolanc, C., Guilln, M., and Rosell, J. (2015). The environmental effects of changing speed limits: A quantile regression approach. *Transportation Research Part D*, *36*, 76–85.

[12] De Blasiis, M., Di Prete, M., Guattari, C., Veraldi, V., Chiatti, G., and Palmieri, F. (2014). The effects of traffic flow conditions on the pollutants emissions: A driving simulator study. *Advances in Transportation Studies*, *2*(SPECIAL ISSUE), 59–70. doi:10.4399/97888548735377.

[13] Panis, L.I., Beckx, C., Broekx, S., Vlieger, I.D., Schrooten, L., Degraeuwe, B., and Pelkmans, L. (2011). Pm, nox and co emission reductions from speed management policies in europe. *Transport Policy*, *18*(1), 32–37.

[14] Carslaw, D.C., Goodman, P.S., Lai, F.C.H., and Carsten, O.M.J. (2010). Comprehensive analysis of the carbon impacts of vehicle intelligent speed control. *Atmospheric Environment*, *44*(23), 2674–2680.

[15] Dijkema, M., Zee, S.C.V.D., Brunekreef, B., and Strien, R.T.V. (2008). Air quality effects of an urban high- way speed limit reduction. *Atmospheric Environment*, *42*(40), 9098–9105.

[16] Li, L., Lv, Y., and Wang, F.Y. (2016). Traffic signal timing via deep reinforcement learning. *IEEE/CAA Journal of Automatica Sinica*, *3*(3), 247–254.

[17] Miles, A., Zaslavsky, A., and Browne, C. (2018). IOT-based decision support system for monitoring and mitigating atmospheric pollution in smart cities. *Journal of Decision Systems*, *27*, 1–12.

[18] Walraven, E., Spaan, M.T., and Bakker, B. (2016). Traffic flow optimization: A reinforcement learning approach. *Engineering Applications of Artificial Intelligence*, *52*, 203–212.

[19] Li, Z., Liu, P., Xu, C., Duan, H., and Wang, W. (2017). Reinforcement learning-based variable speed limit control strategy to reduce traffic congestion at freeway recurrent bottlenecks. *IEEE Transactions on Intelligent Transportation Systems*, *18*(11), 3204–3217.

[20] Chao, L., Chen, H., and Grant-Muller, S. (2013). An indirect reinforcement learning approach for ramp control under incident induced congestion. In *International IEEE Conference on Intelligent Transportation Systems*.

[21] Cruciol, L.L.B.V., De Arruda, A.C., Weigang, L., Li, L., and Crespo, A.M.F. (2013). Reward functions for learning to control in air traffic flow management. *Transportation Research Part C*, *35*(10), 141–155.

[22] Xu, Z., Cao, Y., and Kang, Y. (2019). Deep spatiotemporal residual early-late fusion network for city region vehicle emission pollution prediction. *Neurocomputing*, *355*, 183–199.

[23] Yau, K.L.A., Qadir, J., Khoo, H.L., Ling, M.H., and Komisarczuk, P. (2017). A survey on reinforcement learning models and algorithms for traffic signal control. *ACM Computing Surveys*, *50*(3), 1–38.

[24] Sutton, R.S., and Barto, A.G. *Reinforcement Learning: An Introduction*. MIT Press, 2018. https://mitpress.mit.edu/9780262039246/reinforcement-learning/

[25] Watkins, C.J.C.H., and Dayan, P. Q-learning. *Machine Learning*, 1992, *8*(3–4), 279–292.

[26] Mahadevan, S. (1996). Average reward reinforcement learning: Foundations, algorithms, and empirical results. *Machine Learning*, *22*(1–3), 159–195.

Load prediction of an electric vehicle charging pile

9

Peng Shurong and Peng Jiayi
Changsha University of Science & Technology, Changsha, China

Yang Yunhao
Zhejiang University, Hangzhou, China

Li Bin
Changsha University of Science & Technology, Changsha, China

Contents

DOI: 10.1201/9781003190691-12

9.1 INTRODUCTION

The smart grid is a system of synchronous transmission of information and energy, which is a way to achieve power automation. The development of efficient and clean electric vehicles (EV) is an effective way to reduce oil dependence and alleviate air pollution while transforming energy structure and energy consumption mode and improving energy comprehensive utilization efficiency. According to the 2018 China Statistical Yearbook, in 2016, the power, gas, water production, and supply industry consumed 303.1358 million tons of standard coal, accounting for 6.96% of the annual total energy consumption. The transport, storage, and postal sectors consume 396.5121 million tons of standard coal, accounting for 9.10% of annual total social energy consumption. According to the overall development report of new energy vehicles in 2017, China's s electric vehicle ownership (including pure electric vehicles and plug-in hybrid vehicles) has reached about 1.23 million, accounting for nearly 40% of the global EV ownership [1]. Under the guidance of the Chinese government's macro policy, various industrial technologies are becoming increasingly mature. At present, electric vehicles are booming, and the market share of public and civil new energy vehicles is growing. With the large-scale access of electric vehicles to the grid in the future, the load distribution brought by it has the characteristics of intermittence, volatility, randomness and other uncertainties in time and space [2]. Thus, it is necessary to analyze and predict a large number of node operation data.

In power grid planning, it is necessary to fully consider the temporal and spatial characteristics of the electric vehicle charging load, and weigh the economy and security of power grid construction and operation. The integration of electric vehicles into the power grid will change the power load curve [3], which will have a significant impact on the operation, planning, and control of the entire power grid [4]. Therefore, it is necessary to accurately predict the charging load of electric vehicles in advance, so as to better guide the power system generation, distribution, dispatching, and other work, and do a good job eliminating and protecting the harmonic pollution of the power grid [5, 6]. In general, the establishment of an electric vehicle load forecasting model is complex [7–9], which is affected by many aspects, including user habits, traffic infrastructure conditions, equipment characteristics, the number of electric vehicles, and the distribution of charging pile infrastructure, etc.

At present, the load forecasting methods of electric vehicles are principally divided into two categories. One is to use mathematical models to simulate the charging behavior of electric vehicles to obtain the predicted value of electric vehicle load. The other is to use the model in statistical learning to predict based on historical data.

The Monte Carlo method is a stochastic simulation method based on probability and statistical theory. After determining the probability model of the problem, the computer is used to take the random number according to the probability model in order to obtain the approximate solution of the problem. First, a probability model of the owner's traffic habits is determined according to the database, including charging habits and behavior habits, and a mathematical model with random probability characteristics is established. Next, the Monte Carlo principle is used to predict the charging location, time, and load demand of the car in the future period [10]. The traditional prediction methods of electric vehicle charging load include regression analysis, similar day method, etc. Modern prediction methods include prediction methods based on wavelet analysis, prediction methods based on neural network, and support vector machine (SVM). This chapter uses the deep learning model based on historical data to predict the spatio-temporal dynamic load of electric vehicles.

9.2 CHARGING LOAD CHARACTERISTIC ANALYSIS OF ELECTRIC VEHICLES

Electric vehicle charging load is affected by many factors, among which the main influencing factors are: the charging mode of electric vehicles, the state of charge (SOC), charging and discharging characteristics, charging power, charging time, battery capacity, electric vehicle ownership, and other factors of electric vehicles and users. External factors include weather, temperature, date (holidays, working days), as well as bus schedules. The charging load modeling is to determine the daily mileage and actual parking demand by considering the parking probability model of spatial distribution, and then to predict the load by combining the charging demand model of electric vehicles. These models are affected by the above factors.

With the development of deep learning, recurrent neural networks and convolutional neural networks are used to predict time series problems, and the effect is good. This kind of method can explore the timing characteristics well, which can not only learn the historical law of electric vehicle load but also consider the influencing factors of electric vehicle load in the model.

9.3 QUANTILE REGRESSION MODEL OF DILATED CAUSAL CONVOLUTIONAL

9.3.1 Dilated causal convolutional

Considering the one-dimensional charging load series $x = \left(x_t \right)_{t=0}^{N-1}$, using the past charging load series conditions, the next value $\hat{x}(t+1)$ is predicted by the model with parameter θ, which is the idea of the causal system. The output of the system is only related to the previous value and is independent of the future value. The experiment uses dilated convolution neural network to construct the causal system of charging load, we can define the following:

$$p(x \mid \theta) = \prod_{t=0}^{N-1} p\left(x(t-1) \right) \mid x(0),\cdots,x(t),\theta \tag{9.1}$$

The charging load sequence has long-term autocorrelation. In order to learn this long-term dependence, the structure of stacked dilated convolution layer is adopted, and the characteristic mapping of the output layer of this structure is

$$\left(w_h^l *_d f^{l-1} \right) = \sum_{j=-\infty}^{\infty} \sum_{m=1}^{M_{t-1}} w_h^l(j,m) f^{l-1}(i-d \bullet j,m) \tag{9.2}$$

The dilated factor is d, assuming a layer of dilated convolution L. In order to make the dilated convolution obtain a longer receptive field, the dilated factor of each layer should be exponentially increased by 2 (as shown in Figure 9.1).

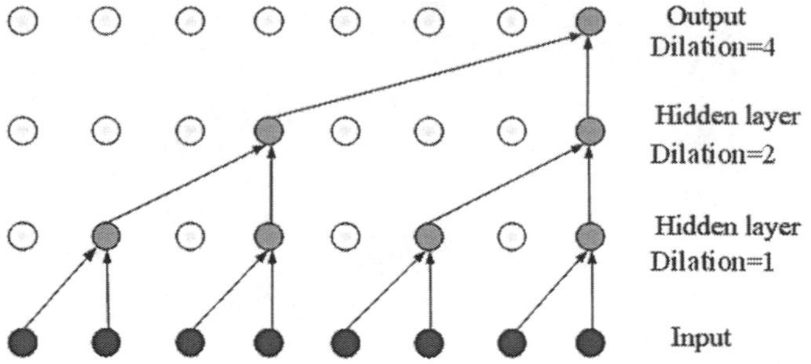

Output
Dilation=4

Hidden layer
Dilation=2

Hidden layer
Dilation=1

Input

FIGURE 9.1   Structure of dilated convolutional neural network.

The receptive field of the network is

$$r = 2^{L-1}k \tag{9.3}$$

where k is the size of the convolution kernel.

For charging load series $x(0)$, $\cdots$, $x(t)$, predict future charging load. The model uses $x(0)$, $\cdots$, $x(t)$ as input and $x(t + 1)$ as output to train the model, that is, to predict the charging load at a one-time point in advance.

The objective function of the prediction model is

$$E(w) = \frac{1}{2N} \sum_{t=0}^{N-1} (y_{pre} - y_{true})^2 + \frac{\gamma}{2}(W,b)^2 \tag{9.4}$$

where W and b represent the parameters of the prediction network structure, y_{pre} and y_{true} represent the predicted and the real values.

9.3.2 Kernel density estimation

Kernel density estimation is a non-parametric estimation method for probability density function. For a sample point z_1, z_2, ..., z_n that is independent and identically distributed, its kernel density estimation is

$$\widehat{f_h}(z) = \frac{1}{n} \sum_{i=1}^{n} K_h(x - x_i) = \frac{1}{nh} \sum_{i=1}^{n} K\left(\frac{x - x_i}{h}\right) \tag{9.5}$$

where $K(\cdot)$ is the kernel function.

The kernel function needs to satisfy the properties of nonnegative and integral 1. There are many kernel functions such as uniform, triangular, biweight, triweight and Epanechnikov, as shown in Figure 9.2. For window width $h > 0$, appropriate window width can fit the probability density distribution of variables better.

9.3.3 Dilated causal convolutional quantile regression

According to the structure of the dilated causal convolutional neural network regression model and neural network quantile regression method, a Quantile Regression Model of Dilated Causal Convolutional

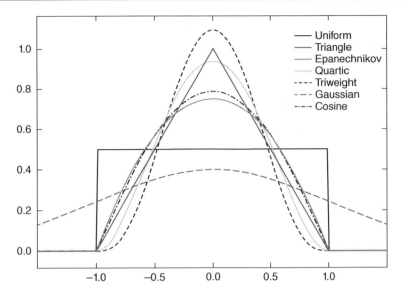

FIGURE 9.2   Kernel function.

Neural Network (QRDCC) is established. The cost function is transformed into the objective function of the quantile regression is given by

$$f_{\text{cost}} = \sum_{i=1}^{N} \rho_{\tau}[Y_i - f(X_i, W, b)] = \sum_{i|Y_i \geq f(X_i, W, b)} \tau |Y_i - f(X_i, W, b)| + \sum_{i|Y_i < f(X_i, W, b)} (1-\tau)|Y_i - f(X_i, W, b)| \qquad (9.6)$$

And parameter estimation is regarded as the optimization problem as follows:

$$\min_{W,b} f_{\text{cost}} + \frac{\lambda}{2}\left|(W, b)\right|^2 \qquad (9.7)$$

where W, b is the weight and bias set of the dilated convolution neural network, respectively, and the optimization problem is solved by the Adma random gradient descent method.

After solving the parameters $\hat{W}(\tau)$ and $\hat{b}(\tau)$, the conditional quantile estimation of Y is obtained by

$$\hat{Q}(\tau \mid X) = f\left(X, \hat{W}(\tau), \hat{b}(\tau)\right) \qquad (9.8)$$

where the value τ is continuously valued on $(0,1)$, the conditional quantile curve is called the conditional distribution (cumulative), and the conditional density prediction is derived from the distribution function $F(F^{-1}(\tau)) = \tau$

$$P\left(\hat{Q}_Y(\tau \mid X)\right) = \frac{d\tau}{d\hat{Q}_Y(\tau \mid X)} \qquad (9.9)$$

Next, perform conditional and discrete operations on Equation (9.9) and finally use density estimation to get conditional density prediction (Figure 9.3).

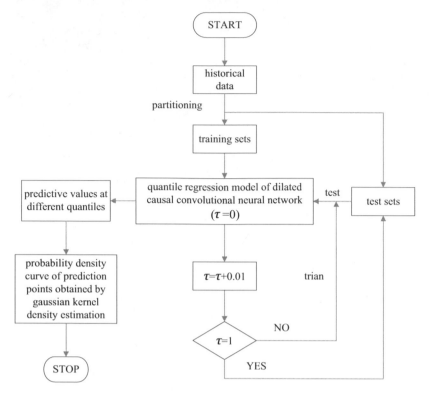

FIGURE 9.3   QRDCC program flow chart.

9.3.4 Model evaluation index

The main commonly used evaluation indexes of the charging load point prediction model include mean absolute error (MAE), mean squared error (MSE)and root mean squared error (RMSE). However, the above evaluation indexes cannot be used to evaluate the results of probability prediction. Considering the strong randomness and wide fluctuation range of charging load, the probability interval evaluation index of reference charging load characteristics is given. Therefore, the following two evaluation indexes are adopted:

(1) Reliability estimation

A total of n prediction intervals under the level of confidence of $1 - \alpha$, reliability indexes can be defined as follows:

$$
\begin{cases}
I_i^\alpha = \left[L_i^\alpha, U_i^\alpha \right] \\
\xi_i^\alpha = \begin{cases} 0 & P^i \notin I_i^\alpha \\ 1 & P^i \in I_i^\alpha \end{cases} \quad i = 1, 2, \cdots, N \\
R_{\text{cov}er} = \dfrac{1}{N} \sum_{i=1}^{N} \xi_i^\alpha
\end{cases}
\tag{9.10}
$$

L_i^α is the lower bound of the ith prediction interval under the above confidence level, U_i^α is the corresponding upper bound, I_i^α is the corresponding interval, and P^i is the position corresponding to the real point. Similarly, ξ_i^α represents whether the ith true value falls within the prediction interval, 1 for true and 0 for false.

R_{cover} represents the reliability estimation, that is, the coverage rate of the charging load forecasting interval to the real value. The probability that the charging load falls within the prediction interval should be equal to or close to the predetermined confidence level. The closer the reliability estimation is to the confidence interval value, the more reliable the prediction model.

(2) Sensitivity estimation

The reliability index cannot fully reflect the quality of probability prediction results, because the reliability is usually higher when the interval width is too large, which will lead to less useful information. Therefore, the sensitivity index is also needed to jointly determine the quality of interval prediction results. The sensitivity indexes are

$$
\begin{cases}
\delta_i^\alpha = U_i^\alpha - L_i^\alpha \\
\delta_{mean}^\alpha = \dfrac{1}{N}\sum_{i=1}^{N}\delta_i^\alpha
\end{cases}
\tag{9.11}
$$

δ_i^α represents the width of the ith prediction interval, the smaller the predictive charging load sensitivity index is, the smaller the charging load interval is, and more effective charging load information in the future period is obtained. However, a single sensitivity index or reliability index cannot fully reflect the quality of the charging load probability prediction model. Only the sensitivity index and reliability index can fully reflect the quality of the probability interval prediction results.

9.3.5 Example simulation based on python

This example is based on the electric vehicle charging piles load data in a certain area of a city in China which has a total of 4320 entries and consists of the hourly charging load in 180 days. The experimental computer conditions for this simulation are as follows: CPU, Core i7-7700; Memory, 16G; GPU, 1050Ti 4G. Before training, the data were normalized first, and then the DCC neural network, the LSTM neural network, and the BP neural network under each quantile are iterated for 100 rounds (epochs) through the Tensorflow and Keras deep learning frameworks. Finally, 96 hours of charging load were predicted using the rolling prediction method (Figure 9.4).

The following information can be obtained by analyzing the diagram:

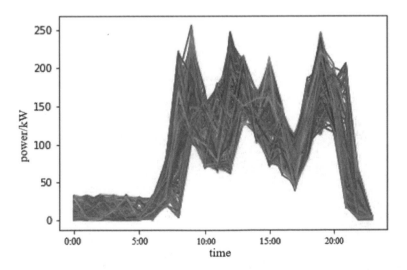

FIGURE 9.4   Daily charging curve.

- The load from 23:00 to 7:00 daily is relatively smooth and below 20% of the maximum. Since this time is the sleeping time of most users and the number of charging is low.
- 9–11, 13–17, and 19–22 are the peak charging periods for users. 9–11 and 13–17 are working hours, and users choose this time to charge mainly because the function of automatic power off after full charge is convenient for users to manage. The users who choose 19–22 o'clock for charging are to make the electric vehicle meet the normal use of the next day.
- Minimal values of charging load occur at 12 and 18 o'clock. This is due to the fact that this time is the peak period of car usage, and the number of charging users decreases first and then increases.

From Figure 9.5, we can see the range of charging volume for each time of the 24 hours and the intervals in which the values are more concentrated. 8:00 to 22:00 is the time when users are more active, so the randomness of charging volume is greater, because of the human randomness factor. The remaining times are more regular in terms of charging volume, which is due to less user activity and less randomness at this time.

Figure 9.6 shows the 24-hour charging load distribution, where the horizontal axis is the amount of charging load and the vertical axis is the probability density. The distribution of charging load is not regular from 8:00 to 22;00, which is the daytime activity time, and the main reason is that the randomness of users is stronger during the daytime. The other hours have less user activity and the distribution is more regular.

After the optimal window width is obtained by the search method, the optimal window width is used for kernel density estimation. Figure 9.7 shows an example plot of the predicted probability density distribution estimation for 24-time points predicted by QRLSTM, and it can be seen that the kernel density estimation is closer to the true distribution than the normal distribution estimation. Therefore, kernel density estimation is chosen as the probability density estimation method.

Figures 9.8–9.10 give the probability density prediction results for the normal distribution estimation (ND) and the kernel density estimation (KDE) at 80%, 85%, and 90% confidence levels, respectively. The results of kernel density estimation have narrower prediction intervals than the normal distribution. And the prediction points falling within the estimation interval differ little, so the kernel density estimation can better reflect the range in which the prediction interval is located, and the kernel density estimation can better approximate the actual distribution of charging load.

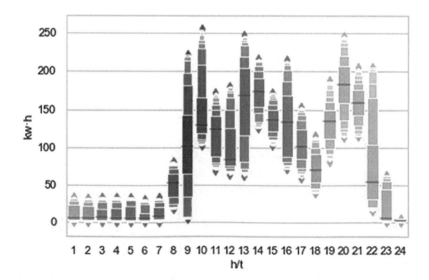

FIGURE 9.5   Daily charging boxenplot.

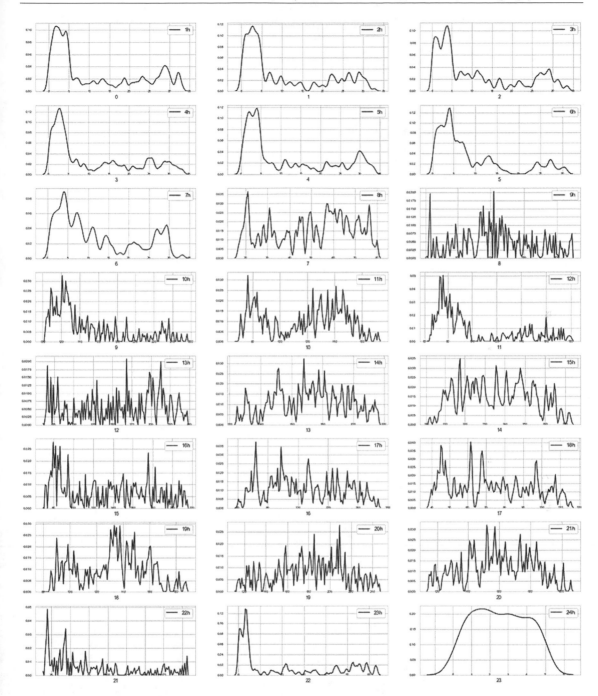

FIGURE 9.6   24-hour charging load distribution.

Table 9.1 further gives a comparison of the reliability and sensitivity of the prediction results under two different estimation methods for the QRDCC and neural network quantile QRNN (Quantile Regression Neural Network) regression models, where the reliability of the normal distribution estimation is generally higher than the confidence level, while the sensitivity is also too high, so the kernel density estimation is chosen.

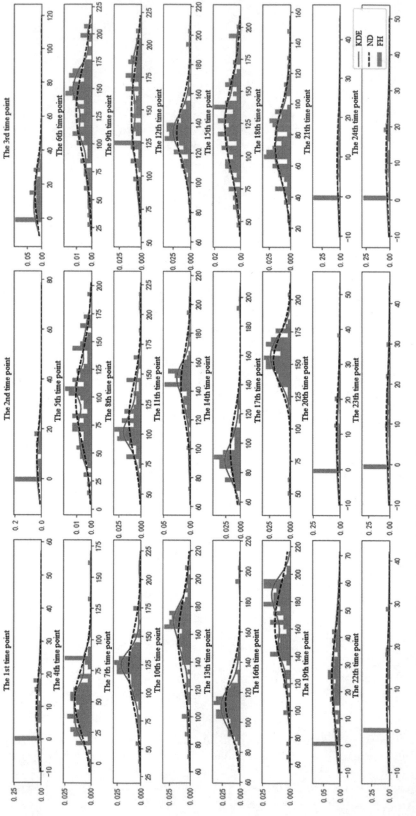

FIGURE 9.7 Comparison of predicted charging load distribution estimates.

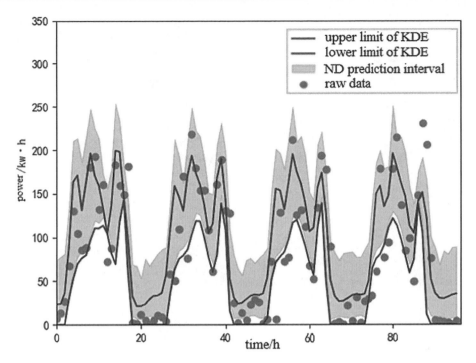

FIGURE 9.8   Charging load prediction intervals at 80% confidence level.

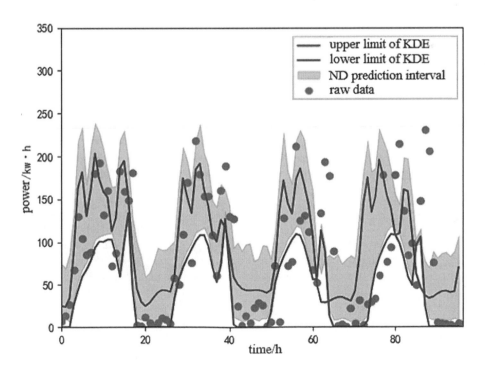

FIGURE 9.9   Charging load prediction intervals at 85% confidence level.

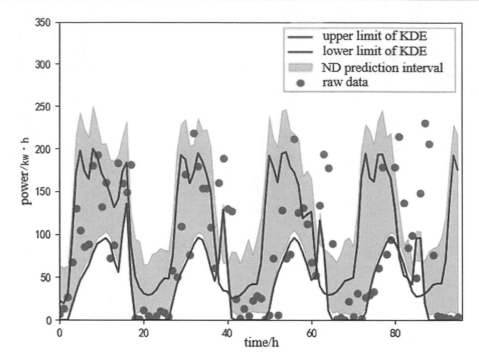

FIGURE 9.10   Charging load prediction intervals at 90% confidence level.

TABLE 9.1   Predictive indexes of QRDCC and QRNN

CONFIDENCE DEGREE(%)	ESTIMATION	RELIABILITY(%)	SENSITIVITY(MW)
80	KDE	81.50	48.65
	Normal Distribution	84.36	79.61
85	KDE	85.80	75.25
	Normal Distribution	87.65	108.97
90	KDE	90.03	87.86
	Normal Distribution	92.64	134.61

To demonstrate the prediction accuracy of the QRDCC regression prediction model, the prediction results obtained from it are compared with those of the QRLSTM and QRNN prediction models. Figures 9.11–9.13 give the prediction intervals for QRDCC, QRLSTM, and QRNN at 90%, 85%, and 80% confidence levels, respectively, and it is clear that the true values fall within the prediction interval of QRDCC regression with a high probability. In comparison with QRLSTM, there is almost no difference in the probability of the true value falling within the prediction interval, but the average width of the prediction interval is significantly smaller than that of QRLSTM; in comparison with the QRNN regression model, the probability of the true value falling within the prediction interval is significantly larger, and the width of the prediction interval is much smaller than that of QRNN. This fully indicates that the proposed QRDCC regression model can predict the charging load volatility well and can predict the charging load volatility for a longer period.

As shown in Table 9.2, the proposed method QRDCC has relatively good reliability at all three confidence levels. QRDCC obtained narrower sensitivity at 80%, 85% and 90% confidence levels: 63.07, 75.25 and 87.86, respectively. The reliability results of the above three methods were not very different, but the smaller the average bandwidth of the prediction interval at the same confidence level, the smaller the

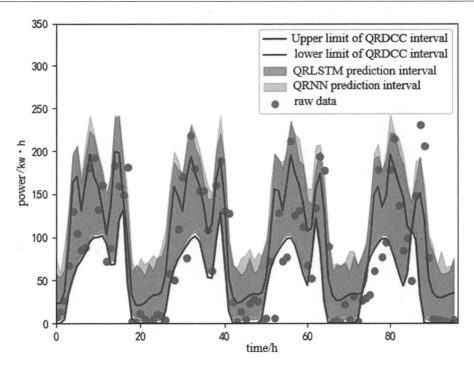

FIGURE 9.11   QRDCC charging load prediction intervals at 80% confidence level.

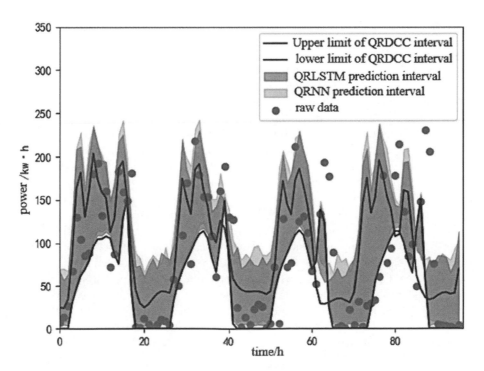

FIGURE 9.12   QRDCC charging load prediction intervals at 85% confidence level.

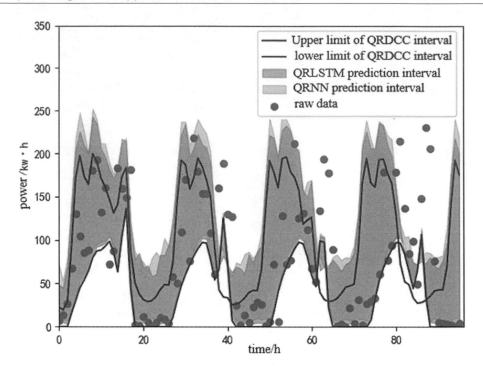

FIGURE 9.13   QRDCC charging load prediction intervals at 90% confidence level.

sensitivity, the higher the prediction accuracy. In conclusion, QRDCC achieved the best prediction results among the three models (Table 9.3 gives the comparison of the prediction indexes).

The probability density distribution of the prediction points that can be obtained using the QRDCC regression method is shown in Figure 9.14, where the QRDCC and QRLSTM box line distribution plots for the 96 prediction points are given. From the predicted box line distribution plots, it is concluded that QRDCC can predict the complete distribution of charging load and the true value falls in the probability region of this prediction interval with high probability. The above example illustrates that the method can give the effective distribution of EV load at the future predicted time point.

The probability density plots for the first QRDCC and QRLSTM prediction time points are given in Figure 9.15, where the horizontal axis is the charging load (kw·h) and the vertical axis is the probability density. It can be seen that the real value falls in the middle region of these two distributions, indicating that both algorithms can predict the probability distribution of the future charging load well. The real value falls at the large probability point of QRDCC relative to the probability density estimate of QRLSTM, and it can be seen that QRDCC can better reflect the future probability distribution of charging load.

The probability density curve of the predicted points can be obtained by using QRLSTM and QRDCC regression methods, and the distribution interval of the probability density function for a total of 96 points of time from prediction point 1 to 96 is shown in Figure 9.16. From the predicted probability density function, it can be seen that QRDCC and QRLSTM can predict the complete probability density distribution of charging load, and the real values all fall in the middle of this density function. Compared with the real value of the charging load, there is a higher probability that falls in the central high probability interval of the density estimate derived by QRDCC. The above example shows that this method can give probability density curves for future predicted time points and that the QRDCC method is closer to the true distribution of the charging load.

Figure 9.17 compares the results of the other three-point prediction with the interval prediction results of QRDCC. Compared with the point prediction method, the interval prediction method has a higher confidence level and can better avoid the risk caused by the error of simple point predictions when using

TABLE 9.2 QRDCC and QRLSTM prediction intervals

QRDCC PREDICTION INTERVALS	QRLSTM PREDICTION INTERVALS	RANGE DIFFERENCE
[113.3,227.5]	[92.0,276.8]	71
[131.6,250.3]	[109.0,296.2]	68
[160.2,258.2]	[135.5,326.3]	65
[160.2,323.0]	[164.5,358.9]	63
[276.4,422.1]	[244.1,447.0]	57
[316.5,467.0]	[281.8,488.0]	56
[322.0,473.0]	[286.9,493.6]	56
[317.2,467.7]	[282.4,488.7]	56
[315.9,466.3]	[281.2,487.4]	56
[300.2,448.9]	[266.5,471.4]	56
[187.6,318.6]	[161.0,355.0]	63
[88.6,196.1]	[69.1,250.5]	74
[47.7,143.2]	[31.3,206.6]	80
[31.8,122.2]	[16.6,189.4]	82
[48.9,144.8]	[32.5,207.9]	80
[87.6,194.9]	[68.2,249.4]	74
[96.6,206.3]	[76.5,258.9]	73
[63.5,163.9]	[45.9,223.6]	77
[34.8,126.2]	[19.5,192.7]	82
[52.6,149.6]	[35.9,211.9]	79
[72.0,174.8]	[53.8,232.7]	76
[94.5,203.6]	[74.5,256.7]	73
[131.9,250.6]	[109.2,296.4]	68
[142.7,264.0]	[119.2,307.8]	67

TABLE 9.3 Comparison of the prediction indexes

CONFIDENCE DEGREE (%)	ALGORITHM	RELIABILITY (%)	SENSITIVITY (MW)
	QRDCC	81.50	63.07
80	QRLSTM	83.36	94.61
	QRNN	79.25	98.76
	QRDCC	85.8	75.25
85	QRLSTM	86.6	106.97
	QRNN	84.3	110.41
	QRDCC	90.03	87.86
90	QRLSTM	91.72	120.06
	QRNN	89.6	123.61

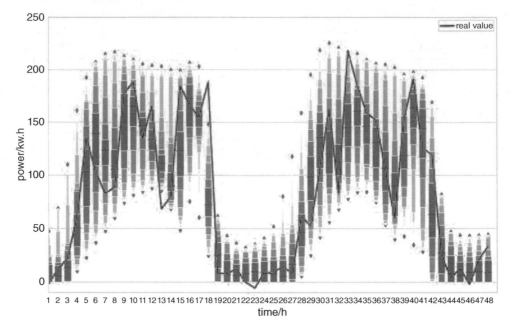

(a)

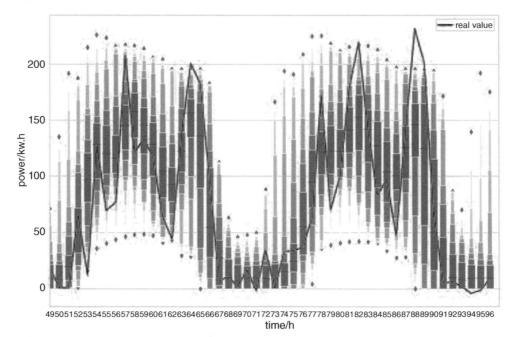

(b)

FIGURE 9.14   Charging load predict box-plot distribution (a) QRDCC box-plot 1–48 (b) QRDCC box-plot 49–96.

(*Continued*)

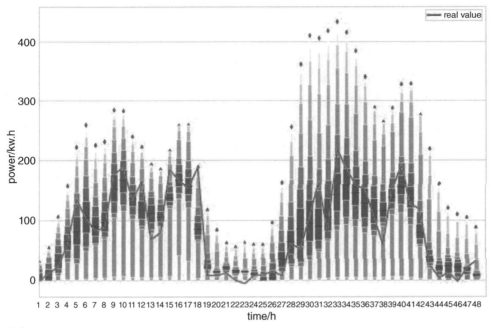

(c)

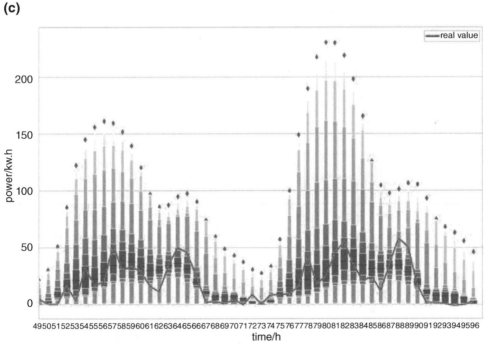

(d)

FIGURE 9.14   (Continued) (c) QRLSTM box-plot 1–48 (d) QRLSTM box-plot 49–96.

the prediction results in practice, and can avoid the phenomenon of misleading information caused by the decrease in prediction accuracy due to the accumulation of errors generated by rolling predictions.

Table 9.4 shows the root mean square error (RMSE) of the three-point prediction models, QRDCC median regression, QRLSTM median regression, and QRNN median regression. The accuracy of QRDCC median prediction is higher than that of QRLSTM and QRNN.

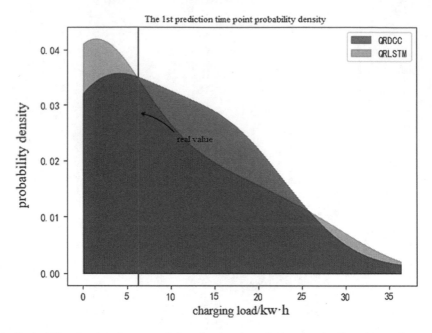

FIGURE 9.15   Probability density diagram of charging load prediction for the first time point.

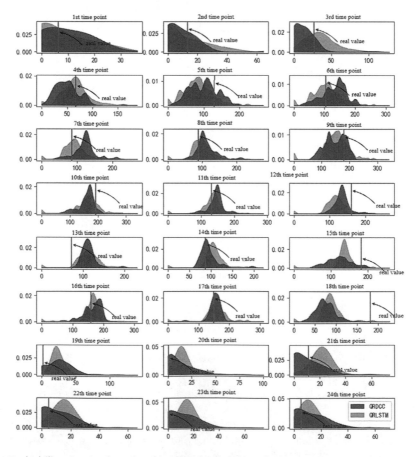

FIGURE 9.16   Probability density function for charging load prediction.

(*Continued*)

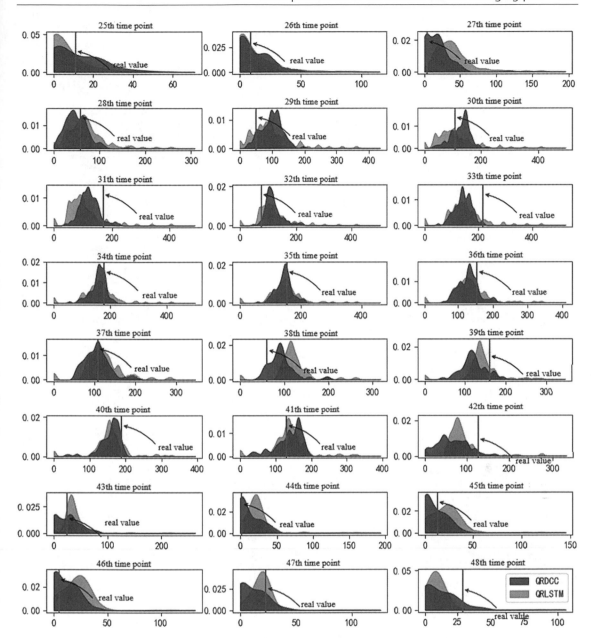

FIGURE 9.16 (Continued)

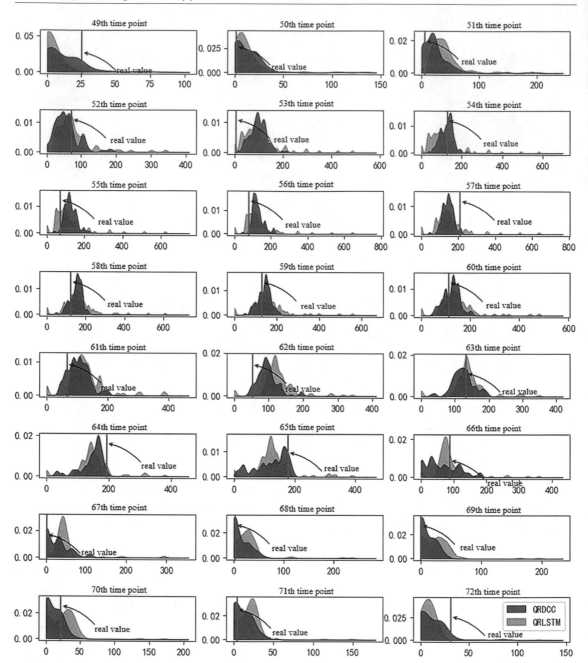

FIGURE 9.16   (Continued)

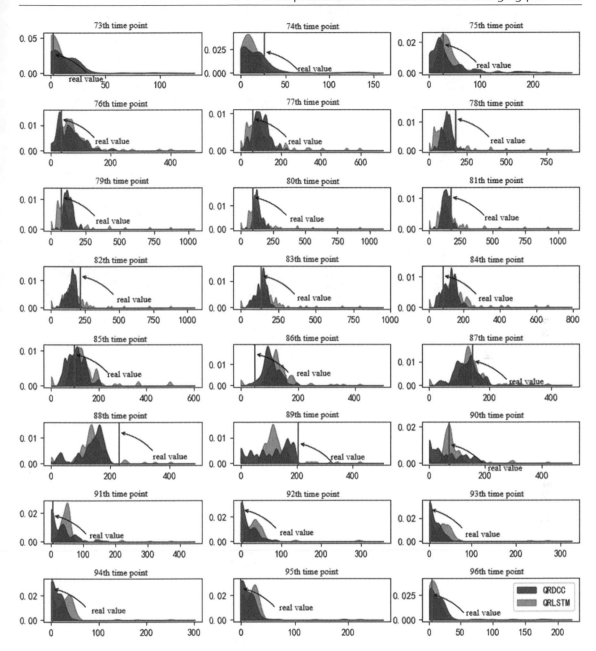

FIGURE 9.16   (Continued)

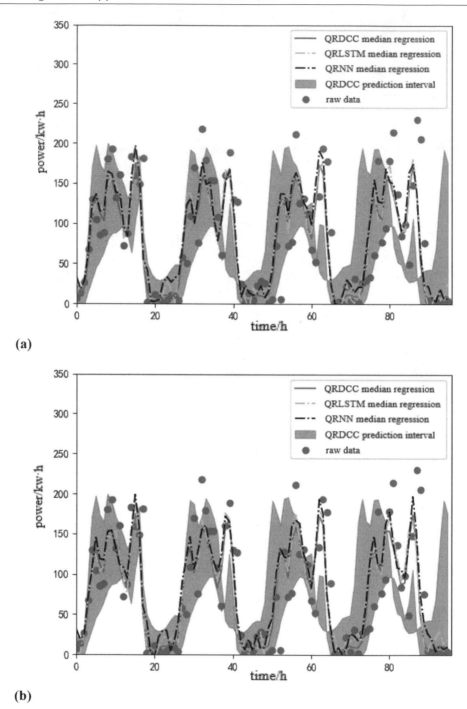

(a)

(b)

FIGURE 9.17 Interval prediction results (a) 80% confidence level interval prediction results (b) 85% confidence level interval prediction results.

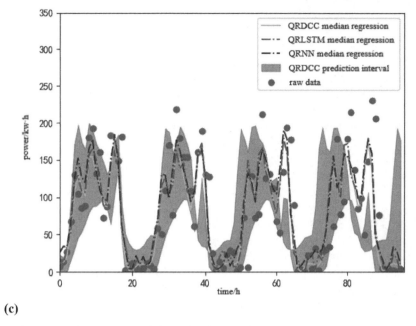

(c)

FIGURE 9.17   (Continued) (c) 96% confidence level interval prediction results.

TABLE 9.4 Comparison of median regression prediction errors

MODEL	RMSE
QRDCC Median Regression	23.86
QRLSTM Median Regression	26.64
QRNN Median Regression	29.16

9.4 SPATIO-TEMPORAL DYNAMIC LOAD PREDICTION OF CHARGING PILE LOAD BASED ON DEEP LEARNING

9.4.1 Spatio-temporal dynamic load prediction of the charging pile

Spatio-temporal dynamic EV load prediction is mainly divided into two categories, one is the method that uses mathematical models to simulate EV charging behavior to derive EV load prediction values [11, 12]; such methods are too complex in mathematical models when considering the spatio-temporal characteristics of charging loads comprehensively, and it is difficult to guarantee the prediction accuracy.

The other is based on historical data using statistical learning models, which use models to learn the potential patterns of historical data to achieve better prediction results. The traditional load prediction methods for electric vehicle charging load prediction include regression analysis, similar day method; modern prediction methods include neural network-based prediction, wavelet analysis-based prediction, and Support Vector Machine (SVM).

The statistical learning methods for EV charging load prediction are considering only the temporal dimension. However, EV charging load also contains a complex spatial nature, and it is necessary to consider both temporal and spatial dynamics of the load in order to better predict the spatio-temporal dynamics. Deep learning (DL), as an important research hotspot in machine learning, has achieved remarkable success in image analysis, speech recognition, natural language processing, video classification, and so on, and has also achieved some success in predicting, and predicting the load in both space and time, a two-dimensional dilated causal convolutional neural network is required. DCC-2D (Dilated Causal Convolution-2D Neural Network) is required to learn the Spatio-temporal dynamic law of the charging pile load [13, 14].

Google has proposed a new audio generation network, WAVENET [15]. This chapter proposes a conditional time series prediction model of a convolutional network based on Google's WAVENET model [16]-Dilated Causal Convolutional Neural Network DCC-2D, which can learn the spatio-temporal dynamic law of charging pile load well. Thus, the load is predicted holistically in space and time.

9.4.2 Spatio-temporal dynamic load matrix construction

Electric vehicle loads are stochastic in time and space, and in order to better predict these spatio-temporal dynamics, the loads on the charging piles need to be portrayed in spatio-temporal dimensions. The charging load at the charging pile is represented by a two-dimensional matrix according to the location of the charging pile and organized into a spatio-temporal sequence of time T is arranged:

$$D = \{D_1, D_2, \cdots, D_T\}, D \in R^{T \times X \times Y} \tag{9.12}$$

where D_t is the space load matrix of the charging pile at time t. The two-dimensional matrix can be defined as follows:

$$D_t = \begin{bmatrix} d_t^{(1,1)} & \cdots & d_t^{(1,Y)} \\ \cdots & \cdots & \cdots \\ d_t^{(X,1)} & \cdots & d_t^{(X,Y)} \end{bmatrix} \tag{9.13}$$

Based on the latitude and longitude distribution of the 10 charging piles we can create a matrix with $X = 40$ and $Y = 40$, and a two-dimensional load matrix is constructed according to the following steps (Figure 9.18):

- Construct the coordinate axes and determine the coordinates of all charging piles.
- Calculate the coverage area of each charging pile load, and the coverage areas of each charging pile load is an L-square centered on its own coordinates.
- Fill in the load coverage of all charging piles with the load of charging piles and accumulate them to obtain the load matrix at that moment.
- Repeat the previous step by moment until all moments are constructed into a two-dimensional load matrix.

To establish a spatio-temporal dynamic load matrix of charging piles for predicting future K time points, it is necessary to build a deep learning model that predicts future K time points based on past S time points observations:

$$\tilde{D}_{t+1}, \cdots, \tilde{D}_{t+k} = \underset{D_{t+1}, \cdots, D_{t+k}}{\arg\max} \, p(D_{t+1}, \cdots, D_{t+k} | D_{t+S+1}, \cdots, D_t) \tag{9.14}$$

where p represents a causal network and $\tilde{D}_{t+k}$ represents the $t + k$th load prediction matrix.

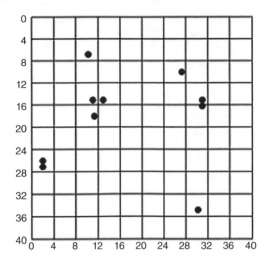

FIGURE 9.18   Charging pile distribution.

Experiments will use SPATIO-TEMPORAL NETWORK's structural spatio-temporal dynamic neural network for constructing this causal system.

9.4.3 Spatio-temporal convolutional networks model

Two-dimensional convolution is usually used on two-dimensional data such as images, and the layer stacking method is used to build a two-dimensional convolutional neural network. The convolution result of the jth convolution kernel (x,y) in the ith layer of the two-dimensional convolutional network is given by

$$v_{ij}^{xy} = h\left(b_{ij} + \sum_m \sum_{p=0}^{P_i-1} \sum_{q=0}^{Q_i-1} w_{ijm}^{pq} v_{(i-1)m}^{(x+p)(y+q)}\right) \tag{9.15}$$

where $h(\cdot)$ represents a nonlinear activation function and b_{ij} represents the bias term. w_{ijk}^{pq} are the values of the convolution kernel parameters with coordinates (p,q), P_i and Q_i are the height and width of the convolution kernel.

Two-dimensional convolution can only capture information in the spatial dimension, while three-dimensional convolution can capture information in both the spatial and temporal dimensions. The three-dimensional convolution kernel is an expansion of the two-dimensional convolution kernel into three dimensions, and the data are stacked into three-dimensional data according to the time dimension and then convolution operation is performed. The convolution result for the jth convolution kernel position (x,y,z) in the ith layer of the 3D convolutional network is given by

$$v_{ij}^{xyz} = h\left(b_{ij} + \sum_m \sum_{p=0}^{R_i-1} \sum_{q=0}^{P_i-1} \sum_{r=0}^{Q_i-1} w_{ijm}^{rpq} v_{(i-1)m}^{(x+r)(y+p)(z+q)}\right) \tag{9.16}$$

where R_i is the temporal dimension in the 3D convolution kernel, P_i and Q_i are the height and width of the convolution kernel, and w_{ijm}^{pqr} is the parameter value of the convolution kernel with coordinates (p,q,r). The comparison plot of the 2D and 3D convolution process is shown in Figure 9.19.

LSTM is usually used to solve the prediction problem of one-dimensional time series and cannot consider spatial correlation. Based on this, we propose ConvLSTM, a network structure that can be used to consider both spatial and temporal dimensions, and ConvLSTM structure can learn long-term

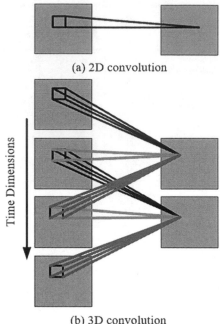

(a) 2D convolution

(b) 3D convolution

FIGURE 9.19   2-D and 3-D convolutions.

two-dimensional data patterns, which is ideal for the prediction of dynamic load matrix of charging piles. It is able not only to retain valid information from previous time nodes and have sequence learning capability like LSTM, but also to extract features and extract spatial features by 2D-CNN like 2D-CNN. This enables to get features in both spatial and temporal dimensions and also switches the state-to-state switching to convolutional computation.

For a time series with a 3-dimensional charging space-time dynamic load matrix of inputs $X_T = \{X_1, X_2, \cdots, X_T\}$ where X_T represents the load matrix at moment t. The specific process of ConvLSTM is

$$
\begin{aligned}
i_t &= \sigma(W_{xi} * X_t + W_{hi} * H_{t-1} + W_{ci} e C_{t-1} + b_i) \\
f_t &= \sigma(W_{xf} * X_t + W_{hf} * H_{t-1} + W_{cf} \odot C_{t-1} + b_f) \\
C_t &= f_t \odot C_{t-1} + i_t \odot \tanh(W_{xc} * H_{t-1} + W_{hc} * H_{t-1} + b_c) \\
o_t &= \sigma(W_{xo} * X_t + W_{ho} * H_{t-1} + W_{co} \odot C_t + b_o) \\
H_t &= o_t \odot \tanh(C_t)
\end{aligned}
\tag{9.17}
$$

where W_{xi}, b_i represents the weight and bias of the input gate and i_t represents the output result of the input gate at time t; W_{xf}, b_f represents the weight and bias of the forget gate and f_t represents the output result of the forget gate at time t; W_{xc}, b_c represents the weight and bias of the update value, C_t represents the update value at moment t; W_{xo}, b_o represents the weight and bias of the output gate, o_t represents the output value at moment t of the output gate; H_t represents the output after the update at moment t; $\sigma(\bullet)$ represents the sigmoid activation function, $\tanh(\bullet)$ represents the hyperbolic tangent activation function, "$*$" represents the convolution computation, and "$\odot$" represents Hadamard multiplication.

9.4.4 Spatio-temporal dynamic load forecasting based on dilated causal convolution-2D

One-dimensional dilated convolution can only be used in one-dimensional time series, which is not applicable when time series in spatial dimension needs to be considered, and the precise consideration of electric vehicle charging load needs to consider the spatio-temporal dynamics. Therefore, the three-dimensional convolutional structure applied in the spatial dimension and the one-dimensional dilated causal convolutional structure are combined to form a two-dimensional dilated causal convolutional neural network, that is, the model replaces the one-dimensional convolution of the one-dimensional dilated convolution with the three-dimensional convolution, where the convolution process is given by

$$v_{lj}^{xyz} = h\left(\sum_m \sum_{p=0}^{R_i-1} \sum_{q=0}^{P_i-1} \sum_{r=0}^{Q_i-1} w_{ijm}^{rpq} v_{(i-1)m}^{(x+r^cd)(y+p)(z+q)} \right)$$

(9.18)

where the convolution kernel size is (2^*w^*h); $d = 2^{l-1}$, $R_i = 2$. d is taken in the same way as the one-dimensional dilated convolution, and the size of the sensory field r is given by

$$r = 2^{L-1}R$$

(9.19)

where R is the size of the first dimension of the three-dimensional convolution kernel, R_i is the time dimension in the three-dimensional convolution kernel, P_i and Q_i are the height and width of the convolution kernel, respectively, and w_{ijm}^{pqr} is the parameter value of the convolution kernel with coordinates (p,q,r). The jth convolution result of the lth layer at position x,y,z is v_{lj}^{xyz}.

The structure when $L=3$ is given in Figure 9.21, which uses historical load heat data from the past 8 moments to predict the load heat at a future moment, thus showing that the model constructs a causal system that uses the past $D = (d_t)_{t=0}^{N-1}$ load heat conditions to predict the next $\hat{d}(N)$ load heat values using a model with parameters.

The objective function of this prediction model is

$$E(w) = \frac{1}{2N} \sum_{t=0}^{N-1} (y_{pre} - y_{true})^2 + \frac{\gamma}{2}(W)^2$$

(9.20)

Where W represents the parameters of the prediction network structure, γ is the weight of the regular term, and y_{pre} and y_{true} are the predicted and true values.

The whole process of the model is shown in Figure 9.21. Firstly, the charging pile plane distribution map will be established according to the charging pile latitude and longitude; then the heat map will be drawn on the distribution map in the order of moments according to the historical load data; then each picture data will be normalized; then the data will be put into the model for training, and the hyperparameters

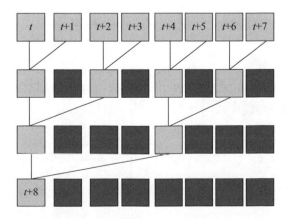

FIGURE 9.20 Two-dimensional dilated convolutional neural network.

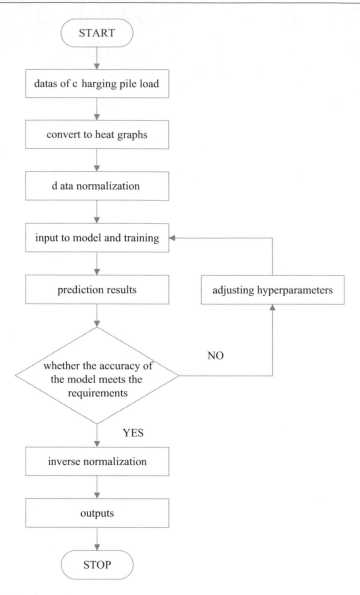

FIGURE 9.21   Algorithm flow chart.

of the model will be adjusted according to the training results until the model training achieves satisfactory results; Finally, the image data are inversely normalized and output to get the final prediction result.

9.4.5 Spatio-temporal dynamic load forecasting based on Spatio-temporal neural network

The spatio-temporal network is used to predict the spatio-temporal dynamic load forecasting of charging piles with a rolling prediction method, which enables the network to output the spatio-temporal dynamic load matrix for multiple time steps simultaneously. Assuming that the input is $D_s=\{D_{t-s}, D_{t-s+1}, \ldots, D_t\}$, the model is represented by M, and all parameters of this model are represented by Θ, the representation of the model is

TABLE 9.5 Algorithm comparison

ALGORITHM	TEST TIMES	MAE	MSE	R^2
DCC-2D	1	1.23	8.18	0.81
	2	1.24	8.21	0.82
	3	1.07	6.56	0.89
	4	1.79	10.30	0.73
	5	1.50	10.14	0.78
	mean	1.37	8.68	0.81
STN	1	1.32	9.44	0.80
	2	1.32	9.22	0.80
	3	1.34	7.63	0.80
	4	1.87	12.96	0.72
	5	1.58	11.36	0.76
	mean	1.49	10.12	0.78

$$\tilde{D}_K = \tilde{D}_{t+1}, \cdots, \tilde{D}_{t+k} = M(\Theta; D_S) \tag{9.21}$$

where $\tilde{D}_{t+k}$ represents the predicted load matrix at the $(t+k)$th moment.

The whole network structure of the model is shown in Figure 9.22, using structural units that merge the ConvLSTM layer and the 3D-ConvNet layer after outputting them separately with a merged layer, which can learn long-term and short-term patterns comprehensively, and the learning ability of multiple unit stacked networks is stronger.

In order to obtain accurate load matrix prediction results, the optimal parameters Θ of the model should be solved, and the objective function of the prediction model is

$$L(\Theta) = \frac{1}{2K} \|M(\Theta; D_S) - D_K\|^2 \tag{9.22}$$

and then the adam adaptive stochastic gradient descent algorithm is used to solve the optimal parameters of the model.

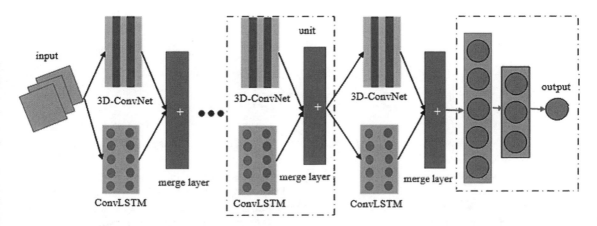

FIGURE 9.22   Three-dimensional convolutional.

9.4.6 Example simulation based on python

This example is based on the electric vehicle charging piles load data in a certain area of a city in China which has a total of 4320 entries and consists of the hourly charging load in 180 days. The experimental platform is conducted on TensorFlow, a deep learning framework from Google Inc. The computer conditions for this simulation: CPU, Core i7-7700; Memory, 16G; GPU, 1070Ti 8G.

Figure 9.23 gives an example of a partial moment charging load heat graph, where the darker color represents the higher load here. And the picture is normalized and then trained and predicted by the DCC-2D model and the Spatio-Temporal Network (STN) model, and the load heat map of the past 200 moments is used as the training set to roll up the load heat map for the next 4 hours.

The prediction result is inversely normalized according to

$$X_i^` = \frac{X_i}{X_{max}} \qquad (9.23)$$

where X_i is the value before normalization, $X^`i$ is the value after normalization and X_{max} takes the maximum of all the charges.

$$X_i = X_i^` \times X_{max} \qquad (9.24)$$

Then the comparison of the predicted results with the real values is shown in Figure 9.24, where the left-hand side of the figure is the predicted graph and the right-hand side is the real graph. From the figure, it can be seen that the real and predicted values have a high similarity, which illustrates the effectiveness and practicality of the algorithm, but it can be seen that the similarity between the predicted and real graphs slowly decreases as the prediction time becomes longer, so the long time prediction needs further research.

To reflect the advantages of this model, it is compared with the STN prediction model. The histogram comparison of the prediction result errors of the two models is shown in Figure 9.25, where the Z-axis indicates the absolute value error generated by each point of the two models, and the red and blue parts represent the prediction errors of the STN and DCC-2D models, respectively. It can also be seen from the figure that the errors of DCC-2D are mainly concentrated in the high load area, which indicates that the model can judge the load concentration area; the errors of the STN model are higher in the low or zero load area in addition to the high load area, and the errors of the STN model are generally higher than those of the DCC-2D model, which fully illustrates the superiority of the DCC-2D model.

Table 9.5 gives the MAE, MSE, and R^2 for the five experiments of the two models, and the corresponding average values are also given. The best average values of all the above three metrics are DCC-2D, and it can be seen that the DCC-2D model has a higher prediction accuracy.

9.5 CONCLUSIONS

1. This chapter uses QRLSTM and QRDCC prediction models first, whose reliability indexes are 9.04% and 5.04% higher and sensibility indexes are 64.08% and 54.08% lower than QRNN, respectively, fully reflecting the advantages of QRDCC and QRLSTM. The models accurately predict the electric vehicle load distribution in detail, and the distribution can better reflect the change of EV load better. The method not only has improved in prediction accuracy, compared with the simple point prediction results, interval prediction can get richer information and a

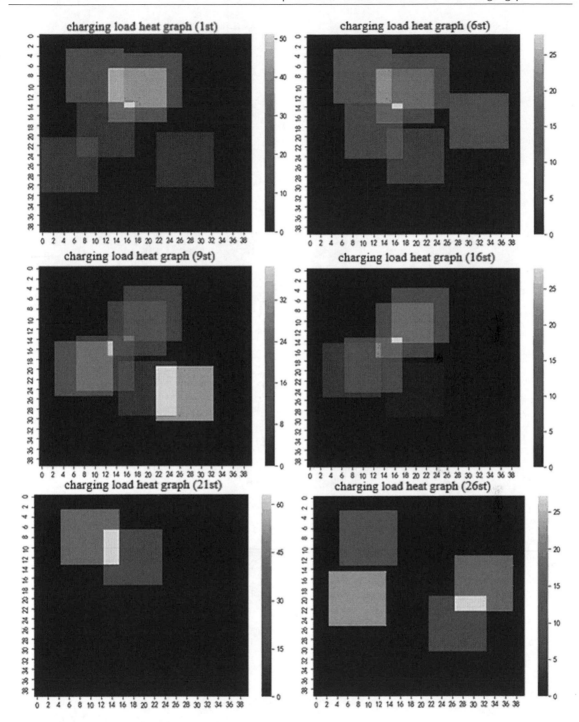

FIGURE 9.23   Charging load heat graph.

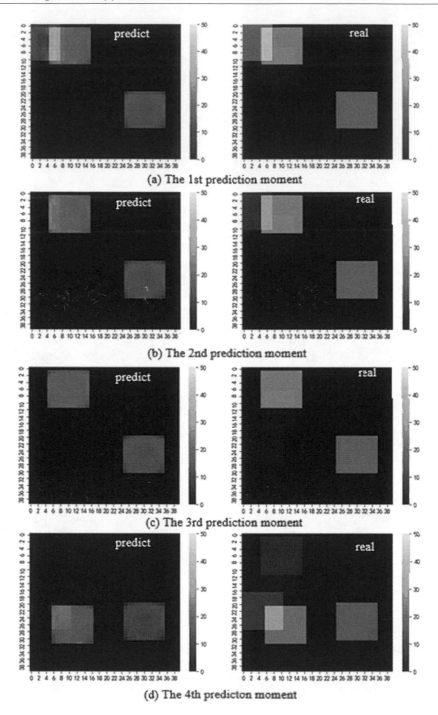

(a) The 1st prediction moment

(b) The 2nd prediction moment

(c) The 3rd prediction moment

(d) The 4th predicton moment

FIGURE 9.24   Prediction results.

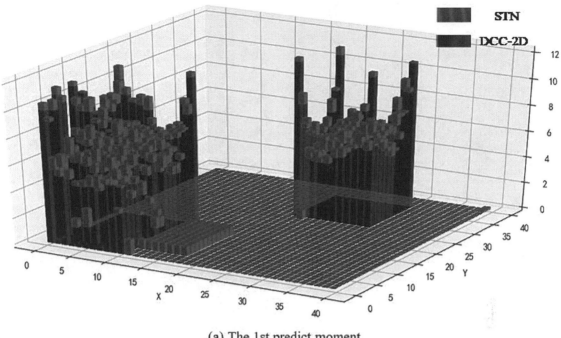

(a) The 1st predict moment

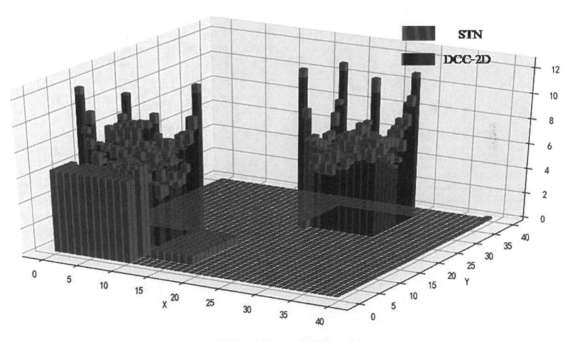

(b) The 2nd predict moment

FIGURE 9.25 Prediction results (a) The 1st predict moment (b) The 2nd predict moment.

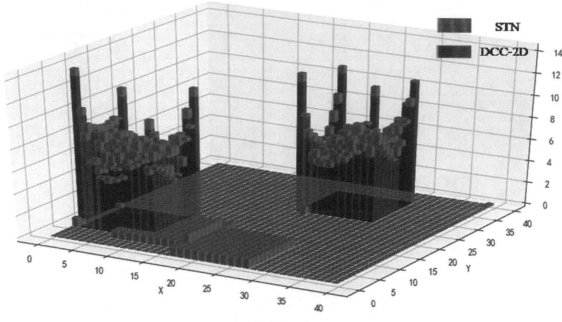

(c) The 3rd predict moment

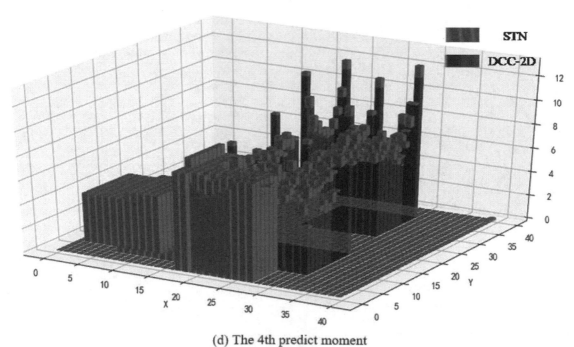

(d) The 4th predict moment

FIGURE 9.25   (Continued) (c) The 3rd predict moment (d) The 4th predict moment

    greater degree of fault tolerance, but also can get the effective prediction of the complete probability distribution of EV load in a certain time in the future, which can provide the grid with a large amount of effective information when the EV load enters the grid.

2. This chapter uses nonparametric kernel density probabilistic prediction models for charging load intervals: dilated causal convolutional neural network quantile regression model and LSTM

neural network quantile regression model. The method estimates the model network parameters under different quantile conditions, and then obtains the predicted values under different quantile conditions, and uses the KDE method to fit the charging load probability intervals. The method used for interval prediction of charging load with the following characteristics:

- The fluctuation range of the charging load, such as the probability interval, can be predicted.
- The structure of the dilated causal convolutional neural network shows that it can learn long-time historical patterns well without using a large increase in parameters.
- The charging load prediction interval is estimated by the Gaussian distribution kernel function, and better reliability and acuity results are obtained comparing QRLSTM and QRNN.

3. The statistical learning methods for EV charging load prediction are based on the temporal dimension. However, EV charging load also contains complex spatial natures, and the dynamic changes of time and space are considered comprehensively for better spatio-temporal dynamic prediction. The average MAE and RMSE errors of DCC-2D are 8.16% and 14.23% lower than those of STN, and the score of DCC-2D is 3.84% higher than that of ConvLSTM. It can be seen that the prediction accuracy of the DCC-2D model has been significantly improved.

When electric vehicles are connected to the grid through charging piles on a large scale in the future, the distribution will inevitably become scattered with users, and coupled with the highly random nature of charging and discharging time, it will make the grid structure more uneven. The volatility of load and power supply, and the heterogeneity of tide distribution will be more prominent, which will have a great impact on the distribution grid network loss, power quality, reliability, and stability, and bring huge challenges to the grid dispatching. The smart grid containing V2G should have the self-adaptive ability to channel this influence correctly and make the storage energy of EVs become the rotating backup, so it is necessary to collect, analyze, and predict a large amount of node operation data.

REFERENCES

[1] Yu Baojun, Yu Wenhan, and Sun Lunjie, "Analysis of strategic planning of pure electric vehicles in China of the 13th national five-year plan," *Auto Industry Research*, vol. 2, pp. 40–48, 2018.

[2] Gao Ciwei, and Zhang Liang, "A survey of influence of electrics vehicle charging on power grid," *Power System Technology*, vol. 35, no. 02, pp. 127–131, 2011.

[3] Yang Fang, Zhang Yibin, He Bo, Bai Cuifen, "Evaluation of impact of large-scale electric vehicle loading on economic value of power system," *Electric Power*, vol. 49, no. 03, pp. 178–182, 2016.

[4] Chen Xin-Qi, Li Peng, Hu Wen-Tang, Xu Jia-Long, and Zhu Jiong et al., "Analysis of impacts of electric vehicle charger on power grid harmonic," *Electric Power*, vol. 9, pp. 31–36, 2008.

[5] Tian Liting, Zhang Mingxia, and Wang Huanling, "Evaluation and solutions for electric vehicles' impact on the grid," *Proceedings of the CSEE*, vol. 32, no. 31, pp. 43–49+217, 2012.

[6] Ma Ling-Ling, Yang Jun, Fu Cong, Liu Pei, and Sun Yuan-Zhang, "Review on impact of electric car charging and discharging on power grid," *Power System Protection and Control*, vol. 41, no. 03, pp. 140–148, 2013.

[7] Huang Xiaoqing, Chen Jie, Chen Yongxin, Yang Hua, Cao Yijia, Jiang Lei, "Load forecasting method for electric vehicle charging station based on big data," *Automation of Electric Power Systems*, vol. 40, no. 12, pp. 68–74, 2016.

[8] Luo Zhuowei, Hu Zechun, Song Yonghua, and Yang Xia, "Study on pluging electric vehicles charging load calculating," *Automation of Electric Power Systems*, vol. 35, no. 14, pp. 36–42, 2011.

[9] Zhanghui Pan, Ciwei Gao, "Rescarch on charging and discharging dispatch of electric vehicles based on demand side discharge bidding," *Power System Technology*, vol. 40, no. 04, pp. 1140–1146, 2016.

[10] Chen Hao, Wan Qiulan, and Wang Yurong, "Refined diebold-mariano test methods for the evaluation of wind power forecasting models," *Energies*, vol. 7, pp. 4185–4198, 2014.

[11] Sungwoo Bae, and Alexis Kwasinski, "Spatial and temporal model of electric vehicle charging demand," *IEEE Transactions on Smart Grid*, vol. *3*, no. 1, pp. 394–403, 2012.

[12] Hao Liang, Isha Sharma, Weihua Zhuang, and Kankar Bhattacharya, "Plug-in electric vehicle charging demand estimation based on queueing network analysis," *Proceedings of IEEE Power and Energy Society General Meeting*, National Harbor, MD. pp. 1–5. http://dx.doi.org/10.1109/PESGM.2014.6939530

[13] Aaron van den Oord, Sander Dieleman, Heiga Zen et al., "Wavenet: A generative model for raw audio," arXiv preprint arXiv: 1609.03499v2 [cs.SD] *19* Sep 2016:1–15.

[14] Anastasia Borovykh, Sander Bohte, Cornelis W. Oosterlee. "Conditional time series forecasting with convolutional neural networks," arXiv preprint arXiv: 1703.04691v3 [stat.ML] 16 Oct 2017:1–19.

[15] Glib Kechyn, Lucius Yu, Yangguang Zang, et al. Sales forecasting using WaveNet within the framework of the Kaggle competition. arXiv preprint arXiv: 1803.04037v1 [cs.LG] *11* Mar 2018:1–6.

[16] Xingjian Shi, Zhourong Chen, Hao Wang, et al. Convolutional LSTM network: A machine learning approach for precipitation nowcasting. arXiv preprint. arXiv: 1506.04214v1 [cs.CV] 13 Jun 2015.

Deep learning for autonomous vehicles **10**
A vision-based approach to self-adapted robust control

Gustavo A. Prudencio de Morais, Lucas Barbosa Marcos, José Nuno A. D. Bueno, Marco Henrique Terra and Valdir Grassi Junior

University of São Paulo, São Carlos, Brazil

Contents

DOI: 10.1201/9781003190691-13

10.1 INTRODUCTION

Visual perception and image-based control are fundamental aspects of autonomous navigation. The first directly represents how the vehicle sees its surroundings and provides information necessary to plan optimal and safe trajectories. The second, on the other hand, ensures that the vehicle performs the desired lateral motion by providing the adequate steering actions. Although lateral and longitudinal control problems and dynamics are topics well addressed in the literature on autonomous navigation, see for instance [1–3], they usually presume exact knowledge of vehicle parameters. However, this assumption does not easily hold, since most of the technical characteristics of the car are kept secret by the manufacturers. In addition, the vehicle is prone to the negative effects of model uncertainties and exogenous disturbances and, therefore, the design of controllers becomes even more challenging.

A possible way to sidestep the aforementioned difficulties is to add available visual information in the control loop. The combination of robust model-based controllers and trained deep neural networks for image processing yields a hybrid vision-based robust control architecture, which is the main topic of this chapter. For this procedure, trained machine learning techniques reproduce the system dynamics through image features and a robust controller guarantees the stability of the closed-loop system. The association of these approaches represents new improvements in computer vision, image processing, and control for the navigation of self-driving vehicles in complex environments.

Uncertainties are common in real applications of autonomous vehicles, such as variations in luminosity, GPS signals, tire friction nonlinearities, and driveline behavior. Thus, this chapter presents methods for the optimal estimation of uncertainty via an evolutionary algorithm that evaluates the reward function based only on measured input and output data.

Interesting achievements regarding hybrid vision-based robust control for autonomous ground vehicles were initially presented in [4]. This chapter extends these results and deepens the application on the main topic.

10.2 REFERENCES SELECTION VIA DEEP LEARNING IMAGE PROCESSING

Understanding or extracting information from images is one of the major points in sophisticated autonomous driving systems. Several deep learning models can be applied for image processing, and one important and classical algorithm for the success of these methods is the Convolutional Neural Network (CNN) [5–6]. Furthermore, variations of CNN (such as CV-CNN, SRCNN, Mask R-CNN, FCN, U-Net, DenseNet, FractalNet, etc.) were presented for different applications [7].

Even though deep neural networks are capable of proposing satisfactory results for this application, they are still processed as a black box, which can tend to diminish the system's reliability. Thus, processing the outcomes of deep neural networks as state variables significantly increases the performance of machine learning methods and the trustworthiness of control systems. In fact, the neural network provides the reference signals instead of representing the plant process as a black box. In this context, this section presents how features detected by CNN can be used as references for robust control methods. To facilitate the understanding of the presented approach, a list of the main used variables is presented in Table 10.1.

TABLE 10.1 Deep learning list of main variables

SYMBOL	MEANING
t	t-th timestep
$l = \{1, \ldots, L\}$	Convolutional layers
$\ddot{I}_t^l = \left[\ddot{i}_{1,t}^l, \ldots, \ddot{i}_{\ddot{o}^l,t}^l \right]$	Output values from the layer l, represented by $\ddot{o}^l$ variables on each timestep t
NS	Total number of simulation steps
P_0, P_1 and P_2	Vehicle possible reference positions
$\overrightarrow{PO_n^l}, \overrightarrow{P1_n^l}$ and $\overrightarrow{P2_n^l}$	Vectors to store the experimental simulation data at P_0, P_1 and P_2, respectively
$\ddot{A}_n^l$	Decision matrices
$\ddot{i}_{\pi^\bullet,t}^l \in \ddot{I}_t^l$	Best output value or values for the control application
x_t	Current measured state variable

10.2.1 CNN analytic outcomes as control references

A CNN is composed of sequential convolutional flow layers, where each layer includes a convolution filter or kernel, pooling layers, nonlinear processing layer and batch normalization [7]. This process results in feature maps and allows the interpretation of an image in different levels of confidence. Finally, these feature maps are processed by fully connected (FC) layers.

The main principle of a CNN is a discrete convolutional operation, on each timestep t, of an input set of matrices $\ddot{I}_t^{l-1}$ with a kernel κ to obtain an output set of matrices $\ddot{I}_t^l$, $\forall l = \{1, \ldots, L\}$ layer. For a more detailed analysis on each layer l, the operational matrices can be defined by a set of scalar independent variables, where the resulting matrix $\ddot{I}_t^l$ has $\ddot{o}^l$ values, as:

$$\ddot{I}_t^0 = \left[\ddot{i}_{1,t}^0, \ldots, \ddot{i}_{\ddot{o}^0,t}^0 \right]$$
$$\vdots$$
$$\ddot{I}_t^l = \left[\ddot{i}_{1,t}^l, \ldots, \ddot{i}_{\ddot{o}^l,t}^l \right] \qquad (10.1)$$
$$\vdots$$
$$\ddot{I}_t^L = \left[\ddot{i}_{1,t}^L, \ldots, \ddot{i}_{\ddot{o}^L,t}^L \right]$$

For example, an input RGB image with 100 pixels, $\ddot{I}_t^0 \in \mathbb{R}^{10 \times 10 \times 3}$ has $\ddot{o}^0 = 10 \times 10 \times 3 = 300$ independent variables on each timestep t. Thus, a convolutional operation involving input matrices $\ddot{I}_t^{l-1} \in \mathbb{R}^{i_1 \times i_2 \times i_3}$, with $\ddot{o}^{l-1} = i_1 \times i_2 \times i_3$ variables, and a kernel $\kappa \in \mathbb{R}^{a_1 \times a_2}$ results in new convolutional maps $\phi^l \in \mathbb{R}^{e_1 \times e_2}$, as:

$$\phi^l = \left(\ddot{I}_t^{l-1} * \kappa \right) = \sum_{x_1=0}^{a_1-1} \sum_{x_2=0}^{a_2-1} \sum_{x_3=1}^{i_3} \kappa_{x_1,x_2} \ddot{i}_{(i_1+x_1,i_2+x_2,x_3),t}^{l-1}. \qquad (10.2)$$

where $*$ indicates the convolutional operation. This procedure provides different feature maps ϕ^l in the L different layers. Next, the resulted feature map is processed as:

$$\ddot{Y}^l = f\left(\phi^l + \ddot{a}^l \right), \qquad (10.3)$$

where $f(.)$ is a non-linear activation function, $\ddot{a}$ is a bias or an intercept added in a linear equation, and $\ddot{Y}^l$ is the input for the pooling layer, as:

$$\ddot{I}_t^l = Pooling\left(\ddot{Y}^l\right), \tag{10.4}$$

where $\ddot{I}_t^l$ is the resulting output matrix.

For vision-based control, a front camera collects the information about the surroundings of the vehicle and provides real-time inputs $\ddot{I}_t^0$ to the CNN. Using a convolutional operation, a set of $a_1 \times a_2$ independent variables on the layer $l-1$ will be reorganized as a single outcome on the layer l. Thus, specific outputs from the layer l can be processed by robust control methods instead of other convolutional or fully connected layers, as discussed in this chapter.

10.2.2 Experimental data

To identify the suitable convolution outcomes for a vision-based control, it is necessary to assess the sensitivity of the state variation in the convolutional matrices $\ddot{I}_t^1, \ldots, \ddot{I}_t^L$, in response to a position variation of the input image $\ddot{I}_t^0$. In this context, the car has a desired position (P_0) on the map that also results in a pixel configuration on $\ddot{I}_t^0$. To verify the displacement variation sensitivity, the car should be moved in two opposite directions on the map (represented by a displacement of Δe_1 to position P_1, and a displacement of Δe_2 to position P_2).

Since P_1 and P_2 denote different positions on the map, they will result in different $\ddot{I}_t^0$ values as well. Furthermore, following the convolutional operation, different outcomes are expected on $\ddot{I}_t^l, \forall l = \{1, \ldots, L\}$ layer, on the different positions P_0, P_1 and P_2. Applications involving lateral control for lane keeping and longitudinal control for keeping a distance from a front vehicle are presented in Figure 10.1.

Since three different positions were proposed, three different simulations should be carried out during a defined number of timesteps, each one collecting NS experimental samples. On the first simulation, the car is driven to the desired map position, so the input image $\ddot{I}_t^0$ results from capturing an image at position P_0. Then, for $l = \{1, \ldots, L\}$ and $t = \{1, \ldots, NS\}$, a group of vectors stores the experimental data, as:

$$
\begin{bmatrix}
\overrightarrow{PO_{1,t}^1} = \{\ddot{I}_{1,t}^1 \mid P_0\} \\
\overrightarrow{PO_{2,t}^1} = \{\ddot{I}_{2,t}^1 \mid P_0\} \\
\vdots \\
\overrightarrow{PO_{\ddot{o}^1-1,t}^1} = \{\ddot{I}_{\ddot{o}^1-1,t}^1 \mid P_0\} \\
\overrightarrow{PO_{\ddot{o}^1,t}^1} = \{\ddot{I}_{\ddot{o}^1,t}^1 \mid P_0\}
\end{bmatrix}
\underbrace{}_{1^{st} \text{ layer}}
\to \ldots \to
\begin{bmatrix}
\overrightarrow{PO_{1,t}^l} = \{\ddot{I}_{1,t}^l \mid P_0\} \\
\overrightarrow{PO_{2,t}^l} = \{\ddot{I}_{2,t}^l \mid P_0\} \\
\vdots \\
\overrightarrow{PO_{\ddot{o}^l-1,t}^l} = \{\ddot{I}_{\ddot{o}^l-1,t}^l \mid P_0\} \\
\overrightarrow{PO_{\ddot{o}^l,t}^l} = \{\ddot{I}_{\ddot{o}^l,t}^l \mid P_0\}
\end{bmatrix}
\underbrace{}_{l-\text{th layer}}
\to \ldots \to
\begin{bmatrix}
\overrightarrow{PO_{1,t}^L} = \{\ddot{I}_{1,t}^L \mid P_0\} \\
\overrightarrow{PO_{2,t}^L} = \{\ddot{I}_{2,t}^L \mid P_0\} \\
\vdots \\
\overrightarrow{PO_{\ddot{o}^L-1,t}^L} = \{\ddot{I}_{\ddot{o}^L-1,t}^L \mid P_0\} \\
\overrightarrow{PO_{\ddot{o}^L,t}^L} = \{\ddot{I}_{\ddot{o}^L,t}^L \mid P_0\}
\end{bmatrix}
\underbrace{}_{L-\text{th layer}}
\tag{10.5}
$$

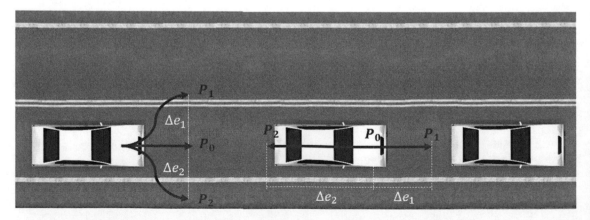

FIGURE 10.1   Desired position P_0 and displacements in two opposite ways, P_1 with Δe_1 from P_0, and P_2 with Δe_2 from P_0, for applications on lateral control and longitudinal control.

In the same way, in the following simulations the car is driven with a displacement position P_1 and P_2 for the second and third simulations, respectively. As a result, for $l = \{1, \ldots, L\}$ and $t = \{1, \ldots, NS\}$, other groups of vectors also store the experimental data as:

$$
\begin{bmatrix}
\overrightarrow{P1_{1,t}^1} = \{\ddot{I}_{1,t}^1 \mid P_1\} \\
\overrightarrow{P1_{2,t}^1} = \{\ddot{I}_{2,t}^1 \mid P_1\} \\
\vdots \\
\overrightarrow{P1_{\ddot{o}^1-1,t}^1} = \{\ddot{I}_{\ddot{o}^1-1,t}^1 \mid P_1\} \\
\overrightarrow{P1_{\ddot{o}^1,t}^1} = \{\ddot{I}_{\ddot{o}^1,t}^1 \mid P_1\}
\end{bmatrix}
\underbrace{}_{1^{st}\ \text{layer}}
\rightarrow \ldots \rightarrow
\begin{bmatrix}
\overrightarrow{P1_{1,t}^l} = \{\ddot{I}_{1,t}^l \mid P_1\} \\
\overrightarrow{P1_{2,t}^l} = \{\ddot{I}_{2,t}^l \mid P_1\} \\
\vdots \\
\overrightarrow{P1_{\ddot{o}^l-1,t}^l} = \{\ddot{I}_{\ddot{o}^l-1,t}^l \mid P_1\} \\
\overrightarrow{P1_{\ddot{o}^l,t}^l} = \{\ddot{I}_{\ddot{o}^l,t}^l \mid P_1\}
\end{bmatrix}
\underbrace{}_{l-\text{th layer}}
\rightarrow \ldots \rightarrow
\begin{bmatrix}
\overrightarrow{P1_{1,t}^L} = \{\ddot{I}_{1,t}^L \mid P_1\} \\
\overrightarrow{P1_{2,t}^L} = \{\ddot{I}_{2,t}^L \mid P_1\} \\
\vdots \\
\overrightarrow{P1_{\ddot{o}^L-1,t}^L} = \{\ddot{I}_{\ddot{o}^L-1,t}^L \mid P_1\} \\
\overrightarrow{P1_{\ddot{o}^L,t}^L} = \{\ddot{I}_{\ddot{o}^L,t}^L \mid P_1\}
\end{bmatrix}
\underbrace{}_{L-\text{th layer}}
\tag{10.6}
$$

for the second simulation. The vectors

$$
\begin{bmatrix}
\overrightarrow{P2_{1,t}^1} = \{\ddot{I}_{1,t}^1 \mid P_2\} \\
\overrightarrow{P2_{2,t}^1} = \{\ddot{I}_{2,t}^1 \mid P_2\} \\
\vdots \\
\overrightarrow{P2_{\ddot{o}^1-1,t}^1} = \{\ddot{I}_{\ddot{o}^1-1,t}^1 \mid P_2\} \\
\overrightarrow{P2_{\ddot{o}^1,t}^1} = \{\ddot{I}_{\ddot{o}^1,t}^1 \mid P_2\}
\end{bmatrix}
\underbrace{}_{1^{st}\ \text{layer}}
\rightarrow \ldots \rightarrow
\begin{bmatrix}
\overrightarrow{P2_{1,t}^l} = \{\ddot{I}_{1,t}^l \mid P_2\} \\
\overrightarrow{P2_{2,t}^l} = \{\ddot{I}_{2,t}^l \mid P_2\} \\
\vdots \\
\overrightarrow{P2_{\ddot{o}^l-1,t}^l} = \{\ddot{I}_{\ddot{o}^l-1,t}^l \mid P_2\} \\
\overrightarrow{P2_{\ddot{o}^l,t}^l} = \{\ddot{I}_{\ddot{o}^l,t}^l \mid P_2\}
\end{bmatrix}
\underbrace{}_{l-\text{th layer}}
\rightarrow \ldots \rightarrow
\begin{bmatrix}
\overrightarrow{P2_{1,t}^L} = \{\ddot{I}_{1,t}^L \mid P_2\} \\
\overrightarrow{P2_{2,t}^L} = \{\ddot{I}_{2,t}^L \mid P_2\} \\
\vdots \\
\overrightarrow{P2_{\ddot{o}^L-1,t}^L} = \{\ddot{I}_{\ddot{o}^L-1,t}^L \mid P_2\} \\
\overrightarrow{P2_{\ddot{o}^L,t}^L} = \{\ddot{I}_{\ddot{o}^L,t}^L \mid P_2\}
\end{bmatrix}
\underbrace{}_{L-\text{th layer}}
\tag{10.7}
$$

store the third simulation data.

Finally, a group of decision matrices $\ddot{A}_n^l \in \mathbb{R}^{3 \times NS}$, $\forall l = \{1, \ldots, L\}$ and $\forall n = \{1, \ldots, \ddot{o}^l\}$, rearranges all the experimental outcomes, as:

$$
\ddot{A}_n^l = \begin{bmatrix} \overrightarrow{P0_n^l} \\ \overrightarrow{P1_n^l} \\ \overrightarrow{P2_n^l} \end{bmatrix}.
\tag{10.8}
$$

The decision matrices $\ddot{A}_n^l$ and the data vectors $\overrightarrow{P0_n^l}$, $\overrightarrow{P1_n^l}$ and $\overrightarrow{P2_n^l}$ are used to measure the outcomes displacement sensitivity and select the best variables, as discussed next.

10.2.3 Multi-objective evaluation

To validate which of the $\ddot{o}^l$ analytic outcomes can be useful for a control application, an evaluation is carried out $\forall l = \{1, \ldots, L\}$. In this context, firstly all matrices $\ddot{A}_n^l$, $\forall n = \{1, \ldots, \ddot{o}^l\}$, are normalized to values between 0 and 1. Next, as presented in [4], the sensitivity for displacement is evaluated using multi-objective optimization for multiple conflicting goals. Also, different constraints can be executed to process only the valid data, as different objective functions can be applied for selection of the outcomes who provided the best $\ddot{A}_n^l$ matrices. Even though different equations can be applied, this section explores examples of constraint conditions and objective functions.

Constraint conditions are applied to select which of the $\ddot{A}_n^l$ represents valid matrices. For example, a constraint condition (CC1) should evaluate whether the $n = \{1, \ldots, \ddot{o}^l\}$ analytical outcomes represent a valid output; therefore the median (**M**) of the simulation vectors should be different from zero, $\forall n = \left\{1,\ldots,\ddot{o}^l\right\}$, as:

$$\text{CC1}: \mathbf{M}\left(\overrightarrow{P0_n^l}\right) \neq 0 \text{ and } \mathbf{M}\left(\overrightarrow{P1_n^l}\right) \neq 0 \text{ and } \mathbf{M}\left(\overrightarrow{P2_n^l}\right) \neq 0 \rightarrow \ddot{A}_n^l \text{ valid.} \tag{10.9}$$

Since the measures from point P_0 represent a desired reference control, another constraint condition (CC2) should ensure that the median $\mathbf{M}\left(\overrightarrow{P0_n^l}\right)$ is a centralized measure between $\mathbf{M}\left(\overrightarrow{P1_n^l}\right)$ and $\mathbf{M}\left(\overrightarrow{P2_n^l}\right)$, $\forall n = \left\{1,\ldots,\ddot{o}^l\right\}$, as:

$$\text{CC2}: \mathbf{M}\left(\overrightarrow{P1_n^l}\right) < \mathbf{M}\left(\overrightarrow{P0_n^l}\right) < \mathbf{M}\left(\overrightarrow{P2_n^l}\right) \text{ or } \mathbf{M}\left(\overrightarrow{P2_n^l}\right) < \mathbf{M}\left(\overrightarrow{P0_n^l}\right) < \mathbf{M}\left(\overrightarrow{P1_n^l}\right) \rightarrow \ddot{A}_n^l \text{ valid.} \tag{10.10}$$

Next, the objective functions evaluate the displacement sensitivity of $\ddot{A}_n^l$, $\forall l = \{1, \ldots, L\}$ and $\forall n = \left\{1,\ldots,\ddot{o}^l\right\}$. Thus, the first and second presented objectives assess difference in the outcomes from the different positions P_0, P_1 and P_2. It is expected that position P_0 provides values that represent the central reference, while P_1 and P_2 provide values spaced from P_0. Then, the best fitness outcomes from this application are the arguments that maximize the distance of the experimental vectors, expressed as:

$$\arg\max\left(f_1\left(\ddot{A}_n^l\right) = \left|\mathbf{M}\left(\overrightarrow{P0_n^l}\right) - \mathbf{M}\left(\overrightarrow{P1_n^l}\right)\right|\right), \tag{10.11}$$

$$\arg\max\left(f_2\left(\ddot{A}_n^l\right) = \left|\mathbf{M}\left(\overrightarrow{P0_n^l}\right) - \mathbf{M}\left(\overrightarrow{P2_n^l}\right)\right|\right), \tag{10.12}$$

while the third objective evaluates the disturbance on the measured experimental vectors. Therefore, the desired arguments have minimal mean square error between the measurement vectors and their median value, as:

$$\arg\min\left(f_3\left(\ddot{A}_n^l\right) = \frac{1}{M}\sum_{j=1}^{M}\left(\left(\mathbf{M}\left(\overrightarrow{P0_n^l}\right) - \overrightarrow{P0_{n,j}^l}\right)^2 + \left(\mathbf{M}\left(\overrightarrow{P1_n^l}\right) - \overrightarrow{P1_{n,j}^l}\right)^2 + \left(\mathbf{M}\left(\overrightarrow{P2_n^l}\right) - \overrightarrow{P2_{n,j}^l}\right)^2\right)\right). \tag{10.13}$$

In sequence, the Pareto Optimality Theory [8] is used for multi-objective comparison, where for each decision matrix $\ddot{A}_n^l$ a vector function is presented as

$$F\left(\ddot{A}_n^l\right) = \left[f_1\left(\ddot{A}_n^l\right), f_2\left(\ddot{A}_n^l\right), f_3\left(\ddot{A}_n^l\right)\right]. \tag{10.14}$$

The Pareto-optimal values are defined by the set of dominant outputs, where an output $o_1 \in \left\{1,\ldots,\ddot{o}^l\right\}$ dominates another vector $o_2 \in \left\{1,\ldots,\ddot{o}^l\right\}$ if and only if

$$f_1\left(\ddot{A}_{0_1}^l\right) \geq f_1\left(\ddot{A}_{0_2}^l\right) \text{ and } f_2\left(\ddot{A}_{0_1}^l\right) \geq f_2\left(\ddot{A}_{0_2}^l\right) \text{ and } f_3\left(\ddot{A}_{0_1}^l\right) \leq f_3\left(\ddot{A}_{0_2}^l\right), \tag{10.15}$$

and for at least one of the three objective functions

$$f_1\left(\ddot{A}_{0_1}^l\right) > f_1\left(\ddot{A}_{0_2}^l\right) \text{ or } f_2\left(\ddot{A}_{0_1}^l\right) > f_2\left(\ddot{A}_{0_2}^l\right) \text{ or } f_3\left(\ddot{A}_{0_1}^l\right) < f_3\left(\ddot{A}_{0_2}^l\right). \tag{10.16}$$

If $\forall n = \left\{1,\ldots,\ddot{o}^l\right\}$ exists any $\ddot{A}_{0_1}^l$, $o_1 \in \left\{1,\ldots,\ddot{o}^l\right\}$, such than o_1 is not dominated for any n value, o_1 is an optimal value, and it will compose the Pareto set (*PS*) and their vector function will compose the Pareto front (*PF*):

$$PS := \{\, \ddot{A}_{o_1}^l \mid \ddot{A}_{o_1}^l \text{ is a Pareto optimal}\},$$ (10.17)

and

$$PF := \left\{\ddot{A}_{o_1}^l \in PS\right\}.$$ (10.18)

For the presented evaluation method, several decision matrices can compose the *PF*. In this sense, in the following step it is necessary to select the best decision matrix or matrices for the control application, represented by $\ddot{A}_{\pi^*}^l$, that correspond to the best output value or values $\ddot{i}_{\pi^*,t}^l \in \ddot{I}_t^l$. Following this, the variable $\ddot{i}_{\pi^*,t}^l$ can be applied as a real-time control state, as presented next. Even though it is possible to choose more than one CNN outcome, the following subsection shows how to interpret a single selected output. Nonetheless, the same principle can be extended to selecting two or more outputs.

10.2.4 Control state variable

Since the selected experimental vector $\overrightarrow{PO_{\pi^*}^l}$ represents an approximation of the desired behavior, the scalar values $\mathbf{M}\left(\overrightarrow{PO_{\pi^*}^l}\right)$ can be assigned as control reference for their respective selected state values $\ddot{i}_{\pi^*,t}^l$. Therefore, a control state variable can be calculated by:

$$x_t = \frac{\ddot{i}_{\pi^*,t}^l - \min\left(\overrightarrow{PO_{\pi^*}^l}\right)}{\max\left(\overrightarrow{PO_{\pi^*}^l}\right) - \min\left(\overrightarrow{PO_{\pi^*}^l}\right)} - \mathbf{M}\left(\overrightarrow{PO_{\pi^*}^l}\right),$$ (10.19)

where x_t is the current measured state variable, and $\max\left(\overrightarrow{PO_{\pi^*}^l}\right)$ and $\min\left(\overrightarrow{PO_{\pi^*}^l}\right)$ are applied to normalize the chosen analytic outcome $\ddot{i}_{\pi^*,t}^l$.

As the selected state variable s_t is influenced by nonlinearities arising from the image-processing method, it is necessary to use robust control techniques to guarantee stability at the desired operating point. In addition, the variables x_t are closely related to robust control procedures as discussed in the following section.

10.3 ROBUST CONTROL DESIGN

Let us consider the discrete-time realization of a linear system given by

$$x_{t+1} = F_t x_t + G_t u_t,$$ (10.20)

or

$$x_{t+1} = \begin{bmatrix} x_t^T & u_t^T \end{bmatrix} \begin{bmatrix} F_t^T \\ G_t^T \end{bmatrix},$$ (10.21)

TABLE 10.2 List of main variables

SYMBOL	MEANING
u_t	Current action
F_t, G_t	Nominal state transition and input matrices
$\delta F_t, \delta G_t$	Parametric uncertainties
Q_t, R_t	Weight matrices
K_t	Quadratic regulator gain

where $t = \{0, \ldots, NS\}$, $x_t \in R^n$ is the state vector, $u_t \in R^m$ is the control input, $F_t \in R^{n \times n}$ and $G_t \in R^{n \times m}$ are known nominal state transition and input matrices. The model matrices F_t and G_t, in addition to the regulator weighing matrices Q_t and R_t, provide a cost function to be minimized. Then, it is necessary to carry out the system matrix identification process, described next.

A list of the main variables explored in this section is presented in Table 10.2.

10.3.1 System identification

Considering a set of sample data with different input and output values, for the definition of the LQR controller, it can be assumed that x_{t+1}, x_t and u_t are known values and, therefore, we can identify the values of the internal matrices F_t and G_t using the method based on mean square error estimation, presented by [9]. For this purpose, suppose that the input and output data of the system are interpreted as:

$$y_t = \Omega_t^T \theta + z_t, \tag{10.22}$$

where y_t and Ω_t^T are known vectors, Θ is a vector whose values will be estimated, and z_t represents errors and disturbances. Then, define a parameter prediction equation as::

$$y'_t = \Omega_t^T \theta. \tag{10.23}$$

The purpose of the estimation process is to minimize the mean square prediction error, represented by

$$E = \frac{1}{N} \sum_{t=1}^{N} \left[y_t - y'_t \right]^2, \tag{10.24}$$

where N is the number of sample data.

Minimizing Equation (10.24) yields the analytical solution

$$\theta = \left[\frac{1}{N} \sum_{k=1}^{N} \Omega_k \Omega_k^T \right]^{-1} \frac{1}{N} \sum_{k=1}^{N} \Omega_k y_k. \tag{10.25}$$

The original purpose of Equations (10.23)–(10.25) is to perform vector identifications. Therefore, they may not seem appropriate to estimate matrices parameters in state–space form. Nevertheless, identifying matrices is possible by rearranging the state-space equation, similarly to what was done in [10]. For example, Equation (10.20) is equivalent to:

$$x_{j,t+1} = \begin{bmatrix} x_t^T & u_t^T \end{bmatrix} \begin{bmatrix} F_{j,t}^T \\ G_{j,t}^T \end{bmatrix} \tag{10.26}$$

for every j-th row of the respective matrices. Therefore, by j consecutive applications of the identification method, the full matrices will be identified, one line at a time.

10.3.2 Robust Linear Quadratic Regulator (RLQR)

Consider the discrete-time system subject to parametric uncertainties described as

$$x_{t+1} = \left(F_t + \delta F_t \right) x_t + \left(G_t + \delta G_t \right) u_t,$$
(10.27)

$$x_0 = constant,$$
(10.28)

where δF_t and δG_t denote parametric uncertainties. The uncertainty matrices are defined as:

$$\begin{bmatrix} \delta F_t & \delta G_t \end{bmatrix} = H_t \Delta_t \begin{bmatrix} E_{F_t} & E_{G_t} \end{bmatrix},$$
(10.29)

where $H_t \in \mathbb{R}^{n \times p}$, $E_{F_t} \in \mathbb{R}^{l \times n}$ and $E_{G_t} \in \mathbb{R}^{l \times m}$ are known matrices and $\Delta_t \in \mathbb{R}^{p \times l}$ is an arbitrary matrix such that $\|\Delta\| \leq 1$.

The RLQR results from the solution of the following least-squares optimization problem [11]

$$\min_{x_{t+1}, u_t} \max_{\delta F_t, \delta G_t} \bar{J}_t^\mu \left(x_{t+1}, u_t, \delta F_t, \delta G_t \right),$$
(10.30)

where $\bar{J}_t^\mu$ is the cost function

$$\bar{J}_t^\mu \left(x_{t+1}, u_t, \delta F_t, \delta G_t \right) = \begin{bmatrix} x_{t+1} \\ u_t \end{bmatrix}^T \begin{bmatrix} P_{t+1} & 0 \\ 0 & R_t \end{bmatrix} \begin{bmatrix} x_{t+1} \\ u_t \end{bmatrix} + \Phi^T \begin{bmatrix} Q_t & 0 \\ 0 & \mu I \end{bmatrix} \Phi,$$
(10.31)

for a fixed penalty parameter $\mu > 0$, positive definite weight matrices $Q_t > 0$, $R_t > 0$, $P_{t+1} > 0$ and

$$\Phi = \left\{ \begin{bmatrix} 0 & 0 \\ I & -G_t - \delta G_t \end{bmatrix} \begin{bmatrix} x_{t+1} \\ u_t \end{bmatrix} - \begin{bmatrix} -I \\ F_t + \delta F_t \end{bmatrix} x_t \right\}.$$
(10.32)

The next paragraphs detail how to solve the robust regularized least-squares problem and how it relates to the robust recursive regulator.

The robust regularized least-squares problem considers the optimization Problem (10.30) expressed in a generic form, where data information, given in matrix A, and measurements provided in vector b, are subject to uncertainties

$$\min_x \max_{\delta A, \delta b} \left\{ J \left(x, \delta A, \delta b \right) \right\}.$$
(10.33)

where

$$J(x) = x^T Q x + \left(\left(A + \delta A \right) x - \left(b + \delta b \right) \right)^T W \left(\left(A + \delta A \right) x - \left(b + \delta b \right) \right).$$
(10.34)

and uncertainties δA and δb are modeled as

$$\begin{bmatrix} \delta A & \delta b \end{bmatrix} = H \Delta \begin{bmatrix} E_A & E_b \end{bmatrix},$$
(10.35)

being A, b, H, E_A, E_b, Q and W known matrices of adequate dimensions, Δ is an arbitrary contraction matrix ($\|\Delta\| \leq 1$) and x is an unknown vector. Lemma 1.3.2.1 [12] brings the optimal solution for the Problem (10.33)–(10.34):

Lemma 1.3.2.1 The solution for the optimization Problem (10.33)–(10.34) is given by

$$x^* = \left(\hat{Q} + A^T\hat{W}A\right)^{-1}\left(A^T\hat{W}b + \hat{\lambda}E_A^T E_b\right),$$ (10.36)

for $\hat{Q}$ and $\hat{W}$ defined as

$$\hat{Q} := Q + \hat{\lambda}E_A^T E_A,$$ (10.37)

$$\hat{W} := W + WH\left(\hat{\lambda}I - H^T WH\right)^\dagger H^T W,$$ (10.38)

with $\hat{\lambda} > \|H^T WH\|$.
Proof: See [12].

Lemma 1.3.2.2 shows an equivalent solution for Problem (10.33)–(10.34), written in terms of matrix arrays.

Lemma 1.3.2.2 If $Q > 0$ and $W > 0$, then the solution x^* for the problem (10.33) – (10.34) can be written as

$$\begin{bmatrix} x^* \\ J\left(x^*\right) \end{bmatrix} = \begin{bmatrix} 0 & 0 \\ 0 & b \\ 0 & E_b \\ I & 0 \end{bmatrix}^T \begin{bmatrix} Q^{-1} & 0 & 0 & I \\ 0 & \hat{W}^{-1} & 0 & A \\ 0 & 0 & \hat{\lambda}^{-1}I & E_A \\ I & A^T & E_A^T & 0 \end{bmatrix}^{-1} \begin{bmatrix} 0 \\ b \\ E_b \\ 0 \end{bmatrix},$$ (10.39)

where $\hat{W}$ and $\hat{\lambda}$ are as in Lemma 1.3.2.1
Proof: See [11] and references therein.

As shown in [11], Lemma 1.3.2.2 allows for solving the optimization problem given in **(10.30)–(10.32)** with $\mu > 0$, according to the following theorem:

Theorem 1.3.2.3

For given initial conditions x_0 and $P_0 > 0$, and chosen positive definite matrices Q_t and R_t the robust recursive regulator is solved as:

$$\begin{bmatrix} x_{t+1}^* \\ u_t^* \end{bmatrix} = \begin{bmatrix} L_t \\ K_t \end{bmatrix} x_t^*, t = 0,\ldots N,$$ (10.40)

with L_t and K_t resulting from the recursion

$$
\begin{bmatrix} L_t \\ K_t \\ P_t \end{bmatrix} = \begin{bmatrix} 0 & 0 & 0 \\ 0 & 0 & 0 \\ 0 & 0 & -I \\ 0 & 0 & \hat{F}_t \\ I & 0 & 0 \\ 0 & I & 0 \end{bmatrix}^T \begin{bmatrix} P_{t+1}^{-1} & 0 & 0 & 0 & I & 0 \\ 0 & R_t^{-1} & 0 & 0 & 0 & I \\ 0 & 0 & Q_t^{-1} & 0 & 0 & 0 \\ 0 & 0 & 0 & \Sigma_t\left(\mu,\hat{\lambda}_t\right) & \hat{I} & -\hat{G}_t \\ I & 0 & 0 & \hat{I}^T & 0 & 0 \\ 0 & I & 0 & -\hat{G}_t & 0 & 0 \end{bmatrix}^{-1} \begin{bmatrix} 0 \\ 0 \\ -I \\ \hat{F}_t \\ 0 \\ 0 \end{bmatrix},
$$

(10.41)

where

$$
\Sigma_t = \begin{bmatrix} \mu^{-1}I - \hat{\lambda}_t^{-1}H_tH_t^T & 0 \\ 0 & \hat{\lambda}_t^{-1}I \end{bmatrix}, \hat{I} = \begin{bmatrix} I \\ 0 \end{bmatrix}, \hat{G}_t = \begin{bmatrix} G_t \\ E_{G_t} \end{bmatrix}, \hat{F}_t = \begin{bmatrix} F_t \\ E_{F_t} \end{bmatrix}.
$$

Proof: Consider the following identifications associating Problem (10.30)–(10.32) with (10.33)–(10.35)

$$
Q \leftarrow \begin{bmatrix} P_{t+1} & 0 \\ 0 & R_t \end{bmatrix}, W \leftarrow \begin{bmatrix} Q_t & 0 \\ 0 & \mu I \end{bmatrix}, x \leftarrow \begin{bmatrix} x_{t+1} \\ u_t \end{bmatrix},
$$

$$
A \leftarrow \begin{bmatrix} 0 & 0 \\ I & -G_t \end{bmatrix}, \delta A \leftarrow \begin{bmatrix} 0 & 0 \\ 0 & -\delta G_t \end{bmatrix}, b \leftarrow \begin{bmatrix} -I \\ F_t \end{bmatrix} x_t, \delta b \leftarrow \begin{bmatrix} 0 \\ \delta F_t \end{bmatrix} x_t,
$$

$$
H \leftarrow \begin{bmatrix} 0 \\ H_t \end{bmatrix}, \Delta \leftarrow \Delta_i, E_A \leftarrow \begin{bmatrix} 0 & -E_{G_t} \end{bmatrix}, E_b \leftarrow E_{F_t}x_t.
$$

By applying the result from Lemma 1.3.2.2 and performing some algebraic manipulations, one obtains Equations (10.40) and (10.41). When $\mu \to \infty$ and the inverse in (10.41) exists, the regulator is optimal and system robustness increases [11].

If the system is not subject to uncertainties, then the solution (10.40)–(10.41) in Theorem is equivalent to the standard nominal LQR. In this case, δF_t and δG_t vanish and the solution to (10.30)–(10.32) becomes:

$$
\begin{bmatrix} L_t \\ K_t \\ P_t \end{bmatrix} = \begin{bmatrix} 0 & 0 & 0 \\ 0 & 0 & 0 \\ 0 & 0 & -I \\ 0 & 0 & F_t \\ I & 0 & 0 \\ 0 & I & 0 \end{bmatrix}^T \begin{bmatrix} P_{t+1}^{-1} & 0 & 0 & 0 & I & 0 \\ 0 & R_t^{-1} & 0 & 0 & 0 & I \\ 0 & 0 & Q_t^{-1} & 0 & 0 & 0 \\ 0 & 0 & 0 & 0 & I & -G_t \\ I & 0 & 0 & I^T & 0 & 0 \\ 0 & I & 0 & -G^T & 0 & 0 \end{bmatrix}^{-1} \begin{bmatrix} 0 \\ 0 \\ -I \\ F_t \\ 0 \\ 0 \end{bmatrix}.
$$

(10.42)

10.3.3 $\mathcal{H}_\infty$ Controller

This section is based on steps from [13] and narrows the contents to the specific class of linear systems. Nevertheless, the reader can easily find a more general description and deeper mathematical analysis for instance in [14, 15], to mention a few well-known references. Therefore, consider the $\mathcal{H}_\infty$ control problem of finding a signal $u_t = K_t x_t$ such that

$$
\sup_{\delta F_t, \delta G_t} \frac{x_{N+1}^T P_{N+1} x_{N+1} + \sum_{t=0}^{N}\left(u_t^T R_t u_t + x_t^T Q_t x_t\right)}{x_0^T x_0 + \sum_{t=0}^{N}\left\|\delta F_t x_t + \delta G_t u_t\right\|_{Q_t}^2} < \gamma^2,
$$

(10.43)

holds for an adequate $\gamma > 0$, where matrices $P_{N+1} > 0$, $Q_t > 0$ and $R_t > 0$ are weights associated to the variables x_{N+1}, x_t and u_t, respectively.

Observe that the problem bounds the worst-case of uncertainties to the quadratic cost in (10.43) through γ. In turn, the parameter γ is usually adjusted off-line and reflects the robustness of the controller with respect to the norm bounded uncertainties $\{\delta F_t, \delta G_t\}$. In this sense, it is desirable to have γ as small as possible to attain a more robust controller. From a project point of view, the choice of γ can be carried out via line search procedures to yield an initial value, which is then adjusted according to the performance requirements of the specific application. Specifically for the autonomous driving application addressed in this chapter, a good practice is to start with an initial, relatively large, γ for which (10.43) holds, and then proceed iteratively to achieve the smallest γ possible.

As discussed in [13] and references therein, a solution exists if, and only if, the following existence conditions hold for some $\gamma > 0$:

$$\lambda\left(I - \gamma^{-2} P_{t+1}\right) > 0, \tag{10.44}$$

and

$$-\gamma^2 I + H_t^T P_{t+1} H_t - H_t^T P_{t+1} G_t \left(R_i + G_t^T P_{t+1} G_t\right)^{-1} G_t^T P_{t+1} H_t < 0, \tag{10.45}$$

where P_t satisfies the recursive algebraic Riccati equation

$$P_t = Q_t + F_t^T P_{t+1} F_t - K_t^T R_c K_t, \tag{10.46}$$

with

$$R_c = \begin{bmatrix} R_t + G_t^T P_{t+1} G_t & G_t^T P_{t+1} H_t \\ H_t^T P_{t+1} G_t & -\gamma^2 I + H_t^T P_{t+1} H_t \end{bmatrix}, \tag{10.47}$$

$$K_t = -\left(R_t + G_t^T P_{t+1} G_t\right)^{-1} G_t^T P_{t+1}. \tag{10.48}$$

In this context, a control law capable of satisfying both (10.44) and (10.45) is given by

$$u_t = K_t x_t \Rightarrow u_t = -\left(R_t + G_t^T P_{t+1} G_t\right)^{-1} G_t^T P_{t+1} x_t. \tag{10.49}$$

At this point, it is adequate to make a few comments regarding the parametric uncertainties. Although $\{\delta F_t, \delta G_t\}$ are assumed to be norm-bounded according to (10.29), different types of structured uncertainties, such as polytopic, can be adopted. In this case, the designer must select the robust control approach accordingly to ensure closed-loop stability. The next section describes how $\{\delta F_t, \delta G_t\}$ are estimated by an evolutionary algorithm and examines the application of the hybrid framework on lateral control.

10.4 CASE STUDY FOR HYBRID CONTROLLER

In this section, we provide a case study for path-following lateral control to illustrate the application of the discussed concepts. First, a simulation environment and the problem objective are discussed. Next, a vision-based Deep Reinforcement Learning (DRL) [16, 17] method, resulting from the combination of the Proximal Policy Optimization (PPO) [18] algorithm with a CNN, is presented as the first control application.

In sequence, the CNN outcomes are used for the design of three hybrid controllers. The first method is a nominal LQR controller. The second and third methods are represented by the robust controllers RLQR and $\mathcal{H}_\infty$, respectively, where the uncertainty variables are estimated using the Evolutionary Algorithm with Numerical differentiation (EAND) [19]. Finally, a performance evaluation is carried out to compare the methods.

10.4.1 Simulation environment and problem objective

The CARLA (Car Learning to Act) [20, 21] is a realistic and open-source simulator, which facilitates the development and implementation of algorithms for machine learning and control of autonomous vehicles in urban environments. The simulator features different weather conditions, with static (buildings, traffic signs, squares) and dynamic (pedestrians and other vehicles) variables. Furthermore, the simulator offers sensor signal measurements as GPS coordinates, speed, throttle and steering actions, collision detection, opposite lane invasion and other traffic violations.

Diverse versions of the simulator have been presented since its launch in 2017. This case study is implemented in CARLA 0.9.3, which presents several cities with different layouts, highways and streets. In these experiments, it is desired to develop hybrid architectures for image-based lateral control, with the minimal path-following error in relation with the center of the road. For this task, a car is initialized at point P_A and should reach its objective at point P_B, as summarized in Figure 10.2. Also, four views of this route in the CARLA simulator are presented in Figure 10.3, where it is possible to note some object

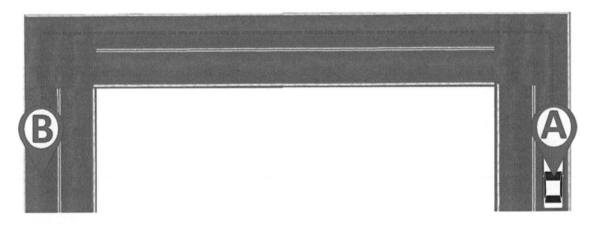

FIGURE 10.2   Route map in the CARLA simulator.

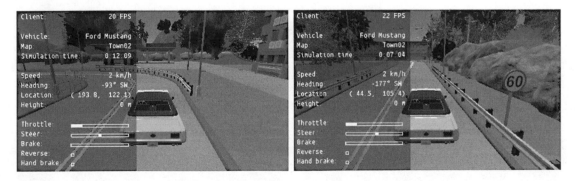

FIGURE 10.3   Views of the route map in the CARLA simulator.

classes that can increase the difficulty for image-based lateral control, such as lane-marking, sidewalk, fence, pole, wall, building, vegetation, etc.

10.4.2 Machine learning design

The DRL algorithm trains a deep neural network based on images in order to increase an associated reward, which translates to an improvement in systems performance. As the reward increases, the neural model better interprets the content of the image, highlighting the pixels configuration more relevant for the control application. For example, for a lateral control application, pixels that describe road elements, as division lines with the opposite lane or sidewalks, should be highlighted in the training procedure.

This section discusses the input image and the output action used by the CNN model. Furthermore, the DRL reward equation and the machine learning design used for the proposed approaches are presented in detail. Finally, the simulation technical details for the training procedure are discussed.

10.4.2.1 Input and output

A real-time RGB image provided by the simulator is resized by 200×100 pixels, as presented in Figure 10.4, and it is considered as the input of all the control architectures developed in this case study. The models' output is a steering action $u_t \in [-0.6, 0.6]$, where negative and positive values represent steering wheel to the left-hand and right-hand sides, respectively, varying up to 60% of the maximum angle for each side.

10.4.2.2 Reward function

Determining the rewards function is a critical and essential step in DRL algorithm development. These functions reflect the quality of the agent's actions in its environment, and indicate behavioral policy resulting from the learning or training process. In the presented context, the agent is represented by a CNN initialized with random weights. As the agent explores its environments, it collects experimental data and the PPO algorithm calculates a cost function based on the reward values.

Therefore, on each timestep t, the neural model selects a steering action u_t based on the input image and, as a result, the simulation environment returns a reward r_t represented by the weighted sum of three terms as:

$$r_t = 50(3 - e_t) + 10d_t - 10c_t, \tag{10.50}$$

FIGURE 10.4   Real-time RGB image as input.

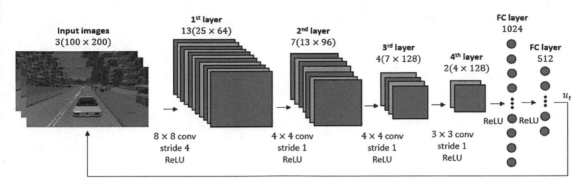

FIGURE 10.5 CNN architecture.

where e_t is the Euclidean distance of the position of the vehicle and the reference path, d_t is the distance traveled and c_t is a collision sensor. The cost function defined by the PPO leads the neural model training in order to maximize the returned reward, which translates to an improvement in systems performance.

10.4.2.3 Neural network design

The PPO algorithm requires two deep neural networks during the training process, represented by the Actor and Critic networks. For testing, only the Actor network selects an action as a function of the current image. This case study considers a CNN with four convolutional layers and two fully connected layers for both Actor and Critic networks. This neural model is summarized in Figure 10.5.

The CNN input is a concatenation of three 200 × 100 RGB images collected in the timesteps t, $t - 1$ and $t - 2$, respectively. Thus, the input image $\ddot{I}_t^0$ is defined by $\ddot{o}^0 = 200 \times 100 \times 3 \times 3 = 180,000$ independent variables on each timestep t. As a result, the proposed CNN presents $\ddot{o}^1 = 20,800$, $\ddot{o}^2 = 8,736$, $\ddot{o}^3 = 3,584$ and $\ddot{o}^4 = 1,024$ independent variables for the output values $\ddot{I}_t^1$, $\ddot{I}_t^2$, $\ddot{I}_t^3$ and $\ddot{I}_t^4$, respectively. Finally, $\ddot{I}_t^4$ is processed by two FC layers with 1,024 and 512 hidden neurons, respectively.

10.4.2.4 Simulation technical details

The machine learning and control algorithms were implemented in Python 3.6, and the development framework for the DRL method was the Tensorblock,[1] defined as a Tensorflow [22] API, that encapsulates the graph variables in blocks or classes, making the access and alterations of the base code simple and faster. To train the CNN, it was considered no dropout, Adam optimizes, ReLU activation function and a learning rate of 5×10^{-4}. The PPO's parameters are defined as a clipping equal to 0.12, a discount factor of 0.99 and a GAE parameter of 0.95. Also, a training episode was performed for each batch size of 1.000 collected experiences, in an NVIDIA GeForce GTX 1050Ti with 4GB memory, Ubuntu 16.04.

The training process was carried out during four hours, with 75,000 collected timesteps. IN this short amount of time, the car is able to complete a straight street without collision, but is not able to complete a curve. This work considers this badly trained neural model to show that it is possible to present a useful hybrid control, as presented next.

10.4.3 Hybrid control design

Considering the trained CNN presented previously, this section explores the combination of this deep learning algorithm with robust recursive controllers in order to enhance performance. The main procedures of this application are discussed, starting with a control reference selection method, followed by a system identification using the selected state variables, the resulting nominal control and, finally, an uncertainty estimation on the previous model via evolutionary search.

10.4.3.1 Control reference selection

An evaluation of displacement variation sensitivity is carried out for control reference selection procedure. Then, the vehicle is manually driven in the positions P_0 (center of the road), P_1 (vehicle displaced to the left side) and P_2 (vehicle displaced to the right side) from point P_A to point P_B (see Figure 4.2). This simulation completed a batch of $NS = 1,000$ timesteps resulting in the decision matrices $\ddot{A}_1^1,\ldots,\ddot{A}_{20,800}^1$ for the 1st layer, $\ddot{A}_1^2,\ldots,\ddot{A}_{8,736}^2$ for the 2nd layer, $\ddot{A}_1^3,\ldots,\ddot{A}_{3,584}^3$ for the 3rd layer, and, finally, $\ddot{A}_1^4,\ldots,\ddot{A}_{1,024}^4$ for the 4th layer, as presented in (10.8). Following, all the elements from decision matrices are normalized to [0, 1] to proceed with sensitivity for displacement evaluation.

The Equations (10.9) and (10.10) were considered as constraint conditions, while the Equations (10.11)–(10.13) were considered as objective functions. As a result, four *PF* with 35, 44, 11 and 35 analytic outcomes were provided by the 1st, 2nd, 3rd and 4th layers, respectively. Following, all the *PF* elements and their neighbors were carefully evaluated in order to select the output that best represents the system dynamics. As a result, the CNN analytic outcome $\ddot{i}_{87,t}^4 \in \ddot{I}_t^4$ was chosen as the control system selected state variable ($\ddot{i}_{\pi^*,t}^l$).

Figure 10.6 shown the selected decision matrix $\ddot{A}_{87}^4$, presenting the plot of the vectors $\overrightarrow{P0_{87}^4}$, $\overrightarrow{P1_{87}^4}$ and $\overrightarrow{P2_{87}^4}$, and the control reference $\mathbf{M}\left(\overrightarrow{P0_{87}^4}\right) = 0.2521$. Since $\max\left(\overrightarrow{P0_n^i}\right) = 16.42471$ and $\min\left(\overrightarrow{P0_n^i}\right) = 0$, the current measured state variable is calculated as:

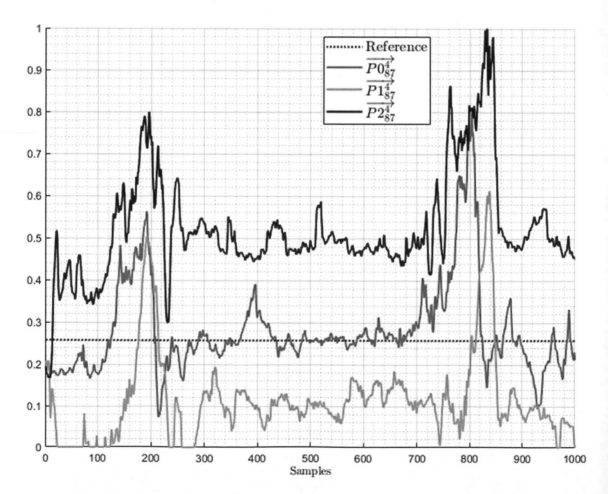

FIGURE 10.6   Selected decision matrix $\ddot{A}_{87}^4$.

$$x_t = \frac{\ddot{i}_{87,t}^4}{16.42471} - 0.2521.$$ (10.51)

An interesting characteristic from the decision matrix $\ddot{A}_{87}^4$ is the fact that all the vectors $\overrightarrow{P0_{87}^4}$, $\overrightarrow{P1_{87}^4}$ and $P2_{87}^4$ presented values greater than the reference for both curve regions, curve 1 $t \in [100, 150]$ and curve 2 $t \in [800, 950]$. This indicates the control system provides an output action consistent with the scenario, since the model indicates a steering action to the left side in all curve regions.

With the state variable x_t presented in (10.51), it is possible to perform the system identification method as following.

10.4.3.2 System identification and nominal LQR

For the system identification method, it is necessary to validate how the current state x_t varies as a function of the current action u_t. Thus, the car was manually driven around the reference in different experiments, with steering action varying from 0 to 60% for both right and left side, and collecting a range of 8,823 experimental samples. Then, the nominal state transition and input matrices are defined based on sample data, as presented in (10.20)–(10.26). The regulator weighing matrices were adjust to $Q_t = 2$ and $R_t = 1$, returning the matrices $F_t = 0.9988$ and $G_t = 0.0486$, and a final feedback gain of $K_N = 1.3420$.

10.4.3.3 Uncertainty estimation via evolutionary search

To apply the robust control methods presented in the previous sections, the parametric uncertainties were estimated by evolutionary search using the EAND algorithm. This case study considered a population with 20 individuals, initialized with random values $X_h \in [-1, 1]$, where each $h = \{1, \ldots, 20\}$ element was represented by

$$X_h = \left[\delta F_{th}, \delta G_{th} \right],$$ (10.52)

where for each individual X_h, a new feedback gain K_{th} is calculated using the values $[(F_t + \delta F_{th}), (G_t + \delta G_{th}), Q_t, R_t]$.

For performance evaluation, a run in the CARLA simulator is defined for the car starting in position P_A and reaching position P_B (or colliding and becoming stuck). Thus, each gain K_{th} is evaluated during a run, and it returns the sum of rewards defined by:

$$Y_h = \sum_{t=1}^{NS} r_t,$$ (10.53)

where r_t is presented in (10.50). Finally, the EAND algorithm adjust the X_h variables to maximize Y_h. The optimization process to define the uncertainties of the control system is summarized in Figure 10.7.

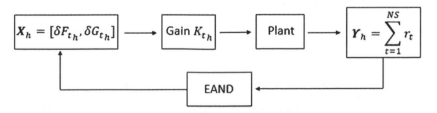

FIGURE 10.7   Optimization process for defining uncertainties of the control system.

TABLE 10.3 Comparison of the models

MODEL	REWARD
Nominal LQR	117.9219 ± 43.7783
RLQR	125.2431 ± 30.1002
$\mathcal{H}_\infty$	124.2740 ± 31.7548

The EAND algorithm was applied for the RLQR and $\mathcal{H}_\infty$ controllers during 300 runs for each one. Assuming $H = 1$ and $\Delta = 1$, then $\delta F_t = E_{Ft}$ and $\delta G_t = E_{Gt}$. The better configuration of uncertainties presented was $\delta F_t = 0.1012$ and $\delta G_t = 0.0610$ for the RLQR, resulting in a gain $K_R = 1.6590$. Finally, the algorithm provided the uncertainties $\delta F_t = 0.9074$ and $\delta G_t = 0.5248$ for the $\mathcal{H}_\infty$, resulting in a gain $K_\infty = 1.7290$.

10.4.4 Performance evaluation

This section presented four models for the control application: (i) DRL algorithm; (ii) nominal LQR ($K_N = 1.3420$); (iii) RLQR ($K_R = 1.6590$); and (iv) $\mathcal{H}_\infty$ ($K_\infty = 1.7290$). The DRL did not complete a simulation, since the CNN was unable to execute a curve. The nominal LQR, RLQR and $\mathcal{H}_\infty$ controllers were evaluated in 25 independent runs and the associated rewards were computed according to (10.50). The mean and standard deviation of these rewards are presented in Table 10.3.

Except for the DRL algorithm, the other three considered control approaches performed well in the simulation scenario. Nevertheless, the rewards returned by the RLQR and by the $\mathcal{H}_\infty$ controller were greater in comparison with the results attained by the nominal LQR. This outcome is expected since both the RLQR and the $\mathcal{H}_\infty$ controller were designed to handle the parametric uncertainties to which the system is subject.

10.5 CONCLUSIONS

This chapter presented a hybrid control method resulting from the combination of deep learning with robust control for autonomous vehicles. This framework can enhance the control performance when compared with standard deep learning control. The system was identified based on visual information available through the embedded camera. Such procedure circumvents the need for an exact description of the vehicle physical model. In addition, the proposed method deals with structured uncertainties, which is essential for autonomous navigation in urban environments. For uncertainty estimation, an evolutionary search method is presented to fine-tune the uncertainty matrices used by the robust controllers. Nonetheless, other methods, such as reinforcement learning and filtering techniques can be applied to estimate the uncertainties in this architecture. At last, the designer can adopt different uncertainty estimation and robust control approaches to compose the overall architecture. This aspect highlights the flexibility and modularity featured by the vision-based control framework.

NOTE

1   Proposed by V.C. Guizilini, TensorBlock — Modular API for Tensorflow, 2017. See https://bitbucket.org/vguizilini/tensorblock/src/master/

REFERENCES

[1] U. Kiencke and L. Nielsen, "Automotive control systems: For engine, driveline, and vehicle," *Measurement Science and Technology*, vol. *11*, no. 12, p. 1828, 2000.

[2] R. Rajamani, *Vehicle Dynamics and Control*, Springer Science & Business Media, 2011. https://link.springer.com/book/10.1007/978-1-4614-1433-9

[3] R. N. Jazar, *Advanced Vehicle Dynamics*, Cham: Springer International Publishing, 2019.

[4] G. A. P. de Morais, L. B. Marcos, J. N. A. Bueno, N. F. de Resende, M. H. Terra, and V. Grassi Jr, "Vision-based robust control framework based on deep reinforcement learning applied to autonomous ground vehicles," *Control Engineering Practice*, vol. *104*, p. 104630, 2020.

[5] A. Krizhevsky, I. Sutskever, and G. E. Hinton, "Imagenet classification with deep convolutional neural networks," In *Advances in Neural Information Processing Systems*, vol. *25*, pp. 1097–1105, 2012.

[6] Y. LeCun, B. Boser, J. S. Denker, D. Henderson, R. E. Howard, W. Hubbard, and L. D. Jackel, "Backpropagation applied to handwritten zip code recognition," *Neural Computation*, vol. *1*, no. 4, pp. 541–551, 1989.

[7] L. Jiao and J. Zhao, "A survey on the new generation of deep learning in image processing," *IEEE Access*, vol. *7*, pp. 172231–172263, 2019.

[8] M. Ehrgott, *Multicriteria Optimization*, Springer Science & Business Media, vol. *491*, 2005. https://link.springer.com/book/10.1007/3-540-27659-9

[9] H. Garnier, L. Wang, and P. C. Young, "Direct identification of continuous-time models from sampled data: Issues, basic solutions and relevance," In *Identification of Continuous-Time Models from Sampled Data*, pp. 1–29. London: Springer, 2008.

[10] L. B. Marcos and M. H. Terra, "Markovian filtering for driveshaft torsion estimation in heavy vehicles", *Control Engineering Practice*, vol. *102*, p. 104552, 2020.

[11] M. H. Terra, J. P. Cerri, and J. Y. Ishihara, "Optimal robust linear quadratic regulator for systems subject to uncertainties," *IEEE Transactions on Automatic Control*, vol. *59*, no. 9, pp. 2586–2591, 2014.

[12] A. H. Sayed, and V. H. Nascimento, "Design criteria for uncertain models with structured and unstructured uncertainties," In *Robustness in Identification and Control*, vol. *245*, pp. 159–173, London: Springer, 1999.

[13] T. Kailath, A. H. Sayed, and B. Hassibi, *Linear Estimation*, Prentice Hall, 2000.

[14] T. Basar, and P. Bernhard, "H_∞-Optimal Control and Related Minimax Design Problems", Springer Science & Business Media, 1991. https://link.springer.com/chapter/10.1007/978-1-4612-0245-5_2

[15] K. Zhou, and J. C. Doyle, "*Essentials of Robust Control*", Prentice Hall, vol. *104*, 1998.

[16] V. Mnih, K. Kavukcuoglu, D. Silver, A. A. Rusu, J. Veness, M. G. Bellemare, A. Graves, M. Riedmiller, A. K. Fidjeland, G. Ostrovski, and S. Petersen, "Human-level control through deep reinforcement learning", *Nature*, vol. *518*, pp. 529–533, 2015.

[17] K. Arulkumaran, M. P. Deisenroth, M. Brundage, and A. A. Bharath, "Deep reinforcement learning: A brief survey", *IEEE Signal Processing Magazine*, vol. *34*, no. 6, pp. 26–38, 2017.

[18] J. Schulman, F. Wolski, P. Dhariwal, A. Radford, and O. Klimov, "Proximal policy optimization algorithms", arXiv preprint arXiv:1707.06347, 2017.

[19] G. A. P. de Morais, B. H. G. Barbosa, D. D. Ferreira, and L. S. Paiva, "Soft sensors design in a petrochemical process using an Evolutionary Algorithm", *Measurement*, vol. *148*, p. 106920, 2019.

[20] A. Dosovitskiy, G. Ros, F. Codevilla, A. Lopez, and V. Koltun, "CARLA: An open urban driving simulator," In *Proceedings of the 1st annual conference on robot learning*, vol. *78*, pp. 1–16, 2017.

[21] F. Codevilla, M. Muller, A. Lopez, V. Koltun, and A. Dosovitskiy, "End-to-end driving via conditional imitation learning," In *2018 IEEE International Conference on Robotics and Automation (ICRA)*, IEEE, pp. 4693–4700, 2018.

[22] M. Abadi, P. Barham, J. Chen, Z. Chen, A. Davis, J. Dean, M. Devin, S. Ghemawat, G. Irving, M. Isard, and M. Kudlur, "Tensorflow: A system for large-scale machine learning", In *12th {USENIX} symposium on operating systems design and implementation ({OSDI} 16)*, pp. 265–283, 2016.

PART IV

DL for information management

A natural language processing-based approach for automating IoT search

11

Cheng Qian, William Grant Hatcher and Weichao Gao
Towson University, Towson, Maryland

Erik Balsch
Air Force Research Laboratory, Wright-Patterson Air Force Base, Fairborn, Ohio

Chao Lu and Wei Yu
Towson University, Towson, Maryland

Contents

11.1 Introduction 238
11.2 IoT search engine 239
    11.2.1 Architecture 239
    11.2.2 Key components 240
    11.2.3 Research challenges 240
11.3 NLP-based query processing 241
    11.3.1 Design rationale 241
    11.3.2 Basic components of NLP 242
    11.3.3 NLP tools 242
    11.3.4 Comparison of NLTK and spaCy 243
11.4 The ACQUISE approach 243
    11.4.1 Baseline strategy 244
    11.4.2 Enhanced static strategy 244
    11.4.3 Enhanced dynamic strategy 245
11.5 Performance evaluation 251
    11.5.1 Methodology 251
    11.5.2 Results 252

DOI: 10.1201/9781003190691-15

11.1 INTRODUCTION

The Internet of Things (IoT) has been thoroughly integrated into our daily lives, establishing a networking communication infrastructure to connect sensors and actuators for massive data collection and to support numerous smart-world systems [1]. IoT is progressing toward full coverage, enabling next-generation smart-world systems via automation and optimization in private and commercial realms, as well as revolutionizing analysis in command and control on an unprecedented scale [2–8]. For example, Ejaz et al. [8] introduced an energy-efficient scheduling algorithm to handle a large number of IoT sensors in smart cities.

IoT devices are important components in dynamic data-driven applications systems (DDDAS) [9] and cyber-physical systems (CPS), which take advantage of a vertical architecture of service, network communication, physical modeling, and sensing and control layers to actualize smart-world systems. IoT devices conduct sensing and actuation by recording or observing the surrounding world and affecting some action on that world. IoT devices can be used in smart infrastructures such as the smart grid, smart transportation, smart health, smart home, and smart city, among others [8, 10–15]. Smart systems also include smart manufacturing, also called 'Industrial 4.0', which enables integration and communication across multiple smart systems (i.e., the system of systems) to expand system abilities and ultimately improve industrial efficacy (reduced cost and loss, increased productivity, etc.) [16–20].

In practice, a variety of IoT systems have been deployed in the world ushering in new concerns, such as the "need to share". Heterogeneous IoT devices monitor dynamic external physical objects and phenomena, resulting in IoT data, which is massively diverse with respect to type, volume, encoding, etc. [2, 21, 22]. As there exist multiple IoT devices belonging to different IoT systems and organizations, which monitor the same physical objects and phenomena, resources can be wasted on redundant collections of IoT data. Moreover, IoT devices deployed in different IoT systems continuously receive and process data and commands; yet, nonetheless, the individual IoT system only provides data and services to its owner, not being required to share and distribute data among different IoT systems and groups. Hence, there is the need for the design of a data-oriented service to enable data sharing among different IoT systems and organizations. To this end, the IoT search engine is one viable approach, one that is intended as an open system for data sharing among different IoT systems, providing data-oriented service to end-users [23, 24].

There are challenges for realizing the IoT search engine with respect to efficiency, intelligence, and security [14, 25]. As an open service for a variety of organizations, users, and machines, the number of queries against an IoT search engine can be massive. The IoT search engine should process queries in a timely manner so that the quality of service (QoS) requirements can be ensured. Also, IoT devices generate a dynamic massive amount of data. The IoT search engine needs to leverage big data analytic techniques to categorize and analyze the data to improve query response and manage efficiency. Additionally, a variety of cost-effective security mechanisms need to be deployed to ensure end-to-end security in the IoT search engine [26].

This chapter focuses on developing the Automatic Coordinated QUery IoT Search Engine (ACQUISE) which leverages machine learning (ML)-based natural language processing (NLP). Nowadays, most queries against search engines are in a human language, and the use of an IoT search engine should be expected to leverage the prevailing semantics, ontologies, and taxonomies. Meanwhile, there can be a massive number of queries to the IoT search engine, which take time for NLP models to understand a query and extract key information from a query to match the target IoT resource in the keyword pool that best responds to the query.

To provide ML-driven query automation, ACQUISE uses a set of strategies and algorithms using the spaCy natural language toolkit [27]. The ACQUISE baseline strategy enables the query processing to extract data from user queries, and then translates the extracted data into a format that can be understood by the IoT search engine. To further improve the efficiency, the ACQUISE design incorporates two enhanced strategies: one refers to the static strategy and the other refers to the dynamic strategy. The static strategy leverages an optimized small keyword pool, which records the most commonly used queries so that the NLP model has less chance to query the original keyword pool, which can be very large, leading to a reduction in query processing time. The dynamic strategy adopts a caching concept and implements several caching update algorithms to dynamically maintain a keyword pool so that the query system can efficiently handle streaming queries over time.

The remainder of this chapter is organized as follows: Section 11.2 briefly illustrates the basic concepts, entities, search techniques, and the architecture of the ACQUISE IoT search engine. Section 11.3 introduces NLP and compares different tools. Section 11.4 presents the ACQUISE approach, including a baseline strategy and two enhanced strategies that can improve the query automation process. In Section 11.5, scenarios and experiments validate the efficacy of the ACQUISE proposed strategies. In particular, human queries are generated to build a keyword pool for the baseline strategy to evaluate the functionality and performance. Using an optimized keyword pool with and without the caching updating algorithms, ACQUISE shows performance improvement. Section 11.6 discusses several open research directions concerning the intersection of ML, data fusion, and IoT naming systems, protocols, and algorithms. In Section 11.7, existing research efforts relevant to ACQUISE are presented. Finally, conclusions are summarized in Section 11.8.

11.2 IOT SEARCH ENGINE

This section introduces the ACQUISE architecture, key components, and research challenges.

11.2.1 Architecture

The basic ACQUISE architecture is shown in Figure 11.1. The IoT search engine consists of multiple IoT service providers with IoT sensors and services within coverage. For each service provider, the IoT devices are registered to the local gateways, and the local gateways are registered to the upper-level gateways (e.g., global gateways) in hierarchical form, facilitating large system scalability. The gateways have the capabilities to locate IoT devices, process user and machine queries, as well as find the target resources by leveraging the gateway's physical addresses to provide geolocation services.

The query processing engine (QPE) module in the ACQUISE system translates human language semantics to machine language syntax. Figure 11.2 illustrates the workflow for the query processing module. From the user side, the user sends the query to the QPE. The QPE translates the human language to machine language, and sends the translated result to the IoT search engine. After the search engine receives the processed query and finds the result, it sends the result directly back to the user. On the machine side, it maps the information to machine understandable language such as the Uniform Resource Locator (URL) to the QPE module. When the QPE module receives the URL, it extracts the information from the URL and sends a request to the IoT search engine so that the target resource can be located. After the search engine obtains the result, it directly sends it back to the user.

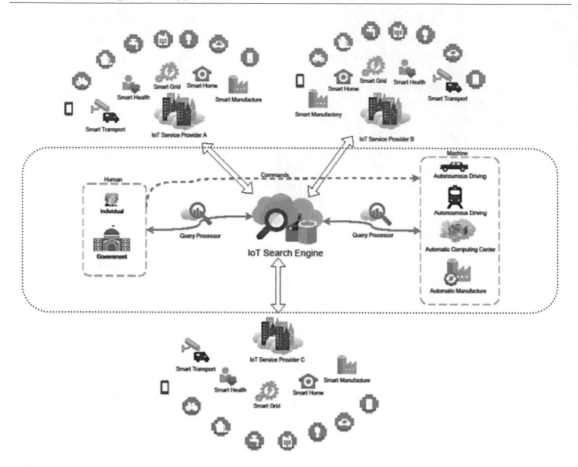

FIGURE 11.1   IoT search engine architecture.

11.2.2 Key components

ACQUISE must manage devices under its discretion, offer the capability to retrieve and present data from the IoT devices, and provide data responses to the user queries that is similar to web search engines.

The following section introduces four critical components of ACQUISE: (i) IoT resources are physical objects that act as IoT devices (sensors, actuators, gateways, and others), where ACQUISE acquires the data from the IoT sensors proactively or passively; (ii) IoT data are generated by the IoT sensors and actuators in a large and time-varying volume. ACQUISE provides the ability to retrieve the requested resources from the massive IoT data based on received queries; (iii) Search Space represents all the IoT resources that it covers. The IoT data can be much larger than typical website data, and can cover a much larger search space than a traditional web search engine; and (iv) query generation not only from humans, but also from automated computing devices. One component in this process is called the query processing engine (QPE) module, which acts as a translator to handle the query process. Together the ACQUISE provides a federated search and query response over networked IoT devices, context, and systems.

11.2.3 Research challenges

Based on our previous work [25], we have identified three existing challenges for IoT search engines: efficiency, intelligence, and security. In terms of efficiency, based on the IoT search engine framework proposed in our prior work [25], ACQUISE needs to accomplish query processing, data discovery, and data retrieval. To improve efficiency, optimization methods improve query processing, data discovery, and information retrieval processes. Intelligence in the IoT search process is a vital requirement for which data mining, machine learning, and information fusion provide viable solutions [28]. Related to security, there are numerous vulnerabilities in IoT devices, as well as a significant lack of security mechanisms in consumer devices [26]. Security examples abound, including a variety of botnets of compromised smart devices, which have been used repeatedly and effectively to launch distributed denial of service (DDoS) attacks. The IoT search engine must ensure users' private information is protected against the disclosure of locations and search habits that can be analyzed and extracted for nefarious purposes.

11.3 NLP-BASED QUERY PROCESSING

This chapter presents the design rationale of applying NLP for query processing, including the basic components and two useful tools.

11.3.1 Design rationale

Recall that an IoT search engine needs to handle multiple types of queries based on location, content, and other information, and can perform heterogeneous search. However, the data that ACQUISE have is different from traditional web search engines. Compared to web search engines, ACQUISE needs to retrieve data from innumerable individual sensors instead of publicly hosted web pages. To illustrate, the web search engine can retrieve data based on what a user inputs and find the target information requested through populated web information updates to users. In the IoT search engine, the goal includes identifying which gateway to ask for a result and which sensor should be the target, which is not always as clear as a web-language.

Generally speaking, NLP is a technique that can assist computers in understanding, interpreting, and processing human language. NLP assists machine processing in performing tasks such as translation, summarization, named entity recognition, relation extraction, speech recognition, and topic segmentation [29]. In addition, NLP can easily understand and derive meanings from the structure of human language. Thus, in ACQUISE, we design an NLP-based approach to assist the query processor in understanding what users are asking for to retrieve the corresponding results.

Figure 11.2 shows the workflow of an NLP model for an IoT search engine. The ACQUISE NLP model mainly focuses on translating a user's original query in human language to a query that can be understood

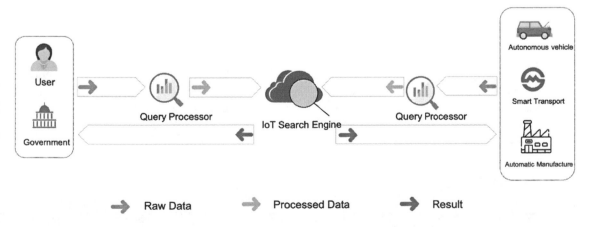

FIGURE 11.2   IoT search engine query processing module.

by the machine. For example, if a user wants to query the weather information in Towson, Maryland, the query processor module first receives a string such as "Weather information in Towson, Maryland." Next, it retrieves the keywords and geolocation information (weather, towson, maryland). Finally, it will translate the extracted information into a URL and send it to the ACQUISE IoT search engine.

11.3.2 Basic components of NLP

According to Bird et al. [30], all NLP libraries have the following four functions: (i) Tokenization, (ii) Part-of-speech tagging, (iii) Sentence segmentation, and (iv) Entity recognition.

Tokenization: Tokenization is a fundamental function for all NLP libraries that splits a piece of text into words, symbols, punctuation, spaces and other elements, thereby creating "tokens."

Part-of-Speech Tagging: Parts of speech (PoS) are specific lexical categories to which words are assigned, based on their syntactic context and role. Usually, words can be categorized into one of the following categories: (i) *Noun*: Typically words that depict some object or entity, which may be either living or nonliving. Examples would include fox, dog, book, and so on. The PoS tag symbol for nouns is *N*. (ii) *Verb*: Words that are used to describe certain actions, states, or occurrences. There are a wide variety of subcategories, including auxiliary, reflexive, and transitive verbs (and many more). Some typical examples of verbs would be running, jumping, reading, and writing. The PoS tag symbol for verbs is *V*. (iii) *Adjective*: Words used to describe or qualify other words, typically nouns and noun phrases. For example, the phrase 'beautiful flower' has the noun *N*, "flower' that is described or qualified using the adjective (*ADJ*) 'beautiful'. The PoS tag symbol for adjectives is (*ADJ*). (iv) *Adverb*: Adverbs usually act as modifiers for other words, including nouns, adjectives, verbs, or other adverbs. For example, the phrase 'very beautiful flower' has the adverb (*ADV*) 'very', which modifies the adjective (*ADJ*) 'beautiful', indicating the degree to which the flower is beautiful. The PoS tag symbol for adverbs is *ADV*.

In addition to the aforementioned four components, there are other components that occur frequently in the English language, including pronouns, prepositions, interjections, conjunctions, determiners, and many others. Furthermore, each PoS tag, such as the noun (*N*), can be further subdivided into components, including singular nouns (*NN*), singular proper nouns (*NNP*), and plural nouns (*NNS*).

The process of classifying and labeling words is called parts of speech (PoS) tagging. PoS software reads text in some language and assigns tags to each word (and other tokens), such as noun, verb, adjective, etc. PoS tags are used to annotate words and describe their PoS, which is helpful to perform specific analysis, such as narrowing down the range of nouns and evaluating the most typical words. PoS tagging can also be used for disambiguation (context) and grammar analysis. For example, the word "reference" has different meaning when it is a noun or a verb. Using PoS, the NLP model can easily identify its meaning, particularly when surrounded by other words.

Sentence Segmentation: Another key step that is commonly performed on text before further processing is sentence segmentation or sentence boundary detection, which means to divide up a running text into sentences. One aspect that makes sentence segmentation less straightforward than it sounds is the presence of punctuation marks, which can be used either to indicate a full stop or to form abbreviations and the like.

Named Entity Recognition: Named entity recognition (NER) is one of the key step toward information extraction, and is the process of locating and classifying named data in text into predefined categories, such as the names of persons, organizations, locations, expressions of times, quantities, monetary values, percentages, and others. NER is used in a number of fields in NLP, and can help in answering numerous real-world questions.

11.3.3 NLP tools

After introducing the key components of NLP, two different toolkits for NLP, which are NLTK and spaCy, will be compared.

NLTK: The Natural Language Toolkit (NLTK) is a suite of libraries and programs for symbolic and statistical NLP for the English Language [30, 31]. NLTK includes graphical demonstrations and sample data. NLTK is a Python library for NLP to support teaching and research in NLP-related areas, including empirical linguistics, cognitive science, artificial intelligence, information retrieval, and machine learning. NLTK supports all the basic NLP functions (e.g., PoS tagging).

spaCy: spaCy is another widely used NLP tool available in Python [32]. spaCy can be used to build chatbots, automatic summarizers, and entity extraction engines. In terms of functions, spaCy has a few more functions than NLTK, including neural network models, integrated word vectors, dependency parsing, and entity linking. To understand how the spaCy actually works, the detailed description of spaCy architecture can be found in [27]. The most important data structures in spaCy are the Doc and the Vocab. The Doc object owns the sequence of tokens and all their annotations. The Vocab object owns a set of look-up tables that make common information available across documents. By centralizing strings, word vectors, and lexical attributes, spaCy can avoid storing multiple copies of duplicated data and save memory. Text annotations are also designed to allow the uniqueness of words. The Doc object owns the data, and Span and Token are views that point into it. The Doc object is constructed by the Tokenizer, and then modified in place by the components of the pipeline. The Language object coordinates these components which takes raw text and sends it through the pipeline, returning an annotated document. Language object can also do the training and serialization.

11.3.4 Comparison of NLTK and spaCy

The key differences between spaCy and NLTK are as follows: (i) NLTK provides a number of algorithms for the researchers and developers to choose from; whereas spaCy keeps the effective algorithms for solving the problem in its toolkit and keep it updated as the improvement. (ii) NLTK supports sixteen languages (Portuguese, Arabic, Danish, Dutch, English, Finnish, French, German, Hungarian, Italian, Norwegian, Portuguese, Romanian, Russian, Spanish and Swedish) [33], while spaCy has models for 19 languages (English, German, Spanish, French, Portuguese, Italian, Dutch, etc.) [32] and supports multi-language named entities. (iii) NLTK is a string processing library. The input and the output of the NLTK are both strings while spaCy uses object-oriented approach. When parsing a text, spaCy returns a document object whose words and sentences are objects themselves. (iv) spaCy has support for word vectors whereas NLTK does not. (v) Since spaCy has the latest developments, it usually has better performance than NLTK.

According to [34], tokenization and PoS-tagging, spaCy performs better than NLTK; but in sentence tokenization, NLTK has the better performance. Taking a closer look at the two different strategies, it appears that NLTK attempts to split the text into sentences. In contrast, spaCy constructs a syntactic tree for each sentence, which can be more robust and gain more information from the text. Also, spaCy consumes less time to perform word organization and PoS tagging. For ACQUISE, these are important functions to assist human queries, thereby spaCy is selected.

11.4 THE ACQUISE APPROACH

This chapter introduces a baseline strategy, and then two enhanced strategies, to efficiently conduct the ACQUISE automate query processing.

For query-based systems, NLP supports translating human language requests into computer scripts. NLP can also assist human users in rapidly performing tasks that would otherwise require a lifetime of study and analysis of large knowledge databases, such as translation, summarization, named entity recognition, relation extraction, etc. Moreover, such a process can be applied to any kind of human language input as long as the base of knowledge has been constructed (i.e., model training or library construction) as well as that of physical interpretation [35]. Thus, ACQUISE uses an NLP-based approach to assist query processing in understanding what the users are asking for and retrieving the corresponding results for users. As denoted above, spaCy is a widely used NLP tool for Python that can be used for chatbots, automatic summarizers, and entity extraction engines [32] that is selected for ACQUISE.

Figure 11.2 shows the workflow of an NLP model in ACQUISE. The ACQUISE NLP model mainly focuses on translating the user's original human language query into a query that can be understood by ACQUISE. For example, consider that a user wants to query weather information for the Towson, Maryland area, the query processing module first receives a string written "Weather information in Towson, Maryland". Then, it will retrieve the keyword and geolocation information (weather, Towson, maryland). Finally, it will transform the extracted information into a URL and send it to ACQUISE.

11.4.1 Baseline strategy

To make the NLP engine assist query processing by converting user queries to URLs, ACQUISE uses a keyword pool that contains multiple keywords organized by nouns, verbs, and adjectives for specific environments. The ACQUISE baseline strategy is based upon the following four steps: (i) *Step 1*: A query processor receives the user query; (ii) *Step 2*: The query processor runs the lemmatization function and identifies PoS and geolocation for the lemmas (base word forms); (iii) *Step 3*: The query processor checks whether the lemmas extracted from the user query matches keywords in the keyword pool; and (iv) *Step 4*: The query processor takes the matching keywords and sends them to ACQUISE so that device information can be retrieved.

Figure 11.3 illustrates how the ACQUISE baseline strategy works. In this example, the query processor receives the user query, say "Traffic Camera in Towson, Maryland." The NLP model will leverage lemmatization, PoS tagging, and NER functions, to extract IoT resource keywords and geolocation from the user's query. Meanwhile, the NLP model will query the keyword pool to determine whether the requested IoT resource exists in the keyword pool. If a match is found, the NLP model will add the keyword and geolocation information to a URL and send it to the IoT search engine.

11.4.2 Enhanced static strategy

Using the ACQUISE baseline strategy, the query processor can map the user query in human language to a URL that a machine can understand and utilize. Hence, when the size of the keyword pool and the number

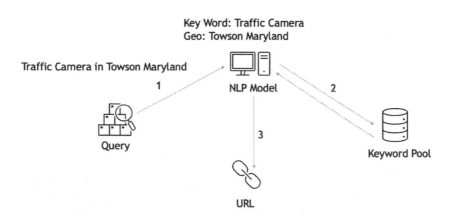

FIGURE 11.3   Baseline strategy.

of queries are significantly large (i.e., 10,000 queries towards one query processor), the processing time will likewise be significant. To deal with the potential for large query volumes, ACQUISE is designed with an enhanced strategy that utilizes a smaller keyword pool that will be searched first, and contains three tables, one each for the most frequently used verbs, adjectives, and nouns, respectively. The enhanced keyword pool is much smaller than the original, storing only the most frequent data. As this smaller keyword pool is searched first, most queries should never access the larger keyword pool described in the baseline strategy. Consequently, the time consumption for a query can be reduced based on the smaller search space, improving the speed of query processing.

The static strategy uses the following six steps: (i) *Step 1*: The query processor receives the user query; (ii) *Step 2*: The query processor runs the lemmatization functions, and identifies PoS and geolocations for the lemmas; (iii) *Step 3*: The query processor determines which category a lemma belongs to, to identify the target pool table (noun, verb, adjective) to search; (iv) *Step 4*: The query processor searches the identified pool table and returns the any matches; (v) *Step 5*: If the keyword not exists in the enhanced pool, the query processor will retrieve the information from the original keyword pool; and (vi) *Step 6*: The query processor sends the matched keywords to the IoT search engine to retrieve device information.

The workflow of the static strategy is shown in Figure 11.4. As in the baseline strategy, the NLP model first extracts keyword from a user query. However, by using a smaller keyword pool segmented by type of word and storing the most frequently used IoT resource keywords, the query processing time in NLP model can be reduced. The NLP model will first process the query using the small keyword pool. If the IoT resource is not stored in the keyword pool, the NLP model will search through the original keyword pool (which is large) to find the target IoT resource keyword. Finally, it sends the translated user request to IoT search engine as a URL.

11.4.3 Enhanced dynamic strategy

Queries in an IoT environment can change over time, fluctuating over the time of day, weather, etc. Thus, the static keyword pool may not be capable of handling continuous queries with different query contents since the static keyword pool does not keep the keyword pool updated. To address IoT query dynamics, ACQUISE implements six caching update algorithms to maintain and update the small keyword pool so that the query time can be further reduced, leading to performance improvement. The caching algorithms in ACQUISE are first-in-first-out (FIFO), last-in-first-out (LIFO), least frequently used (LFU), least recently used (LRU), most recently used (MRU), and random replacement (RR).

The overall workflow for the enhanced dynamic strategy is shown in Figure 11.5. After the NLP model extracts keywords from the user's query, we adjust the size of the small keyword pool and use the caching algorithms to update the small pool based on the popularity of the IoT resource keywords. When the small keyword pool does not contain the requested IoT resource keyword, and after the NLP

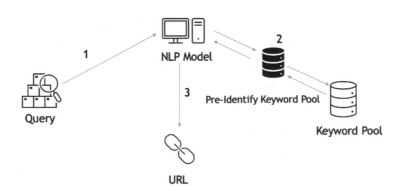

FIGURE 11.4   Static strategy.

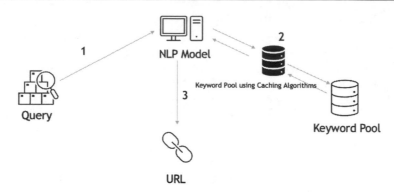

FIGURE 11.5 Dynamic strategy.

model completes query through the original keyword pool; the caching replacement algorithms are used to update the small keyword pool. In the following Section, the aforementioned caching algorithms one-by-one are discussed

1) *FIFO*: The FIFO caching algorithm sets up a buffer for the cached elements. In the ACQUISE approach, the buffer represents the small keyword pool maintained by caching algorithms. Meanwhile, the cached elements represent the elements stored in the buffer. When the buffer is full, the earliest stored element in the buffer will be removed. The detailed procedure is shown in Algorithm 11.1. Here, da, dv, and dn represent the original keyword pool that stores adjs, verbs, and nouns, respectively. The limit means the size of buffer. The ba, bv, and bn are the buffer leveraged by the caching algorithms that store the adjs, verbs, and nouns, respectively. The query represents user queries. The NLP is spaCy's pre-trained convolutional neural network (CNN) model for NLP [36]. The output contains the extracted information from the queries. Also, "geo" represents the geolocation that can be extracted through the spaCy CNN model.

It is worth noting that a noun, verb, and adj are used to store the extracted information of the specific PoS. The query processor first matches the geolocation keyword from each query. Then, it finds out whether there is any keyword already in the buffer. If yes, then the query processor retrieves the keyword for the corresponding variable (noun, verb, adj). If the keyword is not in the buffer, the query processor searches the corresponding keyword pool, retrieves the keyword for the corresponding variable, and puts the keyword into the buffer. If the buffer is full, the cache replacement algorithm is executed. In this case, as in the FIFO caching algorithm, the earliest or oldest data entered in the buffer is popped or removed. Finally, the output will be a string containing keywords and geolocation, which are transformed into URLs.

Algorithm 11.1 Dynamic Strategy with LIFO

1   Initialization: da, dv, dn, LIMIT, ba, bv, bn, query, nip, output, geo, noun, verb, adj
2   **for** *x in query* **do**
3   **if** *x.lable=* "*GPE*" **then**
4   geo=x.text
5   **end**
6   **if** *x.PoS_=* "*NOUN*" *and x in bn* **then**
7   noun=x.text
8   **end**
9   **if** *x.PoS_=* "*NOUN*" *and x not in bn and x in dn and bn not full* **then**
10   noun=x.text
11   bn=x.text
12   **end**

13   **if** *x.PoS_= "NOUN" and x not in bn and x in dn and bn is full* **then**
14   noun=x.text
15   bn.pop()
16   bn=x.text
17   **end**
18   output=noun+verb+adj+geo
19   **end**

2) *LIFO*: The LIFO caching algorithm operates in an opposite way of the FIFO caching algorithm. When the buffer is full, the LIFO algorithm will pop out the latest or most recent element added to the stack. The detailed workflow is shown in Algorithm11.2. In the LIFO algorithm, the keyword pools and buffer are initialized (i.e., the small keyword pool maintained by caching algorithms), and spaCy's CNN model. The query processor first matches the geolocation keyword from each query. Then, it checks for any keyword already in the buffer. If yes, then the query processor retrieves the keyword for the corresponding variable (noun, verb, adj). If the keyword is not currently in the buffer, the query processor searches the corresponding keyword pool, retrieves the keyword for the corresponding variable, and puts the keyword into the buffer. If the buffer is full, the LIFO caching algorithm will pop or remove the last data entered into the buffer. Finally, the system will output a string that contains keywords and geolocation, translated into a URL. The time complexity of this algorithm is $O(n)$, where n represents the total number of words in a query.

Algorithm 11.2 Dynamic Strategy with LIFO

1   Initialization: da, dv, dn, LIMIT, ba, bv, bn, query, nip, output, geo, noun, verb, adj
2   **for** *x in query* **do**
3   **if** *x.lable= "GPE"* **then**
4   geo=x.text
5   **end**
6   **if** *x.PoS_= "NOUN" and x in bn* **then**
7   noun=x.text
8   **end**
9   **if** *x.PoS_= "NOUN" and x not in bn and x in dn and bn not full* **then**
10   noun=x.text
11   bn=x.text
12   **end**
13   **if** *x.PoS_= "NOUN" and x not in bn and x in dn and bn is full* **then**
14   noun=x.text
15   bn.popO
16   bn=x.text
17   **end**
18   output=noun+verb+adj+geo
19   **end**

3) *LFU*: The Least Frequently Used (LFU) algorithm is a caching algorithm, in which the least frequently used cache block is removed whenever the cache overflows. In LFU, if all the items in the buffer have the equal probability of being accessed, the oldest item will be removed. The detailed procedure is shown in Algorithm11.3. In the LFU algorithm, it starts by initializing the keyword pools, buffer (i.e., the small keyword pool maintained by caching algorithms), and spaCy's CNN model. The query processor first matches the geolocation keyword from each query. Then, it determines whether any keywords match in the buffer. If yes, then the query processor retrieves the keyword for the corresponding variable (noun, verb, adj) and increments

the keyword frequency by 1 (the frequency is used to count the number of hits for a word). If the keyword is not in the buffer, the query processor searches the corresponding keyword pool, retrieves the keyword for the corresponding variable, and puts the keyword into the buffer. The frequency of the newly added keyword is incremented by 1. If the buffer is full, then the LFU caching algorithm is executed, removing the element with the lowest frequency from the buffer. Finally, a string is returned containing keywords and geolocation, which are transformed into URLs. The time complexity of this algorithm is $O(n)$, where n represents the total number of words in a query.

Algorithm 11.3 Dynamic Strategy with LFU

1   Initialization: da, dv, dn, LIMIT, ba, bv, bn, query, nip, output, geo, noun, verb, adj
2   **for** *x in query* **do**
3   **if** *x.lable="GPE"* **then**
4   geo=x.text
5   **end**
6   **if** *x.PoS_="NOUN" and x in bn* **then**
7   noun=x.text
8   x.frequency++
9   **end**
10   **if** *x.PoS_= "NOUN" and x not in bn and x in dn and bn not full* **then**
11   noun=x.text
12   bn=x.text
13   x.frequency++
14   **end**
15   **if** *x.PoS_="NOUN" and x not in bn and x in dn and bn is full* **then**
16   noun=x.text
17   **for** *x in bn* **do**
18   **if** *minimal frequency not equal* **then**
19   remove the data with minimal frequency
20   **end**
21   **if** *minimal frequency equals* **then**
22   remove the older one with minimal frequency
23   **end**
24   **end**
25   bn=x.text
26   **end**
27   output=noun+verb+adj+geo
28 **end**

4) *LRU*: The LRU algorithm will remove the least recently used frames when the cache is full. For example, assume the buffer space is 4 and items 1, 3, 2, and 4 are already in the buffer. A counter is used to calculate how long an item exists in the buffer without getting accessed. Assume a new item 5 in entering the buffer. At this stage, item 1 is the item that stays in the buffer for the longest time and does not get accessed. Thus, item 1 will be removed from the buffer in this case. The detailed workflow is shown in Algorithm11.4. In the LRU algorithm, it starts by initializing the keyword pools, buffer, and spaCy's CNN model. The query processor first matches the geolocation keyword from each query. Then, LRU determines whether any keywords match in the buffer. If yes, then the query processor retrieves the keyword for the corresponding variable (noun, verb, adj) and increments the keyword frequency by 1. If the

keyword is not currently in the buffer, the query processor searches the corresponding keyword pool, retrieves the keyword for the corresponding variables, and puts the keyword into the buffer. The frequency of the newly added keyword is incremented by 1. If the buffer is full, the LRU caching algorithm is executed, removing the least recently used data from the buffer. Finally, a string is returned containing keywords and geolocation, which are transformed into URLs. The time complexity of this algorithm is $O(n)$, where n represents the total number of words in a query.

Algorithm 11.4 Dynamic Strategy with LRU

1   Initialization: da, dv, dn, LIMIT, ba, bv, bn, query, nip, output, geo, noun, verb, adj
2   **for** *x in query* **do**
3   **if** *x.lable="GPE"* **then**
4   geo=x.text
5   **end**
6   **if** *x.PoS_="NOUN" and x in bn* **then**
7   noun=x.text
8   x.frequency++
9   **end**
10   **if** *x.PoS_="NOUN" and x not in bn and x in dn and bn not full* **then**
11   noun=x.text
12   bn=x.text
13   x.frequency++
14   **end**
15   **if** *x.PoS_="NOUN" and x not in bn and x in dn and bn is full* **then**
16   noun=x.text
17   remove least recently used data from bn
18   bn=x.text
19   **end**
20   output=noun+verb+adj+geo
21   **end**

5) *MRU*: Compared to the LRU caching algorithm, the MRU algorithm removes the most recently used element from the buffer. For example, consider a scenario where the buffer space is 4, items 1, 3, 4, and 2 are in the buffer, and 7 is to be added. A counter is used to calculate how long an item exists in the buffer without getting accessed. Before item 7 enters the buffer, item 2 is the most recently accessed (most recently enters the buffer). In this case, item 2 will be removed from the buffer. The detailed workflow is shown in Algorithm 11.5. In the MRU algorithm, it initializes keyword pools, buffer, and spaCy's CNN model. The query processor first matches the geolocation keyword from each query. Then, it determines whether any keywords match in the buffer. If yes, then the query processor retrieves the keyword for the corresponding variable (noun, verb, adj) and increments the keyword's frequency by 1. If the keyword is not currently in the buffer, the query processor searches the corresponding keyword pool, retrieves the keyword for the corresponding variables, and puts the keyword into the buffer. The frequency of the newly added keyword is incremented by 1. If the buffer is full, the MRU caching algorithm is executed, removing the most recently used item from the buffer. Finally, a string is returned containing keywords and geolocation, which are transformed into URLs. The time complexity of this algorithm is $O(n)$, where n represents the total number of words in a query.

Algorithm 11.5 Dynamic Strategy with MRU

1   Initialization: da, dv, dn, LIMIT, ba, bv, bn, query, nip, output, geo, noun, verb, adj
2   **for** *x in query* **do**
3   **if** *x.lable= "GPE"* **then**
4   geo=x,text
5   **end**
6   **if** *x.PoS_="NOUN" and x in bn* **then**
7   noun=x.text
8   **end**
9   **if** *x.PoS_= "NOUN" and x not in bn and x in dn and bn not full* **then**
10   noun=x.text
11   bn=x.text
12   **end**
13   **if** *x.PoS_= "NOUN" and x not in bn and x in dn and bn is full* **then**
14   noun=x.text
15   remove most recently used data from bn
16   bn=x.text
17   **end**
18   output-noun+verb+adj+geo
19   **end**

Algorithm 11.6 Dynamic Strategy with Radom Replacement (RR)

1   Initialization: da, dv, dn, **LIMIT**, ba, bv, bn, query, nip, output, geo, noun, verb, adj
2   **for** *x in query* **do**
3   **if** *x.lable="CPE"* **then**
4   geo=x.text
5   **end**
6   **if** *x.PoS_="NOUN" and x in bn* **then**
7   noun=x.text
8   **end**
9   **if** *x.PoS_= "NOUN" and x not in bn and x in dn and bn not full* **then**
10   noun=x.text
11   bn=x.text
12   **end**
13   **if** *x.PoS_= "NOUN" and x not in bn and x in dn and bn is full* **then**
14   noun=x.text
15   remove random data from bn
16   bn=x.text
17   **end**
18   output=noun+verb+adj+geo
19   **end**

6) *Random Replacement (RR) Caching Algorithm*: The RR caching algorithm replaces an item in the buffer at random when a new item is to be added and the buffer is full. The RR algorithm does not require a counter to compute how frequently an item is accessed as it does not need item access time as a reference to update the buffer. The detailed procedure is shown in Algorithm 11.6. In the RR algorithm, it initializes keyword pools, buffer, and spaCy's CNN model. The query processor first matches the geolocation keyword from each query. Then, it determines whether any keywords match in the buffer. If yes, the query processor retrieves the keyword for

the corresponding variable (noun, verb, adj) and increments the keyword frequency by 1. If the keyword is not currently in the buffer, the query processor searches the corresponding keyword pool, retrieves the keyword for the corresponding variables, and puts the keyword into the buffer. The frequency of the newly added keyword is incremented by 1. If the buffer is full, the RR caching algorithm is executed, which randomly removes a data item from the buffer. Finally, a string is returned containing keywords and geolocation, which are transformed into URLs. The time complexity of this algorithm is also $O(n)$, where n represents the total number of words in a query.

11.5 PERFORMANCE EVALUATION

In this section, the evaluation methodology is first shown, including the configuration and scenario for the experiment, datasets, and evaluation metrics. Then, the evaluation results are presented for strategies that we proposed.

11.5.1 Methodology

Configuration: We deployed the ACQUISE query processing model in an emulation environment in Python 3.5, running on Linux (Ubuntu Server v16.04 LTS) OS. The emulation was run on a Dell PowerEdge T640 server (Intel Xeon 2.6 GHz 12 core processor, 192 GB RAM, and 2 TB hard drive).

Scenario: In the evaluation scenario, multiple users utilize the IoT search engine to query for weather and traffic information. The query processing of the ACQUISE IoT search engine needs to use the NLP model to retrieve and understand useful information from the user query. The weather information includes temperature, rain/sunshine, and location. The traffic information includes the location and the device type that is searched for (traffic camera, etc.).

Dataset: We generated 70 queries for weather and 70 queries for traffic information from 110 IoT devices. ACQUISE builds the keyword pool for the query processor to use to match the keyword in user queries. To evaluate the performance of the baseline strategy and the enhanced strategies, we have implemented the strategies with the same size keyword pool. For the baseline static strategy, we use a dataset of 31,262 nouns, 35,452 verbs and 51,064 adjs. For the enhanced static strategy, we use 15,631 nouns, 17,726 verbs, and 25,532 adjs for each category (traffic and weather). Also, we have built a small keyword pool for each category. The size of the keyword pool is ranging from 1000-10000 words for three categories in total. Since the spaCy's pre-trained CNN model is integrated with a geolocation recognition function, we leverage the CNN model to retrieve geolocation keywords for the IoT devices from the queries. For the enhanced dynamic strategy, we use the same original keyword pool as the baseline strategy with a small keyword pool similar to the enhanced static strategy but integrated with caching algorithms to keep the keyword pool updated so that the frequent query keywords are stored.

Performance Metric: To evaluate the efficacy of the ACQUISE strategies, processing time is the key performance metric. Processing time is defined as the time from when the query processor receives the user query to the time the query processor successfully extracts the keyword information from the user query, matches the keyword pool, and returns the response to the user. Recall that we designed the baseline static strategy to ensure that the query processing module can translate a human language query into a machine understandable query. In the enhanced static strategy, we introduced a second, smaller keyword pool of frequently used keywords, to reduce the processing time of query processing. To deal with queries with dynamic contents (i.e., queries for traffic information in different locations), ACQUISE introduces six keyword cache replacement algorithms to update the small keyword pool (keyword pool maintained by caching algorithms) to reflect the contents on more recent searches. Additionally, the size of the small keyword pool maintained by caching algorithm may affect the processing time of the query. Hence, the keyword pool size was set from 1000 to 10000 words to evaluate the relationship between the processing time and pool size.

11.5.2 Results

Baseline Strategy: To ensure that the query processing module can successfully extract key information from the user query, the baseline strategy is shown in Figure 11.6. The first line "Are there any speeding cameras in Germantown, Maryland?" represents the user query. The second line represent the key information extracted by the NLP model. The words "Germantown" and "Maryland" represent geolocation information extracted by the entity recognition method of spaCy, while the "speeding camera" that represents the cameras detecting a "speeding" car is extracted by the part of speech recognition method of spaCy.

   Enhanced Static Strategy: The baseline static strategy enables the NLP model to extract the geolocation as well as IoT resource keywords from a user query. Nonetheless, the original keyword pool contains a massive number of elements, such that query processing can be time consuming. Thus, we design an enhanced static strategy that uses a small keyword pool, which stores the most common queries typically used for the scenario of choice to reduce the NLP model processing time. To evaluate the performance between the baseline strategy and the enhanced strategy, we use different volumes of queries to measure the performance. As shown in Figure 11.7, we set the number of user queries to 140, 280, 560, and 1220. One can observe from Figure 11.7 that the time taken for processing queries increases as the number of queries increases. When the number of queries approaches 1220, the difference between the baseline strategy and the static strategy is 1.21 s.

   Enhanced Dynamic Strategy: Clearly, the enhanced static strategy can reduce processing time from the baseline through intelligent assessment of common queries. Nonetheless, with the static strategy, the small keyword pool does not update rapidly and it only updates in a longer interval (i.e., week or month). Thus, the time-sensitive queries cannot be handled in a timely manner. To deal with real-time dynamics, six cache update algorithms were developed to dynamically update the small keyword pool maintained by caching algorithm, allowing the keyword pool to retain the latest information for handling contemporary queries. Nonetheless, there are two issues in the algorithm implementation. The first is how to define the size of keyword pool. To determine the optimal pool size for NLP efficiency, we conduct an experiment to vary the size of small keyword pool from 1000 to 10,000. The result is shown in Figure 11.8. The latency is the average processing delay of the six algorithms under the same buffer size. The result shows when the buffer size is 4000, the processing time is the smallest. Thus, we set the buffer size to 4000 in our further experiments.

   The second issue is to understand which algorithm can achieve the best performance. To this end, Figure 11.9 shows the performance of the six algorithms under buffer size 4000. From Figure 11.9, one

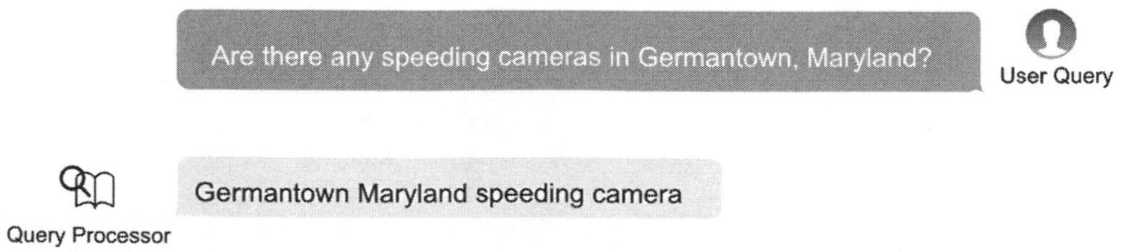

Are there any speeding cameras in Germantown, Maryland?
User Query

Query Processor   Germantown Maryland speeding camera

FIGURE 11.6   Example queries.

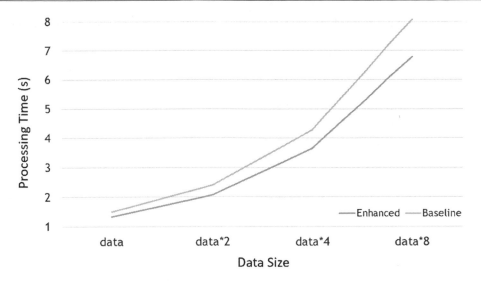

FIGURE 11.7   Performance comparison between baseline and enhanced strategies.

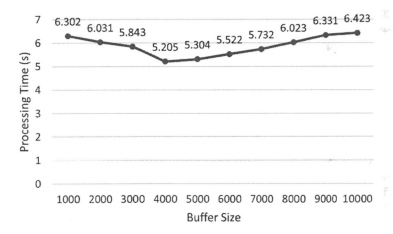

FIGURE 11.8   Buffer size evaluation.

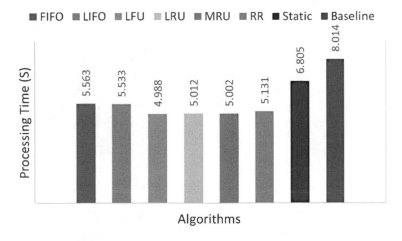

FIGURE 11.9   Dynamic strategy performance evaluation.

can observe that the dynamic strategy indeed improves the processing time performance. In particular, the LIFO and FIFO caching algorithms reduce the processing time to 5.5 s and the LRU, LFU, MRU, and RR caching algorithms reduce the processing time to around 5 s. Among all the caching algorithms, the LFU caching algorithm leads to the best performance, which can reduce the processing time to almost exactly 5 s.

11.6 DISCUSSION

We now discuss several open research questions regarding improving query retrieval for IoT Search.

11.6.1 Machine learning

When there are a massive number of IoT devices and users in the network of the IoT search engine, the complexity of query process increases. There are several ways to improve query efficiency including federated search, relevance hashing, hierarchical networks, and contextual reasoning [37, 38]. In this chapter, we utilize spaCy, which contains a pre-trained Deep Learning (DL) models to carry out entity recognition. Nonetheless, spaCy's pre-trained DL models cannot identify entities that belong to IoT resources without using a dictionary for specific IoT resources. In our future study, we plan to train a different DL model based on an IoT dataset to conduct entity recognition, device identification, and content relevancy which can potentially reduce the query time of the NLP model. Another way to improve query efficiency is the use DL techniques to aggregate IoT data collected by the IoT search engine. Additionally, other DL techniques can provide accuracy in forecasting, regression, and data fusion; which can not only reduce the IoT data size, but also categorize the IoT resources. Thus, the duration of locating a specific IoT resource can be reduced. For example, our prior work leverages an Recurrent Neural Network (RNN) Long Short-Term Memory (LTSM) model to carry out the query prediction [25].

11.6.2 Protocols and algorithms

Because IoT data is massive and dynamic, protocols and algorithms need to be designed to meet the requirements of an IoT search engine. IoT devices have limited power and limited computing resources. To handle such limited computing and networking resources in IoT devices, while providing optimal service, several protocols have been designed. For example, the Constrained Application Protocol (CoAP) [39] is designed specifically for transmitting data between low-power devices. Also, Message Queue Telemetry Transport (MQTT) [40] is an open message protocol that is used for transferring data under high latency and in constrained networks. The MQTT protocol can significantly benefit IoT device communications in rural areas. In addition, the Extensible Messaging and Presence Protocol (XMPP) [41] is designed for real-time communications, including instant messaging, presence, multi-party chat, voice and video calls, collaboration, lightweight middleware, content syndication, and generalized routing of XML data. XMPP has shown promise for query-based sensor fusion systems within Physics-based and Human-Derived Information Fusion (PHIF) systems [35] and could be used to transfer traffic information between IoT resources and gateways to keep all data up to date.

Meanwhile, DL algorithms need be designed and implemented to improve query efficiency. ACQUISE utilized six caching algorithms to reduce the keyword pool query time, leading to the reduction of the NLP processing time of the query. Additional approaches include ranking algorithms, which can improve the performance of the IoT search engine by retrieving the most usable, useful, and requested data for individual search categories [42]. For example, with the ranking algorithm, the IoT search engine can quickly retrieve the most stable and up-to-date weather information based on the IoT device's performance history.

11.6.3 Security and privacy

Recent advances in DL technologies enable accurate translation of human language into machine processing affording enhanced human-machine teaming. However, there exists the potential for adversarial attacks that can compromise DL systems [43]. The most common example is that of a modifying a traffic sign by adding noise to training datasets, such that it cannot be distinguished by a machine, but obvious to the human eyes. Other approaches using the generative adversarial networks (GAN) [44, 45] are perceived by the machine, but fakes are not as discernable to the human as compared to the machine. In addition, how to design cost-efficient data security and privacy-aware techniques to secure communication between IoT devices and gateways remains a contemporary design choice. Furthermore, how to design platforms and algorithms to support data sharing among different IoT search engine equipment and customers at a low cost will drive the adoption of ACQUISE methods.

11.7 RELATED WORK

This chapter reviews relevant research efforts related to the IoT search engine and query processing.

Generally speaking, an IoT search engine retrieves IoT device characterizations, IoT sensed data, and IoT channel communications. Despite widespread application of general web search engines as the primary portals to access content on the Internet, relatively little work has been done toward a fully realized IoT search engine. Relevant to resource discovery in the search of IoT systems, Lunardi et al. [46] proposed a content-based IoT search engine framework to improve data discovery efficiency. Also, Shemshadi et al. [47] designed a crawler for the IoT search engine to discover IoT resources. Likewise, Datta et al. [48] developed a resource discovery framework for IoT devices. Related to data processing in IoT search, Hatcher et al. [25] leveraged the long short-term memory (LSTM) network to predict data to improve the IoT search engine efficiency. Fagroud et al. [49] leveraged exploratory data analysis to analyze the IoT data. Likewise, Makkar et al. [50] implemented deep-learning metrics to remove spam from the IoT search engine results.

In addition to those studies mentioned, some research has been conducted toward providing efficient query processing in different systems [51–54]. For example, related to data-oriented services in sensor networks, Lee et al. [51] used DL techniques to analyze streaming IoT data on a wireless sensor network. Likewise, Sarode et al. [53] leveraged neural networks to perform data aggregation in wireless sensor networks so that the query process efficiency can be improved. Also, Kaur et al. [54] reviewed existing data aggregation methods in wireless sensor networks, to improve energy consumption, network lifetime, delay, energy cost, etc. Related to traditional queries over Internet, Balaji et al. [55] leveraged ML techniques to conduct the web-based query aggregation. Kumar et al. [56] implemented Statistical Machine Translation (SMT) and Neural MT (NMT) models to translate the web queries into natural language questions. Likewise, Barman et al. [57] designed an algorithm based on a recommendation system to respond to user queries efficiently. Hence, there is a growing interest to devise search engines that query IoT knowledge.

Compared with the existing work, ACQUISE primarily focuses on extracting key information from user queries using spaCy and transforms the format to be understood by the IoT search engine, leading to query automation driven by ML-based NLP. Furthermore, both static and dynamic strategies are supported with multiple DDDAS algorithms to improve the efficiency of query processing for IoT search.

11.8 FINAL REMARKS

Automatic Coordinated QUery IoT Search Engine (ACQUISE) is described as automating IoT real-time dynamic knowledge through NLP-based ML approaches. The ability to support human queries and translating them to uncover dynamic IoT knowledge is critical to future "smart" systems control and response such as safety-critical systems. The chapter presents a static baseline strategy with a large dictionary, while the enhanced static strategy introduces a small keyword pool buffer to improve timeliness. To handle dynamically changing query requests over time, six cache updating algorithms demonstrate rapid buffer management, improving performance of query response. Finally, the efficacy of ACQUISE strategies and algorithms show that the dynamic strategy least frequently used (LFU) caching algorithm achieves the best performance in terms of query processing time. Future work will incorporate federated IoT search, channel communication constraints, and security quality of service performance metrics.

ACKNOWLEDGEMENT

This material is based upon work supported by the Air Force Office of Scientific Research under award number FA9550-20-1-0418. Any opinions, findings, and conclusions or recommendations expressed in this material are those of the author(s) and do not necessarily reflect the views of the United States Air Force.

REFERENCES

[1] "Iot growth," https://www.statista.com/statistics/471264/iot-number-of-connected-devices-worldwide/

[2] M. Mohammadi, A. Al-Fuqaha, S. Sorour, and M. Guizani, "Deep learning for IoT big data and streaming analytics: A survey," *IEEE Communications Surveys Tutorials*, vol. *20*, no. 4, pp. 2923–2960, Fourthquarter 2018.

[3] H. Xu, X. Liu, W. Yu, D. Griffith, and N. Golmie, "Reinforcement learning-based control and networking co-design for industrial internet of things," *IEEE Journal on Selected Areas in Communications*, vol. *38*, no. 5, pp. 885–898, 2020.

[4] J. A. Stankovic, "Research directions for the internet of things," *IEEE Internet of Things Journal*, vol. *1*, no. 1, pp. 3–9, 2014.

[5] F. Liang, W. Yu, X. Liu, D. Griffith, and N. Golmie, "Toward edgebased deep learning in industrial internet of things," *IEEE Internet of Things Journal*, vol. *7*, no. 5, pp. 4329–4341, 2020.

[6] S. Mallapuram, N. Ngwum, F. Yuan, C. Lu, and W. Yu, "Smart city: The state of the art, datasets, and evaluation platforms," in *2017 IEEE/ACIS 16th International Conference on Computer and Information Science (ICIS)*, 2017, pp. 447–452.

[7] F. Liang, W. G. Hatcher, W. Liao, W. Gao, and W. Yu, "Machine learning for security and the internet of things: The good, the bad, and the ugly," *IEEE Access*, vol. *7*, pp. 158 126–158 147, 2019.

[8] W. Ejaz, M. Naeem, A. Shahid, A. Anpalagan, and M. Jo, "Efficient energy management for the internet of things in smart cities," *IEEE Communications Magazine*, vol. *55*, no. 1, pp. 84–91, 2017.

[9] E. P. Blasch, F. Darema, S. Ravela, and A. J. Aved (eds.), *Handbook of Dynamic Data Driven Applications Systems*. vol. *1*, 2nd ed., Springer", 2021.

[10] P. Moulema, W. Yu, D. Griffith, and N. Golmie, "On effectiveness of smart grid applications using co-simulation," in *2015 24th International Conference on Computer Communication and Networks (ICCCN)*, 2015, pp. 12679–12693.

[11] Z. Cai and T. Shi, "Distributed query processing in the edge assisted iot data monitoring system," *IEEE Internet of Things Journal*, vol. *8*, pp. 1–1, 2020.

[12] G. Xu, W. Yu, D. Griffith, N. Golmie, and P. Moulema, "Toward integrating distributed energy resources and storage devices in smart grid," *IEEE Internet of Things Journal*, vol. *4*, no. 1, pp. 192–204, 2017.

[13] W. Yu, D. Griffith, L. Ge, S. Bhattarai, and N. Golmie, "An integrated detection system against false data injection attacks in the smart grid," *Security and Communication Netwoks*, vol. *8*, no. 2, pp. 91–109, 2015. [Online]. Available: https://doi.org/10.1002/sec.957.

[14] W. G. Hatcher and W. Yu, "A survey of deep learning: Platforms, applications and emerging research trends," *IEEE Access*, vol. *6*, pp. 24 411–24 432, 2018.

[15] N. Ekedebe, C. Lu, and W. Yu, "Towards experimental evaluation of intelligent transportation system safety and traffic efficiency," in 2015 *IEEE International Conference on Communications (ICC)*, *2015*, pp. 3757–3762.

[16] H. Xu, W. Yu, D. Griffith, and N. Golmie, "A survey on industrial Internet of things: A cyber-physical systems perspective," *IEEE Access*, vol. *6*, pp. 78 238–78 259, 2018.

[17] B. L. R. Stojkoska and K. V. Trivodaliev, "A review of internet of things for smart home: Challenges and solutions," *Journal of Cleaner Production*, vol. *140*, pp. 1454–1464, 2017.

[18] X. Liu, W. Yu, F. Liang, D. Griffith, and N. Golmie, "Toward deep transfer learning in industrial internet of things," *IEEE Internet of Things Journal*, vol. *8*, no. 15, pp. 12 163–12 175, 2021.

[19] H. Xu, X. Liu, W. G. Hatcher, G. Xu, W. Liao, and W. Yu, "Priority aware reinforcement-learning-based integrated design of networking and control for industrial internet of things," *IEEE Internet of Things Journal*, vol. *8*, no. 6, pp. 4668–4680, 2021.

[20] F. Liang, W. Yu, X. Liu, D. Griffith, and N. Golmie, "Towards deep q-network based resource allocation in industrial internet of things," *IEEE Internet of Things Journal*, vol. *9*, pp. 9138–9150, 2021.

[21] X. Zheng and Z. Cai, "Privacy-preserved data sharing towards multiple parties in industrial iots," *IEEE Journal on Selected Areas in Communications*, vol. *38*, no. 5, pp. 968–979, 2020.

[22] M. Bansal, I. Chana, and S. Clarke, "A survey on iot big data: Current status, 13 v's challenges, and future directions," *ACM Computing Surveys*, vol. *53*, no. 6, 2020. [Online]. Available: https://doi.org/10.1145/3419634

[23] F. Liang, C. Qian, W. G. Hatcher, and W. Yu, "Search engine for the internet of things: Lessons from web search, vision, and opportunities," *IEEE Access*, vol. *7*, pp. 104 673–104 691, 2019.

[24] W. Gao, W. Yu, F. Liang, W. G. Hatcher, and C. Lu, "Privacy-preserving auction for big data trading using homomorphic encryption," *IEEE Transactions on Network Science and Engineering*, vol. *07*, pp. 776–791, 2018.

[25] W. G. Hatcher, C. Qian, W. Gao, F. Liang, K. Hua, and W. Yu, "Towards efficient and intelligent Internet of Things search engine," *IEEE Access*, vol. *9*, pp. 15 778–15 795, 2021.

[26] X. Liu, C. Qian, W. G. Hatcher, H. Xu, W. Liao, and W. Yu, "Secure internet of things (IoT)-based smart-world critical infrastructures: Survey, case study and research opportunities," *IEEE Access*, vol. *7*, pp. 79523–79544, 2019.

[27] Explosion. Spacy architecture. [Online]. Available: https://spacy.io/api

[28] S. Y. Nikouei, Y. Chen, A. J. Aved, and E. Blasch, "EIQIS: Toward an event-oriented indexable and query-able intelligent surveillance system," *CoRR*, vol. *abs/1807.11329*, 2018. [Online]. Available: http://arxiv.org/abs/1807.11329

[29] A. Torfi, R. A. Shirvani, Y. Keneshloo, N. Tavaf, and E. A. Fox, "Natural language processing advancements by deep learning: A survey," *CoRR*, vol. *abs/2003.01200*, 2020. [Online]. Available: https://arxiv.org/abs/2003.01200

[30] S. Bird, E. Klein, and E. Loper, Natural Language Processing with Python: Analyzing Text with the Natural Language Toolkit. O'Reilly Media, Inc.", 2009.

[31] https://www.nltk.org/

[32] https://spacy.io/

[33] https://devopedia.org/natural-language-toolkit

[34] A. Malgotra. Nltk and spacy performance comparison. [Online]. Available: https://bit.ly/3mAwByz

[35] E. Blasch, E. Bosse, and D. Lambert, *High-Level Information Fusion Management and System Design*, 1st ed. USA: Artech House, Inc., 2012.

[36] Explosion. Spacy models. [Online]. Available: https://spacy.io/models

[37] L. Snidaro, J. G. Herrero, J. Llinas, and E. Blasch (eds.), *Context-Enhanced Information Fusion: Boosting Real-World Performance with Domain Knowledge*. "Springer", 2016.

[38] H. Sun, Y. Chen, A. Aved, and E. Blasch, "Collaborative multiobject tracking as an edge service using transfer learning," in *2020 IEEE 22nd International Conference on High Performance Computing and Communications; IEEE 18th International Conference on Smart City; IEEE 6th International Conference on Data Science and Systems (HPCC/SmartCity/DSS)*. Los Alamitos, CA, USA: IEEE Computer Society, 2020, pp. 1112–1119. [Online]. Available: https://doi.ieeecomputersociety.org/10.1109/HPCC-SmartCity-DSS50907.2020.00146.

[39] C. Bormann, A. P. Castellani, and Z. Shelby, "COAP: An application protocol for billions of tiny internet nodes," *IEEE Internet Computing*, vol. *16*, no. 2, pp. 62–67, 2012.

[40] R. A. Light, "Mosquitto: server and client implementation of the MQTT protocol," *Journal of Open Source Software*, vol. *2*, no. 13, p. 265, 2017.

[41] P. Saint-Andre et al., "Extensible messaging and presence protocol (XMPP): Core," 2004.

[42] Y. Fathy, P. Barnaghi, and R. Tafazolli, "Large-scale indexing, discovery, and ranking for the internet of things (iot)," *ACM Computing Surveys*, vol. *51*, no. 2, 2018. [Online]. Available: https://doi.org/10.1145/3154525.

[43] U. Majumder, E. Blasch, and D. Garren, 2020.

[44] T. Bai, J. Zhao, J. Zhu, S. Han, J. Chen, B. Li, and A. Kot, "Aigan: Attack-inspired generation of adversarial examples," arXiv preprint arXiv:2002.02196, 2020.

[45] Z. Cai, Z. Xiong, H. Xu, P. Wang, W. Li, and Y. Pan, "Generative adversarial networks: A survey towards private and secure applications," CoRR, vol. *abs/2106.03785*, 2021. [Online]. Available: https://arxiv.org/abs/2106.03785

[46] W. T. Lunardi, E. de Matos, R. Tiburski, L. A. Amaral, S. Marczak, and F. Hessel, "Context-based search engine for industrial IoT: Discovery, search, selection, and usage of devices," in *2015 IEEE 20th Conference on Emerging Technologies & Factory Automation (ETFA)*. IEEE, 2015, pp. 1–8.

[47] A. Shemshadi, Q. Z. Sheng, and Y. Qin, "Thingseek: A crawler and search engine for the Internet of things," in *Proceedings of the 39th International ACM SIGIR conference on Research and Development in Information Retrieval*. ACM, 2016, pp. 1149–1152.

[48] S. K. Datta and C. Bonnet, "Search engine based resource discovery framework for internet of things," in *2015 IEEE 4th Global Conference on Consumer Electronics (GCCE)*. IEEE, 2015, pp. 83–85.

[49] F. Z. Fagroud, L. Ajallouda, H. Toumi, K. Achtaich, S. El Filali et al., "IoT search engines: Exploratory data analysis," *Procedia Computer Science*, vol. *175*, pp. 572–577, 2020.

[50] A. Makkar and N. Kumar, "An efficient deep learning-based scheme for web spam detection in iot environment," *Future Generation Computer Systems*, vol. *108*, pp. 467–487, 2020.

[51] K.-S. Lee, S.-R. Lee, Y. Kim, and C.-G. Lee, "Deep learning based real-time query processing for wireless sensor network," *International Journal of Distributed Sensor Networks*, vol. *13*, no. 5, p. 1550147717707896, 2017.

[52] W. Yu, T. N. Le, J. Lee, and D. Xuan, "Effective query aggregation for data services in sensor networks," *Computer Communications*, vol. *29*, no. 18, pp. 3733–3744, 2006. [Online]. Available: https://www.sciencedirect.com/science/article/pii/S0140366406002258

[53] P. Sarode and T. Reshmi, "Optimized query ordering data aggregation model using neural networks and group search optimization in wireless sensor network." *Adhoc & Sensor Wireless Networks*, vol. *46*, pp. 189–214, 2020.

[54] M. Kaur and A. Munjal, "Data aggregation algorithms for wireless sensor network: A review," *Ad Hoc Networks*, vol. *100*, p. 102083, 2020.

[55] B. S. Balaji, S. Balakrishnan, K. Venkatachalam, and V. Jeyakrishnan, "Automated query classification based web service similarity technique using machine learning," *Journal of Ambient Intelligence and Humanized Computing*, vol. *12*, pp. 1–12, 2020.

[56] A. Kumar, S. Dandapat, and S. Chordia, "Translating web search queries into natural language questions," arXiv preprint arXiv:2002.02631, 2020.

[57] D. Barman, R. Sarkar, A. Tudu, and N. Chowdhury, "Personalized query recommendation system: A genetic algorithm approach," *Journal of Interdisciplinary Mathematics*, vol. *23*, no. 2, pp. 523–535, 2020.

Toward incentive-compatible vehicular crowdsensing

A reinforcement learning-based approach

12

Xinxin Yang and Bo Gu
Sun Yat-Sen University, Guangzhou, China

Contents

12.1 INTRODUCTION

Nowadays, with great advances in transportation systems, intelligent vehicles are equipped with a rich set of sensors (e.g., cameras, radars, thermometers and ultrasonic sensors), triggering the emergence of a new vehicle-centric sensing paradigm, i.e., vehicular crowdsensing (VCS) [1–3], as shown in Figure 12.1. By recruiting sensor-embedded vehicles to accomplish sensing tasks, VCS is able to collect

DOI: 10.1201/9781003190691-16

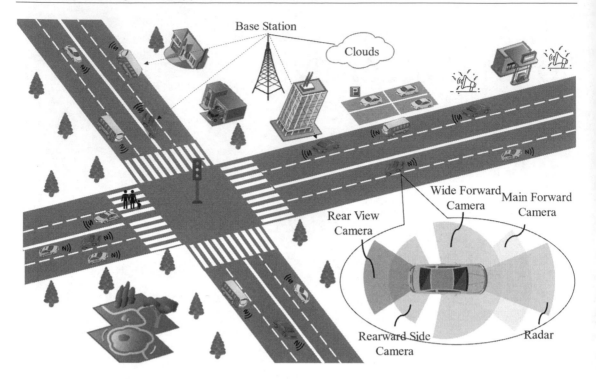

FIGURE 12.1   Vehicular crowdsensing system: an example.

city-scale information in a more efficient way, facilitating a series of smart services, such as environmental monitoring [4], object movement tracking [5], traffic jam alerts [6], noise mapping [7], parking space identification [8], and digital map updating [9].

Generally, a VCS system is composed of multiple task initiators (TIs), sensor-embedded vehicles, and a sensing platform (SP). Typically, the SP acts as a third-party agency to recruit vehicles on behalf of TIs, assign sensing tasks, and analyze the collected data for providing smart services. In traditional cloud-based VCS (CVCS) systems, the SP is deployed on the cloud and operates in a centralized manner, requiring all vehicles to upload their raw sensing data to remote servers [10]. However, due to the increased number of vehicles and sensors, aggregating data on the cloud may consume more bandwidth and incur intolerable delay. Moreover, as sensing data (e.g., road surface quality, high-definition map information, traffic conditions) shows strong spatial locality [11], transmitting data to remote cloud servers is unnecessary and new decentralized frameworks are urgently needed.

Recently, a new computing paradigm, namely edge computing [12], has revolutionized the way of data processing and management. Specifically, edge computing extends the computing ability of cloud servers to network edge layers by leveraging the computing and communicating capabilities of edge nodes, such as roadside units (RSUs), to provide a series of timely and high-quality services like real-time map updating. Great efforts have been devoted to investigating the possibility of integrating edge computing into crowdsensing. In [13], Zhou et al. utilize edge servers to automatically detect forged and irrelevant data with deep learning-based methods. In [14], Li et al. propose a data-deduplication protocol and use edge nodes to detect and remove duplicates. In [15], Zhou et al. leverage edge servers to perform task assignment with the aim of optimizing the sensing coverage under task budget constraints. However, those works pay little attention to how to incentivize vehicles to perform tasks and contribute high-quality sensing data, which is of critical importance to building a successful VCS system.

Designing an efficient incentive mechanism is challenging for the following three reasons. First, due to privacy concerns and energy consumption (e.g., electricity and fuel), vehicles would not perform sensing tasks unless they get fully compensated [16]. Second, a sensing task is generally constrained by a monetary budget and unfair profit distribution may lead to insufficient participation and unsatisfactory task performance [17]. Third, the data quality contributed by vehicles varies due to their heterogeneous sensing ability (e.g., sensor accuracy), and high-quality data contributors deserve more rewards than others [18].

In light of the above challenges, this chapter presents an edge-assisted vehicular crowdsensing (EVCS) framework where a deep reinforcement learning (DRL) [19]-based incentive mechanism is introduced to ensure efficient vehicle recruitment and data collection. Specifically, edge computing utilizes edge nodes, also known as a sub-sensing platform (SSP), to perform distributed vehicle recruitment and data processing. Moreover, the competitive interaction between the SSP and vehicles is formulated as a one-leader multi-follower Stackelberg game, where a multi-agent DRL-based incentive mechanism is developed to assist vehicles to choose optimal bid prices for participation.

12.2 EDGE-ASSISTED VEHICULAR CROWDSENSING

12.2.1 Architecture design

Compared to traditional CVCS systems, EVCS introduces an edge layer to bridge the gap between remote cloud servers and vehicles, where edge nodes act as SSPs to perform distributed vehicle recruitment and data processing. Moreover, a multi-agent DRL algorithm is utilized to assist each vehicle to choose an optimal bidding strategy for participation. As shown in Figure 12.2, EVCS consists of four layers: the application layer, the centralized management layer, the edge intelligence layer, and the sensing layer. In the following sections, the words "vehicles", "participants", and "data contributor" are used interchangeably.

1) **Application layer** is responsible for task initialization and application implementation. According to application requirements, TIs publish a series of sensing tasks along with multiple specifications, such as the monetary budget, the Area of Interests (AoIs), and deadline, to

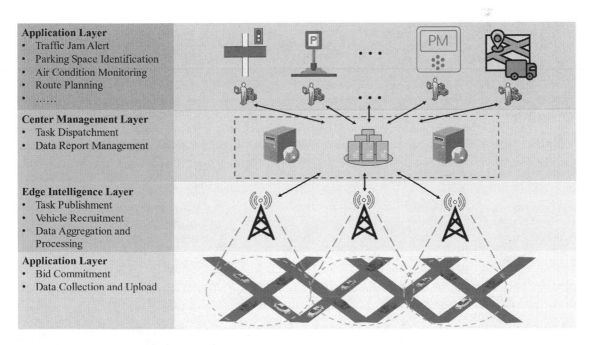

FIGURE 12.2   Architecture of EVCS.

the centralized management layer. With uploaded data, TIs are able to provide various smart applications, such as traffic jam alerts, parking space identification, air condition monitoring, route planning, and so forth.

2) **Centralized management layer** consists of a data broker, also known as center sensing platform (CSP), and a database server. On the one hand, the CSP receives tasks from the application layer and assign them to SSPs. On the other hand, data reports from SSPs are aggregated from SSPs and maintained in the database server.

3) **Edge intelligence layer** is comprised of multiple edge nodes, also known as SSPs, which mainly serve for three purposes: 1) receiving sensing tasks from the CSP; 2) recruiting nearby vehicles to perform tasks and collect sensing data; 3) analyzing collected data (e.g., distilling meaningful information) and sending data reports to the CSP.

4) **Sensing layer** is the place where sensing data are perceived. In order to motivate vehicles to contribute high-quality sensing data, a DRL-based incentive mechanism is proposed to assist vehicles to learn an optimal bidding strategy. Specifically, by observing the historical trade information (i.e., its bid price and the amount of traded sensing time), each vehicle is able to choose a proper bid price to maximize its benefits for participation.

On the one hand, compared with traditional CVCS systems, EVCS substantially improve data-processing efficiency and alleviate the burden of backhaul links through distributed data processing and management. On the other hand, the overall data quality is guaranteed by incentivizing vehicles to contribute high-quality data with a DRL-based mechanism. A detailed feature comparison between CVCS and EVCS is summarized and shown in Table 12.1.

12.2.2 Workflow

A general "many-to-many" scenario is considered where each vehicle can participate in multiple sensing tasks and each task can be allocated to multiple vehicles, simultaneously. The number of tasks and vehicles are denoted by U and V, respectively. Hence, the set of tasks and vehicles are represented by $\mathcal{U} = \{1, 2, ..., U\}$ and $\mathcal{V} = \{1, 2, ..., V\}$, respectively. Moreover, vehicle i's time budget and task j's monetary budget are denoted by t_i and b_j, respectively. It is assumed that there are A AoIs in the system and each AoI consists of exactly one SSP, i.e., edge node. Thus, the set of AoIs and SSPs are denoted as $\mathcal{A} = \{1, 2, ..., A\}$. The workflow of EVCS is elaborated as follows.

TABLE 12.1 Feature comparison between CVCS and EVCS

FEATURE	CVCS	EVCS
Connection	TIs – SP - vehicles	TIs – CSP – SSPs - vehicles
Location of computing resources	Cloud servers	Edge servers
Location of the sensing platform	Cloud servers	Cloud servers (i.e., CSP) & edge servers (i.e., SSPs)
Data processing	Remote	On-site
Traffic load	High	Low
Network delay	High	Low
Vehicle recruitment	Centralized	Distributed
Related incentive mechanism	Evolutionary Heterogeneous Public Good Game (HPGG)-based [20]	1. Bargain Game-based [21] 2. Reverse auction-based [22]

Step 1: Task release. According to application requirements, a group of sensing tasks are initialized by TIs and sent to the CSP.

Step 2: Task distribution. The CSP distributes task j to SSP k with a monetary budget b_{jk} which is proportional to the amount of vehicles (i.e., V_k) in AoI k while satisfying $\sum_{k \in \mathcal{A}} b_{jk} = b_j$ and $\sum_{k \in \mathcal{A}} V_k = V$.

Step 3: Bid commitment. Each candidate vehicle i observes its historical trade information (i.e., bid price and the amount of traded sensing time) and commits its bid price p_i and time budget t_i to the SSP.

Step 4: Vehicle recruitment. Given task budgets $\{b_{jk}\}_{k \in \mathcal{A}}$, vehicles' time budgets $\{t_i\}_{i \in \mathcal{V}_k}$ and bid prices $\{p_i\}_{i \in \mathcal{V}_k}$, SSP k decides how to purchase sensing time from vehicles with the aim of optimizing the overall data quality, which is elaborated in Section 4.3.2.

Step 5: Data collection and management. In each AoI k, each recruited vehicle collects and uploads sensing data to SSP k, where a data reports is generated and sent to the CSP. The CSP gathers data reports from all AoIs and sent them to TIs.

12.3 INCENTIVE MECHANISM FOR VEHICLE RECRUITMENT

This section investigates the competitive relations between the SSP and vehicles, and then presents how they behave to optimize their utilities.

12.3.1 Stackelberg game

Game theory [23] proves to be an effective tool in analyzing the competitive relations among players with conflicting interests. In particular, the Stackelberg game is a two-stage strategic game which involves two parties that act in a sequential manner. One player, who moves first by considering the potential countermeasures of other players, is known as the leader, and the other players, called the followers, observe the leader's action and decide their own actions. Generally, all players are assumed to be rational and self-interested with the aim of optimizing their own benefits. In EVCS, due to the conflicting interests between the SSP and vehicles, the vehicle recruitment problem in each AoI is modeled as a one-leader multi-follower game and formally given as follows.

Player: The SSP is the leader and vehicles are the followers.

Strategy: SSP k decides the amount of sensing time x_{ij} to buy from each vehicle i for each task j; and each vehicle i chooses the bid price p_i for participation.

Utility: For SSP k, its utility equals to the quality of collected sensing data; and vehicle i's utility equals to its payoff, represented by $\sum_{j \in \mathcal{U}} x_{ij}^t \left(p_i^t - c_i \right)$ where c_i is vehicle i's cost per unit sensing time.

12.3.2 Strategy of the SSP

Given $\{b_{jk}\}_{k \in \mathcal{A}}$, $\{t_i\}_{i \in \mathcal{V}_k}$ and $\{p_i\}_{i \in \mathcal{V}_k}$, SSP k decides how to purchase sensing time from vehicles to optimize the overall quality of sensing data, which is formulated as an convex optimization problem and represented as Problem 1.

Problem 1

$$\max_{x} \sum_{j \in \mathcal{U}_k} \log \left(\sum_{i \in \mathcal{V}_k} w_{ij} x_{ij} \right)$$

$$s.t. \quad \sum_{i \in \mathcal{V}_k} p_i x_{ij} \le b_{jk}, \quad \forall j \in \mathcal{U}_k \tag{12.1}$$

$$\sum_{j \in \mathcal{U}_k} x_{ij} \le t_i, \quad \forall i \in \mathcal{V}_k$$

where w_{ij} is the quality of sensing data contributed by vehicle i for task j. With complete information (i.e., $\{b_{jk}\}_{k \in \mathcal{A}}$, $\{t_i\}_{i \in \mathcal{V}_k}$ and $\{p_i\}_{i \in \mathcal{V}_k}$), the optimal solution to Problem 1 is obtained by using convex optimization methods and shown in Theorem 1.

Theorem 1 The optimal solution x_{ij}^* to Problem 1 is given as follows.

$$x_{ij}^* = \begin{cases} \dfrac{b_{jk} w_{ij}}{p_i \sum_{i \in \mathcal{V}_k} w_{ij}}, & \text{if} \quad I \ge 0 \\[4mm] \dfrac{t_i w_{ij}}{\sum_{j \in \mathcal{U}_k} w_{ij}}, & \text{otherwise} \end{cases} \quad \forall i \in \mathcal{V}_k, \forall j \in \mathcal{U}_k \tag{12.2}$$

where

$$I = \sum_{j \in \mathcal{U}_k} \log \left(\sum_{i \in \mathcal{V}_k} \frac{b_{jk} w_{ij}^2}{p_i \sum_{i \in \mathcal{V}_k} w_{ij}} \right) - \sum_{j \in \mathcal{U}_k} \log \left(\sum_{i \in \mathcal{V}_k} \frac{t_i w_{ij}^2}{\sum_{j \in \mathcal{U}_k} w_{ij}} \right).$$

Proof. Proofs are presented in Appendix A.

12.3.3 Strategies of vehicles

Without complete information about the system, e.g., how the SSP accesses its sensing data and other vehicles' bidding strategies, it is difficult for a vehicle to choose an appropriate bid price for performing sensing tasks. To address the above issue, a DRL-based incentive mechanism is developed to assist vehicles to choose optimal bid prices by only observing their historical trades. Specifically, by observing their bid prices and the amount of traded sensing time in previous time slots, vehicles judge how the SSP access their contributed data and choose a proper unit price. For instance, vehicles with high data quality are motivated to increase their bid prices for higher benefits, while others prefer to lower their prices to get recruited due to poor data quality. The proposed algorithm is based on Multi-Agent Actor-Critic (MAAC) [24] where each vehicle is modeled as an agent and competes with each other for higher benefits.

As shown in Figure 12.3, in MAAC each agent consists of four networks, i.e., two actors and two critics. At time slot t, the online actor i take observation of historical trades o_i^t as input, and outputs a bid price a_i^t for participation. The online critic i take the observation o_i^t and actors' action a_i^t as input, and outputs a Q value to indicate the value of action a_i^t. Target actor and target critic are used for computing loss and gradients for online critic. Detailed settings of MAAC are given as follows.

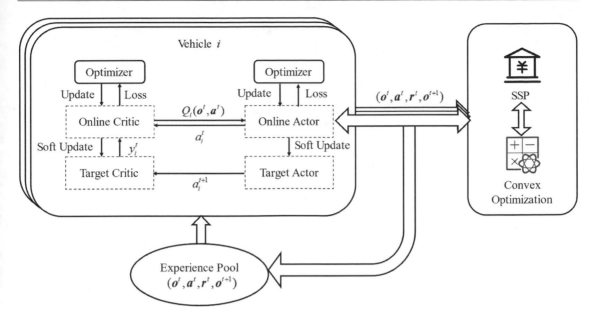

FIGURE 12.3   Stackelberg game between the SSP and vehicles.

Observation: At time slot t, each vehicle i's observation is its trade information in previous L time slots, i.e., bid price $\left\{ p_i^{t-1}, p_i^{t-2}, \ldots, p_i^{t-L} \right\}$ and the amount of traded sensing time $\{x_{t-1}, x_{t-2}, \ldots, x_{t-L}\}$.

Action: Based on its observation at time slot t, vehicle i chooses a bid price p_i^t for participation.

Reward: The reward of vehicle i, denoted by r_i^t, equals to its utility for participation, i.e., $\sum_{j \in \mathcal{U}} x_{ij}^t \left(p_i^t - c_i \right)$.

To accelerate the training process, a lightweight model is constructed for each vehicle. Specifically, each actor or critic is comprised of one input layer, three hidden layers and one output layer. The three hidden layers consists of 128, 64, and 32 neurons, respectively, and takes Rectified Linear Unit (ReLU) as activation. The output layer of actor and critic networks adopts Tanh and ReLU as their activations, respectively.

12.4 CASE STUDY

In this section, simulations are conducted to validate the efficiency of the proposed incentive mechanism. The vehicle recruitment problem in AoI k is considered where there are 8 vehicles and 2 tasks and each task is allocated with a monetary budget of 20. To illustrate the performance of the proposed method, two algorithms have been adopted as benchmarks, i.e., Upper-bound and Random.

- **Upper-bound**: With complete information (i.e., $\left\{ b_{jk} \right\}_{j \in \mathcal{U}}$, $\left\{ t_i \right\}_{i \in \mathcal{V}_k}$, and $\left\{ w_{ij} \right\}_{i \in \mathcal{V}_k, j \in \mathcal{U}}$), each vehicle's bid price is set to be proportional to its data quality while exactly consuming the monetary and time budgets (i.e., $I = 0$), which is impossible in real worlds but can serve as a benchmark.
- **Random**: Each vehicle selects its bid price within the interval of $(0, 1)$.

As shown in Figure 12.4, the proposed method achieves near-optimal performance in terms of vehicles' utilities and welfare in the absence of complete information. Specifically, when the time budget is low, random method cannot fully utilize vehicles' rare time budgets and improve their utilities, whereas in

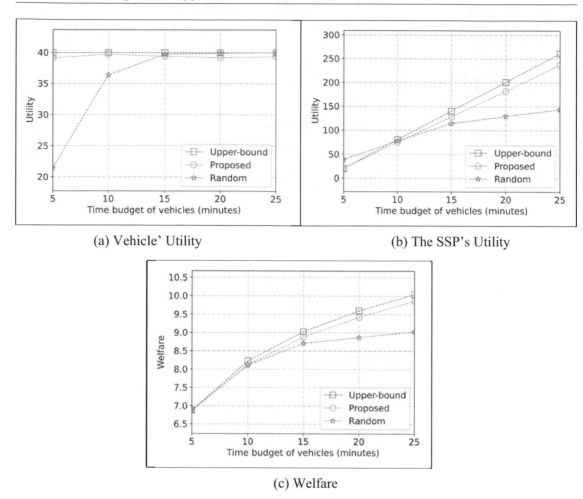

(a) Vehicle' Utility

(b) The SSP's Utility

(c) Welfare

FIGURE 12.4   Performance comparison between the proposed method and other methods for different vehicles' time budget.

our proposed mechanism vehicles are able to intelligently increase their bid prices for higher benefits. Moreover, as the time budget continuously increases from 5 to 25, the SSP's utility and welfare achieved by the proposed method is much higher than that by the random method. The reason behind that is the proposed method motivates vehicles to adaptively lower their bid prices as abundant sensing resources (i.e., time budget) intensify the competition among vehicles. In summary, the proposed method significantly outperforms the random strategy and approximately achieves optimal performance. However, Upper-bound is obtained by assuming that each vehicle acts in a cooperative manner with awareness of other vehicles' bidding strategies, which is impossible in real worlds. In contrast, in the proposed method, vehicles are able to learn an optimal bidding strategy with only local observations.

12.5 CONCLUSIONS

This chapter investigates the vehicle recruitment and data management problem in VCS systems, and presents a hierarchical VCS system, i.e., EVCS, by utilizing edge computing and DRL technologies.

Specifically, the proposed system introduces an edge layer to bridge the gap between clouds and vehicles where edge nodes are utilized to act as SSPs and perform distributed data processing. Moreover, a Stackelberg game is formulated to model the competitive interactions between the SSP and vehicles, where a state-of-the-art DRL algorithm, i.e., MAAC, is utilized to derive optimal bidding strategies for vehicles to participate in sensing activities. Simulation results demonstrate that the proposed incentive mechanism achieves near-optimal performance in terms of vehicles' utilities and welfare.

APPENDIX A

The Lagrangian form of Problem 1 is

$$
L(x,\lambda,\mu) = -\sum_{j\in U}\log\left(\sum_{i\in V_k}w_{ij}x_{ij}\right) + \sum_{i\in V_k}\lambda_i\left(\sum_{j\in U}x_{ij} - t_i\right) + \sum_{j\in U}\mu_j\left(\sum_{i\in V_k}p_ix_{ij} - b_j\right)
\tag{12.3}
$$

where $\lambda = \{\lambda_i\}$ and $\mu = \{\mu_j\}$ are the Lagrangian multipliers.

The Karush-Kuhn-Tucker (KKT) conditions are shown as follows.

$$
\begin{cases}
\dfrac{\partial L(x_{ij},\lambda_i,\mu_j)}{\partial x_{ij}} = 0, & \forall i\in V_k, \forall j\in U \\[3mm]
\lambda_i\left(\displaystyle\sum_{j\in U}x_{ij} - t_i\right) = 0, & \forall i\in V_k \\[4mm]
\mu_j\left(\displaystyle\sum_{i\in V_k}p_ix_{ij} - b_j\right) = 0, & \forall j\in U \\[4mm]
x_{ij} \geq 0, & \forall i\in V_k, \forall j\in U \\[1mm]
\lambda_i \geq 0, & \forall i\in V_k \\[1mm]
\mu_j \geq 0, & \forall j\in U
\end{cases}
\tag{12.4}
$$

By eliminating λ_i, we have

$$
\begin{cases}
\left(\dfrac{w_{ij}}{\displaystyle\sum_{i\in V_k}w_{ij}x_{ij}} - \mu_j p_i\right)\left(\displaystyle\sum_{j\in U}x_{ij} - t_i\right) = 0, & \forall i\in V_k \\[5mm]
\mu_j\left(\displaystyle\sum_{i\in V_k}p_ix_{ij} - b_j\right) = 0, & \forall j\in U \\[4mm]
x_{ij} \geq 0, & \forall i\in V_k, \forall j\in U \\[3mm]
\dfrac{w_{ij}}{\displaystyle\sum_{i\in V_k}w_{ij}x_{ij}} - \mu_j p_i \geq 0, & \forall i\in V_k \\[4mm]
\mu_j \geq 0, & \forall j\in U
\end{cases}
\tag{12.5}
$$

When

$$\frac{w_{ij}}{\sum\limits_{i \in \mathcal{V}_k} w_{ij} x_{ij}} - \mu_j p_i = 0 \tag{12.6}$$

we have

$$\mu_j = \frac{w_{ij}}{p_i \sum\limits_{i \in \mathcal{V}_k} w_{ij} x_{ij}} > 0 \tag{12.7}$$

Since

$$\mu_j \left(\sum\limits_{i \in \mathcal{V}_k} p_i x_{ij} - b_j \right) = 0 \tag{12.8}$$

we have

$$\sum\limits_{i \in \mathcal{V}_k} p_i x_{ij} = b_j \tag{12.9}$$

In summary, in the case where $\sum\limits_{j \in \mathcal{U}} x_{ij} - t_i \neq 0, \quad \exists i \in \mathcal{V}_k$, we get $\sum\limits_{i \in \mathcal{V}_k} p_i x_{ij} - b_j = 0, \quad \forall j \in \mathcal{U}$. Similarly, if $\sum\limits_{i \in \mathcal{V}_k} p_i x_{ij} - b_j \neq 0, \quad \exists j \in \mathcal{U}$, then $\sum\limits_{j \in \mathcal{U}} x_{ij} - t_i = 0, \quad \forall i \in \mathcal{V}_k$. Hence, the solution can be obtained by decomposing Problem 1 into two sub-problems:

Sub-Problem 1

$$\max_{x} \sum\limits_{j \in \mathcal{U}_k} \log \left(\sum\limits_{i \in \mathcal{V}_k} w_{ij} x_{ij} \right)$$

$$s.t. \quad \sum\limits_{i \in \mathcal{V}_k} p_i x_{ij} = b_{jk}, \quad \forall j \in \mathcal{U}_k \tag{12.10}$$

$$\sum\limits_{j \in \mathcal{U}_k} x_{ij} \leq t_i, \quad \forall i \in \mathcal{V}_k$$

The corresponding KKT conditions are presented as

$$\begin{cases} \dfrac{\partial L\left(x_{ij}, \lambda_i, \mu_j \right)}{\partial x_{ij}} = 0, & \forall i \in \mathcal{V}_k, \forall j \in \mathcal{U} \\[4mm] \lambda_i \left(\sum\limits_{j \in \mathcal{U}} x_{ij} - t_i \right) = 0, & \forall i \in \mathcal{V}_k \\[4mm] \sum\limits_{i \in \mathcal{V}_k} p_i x_{ij} - b_j = 0, & \forall j \in \mathcal{U} \\[2mm] x_{ij} \geq 0, & \forall i \in \mathcal{V}_k, \forall j \in \mathcal{U} \\[2mm] \lambda_i \geq 0, & \forall i \in \mathcal{V} \end{cases} \tag{12.11}$$

By eliminating λ_i, we have

$$
\begin{cases}
\dfrac{w_{ij}}{\displaystyle\sum_{i\in\mathcal{V}_k} w_{ij}x_{ij}} - \mu_j p_i \geq 0, & \forall i \in \mathcal{V}_k \\[4ex]
\displaystyle\sum_{j\in\mathcal{U}} x_{ij} - t_i = 0, & \forall i \in \mathcal{V}_k \\[3ex]
x_{ij} \geq 0, & \forall i \in \mathcal{V}_k, \forall j \in \mathcal{U} \\[3ex]
\displaystyle\sum_{i\in\mathcal{V}_k} p_i x_{ij} - b_j = 0, & \forall j \in \mathcal{U}
\end{cases}
\tag{12.12}
$$

According to the complementary slackness and stationarity in Equation (12.11), we have

$$
x_{ij}^* = \begin{cases}
\dfrac{w_{ij}}{p_i \mu_j^* \displaystyle\sum_{i\in\mathcal{V}_k} w_{ij}} & \mu_j^* > 0 \\[4ex]
0 & otherwise
\end{cases}
\tag{12.13}
$$

which can be simplified and represent as

$$
x_{ij}^* = \left(\dfrac{w_{ij}}{p_i \mu_j^* \displaystyle\sum_{i\in\mathcal{V}_k} w_{ij}} \right)^+
\tag{12.14}
$$

with $(\,\cdot\,)^+ = \max(\,\cdot\,, 0)$. Moreover, the primal feasibility in Equation (12.11) induces that

$$
\sum_{i\in\mathcal{V}_k} p_i \cdot \dfrac{w_{ij}}{p_i \mu_j^* \displaystyle\sum_{i\in\mathcal{V}_k} w_{ij}} = b_j
\tag{12.15}
$$

Thus, we have

$$
x_{ij}^* = \dfrac{b_j w_{ij}}{p_i \displaystyle\sum_{i\in\mathcal{V}_k} w_{ij}}
\tag{12.16}
$$

Sub-Problem 2

$$
\max_x \sum_{j\in\mathcal{U}_k} \log\left(\sum_{i\in\mathcal{V}_k} w_{ij}x_{ij} \right)
$$

$$
s.t. \quad \sum_{i\in\mathcal{V}_k} p_i x_{ij} \leq b_{jk}, \quad \forall j \in \mathcal{U}_k
\tag{12.17}
$$

$$
\sum_{j\in\mathcal{U}_k} x_{ij} = t_i, \quad \forall i \in \mathcal{V}_k
$$

The corresponding KKT conditions are presented as

$$
\begin{cases}
\dfrac{\partial L\left(x_{ij},\lambda_i,\mu_j\right)}{\partial x_{ij}} = 0, & \forall i \in \mathcal{V}_k, \forall j \in \mathcal{U} \\[2mm]
\mu_j\left(\displaystyle\sum_{i\in\mathcal{V}_k} p_i x_{ij} - b_j\right) = 0, & \forall j \in \mathcal{U} \\[2mm]
\displaystyle\sum_{j\in\mathcal{U}} x_{ij} - t_i = 0, & \forall i \in \mathcal{V}_k \\[2mm]
x_{ij} \geq 0, & \forall i \in \mathcal{V}_k, \forall j \in \mathcal{U} \\[2mm]
\lambda_i \geq 0, & \forall i \in \mathcal{V}
\end{cases}
\tag{12.18}
$$

By eliminating λ_i, we have

$$
\begin{cases}
\dfrac{w_{ij}}{p_i \displaystyle\sum_{i\in\mathcal{V}_k} w_{ij} x_{ij}} - \dfrac{\lambda_i}{p_i} \geq 0, & \forall i \in \mathcal{V}_k \\[2mm]
\displaystyle\sum_{j\in\mathcal{U}} x_{ij} - t_i = 0, & \forall i \in \mathcal{V}_k \\[2mm]
x_{ij} \geq 0, & \forall i \in \mathcal{V}_k, \forall j \in \mathcal{U} \\[2mm]
\displaystyle\sum_{i\in\mathcal{V}_k} p_i x_{ij} - b_j = 0, & \forall j \in \mathcal{U}
\end{cases}
\tag{12.19}
$$

According to the complementary slackness and stationarity in Equation (12.11), we have

$$
x_{ij}^* = \begin{cases}
\dfrac{w_{ij}}{\lambda_i^* \displaystyle\sum_{i\in\mathcal{V}_k} w_{ij}}, & \lambda_i^* > 0 \\[4mm]
0 & otherwise
\end{cases}
\tag{12.20}
$$

which can be simplified and represent as

$$
x_{ij}^* = \left(\dfrac{w_{ij}}{\lambda_i^* \displaystyle\sum_{i\in\mathcal{V}_k} w_{ij}}\right)^+
\tag{12.21}
$$

Moreover, the primal feasibility in Equation (12.11) induces that

$$
\sum_{j\in\mathcal{U}} \dfrac{w_{ij}}{\lambda_i^* \displaystyle\sum_{i\in\mathcal{V}_k} w_{ij}} = t_i
\tag{12.22}
$$

Thus, we have

$$
x_{ij}^* = \dfrac{t_i w_{ij}}{\displaystyle\sum_{i\in\mathcal{V}_k} w_{ij}}
\tag{12.23}
$$

In conclusion, the optimal solution x_{ij}^* is given as follows.

$$x_{ij}^* = \begin{cases} \dfrac{b_{jk}w_{ij}}{p_i \sum_{i \in \mathcal{V}_k} w_{ij}}, & if \quad I \geq 0 \\ \\ \dfrac{t_i w_{ij}}{\sum_{j \in \mathcal{U}_k} w_{ij}}, & otherwise \end{cases} \qquad \forall i \in \mathcal{V}_k, \forall j \in \mathcal{U}_k \qquad (12.24)$$

where $I = \sum_{j \in \mathcal{U}_k} \log \left(\sum_{i \in \mathcal{V}_k} \dfrac{b_{jk}w_{ij}^2}{p_i \sum_{i \in \mathcal{V}_k} w_{ij}} \right) - \sum_{j \in \mathcal{U}_k} \log \left(\sum_{i \in \mathcal{V}_k} \dfrac{t_i w_{ij}^2}{\sum_{j \in \mathcal{U}_k} w_{ij}} \right).$

REFERENCES

[1] L. Liu, X. Wen, L. Wang, Z. Lu, W. Jing, and Y. Chen, "Incentive-aware recruitment of intelligent vehicles for edge-assisted mobile crowdsensing," *IEEE Transactions on Vehicular Technology*, vol. *69*, no. 10, pp. 12085–12097, 2020.

[2] K. Lou, Y. Yang, E. Wang, Z. Liu, T. Baker, and A. K. Bashir, "Reinforcement learning based advertising strategy using crowdsensing vehicular data," *IEEE Transactions on Intelligent Transportation Systems*, vol. *22*, no. 7, pp. 4635–4647, 2021.

[3] J. Wang, X. Feng, T. Xu, H. Ning, and T. Qiu, "Blockchain-based model for nondeterministic crowdsensing strategy with vehicular team cooperation," *IEEE Internet of Things Journal*, vol. *7*, no. 9, pp. 8090–8098, 2020.

[4] F. Montori, L. Bedogni, and L. Bononi, "A collaborative internet of things architecture for smart cities and environmental monitoring," *IEEE Internet of Things Journal*, vol. *5*, no. 2, pp. 592–605, 2018.

[5] Y. Jing, B. Guo, Z. Wang, V. O. K. Li, J. C. K. Lam, and Z. Yu, "CrowdTracker: Optimized urban moving object tracking using mobile crowd sensing," *IEEE Internet of Things Journal*, vol. *5*, no. 5, pp. 3452–3463, 2018.

[6] R. Du, C. Chen, B. Yang, N. Lu, X. Guan, and X. Shen, "Effective urban traffic monitoring by vehicular sensor networks," *IEEE Transactions on Vehicular Technology*, vol. *64*, no. 1, pp. 273–286, 2015.

[7] Y. Liu, X. Ma, L. Shu, Q. Yang, Y. Zhang, Z. Huo, Z. Zhou , "Internet of things for noise mapping in smart cities: State of the art and future directions," *IEEE Network*, vol. *34*, no. 4, pp. 112–118, 2020.

[2] P. Carnelli, J. Yeh, M. Sooriyabandara, and A. Khan, "ParkUs: A novel vehicle parking detection system," in *AAAI'17*, pp.4650–4656, 2017.

[9] Z. Peng, S. Gao, B. Xiao, S. Guo, and Y. Yang, "CrowdGIS: Updating digital maps via mobile crowdsensing," *IEEE Transactions on Automation Science and Engineering*, vol. *15*, no. 1, pp. 369–380, 2018.

[10] B. Gu, X. Yang, Z. Lin, W. Hu, M. Alazab, and R. Kharel, "Multi-agent actor-critic network-based incentive mechanism for mobile crowdsensing in industrial systems," *IEEE Transactions on Industrial Informatics*, vol. *17*, no. 9, pp. 6182–6191, 2021.

[11] H. Wang, T. Liu, B. Kim, C. Lin, S. Shiraishi, J. Xie, Z. Han, "Architectural design alternatives based on cloud/edge/fog computing for connected vehicles," *IEEE Communications Surveys Tutorials*, vol. *22*, no. 4, pp. 2349–2377, 2020.

[12] Y. Mao, C. You, J. Zhang, K. Huang, and K. B. Letaief, "A survey on mobile edge computing: The communication perspective," *IEEE Communications Surveys Tutorials*, vol. *19*, no. 4, pp. 2322–2358, 2017.

[13] Z. Zhou, H. Liao, B. Gu, K. M. S. Huq, S. Mumtaz, and J. Rodriguez, "Robust mobile crowd sensing: When deep learning meets edge computing," *IEEE Network*, vol. *32*, no. 4, pp. 54–60, 2018.

[14] J. Li, Z. Su, D. Guo, K.-K. R. Choo, Y. Ji, and H. Pu, "Secure data deduplication protocol for edge-assisted mobile crowdsensing services," *IEEE Transactions on Vehicular Technology*, vol. *70*, no. 1, pp. 742–753, 2021.

[15] P. Zhou, W. Chen, S. Ji, H. Jiang, L. Yu, and D. Wu, "Privacy-preserving online task allocation in edge-computing-enabled massive crowdsensing," *IEEE Internet of Things Journal*, vol. *6*, no. 5, pp. 7773–7787, 2019.

[16] G. Ji, B. Zhang, Z. Yao, and C. Li, "A reverse auction based incentive mechanism for mobile crowdsensing," in *ICC 2019 – 2019 IEEE International Conference on Communications (ICC)*, pp. 1–6, 2019.

[17] G. Gao, H. Huang, M. Xiao, J. Wu, Y.-E. Sun, and Y. Du, "Budgeted unknown worker recruitment for heterogeneous crowdsensing using CMAB," *IEEE Transactions on Mobile Computing*, vol. *21*, pp. 1–1, 2021.

[18] C. Dai, X. Wang, K. Liu, D. Qi, W. Lin, and P. Zhou, "Stable task assignment for mobile crowdsensing with budget constraint," *IEEE Transactions on Mobile Computing*, vol. *20*, pp. 1–1, 2020.

[19] R. S. Sutton and A. G. Barto, *Reinforcement Learning, Second Edition: An Introduction*. MIT Press, 2018. https://mitpress.mit.edu/9780262039246/reinforcement-learning/

[20] A. Alamer, Y. Deng, G. Wei, and X. Lin, "Collaborative security in vehicular cloud computing: A game theoretic view," *IEEE Network*, vol. *32*, no. 3, pp. 72–77, 2018.

[21] A. Alamer, S. Basudan, and X. Lin, "A privacy-preserving incentive framework for the vehicular cloud," in *2018 IEEE International Conference on Internet of Things (iThings) and IEEE Green Computing and Communications (GreenCom) and IEEE Cyber, Physical and Social Computing (CPSCom) and IEEE Smart Data (SmartData)*, pp. 435–441, 2018.

[22] A. Alamer and S. Basudan, "An efficient truthfulness privacy-preserving tendering framework for vehicular fog computing," *Engineering Applications of Artificial Intelligence*, vol. *91*, p. 103583, 2020.

[23] D. Fudenberg and J. Tirole, *Game Theory*. Cambridge, MA: MIT Press, 1991.

[24] R. Lowe, Y. I. Wu, A. Tamar, J. Harb, O. P. Abbeel, and I. Mordatch, "Multi-agent actor-critic for mixed cooperative-competitive environments," in *Advances in Neural Information Processing Systems*, pp. 6379–6390, 2017.

Sub-signal detection from noisy complex signals using deep learning and mathematical morphology

13

Jie Wei
The City College of New York, New York, NY

Hamilton Clouse and Ashley Diehl
Air Force Research Laboratory, Wright-Patterson Air Force Base, Fairborn, Ohio

Contents

DOI: 10.1201/9781003190691-17

13.1 INTRODUCTION

In recent years, Artificial Intelligence, especially machine learning, and deep learning in particular, has revolutionized intelligent vehicles considerably. The development of Convolutional Neural Net (CNN) [1], Deep Belief Net (DBN) [2], Stacked Auto-Encoder (SAE) [3], and Long Short-Term Memory (LSTM) based Recurrent Neural Net (RNN) [4, 5] over the last several decades have enabled the pursuit of semi-autonomous/autonomous vehicles and networks of intelligent vehicles. The availability of sufficient and balanced training data is a crucial factor behind every success story of a deep learning approach. One such approach was the deep reinforcement learning-based *AlphaGo* [6]: AlphaGo repeatedly beat reigning human Go champions with ease. The researchers accomplished this feat by using millions of existing Go games to train and re-train itself by participating in thousands of self-playing games per day to improve its policy at each step; this is more games in a day than a human professional player can play for their whole career. Another astounding deep learning approach was a CNN-based skin cancer classifier developed by researchers in Stanford University: The network used nearly 140,000 skin lesion images to achieve expert-level performance when identifying canccrous lcsions [7]. To exploit the immense power of deep learning, great efforts must be made to produce the large, balanced training sets. As it is expensive to collect and label large amounts of representative data, we must also harness transfer learning, i.e., use a small, labeled dataset to re-train and fine-tune a subset of a deep network architecture that has already been trained using *relevant* big data [8].

The increase in intelligent vehicles on the road increases the number of vehicle-to-vehicle and vehicle-to-infrastructure communications. Protecting these communications is becoming increasingly important. This is true whether you have intelligent civilian vehicles on the road or intelligent military vehicles across the ground and sky. In these intelligent vehicles, to effectively protect the drivers, passengers, and facilities and make timely response to potential signals from surrounding environments, we identify and character-ize possible signals, often-times embedded in the signals of complex time series contaminated by severe background noises due to intentional camouflage and information hiding schemes, sensors' and/or air-crafts' unstable and random movements and vibrations, and other unpredictable environment and climate sources. In Figure 13.1, three synthetic signals with known sub-signals are depicted. The rampant noises present in the signals makes a great challenge to reliably detect the presence of sub-signals from within the severe noises. In Figure 13.1a, the step-like sub-signal waveform, depicted in the bottom row, contains sig-nal magnitudes around 0.001 and is contaminated by noise with magnitudes larger than 0.0020; the result-ing magnitudes of the sensed signals, depicted in the middle row, are of magnitudes around 0.0023. In Figure 13c, the sub-signal waveform has extremely high frequency; its separation from surrounding noise is also hard to detect. The sub-signals in both cases shown in columns (a) and (c) are difficult for human operators to identify and characterize; this is especially true when attempting to depict the accurate start and end of the presence of every sub-signal due to the strong noises. The sinusoidal sub-signals loaded in signals shown in Figure 13.1b is probably the easiest to identify by human operators. Using methods such as conventional statistical signal processing or Fourier analysis can often be used to detect these types of sub-signals [9]. Since these types of *"easy"* cases are infrequent, the ad hoc signal processing and Fourier analysis based approaches that are tailored to detect these easy cases will fail in the presence of hard cases, as seen in our experimental studies.

Despite great progresses made in time series analysis [10] and deep learning [11], due to the immense noises, widely varied waveforms of sub-signals, and the lack of a straightforward deep learning approach to process complex numbers directly, the efficient and reliable method to detect these complex sub-signals remains elusive. In response to this challenge, researcher engineers and scientists from the Air Force Research Laboratory and the City College of New York have taken up this problem and worked closely together to apply our prior knowledge and experience in signal processing [12], machine learning and deep learning [13, 14] to detect the sub-signals from among rampant noises. Given that the signals are 1-D complex sequences, it is appealing to apply various mature time series processing and analysis schemes

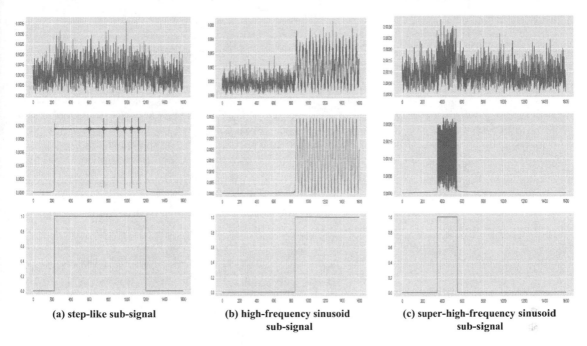

(a) step-like sub-signal   (b) high-frequency sinusoid sub-signal   (c) super-high-frequency sinusoid sub-signal

FIGURE 13.1   Illustrations of noisy nature of signals with sub-signals of different waveforms, from step-like (a) to relatively high-frequency one (b), to super-high-frequency one (c), the magnitudes (|s|) of the complex signal s are shown here. Top Row: Noisy nature of collected signals loaded with various sub-signals. Middle Row: the true sub-signal waveforms. Bottom Row: The indicator function of the presence of sub-signals.

[10, 15] such as Autoregressive Moving Average (ARMA), Autoregressive Integrated Moving Average (ARIMA), spectral analysis, hidden Markov Model (HMM) and dynamic programming [16], which the authors have developed a slew of different methods with varying degrees of success in prior researches [17–20]. However, our initial endeavors to harness these otherwise powerful time series processing and analysis schemes to identify and characterize these sub-signals were unable to combat the challenges posed by this problem, due mostly to the heavy noises innate to the signals, the widely different nature of the waveforms of the sub-signals and irregular and unpredictable presence and absence of sub-signals, and the sophisticated interplays of all these troubling factors.

One major drawback of signal processing methodologies is the reliance on underlying signal and noise models to be addressed, the sub-signals that may arise in practice are so varied that it is impossible and methodologically incorrect if we made any assumptions on the waveforms, the nature of the system, and random noise. The only viable approach is using machine learning techniques [8, 21]; these approaches make as few assumptions as possible regarding the problem in hand and let the data speak for itself. In our previous work, machine learning methods, such as shallow neural networks, logistic regression, and random forests, have been exploited to achieve promising performances in image denoising [22] civilian vehicle engine detection [14], breath signal detection [23], 1D breath signal analysis [24], and MRI super-resolution [25, 26]. However, there are no conventional machine learning methods that can effectively take advantage of the *locally contextual dependencies* in the sub-signals loaded signals, i.e., sub-signals are present as connected clusters, and widely different sub-signals waveforms as illustrated in Figure 13.1. Unlike ordinary neural networks, where the inputs and outputs are considered independent, RNN takes the outputs in prior step (s) as part of the inputs, thus explicitly considering the contextual dependencies in the temporal data. Although theoretically a better network, the recurrent cycle from prior outputs of RNN only has the short-term memory. Only the outputs of the preceding one or several steps can be practically remembered; long-term dependencies, which is far from unusual in time series and language models, cannot be facilitated by this network architecture. The representational and predicting power of RNNs was significantly enhanced with the introduction of LSTMs—a miniature neural network on its own—that can selectively remember and forget previous memories in the local contexts; these keep relatively long-term dependencies with reasonably small additional units [4]. LSTM-based RNNs have been one of the most widely used deep learning methods and have found a great array of utilities in many applications such as natural language processing (NLP) [27] and time series analysis [28, 29] with desirable performance.

After exploring several research avenues, from statistical signal processing to shallow machine learning with subpar results, we eventually set out to apply LSTM-based RNN (LSTM-RNN) in our sub-signal detection work. After careful problem formulation and data pre-processing, the original noise-loaded signals are turned into a large volume—from hundreds of signals to the order of ~100,000—of *balanced* sub-signals training instances, the LSTM-RNN N is trained to enhance and predict the presence of sub-signal in each location. For each incoming signal segment s, after going through the same data pre-processing step as done in N training phase, s is enhanced by the use of N. The resulting signal enhanced the sub-signals signals while suppressing noises in the original data thus significantly increased the signal to noise ratios. A post-processing procedure based on mathematical morphological (MM) operators such as watershed, run-length encoding and size filtering, can be applied to segment s to arrive at the global shape/signature of the sub-signals in s. These MM operators can effectively encode the global properties of sub-signals in the data segment s. As observed from the sub-signals simulation procedure we were provided, this new combination of LSTM-RNN's immense learning power to predict *local* presence of sub-signals and MM's prowess to enforce *global* signature has given rise to encouraging results of primary interest to ensure the security of civilian or military intelligent vehicles.

In the next section, the technical details of the sub-signals detection algorithm are described. The algorithm components described include pre-processing, LSTM-RNN training, and MM-based global post-processing. Experimental results for signals generated by sub-signals simulation procedures are reported and analyzed in Section 13.3. We conclude this paper in Section 13.4 with more remarks on possible new directions to be taken in the near future on this sub-signal detection work for intelligent vehicles.

13.2 LSTM-RNN AND MATHEMATICAL MORPHOLOGY-BASED ALGORITHM TO DETECT SUB-SIGNALS FROM NOISY COMPLEX SIGNALS

In this section, we outline the technical details of our LSTM-RNN and MM-based algorithm to detect sub-signals from noisy complex signals. The sub-signals signals used in this study are generated using simulation functions that serve as faithful proxies of practical sub-signals signals based on extensive prior exploratory data analysis over sub-signals signals. To represent the real-world situations as closely as possible, the simulation procedure in MATLAB was made available to this research team, where the specific waveforms and durations, Gaussian smoothing factors, and noise levels that may arise in practical signals of interest are generated by random sampling [30]. Each simulated data segment s generated by these simulation functions is a sequence of 1,600 complex numbers, the ground truths of the sub-signals in each s, namely, the waveform and precise duration of each sub-signal are also available for ease of algorithmic developments.

Three such segments are illustrated in Figure 13.1, where the top row are the simulated signals, and the next two rows provide the known ground truths about the waveforms – middle row – and the presence of sub-signals, bottom row. *The objective of our algorithmic development is to take signals s as inputs to generate outputs corresponding to the presences $t(s)$ of sub-signals, where s is a 1600-dimension vector, and $t(s)$ is the corresponding 1600-dimension Boolean (indicator) vector indicating the presence of sub-signal at each location in signal s.* The overall logic flow chart of the proposed algorithm is diagrammatically depicted in Figure 13.2. Technical details of each step in both training (colored in red or green) and testing (in green or blue color) phases are expanded in detail in the sequel.

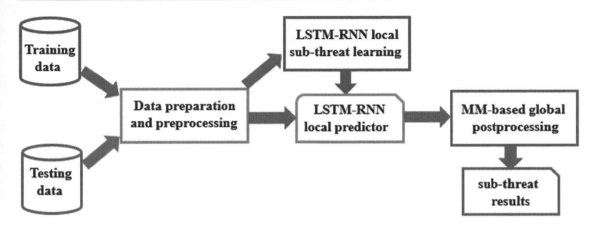

FIGURE 13.2 Logic flow chart of the proposed algorithm. Training phase (red data flow): training data go through *data preparation and preprocessing* and *LSTM-RNN local sub-signal* step to deliver the *LSTM-RNN local predictor*. In testing phase (blue data flow), the testing data first go through *data preparation and preprocessing* procedure and then the signal is enhanced by the trained *LSTM-RNN local predictor*; the final sub-signal detection results are declared by the *MM-based global post-processing* step. Color designations: Data and procedure associated with training phase only are colored in red; while those corresponding to testing phase only are in blue color. Procedures involved in both phases are colored in green

13.2.1 Data preparation and pre-processing

As briefly introduced in Section 13.1, to effectively harness the great power of deep learning that is extremely data-hungry, it is crucial to have a *large* and *balanced* data as the training data. Our data preparation and preprocessing step is developed to generate large and balanced training data that can effectively reflect the targeted sub-signals for effective following processing.

By *large* data, for every class to learn, sufficient number of instances should be available. For instance, in LeCun et. al.'s seminal effort of digit recognition using CNN [31], to learn the ten digits 60,000 28x28 training digits were provided as the now-standard MNIST dataset. As reported by Stanford's skin cancer detection using CNN [7], their excellent skin cancer performance, better than or at least in par with human dermatologists, are only possible after they have adequate training skin lesion images in the order of a hundred thousand (~140,000 to be precise). In our sub-signal detection work, it is *impossible* to learn the 1600-dimension sub-signal indicator $t(s)$ directly from 1600-dimension signal s: the extremely high dimension (1600) of the objective to-be-learned targets will, in theory, demand prohibitively more training data, and, more importantly, the sub-signals, as shown in bottom row of Figure 13.1, can present essentially everywhere in s with totally random duration, which is determined by drawing a random variable in the simulation procedure, except for a few weak constraints about the behavioral property of the sub-signals to be described at length in Section 13.2.3—which will be exploited in the global post-processing phase—there is no global regularities or interplays among the presence or absence of sub-signals and different waveforms that can be learned from the training data, however big they may be. Therefore, it is an ill-posed problem to learn the entire 1600-dimension $t(s)$ directly from s as the space spanned by possible $t(s)$ could be in an order exponential to 1600 as the presence and absence of sub-signal is randomized.

A problem re-formulation is thus needed to pose the sub-signal detection problem as a viable deep learning problem: if there is little global regularity to be learned for the entire $t(s)$ from the global data segment s, we can then single out the individual Boolean indicator t_i from $t(s)$, i ranging from 1 to 1600, and try to learn the 1D Boolean value from s, again due to the random nature of the signal s in real sub-signals signals and reflected in the available simulation functions, it is unlikely t_i is determined by the entire s. Conversely, the Markovian neighborhood can be safely assumed [17], i.e., t_i can be viewed as a function of its local neighborhood N in signal s only: $s[i-k_1: i+k_2]$, that is, the vector of size k_1+k_2 centered at location i, the position of t_i. Because the signal is non-causal, the reversal of s remains a legitimate signal; in this work we thus have no reason to have different k_1 and k_2 values, hereafter they are denoted by one value k. After intensive empirical studies, we found that setting k at 20 gives rise to good overall performances for datasets generated by the simulation function. In consequence, the new learning problem is *to learn a Boolean indicator function f for scalar t from 2k vector **v*** (= s[i − k, i + k]), as dictated by the equation below.

$$t = f(v) \tag{13.1}$$

From this problem formulation, each 1600-dimension signal **s** can yield up to 1600-2k (by trimming the start and ending positions in **s**), given that the k is set at 20, 1560 training instances can be formulated to learn f for Equation (13.1). Since there are only two classes, i.e., presence of absence of sub-signal, following the example of other deep learning applications, e.g., [1, 31], one hundred typical **s** will give rise to sufficient training data for deep learning purposes, with an order of ~100,000 available training instances. Thus, the large data size requirement for deep learning can be facilitated with this problem formulation.

The other requirement for effective deep learning is the *balance* of training data. In our problem as dictated by Equation (13.1), the positive and negative responses of t, the actual presence and absence of individual sub-signal, should be roughly balanced: if there are too many positive (negative) instances, the learned deep net will unfairly favor positive (negative) instances, thereby reducing the quality of the net considerably. In our signals, there are many cases that the sub-signals are only present in a very small portion of the signal **s**, as seen in Figure 13.1c, only about 10% of **s** are positive instances for t. Even worse, there are many more signals where there is no sub-signal at all, which is the norm in practical scenarios. To avoid this imbalance problem, in preparing the training data, instead of using all **s** to obtain t's and **v**'s, cf. Equation (13.1), the following two *choice rules* are applied to enforce the rough balance of positive and negative training instances:

Choice rules:
1. *s is discarded if there is no sub-signal*
2. *for every positive sub-signal chunk ss-$_i$ of length L, only keep possible 0.6*L prior and post non sub-signal locations in **s***

Rule 1 ensures that those signals with no sub-signal presence should not be employed for training at all. Rule 2 makes certain that the number of positive and negative t's are roughly of the same number: we intentionally keep 60% prior and post non sub-signal positions because the following two factors will reduce the actual number of negative instances: 1. If a sub-signal chunk is close to the starting or end of signal s, there will be fewer negative instances; 2. the next skipping in the leading and ending locations in forming the local neighborhood **v** for each t will reduce the number of actual negative instances. The potential imbalance trouble in training data is thus resolved. Because of these choice rules which reduced the number of instances, to ensure sufficient number of training instances, two to three hundred 1600-dimension signals are generally enough to produce ~100,000 balanced training instanced. In our tests, ~250 signals are harnessed to train our LSTM-RNN to predict local sub-signal.

Mathematically, the procedure to find t from v as dictated by Equation (13.1) is a typical *inverse* problem [32], whereof special care should be taken to avoid troubles of this generally ill-posed problem. In view of the severe and rampant noises present in the sub-signal signals, to effectively enhance sub-signals while suppressing noises, the *regularization* technique, which was developed in applied mathematics to help solve inverse problems, has been widely used in image processing [33] and machine learning [34] with promising results. The key to the regularization technique is the introduction of additional information of the desirable properties of the objectives. For instance, in the celebrated *snakes* or *active contour models* [34], the *internal* energy is added in the optimization process to enforce the continuity and smoothness, the gradients (first partial derivatives) and curvature (second partial derivatives) of the desirable contour to be sought after. In our detection problem, along the line of the internal energy addition in active contours, the desirable and/or known property of sub-signals should also be encoded as a regularization term to achieve better detection results. The 2k-dimension data segment **v** in Equation (13.1) is the sum of the contribution of sub-signal 2k-dimension **st** and system and/or 2k-dimension random noises **n**:

$$v = st + n \tag{13.2}$$

The additional regularizing terms should emphasize the property of sub-signals that are significantly different from noises. After checking all cases of the available simulation functions Gen00 to 05, as illustrated in Figure 13.1, we found the common property shared by all sub-signal signals: although of varying frequencies, the sub-signals **st** are still *smoother* than those noises **n** within the relatively short duration 2k, notice that k is ~20. To encode the smoothness contributed by **st**, the Fourier transform fits in perfectly: now that **st** is smooth, its corresponding Fourier transform should be mostly dominated by its low-frequency components; conversely, noise vector **n**'s Fourier transform should contribute far more high-frequency components, that is, if we take the Fourier transform on both sides of Equation (13.2), the linearity of Fourier transform will result in the equality below:

$$F(v) = F(st) + F(n) \tag{13.3}$$

Since the low-frequency components of **F(v)** mostly come from **F(st)**, if only the top *m* AC components are kept—the signals used in this work are zero-mean, hence the DC component F(v)[0] is always 0 and thus ignored—the following approximation is obtained:

$$ACm(v) \approx ACm(st) \tag{13.4}$$

where $AC_m(x) = F(x)[1:m]$, the first *m* AC components of x. Hence the smoothness regularization term due to sub-signal **st** can be safely represented by the leading *m* AC components of the Fourier transform of **v**. The resultant regularized term **r**(p) at a position p is below

$$r(p) = \left[v(p), ACm(v(p)) \right] \tag{13.5}$$

which is a vector of 2k+m dimension. From our experiments, optimal detection performance occurs when *m* takes value 3, hence for each position p, as *k* = 20, we need 43-D vector in order to train a learner for sub-signal t. Because in our following LSTM-RNN training process, the L_2 norm is used, *Parseval's theorem* [10] ensured that the sum of squares of $AC_m(v(p))$ is (approximately) equal to that of *st*, *r(p)* is therefore a viable regularized representation at location p to be optimized and learned with desirable smoothness of sub-signals effectively encoded. Although in theory different weights should be assigned to different AC coefficients given their different nature. From our tests, likely due to the widely different sub-signals, putting these weights higher or lower than 1 cannot yield better performances over all six different simulation signals. In this work we simply assign all three weights to 1.

One more important issue needs to be addressed before engaging LSTM-RNN learning: the type of number system. As mentioned in Section 13.1, all signals in the sub-signal identification and characterization tasks are complex, thus the 43-D vector **r**(p) for each position p is complex as well. However, so far there is no readily available support for the use of complex numbers available in *TensorFlow*, likely due to the lackluster performances. Despite the theoretical advantage the complex representations can offer, as reviewed in Bengio et al.'s recent unpublished manuscript [29] (submitted to NIPS in May 2017), most recent deep learning work using complex numbers directly can only handle toy tasks, with very few exceptions [35]. In the work reported here, two different approaches are adopted to convert the 43-D complex vector **r**(p) to real numbers that can be handled by current *TensorFlow* backend that we have been using in this work. 1) The first one is to use the magnitude of a complex representation:

$$ra(p) = \left\| \left[v(p), ACm(v(p)) \right] \right\|$$
(13.6)

where $| c |$ is the magnitude, $\sqrt{c_{real}^2 + c_{imag}^2}$, of a complex number $c = c_{real} + c_{imag} \, i$. Thus the real value vector $r_a(p)$ consists of 43 *positive* real numbers that are the corresponding magnitudes of the complex numbers. 2) The second one is to use the *absolute* values of both the real and the imaginary components of a complex variable:

$$rb(p) = abs\left(\left[real(v(p)), imag(v(p)), real(ACm(v(p))), imag(ACm(v(p))) \right] \right)$$
(13.7)

where **real**(c) and **imag**(c) are the **real** (c_{real}) and imaginary (c_{imag}) part of a complex variable $c = c_{real} + c_{imag} \, i$. The **abs**($\circ$) operator takes the absolution value of the real numbers. The vector $r_b(p)$ is composed by 86 *positive* real numbers for the corresponding 43-D complex vector. According to the meaning of complex representations, each component in $r_a(p)$ indicates the radius of the complex number, thus all complex numbers of the same radius are mapped to the same value; whereas in $r_b(p)$ the absolute values of the real and imaginary part are used in the representation: only four complex numbers can be mapped to the same two values in this case—by folding four quadrants to the first quadrant, therefore, the many-to-one transform employed in representation $r_b(p)$ is not as drastic as that in $r_a(p)$, thus the former can potentially load more information. As to be reported in Section 13.3, without the **abs** operator the detection accuracy is unacceptably worse probably due to the numerous periodic sudden phase changes in the complex representations that are irrelevant to the presence or absence of sub-signals, which could indicate some complications in direct complex number usage. Sub-signal detection performances for both representations based on Eqs. (6, 7) will be reported in Section 13.3.

13.2.2 LSTM-RNN local sub-signal learning

The careful data preparation and pre-processing step as described in the preceding section generated a big, balanced and regularized dataset, namely the r_a's and r_b's, which are 43- or 86-D real vectors, respectively, that can be processed by all deep learning packages. In view of the new regularized data representation, in place of Equation (13.1), for each position p, the sub-signal t(p) is a function g() of $r(p)$, which is to be learned by a deep learning process:

$$t(p) = g(r(p))$$
(13.8)

where r is either r_a or r_b. The memory unit (forget/remember gate) introduced in LSTM is the only means to fully take advantage of the potential long-term temporal dependencies among the sequential data in $r(p)$, a 43- or 86-dimension vector. Because of this, LSTM-RNN, the LSTM unit-based RNN, has been widely used in temporal/sequential data processing. In this work, after trying out other deep learning schemes, LSTM-RNN is found to yield optimal performances consistently, which indicates that there indeed exist long-term dependencies in the sub-signal signals which can be only captured by the LSTM memory units. This specific net is thus employed in this work as the workhorse.

The next two choices to be made on the nature of LSTM-RNN are the number of layers and regression or classification for the target t, as dictated by Equation (13.8). Unlike visual object classification tasks taken up by CNN or RNN [1, 7], where a lot of layers are needed to find edges, contours and local semantically meaningful shapes that contribute to the formulation of a visual object, in our sub-signal signals within a relatively short span of 43 or 86 numbers, the hidden sub-signals do not have sophisticated composite curves or shapes to be discriminated; therefore the number of layers, generally accounting for contextual structures of different semantics, needed for this sub-signal detection task is not too large.

From our empirical studies, we found one layer of LSTM is adequate in this RNN, additional layer(s) of LSTM cannot yield better performances.

The other important choice is 1) *direct classification*: to set the LSTM-RNN to directly learn class label, presence or absence of sub-signal, for t(p) from **r**(p), thus yielding an essential full-fledged classification machine; or 2) *regression as a data enhancement procedure*: to use the LSTM-RNN as a regression machine to enhance the hidden sub-signal signals while suppressing the rampant noises that will be relayed to the next post-processing step for final sub-signal classification. Due to the significantly different sub-signal waveforms—ranging from step curves to sinusoidal of different frequencies and Gaussian shapes—and even more different noise levels—from Gaussian, uniform to flicker noises of entirely different seriousness, as evidenced by our intensive empirical studies, the direct classification scheme can only generate subpar performances for our data.

In the second option the LSTM-RNN plays a role as a regression step to enhance the targeted sub-signal signals while suppressing the severe noises, thus achieving data enhancement, this seemingly modest approach of the LSTM-RNN application has been employed recently by several groups for effective signal enhancement purposes recently with promising performances [36, 37]. From our empirical studies, we observed that while it is extremely difficult to train a LSTM-RNN to come up with acceptable sub-signal classification labels for different types of sub-signal signals which is highly correlated to the local sub-signal waveforms and noise natures, the local long-term dependencies captured by the LSTM units can enhance the sub-signals and suppress noises by varying orders of magnitude: in some cases, the LSTM-RNN can almost boost sub-signals to 1 and suppress background noise to 0, thereby behaving like a great classifier; whereas in many cases the sub-signals are elevated to modestly larger values than those of background noise, e.g., ~0.035 for sub-signals and ~0.025 for background signals. This LSTM-RNN enhanced data will provide a solid foundation for our next post-processing step to finally classify sub-signals by taking account of the global behavioral properties of sub-signals in the signal segments, which is impossible to be effectively learned by LSTM-RNN given that this global properties are related to dependencies of distance in terms of up to several hundred even a thousand data points, well beyond the dependencies a LSTM-RNN can effectively handle and thus making this line of work impractical. In addition, we believe for this type of global analysis classic signal processing, especially mathematical morphological [38], fits in perfectly and thus should be exploited.

The layout of the training phase of the LSTM-RNN regression model for data enhancement, the actual *main graph* generated by *TensorBoard* coupled with the *TensorFlow* package, is shown in Figure 13.3, the input 43- or 86-D data are fed to the LSTM layer; the outputs of this layer are fed to a fully connected logistic neural net (tanh activation function is used in place of the default sigmoid with faster convergence time and similar results). The target data are compared with the output of the net to update the learned parameters. This rigorously learned model will be employed in the testing and detection phase to enhance data quality thus laying a solid foundation for the next global sub-signal detection step, as empirically proved by our experimental studies presented in Section 13.3. The two different conversion methods for complex numbers have almost the same architecture except the dimensionality of the input data. This trained model is saved as the sub-signal local predictor depicted in Figure 13.2, to be used in the detection phase. The training phase, the red colored flow in Figure 13.2, is now complete.

13.2.3 Mathematical morphological global sub-signal detection

The sub-signal detection task is performed over the *testing data*, the data flow designated in blue color in Figure 13.2 by using the LSTM-RNN predictor for data enhancement. The incoming 1600-D data first go through the pre-processing step—without applying the two *choice rules* which are called upon for the sole purpose of balanced training data and should thus be skipped in the detection phase—to generate the 43- or 86-dimension representation vector **r**(p)'s, cf. Equation (13.5). These **r**(p)'s are next fed to the trained *LSTM-RNN local predictor* for data enhancement, which can effectively suppress noise while boosting sub-signal signals. The signals enhanced by the LSTM-RNN model for the three noisy signals based on $\mathbf{r_b}$

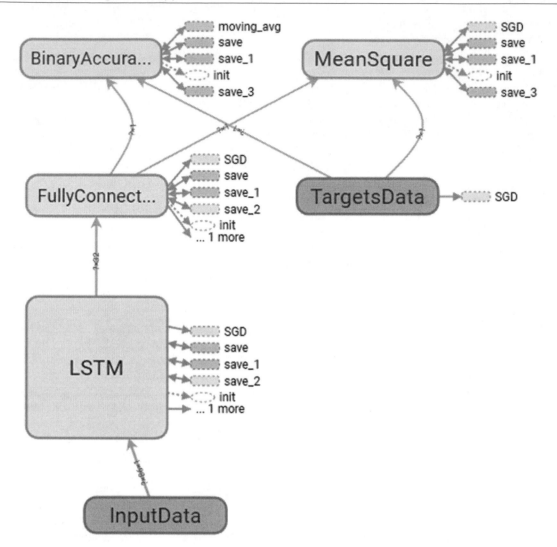

FIGURE 13.3 Architecture of the trained LSTM-RNN model, the actual *main graph* generated by *TensorBoard* coupled with the *TensorFlow* package. The SGD (stochastic gradient descent) is used as the optimization approach.

shown in Figure 13.1 are displayed in Figure 13.4, the three sub-signals revealed themselves more clearly from the background noise more easily than the original ones.

Because in the training process the presence and absence of local sub-signal takes values 1 and 0, respectively, and the addition of three leading AC coefficients in the trained representational vector $r(p)$'s, as evidenced in the three enhanced signals, the values corresponding to sub-signals tend to have higher values than those associated with background noises. The detection of sub-signals is thus the separation of *foreground* from the *background* from the 1600-D data segment using certain global properties of the foreground, mathematical morphological (MM) operators fit perfectly in this task, which the authors have utilized expansively in lots of image processing [22, 39, 40], computer vision [40, 41], and medical imaging applications [9, 13, 26] with promising performances to segment out moving objects, human beings, brain vessels, and lungs. To effectively apply MM approaches, the global nature of the sub-signals should be first laid out. As briefly discussed in Section 13.2.1, although the sub-signals did not exhibit too much global regularities given their randomized nature, they nonetheless have some weak but useful statistical properties for MM operators to exploit effectively for detection purposes:

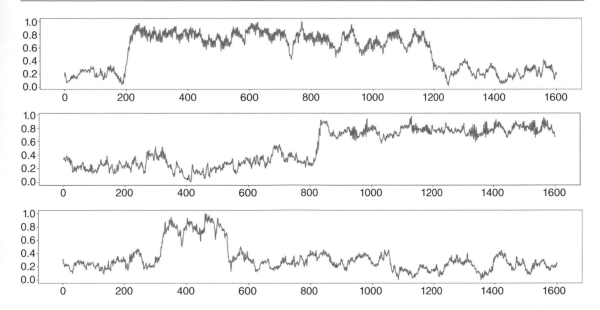

FIGURE 13.4 The three signals shown in top row of Figure 1 are enhanced by the learned LSTM-RNN local predictor using r_b, the sub-signals whose ground truths given in bottom row of Figure 1 in the middle, left, and right parts, respectively, are far more outstanding than the original ones after this process. The values are normalized for each 1600-D segment.

1. *Size property*: to convey meaningful information, the length of each sub-signal is of considerable size. Indeed, after running the simulation functions multiple times, on average more than 99.9% sub-signals are of length larger than 60, hence any cluster of foreground whose length is less than 60 can be dismissed as background.
2. *Sub-signal sparseness property*: the sub-signals did not present themselves as dense pulses or sinusoidal curves. If the gaps between two possible foregrounds are too small, then these two neighboring sub-signals should be merged as one because of the sparse nature of sub-signals. In addition, the sparseness property also demands that, within a signal segment, if there are many candidate sub-signal detection results, the one with the smallest number of sub-signals should be preferred. This rule of thumb can effectively combat the false positives caused by severe noises present in sub-signal signals.

The foregoing two statistical properties are justified by the available sub-signal simulation functions and researchers with knowledge of real sub-signal signals from applications. They serve as guidelines to the ensuing MM based sub-signal detection processing, a 1-D *watershed based segmentation based on run-length encoding*.

Given the different foreground sub-signal waveforms and noise levels, it is impossible to find a global threshold to classify the enhanced signals. Instead, careful considerations should be given to the nature of each segment individually. The two foregoing properties of authentic sub-signals point to a powerful MM segmentation methodology, the *watershed transform* [42]. Simply put, the idea is to tentatively *flood* the landscape from minimum values and find a set of *barriers* when different sources of flooding meet, the segmentation from this set of barriers that optimizes the objective is the resultant segmentation. To speed up the segmentation, which is crucial for practical use, a simplified procedure[1] is applied: the possible flood levels δ, the actual sought-after thresholds, are chosen from the range of minimum and maximum values of the segment with equal intervals (0.05), e.g., if the minimum and maximum are 0 and 1, respectively, possible levels to be tried out will be 0.05, 0.10, ..., 0.95, 19 in total. For each δ, the signal binarization is applied over the LSTM-RNN enhanced 1600-D signal s_{enh}:

$$tp(\delta) = senh \geq \delta \tag{13.9}$$

The possible classification result $\mathbf{t}_{p(\delta)}$ due to δ is a 1600-D binary vector. The ideal classification result $\mathbf{t}$ should be the one best satisfying the two above-mentioned sub-signal properties. To determine the optimality of a candidate $\mathbf{t}_{p(\delta)}$, the tentative foreground and background sequences declared by δ in $\mathbf{t}_{p(\delta)}$ should be checked: 1) the size of declared sub-signals, that is, the continuous foreground clusters, should have considerable size (due to the *size property*); 2) if two foreground clusters are too close, or put another way, a background sequence in-between two foreground clusters is too short, then the two foreground clusters should be merged as one (due to *sparseness property*). The run-length encoding (RLE), a powerful binary encoding algorithm widely used in signal processing and image compression, is employed to facilitate the foregoing optimality checking: after performing RLE procedure, the nature (0 or 1) **symbol** of each run and the corresponding number **count** of positions for each are available: if there are n runs in $\mathbf{t}_{p(\delta)}$, **symbol**[i], i = 0..n−1 stores the ith run is 0 or 1, while count[i] stores the length of the ith run. The following steps are conducted in order for optimality checking:

Procedure Optimality checking of $\mathbf{t}_{p(\delta)}$:
1. Apply binary MM *opening* and *closing* operators to cleanse isolated foreground and background chunks (to result in shorter RLE codes);
2. Perform RLE to obtain run length array **symbol** and **count**.
3. if **symbol**[i] = 0 and **count**[i] < min(**count**[i−1], **count**[i+1]), merge three runs No. $i−1$, i, and $i+1$ to a single 1 run;
4. if **symbol**[i] = 1 and **count**[i]<60, merge three runs No. $i−1$, i, and $i+1$ to a single 0 run.
5. Conduct another RLE and return the new **symbol** and **count** arrays as outputs.

The $\mathbf{t}_{p(\delta)}$ that yield the smallest number of foreground cluster(s), evaluated by use of the symbol and count arrays returned by the preceding procedure, is chosen to be the best classification results $\mathbf{t}$, this rule is applied due to the second part of the sparseness property. If there is more than one δ yielding the smallest number of foreground clusters, the one corresponding to the largest δ is opted for, which is based on the heuristic that results due to larger δ is less likely to be disturbed by severe noises. The sub-signals for the three signals detected by this MM-based post-processing procedure using $\mathbf{r_b}$ are presented in Figure 13.5,

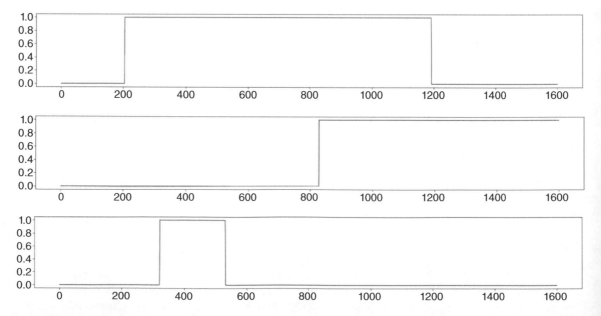

FIGURE 13.5 The final sub-signal detection results for the three noisy signals shown in Figure 1 reached by the MM-based post-processing procedure using r_b described in Section 13.2.3 based on the enhanced signals illustrated in Figure 13.4.

the *accuracy*, *precision*, *recall*, and *f1* scores of these three detection results are (0.99, 0.99, 1.0, 0.99), (0.99, 0.92, 1.0, 0.96), (1.0, 1.0, 1.0, 1.0).

13.3 EXPERIMENTAL RESULTS

To inspect the performances of the proposed algorithm developed in the preceding section and summarized in the flow chart of Figure 13.2, the simulation function available to us are employed to generate the training and test cases. It is worth noting that these simulation functions are entirely *stochastic*, i.e., the specific waveforms, start time and duration, and noise type and levels are all randomly drawn; the only parameter that can be deterministically controlled is the number of instances to be generated. In consequence, every different call of these functions will yield entirely different sub-signal data contaminated by different noises. We first call it to generate sub-signal signals as the training data. As described in Section 13.2.1, 200 to 300 data files will be sufficient for the purpose of producing a big and balanced data representation $\mathbf{r}(p)$'s for deep learning. We thus generate 250 sub-signal signals to serve as the training set. After going through the choice rules and transforms dictated by Equations (13.3–13.5), which is the red data flow in Figure 13.2, ~140,000 43 complex valued instances are available for the training phase delineated in Section 13.2.2, using either the complex magnitudes $\mathbf{r}_a$ or the absolute values $\mathbf{r}_b$ of the real and imaginary components, dictated by Equations (13.6) and (13.7), respectively. In this work, *python* 3.6.1 from *Anaconda* 4.4.0 platform, *TensorFlow* 1.1.0 with GPU support and *TFlearn* 0.3.2 API are used for coding development. The two trained LSTM-RNN data enhancement model for both complex value-encoding schemes are saved for the testing phase. The experiments reported in this section are conducted over a Dell Precision T7610 desktop computer with Intel Xeon CPU E5-2630 v2 with 2.60GHz and 32.0 GB on Windows 10 OS. The training of the LSTM-RNN with 150 epochs for the two proposed algorithm costs 95 min. and 219 min. for $\mathbf{r}_a$ and $\mathbf{r}_b$ methods, respectively. The average detection time for one 1600-D test data item is around 0.06 sec. and 0.15 sec., respectively. If code optimization techniques such as *Numba* and *Cython* and more powerful computers are used, the detection performance can be further reduced by order of magnitudes.

The test data are produced by calling the randomized simulation function with size 1024 (2^{10}), each test folder having 1024 sub-signal 1600-D signals. Notice that due to the randomized nature of these data generation functions, a different call with the simulation function, which was harnessed to produce the ~140,000 training instances, will yield different test data different from the previous run for training data generation as the waveforms and noise levels are controlled by random numbers drawn *on the fly*, the test and training data therefore are different. As described in Section 13.2.3 and illustrated as the blue data flow in Figure 13.2, all test data are first pre-processed to generate the corresponding $\mathbf{r}_a$ or $\mathbf{r}_b$ representations, which are then enhanced by the learned LSTM-RNN sub-signal predictor, the final sub-signal detection results are declared by calling the MM-based post-processing procedure described in Section 13.2.3, esp. the procedure of *optimality checking for* $\mathbf{t}_{p(\delta)}$, from candidate results generated by Equation (13.8).

In Figure 13.6, sub-signal detection results for eight typical signals generated by the simulation function produced by the proposed algorithm are illustrated. Each panel consists of four images corresponding to the original simulation signals, data enhanced by the trained LSTM-RNN models, the final sub-signal detection results, and the known ground truths for sub-signals, respectively, are illustrated. To provide a comparison between these two different complex number conversions, detection results for the same eight signals are shown in the upper and lower part for both methods on Figure 13.6, with the same layout. The four numbers are the measures widely used to evaluate the classifier qualities: *accuracy, precision, recall* and *f1* scores, based on *True Positive* (TP): predicted sub-signals are actual sub-signals per ground truths, False Positive (FP): predicted sub-signals are not actual sub-signals, *False Negative*: the actual sub-signals are not predicted, and True Negative (TN): the actual non-sub-signals are predicted correctly, the formulas for all four measures are tabulated in Table 13.1. As briefly discussed in the preprocessing step at Section 13.2.1, this sub-signal detection problem is *uneven* in the following two aspects:

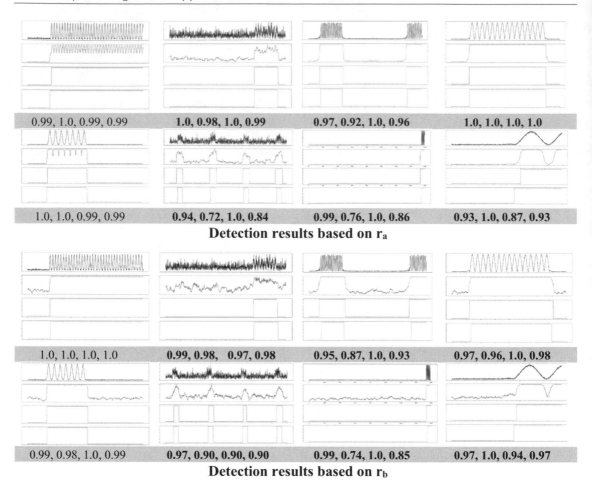

Detection results based on r_a

Detection results based on r_b

FIGURE 13.6   Detection results by the proposed sub-signal algorithm using r_a and r_b. Each panel consists of four graphs: row 1: original signals; row 2: signals enhanced by LSTM-RNN model; row 3: sub-signal detection after post-processing; row 4: sub-signal ground truths. The four numbers under each panel are accuracy, precision, recall and f1 score, respectively, for the 1600 positions. The panels for r_a and r_b detection results are put in the same layout for ease of comparisons.

1. *Unbalanced occurrences*: the positives, namely, the presence of sub-signals, are not as many as the negatives, only about 30~40% are sub-signals in each 1600-D signal by running the simulation function, which is the reason we developed the *Choice rules* to insure the balance of training data.
2. *Different importance in positives and negatives*: in practical applications, the presence of sub-signals is far more important than their absence because urgent reactions are needed should sub-signals make their appearance. Furthermore, missing an actual sub-signal is a far more serious mistake than missing a negative.

In view of the foregoing two unevenness of this detection problem, let us check the properties of the four quality measures tabulated in Table 13.1 to see if they serve our needs.

1. *Accuracy* is defined by treating both positives and negatives equally, the unbalanced nature of sub-signals alone will seriously bias its usefulness: if in a signal the size of the sub-signal is short, e.g., the one in Row 2 Column 3 of Figure 13.6, a detection algorithm totally missing the

TABLE 13.1 Definitions of quality measures

$$accuracy = \frac{TP + TN}{TP + TN + FP + FN} \qquad precision = \frac{TP}{TP + FP}$$

$$recall = \frac{TP}{TP + FN} \qquad f1 = \frac{2 * precision * recall}{precision + recall}$$

short sub-signal will still result in a 97% accuracy, which is inappropriate to fairly measure the quality of our sub-signal detection.

2. *Precision* measures the ratio of true positives from the positives predicted by the classifier, it unfairly favors those "*thrifty*" classifiers that declare presence of positives only when very strong evidence presents: the precision is always 1.0 if the declared sub-signals are always a subset of the actual ones. Due to the higher price of missing actual positives in sub-signal detection tasks, precision's usefulness is rather limited.

3. *Recall* indicates how many actual sub-signals are really predicted, since it focuses on positions with true sub-signals, the relative sparseness of sub-signals is resolved. Furthermore, it directly measures how many actual sub-signals are missed, which is of crucial importance in practical applications. Therefore, recall is a valuable quality indicator of our problem and should be employed. It must be remarked that recall is imperfect either: an over "*generous*" classifier that predicts many more positives will have a high recall value, which is problematic.

4. *F1 score* is the harmonic mean of precision and recall, because of the limited usefulness of precision compared with recall and recall's own shortcoming, this measure should be used. It is however not a perfect fit for our task in hand. Given that in practical applications the danger of a false negative is much higher than that of false positive in sub-signal detection problem, probably a better indicator could be a weighted sum of recall and precision with heavier weight goes to recall. Despite its over-emphasis on precision, we still use it as one measure of classifiers, just keep in mind its potential weakness.

To learn the performance of these two different schemes, a Monte Carlo study is conducted: we run the randomized simulation function 20 iterations independently, and each iteration generates 2^{10} test instances. The proposed detection algorithm, that is, the blue flow depicted in Figure 13.2, is then performed to obtain the detection results, for **ra-** and **rb-** based methods. The accuracy, precision, recall and f1 scores for three representative tests of this Monte Carlo study is shown in Figure 13.7. To illustrate the difference made by the introduction of LSTM-RNN data enhancement step, detection results based on r_a and r_b skipping the LSTM-RNN step in Figure 13.2 are also collected where only the conventional signal processing techniques are employed. In our **rb-**based method, the real and imaginary parts of a complex number went through an absolute operator to be converted to positive real numbers. To inspect what may happen when this absolute operator, Equation (13.7), is skipped, i.e., using the real and imaginary parts as two real numbers in the 86-D representation, the detection results by this method are also collected and compared. As seen from Figure 13.7, the overall performances, per all four quality measures, achieved by these two complex number conversion approaches are of similar performances. The other three comparison methods failed to deliver consistent performances. Interestingly, the r_a without RNN algorithm delivered comparable performances based on *accuracy* and *precision* measures, it is even the best overall (0.95) in precision. However, all these three methods have trouble based on *recall*: for the randomly generated data set No. 3, all three comparison methods failed gravely with *recall* values less than 0.4. Even for this "worst" test data set, r_a without RNN has the best *precision*, 0.98, while getting a mere 0.28 *recall*. Hence without LSTM-RNN data enhancement step, the sub-signals announced by the conventional signal processing method are almost all true signals, however, without data enhancement most actual sub-signals, 78%, are

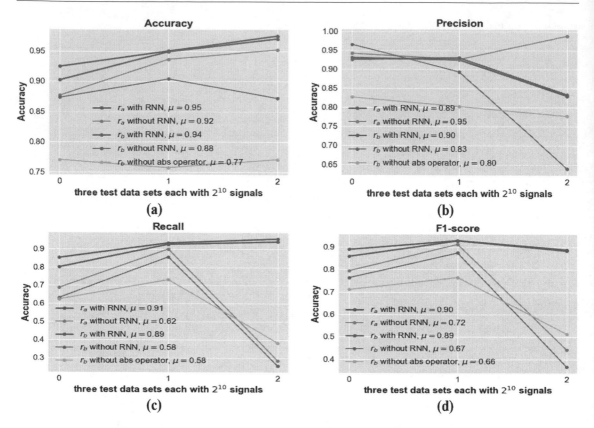

FIGURE 13.7   Performance measures attained by r_a and r_b for three representative simulation data sets for the two proposed algorithms and three comparison methods.

missed, thus a total failure. But per *accuracy* (0.86) and *precision* (0.98), this dire situation is not reflected at all. This confirmed our foregoing discussion about these two quality measures, only the *recall* and *f1* scores can properly represent the performances of the sub-signal detection algorithms, and *recall* should be given most attention.

In Figure 13.8, the *recall* and *f1* boxplots of all five methods for the Monte Carlo study are presented. The two proposed algorithms are better than the other three contrasting approaches by a large margin. The performances achieved by these two algorithms are promising given the practical nature of the simulation functions. In addition, while the other three methods have two or three total failures, the two proposed algorithms perform quite robustly in all cases, $\mathbf{r_a}$ based method is slightly better than the $\mathbf{r_b}$ based one, but statistically insignificant. The data enhancement achieved by LSTM-RNN is thus crucial to robustly detect sub-signals. However, the use of original real and imaginary component of complex numbers delivers consistently the worst performance—worse than the two relatively simple methods without going through the LSTM-RNN enhancement procedure, thus the careful choice of data representation is crucial for sub-signal detection tasks. The phase information carried by using the original values of the real and imaginary parts thus hampers the classification, more investigations are still needed on this issue soon.

In view of the extremely similar performance attained by *ra-* and *rb-*based methods as shown in Figures 13.7 and 13.8, if their detection results are mostly the same, then they are likely to get hold of the same information from the sub-signals and thus there is no need to have both approaches. However, as already hinted at from Figure 13.6, this is not the case: the detected sub-signals by these two methods are not photocopies of the other. Indeed, due to their different ways of encoding the underlying complex variables, one mapping all complex number of the same magnitudes to the same real number, the other mapping four points in the four quadrants to one pair of real positive number, the information they captured

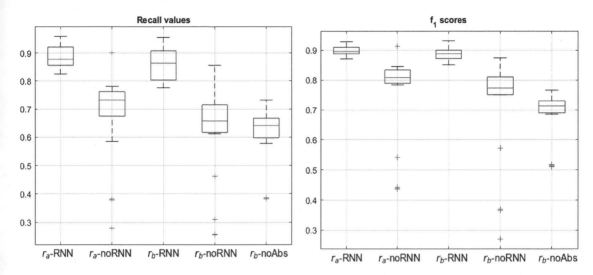

FIGURE 13.8   The box plots of the Recall (Left) and f1 scores for the Monte Carlo studies. The two LSTM-RNN (Columns 1 & 3) based approaches r_a and r_b are significantly better than the other three comparison methods: without RNN enhancement procedure (ra-noRNN and rb-noRNN) and r_b without taking the absolute operator.

should be different. As shown Figure 13.9, four new pairs of signals are provided to showcase the differing performances of r_a and r_b based methodologies. In cases where the noises are exceedingly severe, these two methods responded differently. Hence these two methods could complement each other by taking account of different aspects of the noisy sub-signal signals. A simple combination of the detection results by these two methods, e.g., a simple OR as seemingly suggested by Figure 13.9, is not working. Cases shown in Figure 13.9 suggest this simplistic scheme works. For many more cases, false positives and false negatives by both methods add up and result in worse accuracy. The average accuracy for all simulation sets used in Monte Carlo studies reported in Figures 13.7 and 13.8. This over-simplistic OR combination results in slightly but consistently worse performances than the minimal of the two original approaches. More methods are still needed if the ensemble methodology [21] can be seriously evaluated.

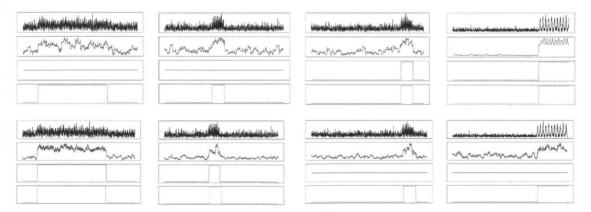

FIGURE 13.9   Different performances of r_a (Row 1) and r_b (Row 2) based detection results: while r_a method failed to detect the two sub-signals due to severe noises (Columns 1 & 2 in Row 1), r_b based method has no trouble picking up the sub-signals. Conversely, while r_b missed the two sub-signals in the last two columns (Columns 3 & 4 in Row 2), r_a based method detected them perfectly.

13.4 CONCLUSION

To detect complex sub-signals severely contaminated by noises for the security of intelligent vehicles, we developed a new deep learning approach combined with a signal post-processing algorithm. In this work, the uneven and unbalanced signals are first pre-processed and regularized as a local vector for proper training and testing by deep learning. The complex numbers are converted to real ones using two different schemes: one using the magnitude of the complex number, the other using the absolute value of a complex number's real and imaginary component. The LSTM-RNN was exploited to enhance the sub-signals that otherwise are buried by background noises. The enhanced data are next classified by use of a global signal analysis procedure based mostly on mathematical morphology. These two algorithms were tested rigorously using the simulation functions made available to us, the performances achieved are encouraging. The great power of the deep learning and conventional signal processing are effectively harness to achieve valuable detection results.

This is our first effort to detect sub-signals from noisy and complex signals by combining the prowess of conventional signal processing techniques with deep learning approaches and this is an on-going endeavor. Next, three different directions will be explored to gain deeper insights into this task and attain better results:

1. Change simulation functions to expose more parameters for us to control, so that in our Monte Carlo studies, we can fine-tune these parameters to have better knowledge about when and why our algorithms succeed or fail. This way more fine-tuning can be conducted to improve and generalize our algorithms.
2. Use different deep learning methods for data enhancement. In this work, we only used LSTM-RNN for data enhancement, CNN-based method, given its great power of exploiting local dependencies with multiple resolutions, will be examined to detect sub-signals. The sub-signal detection may benefit from the higher-dimensions involved in the CNN framework.
3. Explore direct complex number representation-based methods. In this work we relied on *TensorFlow*'s backend for LSTM-RNN training, which has no support for complex numbers so far. We thus formulate two different ways to load the complex information by real numbers: one using complex magnitude; the other using absolute values of the real and imaginary components. We have proved empirically that the literal use of the real and imaginary components of complex numbers cannot yield desirable results. In parallel to our ongoing research and development, Bengio's group made impressive progress in deep learning using complex numbers directly [29] based on their *Theano* backend, whereof they reported ~3% performance gains due to the direct use of complex numbers. Next, we will study how to plug this deep complex net in our data enhancement framework with improved performance.

ACKNOWLEDGMENT

This document was approved by Air Force Research Laboratory for public release via 88ABW- 2019-3993.

NOTES

1   This is more like the exhaustive threshold searching procedure in optimal threshold discovery, the difference is, instead of minimizing the weighted sum of variances in Ostu's method, we used *size property* and *foreground sparseness* as the objective function.

REFERENCES

[1] Y. LeCun, Y. Bengio, and G. Hinton, "Deep learning," *Nature*, vol. *521*, p. 9, 2015.

[2] G. E. Hinton and R. R. Salakhutdinov, "Reducing the dimensionality of data with neural networks," *Science*, vol. *313*, pp. 504–507, 2006.

[3] Y. Bengio, *Learning Deep Architectures for AI (Foundations and Trends in Machine Learning, Book 2)*. Now Publisher Inc., 2009. http://dx.doi.org/10.1561/2200000006

[4] S. Hochreiter and J. Schmidhuber, "Long short-term memory," *Neural Computation*, vol. *9*, pp. 1735–1780, 1997.

[5] C. Bishop, *Pattern Recognition and Machine Learning*. Springer, 2007. https://link.springer.com/book/9780387310732

[6] D. Silver, A. Huang, C. J. Maddison, A. Guez, L. Sifre, G. van den Driessche, et al., "Mastering the game of Go with deep neural networks and tree search," *Nature*, vol. *529*, pp. 484–489, 2016.

[7] A. Esteva, B. Kuprel, R. A. Novoa, J. Ko, S. M. Swetter, H. M. Blau, et al., "Dermatologist-level classification of skin cancer with deep neural networks," *Nature*, vol. *542*, pp. 115–118, 2017.

[8] K. Murphy, *Machine Learning: A Probabilistic Perspective*. The MIT Press, 2012. https://mitpress.mit.edu/9780262018029/machine-learning/

[9] J. Wei and G. Li, "Automated lung segmentation and image quality assessment for clinical 3D/4D computed tomography," *IEEE Journal of Translational Engineering in Health and Medicine*, vol. *2*, pp. 1–10, 2014.

[10] A. Oppenhaim and R. Schafer, *Discrete-Time Signal Processing*. Prentice Hall, 2009. https://www.bookdepository.com/Discrete-Time-Signal-Processing-Alan-Oppenheim/9780131988422?ref=grid-view&qid=1672983198725&sr=1-7

[11] I. Goodfellow, Y. Bengio, and A. Courville, *Deep Learning*. Cambridge, MA: MIT Press, 2017.

[12] J. Wei, "Video content classification based on 3-D eigen analysis," *IEEE Transactions on Image Processing*, vol. *14*, pp. 662–673, 2005.

[13] J. Wei, B. Cai, L. Zhang, and B. M. Fu, "Automatic classification and quantification of cell adhesion locations on the endothelium," vol. *43*, p. 12, 2015.

[14] J. Wei, K. Vongsy, O. Mendoza-Schrock, and C. Liu, "Vehicle engine classification using spectral tone-pitch vibration indexing and neural network," *International Journal on Surveillance & Monitoring Reserach Technologies, Special issue on Machine learning and sensor fusion techniques*, vol. *2*, p. 29, 2014.

[15] J. P. Brockwell, *Introduction to Time Series and Forecasting*. New York, NY: Springer Science+Business Media, 2016.

[16] R. E. Bellman, *Dynamic Programming*. Princeton University Press, 2003. https://press.princeton.edu/books/paperback/9780691146683/dynamic-programming

[17] J. Wei, "Markov edit distance," *IEEE Transactions on Pattern Analysis and Machine Intelligence*, vol. *26*, pp. 311–321, 2004.

[18] J. Wei, "Numerical sequence matching based on local sum functions," *Pattern Recognition Letters*, vol. *31*, pp. 600–608, 2010.

[19] J. Wei, "On Markov Earth mover's distance," *International Journal on Image and Graphics*, vol. *14*, p. 1450016, 2014.

[20] A. Yuan, J. Wei, C. P. Gaebler, H. Huang, D. Olek, and G. Li, "A novel respiratory motion perturbation model adaptable to patient breathing irregularities," *International Journal of Radiation Oncology, Biology, Physics*, vol. *96*, pp. 1087–1096, 2016.

[21] K. P. Manning, *Machine Learning: A Probabilistic Perspective*. MIT Press, 2012. https://mitpress.mit.edu/9780262018029/machine-learning/

[22] J. Wei, "Lebesgue anisotropic image denoising," *International Journal of Imaging Systems and Technology*, vol. *15*, pp. 64–73, 2005.

[23] M. Chao, J. Wei, T. Li, Y. Yuan, K. E. Rosenzweig, and Y. C. Lo, "Robust breathing signal extraction from cone beam CT projections based on adaptive and global optimization techniques," *Physics in Medicine & Biology*, vol. *61*, pp. 3109–3126, 2016.

[24] G. Li, J. Caraveo, J. Wei, A. Rimner, A. Wu, K. Goodman, et al., "Rapid estimation of 4DCT motion-artifact severity based on 1D breathing-surrogate periodicity," *Medical Physics*, vol. *41*, p. 111717, 2014.

[25] G. Li, J. Wei, M. Kadbi, J. Moody, A. Sun, S. Zhang, et al., "Novel super-resolution approach to time-resolved volumetric 4-dimensional magnetic resonance imaging with high spatiotemporal resolution for multi-breathing cycle motion assessment," *International Journal of Radiation Oncology, Biology, Physics*, vol. *98*, pp. 454–462, 2017.

[26] G. Li, J. Wei, D. Olek, M. Kadbi, N. Tyagi, K. Zakian, et al., "Direct comparison of respiration-correlated four-dimensional magnetic resonance imaging reconstructed using concurrent internal navigator and external bellows," *International Journal of Radiation Oncology, Biology, Physics*, vol. *97*, pp. 596–605, 2017.

[27] R. Socher, C. Y. Lin, A. Y. Ng, and C. D. Manning, "Parsing natural scenes and natural language with recurrent neural networks," *Presented at the 28th ICML*, 2011.

[28] H. Jaeger and H. Haas, "Harnessing nonlinearity: predicting chaotic systems and saving energy in wireless communication," *Science*, vol. *304*, pp. 78–80, 2004.

[29] C. Trabelsi, O. Bilaniuk, D. Serdyuk, S. Subramanian, J. F. Santos, S. Mehri, et al., "Deep complex networks," *submitted to NIPS*, 2017.

[30] G. E. P. Box and G. C. Tiao, *Bayesian Inference in Statistical Analysis*. Reading, MA: Addison-Wesley Pub. Co., 1973.

[31] Y. LeCun, L. Bottou, Y. Bengio, and P. Haffner, "Gradient-based learning applied to document recognition," *Proceedings of the IEEE*, p. *46*, 1998.

[32] A. Tarantola, *Inverse Problem Theory and Methods for Model Parameter Estimation*. Philadelphia, PA: Society for Industrial and Applied Mathematics, 2005.

[33] R. C. Gonzalez, R. E. Woods, and S. L. Eddins, *Digital Image Processing Using MATLAB*. 2nd edition: Gatesmark Publishing, 2009. https://www.mathworks.com/academia/books/digital-image-processing-using-matlab-gonzalez-in.html

[34] R. Szeliski, *Computer Vision: Algorithms and Applications*. Springer, 2011. https://link.springer.com/book/10.1007/978-1-84882-935-0

[35] E. Oyallon and S. Mallat, "Deep roto-translation scattering for object classification," *Presented at the IEEE CVPR'15*, 2015.

[36] H. Erdogan, J. R. Hershey, S. Watanabe, and J. Le Roux, "Phase-sensitive and recognition-boosted speech separation using deep recurrent neural networks," *Presented at the 2015 IEEE International Conference on Acoustics, Speech and Signal Processing (ICASSP)*, 2015.

[37] F. Weninger, J. R. Hershey, J. Le Roux, and B. Schuller, "Discriminatively trained recurrent neural networks for single-channel speech separation," *Presented at the 2014 IEEE Global Conference on Signal and Information Processing (GlobalSIP)*, 2014.

[38] J. P. Serra and P. Soille, *Mathematical Morphology and its Applications to Image Processing*. Dordrecht; Boston: Kluwer Academic Publishers, 1994.

[39] J. Wei, "Color object indexing and recognition in digital libraries," *IEEE Trans. on Image Processing*, vol. *11*, pp. 912–922, 2002.

[40] J. Wei, "Shape indexing and recognition based on regional analysis," *IEEE Transactions on Multimedia*, vol. *9*, pp. 1049–1061, 2007.

[41] J. Wei, "Small moving object detection from video sequences," *International Journal of Image and Graphics*, vol. *14*, 2013.

[42] R. C. Gonzalez and R. E. Woods, *Digital Image Processing*. New York, NY: Pearson, 2018.

PART V

Miscellaneous

The basics of deep learning algorithms and their effect on driving behavior and vehicle communications

14

Abdennour Najmeddine, Ouni Tarek and
Ben Amor Nader
University of Sfax, Sfax, Tunisia

Contents

DOI: 10.1201/9781003190691-19

14.1 INTRODUCTION

Deep learning (DL) is considered now one of the most important fields in computer science for its capability to deliver the best results from enormous quantities of data and really complex information. When it comes to intelligent vehicle networks, deep learning can play an important factor in improving the communication between vehicles and improving road safety conditions. The analysis of vehicle communication is the analysis of all available data and features from the vehicles in order to decide on the best outcome and traffic route for a road-based scenario. This operation can seem complicated and challenging, especially when dealing with the unpredictability and the inescapable human error factor in the decision-making process that still interferes with the roads and traffic structures of our days. However, the evolution of deep learning algorithms is undeniably an exciting prospect to deal with these challenges, from the basic principles of artificial neural networks, convolutional neural networks and recurrent neural networks to the newest state-of-the-art solutions of variational auto-encoders, generative adversarial networks and transformers. These principles, alongside the variant nuance architectures, combined with the powerful computing powers available in our time are on the edge of delivering the futuristic vision of totally autonomous vehicles and road networks that we thought is still too far to achieve. In this chapter, we are going to discuss the basics of deep learning algorithms, the pros and cons of every method and the pre-processing steps and refinement of the hyperparameters. Then, we are going to describe and elaborate more, with some examples, the effect of these principles on driving behavior and vehicle communication.

14.2 BASICS OF DEEP LEARNING ALGORITHMS AND SUPERVISED LEARNING

In order to apprehend the concept of deep learning, we first have to begin with machine learning, which is the origin and the basis that deep learning emerged from. A simple and basic definition of machine learning is to define it as the practice of making predictions, decision-making, and pattern recognition based on data analysis and computer learning algorithms instead of the traditional condition statements used by normal computing algorithms. Deep learning is a subdivision of machine learning which makes this definition applicable to it as well, although it is still considered as a more advanced and complicated concept than the latter. While machine learning includes a variety of statistical analysis algorithms, deep learning targets, in particular the Artificial Neural Networks (ANN) algorithms, and develop it even further by integrating other complex concepts such as stacking more layers and exploring different model architectures and diving into details in hyperparameters tuning. This affirmation leads us to one of the simplest definitions of deep learning, which is to consider it as an Artificial Neural Networks that has more than three layers of neural networks. The most primitive and abstract algorithms that ANN inspired from and managed to refine and develop them are linear regression and logistic regression. The simplicity of these regression algorithms, and their importance, makes them the perfect algorithms to start exploring the artificial intelligence field and master these machine/deep learning algorithms.

14.2.1 Linear regression and logistic regression

Linear regression is one of the most famous and basic machine learning algorithms, it is commonly used in continuous values predictions and regression based on the conjecture that the relationship between the concerned variables is linear, as the name suggests. The simplicity of this algorithm lays in the basic polynomial function used for its implementation as the output vector or also known as the predicted values vector Y_{lin} delivered by Equation 14.1:

$$Y_{lin} = a\,X^T + b \tag{14.1}$$

Where a as the parameter vector or the coefficient vector, b is the basis correction vector and X^T is the input variables vector transposed.

On the flip side, the logistic regression algorithm is a very prominent binary classification method to segregate between different categories of data. When it comes to mathematical theories, the only differentiating factor between logistic and linear regression is the sigmoid function applied to the previous linear regression polynomial equation. This function helps transform the output values into probabilities between zero and one on a logistic curve, as shown in Figure 14.1 and demonstrated by Equation 14.2:

$$Y_{log} = S\left(Y_{lin}\right) = S\left(a\,X^T + b\right) \tag{14.2}$$

Where $S(x) = 1/\,1+ e^{-x}$ is the sigmoid function and Y_{lin} is the same equation of the linear regression algorithm.

14.2.2 Artificial Neural Networks

Artificial Neural Networks are computational units connected to each other through other layers of units. These computational or processing units transform the information in their inputs and redistribute it again

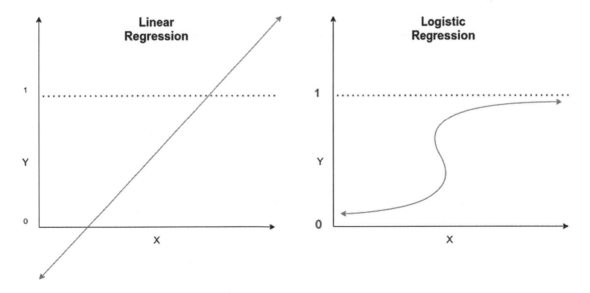

FIGURE 14.1 The difference between linear and logistic regression with regards to the output Y given the same input X.

to other processing units. The processing units are called neurons which can explain the name Artificial Neural Networks, which was initially inspired by the human brain neural networks in the first place. If we dive even more into the details of how ANN works, we can find a clear similarity with logistic regression when it comes to the individual neurons as every neuron can serve as a logistic regression algorithm when the activation function is sigmoid. We can also consider every distinct neuron in an ANN as a linear regression algorithm with an additional activation function that can range from Sigmoid, ReLu, Tanh, Softmax or any other customized activation function. We can elaborate more and demonstrate that with a simple representation of an ANN in Figure 14.2.

As we can observe, we have the X vector with 3 values as the input, Y with 2 values as the output and S as the hidden layer vector with 4 values. The F1 and F2 are, respectively, the activation functions for S and Y, W1 and b1 are the weights and the biases for the hidden layer represented by S, the same applies for W2 and b2 with regard to the output vector Y.

The accuracy of output Y is dependent on all the elements and parameters in this network from weights, biases and activation function to the learning rate, batch size, and number of layers or neurons. The purpose and the inspiration of the learning process of these algorithms comes from the fact that the weights get updated through backpropagation in order to reduce the error rate of the output prediction [1]. What this basically means is that these feed forward networks can generally be trained using the difference between the real value of the output and the predicted ones by calculating the derivation of this cost function with respect to the weights in a chain rule. The backpropagation gradient or derivative calculations can also benefit from various different training methods; however, the gradient descent with its variations is the most common and most efficient one. These postulations apply in the same way to a simple

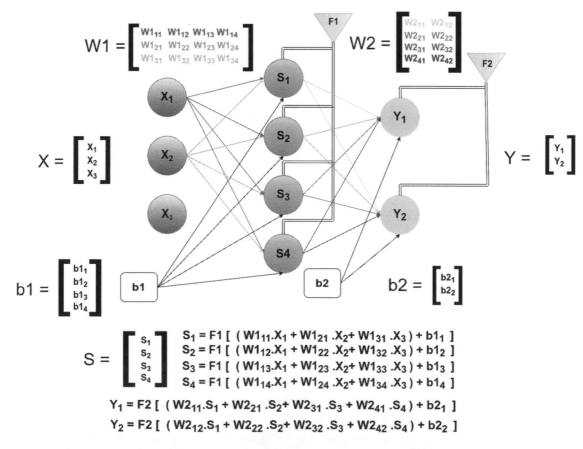

FIGURE 14.2 A detailed presentation of a simple ANN (example of multilayer perceptrons).

Multilayer Perceptron, which can be perceived as a machine learning algorithm, and to a deep learning artificial neural network with stacks of layers and a complicated design. One of the downsides of these deep learning networks is the high computational demand and processing power for the gradients calculation of these networks whenever they contain a big number of layers or neurons which means a longer training time, especially for large quantities of data. However, the use of deep learning is almost necessary for big databases and for complicated problems to achieve better results and the greater optimization that we can only reach through the existence of substantial numbers of parameters and layers.

14.2.3 Convolutional Neural Networks

Convolutional Neural Networks (CNN) are another evolution and another progress achieved in the artificial intelligence field after the use of ANNs with deep architectures and stacked layers. Even though ANNs are really powerful algorithms, they are unable to produce efficient performance and illustrate sustainable capabilities for computer vision and image processing, which opened the way for CNNs to shine. CNNs have the same basic principles as ANNs, yet the unique trait of a convolutional layer is the use of filters (also called kernels) that can select and extract a unique feature from the data or the image and pass it to the next layer. This trait can offer a huge advantage and evolve the potential of the neural network by identifying patterns of increased complexity using a scaled-down and small extraction of data details. This function can help additionally reduce the complexity of the algorithm in order to apprehend all the data. Furthermore it can accelerate the process by reducing the huge quantities of data coming from images or other types of sources to the specific patterns and features that can lead our network to make the right decisions or predict the correct outcome. The convolutional layer of CNN performs convolution between this filter and the input data, this kernel slides through the input data matrix conducting dot product operations to produce what is called feature map which is the output generated by this proceeding. In Figure 14.3, we

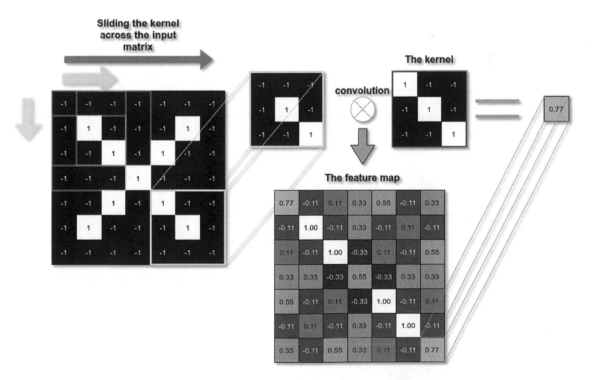

FIGURE 14.3 A Flowchart explanation of the function of a convolution layer using one kernel on an X black and white image.

demonstrate an extraction of the main diagonal feature from a black and while x sign using convolution with a single filter.

Typically, convolutional layers are followed by pooling layers to reduce the dimensionality of the data. In Figure 14.4, we illustrate the pooling operation after the feature map extraction of the convolutional layer. However, most CNN-based architectures usually include a layer or two or sometimes even more of ANNs at the output of the model. These layers can serve the purpose of translating the feature extraction process of CNNs to achieve the required results from the model.

14.2.4 Recurrent Neural Networks

Recurrent Neural Networks (RNN) are a different type of ANN; they are the results of an innovative idea that has a completely different concept behind it compared to CNN. RNNs are neural networks that are capable of grasping the relationship between the different inputs in a significant manner; they use the previous outputs as inputs while having hidden states. RNNs are characterized by this memory feature, which allows them to remember the past and make decisions based on what they learned, which gives them a huge advantage compared to ANNs and CNNs when it comes to time series dependent data or sequential data. Typically, RNNs are used for speech recognition, natural language processing and language translation. The input vector of an RNN can be in whatever size and the same input vector can produce different output in a network due to the dependence of the results on the previous inputs and previous state. Figure 14.5, demonstrates the difference between simple ANNs and RNNs, while also presenting an example on unrolled (unfolded) RNN as a function of time. In the unrolled flowchart, we notice that all the network with the weights and biases remain the same in every step affiliated to time, except the inputs in each time step that get concatenated in the hidden units (hidden layer) with the state of the previous step before passing through the network. This property requires taking the backpropagation as well through time with the gradient calculations conducted at every point in time. Although RNNs are a great and powerful tool for time series dependent data, they have been overtaken recently in language processes by transformers and attention mechanism algorithms, which are more complex and mature methods. One of the most important disadvantages of using RNNs is their computational cost, slowness, and instability in backpropagation

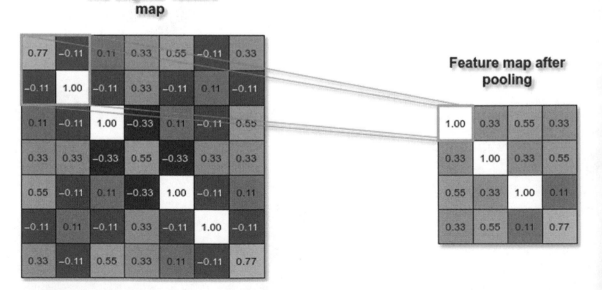

FIGURE 14.4   Max pooling of a feature map with a window size of 2 and a stride of 2.

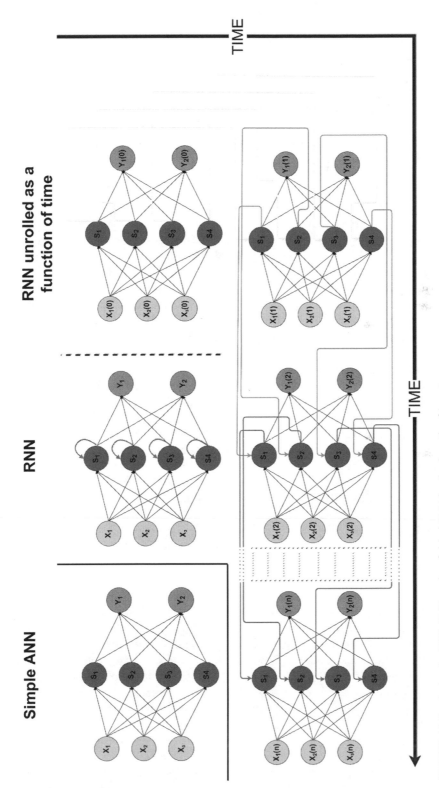

FIGURE 14.5   A simple ANN, RNN and unfolded RNN by the length of input sequence n.

calculations leading to some cases of vanishing gradient and problems with the exploding gradient, especially for long-term dependencies. However, RNN remains as one the most powerful deep learning algorithms, especially with the numerous variants generated from it such as Gated Recurrent Unit (GRU) and Long Short-Term Memory units (LSTM). These variants were initially created to solve the vanishing gradient problems of the traditional RNNs and reduce their training parameters.

14.2.5 Deep learning architectures

One of the first convolutional networks and the initial building block for the foundation of deep learning is the LeNet network molded by LeCun between 1988 and 1998 [1]. LeNet, and especially LeNet5, which can be recognized as the origin of most of the deep learning architectures of today, was ahead of time work that managed to exploit convolutions, backpropagation, learnable weights, and biases even before having the GPUs and the computational power. This network managed to extract features from images and recognize handwritten digits. After the accomplishment of LeNet in this area as early as 1998, the field achieved only slow progress, which lasted until 2010. This hibernation period was happening alongside the development and progress in computational power, GPUs and the availability and growth of collected data. In the years after this dwindling phase, the scope of deep learning gained an exponential boost, which began with Dan Ciresan Net [2] and the famous AlexNet (which managed to win the ImageNet competition challenge of 2012 outshining all the other contestants) [3]. Alex Krizhevesky et al. [3] created a network that offered a deeper and more extensive outlook on CNNs than LeNet by presenting new concepts such as the use of ReLU as and activation function, dropout regularization, and overlapping max pooling. This network became the crown jewel and the keystone of the research in this field, while also being the reason for the deep learning revolution that we have lived through in the past decade and also the upcoming one. AlexNet outperformed all traditional machine learning and statistical methods, alerting researchers to how powerful these networks can be and offering a perception of the possibilities, development and progress that can be achieved in this field. The following year, the work of Matthew Zeiler and Rob Fergue, who produced ZFNet [4], followed by Pierre Sermanet from Yan LeCun's NYU laboratory with Overfeat [5], were both derived from AlexNet and direct descendants of the earlier system. These networks included a reduction in the computational complexity and the parameters needed with some optimization and improvements in networks design and overall accuracy. In the same year (2013), the work of Min Lin, which introduced the concept of Network in Network (NiN), also offered a different perspective and featured new concepts [6]. NiN used a multilayer perceptron convolution (1×1 filter) which reinforced the nonlinearity of the network and also introduced the notion of replacing fully connected layers with the Global Average Pooling (GAP). GAP reduced the number of parameters and produced a feature vector with low dimension from big feature maps without reducing their dimensions. In Figure 14.6, we show the difference and the evolution of network architectures from 1988 to 2013.

The year 2014 witnessed the rise of two important networks, the visual geometry group or VGGNET built by Simonyan and Zisserman [7] and the winner of the 2014-ILSVRC competition GoogleNET, also called Inception-V1 [8]. VGG was one of the first models that largely expanded the depth of the network. This network had the precedent of stacking more layers using smaller-sized filters of 3×3 in sequences instead of the commonly used size of 5×5, 7×7 and 11×11. This method improved the learning capacity of the network by mimicking the effect of big filters while replacing them with smaller consecutive filters, allowing the extraction of more complex features and the reduction of the computational complexity. GoogleNet is considered the first of the inception architectures and the first to present the idea of inception blocks in neural networks. The novel concept of inception blocks offered new information extraction transformations such as splitting and merging the features to different convolutional channels with different filter sizes in order to achieve diverse spatial resolution in the features. This means that the normal convolutional layer of the network is replaced with blocks of sparse convolutional connections

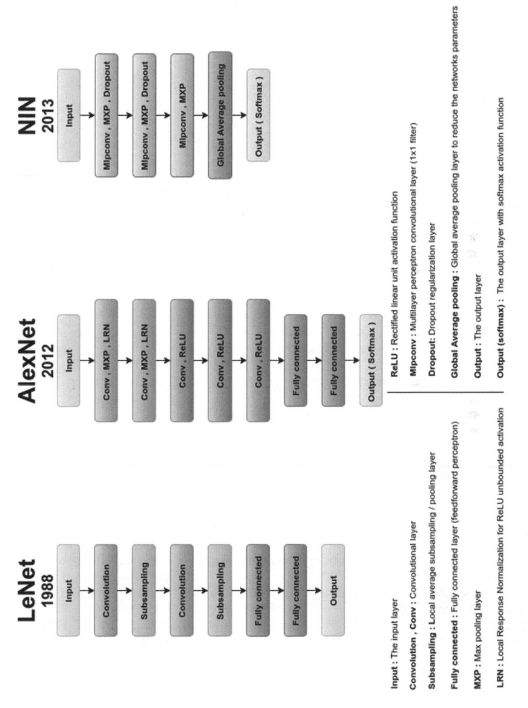

LeNet
1988

Input

Convolution

Subsampling

Convolution

Subsampling

Fully connected

Fully connected

Output

AlexNet
2012

Input

Conv , MXP , LRN

Conv , MXP , LRN

Conv , ReLU

Conv , ReLU

Conv , ReLU

Fully connected

Fully connected

Output (Softmax)

NIN
2013

Input

Mlpconv , MXP , Dropout

Mlpconv , MXP , Dropout

Mlpconv , MXP

Global Average pooling

Output (Softmax)

Input : The input layer

Convolution , Conv : Convolutional layer

Subsampling : Local average subsampling / pooling layer

Fully connected : Fully connected layer (feedforward perceptron)

MXP : Max pooling layer

LRN : Local Response Normalization for ReLU unbounded activation

ReLU : Rectified linear unit activation function

Mlpconv : Multilayer perceptron convolutional layer (1x1 filter)

Dropout: Dropout regularization layer

Global Average pooling : Global average pooling layer to reduce the networks parameters

Output : The output layer

Output (softmax) : The output layer with softmax activation function

FIGURE 14.6   Comparison of the first important CNN architectures (between 1988 and 2013).

operating in parallel to avoid the extraction of redundant information in the normal consecutive convolutions. GoogleNet also used the bottleneck convolution sections (1×1 filter) inspired from NiN for dimensionality reduction to decrease computational cost. These characteristics reduced the network parameters and computational burden of GoogleNet to more than ten times of their forerunners, VGG or AlexNet, while improving the state-of-the-art accuracy and learning capacity [9]. The GoogleNet team went as far as producing five more networks in the following years, labeling them respectively Inception-v2, Inception-v3 [10], Inception-v4, Inception-ResNet v1 and Inception-ResNet v2 [11]. These networks offered a variety of different concepts and improvements that have heavily impacted the field and contributed to his development. We briefly mention batch normalization [12], which is one of the widely used and heavily praised techniques to accelerate convergence and mitigate the covariate shift of non-normalized data between layers during the network training. Batch normalization is arguably also used as regularization techniques. The winner of the 2015-ILSVRC competition was also one of the most influential networks in the field; we are talking about the residual network architecture ResNet [13]. This network is one of the best architectures dealing with the vanishing gradient problem, especially with a depth of over a hundred trainable layers, and reached more than a thousand in the following model iterations. The secret to the success of ResNet lies in a new concept that instructs passing the features to two successive convolutional layers and a bypass pathway of the same features to meet in an output that guarantees cross-layer connectivity. The ResNet block is the connection of the features processed by the two convolutional layers to have detailed extractions and the direct feature bypass also referred to as a residual connection that accelerates convergence while providing another reminder of the previous extractions to the network. In Figure 14.7, we present the previously mentioned networks as they constitute the most important architectures in deep learning and the main source of inspiration to every architecture that succeeded them. After the release of ResNet, the trend of the following years focused on capitalizing on the success of ResNet and GoogleNet. Various validated networks integrated their influential concepts such as the previously mentioned versions of Inception or the SqueezeNet architecture which significantly reduced the number of parameters [14]. With the rise of these advanced networks, the challenge to alleviate was how to reach a tradeoff between the accuracy and speed of convergence. Xception [15], DenseNet [16], and CapsuleNet [17] were also other heredities of the previous networks taking the creative perceptions of AlexNet, NiN, VGG, GoogleNet and ResNet to the extreme and displaying remarkable ingenuity in architecture building. While the success of these networks is undeniable, some specific tasks could not benefit from these networks as much as others. Natural language processing, object detection, and segmentation tasks are very different to computer vision and classification problems. This fact forced the development of other networks that relied on a fusion of recurrent neural networks and convolutional neural networks to address these needs. One of the first hybrid networks to use recurrent convolutional layers was the recurrent convolutional neural network (or RCNN) [18], followed by an improved version inspired by ResNet named inception convolutional recurrent neural network IRCNN [19]. Furthermore, the first network specialized in segmentation tasks was the fully convolution network FCN [20], which was upgraded later to the SegNet [21]. These networks demanded encoding and decoding operations that perform convolution and sub-sampling followed by deconvolution and up-sampling. For object detection tasks, many networks have been created and developed, most notably the region-based convolutional neural network Region CNN [22] that afterwards inspired faster RCNN [23], fast RCNN [24] and mask-RCNN [25]. These detection-focused networks were also succeeded by other more sophisticated and advanced networks, in particular the focal loss for dense object detection [26], you only look once (YOLO) [27] and single-shot multibox detector SSD [28] with all their iterations such as YOLOv3 [29], deconvolutional single-shot detector (DSSD) [30], and deeply supervised object detectors (DSOD) [31]. Object detection-focused networks train two interdependent loss functions: one for the standard classification function and the other for the regression function responsible for the detection of the object's location.

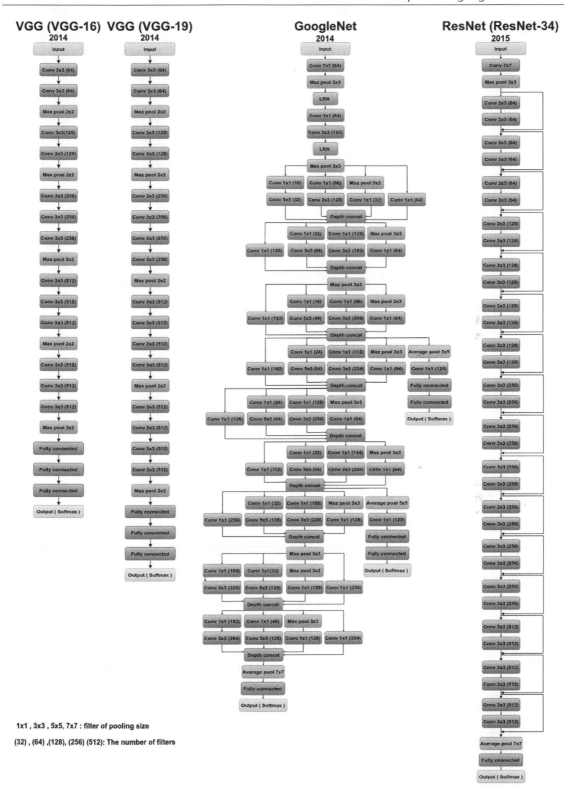

FIGURE 14.7 Deep learning architectures that revolutionized and inspired the current state of the art networks.

14.3 DEEP UNSUPERVISED AND SEMI-SUPERVISED LEARNING

After all the breakthroughs that this field has witnessed, from the first convolution neural networks and recurrent neural networks to all the different network architectures that revolutionized and shook the foundation of the domain, the inspiration and creativity never faded. Deep learning kept evolving and developing, creating new ideas and concepts that pierced through the problems faced by the researchers in every field and adapted to reach its current progress and reputation. Moving away from the standard notion of deep learning and popularity of supervised learning algorithms, other unsupervised and semi-supervised learning methods shined as well and took over the scene to create a new plateau that presents the current state of the art of deep learning.

14.3.1 Restricted Boltzmann Machines and deep belief nets

Restricted Boltzmann Machines (RBM) is a feature extraction and dimensionality reduction algorithm, which was originally known as harmony theory and created by Paul Smolensky in 1986 [32]. A simple description of RBMs is that they are generative models composed of two layers: an input and hidden layers with restriction over the connection between units of the same layer, hence the use of 'restricted' in the naming. Unlike AEs which are deterministic models meaning that they always produce the exact same predictions in their outputs, RBMs have a stochastic process using contrastive divergence to extract the probability distribution of the input constituting the fundamental distinction between RBMs and AEs. The other fundamental distinction is the aspect of having two biases instead of one with each bias corresponding to each layer.

RBMs are also the building blocks to deep belief net (DBN). DBNs use stacked blocks of RBMs in the pretrain phase and a standard feed-forward multilayer perceptron network for the fine tuning phase [33]. DBNs are a semi-supervised networks with the first phase considered as unsupervised pre training while the second phase is supervised fine tuning achieved through the output layer classification network. DBNs are a generative models and can be easily described by Figure 14.8.

14.3.2 Autoencoders & variational autoencoders

Autoencoders (AE) are one of the most common unsupervised learning algorithms [34]. They are used for encoding rather than predicting outcomes starting from the inputs. The benefit of this operation is mostly dimensionality reduction, denoising or compression. These networks first encode the input by extracting low dimensional features in the hidden layers to reach a compact feature representation. Then in the decoding phase, these compact features reversely generate the inputs while trying to minimize the reconstruction error.

Building on the success of its predecessor, the idea of variational auto-encoders (VAE) rose to existence creating a generative model out of the simplicity of autoencoders [35]. VAE is an auto-encoder that extracts a latent space distribution using a probabilistic approach to sample the compact feature used in the reconstruction process. In Figure 14.9, we showcase that the difference between AE and VAE is that VAE extracts a distribution over the latent space instead of a simple compact feature. This latent space distribution is later used to generate compact features that finally get decoded into a reconstructed input. VAE were also used and developed for time series data through the emergence of variational recurrent autoencoders [36].

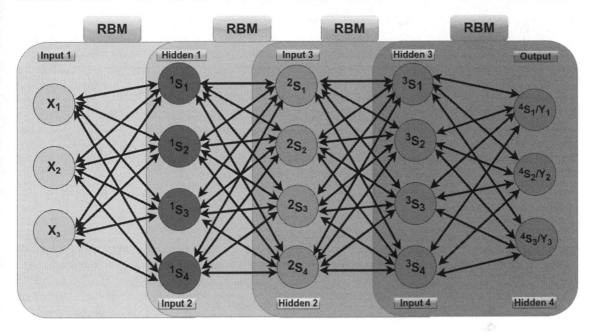

FIGURE 14.8   DBN architecture with RBMs building blocks.

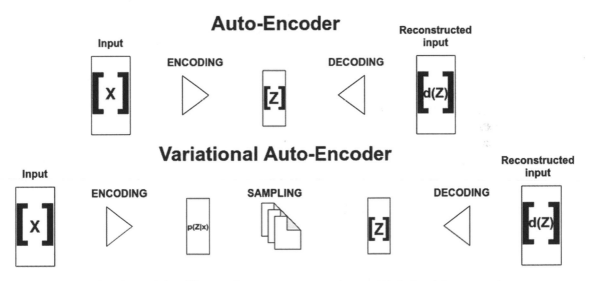

FIGURE 14.9   Flowchart of the difference between auto-encoders and Variational Auto-encoders.

14.3.3 Generative adversarial networks

Generative adversarial networks (GANs) are a popular generative model [37], as Yann LeCun has said, GAN is the best thing to happen to the field of deep learning in the last decade. They are an unsupervised learning system of two networks that are trained simultaneously in an adversarial way presenting a replacement to the maximum likelihood estimation methods. A GAN is basically split to a model that starts generating data called generative model and another model that's called discriminator that attempts to differentiate between the generated data (fake) and the original data (real). The loss function of these generated data tagged as fake by the discriminator, trains our generative model to improve the generated data in an attempt to fool the discriminator into perceiving them as real data instead of fake. This novel concept of placing two networks training against each other is what makes GANs one of the most influential networks in the field. GANs were and still are a very successful networks especially with image based data, which opened the door for numerous networks to emerge succeeding GANs such as conditional generative adversarial nets (CGANs) [38], deep convolutional generative adversarial networks known as DCGAN [39], StackGAN [40] and Style GAN [41]. Dozens of other GAN variants came to light in the past decade, which is another indicator for their success and potential worth.

14.3.4 Transformers

Moving on to another novel and influential modern state of the art approach, Transformers are a self-attention mechanism networks that were initially developed for natural language processing tasks. Being the latest installment of semi-supervised learning networks and a revolutionary proposition by the Google Brain team in 2017 with the paper Attention is all you need [42], they implied to changed everything. The tasks of natural language processing were overtook by the RNNs and their already mentioned variations LSTMs and GRUs. Although they were powerful algorithms RNNs and their variants failed to escape the sequential nature of their process that restricted them from taking advantage of parallelizing the operation with GPUs. This problem affects their performance alongside the gradient explosion problem and limited their development. The Facebook AI team tried to solve this problem first with convolution and Seq2seq network [43], by offering hierarchical presentation of the input into a fixed size vector, positional embeddings to capture the order of the sentence and multi-step attention. Transforms dropped the convolution and recurrence, proposing to encode each word position and applying a multi-head attention mechanism that managed to capture dependencies regardless of their position in the input or the output sentence. As presented in Figure 14.10, transformers encode the whole input sequence at once into a continuous representation that gets decoded one token at a time generating an output vector of translated or transformed words coupled with the probability of each of them. We note here that the encoding could be repeated several times to extract relevant information.

In 2020 Transforms entered the domain of images and computer vision with Google's vision transformers [44]. In 2021 and as transformers evolved with the emphasis on the significance of the new self-attention mechanism, came the confirmation on the importance of the feed forward layers and the residual connection proving their need to attain an efficient performance [45]. In the same year, Facebook AI's TimeSformer was released applying the transformers approach to videos [46]. This success opens doors for transformers to enter other domains like driving behavior and vehicle communications.

14.4 HYPERPARAMETERS, PRE-PROCESSING AND OPTIMIZATION

No matter how strong and powerful a neural network and its architecture, if it is not matched with carefully picked hyperparameters and pre-processing steps, the results will reflect directly on the performance and in a negative manner. Every neural network has some kind of problem or weak point that we can address and soften the impact of with some simple parameter tweaks or pre-processing that boosts the efficiency of the chosen architecture. Most network weaknesses can be traced down to a handful of popular problems, such as underfitting, overfitting, vanishing or exploding gradient problems, local minimum or flat regions, and long training time or lack of parallelization. These problems always play tug of war between them. If we are not careful enough, trying to solve one of them can cause the appearance of one or more other problems. In this section, we illustrate the most successful and common hyperparameters and optimization practices through the examination of the problems that they solve.

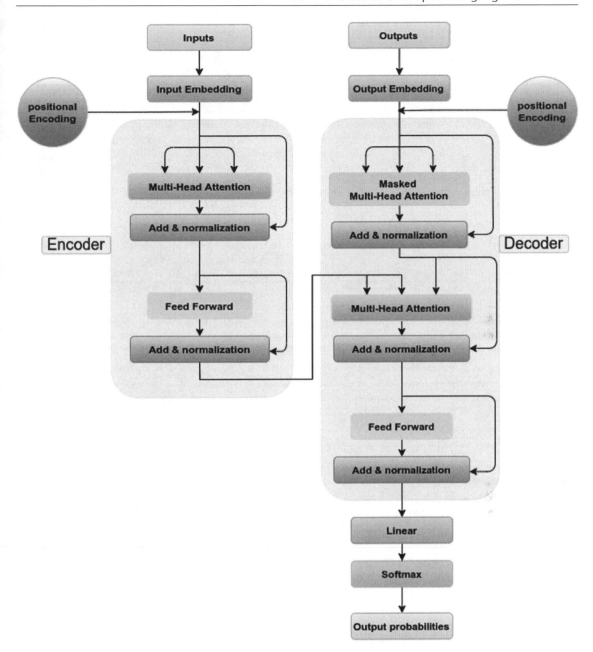

FIGURE 14.10   Architecture of the first iteration of transformers (with single encoding phase).

14.4.1 Data augmentation and transfer learning

The only confirmed fact here is that the most shared flaw and the number one rule for all deep learning algorithms is the need for large amounts of data. Not having enough data as input can lead to underfitting or overfitting the network, which means, in both cases, performance deficiency with either high error rate or inability to generalize. This problem can be resolved by the simplest solution of acquiring more data or as a last resort we turn to other methods such as data augmentation, artificially generated data and even transfer learning. When it comes to data augmentation, if we take computer vision as an example, we can flip the images, crop, scale, rotate, translate them, lose some of their information or even add some noise to them. These simple methods may seem useless since we are repeating the same images but in a different form; however, they help the networks not to rely on obvious naive features and add to the number of data available for training. Artificially generated data or also called synthetic data are products of the generative models that we discussed in the unsupervised and semi-supervised learning algorithms section. Whether it is RBMs, DBNs, VAEs or GANs, these models are capable of generating data based on the original data very efficiently and consistently, as well as data in the same probability or latent space distribution. The lack of a large dataset or the shortage of data can also be tackled by transfer learning, which saves us the trouble of building our deep learning model from scratch or extensively training them for long periods of time. Transfer learning is the effortless act of using pretrained models by other actors on extremely large datasets, updating their weights coefficients using our available new data while sometimes including other customization to the network for it to match our needs. The network can start learning with weights pre-trained on similar data then to be updated by the data that we have, conserving time and effort on repeating the same actions with unavailable data.

14.4.2 Weight initialization, activation functions and optimizers

When it comes to training deep learning models, the choice of our optimizer, weight initialization and activation functions can mean the difference between a model that converges to the required results and another that fails to reach half of its potential. These factors, although correlated, can individually affect the outcome of our training session. One of the main weak points of CNNs is their demanding need of proper weight initialization refinement in order to elude local minimum points. Weight initialization was always a confusing subject for researchers due to the possible consequences and lack of clear methodology for many years [47]. One of the first and well-known weight initialization methods is the Xavier initialization that promised to preserve the variance of the activation and gradients throughout all the layers of the network [48]. In 2015, another very successful initialization method was created that insinuated that the initialization method does not depend solely on the number of layers, but it should consider the activation function and take it into account, this method is the He initialization [49]. He initialization proved that it is the best initialization option for ReLU and leaky ReLU activation, while the Xavier weight initialization method is preferred to Tanh activation functions.

These conclusions led us to another factor that should be considered in preparing the network for training which is activation functions. Activation functions manage the way hidden layers learn and the type of prediction in the output layer which make them critical for our network success. Sigmoid and Tanh are considered the traditional activation functions that were used for years, while the ReLU, leaky ReLU and ELU are the new generation. Conceivably, ReLU is now regarded as the most popular and used activation for hidden layers due to its simplicity and its ability to overcome the limitation of the legacy activation functions [50]. ReLU and its variants are the best solution for ANNs in general and especially CNNs preventing these networks from falling into vanishing gradient problems. Unlike Sigmoid and Tanh activation that are more suitable for RNNs in general that come with the inconvenience and price of susceptibility to the vanishing gradient problems. When it comes to the output layer that normally has a different activation function from the other layers, Sigmoid and Softmax are mostly used for classification while regression problems tend to use a linear activation function. In Figure 14.11, we display the most common activation functions alongside their mathematical expressions that produce them.

Training algorithms (also called optimizers) evolved over time in an attempt to solve vanishing gradient and exploding gradient problems while converging quickly to the optimum solution. The vanishing gradient problem can stop the algorithm from training or delay it, while the exploding gradient problem can cause the algorithm to miss the convergence point altogether and overshoot to another local minimum. The efficiency of every optimizer is measured by their ability to overcome these two issues. Many training algorithms have been used over the years for deep neural networks, their target is to find the best combination of weights to minimize the error equation or also called loss function of a model. We have

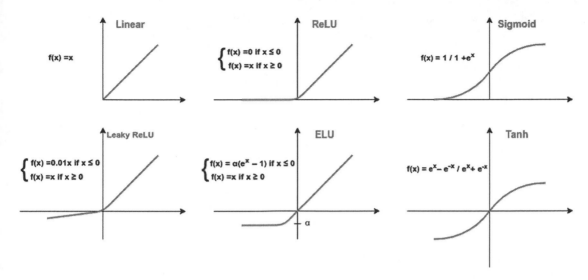

FIGURE 14.11   The most common activation functions.

various optimizers with different pros and cons available to train a neural network, which makes selecting the right fit for our model a significant process. Gradient descent is an easy-to-understand and implement optimizer since it depends only on the derivative of the loss function but requires large memory because the derivative calculation is done for the whole dataset in a single update which makes it slow for large datasets. Stochastic gradient descent (SGD) is another variation of gradient descent that gets an update with every dataset sample; this makes it flexible working with large datasets and reduces the need for large memory. However, the high frequency of the updates for SGD can cause high variance and noisy gradients that can have a reverse effect on the error. Mini-batch gradient descent is proposed to solve that by creating the combination of the previous two optimizers, which makes it a good compromise between them. The Nesterov accelerated gradient (NAG) added a momentum term to SGD, which made the optimizer take into account the history of the updates, improving the stability but adding another hyperparameter that needs to be carefully tweaked to get the desired results. Adaptive gradient descent (AdaGrad) introduced adaptive learning rates that change automatically with every iteration which made it a good solution for sparse data; however, it is computationally expensive through the need of the second-order derivative calculation. AdaDelta is the same as AdaGrad while removing the obligation of the automatically decaying learning rate. Root mean square propagation (RMS-Prop) is another version of AdaGrad with a learning rate taking the value of the exponential average of the gradients which adjust it automatically, making it a combination of AdaGrad with momentum. Finally, Adaptive moment estimation (also known as Adam) is one of the most successful and popular optimizers. It comes with an adaptive learning rate and combines the advantage of AdaDelta and RMS-Prop using both the decaying average of the past gradient and the squared decaying average of the past gradient which make it fast, rapidly convergent, resistant to vanishing gradient and high variance but computationally expensive [51].

14.4.3 Training time, pre-processing and architectural refinements

Deep learning algorithms in general require a lot of computational power which requires the availability of hardware resources like CPUs and GPUs and affects the speed of convergence with some algorithms taking days or months of training before producing tangible results. CNNs are known to be fast algorithms to train relatively speaking compared to RNNs when GPUs are available. This is due to their aptitude to use the GPUs' power to parallelize the workload improving the training time up to ten or hundred times faster. However, RNNs have a sequential nature in their architecture and training process, which makes it impossible for them to parallelize the training resulting in a slow architecture to train relatively to CNNs.

Another factor responsible for the training time value is the size of trained data and their utility to model training. Having large data is great for training any deep learning network, unless the quality of data is compromised and includes contaminated samples or useless information for our objective. For this problem, data pre-processing is done through data cleaning, data scaling, feature selection, dimensionality reduction. Data cleaning involves organizing the data, missing value treatments either by regression, interpolation or the elimination of some data sectors all together, and also the deletion of redundancy and repetition that can influence the bias of the model. Data scaling, on the other hand, is the standardization or normalization of data, eliminating any kind of bias that the network can fall for by forcing the comparison of different features on the same scale, adjusting the distribution of features for better performance and accelerating the training process. Feature selection and dimensionality reduction are also techniques that change the feature distributions and eliminate bias, allowing better reception of data as the network input. There are various dimensionality reduction techniques that offer better feature management, including principal component analysis (PCA), which is a statistical procedure that help express the data in more condensed and interpretable form, and other methods such as autoencoders that we already discussed before in the unsupervised learning section. Unsupervised learning has more importance in current time due to the emergence of big data and the wide availability of raw unlabeled or non-categorized data.

There are other practices that can help speed up the training time of a network, such as learning rate adjustment and architecture refinements that involve additional optimization functions and layer manipulation. The learning rate is what controls the weight updating pace, which has a direct effect on the training time and convergence. As we have seen with different optimizers, some of these training algorithms have the possibility of applying an adaptive learning rate, which can reduce the training time and improve convergence with the learning rate changing during the training. One of the most famous additions to architecture refinements is batch normalization and dropout regularization layers. Batch normalization is another normalization applied to the data in the hidden layers of the network rather than only applying it in the input layer. This additional function has been proven to accelerate our training process and improve the convergence [12]. Eventually, if we investigate further on training time or the ability to converge in a model while avoiding overfitting and vanishing or exploding gradient, we need to consider the number of layers in a model and their effect and other hyperparameters, such as the number of filters or pooling layers for CNNs. Overfitting, and the ability of the network to generalize, can also be challenged by choices in the network architect, either by using residual connections as established by the ResNet architecture or through the use of dropout regularization layers. Dropout is a regularization technique that involves resetting a percentage of random neurons in a layer to zero which cancels their activation, teaching the network not to rely on a specific neuron or set of neurons [52].

14.5 APPLICATIONS OF DEEP LEARNING IN DRIVING BEHAVIOR ANALYSIS AND VEHICLE COMMUNICATION

The term driver behavior analysis emerged in the 1960s and it was initially founded on psychological advancement in information processing models. Driver behavior analysis is the use of data extracted from vehicles or the environment to identify the driver or to classify his driving style into aggressive and normal in order to assess his dangerous habits and the risky situations that he can run into. This classification is later used to offer guidance and warn the driver to his surroundings in case of incoming danger. In 1995, one of the first review papers done by Dougherty et al. [53] documented in detail the work done with artificial neural networks in all fields of transportation. This offered us a look at the first two papers that used

ANN in driver behavior which came out in the same year of 1992: Yang et al. [54] and Doughtery et al. [55]. This initial appearance of ANN in the driver behavior and vehicle communication world coincided with a period that witnessed the emergence of the first deep learning model. After the emergence and standardization of the On-Board diagnosis II (OBD-II) in cars between 1996 in the US and 2001 in Europe, the field was liberated to other domains rather than being restricted to the psychology research and car manufacturers. The liberation of this field coincided with the rise of deep learning, which opened a lot of opportunities to invest the deep learning gains in driver behavior analysis. Although this event could have been a sign to move this field to deep learning, the DL domain was not mature enough to lift the weight of an already progressive field. The field of driver behavior, with all the sub-branches such as identification, driver state detection, and event prediction, used other rule-based algorithms, statistical algorithms and even machine learning for the next decade. This stagnation lasted until the deep learning revolution that got ignited by AlexNet in 2012 [3]. This fact is confirmed by the 2013 comparative study of Singh et al. [56] which compared other machine learning algorithms to DL. This work concluded the superiority of DL algorithms in the driver stress level analysis from physiological signals to classical machine learning. In 2014, Del Campo et al. [57] used deep ANN in a driver identification system. The same year realized the use of deep sparse autoencoders (DSAE) in driver behavior visualization by Lui et al. [58]. In 2016, a model for driver activity anticipation based on LSTMs' recurrent architecture was created by Jain et al. [59], LSTMs were also used for driver intention prediction by Philips et al. [60]. In 2017, De Naurois, C et al. [61] applied deep ANN for driver drowsiness detection and prediction, the same year that Carvalho et al. [62] used LSTMs and GRU to detect aggressive driving. Kuefler et al. [63] used generative adversarial networks in human driving behavior simulation, data generation and prediction process that compete with rule-based controllers and outperforms behavior cloning that also utilized deep learning in its method. In 2018, Baheti et al. [64] used transfer learning on the VGG model [7] with additional dropout and batch normalization layers to detect distracted drivers from a camera sensor. Although most of the event detection and action recognition studies benefited from transfer learning in order to obtain tangible and admissible results for their tasks, such as Baheti et al. [64], some researchers preferred using their own architecture as Jeong et al. [65] did for real-time driver identification systems. Lee et al. [66] used deep CNN for driver emotion classification through aggressive and untroubled driving, relying on the images from the driver's face instead of the previous methods that operated on physiological and inertial measurement unit signals. In 2019, Bian et al. [67] created a deep neural network (DNN) model for driver risk assessment identifying aggressive driving behavior from GPS and OBD-II signals and proving that their results surpass classical machine learning algorithms. The same year Zhang et al. [68] created multiple hybrid models of CNNs and attention-based RNNs that used LSTMs and GRUs for driver behavior identification. In 2021, Abdennour et al. [69] introduced a deep learning model that employed residual connections inspired from ResNet [13] for driver identification that outperforms the previous hybrid models of Zhang et al. [68]. As we can notice by these various studies, which included different tasks such as identification, event and state detection, visualization and prediction, DL, with its diverse applications of supervised and unsupervised learning, is heavily used in driver behavior.

As for vehicle communication, they have witnessed a big leap of evolution. Vehicles are coming from a state of basic individual entities that function without any correlation to mobile operating smart computers that are able to communicate and interact with each other in a homogenized way. Vehicle communication has become necessary for traffic efficiency and road safety. Whether it is in wireless communication networks, trajectory prediction or traffic flow forecasting, the use of deep learning in these cases increased dramatically in order to solve the imminent rise of vehicle populations on our roads and their complicated environmental interactions. This field is enormously intertwined with various other fields that succeeded with DL, such as computer vision, autonomous driving, and wireless communication. In this study we try to focus on the direct influence of DL on vehicle communications instead of capitalizing on the work of other fields and discussing them. Our aim is to highlight the cases that the DL algorithms were suitable and justifiable for their solution. Vehicle communication is currently achieved through three main methods; the wireless IEEE 802.11p communication protocol known as WAVE (wireless access in vehicular environments); the optical camera communication (OCC); and the visible light communication (VLC).

DL is applied for WAVE, by learning the dynamics of high mobility networks and Channel estimation. DL can be used to predict the channel statistics and enhance instantaneous channel estimation for operating vehicular links. In the 2008 paper, Potter et al. [70] RNNs were used to predict the instantaneous channel state information (CSI) for a Multiple-input multiple-output (MIMO) wireless communication systems. In 2011, Shi et al. [71] presented a deep learning neural network that approximated the weighted minimum mean-squared error (WMMSE) algorithm to create a linear transceiver algorithm for weighted sum-rate maximization. Fast-forward to 2017, and Ye et al. [72] created a deep neural network that predicts CSI and detects orthogonal frequency-division multiplexing (OFDM) systems signals. In 2018, Luo et al. [73] used a hybrid CNN and LSTM deep learning model to predict the CSI for efficient 5G wireless communication. In 2019, Joo [74] applied a Deep LSTM network for CSI prediction in a realistic vehicle communication environment.

Moving on to the optical camera communication (OCC) and visible light communication (VLC), we could not help but notice that most of these visual communication systems that use a camera sensor for their objective have been using transfer learning or the object detection and object recognition algorithms that we already mentioned, including Region CNN [22], faster RCNN [23], fast RCNN [24], mask-RCNN [25], YOLO [27], SSD [28] and their iterations such as YOLOv3 [29], DSSD [30], DSOD [31] and YOLOv4 [75].

Vehicle communications also included trajectory prediction and traffic pattern analysis that can insure traffic efficiency and road safety, as we have already stated. We mention here the 2016 paper by Khosroshahi et al. [76] that used RNNs for the trajectory analysis of surrounding vehicles. The same year, Ondruska et al. [77] built a deep encoder decoder RNN used in one of the first end-to-end object racking methods from raw sensors without any feature manipulation. In 2017, Lee et al. [78] used a deep CNN in a lane-change prediction model of surrounding vehicles for an adaptive cruise control assistance system. In the same year, an LSTM model was also used for trajectory prediction, the Kim et al. [79] RNN architecture for a probabilistic vehicle trajectory prediction in a high-velocity traffic location. 2018 saw the materialization of three other LSTM-based networks for trajectory prediction with different architectures: Park et al. [80] used an encoder decoder LSTM architecture in a sequence-to-sequence prediction of vehicle trajectory, and analyzing past sensor measurements to generate the future trajectory of a vehicle; Deo et al. [81] chose an LSTM-based novel architecture for multi-lane trajectory maneuver prediction after comparing it to a generative adversarial imitation learning model based on GRUs; And Xin et al. [82] proposed a long-term trajectory prediction that can reach up to five seconds for highways using LSTMs that outperformed the Kim et al. [79] network. In 2019, Dai et al. [83] created a modified spatial temporal LSTM with residual connections inspired by ResNet [13] to model vehicle interaction via trajectory prediction. The same year Ma et al. [84] proposed Trafficpredict, which is a real-time trajectory predictor using an LSTM-based model with a self-attention mechanism. In 2020, Djuric et al. [85] developed a hybrid CNN/LSTM model that determines the uncertainty and the future trajectory estimation with the actors' positions for self-driving vehicles.

When it comes to vehicle-to-infrastructure communication and traffic flow forecasting that can ensure efficient traffic management, a variety of methods have been used. Dating back to 1979, when Ahmed et al. [86] worked with the autoregressive integrated moving average (ARIMA) model in one of the first traffic flow predictors for short-term freeway traffic. This helped the rise of many variants of ARMA to be used for traffic flow forecasting, such as the use of ARIMA for urban areas instead of freeway, the accuracy prediction improvements brought away by KARIMA, ARIMAX and SARIMA. These models were succeeded by the Kalman filter and other machine learning models, such as support vector machines (SVM) and hidden Markov models. Next, they were followed by one of the first ANN use for traffic flow by Park et al. [87]. The use of ANN continued with the development of DL, such as Kumar et al.'s [88] deep learning network that predicts traffic flow for non-urban highways. In 2014, Huang et al. [89] proposed a deep belief net of RBMs for traffic flow prediction using multitask learning. The same year Lv [90] used a deep-stacked autoencoder to learn generic traffic flow features that eventually got used for prediction. The following year, LSTMs were also used by Ma et al. [91] for traffic speed prediction in a traffic flow monitoring environment after a comparative study that proved their superiority to other models that used ANNs, SVM, and the Kalman filter. In 2016, Koesdwiady et al. [92] improved traffic flow prediction using the weather information with the DBN model. The same year, Fu et al. [93] delivered the GRU model for a real-time traffic flow predictor, in one of the first times GRU is applied for this task. In the year 2017, Liu et al. [94] performed a short-term traffic flow prediction using a hybrid CNN/LSTM model and Zhang et al. [95] predicted the city-wide crowd flow using a spatio-temporal residual network based on ResNet [13]. In 2018, a pre-processing normalization and a cascaded ANN (CANN) were used by Zhang et al. [96] for traffic flow prediction, while Du et al. [97] used a hybrid CNN/GRU model for the same task. The same year, Lin et al. [98] and Liang Y [99] both used generative adversarial networks in a traffic state estimation and a pattern-sensitive traffic flow forecasting. The year 2019, Cui et al. [100] built a traffic graph convolutional recurrent neural network that was used for a network-scale traffic learning and forecasting benefiting from the spatial convolution. Xiao et al. [101], proposed a hybrid LSTM model that added dropout layers and ANNs for the short-term traffic flow prediction task. The same year Zang et al. [102] presented a residual deconvolution-based deep generative network (RDBDGN) for long-term traffic flow forecasting. Wei et al. [103] produced a combination of autoencoders and LSTM (AE-LSTM) for traffic flow prediction. Similar to the case of driver behavior analysis, vehicle communication has become (and still is) a field that heavily relies on DL in a mutually beneficial relationship, that helped develop DL as much through the advancement of the vehicle communication domain.

14.6 CONCLUSIONS

Deep learning went through an incredible evolution in the past two decades making one breakthrough after another and invading every possible field, and each promising domain. In this chapter, we introduce deep learning, then we go through the evolution of deep learning from its humble beginnings and the problems that this field faced to the sophisticated architectures and revolutionary models of these current days. We detail this journey and explain the advantages and disadvantages of this variety of networks while also showcasing the huge possibilities of hyperparameter refinement and pre-processing that can contribute directly to the success or the failure of an architecture. Finally, we present the applications of deep learning in driver behavior analysis and vehicle communication to conclude with the huge dependence of these fields on deep learning that directly contributed to their success.

REFERENCES

[1] LeCun, Yann, et al. "Gradient-based learning applied to document recognition." *Proceedings of the IEEE* 86.11 (1998): 2278–2324.
[2] Cireşan, Dan Claudiu, et al. "Deep, big, simple neural nets for handwritten digit recognition." *Neural Computation* 22.12 (2010): 3207–3220.
[3] Krizhevsky, Alex, Ilya Sutskever, and Geoffrey E. Hinton. "Imagenet classification with deep convolutional neural networks." *Advances in Neural Information Processing Systems 25* (2012): 1097–1105.
[4] Zeiler, Matthew D., and Rob Fergus. "Visualizing and understanding convolutional networks." *European Conference on Computer Vision*. Springer, Cham, 2014.
[5] Sermanet, Pierre, et al. "Overfeat: Integrated recognition, localization and detection using convolutional networks." arXiv preprint arXiv:1312.6229 (2013).
[6] Lin, Min, Qiang Chen, and Shuicheng Yan. "Network in network." arXiv preprint arXiv:1312.4400 (2013).
[7] Simonyan, Karen, and Andrew Zisserman. "Very deep convolutional networks for large-scale image recognition." arXiv preprint arXiv:1409.1556 (2014).
[8] Szegedy, Christian, et al. "Going deeper with convolutions." *Proceedings of the IEEE Conference on Computer Vision and Pattern Recognition*. 2015.

[9] Canziani, Alfredo, Adam Paszke, and Eugenio Culurciello. "An analysis of deep neural network models for practical applications." arXiv preprint arXiv:1605.07678 (2016).

[10] Szegedy, Christian, et al. "Rethinking the inception architecture for computer vision." *Proceedings of the IEEE Conference on Computer Vision and Pattern Recognition*. 2016.

[11] Szegedy, Christian, et al. "Inception-v4, inception-resnet and the impact of residual connections on learning." *Thirty-first AAAI Conference on Artificial Intelligence*. 2017.

[12] Ioffe, Sergey, and Christian Szegedy. "Batch normalization: Accelerating deep network training by reducing internal covariate shift." *International Conference on Machine Learning*. PMLR, 2015.

[13] He, Kaiming, et al. "Deep residual learning for image recognition." *Proceedings of the IEEE Conference on Computer Vision and Pattern Recognition*. 2016.

[14] Iandola, Forrest N., et al. "SqueezeNet: AlexNet-level accuracy with 50x fewer parameters and< 0.5 MB model size." arXiv preprint arXiv:1602.07360 (2016).

[15] Chollet, François. "Xception: Deep learning with depthwise separable convolutions." *Proceedings of the IEEE Conference on Computer Vision and Pattern Recognition*. 2017.

[16] Huang, Gao, et al. "Densely connected convolutional networks." *Proceedings of the IEEE Conference on Computer Vision and Pattern Recognition*. 2017.

[17] Sabour, Sara, Nicholas Frosst, and Geoffrey E. Hinton. "Dynamic routing between capsules." arXiv preprint arXiv:1710.09829 (2017).

[18] Liang, Ming, and Xiaolin, Hu. "Recurrent convolutional neural network for object recognition." *Proceedings of the IEEE Conference on Computer Vision and Pattern Recognition*. 2015.

[19] Alom, Md Zahangir, et al. "Inception recurrent convolutional neural network for object recognition." *Machine Vision and Applications 32*.1 (2021): 1–14.

[20] Long, Jonathan, Evan Shelhamer, and Trevor Darrell. "Fully convolutional networks for semantic segmentation." *Proceedings of the IEEE conference on computer vision and pattern recognition*. 2015.

[21] Kendall, Alex, Vijay Badrinarayanan, and Roberto Cipolla. "Bayesian segnet: Model uncertainty in deep convolutional encoder-decoder architectures for scene understanding." arXiv preprint arXiv:1511.02680 (2015).

[22] Girshick, Ross, et al. "Rich feature hierarchies for accurate object detection and semantic segmentation." *Proceedings of the IEEE Conference on Computer Vision and Pattern Recognition*. 2014.

[23] Ren, Shaoqing, et al. "Faster R-CNN: Towards real-time object detection with region proposal networks." *IEEE Transactions on Pattern Analysis and Machine Intelligence 39*.6 (2016): 1137–1149.

[24] Wang, Xiaolong, Abhinav Shrivastava, and Abhinav Gupta. "A-fast-RCNN: Hard positive generation via adversary for object detection." *Proceedings of the IEEE Conference on Computer Vision and Pattern Recognition*. 2017.

[25] He, Kaiming, et al. "Mask R-CNN." *Proceedings of the IEEE International Conference on Computer Vision*. 2017.

[26] Lin, Tsung-Yi, et al. "Focal loss for dense object detection." *Proceedings of the IEEE International Conference on Computer Vision*. 2017.

[27] Redmon, Joseph, et al. "You only look once: Unified, real-time object detection." *Proceedings of the IEEE Conference on Computer Vision and Pattern Recognition*. 2016.

[28] Liu, Wei, et al. "Ssd: Single shot multibox detector." *European Conference on Computer Vision*. Springer, Cham, 2016.

[29] Redmon, Joseph, and Ali Farhadi. "Yolov3: An incremental improvement." arXiv preprint arXiv:1804.02767 (2018).

[30] Fu, Cheng-Yang, et al. "DSSD: Deconvolutional single shot detector." arXiv preprint arXiv:1701.06659 (2017).

[31] Shen, Zhiqiang, et al. "DSOD: Learning deeply supervised object detectors from scratch." *Proceedings of the IEEE International Conference on Computer Vision*. 2017.

[32] Smolensky, Paul. *Information Processing in Dynamical Systems: Foundations of Harmony Theory*. Colorado Univ at Boulder Dept of Computer Science, 1986. https://apps.dtic.mil/sti/citations/ADA620727

[33] Hinton, Geoffrey E. "Deep belief networks." *Scholarpedia 4*.5 (2009): 5947.

[34] Vincent, Pascal, et al. "Extracting and composing robust features with denoising autoencoders." *Proceedings of the 25th International Conference on Machine Learning*. 2008.

[35] Kingma, Diederik P., and Max Welling. "Auto-encoding variational bayes." arXiv preprint arXiv:1312.6114 (2013).

[36] Fabius, Otto, and Joost R. Van Amersfoort. "Variational recurrent auto-encoders." arXiv preprint arXiv:1412.6581 (2014).

[37] Goodfellow et al. "Generative adversarial networks." arXiv preprint arXiv:1406.2661 (2014).

[38] Mirza, Mehdi, and Simon Osindero. "Conditional generative adversarial nets." arXiv preprint arXiv:1411.1784 (2014).

[39] Radford, Alec, Luke Metz, and Soumith Chintala. "Unsupervised representation learning with deep convolutional generative adversarial networks." arXiv preprint arXiv:1511.06434 (2015).

[40] Zhang, Han, et al. "Stackgan: Text to photo-realistic image synthesis with stacked generative adversarial networks." *Proceedings of the IEEE International Conference on Computer Vision.* 2017.

[41] Wang, Xiaolong, and Abhinav Gupta. "Generative image modeling using style and structure adversarial networks." *European Conference on Computer Vision.* Springer, Cham, 2016.

[42] Vaswani, A., Shazeer, N., Parmar, N., Uszkoreit, J., Jones, L., Gomez, A. N., … and Polosukhin, I. (2017). Attention is all you need. *Advances in Neural Information Processing Systems* (pp. 5998–6008).

[43] Gehring, J., Auli, M., Grangier, D., Yarats, D., and Dauphin, Y. N. (2017). Convolutional sequence to sequence learning. *International Conference on Machine Learning* (pp. 1243–1252). PMLR.8).

[44] Dosovitskiy, Alexey, et al. "An image is worth 16 × 16 words: Transformers for image recognition at scale." arXiv preprint arXiv:2010.11929 (2020).

[45] Dong, Yihe, Jean-Baptiste Cordonnier, and Andreas Loukas. "Attention is not all you need: Pure attention loses rank doubly exponentially with depth." arXiv preprint arXiv:2103.03404 (2021).

[46] Bertasius, Gedas, Heng Wang, and Lorenzo Torresani. "Is space-time attention all you need for video understanding?." arXiv preprint arXiv:2102.05095 (2021).

[47] Sutskever, Ilya, et al. "On the importance of initialization and momentum in deep learning." *International Conference on Machine Learning.* PMLR, 2013.

[48] Glorot, Xavier, and Yoshua Bengio. "Understanding the difficulty of training deep feedforward neural networks." *Proceedings of the Thirteenth International Conference on Artificial Intelligence and Statistics. JMLR Workshop and Conference Proceedings,* 2010.

[49] He, Kaiming, et al. "Delving deep into rectifiers: Surpassing human-level performance on imagenet classification." *Proceedings of the IEEE International Conference on Computer Vision.* 2015.

[50] Nair, Vinod, and Geoffrey E. Hinton. "Rectified linear units improve restricted boltzmann machines." ICML. 2010.

[51] Kingma, Diederik P., and Jimmy Ba. "Adam: A method for stochastic optimization." arXiv preprint arXiv:1412.6980 (2014).

[52] Ioffe, Sergey, and Christian Szegedy. "Batch normalization: Accelerating deep network training by reducing internal covariate shift." *International Conference on Machine Learning.* PMLR, 2015.

[53] Dougherty, Mark. "A review of neural networks applied to transport." *Transportation Research Part C: Emerging Technologies 3.*4 (1995): 247–260.

[54] Yang, Hai, Takamasa Akiyama, and Tsuna Sasaki. "A neural network approach to the identification of real time origin-destination flows from traffic counts." *International Conference on Artificial Intelligence Applications in Transportation Engineering,* 1992, San Buenaventura, California, USA. 1992.

[55] Dougherty, Mark S., and Matthew Joint. "A behaviourial model of driver route choice using neural networks." *International Conference on Artificial Intelligence Applications in Transportation Engineering (1992: Ventura, Calif.).* Conference preprints. 1992.

[56] Singh, Rajiv Ranjan, Sailesh Conjeti, and Rahul Banerjee. "A comparative evaluation of neural network classifiers for stress level analysis of automotive drivers using physiological signals." *Biomedical Signal Processing and Control 8.*6 (2013): 740–754.

[57] Del Campo, Ines, et al. "A real-time driver identification system based on artificial neural networks and cepstral analysis." *2014 International Joint Conference on Neural Networks (IJCNN).* IEEE, 2014.

[58] Liu, HaiLong, et al. "Visualization of driving behavior using deep sparse autoencoder." *2014 IEEE Intelligent Vehicles Symposium Proceedings.* IEEE, 2014.

[59] Jain, Ashesh, et al. "Recurrent neural networks for driver activity anticipation via sensory-fusion architecture." *2016 IEEE International Conference on Robotics and Automation (ICRA).* IEEE, 2016.

[60] Phillips, Derek J., Tim A. Wheeler, and Mykel J. Kochenderfer. "Generalizable intention prediction of human drivers at intersections." *2017 IEEE Intelligent Vehicles Symposium (IV).* IEEE, 2017.

[61] de Naurois, Charlotte Jacobé, et al. "Detection and prediction of driver drowsiness using artificial neural network models." *Accident Analysis & Prevention 126* (2019): 95–104.

[62] Carvalho, Eduardo, et al. "Exploiting the use of recurrent neural networks for driver behavior profiling." *2017 International Joint Conference on Neural Networks (IJCNN).* IEEE, 2017.

[63] Kuefler, Alex, et al. "Imitating driver behavior with generative adversarial networks." *2017 IEEE Intelligent Vehicles Symposium (IV).* IEEE, 2017.

[64] Baheti, Bhakti, Suhas Gajre, and Sanjay Talbar. "Detection of distracted driver using convolutional neural network." *Proceedings of the IEEE Conference on Computer Vision and Pattern Recognition Workshops*. 2018.

[65] Jeong, Daun, et al. "Real-time driver identification using vehicular big data and deep learning." *2018 21st International Conference on Intelligent Transportation Systems (ITSC)*. IEEE, 2018.

[66] Lee, Kwan Woo, et al. "Convolutional neural network-based classification of driver's emotion during aggressive and smooth driving using multi-modal camera sensors." *Sensors 18*.4 (2018): 957.

[67] Bian, Yiyang, et al. "A deep learning based model for driving risk assessment." *Proceedings of the 52nd Hawaii International Conference on System Sciences*. 2019.

[68] Zhang, Jun, et al. "A deep learning framework for driving behavior identification on in-vehicle CAN-BUS sensor data." *Sensors 19*.6 (2019): 1356.

[69] Abdennour, Najmeddine, Tarek Ouni, and Nader Ben Amor. "Driver identification using only the CAN-Bus vehicle data through an RCN deep learning approach." *Robotics and Autonomous Systems 136* (2021): 103707.

[70] Potter, Chris, Kurt Kosbar, and Adam Panagos. "MIMO channel prediction using recurrent neural networks." *International Foundation for Telemetering*, 2008.

[71] Shi, Qingjiang, et al. "An iteratively weighted MMSE approach to distributed sum-utility maximization for a MIMO interfering broadcast channel." *IEEE Transactions on Signal Processing 59*.9 (2011): 4331–4340.

[72] Ye, Hao, Geoffrey Ye Li, and Biing-Hwang Juang. "Power of deep learning for channel estimation and signal detection in OFDM systems." *IEEE Wireless Communications Letters 7*.1 (2017): 114–117.

[73] Luo, Changqing, et al. "Channel state information prediction for 5G wireless communications: A deep learning approach." *IEEE Transactions on Network Science and Engineering 7*.1 (2018): 227–236.

[74] Joo, Jhihoon, et al. "Deep learning-based channel prediction in realistic vehicular communications." *IEEE Access 7* (2019): 27846–27858.

[75] Bochkovskiy, Alexey, Chien-Yao Wang, and Hong-Yuan Mark Liao. "Yolov4: Optimal speed and accuracy of object detection." arXiv preprint arXiv:2004.10934 (2020).

[76] Khosroshahi, Aida, Eshed Ohn-Bar, and Mohan Manubhai Trivedi. "Surround vehicles trajectory analysis with recurrent neural networks." *2016 IEEE 19th International Conference on Intelligent Transportation Systems (ITSC)*. IEEE, 2016.

[77] Ondruska, Peter, and Ingmar Posner. "Deep tracking: Seeing beyond seeing using recurrent neural networks." *Thirtieth AAAI Conference on Artificial Intelligence*. 2016.

[78] Lee, Donghan, et al. "Convolution neural network-based lane change intention prediction of surrounding vehicles for ACC." *2017 IEEE 20th International Conference on Intelligent Transportation Systems (ITSC)*. IEEE, 2017.

[79] Kim, ByeoungDo, et al. "Probabilistic vehicle trajectory prediction over occupancy grid map via recurrent neural network." *2017 IEEE 20th International Conference on Intelligent Transportation Systems (ITSC)*. IEEE, 2017.

[80] Park, Seong Hyeon, et al. "Sequence-to-sequence prediction of vehicle trajectory via LSTM encoder-decoder architecture." *2018 IEEE Intelligent Vehicles Symposium (IV)*. IEEE, 2018.

[81] Deo, Nachiket, and Mohan M. Trivedi. "Multi-modal trajectory prediction of surrounding vehicles with maneuver based lstms." *2018 IEEE Intelligent Vehicles Symposium (IV)*. IEEE, 2018.

[82] Xin, Long, et al. "Intention-aware long horizon trajectory prediction of surrounding vehicles using dual lstm networks." *2018 21st International Conference on Intelligent Transportation Systems (ITSC)*. IEEE, 2018.

[83] Dai, Shengzhe, Li Li, and Zhiheng Li. "Modeling vehicle interactions via modified LSTM models for trajectory prediction." *IEEE Access 7* (2019): 38287–38296.

[84] Ma, Yuexin, et al. "Trafficpredict: Trajectory prediction for heterogeneous traffic-agents." *Proceedings of the AAAI Conference on Artificial Intelligence*. vol. *33*. no. 01. 2019.

[85] Djuric, Nemanja, et al. "Uncertainty-aware short-term motion prediction of traffic actors for autonomous driving." *Proceedings of the IEEE/CVF Winter Conference on Applications of Computer Vision*. 2020.

[86] Ahmed, Mohammed S., and Allen R. Cook. Analysis of freeway traffic time-series data by using Box-Jenkins techniques. No. 722. 1979.

[87] Park, Byungkyu, Carroll J. Messer, and Thomas Urbanik. "Short-term freeway traffic volume forecasting using radial basis function neural network." *Transportation Research Record 1651*.1 (1998): 39–47.

[88] Kumar, Kranti, Manoranjan Parida, and V. K. Katiyar. "Short term traffic flow prediction for a non urban highway using artificial neural network." *Procedia-Social and Behavioral Sciences 104* (2013): 755–764.

[89] Huang, Wenhao, et al. "Deep architecture for traffic flow prediction: Deep belief networks with multitask learning." *IEEE Transactions on Intelligent Transportation Systems 15*.5 (2014): 2191–2201.

[90] Lv, Yisheng, et al. "Traffic flow prediction with big data: A deep learning approach." *IEEE Transactions on Intelligent Transportation Systems 16*.2 (2014): 865–873.

[91] Ma, Xiaolei, et al. "Long short-term memory neural network for traffic speed prediction using remote microwave sensor data." *Transportation Research Part C: Emerging Technologies 54* (2015): 187–197.

[92] Koesdwiady, Arief, Ridha Soua, and Fakhreddine Karray. "Improving traffic flow prediction with weather information in connected cars: A deep learning approach." *IEEE Transactions on Vehicular Technology 65*.12 (2016): 9508–9517.

[93] Fu, Rui, Zuo Zhang, and Li Li. "Using LSTM and GRU neural network methods for traffic flow prediction." *2016 31st Youth Academic Annual Conference of Chinese Association of Automation (YAC)*. IEEE, 2016.

[94] Liu, Yipeng, et al. "Short-term traffic flow prediction with Conv-LSTM." *2017 9th International Conference on Wireless Communications and Signal Processing (WCSP)*. IEEE, 2017.

[95] Zhang, Junbo, Yu, Zheng, and Dekang Qi. "Deep spatio-temporal residual networks for citywide crowd flows prediction." *Thirty-first AAAI Conference on Artificial Intelligence*. 2017.

[96] Zhang, Shaokun, et al. "Traffic flow prediction based on cascaded artificial neural network." *IGARSS 2018-2018 IEEE International Geoscience and Remote Sensing Symposium*. IEEE, 2018.

[97] Du, Shengdong, et al. "A hybrid method for traffic flow forecasting using multimodal deep learning." arXiv preprint arXiv:1803.02099 (2018).

[98] Lin, Yilun, et al. "Pattern sensitive prediction of traffic flow based on generative adversarial framework." *IEEE Transactions on Intelligent Transportation Systems 20*.6 (2018): 2395–2400.

[99] Liang, Yunyi, et al. "A deep generative adversarial architecture for network-wide spatial-temporal traffic-state estimation." *Transportation Research Record 2672*.45 (2018): 87–105.

[100] Cui, Zhiyong, et al. "Traffic graph convolutional recurrent neural network: A deep learning framework for network-scale traffic learning and forecasting." *IEEE Transactions on Intelligent Transportation Systems 21*.11 (2019): 4883–4894.

[101] Xiao, Yuelei, and Yang Yin. "Hybrid LSTM neural network for short-term traffic flow prediction." *Information 10*.3 (2019): 105.

[102] Zang, Di, et al. "Traffic flow data prediction using residual deconvolution based deep generative network." *IEEE Access 7* (2019): 71311–71322.

[103] Wei, Wangyang, Honghai, Wu, and Huadong Ma. "An autoencoder and LSTM-based traffic flow prediction method." *Sensors 19*.13 (2019): 2946.

Integrated simulation of deep learning, computer vision and physical layer of UAV and ground vehicle networks

15

Aldebaro Klautau, Ilan Correa, Felipe Bastos, Ingrid Nascimento, João Borges and Ailton Oliveira
Federal University of Pará, Pará, Brazil

Pedro Batista
Ericsson Research, Torshamnsgatan, Kista, Sweden

Silvia Lins
Innovation Center, Ericsson Telecomunicações, São Paulo, Brazil

Contents

DOI: 10.1201/9781003190691-20

15.1 INTRODUCTION

Modern mobile networks rely on multiple antennas and algorithms collectively called MIMO (multiple input multiple output). The sixth generation (6G) and beyond will adopt large antenna arrays to enable MIMO systems and higher-frequency bands than the ones currently in use. Before application-specific integrated circuits (ASICs) are available, similar to the situation faced with 5G, the 6G measurement campaigns will require expensive equipment in order to support ultra-massive MIMO and terahertz frequency bands. In this case, proper simulation methodologies for the generation of communication channels can produce abundant data in controlled conditions and fill the gap until measurements are available.

When considering terrestrial and aerial vehicular networks, another trend in 6G is that many relevant use cases rely on machine learning (ML) or, more generally, artificial intelligence (AI), and computer vision. For instance, collaboration among autonomous vehicles strongly depend on computer vision, ML/AI and a reliable communication network. These three distinct domains can be independently simulated, but this chapter will present the advantages and issues when integrating distinct simulation tools in an integrated simulation, as proposed in [1].

The scope of applications that benefit from integrated multidomain simulations is large, and we will focus in this chapter on simulations with the following features:

- Based on realistic **3D computer generated imagery** (CGI) such as those created with the Unreal[1] and Unity[2] engines, and NVIDIA's Omniverse platform.[3]
- Support to **computer vision** given the availability of simulated sensors that collect information from the CGI 3D scenario, such as cameras collecting images or videos.
- Enhanced **mobility** modeling. The 3D scenes are composed by static and mobile objects (UAVs, trains, pedestrians, etc.). The trajectories of the mobile objects are either pre-determined and do not change along the evolution of the simulation or are generated on-the-fly.
- Artificial intelligence/machine learning (**AI/ML**) for optimizing the communication network or as part of the application. In the latter case, the AI/ML can be used, for instance, for object detection and UAV path planning.
- Modeling the **communication channel** based on site-dependent and time-varying communication channel, with special focus on MIMO channels due to the importance of multiple antennas in 5G/6G networks. Instead of using stochastic channel models that aim at capturing the behavior in any scenario (site-independent), we use ray-tracing to obtain realistic characterization of a channel that actually corresponds to given 3D scenario and positions of all mobile objects.

We call a simulation that supports the features mentioned above as CAVIAR (*Communication networks, Artificial intelligence and computer VIsion with 3D computer-generAted imageRy*). A CAVIAR simulation is capable of generating not only communication channels, but also the corresponding sensor data, matched to the scene. The sensors include cameras that capture parts of the 3D scenario, mimicking the images or videos obtained by real cameras in support to computer vision systems. A ML/AI system is also a constituent part of a CAVIAR simulation, and can be used for distinct purposes but the focus here is on deep learning applied to vehicular networks. Such integrated simulation of vehicular networks can be computationally expensive, especially due to the time-varying characteristics imposed by mobile objects such as pedestrians, cars, and UAVs, which compose the computer-generated imagery scenario together with buildings and other fixed-position objects.

As the generation of real data to train AI/ML models is a laborious task, a valid alternative is to leverage synthetic data, such as the ones provided by simulators. However, finding software that simulates different domains, for instance, vehicles physics and communication systems, is not straightforward.

CAVIAR has been originally proposed in [1] and further discussed in [2]. It builds upon the Raymobtime methodology presented in [3] for generating *episodes* of communication channels via ray-tracing to facilitate AI/ML for the 5G physical layer (PHY). CAVIAR is under development and its source code is publicly available.[4] Previous works incorporate some of the features of a CAVIAR simulation [4–6, 7–9]. For instance, an important related work is the Veneris system presented in [5], which uses the Unity engine, an in-house ray-tracing software and the Omnet++ network simulator. The main difference of our CAVIAR simulations and Veneris is the integration of AI/ML and computer vision in CAVIAR, as will be discussed in this chapter. Another distinguishing feature is that CAVIAR relies on the widely adopted and validated commercial ray-tracing software Wireless InSite by Remcom [10–12]. While some ray-tracing packages are specialized in visible light applications, Wireless InSite supports advanced features for frequency bands adopted in wireless communications, such as diffuse scattering when millimeter waves (mmWaves) are used. The ray-tracing tool used in [5] does not support diffuse scattering nor diffractions, being limited to modeling signal propagation via reflections.

The trend toward more realistic and integrated simulations can be observed not only in academia, but also in industry. For instance, NVIDIA's Omniverse platform has been used to enhance Ericsson's radio propagation tools.[5]

This chapter discusses the current status of CAVIAR simulations based on two applications: beam-selection for vehicle-to-infrastructure (V2I) communications; and a vehicle tracking application that relies on computer vision and reinforcement learning for trajectory calculation. Section 15.2 discusses these two applications and related concepts. Section 15.3 discusses integrated simulation methodologies based on Raymobtime and CAVIAR. Section 15.4 presents simulation results and Section 15.5 concludes the chapter.

15.2 APPLICATIONS THAT CAN BENEFIT FROM CAVIAR SIMULATIONS

This section discusses some applications that can benefit from CAVIAR simulations. Given the wide scope of possible applications and to make the discussion concrete, the next section describe two categories of simulations: beam-selection applied to V2I and computer vision application with a UAV-enabled communication network [13]. In the former, the ML/AI system is responsible for optimizing a communication network module: beam-selection. In this case, the trajectories of mobile objects (cars and buses) are predefined. In the latter application, the ML/AI module is part of the application itself, implementing object detection and tracking, and also perform trajectory calculation, with the UAV trajectories changing according to the ML/AI module decisions. In summary, we discuss an example of ML/AI to optimize V2I communications and another in which a ML/AI application relies on a communication network. Before delving in these two examples, we discuss UAV applications in general, with the goal of positioning them with respect to CAVIAR simulations.

15.2.1 Simulation of UAV-enabled AI/ML

Unmanned aerial vehicles (UAVs), popularly known as drones, have emerged as an alternative technology in many fields, such as robotics, traffic surveillance, mineral exploration, Internet drone delivery systems, military, and telecommunications. The growing usage of these devices are evident due to their unique characteristics such as flexibility, mobility, adaptive altitude, and its applicability in wireless networks. Despite these advantages, researchers need to face a key challenge when simulating UAV missions.

An important aspect for simulation regards the UAV autonomy and the placement of functionality in case the UAV is not fully autonomous and part of the processing is executed at the edge or cloud. For instance, the trajectory calculation can be performed by the UAV, but the overall mission may still depend on computer vision for finding targets (e.g., tracking a vehicle based on a video camera and deep learning). In this chapter, we are mainly interested on use cases in which the UAV is not fully autonomous and relies on a communication channel with a terrestrial or aerial base station.

The UAV trajectory and autonomy depends on the *path planning* module. Path planning refers to the movement of an object from a start position to a destination through an optimal route [14]. Also, UAV path planning can be defined as a collision-free optimal path that takes into account drone's maneuverability and environment constraints to move a drone from a start node to an ending point [14, 15].

Path planning should be incorporated in a UAV-based CAVIAR simulation. For instance, in applications in which UAVs are used for the autonomous inspection of large geographical areas, an energy-efficient path planning strategy is essential to maintain communication with the base station(s), eventually also taking in account the cost and reliability of data transmission to the terrestrial base station.

Another component of some simulations is an efficient obstacle avoidance system, because the drone needs to perceive its surrounding and customize its flight pattern for safe operations [16]. In this case, small response time and rapid adjustments are important requirements for trajectory control in real or simulated scenarios.

When UAVs are used as Aerial Base Stations (ABS), there are additional requirements for determining their positioning. The UAV trajectory can be determined to minimize delay and interference between UAV-BSs and for optimal data distribution [17].

One promising approach for determining UAV trajectories is reinforcement learning (RL) [18, 19], which will be briefly discussed here. The majority of RL approaches consider regular exploratory policies for search paths in autonomous flight, which is not suitable for rapid algorithm convergence in environments where rewards are sparse. In this type of environment, actions taken by the RL agent do not bring immediate rewards, which is the case with UAV missions, where drone departure from a start position, need to achieve a specific goal and only receives feedback from the environment when it arrives in the destination.

In this context, intrinsic motivated RL becomes an alternative to solve the reward sparsity problem, where intrinsic rewards are introduced as intermediate rewards used to guide agent and help to accelerate algorithm convergence [20]. Results of intrinsic motivation applied to computational vision presented performance improvement of DRL methods in addition to solutions for sparse rewards settings [20]. Therefore, we can say that intrinsic motivated RL has the potential to tackle problems of trajectory generation in complex scenarios, such as autonomous flight in urban areas where blockage elements are usual, multiple UAV base stations (UAV-BSs) interference scenarios and path planning for long missions.

In summary, there are several possible architectures when adopting solutions based on AI/ML for the mentioned UAV-enabled applications. Some of these solutions are cloud-centric and require frequent data exchange between the UAV and a central-entity [16]. When evaluating a solution, it is sometimes important to conceive an integrated simulation that allows to observe the tradeoffs among the several subsystems. A CAVIAR simulation enables such evaluation as will be discussed in future sections. The next subsection discusses beam-selection.

15.2.2 Beam-selection for V2I

There is a clear trend toward smarter and more automated vehicles, which pushes the deployment of a variety of sensors, such as cameras, LIDAR, GPS, etc. These sensors are related, for example, with detection of pedestrians and other vehicles, interpretation of signaling on the streets, automatic and semi-automatic driving, and so on. In a standalone vehicle, these sensors are limited in range, as they are, in general, able to detect only objects that are in the line of sight of the vehicle. These restrictions motivate the increasing connectivity of these vehicles, which, in turn, motivate more applications of vehicle-to-vehicle (V2V), V2I, and even vehicle-to-everything (V2X) communications. These connectivity options allow a vehicle to bypass the line-of-sight limitation of their sensors, as it is possible to "view" the environment by the "eyes" of other vehicles, which is known as cooperative perception. Moreover, it is also possible to have a centralized entity, such as a server in the core of a mobile network controlling the vehicles with an overview of the environment provided by the sensors of several vehicles.

One of the connectivity options that can be integrated into vehicles is the dedicated short-range communications (DSRC), which is based on the IEEE 802.11p-Wireless Access for Vehicular Environments (WAVE), and allows data rates in the order of dozens of Mbps over a range of up to 1000 meters [21]. However, this technology may be insufficient to allow exchanging all the required sensors data on a large scale. For example, sensors have distinct data rate requirements: radars require less than 1 Mbps; cameras require 100–700 Mbps for raw images, and 10–90 Mbps for compressed images; while LIDARs require 10–100 Mbps [22]. In contrast, mmWave 5G communication is a technology with the potential to fulfill these data rate requirements. The requirements of V2X scenarios have been defined in 3GPP's technical specifications TS 22.185 and TS 22.186. In Cellular V2X (C-V2X), one of the applications refers to intelligent transportation systems (ITSs), which aim to improve traffic safety and increase efficiency. This can be referred to as platooning, where several trucks drive very close to each other and follow the first truck in the platoon, thereby saving fuel and reducing CO_2 emissions. There are several other applications as 5G uses cases, comprising eMBB, URLLC, and mMTC [23].

The two mmWave standards that are used in V2X scenarios are IEEE 802.11ad, with a peak data rate of 6.75 Gbps, and 5G, with a peak data rate of 20 Gbps. These data rates allow the exchange of the huge amount of information generated by the sensors in the newer vehicles. However, a drawback of the mmWave bands is the higher attenuation in comparison to sub-6 GHz frequencies. Thus, multiple-input multiple-output (MIMO) techniques at mmWave bands are one of the main technologies considered in the development of 5G, since they provide better directionality of the electromagnetic wave, allowing to circumvent the high path attenuation. Moreover, MIMO can also allow increasing system capacity over the same available time-frequency resources, thus increasing significantly the spectral efficiency.

A challenge of massive MIMO at mmWave frequencies is that the beams formed by the beamforming techniques can be very narrow, requiring that the beams of the transmitter and the receiver point to each other accurately. A process called beam training is part of standards such IEEE 802.11ad, 5G, and other wireless networks [24]. Due to the high number of possible beams, the search for the best beam pair for the transmitter and the receiver can be a time-consuming process. As a means to solve this issue, many recent works are applying machine learning techniques to predict the beams [25]. Some works rely on pilot signals, which are exchanged to allow channel estimation and the prediction of the beam pair [26]. The option of using pilot signals is also challenging due to the high number of antennas, which requires a high number of pilots to be exchanged, consuming wireless resources.

To overcome the issues of finding the optimum beam pair and the exchange of pilots previously discussed, other works evaluate the prediction of the beam pair by using information available only on one side, to avoid the need of exchanging pilots. For example, in a mobile network in which vehicles are connected to the network, and have distinct sensors, these data can be used to predict the beam based on its surroundings. These distinct types of input data may impact the prediction performance. Examples of data available from the sensors are GPS data, images captured from cameras, and data from LIDAR sensors. From the BS side, the positions of several vehicles in the cell could be used to construct a position matrix [3, 27]. The position matrix represents a scenario in which a vehicle that contains the receiving antenna (RX), which is the target of the current packet, while the other vehicles are potentially blocking the LOS of the RX. Thus, this position matrix could provide to an ML algorithm the information required to predict the beam pair.

Mathematically, the beam selection problem can be modeled as follows. The MIMO system corresponds to a transmitter with N_t antenna elements at the BS and the receiver vehicle with N_r antennas.

FIGURE 15.1   Generic representation of a fully digital MIMO architecture.

Both the BS and the vehicle can adopt distinct antenna array configurations, such as a Uniform Linear Array (ULA), a Uniform Planar Array (UPA), or a Uniform Circular Array (UCA). Moreover, the BS and the vehicle can adopt analog, hybrid, and digital MIMO architectures. For example, Figure 15.1 shows an example of the processing chains in the transmitter and receiver, both with a fully digital MIMO architecture, which consists of several Radio Frequency (RF) chains composed by a digital-to-analog converter (DAC) in the transmit chain or an analog-to-digital converter (ADC) in the receiver chain, connected to an RF chain and an antenna. In all the MIMO architectures options, the MIMO channel between the BS and the vehicle is represented by an $N_r \times N_t$ matrix H. In the beam-selection problem, the goal is to find the best indexes of the transmitter and receiver codebooks. Figure 15.1 also depicts the beams of the transmitter and receiver.

In a digital MIMO architecture, the codebooks could be obtained, for example, from the Discrete Fourier Transform (DFT) matrices and denoted by $C_t = \{\bar{w}_1, \ldots, \bar{w}_{N_t}\}$ and $C_r = \{\bar{f}_1, \ldots, \bar{f}_{N_r}\}$. They are used at the transmitter and the receiver sides, respectively. Thus, the beam-selection goal is to choose the beam pair $[p, q]$ for the transmitter and the receiver. This pair can be represented by a unique index $i \in \{1, 2, \ldots, M\}$, where $M \leq N_t N_r$, with each index p (or q) generating a specific radiation pattern. For the i-th index, the equivalent channel can be calculated as:

$$y_i = w_i^* H f_i, \tag{15.1}$$

and the optimal beam index $\hat{i}$ is given by:

$$\hat{i} = \arg\max_{i \in \{1,\ldots,M\}} |y_i|. \tag{15.2}$$

Instead of estimating $\hat{i}$ by beam sweeping or similar methods that require overhead signaling, in this chapter we assume that an estimate of $\hat{i}$ is provided by an AI/ML module, such as a deep neural network [3, 27].

In order to assess the solutions to problems discussed in this section, realistic and consistent channels H are required. The next section discusses Raymobtime, a methodology to create such channels, and CAVIAR, the simulation architecture which integrates the communication network with vehicular networks, computer vision and AI/ML.

15.3 MULTI-DOMAIN INTEGRATED SIMULATORS

This section discusses the Raymobtime and CAVIAR multidomain integrated simulations. Before discussing them, this section introduces some tools to create the multidomain simulations. These tools include options to generate realistic virtual-world scenarios from real places, mobility simulators, sensors, and communication channels. Each mentioned tool is briefly discussed in the following paragraphs.

- **Realistic maps**: Both methodologies presented in this chapter are based on simulations in a virtual world, in which the mobile receivers, such as pedestrians and vehicles are inserted. The mobile receiver can interact with the environment of the virtual world, as well as the simulated telecommunication signals. One option to generate such virtual worlds is gathering data from real places via databases such as OpenStreetMaps. The software called Cadmapper allows generating an initial 3D virtual world from the 2D data from the map. Another option is to rely on 3D scenarios available on game engines, such as Unreal and Unity. An advantage of using maps from game engines is that they are, in general, more detailed than the ones from OpenStreetMaps and Cadmapper, as the developers can polish the scenario. Scenarios from OpenStreetMaps and Cadmapper can also present the same level of details, but it would be needed to include the details, while maps from game engines are readily available. One disadvantage of maps from game engines is that they may not be freely available. Another tool is the Cesium plug-in for Epic Game's Unreal Engine, which integrates photogrammetric information obtained from drones into 3D models available via Cadmapper and other sites. This plug-in complements tools such as Twinmotion, which facilitate the construction of 3D virtual worlds.
- **Mobility simulators**: Simulators of vehicle and pedestrian mobility provide flexibility to investigate the impact of mobility in V2I and related applications. The main role of a traffic simulator is to facilitate modeling mobility, especially the motions of both transceivers and potential scatter in the environment. Traffic simulators are specialized tools with plenty of features to describe vehicles with distinct characteristics, interaction with pedestrians, and infrastructure, such as traffic lights, etc. They enable the user to depart from simplistic scenarios, such as those in which all vehicles have a constant speed, and simplifies the experiment configuration, and grants the user flexibility, for instance, to impose trajectories to any object or person, use distinct speeds, etc. For example, the open-source Simulation of Urban Mobility (SUMO) [28] is a traffic simulator that facilitates modeling mobility. Another tool is Airsim, which is a plug-in for Unreal Engine 4 that offers physically and visually realistic simulations. Airsim has sensor models, such as GPS, and the possibility to register trajectories from UAVs and cars. It allows the use of hardware-in-the-loop (HITL) simulations, in which a real drone flight controller is connected to the machine running the simulation, improving the realism of the UAV dynamics [29]. Moreover, Airsim also includes a physics engine that models some physical phenomena related to ground and aerial vehicle dynamics, for instance, gravity, magnetic field, air pressure and density, linear and angular drag, etc.
- **RGB cameras**: Nowadays, the presence of one or more cameras in vehicles is common. For example, cameras can be used for parking assistance or can substitute rearview mirrors in vehicles, providing a view of the surroundings to the driver on a display. Other cameras could also be used, for example, to detect lanes and cameras to interpret signs on the streets. Thus, realistic simulation of V2X scenarios should integrate cameras, mainly in the vehicles, as previously discussed, but also cameras can be integrated with pedestrians and infrastructure objects in the virtual world. An example of software that supports images generation is the mentioned Airsim. Airsim has an API to position available cameras in any arbitrary pose, and collect images such as depth, disparity, surface normal, or object segmentation.
- **LIDAR**: Modern vehicles may also include other sensors, such as LIDAR. The software that allows simulate sensor data is the Free Open-Source Simulation Package for Light Detection and Ranging (LIDAR/LADAR) and Kinect sensors, which is known shortly as BlenSor.[6] It is a plug-in for the Blender[7] software and allows to simulate ranging technologies, such as time of flight, line laser, and rotating laser scanners. This conveniently allows the development of algorithms for those sensors without the need to possess a real sensor.
- **Ray-tracing-based communication channels**: Ray-tracing (RT) is considered a promising simulation strategy for wireless communication channels. RT is specially of interest for 5G and 6G systems due to the frequency bands involved. Before application-specific integrated circuits (ASICs) are available for 6G, similar to the situation faced in 5G, the 6G measurement

campaigns will require expensive equipment to characterize mmWave and terahertz frequency bands for MIMO transmissions. In this context, realistic simulators provide very accurate insights of the signal transmission for generating abundant data in controlled conditions and fill the gap until measurements are available. RT can provide very accurate results [30, 31] but its computational cost increases exponentially with the maximum allowed number of reflections and diffractions [32]. Another issue of RT is that the generated channels are site specific, depending on the specific propagation environment. The site-dependency can be an advantage or disadvantage, depending on the adopted assessment methodology.

15.3.1 Wireless channel generation with Raymobtime

Raymobtime is a methodology for collecting realistic datasets for simulating wireless communications. It uses ray-tracing and 3D scenarios with mobility and time evolution, for obtaining consistency over time, frequency and space. For instance, a 3D outdoor scenario can be exported from Cadmapper,[8] and imported to Wireless InSite.[9] The traffic simulation can be made using Simulator for Urban Mobility (SUMO), combining the information from the Cadmapper 3D model and the location of streets from OpenStreetMaps.[10] The channels generation methodology is described in [3], and relies on Remcom's Wireless InSite ray-tracing simulator.

SUMO and InSite operate in a unified scenario, where SUMO is invoked to generate the positions of the mobile users (vehicles and pedestrians). Those positions are imported in a three-dimensional (3D) scenario along with their 3D models. Then, InSite performs ray-tracing in the scenario, and the L strongest rays are stored for each transmitter–receiver pair. The stored information includes path loss (α_l), delay (dl), transmitter and receiver's angles of departure and arrival in azimuth (φ^D_1 and φ^{DA}_1) and elevation (θ^D_1 and θ^A_1), and phase. The combination of SUMO and InSite allows the generation of accurate and time-correlated channels, including effects from the mobility of the scenario components, such as receivers, vehicles, and scatterers, representing, for example, V2I and FW communication scenarios. Raymobtime also incorporates simulations of LIDAR (via BlenSor), cameras (via Blender), and positions to enable investigations in which machine learning and other techniques rely on such features.

The nomenclature defined in [3] consists of scenes s and episodes e. An episode e of T_{epi} seconds is composed of a set of $N = T_{epi}/T$ scenes separated by T seconds. Before starting the first episode, SUMO is invoked until the configured number of mobile users "arrive" in the scenario. After an episode, several scenes are skipped before starting a new episode to improve scenario diversity. The spatial consistency relies on keeping the mobility history of the mobile users and the simulators are invoked for each scene. Once the mobile objects are positioned in the scenes, the InSite simulator can be invoked to perform the ray-tracing on the scenario.

The Raymobtime methodology is based on a Python orchestrator code to repeatedly invoke the traffic simulator, which works as shown in Figure 15.2. The orchestrator converts the vehicles' position to a format that can be interpreted by the Wireless InSite RT simulator, which is, then, invoked to generate the ray-tracing simulations. Lastly, post-processing is made on the RT results to create episodes, as depicted in Figure 15.2.

The main steps of the Raymobtime methodology can be organized into configuration and simulation stages. In the configuration stage (elements on the left in Figure 15.2), the user provides, e.g., information to enable conversion of coordinates between the two main software. To facilitate the interaction with the traffic simulator, the orchestrator associates each mobile transmitter or receiver to a mobile object (MOBJ). A MOBJ can also simply play the role of a blocker or scatterer, with no associated transceiver. In the configuration stage, for each episode, the user specifies the base scenario files. The base scenario files, together with positions for all MOBJs, specified by the traffic simulator, compose all information required for a complete RT simulation.

In the simulation stage, the orchestrator invokes the traffic simulator and then positions the MOBJs to compose a scene. Based on the output of the traffic simulator, some files of the base scenario are modified

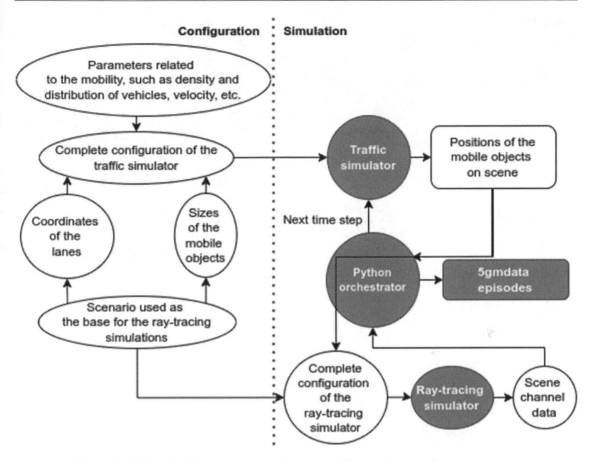

FIGURE 15.2   Methodology that integrates ray-tracing and traffic simulators.

and stored in a unique folder. For each scene, this folder path is stored to allow reproducing the RT simulation of that scene. This enables the user to later extract additional information through customized software routines, as well as visualize results for a scene using the RT and traffic simulator's GUIs. Similarly, the corresponding information about the traffic simulation is recorded. For instance, this allows retrieving the positions (x, y, z) and dimensions (l, w, h) of all MOBJs in a given time instant. The Raymobtime methodology results in the creation of simulation data of 5G mmWave MIMO systems involving mobility (or 5GMdata) that can be used in different applications. The following paragraphs describe each type of data generated by the Raymobtime methodology.

Figure 15.3 shows an example of the ray-tracing simulation in a 3D scenario. The generated channel data is organized in a 4D structure ($N \times N_R \times N_L \times N_p$), which are the number of scenes, the number of receivers, the maximum number of rays (paths), and the rays' parameters. Each ray has eight path parameters, which are the received power (dBm), time of arrival (seconds), angle of arrival and departure (both azimuth and elevation), flag '1'for a line-of-sight ray or '0' for non-line of sight, and path phase (degrees). The position of each vehicle in the dataset is available, as well as an angle indicating their current instantaneous movement direction.

Raymobtime datasets may also include simulated LIDAR data obtained with the software BlenSor. The process consists of placing the vehicles in the 3D scenario for each scene, then LIDAR sensors are added for each vehicle that is received in the ray-tracing simulation. The LIDAR scan is performed and saved in a .pcd file, which stores the coordinates of the spots where the light reflected. Figure 15.4 shows an example of LIDAR data that is obtained in Raymobtime with the Blender Sensor Simulation (BlenSor) [33].

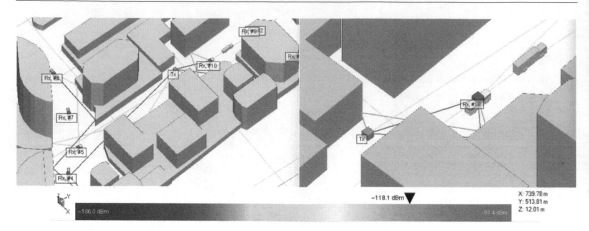

FIGURE 15.3   An example of ray-tracing with InSite.

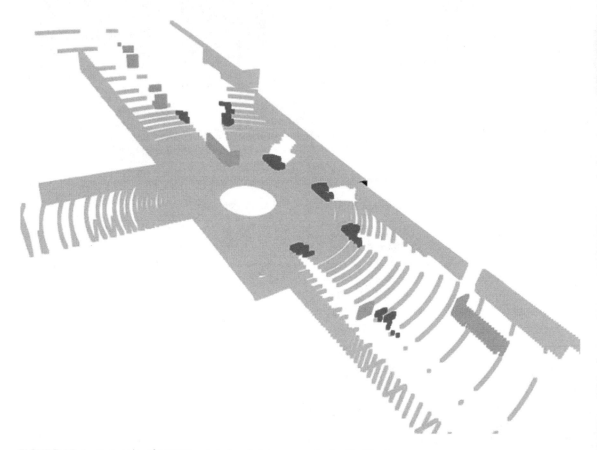

FIGURE 15.4   Example of LIDAR point cloud data generated with BlenSor.

Raymobtime dataset may also include RGB images, which are extracted with photo-realistic textures added to the 3D objects. Four cameras are positioned on the top of each vehicle, such that each camera is directed to one end of the vehicle. The cameras were positioned at an angle of 90 degrees. Figure 15.5 shows the cameras positioned in a vehicle and an example of images obtained by each camera in a given vehicle. This way, during a simulation, due to temporal mobility, each vehicle that is a receiver has its position varied and there are four images, one for each camera and scene.

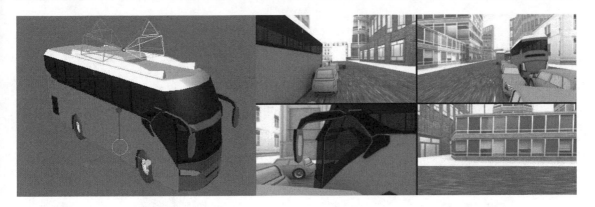

FIGURE 15.5   An example camera positioning on the top of a bus and images captured by a camera mounted on the top of a car.

15.3.2 Caviar simulations

The two main architectures of a CAVIAR simulation [1] are depicted in Figure 15.6 and Figure 15.7. These architectures differ by the position of the AI/ML engine. In Figure 15.6, the AI/ML engine is within

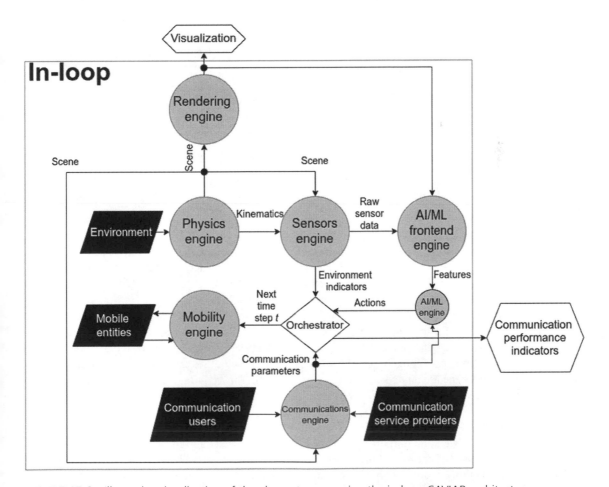

FIGURE 15.6   Illustrative visualization of the elements composing the in-loop CAVIAR architecture.

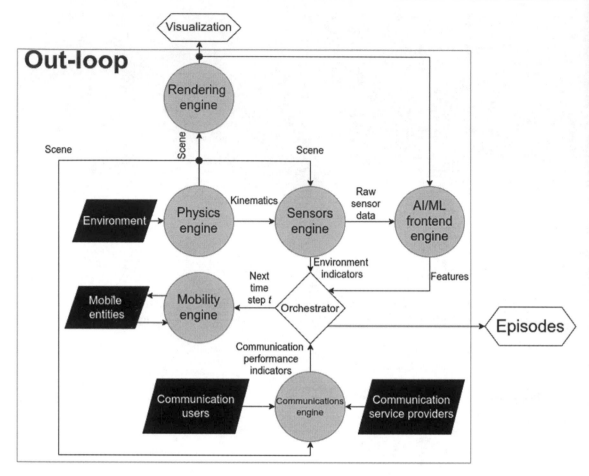

FIGURE 15.7   Example of the elements composing an out-loop CAVIAR simulation. Note the absence of the "AI/ML engine" element.

the simulation loop, which advances every time step t. In contrast, this AI/ML engine is not part of Figure 15.7, because it is executed offline, based on the data *episodes* generated by the simulation. Therefore, we call "in-loop" and "out-loop" the architectures in Figures 15.6 and 15.7, respectively. The out-loop is simpler in the sense that the trajectories of all mobile entities are pre-determined and do not depend on the AI/ML engine. This implies that the communication channels can be calculated along the CAVIAR simulation and all pertinent data stored as episodes for subsequent processing.

An out-loop CAVIAR simulation can be considered as a mean to generate rich datasets, with paired information [1]. However, some applications require an in-loop CAVIAR. For instance, consider the problem in which the ML/AI engine implements a RL agent that tries to optimize a vehicle (e.g. UAV) trajectory. At each time step t, the RL agent decides for an action that modifies the environment, repositioning the UAV and changing the associated communication channel. This requires an in-loop CAVIAR simulation, such that the agent actions can properly affect the simulation flow. The following paragraphs provide more details about the features that the two architectures have in common.

Taking as reference the in-loop CAVIAR in Figure 15.6, its engines interact with each other in an orchestrated fashion, generating outputs that can be further processed and returned during the simulation. The digital **environment** is composed of a 3D scenery with fixed and mobile objects. These objects can be created with specialized tools, such as Blender, and with data from collaborative and/or open-source databases of geospatial information, for example, OpenStreetMap (OSM). The positions and influences of the mobile objects in the simulation are determined by a **physics engine** (for instance, using the Unreal Engine) and a **mobility engine** (e.g., the Simulation of Urban MObility (SUMO)). The models and positions of all entities compose a "scene." Once the scene is complete, it can be represented via sensors (such as GPS or cameras). A ray-tracing application (e.g. Remcom's Wireless InSite) acts as part of the **communications engine** and estimates the channel for the given scene. Based on this channel, scripts executed by the communications engine can use models to generate all parameters and metrics of interest. The **sensors engine** output constitutes the input to the **AI/ML frontend engine**, which is an optional block that preprocesses the data before being sent to the **AI/ML engine**, which is expected to implement the AI model that generate actions based on the acquired features. The actions suggested by the AI/ML engine are then implemented by the **orchestrator**, that also considers parameters from the communications engine and environment. This orchestrator can output predicted performance indicators and actions to optimize the network performance. An example of output in the context of beam selection, for instance, would be a list of codebook indices to be tried to avoid a full beam sweeping.

15.4 SIMULATIONS RESULTS

This section presents results for two distinct simulations. The main goal is to contrast the different requirements and highlight the involved issues with respect to computational time and accuracy.

15.4.1 Beam selection for V2I with lidar as input

The results discussed in the next paragraphs were obtained with an out-loop CAVIAR simulation, for which all mobile objects were positioned by the mobility software SUMO. The BlenSor plugin was used to obtain simulated LIDAR data from the 3D scenario. Moreover, LIDAR data was used as input of a DNN model, as it can be used to decrease the overhead of communication systems [33]. The strategy is to collect LIDAR raw data (a point cloud) and extract features that can feed a deep neural network (DNN). The raw data was transformed in parameters to the DNN using a multidimensional histogram, as detailed in [33].

The topology of the DNN is described in Table 15.1. The DNN is trained to select a good subset of beam indices. An important aspect is that the DNN is trained in matched conditions, in the sense that the 3D scenario used for training is also the one adopted for testing. In this case, the DNN model is capable of learning prior information imposed by the 3D scenario, such as preferred signal propagation directions. Adapting the model to other (mismatched) scenarios using transfer learning or similar technique is an important research area, but out of the scope of this chapter.

In the simulations, both BS and UE have uniform linear arrays (ULAs), with $N_t = 32$ and $N_r = 8$ antennas, respectively. We used the ray-tracing data to generate the communication channel, as shown in [3]. The carrier frequency of 60 GHz was used, a narrowband MIMO communication channel was adopted, which is equivalent to evaluating the transmission in a single ($K = 1$) subcarrier of an Orthogonal Frequency Division Multiplexing (OFDM) signal. The ray-tracing data used in the simulations had up to 25 multipath components (MPCs), which means that the ray-tracing simulation from InSite can save up to 25 rays if such a quantity can arrive at the receiver with significant power, according to the configurations of the RT simulations. Table 15.2 summarizes the parameters adopted for the communication system.

The rays from the RT simulation were converted to a MIMO channel [3] considering a Uniform Linear Array (ULA). The codebooks were generated as described in Section 15.2.2. To generate the labels for supervised learning, all codewords of the codebook were analyzed to find the one that results in the largest combined channel magnitude of Equation (15.1), which is equivalent to the largest received power, and the results were assessed accordingly. Thus, the beam indexes $[p, q]$ that generate the greatest magnitude is the optimum beam (top-1). Figure 15.8 depicts the histograms for the optimum pair of indices

TABLE 15.1 Parameters of the convolutional deep neural network adopted in the simulations

LIDAR – DNN PARAMETERS		
Input shape	20 × 200 × 10	relu
Conv2D #1	kernel size: 13 × 13	relu
Conv2D #2	kernel size: 11 × 11	relu
MaxPooling2D and Dropout	pool size: 2 × 1	relu
Conv2D #3	kernel size: 7 × 7	relu
MaxPooling2D	pool size: 1 × 2	relu
Conv2D #4	kernel size: 5 × 5	relu
Dropout		
Conv2D #5	kernel size: 3 × 3	relu
Conv2D #6	kernel size: 1 × 1	relu
Dense	M neurons	softmax

TABLE 15.2 Parameters of the communication systems adopted in the simulations

SIGNAL AND MIMO PARAMETERS	
Number N_r of antennas at receiver	8
Number N_t of antennas at transmitter	32
Carrier frequency	60 GHz
Subcarriers	K = 1
Maximum number of MPCs	25
Antenna array	ULA
Transmitter codebook	m = N_t and n = N_t
Receiver codebook	m = N_r and n = N_r

(top-1), when combining the transmitter and receiver indices in a single index. There is a total of 256 possible pairs in this case and the ones close to 150 are the ones that are the optimum more often due to their preferred directions coinciding with the geometry of the 3D scenario.

The performance of the convolutional deep neural network model was compared with two baselines, which are referred to as *Occurrence* and *Dummy*. The performance for the DNN and of the *Occurrence* and *Dummy* baselines are shown in Figure 15.9. The *Occurrence* baseline chooses the beam pair randomly, but it considers a weighted probability according to percentages of occurrences in the histogram of Figure 15.8. Thus, the *Occurrence* baseline presents a very high likelihood of choosing the beam pair number 151 or close numbers. The *Dummy* baseline simply randomly picks a number from 1 to 256. The DNN uses the LIDAR data and outputs the likelihood of each beam pair to be the top-1. Figure 15.9 shows the validation performance during the training per epoch and for top-1 (categorical accuracy), top-5, top-10, top-30, and top-50. The higher the k of the top-k classification presented in Figure 15.10, the easier is to predict correctly. It happens because in top-k classification, the model picks k candidates and this prediction is considered correct if the optimum beam pair as in Equation (15.2) is among these k selected pairs. Figure 15.9 shows the DNN model always performs better than the other baselines. When the model is deployed, an exhaustive beam-sweeping search can be adopted only for the top-k pairs, which represents a smaller overhead when compared to sweeping over all 256 pairs.

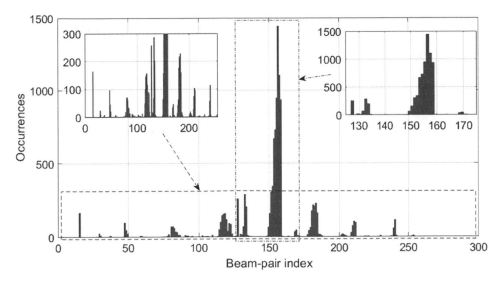

FIGURE 15.8   Histogram of the occurrences of the beam pair index as the one (top-1) that leads to the combined channel with the largest magnitude.

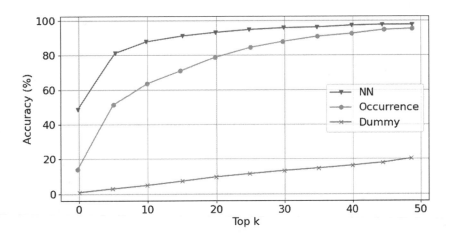

FIGURE 15.9   Accuracy of the top-k beam pair prediction for the DNN and the baselines.

Figure 15.10 provides a more detailed view of the convergence along training epochs of the DNN models. In Figure 15.9 a test set that is disjoint from the training set was adopted, while in Figure 15.10, the accuracy was obtained with the training set itself.

15.4.2 In-loop CAVIAR simulation of a computer vision application

This subsection discusses a computer vision simulation in which a UAV, equipped with a camera, must follow a vehicle. This can be associated to a robbery situation and has similarities to many other security-related applications of object tracking [34, 35]. In this specific case, the drone with the camera, denoted as UAV-A, can communicate with the cloud with the assistance of another drone, which plays the role of a wireless base station and is called UAV-BS. AI/ML is adopted for two main tasks: a) vehicle tracking using computer vision and b) determining the UAV trajectories via reinforcement learning. The simulation must provide information about the following key performance indicators: a) the accuracy of object detection,

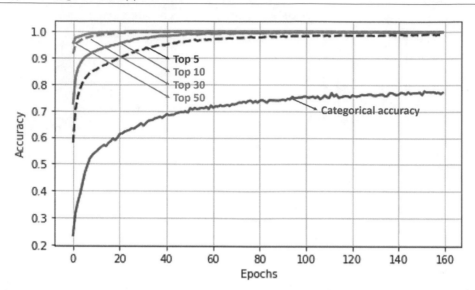

FIGURE 15.10   Progress over epochs of training a DNN with several top-k curves indicated.

FIGURE 15.11   UAV-based vehicle tracking: image from a 3D CGI collected by UAV. It shows a car with the surrounding bounding box indicated by a Yolo deep neural network.

b) demanded bit rate, c) UAVs' energy consumption and d) total mission time. Figure 15.11 depicts an object detection result. The adopted 3D scenario for this simulation is the same as used in the 2021 ITU Machine Learning for 5G Challenge,[11] and there is a video illustrating it.[12]

The application represented in Figure 15.11 is an example of connected AI/ML, in which the object detection algorithm and trajectory planning are not executed on the UAVs, but on the cloud. Therefore, the performance of these algorithms strongly depends on the communication channel. For instance, in [36], it has been shown that a severely impaired communication link may eliminate the chance of executing object detection or the UAV capability to follow a trajectory without deviations.

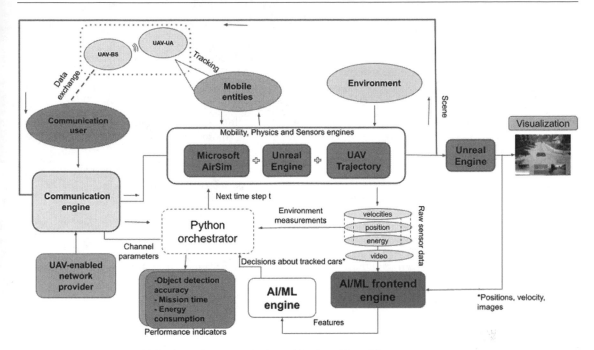

FIGURE 15.12   UAV vehicle detection scenario based in CAVIAR architecture.

In applications in which UAVs are used for vehicle detection, image data containing valuable information about vehicle dynamics, such as position and velocities, is collected by the UAV. However, the hardware available on the drone is not always capable of performing complex analysis. So, to process this information, the image data must be sent to the cloud, where it can pass through a process of feature extraction and shape detection to enable vehicle tracking. In the implemented CAVIAR simulation, this is achieved with the support of a UAV-BS as shown in Figure 15.12.

In this scheme, the UAV-A trajectory and the mobile entities' dynamics, such as the cars, are reproduced with the mobility, physics, and sensors engines, composed by AirSim and Unreal Engine. During the simulation, all the relevant raw data are sent to AI/ML frontend engine to be pre-processed, and later follows to the AI/ML module implemented using Keras and Tensorflow libraries. In this module, decisions, such as the trajectory to follow, will be determined from the positions, velocity, and images of the tracked cars. The Python orchestrator implements these decisions and also considers measurements from the environment to adjust actions accordingly. To consider the impact of the quality of the communication link on the application performance, ray-tracing is used to obtain consistent channels. Wireless InSite works as a communication engine and provide channel parameters to the orchestrator, which is extracted from every scene of the simulation. These channel parameters determine the data rate that can be achieved by the drone during the mission, which can affect its capability of concluding the mission.

15.4.3 Impact of 3D model accuracy on wireless channels

The described in-loop CAVIAR simulation validated the benefits of an integrated simulation, but uncovered a key issue: the ray-tracing simulation of a single scene for the adopted 3D scenario required, on average, 19.7 minutes in a personal computer with a GPU board. In this case, it is prohibitive to adopt a small sampling interval. On the other hand, the communication channel can change substantially over seconds and a complete episode may last for several minutes. Due to its importance, this subsection discusses this fundamental tradeoff between the level of details adopted in the descriptions of the 3D scenario and the accuracy of the corresponding communication channel. Because in 5G and 6G the simulations are used before plenty of measurement data are available, the question is how much details should be incorporated at each stage of the integrated simulation.

It is useful to make an analogy between the current status of simulations and datasets generation in 5G/6G with what happened in automatic speech recognition (ASR). ASR history proved that, sometimes, refining a specific aspect of the simulation methodology aiming at realistic experiments ends up not being necessary. The TIMIT speech corpus developed in 1986 had carefully time-aligned phonetic transcriptions, which took 100 to 1000 hours of work to transcribe each hour of speech. But training current ASR systems with machine learning does not require phonetic transcriptions and simply use an orthographic transcription that is not time-aligned.

In order to reach 5G/6G simulation results that can be trusted, this sort of "overzealousness" when designing TIMIT should be repeated in communications, while datasets and measurements for 6G are being developed. The experiments that will be described here are steps along this direction. Our hypothesis is that we can start with very sophisticated models, leading to high computational costs, and incrementally simplify them by continuously monitoring the accuracy and key performance indicators until the point that there is sensible discrepancy between the simpler model and its predecessors.

The proposed strategy to deal with the cost of ray-tracing simulations is to continue using realistic 3D models (vehicles, environment, buildings, etc.) in CAVIAR simulations while executing engines such as Unreal, but use a paired simpler model when switching to ray-tracing. In fact, Wireless InSite has a tool that allows to choose the level of details when importing a 3D model. It is well known that the complexity of 3D objects increases the duration of the ray-tracing simulation. In [37], some experiments were done in order to measure how the levels of details of 3D models can affect a ray-tracing simulation. We complement these results with newer ones here.

The simulations generated communication channels for serving a UAV flying over an urban canyon. We created three variations of this urban canyon and related models, as depicted in Figure 15.13. The first variant, called large (L), uses a more elaborated drone model and detailed buildings and street objects, such as traffic lights and garbage cans, trying to faithfully replicate the diverse environment of a real city. The second one, medium (M), also uses detailed models but removes the street objects. Finally, in the third one, small (S), all buildings are modeled as simple boxes and a cube represents the drone.

The experiments also used three levels of electromagnetic materials diversity: large (L), medium (M), and small (S), to verify if it also impacts the simulations. The level L uses 10 different materials, the level M 5 different materials, and the level S just 2 different materials (for instance, concrete and metal, as defined by Wireless InSite). In the following plots, SL means the "small" variation with respect to details in 3D models and the "large" diversity in electromagnetic materials. The other combinations (SS, SM, LM, etc.) follow the same convention: the second letter refers to the materials diversity.

Figure 15.14 shows that the level of details of 3D models (number of faces, etc.) affect the result of simulations significantly. In this study, it had a greater impact than the material diversity. Each simulation presented different results, but the simulations with very simple 3D models (S) presented completely different behavior from the other experiments, which is an indication that our suggested strategy of starting by very complex models can be useful.

In Figure 15.15 it can be noticed that the simpler models have a lower delay spread, especially when the UAV is at lower heights. Due to the low level of detail, simulations with fewer faces produce less ray

L   **M**   **S**

FIGURE 15.13   3D scenario variations.

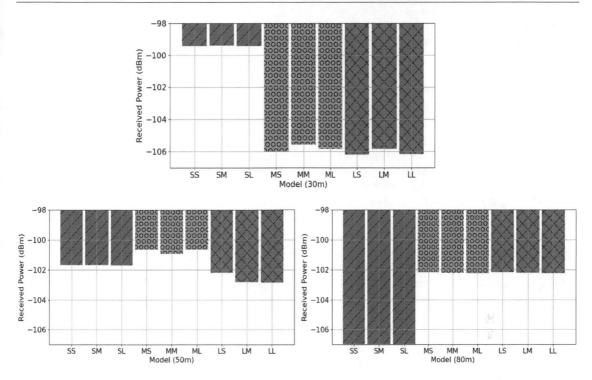

FIGURE 15.14   Received power by the UAV.

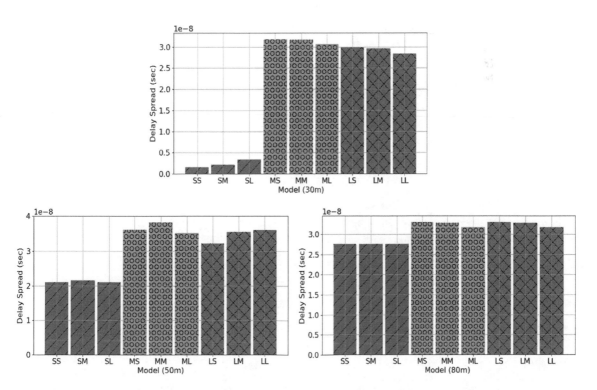

FIGURE 15.15   Delay spread of the simulations with the UAV.

scattering, thus reducing the number of rays reaching the receiver. We conclude promoting the strategy of obtaining ray-tracing channels with a lower computational cost by simplifying the 3D models, while guaranteeing that the results are not discrepant.

15.5 CONCLUSIONS

We discussed CAVIAR simulations within the context of beam selection for V2I and UAB-enabled vehicle tracking. CAVIAR is an architecture that promotes the integrated simulation of a communication network with AI/ML applications, leveraging on 3D scenarios that enable computer vision applications.

It has been shown that out-loop simulations are easier to implement, but not as flexible as the in-loop ones. As an example, the beam selection for V2I can rely on MIMO channels and LIDAR point clouds that are computed once and used to generate the outputs and inputs for training a DNN model. Once these input features and desired outputs are defined, they can be repeatedly used to train several distinct AI/ML models and tune their parameters via automatic model selection. On the other hand, simulations in which the environment changes based on decisions of the AI/ML models that are being assessed, require the more complex in-loop simulations.

Using the vehicle tracking as the target application, we explored the simulators that were integrated in order to enable assessing the tradeoffs among object detection and trajectory calculation. The combined usage of Unreal and AirSim brings a good level of realism in terms of 3D scenario and physics. But the relatively large number of details in scenes strongly impact the computational cost of ray-tracing. For instance, the ray-tracing simulation of a single scene for the adopted scenario required approximately 20 minutes in a personal computer with a GPU board. Taking in account that applications that require a sampling interval in the order of milliseconds and total durations of several seconds, it becomes clear that the cost of ray-tracing would be prohibitive.

It is clear that integrated simulations will evolve and enable sophisticated evaluations of new algorithms. Faster hardware and software will contribute for that. But it is also important to tune the simulations parameters to avoid using too much details in case they are not necessary. Along this direction, future work includes decreasing the computational time by finding the proper tradeoff between 3D scene details and the accuracy of the corresponding communication channel when this 3D scene is imported by the ray-tracer.

ACKNOWLEDGMENTS

This work was supported in part by the Innovation Center, Ericsson Telecomunicacões S.A., Brazil, CNPq and the Capes Foundation.

NOTES

1   https://www.unrealengine.com/
2   https://unity.com/
3   https://www.ericsson.com/en/blog/2021/4/5g-simulation-omniverse-platform
4   https://github.com/lasseufpa/ITU-Challenge-ML5G-PHY

5   https://www.ericsson.com/en/blog/2021/4/5g-simulation-omniverse-platform
6   https://www.BlenSor.org/
7   https://www.blender.org/
8   https://cadmapper.com/
9   https://www.remcom.com/
10 https://www.openstreetmap.org/
11 https://challenge.aiforgood.itu.int/match/matchitem/39
12 https://www.youtube.com/watch?v=6o6PUsbaWnA&ab_channel=LASSE-UFPA

REFERENCES

[1] A. Klautau, A. de Oliveira, I. Pamplona Trindade, and W. Alves, "Generating MIMO channels for 6G virtual worlds using ray-tracing simulations," *IEEE Statistical Signal Processing Workshop (SSP)*, 2021, pp. 595–599, doi: 10.1109/SSP49050.2021.9513861.

[2] A. Oliveira, F. Bastos, I. Trindade, W. Frazão, A. Nascimento, D. Gomes, F. Müller, and A. Klautau, "Simulation of machine learning-based 6G Systems in virtual worlds," *ITU Journal on Future and Evolving Technologies*, 2021. doi: 10.52953/SJAS4492.

[3] A. Klautau, P. Batista, N. González-Prelcic, Y. Wang, and R. W. Heath, "5G MIMO data for machine learning: Application to beam-selection using deep learning," *2018 Information Theory and Applications Workshop (ITA)*, 2018, pp. 1–9, doi: 10.1109/ITA.2018.8503086.

[4] D. Garcia-Roger, D. Martin-Sacristan, S. Roger, J. F. Monserrat, A. Kousaridas, P. Spapis, S. Ayaz, and C. Zhou (2018). 5G multi-antenna V2V channel modeling with a 3D game engine. *2018 IEEE Wireless Communications and Networking Conference Workshops, WCNCW 2018*, 284–289. https://doi.org/10.1109/WCNCW.2018.8369016

[5] E. Egea-Lopez, F. Losilla, J. Pascual-Garcia, and J. M. Molina-Garcia- Pardo (2019). Vehicular networks simulation with realistic physics. *IEEE Access, 7*, 44021–44036. doi: 10.1109/ACCESS.2019.2908651 (Software: http://pcacribia.upct.es/veneris)

[6] S. A. Hadiwardoyo, C. T. Calafate, J. C. Cano, Y. Ji, E. Hernandez-Orallo, and P. Manzoni (2019). 3D simulation modeling of UAV-to-car communications. *IEEE Access, 7*, 8808–8823. doi: 10.1109/ACCESS.2018.2889604.

[7] A. Mairaj, A. I. Baba, and A. Y. Javaid (2019). Application specific drone simulators: Recent advances and challenges. *Simulation Modelling Practice and Theory, 94*, 100–117. doi: 10.1016/j.simpat.2019.01.004.

[8] D. Jia, J. Sun, A. Sharma, Z. Zheng, and B. Liu (2021). Integrated simulation platform for conventional, connected and automated driving: A design from cyber–physical systems perspective. *Transportation Research Part C: Emerging Technologies, 124*. doi: 10.1016/j.trc.2021.102984.

[9] M. Calvo-Fullana, D. Mox, A. Pyattaev, J. Fink, V. Kumar, and A. Ribeiro, "ROS-NetSim: A framework for the integration of robotic and network simulators," in *IEEE Robotics and Automation Letters*, vol. 6, no. 2, pp. 1120–1127, 2021, doi: 10.1109/LRA.2021.3056347.

[10] B. Antonescu, M. T. Moayyed, and S. Basagni, "Diffuse scattering models for mmWave V2X communications in urban scenarios," *2019 International Conference on Computing, Networking and Communications (ICNC)*, 2019, pp. 923–929, doi: 10.1109/ICCNC.2019.8685661.

[11] S. Z. Tariq and H. Al-Rizzo, "Investigation of MIMO channel capacity using stochastic and ray-tracing techniques for Wi-Fi 6 applications," *2021 IEEE-APS Topical Conference on Antennas and Propagation in Wireless Communications (APWC)*, 2021, pp. 087–087, doi: 10.1109/APWC52648.2021.9539667.

[12] M. T. Moayyed, L. Bonati, P. Johari, T. Melodia, and S. Basagni, "Creating RF scenarios for large-scale, real-time wireless channel emulators," *2021 19th Mediterranean Communication and Computer Networking Conference (MedComNet)*, 2021, pp. 1–8, doi: 10.1109/MedComNet52149.2021.9501275.

[13] J. Hu, C. Chen, L. Cai, M. R. Khosravi, Q. Pei and S. Wan, "UAV-assisted vehicular edge computing for the 6G internet of vehicles: Architecture, intelligence, and challenges," *IEEE Communications Standards Magazine*, vol. 5, no. 2, pp. 12–18, 2021, doi: 10.1109/MCOMSTD.001.2000017.

[14] N. Yu, *Research on Key Technology of Path Planning of UAV*, Beijing, China: Beihang University, 2011.

[15] C. Mao and P. Wu, "Obstacle avoidance algorithm of UAV path planning based on artificial potential field method," *Electronic Science and Technology*, vol. 7, pp. 314–320, 2019.

[16] B. Brik, A. Ksentini and M. Bouaziz, "Federated learning for UAVs-enabled wireless networks: Use cases, challenges, and open problems," *IEEE Access*, vol. 8, pp. 53841–53849, 2020, doi: 10.1109/ACCESS.2020.2981430.

[17] D. Kwon and J. Kim, "Optimal trajectory learning for UAV-BS video provisioning system: A deep reinforcement learning approach," *2019. International Conference on Information Networking (ICOIN)*, 2019, pp. s372–374.

[18] Y. Li et al., "Fast and accurate trajectory tracking for unmanned aerial vehicles based on deep reinforcement learning," *2019 IEEE 25th International Conference on Embedded and Real-Time Computing Systems and Applications (RTCSA)*, 2019, pp. 1–9, doi: 10.1109/RTCSA.2019.8864571.

[19] R. Wu, F. Gu, and J. Huang, "A multi-critic deep deterministic policy gradient UAV path planning," *2020 16th International Conference on Computational Intelligence and Security (CIS)*, 2020, pp. 6–10, doi: 10.1109/ CIS52066.2020.00010.

[20] N. Dilokthanakul, C. Kaplanis, N. Pawlowski, and M. Shanahan, "Feature control as intrinsic motivation for hierarchical reinforcement learning," *IEEE Transactions on Neural Networks and Learning Systems*, vol. *30*, no. 11, pp. 3409–3418, 2019, doi: 10.1109/TNNLS.2019.2891792.

[21] J. B. Kenney, "Dedicated short-range communications (DSRC) standards in the United States," *Proceedings of the IEEE*, vol. *99*, no. 7, pp. 1162–1182, 2011, doi: 10.1109/JPROC.2011.2132790.

[22] J. Choi, V. Va, N. González-Prelcic, R. Daniels, C. R. Bhat, and R. W. Heath, "Millimeter-wave vehicular communication to support massive automotive sensing," *IEEE Communications Magazine*, vol. *54*, no. 12, pp. 160–167, 2016, doi: 10.1109/MCOM.2016.1600071CM.

[23] A. Alalewi, I. Dayoub, and S. Cherkaoui, "On 5G-V2X use cases and enabling technologies: A comprehensive survey," *IEEE Access*, vol. *9*, pp. 107710–107737, 2021, doi: 10.1109/ACCESS.2021.3100472.

[24] J. Kim and A. F. Molisch, "Fast millimeter-wave beam training with receive beamforming," *Journal of Communications and Networks*, vol. *16*, no. 5, pp. 512–522, 2014.

[25] W. Ma, C. Qi, and G. Y. Li, "Machine learning for beam alignment in millimeter wave massive MIMO," *IEEE Wireless Communications Letters*, vol. *9*, no. 6, pp. 875–878, 2020, doi: 10.1109/LWC.2020.2973972.

[26] Q. Hu, F. Gao, H. Zhang, S. Jin and G. Y. Li, "Deep learning for channel estimation: Interpretation, performance, and comparison," *IEEE Transactions on Wireless Communications*, vol. *20*, no. 4, pp. 2398–2412, 2021, doi: 10.1109/TWC.2020.3042074.

[27] Y. Wang, A. Klautau, M. Ribero, A. C. K. Soong, and R. W. Heath, "MmWave vehicular beam selection with situational awareness using machine learning," *IEEE Access*, vol. *7*, pp. 87479–87493, 2019, doi: 10.1109/ ACCESS.2019.2922064.

[28] D. Krajzewicz, J. Erdmann, M. Behrisch, and L. Bieker, "Recent development and applications of SUMO - simulation of urban mobility," *International Journal on Advances in Systems and Measurements*, vol. *5*, no. 3&4, pp. 128–138, 2012.

[29] S. Shah et al. "Airsim: High-fidelity visual and physical simulation for autonomous vehicles," *Field and Service Robotics*. Springer, Cham, 2018. https://link.springer.com/chapter/10.1007/978-3-319-67361-5_40

[30] T. S. Rappaport, R. W. Heath, R. C. Daniels, and J. N. Murdock, *Millimeter Wave Wireless Communications*. Prentice Hall, 2014. https://www.pearson.com/en-us/subject-catalog/p/millimeter-wave-wireless-communications/ P200000007616/9780137582174

[31] S. Oliver, and R. Hoppe. "MIMO channel capacity computed with 3D ray tracing model," *2009 3rd European Conference on Antennas and Propagation*. IEEE, 2009.

[32] S. Arikawa and Y. Karasawa, "A simplified MIMO channel characteristics evaluation scheme based on ray tracing and its application to indoor radio systems," *IEEE Antennas and Wireless Propagation Letters*, vol. *13*, pp. 1737–1740, 2014.

[33] A. Klautau, N. González-Prelcic and R. W. Heath, "LIDAR data for deep learning-based mmWave beam-selection," *IEEE Wireless Communications Letters*, vol. *8*, no. 3, pp. 909–912, 2019, doi: 10.1109/ LWC.2019.2899571.

[34] M. Lee and S. Yeom, "Tracking of Moving Vehicles with a UAV," *2018 Joint 10th International Conference on Soft Computing and Intelligent Systems (SCIS) and 19th International Symposium on Advanced Intelligent Systems (ISIS)*, 2018, pp. 928–931, doi: 10.1109/SCIS-ISIS.2018.00154.

[35] R. Sun, L. Fang, X. Gao, and J. Gao, "A novel target-aware dual matching and compensatory segmentation tracker for aerial videos," *IEEE Transactions on Instrumentation and Measurement*, vol. *70*, pp. 1–13, 2021, Art no. 5015613, doi: 10.1109/TIM.2021.3109722.

[36] S. Lins, et al. "Artificial intelligence for enhanced mobility and 5G connectivity in UAV-based critical missions," *IEEE Access 9* (2021): 111792–111801.

[37] F. Bastos, et al. "Effects of environment model complexity in UAV channel estimation using ray-tracing," *X Conferência Nacional em Comunicações, Redes e Segurança da Informação (ENCOM)*, Natal – RN, Brazil, 2020.